pground Common Area Thorsmork Iceland

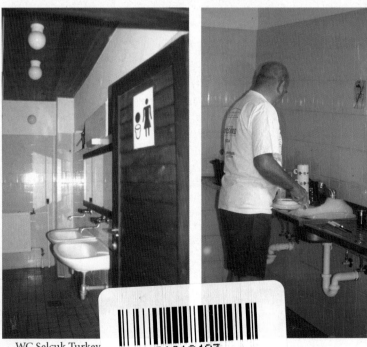

pground Pool
Galini Crete

WC Selcuk Turkey

Amsterdam The Netherlands

Bike Ready for Airline Transport

Braising Meat

Camp Cooked Meal

...na Italy

...sterdam The Netherlands

Paris France

...ohora Crete

Tirol Austria

Pyrennes Spain

Pelion Peninsula Greece

Azores Portugal

Bavarian Alps Germany

Rondane National Park Norway

Jotunheimen National Park Norway

Campground Pool Akureyri Iceland

Lake Sauna, Dalarna Sweden

Bothnian Coast Sweden

Lake Myvatn Iceland

Ruunaa Finland

Skaftafell National Park Iceland

ry to Islands Croatia

opane Poland

is Area Croatia

Carpathian Mountains Poland

Tatra Mts Slovak Republic

Julian Alps Slovenia

Plzen Czech Republic

Vltava River Czech Republic

...s Turkey

Sakikent Gorge Turkey

...garas Mts Romania

...rquoise Coast Turkey

Bucovina Romania

Turda Gorge Romania

Matsalu Nature Reserve Estonia

Camping Europe

By Carol Mickelsen
Cartography By Dion Good

To My Sons
Gregory and Ashley

Publishedby: by:
   Affordable Travel Press
   PO Box 3296
   Half Moon Bay, CA 94019
   carol@campingeuropeguide.com
   www.campingeuropeguide.com

Distributed to the book trade by Publishers Group West through::
   Carousel Press
   PO Box 6038
   Berkeley, CA 94706-0038
   510-527-5849
   info@carousel-press.com
   www.carousel-press.com

This is the enlarged and updated **third edition** of **Camping Europe**
This book was previously published in 2001 as **Camping Europe** and in 1996 as **Camping Your Way Through Europe**.

Library of Congress Cataloging-in-Publication Data:
Mickelsen, Carol
   Camping Europe/ by Carol Mickelsen/ 3rd edition
   Includes indexes
   ISBN 10 0-917120-20-5
   13   978-0-917120-20-6
      1. travel/Europe 2. Budget travel Europe/Camping 3. Driving/Europe

Cartographer: Dion Good
Editor: Carole Terwilliger Meyers
Design and Production: Hayden Foell
Cover Design: Michael Wong
Cover Photos: Front/Top: Francesco Survara
                       Front/Bottom: Carol Mickelsen
                       Back: Carol Mickelsen
                       4881720

Manufactured in China

Author's Note

This book is my joyous response to 30 years of car-camping alongside relaxed and unpretentious camping Europeans. My travels have taken me throughout 25 European countries where English is not the local language. I love the major cities and well-known sights, but I also look for out-of-the-way fun and interesting things to do that appeal to my adventurous and curious spirit.

For years I've struggled with camping guides and country campground lists from tourist offices. They commonly use only symbols for descriptions and include little information on how to drive to the campgrounds. I've also struggled with travel books that don't tell readers how to *drive* to points of interest. The goal in writing this book is to give you the detailed information needed to experience Europe easily and affordably while car-camping.

Because of the large number of countries covered in this book, full descriptions, detailed maps, accent marks, and exact mileage is impossible for me to provide. I recommend securing additional guidebooks and maps for the areas you'll be traveling in. The opening and closing dates of the campgrounds are conservative; call ahead if you are traveling early or late in the season. The closed days for museums refer to summer months. Europeans use the word *caravan* for what Americans call an RV so in this book I use the word caravan.

ABOUT THE AUTHOR

Carol Mickelsen is a professional chef. She bought and restored a dilapidated but historic hotel with restaurant and bar in Half Moon Bay California, a small town on the Pacific Coast, south of San Francisco. She named it the San Benito House. The restaurant has received rave reviews from Gourmet and National Geographic Traveler magazines. She sold the business to her oldest son giving her time to travel and write.

She has traveled throughout the world and finds budget travel fascinating, fun, and easy. Readers are encouraged to ask questions, give suggestions, pass on new information; and even complain. Carol@campingeuropeguide.com. Visit www.campingeuropeguide.com

ABOUT THE CARTOGRAPHER

Dion Good has been a professional cartographer for 10 years. He has a B.A. and M.A. in Geography and Certificate in GIS. He has produced maps for Lonely Planet Publications, Art-Sites Press, Cork Hill Press, Travel Host East Bay, the San Francisco Neighborhood Parks Council and the American Land Conservancy. He is also the creator of A Jazz History Map of the United States, which can be ordered directly from the cartographer. d.good@yahoo.com He has traveled widely in the U.S., Mexico, and Turkey. He and his wife Tulin are based in Oakland, California.

1

CONTENTS

2

WESTERN EUROPE

Italy   150

Luxembourg

Portugal

SCANDINAVIA

CENTRAL EUROPE

WHY TRAVEL?

I regard travel as an essential part of an adventuresome life. Much more than just recreation, it is one of the finest ways to become educated. It's presents challenges that make you think.

Although spending time studying a country's history, culture, and language before a trip is important, do try to venture out with a beginner's mind and leave preconceptions behind. Train your eyes to be attentive, to drink in every moment. No matter how many photos you look at, how many words you read, or how many conversations you have about a place, you will never have even the tiniest understanding of it until you've personally exposed yourself to it.

I enjoy being around cheerful, upbeat, and indomitable people. Traveling, particularly car-camping, has helped me become more like this myself. Just the simple pleasure of facing the unexpected, accepting what comes along, and being able to follow my curiosity wherever it leads me has paid me back in invigoration, easy laughter, and a sense of being profoundly alive.

WHY CAMP?

Money matters. Let's face it, root of evil or not, you need money to travel. Where can you get off the tourist track, spend time absorbing the local culture, and not spend a lot of money? Car-camping for two or more persons costs much less than staying in inexpensive hotels or hostels, eating at inexpensive cafes or fast-food places, and taking public transportation. Sizably less! The luxury of a car enables you to go wherever whim takes you, whether it's to a local festival, a breathtaking location, or better weather. Instead of just looking at all the delectable food in open markets and grocery stores, you can purchase some and fix yourself a delicious meal for very little expense at a scenic campground.

Middle-class Europeans often camp when they're on a vacation so joining them is easy. They are relaxed and unpretentious and enjoy laughing and talking with you at the common cooking and washing-up areas. You share with them the experience of savoring the sunset from the campground's terrace. You find yourself pouring over maps together, exchanging funny travel stories, and sharing details on what's fun to do.

Catering to demanding Dutch, German, French, and British campers, popular campgrounds must have well maintained warm showers, clean toilets, common kitchen and laundry facilities, a well-equipped children's playground, grass, shade, and if close to a city, nearby public transportation. Location is important to popularity, so many are close to the lakes, rivers, or the sea, or are on a hillside with a view. They are generally large grassy lawns under shade trees. Safety and theft are simply not issues. You are camping alongside people who have their own equipment and are not interested in yours.

Contemporary camping equipment is very comfortable and easy to assemble and pack. Go to a sports store and lie down on the new self-inflating mattresses and see the new easy-to-put-up rainproof tents. You'll be surprised how comfortable, easy to pack, and set up the new equipment has become.

Europeans love to cycle and I like to join them. Taking your bike and a bike-rack is easy when you car-camp.

Take the Kids to Europe

Giving a little sip of travel to your children, grandchildren, or school/church-group can open up immense vistas, stimulate curiosity, and provide an appreciation of life beyond oneself. Travel changes people. It broadens their perspective of the world and their understanding of their place in it. Upon returning from travel, you'll notice that thinking and problem-solving abilities are sharper and children will find schoolwork is more interesting.

Savvy travelers know that a good travel experience must be approached delicately, without preconceptions. They never stint on good planning and preparation, and they know that flexibility, optimism, and joie de vivre must be carried just like a cash card tucked into their money belt. Being able to look ahead, to step over problems like stones in a creek, and to continue with optimism and a belief in yourself is one of the greatest gifts a person can give or receive. Teaching this is best done by example. Car-camping is one of the easiest and most relaxing ways to appreciate Europe with kids and young people. Its relaxing pace makes it easy to take time out to stop and reflect on everyone's ideas for a solution and to provide the opportunity of finding humor, or least patience, during mishaps.

Use mornings for learning and afternoons for playing. Open up the guidebook and make a list of possible activities for the day. Take turns planning chunks of time, and abide by the choices. Every two hours, interlace activities with some wind-down time. Allow some independence within boundaries. Come to an agreement on what happens when someone goes "out of bounds." Have a "meet back here in 20 minutes" agreement. Synchronize watches.

Play some pranks. Laugh at each other. Be silly. Take funny photos and have them printed enroute so you can savor them along the way. Have everyone write down their version of the same story in their trip journal and then read them aloud together later. It's easier to be organized but not rigid if you keep your plans simple. Relish the unexpected and spontaneous. Spend several hours each day in a physical activity that isn't just walking to see sights. Rent bikes, roller blades, or a canoe. Walk across a bridge, build an elaborate sandcastle, or swing in a park. Look for goulish things as you walk as well as the beautiful and historic.

Your kids will join European kids having fun at the swimming areas and playgrounds. Adults will make new friends with Europeans as they hang-out together watching the kids. Make meal preparation easy. Let each person take turns at being chef, assistant, or dishwasher. Let the chef chose what they will prepare. Lavish compliments. European markets are filled with plenty of easy-to-fix foodstuffs, and deli-cases are loaded with mouth-watering choices that make meal preparation easy and doable even for the very young. Let your desire for family togetherness be met. Give vent to a feeling of adventure. Take the kids to Europe.

Car-Camping in Retirement Years

I am 65 and my partner is 69. We love car-camping and plan to continue doing it for many more years. Our new, comfortable, easy-to-set-up and pack equipment let's us set up a very comfortable campsite in just a few minutes. We have all the motions memorized. Now we have the time and car-camping is so affordable, we go often. After a trip we clean up the equipment and repack it immediately, making notes about what needs to be replenished. We're always ready for the next a trip.

When traveling we love meeting European campers who are retired like ourselves. There's no rush to be somewhere else. There's time to play some cards, examine maps and brochures, walk together to the village, and even take a nap. Younger campers often come up to us and say, "Boy, you guys (meaning old folks, I guess) do all right! I hope I can do it like you guys do when I get to your age!"

Solo Car-Camping

I started solo car-camping a few years ago when my travel companions wanted to stop and stay for a while in the beautiful places we found. In order to research this book, I needed to cover more countryside, so I decided to go alone and fell in love with solo car-camping. I was released from worrying about whether someone else was having fun. I could get up early and continue traveling until early evening. Relaxed and carefree, I didn't measure time-I lived it. I stopped whenever I felt like it. I took naps at rest-stops, made coffee, and continued on. I was never bored or lonely. I lost myself in a lightheartedness that relished simple things and discovered that all serious daring and adventurous experiences start from within. I took pride in simple accomplishments. I hiked and walked in companionable silence with myself. I met people and places with a steady, open gaze. Each day I awoke with anticipation, having no idea how it might unfold. I would just let myself go with the flow. I wasn't worried about "success or failure" or whether or not I looked foolish. It was all about having fun following my curious nature.

I hike with walking sticks. I know these have prevented sprained ankles and falls on the trail. When I am hiking alone, I appreciate this security. I can set up my tent in just minutes. Everything is arranged in the car so it is convenient. I am never afraid alone in my tent. I have books to read, journals to write in, brochures and maps to study. I bring music and books-on-tape that I listen to with a headset. I make myself a little dinner and put it in a picnic basket along with a good book, grab my collapsible chair, and head joyfully to a scenic spot close to the campsite to watch the sunset.

Some of my most enjoyable experiences have occurred when I am doing nothing more than wandering by foot or bicycle through historic centers and neighborhoods, breathing in the atmosphere. I keep my mind alive by looking for photo shots: a cat sunning on a stoop, a polished doorknob, a bicycle tethered to a railing, wisps of vine on an open gate, or light chasing water. I take my journal and my binoculars so that if I find a park I can sit and listen for the buzz of hummingbirds and watch the birds swoop home to their nests or perching places. Flea markets are great for people watching and soaking up a scene. It's fun to watch others examine the amazing bits and pieces of crockery and enamelware, old books, or a maybe-useful tool. I've joined inexpensive bicycle and walking tours of the historic areas when I felt the need for some conversation. I've sought out tiny museums appealing to a special interest and had fascinating conversations with staff. I've gone to the open markets for a delicious assault on my senses and to smile at the hardworking crew of vendors and their scurrilous banter.

At the end of the day, if I feel a need for conversation, I walk around the campground and look at license plates. Dutch?...They all speak English. French?...Just start out with some complimentary French words they'll appreciate, and they will start speaking English. German?...Just a couple of words in German and one of them will start speaking English. Brits?...Oh, we'll talk for a long time! On the trail I often stop other hikers. They enjoyed talking for a few minutes. Sometimes we fall in step together. Nothing is a more useful bridge however, than children. My interest in children unlocks every parent's heart. I even connect with people whose language I don't speak. We laugh and smile, gaily speaking our own languages without either understanding the other's words.

I have learned to make the most out of the here and now, to enjoy the unpredictable, and to not sweat the small stuff. I try to approach a landscape with a fresh point of view, to look for small ways in which it is radiant, glorious, and maybe even surreal. I revel in the joy of just being there.

Hints for a Smooth and Enjoyable Trip

Set-up and Take-Down Campsite Routine.

- One person unrolls the inflatable mattresses onto the car hood or roof. (The warmth will cause them to inflate by themselves.)

- The other person starts looking at the ground to select the area for setting up the tent. If there's a slight slope, plan to have your heads on the up-slope. If there's a chance of rain, don't choose a spot where water from an up-slope can flow down under your tent.

- Unroll the tent. One person can snap the structuring poles together while the other lays down the 'footprint' and the tent with the door in the right direction. Standing on opposite ends of the tent, thread the structuring poles through the loops to each other. Take turns placing the structuring poles in the final grommets. Throw the rainfly over the tent making the correct arrangement for the door.

- One person starts hammering in the tent stakes using a plastic hammer (sold in sports stores) Pound, half-way only, four corner stakes. This trick allows for easy adjustments for evenly cover the tent with the rainfly. Finish pounding the 4 corner stakes further into the ground and continue with the other stakes, stretching the rainfly out from the tent so there can be good air movement inside the tent. Store tent/stake bags by the door of the tent so they are easy to find for convenience at take-down.

- The other person blows a couple of times into each of the air mattresses and then slides them into their 'mattress pillowcases' (see Recommended Camping Equipment). This person continues to place bedding into the tent while the other person stakes the tent. Bedding stuff-bags are placed inside the tent for ease in using on take-down. (This set-up procedure will take about 10 minutes when you get into the routine.)

- Before quitting the tent after waking up in the morning of take-down, each person deflates their own mattress enough so it stays folded in half and puts their own bedding into their stuff-bag.

- One person starts breakfast while the other takes down the tent. Both help to get things stored back into the car.

Storing Camping Equipment and Personal Things in the Car

Being organized is essential to make car-camping easy. Here's how I do it:

* At my first campsite, I throw down a ground tarp and arrange all the camping equipment and personal things in categories for the duration of the trip.

* I use the back seat for personal stuff. Each person gets a "side", using duffels or grocery store boxes to keep things organized. Folded air mattresses are placed over the personal stuff in the backseat of the car.

* I fold up the empty duffels and put them in back/bottom of the trunk with things I'm not going to use for awhile. The tent and bedding are stored over these. I use discarded boxes from the grocery store to arrange my kitchen equipment and foodstuffs, placing them along the front of the trunk for easy use.

Hints for Harmony

Rituals engender feelings of comfort and safety. They bring a welcome consistency to an otherwise unstructured life. Establish a morning and evening routine. In the morning you might do stretching or yoga exercises, drink a leisurely cup of coffee, walk to the camp-store for fresh bread and yogurt, read a book or guidebook, study the map taking notes, take a walk, visit the market. In the evening you might write in your journal, read a book, listen to music or books on tape, take a stroll.

I keep a journal. It is a sort-of portable support system. It allows an active relationship with my inner self, is a repository of lists, and a place to record notes for memoirs of unique moments in time. A journal can become your companion and confidante. It can help you handle difficult moments, to remind you to be confident and decide for yourself what you want in life. It encourages you to think about what makes you happy. It helps keep you centered. The sense of order it brings is comforting.

It is a myth that vacations occur without conflict with your companion. We all need to learn to cope with disagreements and difficulties and to be creative in solving problems that emerge. When divergent desires emerge, take time to brainstorm creative solutions to the dilemma. See if there's a way for each to get what they want without too many compromises. Try these ground rules for discussion. Each person must:

* Explain their proposal and why they think it will work, offering trade-offs when a companion has to give up something.

* Stick to the facts when discussing the options, maintain a positive attitude and *a sense of humor.*

* Set a time limit for reaching a compromise.

* Create new options to break an impasse.

* Honor agreements, avoiding the desire to renegotiate.

Money, Money Money

Money is an easy source of conflict. I recommend a "common purse" where each person antes up an equal amount of money for the day. Take turns being the banker. Use the purse for paying for common activities: groceries, museum entrance fees, bus fare, gas, campground fees. For personal expenses. each person pays on their own. If one traveler consistently wants to spend more for groceries than another, discuss it and come up with a budget.

Find interesting inexpensive things to do:

- Look for posters advertising concerts in cathedrals, special art shows, festivals, events.
- Talk to staff at the campground or tourist office about fun and inexpensive things to do.
- Take the recommended walk offered in a guidebook or tourist office.
- Sit in a park and, using your journal or a sketchpad, record what you see and hear.
- Take a public bus without worrying about its destination. Get off when it looks interesting. Return on the same bus number going in the opposite direction.
- Walk or cycle down tiny roads and into neighborhoods.
- Visit to the local library.
- Step off the beaten tourist track.

Hints for Facing New Situations

Develop the habit of looking back. When you leave a space you've sat down or spent time-public transportation, bathroom, hiking trail, etc-look around carefully to see if you have left anything. Count the number of items you are carrying, and recount them every time you move. Losing things is especially difficult when you are also facing new experiences. Take time to be careful.

On walks, turn around and look back. Write down landmarks so finding your way back is easier. Increase your level of exercise before your trip. Walk an hour or two a day. Go hiking or cycling. Do exercises or work that increases your upper and lower body strength and energy level.

See a place and its people through your own eyes before peering through the lens of a camera. Don't reach for your camera until you are almost ready to leave a scene unless you are capturing a momentary scene. Establish a rapport with people you wish to photograph close up. Take a few minutes to discuss the weather, admire the flowers or birds. Then slowly take your camera out and ask for permission to photograph them. Be prepared to accept a refusal. Don't fight the serious pose-just snap more pictures right after, when smiles of relief and natural poses emerge. Learning a few conversational phrases in the local language will go far to demonstrate your respect for the culture and for them. Have fun with your camera. Photograph other people taking photos, a crowd waiting for a bus, children on the way home from school, people eating at food stalls. Study the work of other photographers by checking out books from the library. Then relax and experiment on your own.

Leave behind your expensive possessions, your pride, and your assumptions. Instead carry simple humanity. Learn to laugh at yourself in front of other people. Generally, folks will laugh *with* you and be friendlier afterwards. Talk through sign language, through smiles, and through gentle laughter. Be quick to forgive. There's an unspoken camaraderie between campers, even if you don't speak the same language. The hospitality and warmth are lovely to be around.

Adventure means learning. It means encountering things you cannot foresee but must figure out how to address. If it's scary, you must figure some way to get through it. If it's a mundane obstacle, take a novel approach. Aim to make it interesting, and maybe fun or at least memorable. You never know what you can do until you try. Learn to trust yourself to find a way when you face something unexpected. And, importantly, ask for help, even from people who don't speak your language. People generally enjoy being helpful.

When you put yourself in a place that is totally new to you, you reveal yourself. It gives you a chance to feel confident in your ability to take care of yourself. And this feels good. You blossom when you encounter challenges and rise to meet them. You'll say, "I didn't know I could do that!" Returning home, don't be surprised if you view your life from a different perspective. What was once important to you may no longer be so. You'll discover that you have more confidence in yourself and more courage to tackle new things.

Budgeting for the Trip

Groceries and *gas will cost close to what you spend for them at home. The car rental business is highly competitive. Good deals are out there. (see the appendix for recommended companies) Plan to spend 7 to 10 euros for admission to most major museums and historic sites in Western Europe. In Central and Eastern Europe the cost is 25 to 50 percent less. Students and seniors get sizable discounts on museum tickets and transportation. Bring a few extra passport-like photos for transportation passes and show your passport when buying tickets to museums and exhibitions. Plan an average of 20 euros for a camp-site per night (includes 2 persons, car, and tent) in Western and Scandinavian Europe. In Central and Eastern Europe, you'll pay less. Your biggest expense is getting there (unless you can use frequent flyer miles) and renting a car. (European cars are gas efficient and distances between sights aren't great)

Keeping Money Safe

Use a cash card to get local money. Cash machines are in the same locations they are at home: bank, shopping center, airport, tourist areas. Transactions from machines at banks give the best rate. Be sure your pin number is only four digits and is numerical. Change enough money for several days or a week. Put most of the money in a money belt with the strap safely tucked underneath your clothing. Put the day's cash in a safe, but easily accessible, location. Keep change available for parking meters, toll roads, illuminating art in churches, and restrooms.

Using the Phone and E-Mail

Phone cards and multilingual instructions in phone booths make using the phone in Europe easier than ever. Phone cards are available wherever newspapers and magazines are sold. You just slide the card into the slot in the phone and press in the phone number. An electronic readout tells you how much value is left on the card. Buy a phone card at home and practice using it before the trip if you have never used one before. To make an international call: press the international access number of the country you are calling from (it's usually 00) the country code of the country you are calling, the area code, and number. For calls within the country, do like you do at home: press in the area code and the number. If you want to use a direct phone service, use a phone card to call the toll-free access number listed on the back of your calling-card and an English speaking operator will assist you. Within Europe using a phone card is cheaper than using a direct service. If you have trouble, ask a local to help. Some phone cards require you to remove a perforated corner in order to activate the card. Always press the phone number in slowly and deliberately. If you have trouble getting your call to go through, try another phone or ask for help.

At a calling call center you can place your call from a quiet phone booth, get assistance from staff if you're having problems, and pay when you're finished without using a phone card. Cyber cafes can be fun if you want to stay in touch via e-mail. Campground staff, tourist offices, computer stores, and major hotels can direct you to the nearest one. To send a fax or call abroad from the USA, dial the international access code 011 first, then the area code and number.

Tourist information

The local tourist office is the best place to get information about what's happening in town. At least one staff person will speak fluent English, and racks of colorful brochures will offer a host of things to do or see. Most major cities publish a monthly magazine that lists the current open hours of sights and museums as well as information about current performances, festivals, and exhibitions. This valuable information can enhance your trip beyond your guidebook. Offices invariably have a line in major cities, so understand that to accommodate everyone staff must be fairly brisk with their answers. Write down the questions you want to ask the staff, and then, as they speak, write down their answers so you don't forget details.

Europe uses at 24-hour clock. This means that after 12 o'clock noon the naming of hours continues on rather than starting again with a PM. In other words, 2 PM is written as 14:00, etc. Most cars take unleaded gas. A liter is about a quart. A kilometer is about $1/6^{th}$ of a mile. To convert kilometers to miles just divide the kilometer distance by two and add 10 percent. So 100km=50+10=60 miles.

Camping and Cooking Equipment

- Tent with rain fly

- Tarp for outside the tent

- Inflatable sleeping mattresses (Self inflating are best because you can put them on top of the car when you arrive at the campsite and they will be inflated in minutes)

- Bedding for summer travel (June-August): Except for Scandinavia or mountainous regions, I find my down-sleeping bag too warm for summer camping. I prefer to make a pillowcase for each thermal mattress from twin bed sheets by folding the sheet in half lengthwise and sewing the bottom and the open side. I lay the inflated mattress on the car and slip it into its "pillowcase". For each person I take along an additional twin bed sheet for the top sheet (sew the bottom and part way up the side) and a thermal blanket. This bedding makes sleeping more home-like. In May and September, I take one down sleeping bags that unzip to make coverings for the cooler months.

- Inflatable pillows and pillow cases

- Collapsible ground chairs and/or small standing chairs with backs that fold and pack easily; Roll-up camping table.

- Stove: I love my Campingaz Turbo 270, a small burner that twists on top of canned fuel called Campingaz. I especially like it because Campingaz fuel produces an excellent clean hot flame. The storage case for the stove is only 5 inches by 3 inches and it weighs less than a pound. The stove is available at major sports stores and at www.campingaz.com. Consumer service in English: 44-1275-845-024, fax 44-1275-849-255 Bristol England. You cannot take fuel aboard a plane, so plan on buying it on arrival. You'll find the fuel, in its signature blue canisters, at hardware stores and sports stores throughout Western Europe. If you are traveling in Central or Eastern Europe, contact Campingaz to find out if they have a distributor in the major city where you'll arrive.

- Alternate Stove: Mountain Safety Research's Dragonfly Multi-Fuel stove is another good choice. It uses white gas best but can also operate on unleaded gas available at gas stations. It also has easy maintenance features.

- Stove board: I make this at home to keep the stove level if I'm not cooking on a table. To make one. To make a cut a 1/4 inch piece of playwood about 12" by 24". Cover it with contact paper.

- One 8" sauté pan: ideally heavy aluminum or calphlon with sloping sides and lid

- One 1 1/2-quart lightweight pot with lid
- Thermos or thermos cups with filter for making coffee or tea
- One 8-inch and two 4-inch metal bowls
- One slotted and one unslotted cooking spoon
- One rubber and one metal spatula
- Can opener and vegetable peeler
- One 8-inch and one 4-inch good quality knife
- Small jar with lid for salad dressings
- One quart-size storage container
- Plastic cups, bowls, plates and silverware
- Sponge, scrubber, two dish-drying towels
- Plastic bowl for washing dishes
- Two table cloths for roll-up table.
- Foldable insulated bag to store fish when shopping in open markets
- One flashlight per person
- Battery-operated mini table or tent light; optional
- Plastic shower bag for handy warm water, optional (store on back shelf of car to warm while driving).
- Inner tube or inflatable mattress for river floats; optional

All of the above fits easily into three duffels. This allows two persons an extra duffel plus some extra space here and there for personal items without going over the allowable luggage limit for air travel. When you pack the duffels, keep the weight fairly equal. Because of potential back problems with baggage-loading airline staff, airlines no longer consider the total weight of baggage. Each bag is checked individually.

Camp Cooking Hints

Make meal preparing easy by purchasing just what you need for that day's meals.

Buy a small inexpensive cooler on your first grocery-shopping trip. European markets and deli-cases are filled with plenty of easy-to-fix foodstuffs. If you are shopping in the morning, you may want to buy your meat frozen so it is defrosted by dinnertime.

I use the car trunk for my "kitchen cupboard and refrigerator". I get discarded boxes at the grocery store and arrange all my equipment, utensils and food so that it is orderly and easy to access. I store the cooler here, too.

When it's time to cook, start by gathering all food ingredients, spices, packaged mixes, utensils, pots and pans, and eating utensils that you need for the meal. Wash all the produce bought that day. Store what you won't be using for this meal. Start your vegetable and fruit preparation, placing what will be cooked together in one bowl.

Braising is an excellent way to use a less expensive and less tender, yet flavorful, piece of meat. Trim off excess fat and membrane. Cut the meat into 1 1/2 inch pieces. Put one to two tablespoons of oil in the sauté pan. Over high heat, let the oil get smoking hot. Place the meat in the pan a little at a time, allowing enough room around each piece so it will brown well. This seals in the juices. If you put in too much meat at one time the juices will run from the meat and the color will be gray instead of brown. If you are including veg-etables with the meat remove the meat when browned. Add one or two tablespoons of oil to the pan and heat it to medium hot. Saute the vegetables (*see below for additional notes on vegetables). The particles of meat left in the pan add flavor so don't throw them away. When the meat and vegetables are cooked remove them from the pan. Over medium-low heat, pour enough water, wine/beer, chicken stock, fruit juice or a combination to make one inch of cooking liquid in your pan. Stir in bouillon cubes, packaged mix, or spices. Scrape the bottom of the pan to incorporate the leftover cooked particles into your sauce. Taste and adjust spices accordingly. Return the meat and cover with lid and cook over low heat until meat is tender. Add the cooked vegetables when the meat is done and cook uncovered until hot. Bon Appetite!

Marinating meat and fish enhances the end result. Meat benefits from 3 to 4 hours of mari-nating. Fish needs only a few minutes. Curing pork is easy to do and makes a world of dif-ference in taste. *See below for recipes

*Some vegetables such as green beans, broccoli, or potatoes need blanching before you sauté them. Bring a pot of boiling salted water to a boil. Add the vegetables and cook until they are softened but still have a bit of firmness. Remove them with a slotted spoon. Save the hot water for cooking pasta, rice, or polenta, or use it for cleaning up.

To sauté vegetables, place a small amount of oil in a frying pan over moderate heat. When it is almost smoking hot, add the vegetables, turning them as they brown. To sauté meat or fish, proceed as above but allow space between each piece so the juices are sealed by brown-ing.

To cook pasta, place about four times as much water in the pot as the amount of pasta you are cooking. Add enough salt so the water tastes salty. Cover the pot and bring the water to a boil. Add the pasta stirring occasionally to keep it separated. When it is almost cooked, take it off the heat. Cover and set aside. While it rests and stays warm, it will finish cooking. When you are ready to serve, drain the pasta. Add sautéed vegetables, meat, or packaged sauce.

Polenta is a wonderful, flavorful, and filling starch. Serve it like you would potatoes. You'll probably find it in the same section in the store where rice is shelved. It swells in cooking to the amount of liquid it is cooked in. For one cup of dry polenta bring four cups water to a boil. Pour in the polenta stirring constantly. Turn down the heat and let it bubble slowly. Stir frequently to avoid lumps. When it is thick and smooth remove it from the heat and cover with a lid or towel until you are ready to serve.

Couscous is also a healthy starch choice. For 2 cups of dry couscous, heat 2 cups of liquid (water, chicken or vegetable stock, fruit juice). When the liquid is hot pour in the cou-cous. Stir for only a moment to incorporate, cover with tight fitting lid, remove from heat. Couscous will swell and cook in 10 minutes.

Clean up as you cook. I use paper towels for drying because they are sanitary and don't have to be 'hung-out' to dry. Keep a plastic bag in your cooking area for throwaway stuff. Keep a basin of warm water close to where you are cooking and wash and dry equipment as you cook. I use the warmed water from a plastic "camping shower-bag" that I have put on the ledge above the back seat each day. I either hang it from a tree or the car. This gives me a source of warm water right at my campsite. I try to have everything washed or soaking before I sit down to eat so that the after-meal clean-up is minimal.

Marinating Oil for Meat and Fish

Stir together: 1/2 cup olive oil, 2 teaspoons lemon juice, salt and pepper; optional: garlic, fresh or dried herbs, teriyaki sauce, sugar, lemon zest, or mustard.

Rub flavored oil into meat and let it rest for 30 minutes. Less tender cuts of meat profit from longer marination.

Curing Liquid for Pork

Simmer together for five minutes: 3 cups water, 1/2 cup lemon juice, 2/3 cup sugar or 1/2 cup maple syrup, 1/4 teaspoon cinnamon, 1 tablespoon salt. Let cool. Place pork into a storage container and pour cooled curing liquid over it just to cover. Keep in cool box with ice for 24 hours. Remove the pork from the curing liquid. Dry with paper towel. Discard the used liquid.

Driving in Europe

NAVIGATING HINTS

Driving in Europe is just like driving at home. At home when you drive in a major city you've never been to before, you buy a good map. You also get *written* directions at the car rental desk on how to get to your first destination. (free car-rental maps aren't detailed enough).

And that's what you also do in Europe. Your most challenging moments will be getting out of the airport and onto the right road to your first destination. Have the car rental agent draw a map for you, detailing the directions in writing. Be sure all the exits and the distances between them are shown.

Before you drive out of the airport, both the driver and the navigator need to compare the agent's drawn map with the purchased map. You will both need to have a concept of the route. Make an easy-to-read list of the exits. Note the large cities on your route so you can predict what the signposting will be. Know where you *don't* want to go. Once you are on the road with heavy traffic, your time to look at the map will be limited.

If you see a road sign listing places you don't recognize, pull over and find each place name on the map. Pulling over in front of signs is a good habit. Use the map's index if you don't find the place readily. Before entering a roundabout, read the road sign and note whether you want the first, second, or third exit. Going around again until you are certain where to exit is *not* a waste of time. Never continue on when you are uncertain. Instead, turn around and go back to the last sign. This effort will save you time, money, and frustration.

Stay calm. Don't let angry drivers bother you. Anticipate heavy, fast-moving traffic. Drive in the slow lane for the first few days. The navigator should know where you are on the map at all times. Use a highlighter to mark the route. The navigator needs to anticipate the signs ahead and inform the driver. European drivers are alert, make quick decisions, and check their mirrors constantly so they know what is happening around them. You'll need to do the same.

Realize that being either the driver or the navigator is difficult, and keep peace between you. Learn from your mistakes. Congratulate each other on their expertise. Celebrate your skills.

Advantages of Driving

Having your own car gives you the freedom to go where you want, when you want. It enables you to stop for spur-of-the-moment pleasures. Time isn't spent on getting ticketed and then waiting for buses and trains. You don't have to lug bags or backpacks. Your things are organized so that you can set up your campsite in just a few minutes. At the morning market, you can purchase wonderful foodstuffs inexpensively and store them in the cool box in your car (cool boxes are inexpensive and can be purchased at the same places you'd find them at home). Lunches and dinners made at the campground or at special stops along the way will be memorable and cost just a fraction of what it would cost to eat even at inexpensive places.

The Car and Its Expenses

As companies compete for business, the cost of renting or leasing a car seems to go down rather than up. When you rent for 21 days or more you qualify for lease terms, decreasing the daily rate considerably. There is a sizable difference in car rental rate from one country to another. Generally it costs less if you return the car where you picked it up. For the best rate, make your reservation at home. Use your credit card so you can dispute the charge if there is a problem. Don't use the rental company for collision damage waiver (CDW) insurance. If you rent a car and purchase insurance from the same company, it is a conflict of interest. You can get this same insurance from less expensive sources. The rental/lease cost generally includes third party insurance (damage to the other party) but be sure this is written in your agreement. It's a good idea to have theft insurance. If you have a home policy, it might cover you on your trip. Be sure to check. See the appendix for rental and insurance companies.

Unleaded fuel is called petrol or benzine. Diesel is gasoil. Tolls can be expensive, but if you want to get somewhere fast, pay them. In countries that have a highway-user tax, you can be pulled over for not having the sticker and must pay on the spot, sometimes with an additional penalty. Inform the car rental agent when you pick up the car, what countries you might travel in. They will be able to research the roadway taxes that apply. Purchase the sticker at a gas station when you enter that country.

Getting Directions

Signage in Europe is very good. Europeans are used to directing foreigners, so they use international graphic signs rather than linguistic ones. Fellow travelers and locals you meet in gas stations can be helpful. Be sure to have your map and a piece of paper and pencil with you when you ask for directions. Use your phrase book to write your questions down in the local language if you don't feel confident about your skill in speaking the language. Always start by saying "Hello, Can you help me?" in *their* language. Show them your paper with the name of the place you want to go printed in large letters. Hand them a paper and say, "Please" in *their* language and indicate you want them to draw a map or write down directions.

On a town's outskirts, stop at a gas station and buy a good city map. Locate your destination on the map. Ask someone to direct you to your next exit. Keep pulling off to ask for directions as you need them or to reconfirm what the last person said. Keep in mind that every time you ask for directions, you have a small conversation with a local. The smiles and "thank-yous", in *their* language feel good.

Parking and Tolls

Many cities have parking areas adjacent to historic areas. Look for a ticket dispenser in the area. Feed coins into the dispenser for the time you plan to be gone. Display the ticket on your dashboard. Keep change available for this. Always look at how the other cars are parked and follow suit. Parking costs and time limits are the same as at home. The closer you get to historic areas of large cities, the more expensive and limited in time the parking will be.

In large underground parking garages, push the button to receive a ticket upon entering. Before you get back in your car to leave, take the ticket to a central processing machine and insert the amount of local currency indicated on the screen. When you leave with the car, insert the paid ticket into the machine to lift the bar.

Clamping a lock onto a tire of an illegally parked car is common in Eastern Europe. To release the clamp you must go to the police station, pay the fine, and wait for them to unlock the clamp. In Western Europe tickets for illegally parked cars are paid with stamps you buy in a kiosk. Affix the stamp to the ticket and mail it promptly or you will have to pay for the ticket plus penalties when you settle your car rental bill.

If you bring your bike you can park outside the conjested area and pedal in. It's a great way to get a sense of a city. I enjoy pedaling almost as much as prowling through the monuments and museums. If you haven't brought your bike, consider renting one. Many cities and towns throughout Europe encourage tourists to cycle. Rentals are now usually readily available close to tourist areas, trains stations, and campgrounds. Ask at the tourist office.

When you enter a toll road, a machine issues a ticket. Keep it handy, always putting it in the same place in the car. When you leave the toll road, hand your ticket to the agent at the station. Your charge will be shown on the screen. Tolls can be paid with charge cards as well as local currency. Some toll-stations have separate toll booths for trucks. Don't enter these. The ticket dispenser is raised up for truck drivers to reach.

Road Signs and Rules

Round signs with red borders indicate prohibitions. Triangular signs with red borders warn of dangers. Blue indicates positive information that you can take advantage of. In all cases graphics inside the sign tell more. Parking areas are signposted with a "P", campgrounds with a tent, and airports with an airplane. The word "*stop*" is used for stop signs throughout Europe. A yellow blinking or steady light means that a red light is imminent. Street signs are usually posted on buildings and have an unnerving way of changing names on the same route. To leave a city, follow the signs that say *all directions*. (see the appendix for more details).

Be cautious around trams and never overpass them when they are stopped. Pedestrians have the right of way in crosswalks, as do cyclists in bike lanes. A fixed green arrow on a red traffic light indicates you can turn in that direction after coming to a full stop. In a roundabout you must yield to traffic that is already in it. If two lanes enter a roundabout, you need to stay in the lane you are in and use your blinker to change lanes. Public buses have the right of way and you must obey any signal they give. In many countries headlights are required to be on whenever driving.

It is compulsory to carry driving license, vehicle registration, and evidence of third-party insurance at all times. Persons in both front and back seats must wear seat belts. Maximum level of alcohol in the blood is usually 0.05, and after an accident all drivers must undergo a breath test. A warning triangle must be used when you must pull over because your car isn't operating properly or you have had an accident. They should be placed 50 meters behind the car. Rental cars will have them in the trunk.

Credit cards are accepted at most gas stations, but check first by showing your card. Sometimes the station only accepts within-the-country charge cards.

Traveling Smart and Safe

Although most places are very safe it's important not to be naive. The following tips will keep you safe while traveling in areas where theft is a problem. Most importantly, be aware that distraction is the con artist's tool and that thieves often are friendly and don't look menacing. In some cities where the mafia is powerful, thieves have reached a new level of sophistication. They may even look like tourists-with a camera, map, and sandals. Don't allow yourself to be distracted. Avoid crowds. Keep your camera in a nondescript local bag that you wear with the strap over your head and across your body. Then just casually keep you hand on the strap to cover the bag. Keep your lunch and jacket in an inconspicuous, inexpensive daypack.

When you are in an area known for petty theft, you want to be inconspicuous. You want to look like a local. Walk with purpose. Be serious, quiet, and know what's happening around you. Don't reveal your native language by talking to your companion or reading a book. Use eye contact and hand gestures instead of language. Sit rather than stand in the bus or metro if possible. Don't get on if it is going to be very crowded. Don't give a thief advance notice that you are departing the bus or subway by standing early at the door. You are less vulnerable if you stand against a wall when you look at a map. Talk softly. If someone approaches you, don't speak or respond in any way except to move on. Step into a store if you feel unsafe. Congestion and confusion are a thief's friend, and a thief can be well dressed and approach in a friendly manner.

Always remove your car keys from the ignition or trunk. Keep them with you even if you are getting out of the driver's seat for just a moment. Consult your guidebook and if car theft is a problem you might consider bringing a steering wheel lock from home. In high theft areas, one adult passenger should always stay with the car. Keep the car locked even when passengers are inside. Thieves want the car vacant. They will try to get you out of the car. An old trick is to put plastic bottles in between the tire and fender in hopes that when you start driving the noise will get you out of the car to see what is wrong. Making tires look damaged is another standard trick. If someone tries to distract you, don't get out of the car. Keep the doors locked and the windows rolled up. Act as if they aren't there, and drive away. While driving through a city where car-theft is problem, keep all the doors locked, windows rolled partway up, and valuables out of sight.

Make your car look local. Buy a local paper or magazine and keep it visible. Add a local sports club sticker to the fender. Dangle something from the rearview mirror like other locals do. Keep the backseat kind of junky. *Never* leave anything visible that announces you speak English or that you are a tourist, like books and maps. Look inside local cars to get an idea of what is left visible and copy what you see. Let the car get dirty. Park where there is pedestrian traffic. In an attended parking area, choose a spot that is easily visible by the attendant.

Don't rent or lease an expensive car. A free upgrade is not an advantage in countries where car theft is a problem. If you are planning to drive into Central and Eastern Europe, it's important to tell the car rental office. They will rent you a car that car-theft experts aren't interested in. In cities where car theft is a problem, remove the car registration and ID papers and carry them in your money belt while you away from the car. You probably won't have a collision, but in case you do, lock the car when you get out and put your keys away before you approach the other party. Never sign anything that hasn't been translated to English. Sign only if the information is acceptable. Make sure the other party prints information legibly. Report the accident immediately to your rental or lease company. Emergency road phones, with directions for use, are common on major highways throughout Europe.

Wear a money-belt that you tuck into your clothes or wear around your neck. Your passport, credit cards, cash card, currency, traveler's checks, car vehicle numbers, and airline ticket should be kept here. Your companion should have a different ATM card and charge card in case one is lost and must be cancelled. Put your money in your money-belt before you leave a cash machine or bank. Keep enough currency handy so that you don't have to get into your money-belt in public. Leave expensive rings, watches, and jewelry at home.

Though campgrounds are very safe and filled with families and couples relaxing and having fun, for ease of mind lock valuable camping equipment in the car before leaving for the day.

Using Public Transportation

Ask how to board and validate your ticket. Board buses where the validation box is located, usually at the rear. Metro and train validation boxes should be obvious, if not stand aside and watch others. If you don't see locals validating their ticket, it is probably because they have a monthly or weekly ticket. Inspectors, in plainclothes, check tickets for validation. They get part of the violation fee and consider tourists easy prey. You must pay for a violation on the spot.

Ask a fellow camper for details about the bus or metro stop. Have them write down the name of the place you want to get off and the name of the stop for returning to the campground. Be sure this is in large, bold letters so a fellow passenger, who might not have their glasses, can easily read it. Show the name of the stop you want to a fellow passenger. They will help you. For safety reasons, bus drivers don't want to be distracted by reading.

If you aren't used to taking a metro or subway, there are a few things you need to know. Metro "lines" or routes are named, numbered, or color-coded. A train doesn't deviate from this route. The direction the train is going to be its last station. A large map of the entire metro system is posted in the station. Plan your route. Transfer stations have good directional signs to the other lines. Inside the train, the route is posted over a door. When you are on a train, watch for the names of the stations as you pass them and check these with the posted route. If you're going in the wrong direction, just get out at the next station and follow directional signs to trains going in the right direction.

Taking Your Bike

I take my bicycle to Europe wherever possible. Europeans are avid pedalers, so dedicated cycle paths and locking bike racks are common. I enjoy pedaling around historic areas, down grand boulevards, into small neighborhoods, and along country roads. The fresh air and exercise are invigorating. Whenever I have a whim for a ride, my bike is there.

Most, but not all, major airlines sell cardboard "bike boxes" for just a few dollars. They are purchased at the ticket counter, and you must be ticketed with that airline to buy one. Because I don't have a place to store the box while I'm traveling, I discard it after use and buy a new one when I am departing for my return trip home.

Take your bicycles to the airport on the same bike rack you'll use on the trip. Allow yourself plenty of time to pack them. I bring foam sheeting, extra cardboard, and plastic-covered wire to cover the gear and sprocket areas. I pre-measure these and cut them at home, save them for the return, and reuse on other trips. I also bring two rolls of duct tape and scissors.

Find a quiet area, close to the oversize luggage area check-in, to pack your bikes. Take the pedals off, loosen the handlebars, and deflate the tires. Protect the socket and gear areas with foam and cardboard. Attach helmets, bike locks, the bike rack, a tool kit, and extra small duffles of miscellaneous items to the bicycles. Slide the bicycles into their boxes. Secure the boxes with lots of duct tape, reinforcing the handling holes so the cardboard doesn't rip. If you need to get to another level, ask to use the freight elevator if the regular passenger elevator is too small.

When you make your airline reservation, check with the agent about the cost of bicycle transport and the availability of boxes. Check again several days before leaving. Upon arrival in Europe, check with the airline you'll go home on about box availability for your return. When none are available, airline personnel can usually get one from another airline. Airlines no longer let you claim the bike as part of your allowable luggage.

Schedule for Preparation and Packing

I like to get ready for a trip in a relaxed manner. Here's how I do it:

4 months before departure: I purchase airline tickets and arrange for seat assignment. I examine the tickets carefully to make sure they are correct. I mark my calendar with departure time, return times, and flight numbers. I check the expiration date on my passport because custom officials want it to be valid for 6 months beyond my return-home date. I make sure the magnetic strips on my credit cards aren't overused and order new cards if needed. I check to see that my driver's license will be valid during my trip. I obtain an international camping card for the reasons, and from the source, listed in the appendix. I arrange for rental car and insurance.

3 months before departure: I purchase maps and guidebooks. Using the suggested reading sections of the guidebooks, I check out books from the library and start researching so that what I am seeing and experiencing while I travel means more. I start studying the local language.

2 months before departure:I check my camping equipment, duffels, camera, and carry-on bag so I can leisurely purchase or borrow things I will need. I decide what clothing and personal items I will take. I make the foam padding for the parts of the bicycle that will need protection during transport. I photocopy all tickets, car rental confirmations, insurance confirmations, passports, addresses and phone numbers for family and friends, and service numbers for credit cards, cash card, and insurance. I keep one set for myself and give one set to someone I can call in an emergency. I add to *their* copy, not mine, credit card, cash card, and pin-numbers.

1 month before departure: I pack. I leave notes on duffels, carry-on, purse, and money-belt to remind me to include things I am still using or need to purchase. I reconfirm my rides to the airport and pickup on return.

2 weeks before departure: Everything I am going to take is packed and placed in one location. Reminders about including drivers license, credit cards, cash card, airline tickets, passports, and money are attached to carry-ons. I am ready to go. My mind is free to concentrate on arrangements for work and home while I am gone.

Preparing for Your Trip
Buying Your Airline Ticket
Go to several airfare on-line booking sites and compare results. Contact travel agencies specializing in budget travel. Consider reputation for reliability and restrictions.

Sites on the Web
The largest and most reliable companies, listed alphabetically:

Expedia www.expedia.com Orbitz www.orbitz.com Travelocity www.travelocity.com

Reliable, but tickets are more restricted. The fares have been discounted for reasons listed below in agencies specializing in budget travel:

Cheap Tickets wwwcheaptickets.com Council Travel www.counciltravel.com Last Minute Travel www.lastminutetravel.com Low Airfare www.lowairfare.com STA Travel www.statravel.com

Major Airlines that post web-only bargains. Look for their link "special savings", etc:

Alaska Airline www.alaskaair.com American Airlines www.aa.com Delta Air Lines www.delta.com Northwest Airlines www.nwa.com United Airlines www.ual.com US Air www.usairways.com

Others:
Air Treks www.airtreks.com Easy Jet www.easyjet.com Europe By Air www.europebyair.com Go Fly www.go-fly.com Global Fare www.globalfare.com Iceland Air www.icelandair.com Ryan Air www.ryanair.com Travel Select www.travelselect.com Virgin Blue www.virginblue.com.au

Budget travel agencies that you can call and talk to an agent:

- STA Travel (student/young travelers) 800-777-0112; www.sta-travel.com Specializing in world-wide travel, this agency's tickets are very flexible. Making a change in plans or arranging for "open jaw" (flying in and out of different airports) travel is easy and penalty free.

- Council Travel (for the general public) 800-2-Council; www.counciltravel.com Founded in 1947, this non-profit agency is dedicated to international exchange programs. Popular with students, they work with the general public as well.

- Consolidator/Bucket Shop Tickets

Consolidators, or "bucket shops" are wholesalers. They buy a large number of tickets from regularly scheduled airlines and then sell them at a lower price than the airline. If you decide at the last minute to take a trip, this could work well for you. Ask if your ticket can be exchanged for a ticket on another airline, because if there is a problem with the flight you might need to take another carrier. Usually these tickets have unusual schedules with multiple stops, which is why the airline has made them available to the consolidator. The seat selection won't be as good as at full fare, but all other amenities are the same. To find a consolidator, check the travel section of your Sunday newspaper.

Charter Flights

Charters flights follow the high-season traffic. They usually fly full, often with tighter seating and fewer amenities than on a commercial carrier. Their ticket has no value with another airline or even with the airline it has contracted with. It has value only with the charter company. If seats are still available close to departure, the company might discount the ticket even further to assure that the flight goes out full. Stand-by tickets are also available. To find charter flights check the travel section of your Sunday newspaper.

Apex Tickets (Advanced Purchase Excursion Fare)

Offered by regularly scheduled airlines, these are considerably cheaper than the full economy fare. You can reserve and select your seat in advance and then pay just 21 days in advance of departure. You must travel as ticketed to avoid extra charges. The advantage of these tickets is that they will be honored by another airline if your airline has unforeseen problems, and you can travel in the high season without the inconveniences of a charter or consolidator ticket. Seating choices and amenities are the same as if you paid full fare. Departure and arrival times are good, and flights are often nonstop. Ticketing on line or with an agent indicate you are interested in traveling as cheaply as possible and that you are flexible on the departure and return dates. It is cheaper to fly mid-week or on the weekend. Highest prices occur at the beginning and end of the week, when business travel is at its peak. After you are quoted a price, call a budget travel agent and see how the price compares. They will know about current consolidator and charter flight offers.

Open Jaw Tickets

These tickets allow you to start your trip in one place and end it in another. They cost more but can be worthwhile if you don't want to make a loop in your route to return to where you started. Note that your car rental will also usually incur additional costs if you don't return it where you picked it up, particularly if you want to return it in a different country.

Other Important Details

Always use your charge card for payment. This protects you if there is a dispute. *Never* pay with cash or check. Ask how many stops your flight makes before it reaches your destination. Each time it stops, there is a chance for delay. The most desirable flight goes nonstop to your destination. Request your seat assignment for both legs of your journey when you are making the reservation. Reconfirm the reservation and seat number by asking for a faxed or e-mailed confirmation. Carefully examine this immediately. Mistakes are made. Unless you catch a mistake immediately, you might be charged a re-ticketing fee. It is your responsibility to make this final check. Understand that you can "lose" a day going to Europe and can "gain" one on the return, because you'll be traveling through time zones. Mark your calendar and reconfirm the flight at least 72 hours before departure.

Getting Your Documents

Apply several months in advance for the documents you will need: passport, visa, senior citizen card, international camping card, international, and student, teacher, or youth identification cards (see appendix). Check the expiration date on your driver's license because you need it to valid beyond your trip. If the magnetic strips on your cash cards and charge cards are worn, get new ones.

Getting Vehicle Rental/Lease Information

Renting or leasing your car from home is much cheaper than making arrangements in Europe. For safety, it's best to have a separate and lockable trunk, not a hatch-back or 3-door. However, I've traveled with a 3-door without a problem. Make a list of questions to ask each company and keep track of the answers. If you are booking a vehicle for 3 weeks or more, you'll probably qualify for a cheaper lease program. They will need to know where you are picking up and dropping off the vehicle. If you do this at the same airport, the rate is usually less. Make sure the VAT (value added tax) is included in their quote. Inform them you'll be getting CDW insurance from another company.

Ask:

- Does the country where you are picking up the car have a highway tax? Is it included in the cost?

- Is unlimited mileage included?

- Is third-party (damage to the other car and persons) insurance included?

- What is the minimum and maximum age limit for drivers?

- What is the cost for an additional driver?

If you want a particular car, be clear that you don't want a substitute and have it noted on the agreement. When the transaction is completed, ask for a fax of the agreement and check it carefully. You'll want any mistakes corrected so the right car is waiting for you. If you plan to rent a RV or caravan, check to see if bike racks and a table with chairs can be rented. Some RV companies carry these, but you need to reserve ahead. Ask them to fax or e-mail a confirmation along with a map to their pick-up area, which is usually in a suburb.

Arranging Insurance

CDW (collision damage waver) insurance is compulsory in most countries. This covers you for loss of or damage to the car you rent. Purchasing the car rental company's CDW insurance is not advisable. If you rent a car and purchase insurance from the same company, making a claim becomes a conflict of interest. Other sources are cheaper (see appendix). Keep your car rental voucher and CDW insurance verification together with your hand-held luggage so they are easily accessible when you pick up your car. Have the rental company mark your vehicle papers to show that you have "green card" insurance. Theft insurance for your personal belongings is a good idea. You might be covered by a home insurance policy.

Purchasing Maps and Guidebooks

It's fun to look at maps before a trip. Visit your local or online bookstore or map source. Maps and atlases with a scale of 1/400 000-1 cm: 4 km will show the detail you need to find camping places. Check to see if the major cities you'll be driving into are expanded on the maps you have. If they are not detailed enough, you should buy an additional map. Check the publication date to confirm the map is current. High quality detailed maps are a good investment. They make it easy to plan routes and find campgrounds and they save time, gas money, and frustration.

A good guidebook is essential. To select one suited to your interests, read about the same city and a particular sight in several guidebooks, then decide which approach you like best.

The bookstore at your arrival airport will usually have a good selection maps and guidebooks if you haven't bought ahead. I always like to visit it before I leave the airport.

Learning About the Country and Its Language

Use your library. Your trip will be more rewarding if you spend time getting to know the important historical events and important artistic persons of the countries you will be visiting.

Learning some words of the local language will help you have more fun. There is a remarkable difference in the response from locals when I approach them using their language, even if it is just a few words. They appreciate my effort and exert more energy in helping me. Several months ahead of a trip, I purchase language tapes that include a phrase book. I play them in the car and use a headset to listen while I do housework, cook, and garden. At first, I just listen and repeat back, even if I don't know what I am saying. Then I start attaching meaning to the words. Finally, I write down little quizzes for myself. Even though learning another language can be difficult, I keep reminding myself that I will have more fun if I learn some basic phrases. Finally I make a list of commonly used words and phrases that I can keep handy in my pocket. I waterproof the card with plastic tape. Before approaching locals I scan the card and practice. It works great!

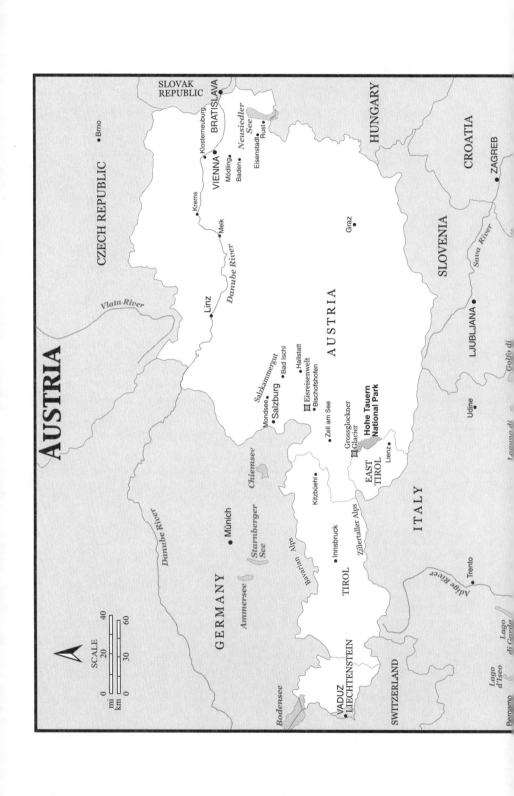

AUSTRIA

SCALE

mi: 0 20 40

km: 0 30 60

GERMANY

CZECH REPUBLIC

SLOVAK REPUBLIC

HUNGARY

CROATIA

SLOVENIA

ITALY

SWITZERLAND

LIECHTENSTEIN

AUSTRIA

TIROL

EAST TIROL

- Brno
- BRATISLAVA
- Klosterneuburg
- VIENNA
- Mödling
- Baden
- Eisenstadt
- Rust
- Krems
- Melk
- Linz
- Graz
- ZAGREB
- LJUBLJANA
- Udine
- Trento
- Munich
- Mondsee
- Salzburg
- Bad Ischl
- Hallstatt
- Eisreisenwelt
- Bischofshofen
- Zell am See
- Grossglockner Glacier
- Lienz
- Kitzbüehl
- Innsbruck
- VADUZ

Neusiedler See

Danube River

Vlata River

Chiemsee

Starnberger See

Ammersee

Bavarian Alps

Zillertaller Alps

Salzkammergut

Bodensee

Sava River

Adige River

Lago d'Iseo

Lago di Garda

Golfo di

Laguna di

Bergamo

Hohe Tauern National Park

AUSTRIA

www.austria-tourism.com

At the turn of the 19th century, when the Hapsburg empire was dying, Austria, and Vienna in particular, witnessed an outburst of creativity so rare in a moment of history that one is reminded of the Italian Renaissance or ancient Greece. It set an amazing pattern and pace in literature and music, in arts and architecture, in science and politics, in cinema and design, and became an extraordinary center of creative activity.

Sustained by trade and navigable Danube River, the Romans claimed the land that is now Austria from the Celts and held power here until the end of the 4th-century. After a series of barbarian invasions, the authoritarian Hapsburg dynasty clung to power for 640 years, from 1278 to 1918. They extended their rule throughout present day Austria, Hungary, Slovenia, Croatia, and the Czech and Slovak republics finally dying under the tensions of nationalism and World War I. Much remains today from this imperial dynasty.

The country remains a mecca for musicians, hosting world-renown music concerts ranging from classical to jazz. Its atmosphere drew the likes of Mozart, Haydn, Beethoven, Schubert, Brahms, Mahler, Schoenberg, and Bruckner. At the turn of the 19th century, Austrians Klimt, Schiele, and Kokoschka were Europe's most powerful painters of sensitivity and anguish. Loos influenced the path of modern architecture. Stroheim and Lang pioneered the transformation of cinema into art and Freud transformed a way of thinking. Austrians have long had almost an obsession with culture. Their heroes are actors, artists, and composers-not politicians. These artists and intellectuals don't work in isolation but know each other. They keep abreast of world affairs and exchange ideas in the coffeehouses, just as they did at the turn of the century.

Austrians love drama, theatre, music, and a good time. The country is staggeringly beautiful, and Austrians get outside and enjoy it. Walking and cycling trails web magnificent mountainsides, flower-filled meadows, and picturesque villages that hug grand river banks. Yet sophisticated cities, in love with the best of the European music and Baroque architecture, are always nearby.

Adoring the outdoors, the Austrians are avid campers. From among the country's hundreds of campgrounds, I've selected those that are scenic and not resort-like. Well-maintained campgrounds with warm showers are de rigeur. Most have covered common areas and children's playgrounds that are great places to chat with locals on vacation and to share stories and information with fellow international travelers. Austrians love their country and will happily help you enjoy it too. Campgrounds are moderately priced considering their excellent maintenance and scenic locations. Camping for two persons, a car, and a tent is around 20 euros per night in the listed campgrounds noted here as $$. Excellent campgrounds close to major tourist areas or resort-like campgrounds will charge around 25 euros noted here as $$$. Plan to arrive by 11 AM or after 2 PM. During lunch and afternoon rest time, the office is closed. Stores in small towns and villages also observe these hours.

Driving is a pleasure through such fabulous scenery. Take your time; follow whims down side roads. Good signposting and excellent roadways makes the country driver-friendly, so it's no suprise Austria has a highway tax for all motorists. Car-rental companies within the country automatically include the tax payment. If you arrive in Austria from another country, purchase the tax-stamp at a gas station when you cross the border. Post your stamp immediately on the windshield. The tax is based on the length of your stay and is under 20 euros for a week. Expect additional tolls or *mauts* for long tunnels or special Alpine roadways. Blue parking zones indicate limited-time parking. Look carefully for the ticket dispenser. If the parking is free but timed, use the rental car's clock disc in your glove compartment to show the time you left. Buses have priority on mountain roads, as do cars coming downhill. Circular blue signs with a cross and red border mean no stopping. A diagonal slash means a stop is permitted for the length indicated in the sign. Parking and road tax stamps are closely regulated, and stiff fines are added to your car rental bill if you don't pay on the spot. Austrian police accept credit cards for payment.

Cycling is a popular sport. Pedaling along backroads through the magnificent scenery and through charming historic villages and towns is a wonderful way to have a closer touch with the people and the countryside. Bringing your own bike and a bike rack is recommended, however many town train stations rent bikes and so do campgrounds. One of Europe's most popular bike routes follows the Danube River from Passau Germany to Vienna, then on to Bratslavia, Slovakia. Called the Donauradweg, it is almost free of motorized traffic and practically flat. Campgrounds line the route, as do bike rental companies. Bicycles can be carried on the U-bahns for half fare. The campgrounds also have information on rentals and routes. For a maps and bike rental companies go to **www.danube.com**.

VIENNA

The showy elegance of the Viennese waltz, with it's curving and evasive movements, makes a perfect match for Vienna and its love of a carefree life. The music still pulls on the heart, filling the mind with romantic imaginings and longings. Rich endowments and patronage have long allowed Vienna's support of the major proponents of classical music. In such an atmosphere, Haydn, Mozart, and Beethoven were able to achieve musical perfection, as did Schubert, Strauss, Bruckner, and Mahler. It was, and still is, a world-renowned center for music. To stand in a narrow street, and whisper reverently, "That's where Mozart lived when he wrote *The Marriage of Figaro*" or "That's where Beethovan wrote *Fidelio*", is magical. But Vienna's streets are not just a quaint setting for tourists or a walk through time. They are the setting for a way of life.

With a flair for harmony and design, the city's architecture is like a melody from a heritage of diverse cultures and races. Tiny streets, some almost alleyways, are lined with red, steeply pitched roofs and charming wrought-iron signs announce sidewalk cafes. Roses wind around street lamps, pigeons swoop down for food, music drifts out through upper-story windows, and the air is laden with sweet aromas of pastries. Purchasing the Vienna Card-with transportation and museum discounts-at the campground makes sense if you are spending a few days. The inner city streets that are pedestrian zoned are paved in attractive fan-shaped cobblestone. The city promotes cycling with extensive bike-only paths. You can rent a bike at one train station and leave it off at another.

The Ringstrasse, Vienna's circular grand boulevard shaded by leafy chestnut trees, is a hallmark of Viennese culture. Architects were given free reign to historic interpretation and worked like stage designers sparing no cost. Inside the grandiose buildings, walls and ceilings are covered with giant paintings of Greek mythology. Statues, in complex poses, accent grand stairways. It's a colossal festive pomp of exuberant colors and shapes designed to give the city a pedigree. Trams 1 and 2 both circle the Ringstrasse.

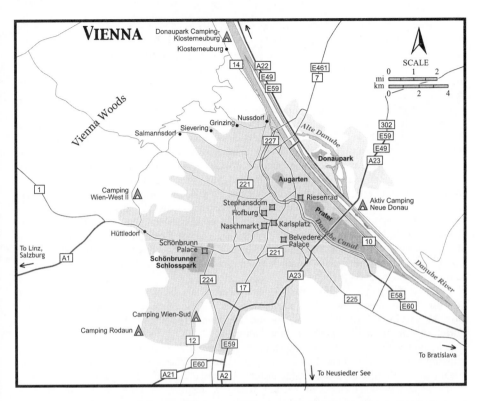

Start your exploration at the Stephansdom. This cathedral, with its vast multicolored roof and ornate towers, is the heart of the city. Elaborately carved pillars guard the impressive net and star-ribbed vaulting of the nave. Begin your exploration with a climb or elevator ride to the tower's observation areas for panoramic views of the Danube canal, the Belvedere, the Vienna Woods, and the Imperial Palace; open daily. Directions: U-bahn 1 or 3 to Stephansplatz.

Walk over to the Figaro House, just east of Stephansplatz at Domgasse 5, and climb the stairs as Mozart did when this was his residence for over two years. To stand in the room where he lived with his lively family and composed the opera *The Marriage of Figaro* and the *Hayden Quartets* is exhilarating and eerie at the same time; closed Monday.

Living long in close contact with the imperial family, the Viennese developed a love of ceremony and intrigue. Every emperor tinkered with the Imperial Palace, the Hofburg, making it a city within a city. After viewing the staggering treasures of gold, silver, and jewels in the Schatzkammer, or treasury, you will understand the power of it's royal occupants; closed Tuesday. Up the stairs above the entrance to the Schatzkammer, is the Bugkapelle, where on Sunday mornings the renowned Vienna Boys' Choir sings. Purchase tickets months ahead by e-mail: Hofmusikkapelle@asn-wien. ac.at, or fax: 431 533 99 2775. The Chapel of the Imperial Palace box-office sells last-minute tickets on Friday for the next Sunday's Mass.

Then wander over to the Royal Stables, or Stallburg. This lovely Renaissance building was converted to stable the royal stud during the hey-day of haute-ecole horsemanship. The parentage of the famous snow-white Lipizzaner horses stems from the Moorish occupation of Spain, and their beauty is a blend of unusual physical strength and graceful lightness. Saved from war, sickness, and fire, the Lippizzaner horses have a special place in the Austrian heart. You can look into the stables through sound-proof observation window in the Lipizzaner Museum in the Stallburg; open daily.

To purchase tickets for that day's morning training session at 10 AM go to the entrance of the Spanish Riding School on Josefsplatz. Tickets aren't sold ahead. To get tickets to either a performance or rehearsal of their unforgettable equestrian ballet performed in a chandelier-lit Baroque hall, that is as white as the steeds themselves, requires ticketing months ahead. Contact the ticket office by e-mail: office@srs.at, or by fax: 431 535 0186.   Directions: U-bahn 3 to Herrengasse, then walk south on Herrengasse to Michaelerplatz.

The amazing collection in the Kunsthistorisches Museum is on par with the Louvre or the Hermitage. It is home to works by Vermeer to Raphael to Velaquez, with unrivaled collections of Rubens and Bruegel the Elder. The structure itself is a work of art. Each room is lavishly decorated with ceiling cherubs, fanciful flora, and mythic beasts. Don't miss the Egyptian halls where ancient treasures are surrounded by hieroglyphed walls; closed Mondays. Directions: On Maria-Theresien-Platz. Trams 1 or 2 or U-bahn 2 to Mariahilfer Str. The Museu fur Angewandte Kunst (MAK), or applied arts, has some terrific exhibits in glass and furniture that speak of the gay, lighthearted spirit that characterized the end of the century as well as a stunning and provacative freize by Klimt; closed Monday. Directions: Trams 1 or 2 or U-bahn 3 to Stubentor.

Reflecting the city's love of glorified burials, the crypt of Kapuzinerkirche houses over 140 Hapsburgs in haunting, now blackened, sarcophagi. The figures, raised on their elbows and gazing out at their companions, bristle with extravagance; open daily. Directions: Walk south Karntinerstrasse from Stepansplatz.

The Neue Hofburg houses four very impressive museums: the National Library, the Collection of Musical Instruments, the Collection of Weapons, and the Ethnographical; all closed Tuesday. Don't miss seeing at least one or two. Directions: U-bahn 2 to Museumplatz, or take trams 1 or 2 to Heldenplatz and walk 100 meters to the southwest.

In keeping with its historic role as apex for European music, Vienna's interactive and high tech museum, the House of Music, puts a new spin on an old theme by inviting visitors to personally interact with music. Housed in the historic Archduke Charles' Palace, your musical journey through the museum includes an exciting tribute to historic composers and conductors, an experience with the tones and sounds that create music, a chance to pick up a baton and direct an orchestra, and finally a chance to create new music yourself; open daily, including evenings. Directions: U-bahn 1 to Oper, then trams 1 or 2 to Schwarzenbergplatz. Then walk or take trams D or 71 north 3 blocks to the end of Schwarzenberstrasse.

Visitors to the Albertina, which houses one of the greatest graphic art collections in the world, are treated to an intimate contact with Michelango, Raphael, Rembrandt, and Durer, that doesn't come when you see the final work. It's a thrill to stand so close to drawings on paper the artist handled as he made studies for larger works. Directions: On the southeast corner of the Hofburg.

Revolting against the Baroque splendors of Imperial Vienna, the new age thinkers of the early 1900s shocked Vienna by stripping away nonessential ornaments to expose only proportion. Stop in front of the Michaeler Platz entrance to the Hofburg, and turn to look across at the Loos House. Nicknamed the building without eyebrows, the four huge slabs of marble stand like modern versions of Greek columns. Unwilling to compromise, the young thinkers caused a great stir in the city and coffeehouses, the fulcrum from which the Viennese operated, buzzed with heated arguments.

At Karlsplatz, take time to admire the old station buildings designed by Otto Wagner. Their curving lines and rosette patterns on the iron railings, the green copper roofing, and the gold trim all represent the elegance of the turn-of-the-century Jugendstil art movement. Turn to view the twin marble columns and green copper dome of Karlskirche, a monument of imperial greatness. Walk over to see the magnificent fresco spread inside its soaring cupola. Directions: U-bahn 1, 2 or 4 to Karlsptatz

Devoid of unnecessary frills both inside and out, the turn-of-the-century Secessionist Building and the art that it houses was an affront to the Viennese sensibilities at the turn of the century. An open filigree bronze ball of laurel leaves and berries graces the top of this geometric building. A famous freize by Klimt, honoring Beethoven's *Ninth Symphony*, is downstairs; closed Monday. Directions: On the west side of Karlsplatz. Vienna and its environs are filled with delightful art nouveau treats. Buffs can get a special brochure from the tourist office and seek out its finest addresses.

The world's largest collection of works by a master of psychological penetration and frank sensuality, Egon Schiele, is housed in the Leopold Museum, part of the new Museumsquartier. Rounded out by other works of sensitivity and anguish by Klimt, Kokoschka, Loos, and Otto Wagner, it's an exciting place; closed Monday. Understanding modern art becomes easier after you visit the Museum Moderner Kunst's collection, which is curated in movements of expressionism, cubism, photo-realism, and Viennese actionism; closed Monday. Directions: U-bahn 2 Museumquartier.

Reminiscent of the old Halles Market in Paris, the huge outdoor Naschmarkt is feisty and humorous. Perfuming the air, the wurst and pastry stalls are plentiful and not indulging would be sinful; closed Saturday afternoons and all day Sunday. The adjoining Flohmarkt, or flea market, is a memorabilia bridge from past to present. Here a new generation finds meaning and continuity with the older generations; Saturday is best. Directions: U-bahn 4 to Kettenbruckengasse. Taking a ride on Vienna's famous giant ferris wheel, the Riesenrand, in the Prater, a large parkland, is an integral part of seeing Vienna for me. The ride itself is slow, providing a chance to view the city from a unique angle. Directions: U-bahn Praterstern.

Austrian Baroque is triumphant in the magnificent stairway, grandiose halls, and gilded and painted ceilings of the Hildebrandt-designed Belvedere Palace. Built on a slope in the southeast corner of the city in the early 1700s, it was the summer palace for Prince Eugene, the military hero in the wars with the Turks. Graceful gardens flow down the slope joining the former residence with the reception hall. The stunning gilded masterpiece *The Kiss* by Klimt, is housed in the Oberes Belvdere along with other exciting works by Schiele, Kokoschka, and Makart; closed Monday. The lower palace houses an extensive collection of sculptural works; closed Monday. Directions: U-bahn to Karlsplatz, then Tram D to Schloss Belvedere.

Not to be outdone by the glamour of Louis IVX's Versailles, the Habsburgs built Schonbrunn Palace. The views of Vienna from the colonnaded pavilion, Gloriette, are superb. The park is an exuberance of theatrical Baroque art, with elaborate fountains, symmetrical gardens, statuary, and reproductions of Greek ruins. The opulent gilded interior includes the Millionenzimmer decorated in priceless Indian and Persian miniatures, a grand ballroom, the piano and room where six-year-old Mozart played, and a dining table mechanically drawn up through the floor. This is a popular tourist destination. Purchase tickets for the interior, then enjoy the gardens until your tour time; open daily. Directions: U-4 to Schloss Schonbrunn. It's on the southwest edge of the city and well signposted off A1.

Vineyards embroider the hillsides of northwestern Vienna, and it's a Viennese custom to enjoy time off in their congenial heurigen, or wine gardens. A pine tuft hung from the end of a pole jutting out from one indicates that the young wine is being served. The wine gardens also offer tasty picnic fare. A paved walking path from Nussdorf to Grinzing traces a favorite walk of Beethoven's. It follows a creek passing through a tiny park named after him, then meanders through vineyards to Grinzing where it's fun to stop and join others toasting the new wine at one of the numerous outdoor wine gardens. Park in Nussdorf at the train station close to the Danube. Walk west on Zahnradbahnstrasse to the path marked Stadt Wanderweg 1 and follow the trail along the creek. There is good signposting along the route. Afterwards, take the bus back to Nussdorf and your car. Directions: Drive northwest of the city on 14 in the direction of Klosterneuberg to Nussdorf, which is just south of Klosterneuberg. If you prefer to drive, there is good signposting from here for scenic little roads that wind through the woods and villages.

Vienna's festivals are legendary. Throughout the summer there is a wide range of vibrant concerts, exhibitions, and theater-many avant garde. The Vienna Festival Weeks of mid-May through mid-June are particularly extravagant. Visit **www.austria-tourism.at** or contact the National Austrian Tourist Office for a calendar of events and information on advance ticket purchases for the most notable performances. However, in this musical city tickets for lesser-known performances are available for that night's performance and attending one doesn't have to be costly.

▲**Camping:** • Northwest of the city, close to the Danube, in Klosterneuburg off 14. Drive east of Klosterneuburg to the train station. Turn east, following signposting under the train tracks and across the small bridge to the campground. Donaupark-Camping Klosterneuburg (022 432 5877); large, in a recreational area with large swimming pool and tennis courts; a doable but lengthy ride by bike along the Danube to the historic area; closeby public transport to the historic center; especially nice café, internet access, and children's playground; all the amenities; open all year; $$$. • Closest to the city. On the east side of the Danube, close to the intersection of A22 and A23 exit Olhafen Lobau. Aktiv-Camping Neue Donau (01 202 4010); large; traffic noise; little shade; public transport close by; all amenities; open mid-May-Sept; $$$. • West of the city in the suburb of Hutteldorf. On A1 follow signs to centrum and then Hilleldorf. Turn left on Huttelburg Str., and continue to the campgrounds. Camping Wien-West II (01-914-2314); large, cabins; all amenities; public transport close by; open all year; $$$. • Close to southern end of the Vienna Woods. Eight kilometers southwest of the city, exit A2/E59 for Atmannsdorf. Or from A21/E60 take exit 36. Camping Wein-Sud (01 867 3649); close to the Schlosspark; traffic noise; open May-Sept; $$. • In the same area. Exit off A2/E59 for Rodaun. Camping Rodaun (01 888 4154); smaller; traffic noise; open Apr-Oct; $$.

Danube Valley

For as far as you can see, vineyards blanket the steep and rocky terraced hillsides in Austria's most famous wine-producing region. The fruity aromas of grapes, peaches, and apricots produce a heavy elixir in the air. The region's ancient towns date to Roman times, following the Danube and crowning their hillsides with castles, monasteries, and fortresses. The attractive squares, narrow cobblestone streets, and 15th-century buildings are charming. Friendly cafes are filled with flowers and wine tasters. The route follows the Danube between Krems and Melk. One of the most romantic towns is Durnstein, the ruins of a castle, in which Richard the Lionheart was imprisoned, crowns her terraced hillside and are in remarkable condition. At the south end of the route, the vast and famous Benedictine abbey of Melk sweeps majestically up from the Danube. Its sandy colored walls, red-tile roof, and twin church towers punctuate the skyline. Heavily Baroque and staggeringly beautiful, the sunlight pours over an enormous riot of gold. The monastery has a rich and colorful history so, although you can wander around on your own, the tour

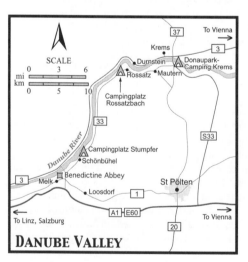

DANUBE VALLEY

is fascinating. Directions: Krems is 83km west of Vienna on highway 3. From Krems to Melk there are picturesque small roads on both sides of the Danube. And best of all there is a terrific cycle/walking route along the river through valley's length that is almost flat and separate from motorized traffic. Called the Donauradweg, it's part of a longer route from Passau, Germany in the north to Bratislava in the south. It's very popular with cyclists from all over Europe and is a wonderful way to meet fellow travelers. Rentals are readily available in the towns along the route. **www.danube.at** or e-mail:info.donau@oberoesterreich

▲Camping: • In Rossatz, close to Durnstein, at the north end of the route. Campingplatz Rossatzbach (02-714-6317). • In Schonbuhel, at the south end of the route. Camping Stumpfer (02-752-8510). Both are: small; with nice locations on the river; popular with cyclists; open Apr-Oct; $$. • Two kilometers south of Krems on the river. Donaupark-Camping Krems (02732 844 55); in the river park; some traffic noise; open Apr-Oct; $$.

Neusiedler See

Salt marshes and reed beds characterize the spring-fed lake of Neusiedler See, making it an important bird-watching area. Searching for frogs, tadpoles, and fish, great white herons and egrets quietly forage alone, occasionally taking flight on long, broad, slowly flapping wings. Tranquil ducks dabble and dive, then explode suddenly in the air with a burst of flapping cacophony. Swans float regally followed by a line of their charming youngsters. Storks nest on rooftops in the village of Rust, where birders often spot collared flycatchers in the nearby woods. There are only a few places to bird near the shallow water and open sea. These include the north shore by Neusiedl-am-See, the west shore near Oggau, and the east shore between Podersdorf-am-See and Illmitz, where in the steppe farmland snaker falcons are spotted. Expert birders will be happy to know that the vast reedbeds support the delightful reeding, the only representative of the parrotbill family in Europe.

Colorful sails of wind surfers dot the lake when the wind picks up. When just a soft wind blows it's a good place for beginners since the lake is shallow. Rentals are available. Cyclists enjoy the cycle path that winds through the reed beds along the lake. Once this region was Hungarian, but now only the southern edge is. A Magyar, or Hungarian, air still hangs prettily in the village squares. The warm water and swimming beaches are perfect places for sunbathing and children's play.

▲Camping: • On the westside of the lake in Rust. Off A3 or A4 exit for Eisenstadt, then exit east onto 52 and drive 15km to Rust. Camping Rust (026-85-595); nice setting on the lake; popular with families; open May-Sept; $$. • In Oggau, 4km north of Rust. Camping Oggau (026-85-7271); large; popular with families; open May-September; $$. • On the east side of the lake in Podersdorf. Exit A4 or 50 onto 51 at the north end of the lake, and drive 20km south to Podersdorf. Signposted north of town. Camping Podersdorf am See (021-77-2279); nice location on the lake; resort-like; thermal swimming pool; open May-Sept; $$$.

Salzburg

Playful Mozart, whose flowing melodic music is a tapestry of both radiance and drama, is a perfect idiom for this beautiful city that was his birthplace. Soaring upward, like his music, is one of the greatest castle-fortresses in Europe, the Hohensalzburg. Its looming presence is in harmony with the grandeur of the surrounding Alpine landscape. Dramatic, massive, and sober on the outside, it is lavish with ornamentation and pleasing color inside. Start your city exploration from the ramparts of Hohensalzburg with its spectacular views of Alpine peaks, the winding Salzach River, and the lantern-topped cupolas of the Dom. Aristocratic life during the Middle Ages comes alive on the castle tour, which winds through princely state rooms, a lookout tower, and torture chambers; open daily. Directions: Behind Kapitelplatz, walk up tiny Festungsgasse to the cable car, or continue walking up the steep hill on your own. Return is by an elevator built in solid rock, or take a more leisurely walk down enjoying the views.

The massive Dom stands majestically between the city's three main squares. Bright sunlight floods through its monumental barrel-vaulted nave and heavy stucco ornamentation graces its ceiling frescoes, making it a very elegant setting for the opening of the famous Salzburg Festival. Mozart was christened here and later filled it with the passionate tenderness of his music as he played on its great organ. Check the calendar at the doorway and make sure you take in one of the free, almost daily performances by excellent visiting choirs; open daily. How often can you play a game of chess with huge chess pieces? Join the fun at Kapitelplatz, just behind the cathedral. The friendly tourist bureau is conveniently located on the main street, Getreidegasse, so stop by to find out what's happening. In the evening, stand along the Salzach River and enjoy the moonglow, spotlights, and stones glittering in the reflection. A haze of nostalgia will come over you as you are serenaded by a myriad of street musicians and the clip-clop of horses' hooves, all part of the charms in this the ancient UNESCO-listed old town.

Take a break from culture and visit the fun Haus der Natur. Arranged thematically into huge aquariums, terrariums, and simulated habitats, it is a fascinating mix of both existing and lost worlds of creatures from around the world; at Museumsplatz 5; open daily. Later, walk across the bridge to the rose-scented gardens of Mirabellgarten. This lovely rosy-hued palace is also the setting for many musical performances but it also is a sheltered niche for a picnic or snooze.

▲**Camping:** • South of Salzburg in the suburb of Aigen. Exit off A1/E55 at exit 8 for Anif und Glasenbach and follow signposting. Camping Schloss-Aigen (0662-2079); lovely location on a small hill with views of the Alps; adjacent to forest preserve with creek and hiking trails; public transport close by; small; open May-Sept; $$. • Closer to the city, doable by bike to the historic center; public transportation close by. On the n orth side of Salzburg exit E55 at exit 288 for Salzburg-Nord and centrum. Follow campground signposting in the suburb of Stadblick-Rauchenbichl. Camping Panorama Stadblick (0662 45 0652); scenic location; terraced sites; open May-Sept; $$. • In the same area but in the suburb of Nord Sam. Camping Nord-Sam (0662 6604 94); small pool; some traffic noise; open May-Sept; $$.

SALZKAMMERGUT

Looking like gigantic castles with turrets and battlements, the mighty Alps of Salzburger Land cradle gleaming deep-blue lakes that mirror their peaks. Valleys smile openly with lush green meadows joyfully abloom with larkspur and daisies, while shadowy forests are tranquil and secretive. Southeast of Salzburg, the winding roads of the region lead through rich pastoral countryside punctuated with picturesque little towns and villages, through sophisticated spa towns, and through lakeside villages that cling to ledges below towering rocks. Chairlifts and well-trodden walking paths make hiking easier and provide breathtaking views while little mountain cafes provide delectable Austrian treats.

Eisriensenwelt Ice Cave

Experiencing this spectacular show of frozen rivers, eerie shadowy walls, and icicles built over thousands of years is well worth going out of your way for. The cave is forty kilometers south of Salzburg and five kilometers above the village of Werfen. The road is narrow and steep and doable in your own car but many prefer to take the bus from the train station. From the parking area where the bus stops, follow the path to the cable car for a short whisk up the nearly vertical slope to the mouth of the cave. Directions: Drive south of Salzburg 40km on A10 in the direction of Bischofshofen and follow signposting for Werfen.

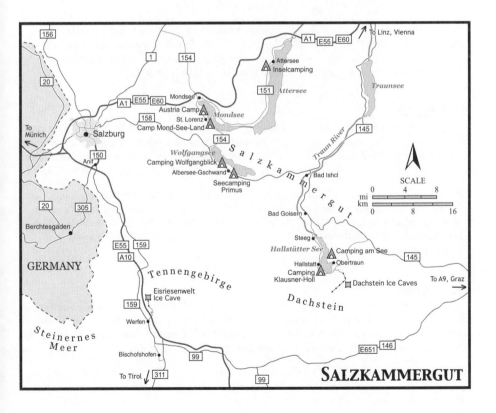

Hallstatt

Clinging prettily to sheer rocky cliffs, Hallstatt has almost a Mediterranean feel. One of the oldest towns in Austria, it has been a center of salt mining in this area since 1000 BC. Excavated amber beads, ivory-inset sword sheaths, and leather shoes prove that a flourishing salt trade took place with the Baltic region. Filled with flowers, this picturesque village is tightly packed with cafes and inns making it a popular daytrip for vacationers. Make your way along the narrow streets and up the ancient steep steps to the church, or Pfarrkirche, overlooking the lake. A miniscule cemetery there is filled with wrought iron crosses and colorful flowers. Because there is little room for cemetery plots, the skulls of loved ones are exhumed and carefully decorated; open daily. Walk farther up the steep steps to reach the ancient salt mine; open daily. (a tram ride is available from the village) A lakeside-walking path running along the east bank, from the Steeg Gosau train station to the resort village of Obertraun, provides spectacular views of the lake. Take the gondola ride from Obertraun to see the famous Dachstein Ice Caves, whose gargantuan curtains of ice in this subterranean world are errie and fun; open daily. Arrive by noon to join an English tour and remember ice means cold; bring a jacket. If you feel like hiking or if it's a clear day, buy tickets on the gondola ride for the third stop, the summit. Here are panoramic views of the incredible mountain scenery plus trailheads down to the valley. Ferries cross the lake, stopping at various villages. Splendid walking paths pass through gorges, alongside thundering waterfalls, and on up to wildflower-splashed hillsides. Purchase a map from the campground. The region is UNESCO listed. Directions: Drive east of Salzburg on 158 for 55km. Exit south at Bad Ischl onto 145, and drive 11km, going just beyond Bad Goisern. Then exit south onto a small road in the direction Hallstatt and drive 9km.

▲**Camping:** • South of the Hallstatt-Tunnels, follow signposting for Lahn. Camping Klausner-Holl ((06 134 8322); small and popular; reserve ahead; open May-Sept; $$$. • West of Obertraun in the village of Winkl. Camping am See (06131 256); beautiful location close to the lake; small and popular; reserve head; open May-Sept; $$$.

Bad Ischl

Once the destination for vacationing Emperor Franz Joseph, today Bad Ischl is a sophisticated mountain resort. Vacationeers enjoy the Biedermeier-style facades, Franz Lehar's home, and Franz Joseph's hunting lodge-Kaiservilla. Good cycle paths follow the Traun River, and the summer calendar is filled with various musical events. Directions: Drive east from Salzburg on 158 for 55km.

▲**Camping:** • 17km west of Bad Ischl exit off 158 at km 32 for Abersee-Gschwand, and drive to the lake. Camping Primusbauer (062 27 3207); lovely location on the lake; open May-Sept; $$$. • In the same area. Seecamping Primus (06227 3228); lovely location; open May-Sept; $$. •A bit farther, at km 34. Camping Wolfgangblick (06227 3475); lovely location; open May-Sept; $$.

Mondsee

The warm lake waters make lessons at the sailing and wind surfing schools in Mondsee enticing. Attersee, the lake just east of Mondsee, enchanted the Secessionist painter Klimt, and Mahler composed some of his greatest symphonic works in the richly evocative countryside. Directions: 30km east of Salzburg exit south off A1 at exit 265 onto 154 for Mondsee.

▲**Camping:** •Exit 154 at km 21.4 and drive to the village of St Lorenz and the lake. Austria Camp (062 32 2927); nice location on the lake; open May-Sept; $$. •In the same area in the village of Tiefgraben. Camp Mond-See-Land (06232 2600); tranquil setting; open Apr-Oct; $$.

The Tirol
In this area featuring the dramatic Alps as a backdrop, wood-fronted houses drip with bright, well-tended, geranium-filled window boxes. Charming chapels sit prettily in flower-flecked meadows, and a network of walking paths allows you to enjoy bird songs and pure Alpine air.

Zillertaller Alps
Cradling lush green valleys, these towering mountain ranges host a wide range of well-known walking trails over wonderful Alpine pastures blanketed in brilliant summer bloom. Lifts to higher elevations via cable cars and chairlifts make the walking easier. In Mayrhofen, pick up the free "Mayrhofen A-Z" brochure for details on paragliding, river rafting, glacier walking, summer skiing, and folk-singing festivals, plus walking-trail maps. Directions: 40km east of Innsbruck exit A12 south onto 169 and drive for 23km. At the fork of 169 and 165 continue on 169, the smaller road, for another 9km.

▲**Camping**: • In Zell am Ziller. Cross the river at the fork of 169 and 165 and follow sign-posting. Camping Hofer (05282 2248); pleasant meadow setting; open all year; $$.

The resorts of Kitzbuhel, Kirchberg, and St. Johann at the eastern end of the Tirol are beautifully manicured and photogenic. Directions: 58km east of Innsbruck exit A12 onto 312, and drive east 34km in the direction of St. Johann. For Kitsbuhel, exit south at St Johann onto 161 and drive 10km farther.

▲**Camping**: • In St. Johann, just over a kilometer south of town on 161 towards Kitzbuhel. Camping Michel'hof (05352 62584); beautiful view of the Alps; open all year; $$$.

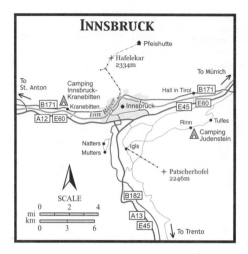

INNSBRUCK

- 14km west of Kitzbuhel on 170 in the village of Westendorf. Panorama-Camping (05334 6166); scenic location; sauna; open all year; $$$. • In the same area, just a bit west, close to the village of Hopfgarten off 170. Camping Reiterhof (05335 3512); nice setting; open all year; $$$.

INNSBRUCK

Set in the narrow east-west valley of the Inn River, with precipitous mountains rising on both sides, Innsbruck is a hiker's paradise. Two base tram stations, one on each side of the river, are close to the center of town, so in minutes you are far above the bustle of the city. Catering to hikers, the city runs free guided hikers for people staying at least 3 days in the area. However, the trails are well marked, and maps and advice from the tourist office close to the train station will arm you with what you need to go on your own. Summer rainfall comes and goes without advance warning so include a waterproof jacket and hat in your daypack. Check the weather prediction before going on a hike above timberline, where conditions can deteriorate rapidly in a storm.

Innsbruck was once a wealthy mountain mining town and later became the home of archdukes, including Maximilian I. Today it is a very likable and fashionable city. Start enjoying the old town by climbing up the Stadtturn, a 14th-century tower, to gaze down on the Baroque facades along the main street, Herzog Friedrich Strasse. Look across at the Goldenes Dachl, the gilded, copper-tiled cap of the famous balcony where Emperor Maximilian once enjoyed singers and dancers performing in the street below; open daily. Directions: Follow signs for Altstadt and parking. If you love maps as I do, check out the Freytag-Berndt und Artaria store two blocks from the Hauptbahnhof, their collection is immense. A visit to Alpenzoo, carefully housing over 150 species of fauna in especially nice natural settings, is a real treat; open daily. Directions: At the north end of town, on the west bank of the Inn River follow signposting on Weiherburgasse or arrive by cable car from the Hungerburgbahn funicular. The Renaissance castle Schloss Ambras and its beautiful grounds are a good place to while away time if the weather isn't good for hiking. Directions: Drive east of the city on A12/E60. It's well signposted just outside the city center.

The exciting, above-timberline hike from Goetheweg to Pfeishutte is a classic ridge hike with extraordinary views. The mostly rocky trail is well maintained but sometimes quite narrow, with parts clinging to the sides of cliffs with almost vertical face (cables are secured in these areas). Although not dangerous for experienced hikers, it is not recommended for those who suffer from vertigo. It also poses serious hazards in bad weather. Park at the Hungerburgbahn funicular railway where you board for the Seegrube station. After enjoying the marvelous view at Seegrube, purchase tickets for the cable car to Hafelekar, where the trailhead to Goetheweg to Pseishutte #219 begins. Unless you are a very experienced hiker, you will not want to hike down the very steep rubble and scree side of the mountain from Pseishutte. Most hikers return the way they came, taking the same cable car down that they came up on.

An easier hike, the Zirbenweg on the Patscherkofel Mountain, starts on the south side of the Inn River. Interpretive nature signs-German and scientific Latin names-describe the flora along the trail through forest and timberline scrub. Named after the arolla pine, the trail meanders through larch and alpenrose with wonderful views of wild and craggy peaks. A part of the trail is on talus slope, and there are various branches to shorten or lengthen your hike. Here and there friendly little cafes make pleasing rest stops for treats and leisurely enjoyment of the mountain ambiance. Directions: Exit A12 south for Igls and follow signposting for Patscherkofelbahn and parking. Purchase tickets to the upper station, Patscherkofel. Using a map, follow signs for Zirbenweg then Rote Wand. Stay on the Zirbenweg for the cable car at Tulfein, unless you'd rather take the very steep and narrow red-white marked trail. When you return to the valley at Tulfes, you can take the bus back to Igls and your car.

▲**Camping**: • 12km east of the city, exit A12/E60 at exit 68 at Hal in Tirol, and drive south on the small road toward Tulfes, pass through the village and continue to Rinn. Camping Judenstein (05223 8620); lovely location in a pristine village; open May-Sept; $$. • Take the Innsbruck-Kranebitten exit off A12/E60 close to the junction with B171. Camping Innsruck-Kranebitten (0512 28 4180); convenient; traffic noise; open all year; $$.

Hohe Tauern National Park

Dazzling capes of ice drape from the rugged shoulders of the enormous Hohe Tauern Mountains even in summer. Thundering falls cascade wildly down through boulder-choked gorges, and crystal-blue waters are clasped in bowls of rock carved out by giant rivers of ice. Trails, from easy to difficult, wind up and down the mountains that face Grossglockner, Austria's highest mountain. Tourist offices in lakeside picture-postcard-beautiful Zell am See and its riverside neighbor Kaprun provide advice, maps, and rentals for hikers, wind surfers, and white-water enthusiasts. Directions: Drive 47km south of Salzburg on A10 in the direction of Bischofshofen. Exit west onto 311 and drive 48km to Zell am See.

Take the gondola up to Kitzsteinhorn and the Alpincenter from Kaprun, for summer skiing and hiking trails. From here you can take a cable car to the top station for breathtaking views of the Grossglockner. If the weather is good, there is a terrific downhill hike from the Alpinecenter called the Alexander Enzinger Weg. From the Alpinecenter follow signposting to the Kreefelder Hut, then Stangenhohe, and finally the Maiskogel cable car that takes you down to the valley floor. Catch a bus back to Kaprun.

▲**Camping**: •Just south of Kaprun. Camping Gasthof zur Muhle (06547 8254); convenient for hiking; open all year; $$. • In Thumersbach. Camping Sudufer (06542 56228); nice location; smaller; open all year; $$. • Just north of Zell am See. Seecamp Zell am See (06542 72115); larger; nice location; open all year; $$.

The famous scenic and expensive toll road, Grossglockner Hochalpenstrasse, begins in valleys where cows graze in lush green meadows, then climbs up steeply, affording eye-popping views of the Grossglockner Glacier. Large viewing/parking areas are often coupled with cafes. The road is broad, the turns are wide and driving in low gear is necessary. The side road Gletscherstrasse, close to the Hochtor tunnel, to Franz-Josef's-Hohe provides the trip's most exciting view of the Grossglockner and the Pasterze glacier. Many sightseers prefer to sit back and relax in the Bundesbus leaving from Zell am See at the north end or Lienz in the south, which also stops at Franz-Josefs-Hohe. At the north end of the road, stop at Wildpark Ferleiten for a closer look at the Alpine animals that inhabit the mountains and at the free Alpine Naturschau Museum, which has a small but interesting exhibit on the ecology, flora and fauna of the region. Directions: Follow highway 107 between Lienz and Zell am See.

Equally famous are the Krimmel Falls, a series of giant falls and cascades dropping 380 meters. Hike up the exciting Wasserfallweg, a twisting four-kilometer trail through the surrounding forest with magnificent vistas and mounting thunder of the falls. Arrange your hike so you are at the top at midday, when the sun is behind the falls, making them extra brilliant and iridescent. Bring a waterproof jacket. Tickets must be purchased for both the trail and parking. Directions: 55km west of Zell am See. Drive west out of Zell am See in the direction of Mittersill for 23km on 168. Continue west for 31km to the Gerlos Pass. There is parking by the trailhead.

▲**Camping**: • On the east side of the Krimmel in Wald im Pinzgau. SNP Camping (06565 84460); small; nice setting; open all year; $$.

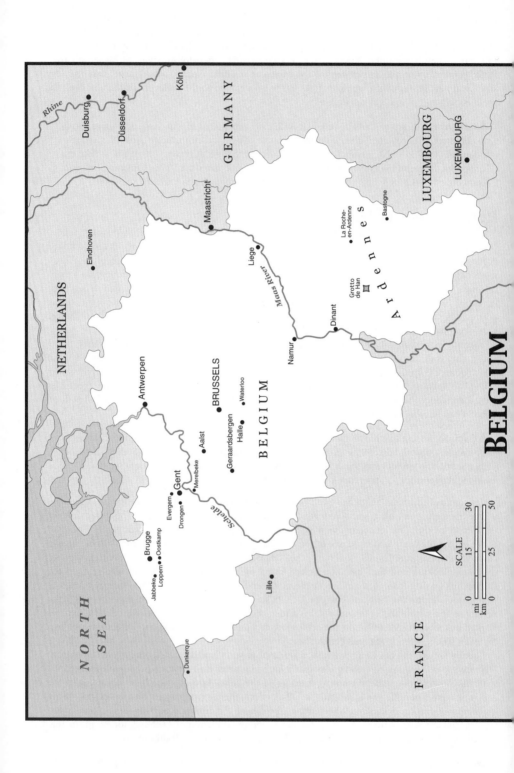

BELGIUM

www.visitbelgium.com

Peals of laughter, raucous music, and wild stomping bursts from Pieter Brueghel's The Wedding Dance. Painted in the 1500's, it still exemplifies the spirit of today's Belgian. In love with carnivals and festivals, the Belgian summer calendar is full of color and music. The belle of the ball in the 15th and 16th-centuries, Belgium lavished herself with fine silks, jewels, and paintings paid for with monies from her lucrative trade business and her extraordinarily skilled craftsmen. Lured by the riches that could be made from taxation, the Duke of Burgundy, known for his arrogant and flamboyant ways, made her his home. Talented Flemish painters, sculptors, musicians, and architects were encouraged, bringing forth a Golden Age of art that rivaled Florence and Venice in splendor. Today the painstaking craftsmanship is on view in museums and churches. The attention to detail is almost beyond belief in today's art world.

Belgium's proud, energetic, and quick-tempered citizens bristled under the weight of heavy taxes and heroically resisted outside authority. Throughout history, Belgium has continued to face unsolicited outside involvement. Nicknamed "the cockpit of Europe," she has served as a battle zone for Europe, receiving in return enormous architectural, economic, and social devastation. In an attempt to free herself from this position, she declared neutrality. Belgium rose from the ruins of World War I with heroic determination and restored the economy with rapid industrialization. But the German invasion in 1940 brought harsh rationing and strict control over everyday living. After World War II, faced again with destruction, the citizenry reevaluated their position and promoted a political alliance system and active foreign policy that lead to the formation of NATO, with Brussels as its administrative headquarters.

Belgium's toll-free highways are in good condition and are well signposted. A detailed current map is essential; purchase one at gas station. Major gas stations have mini-markets. It is important to know that near Brussels bilingual road signs show the place name in both Flemish and French. So what might seem a place name for two places is often just one. Public parking close to historic areas is available with time limits and costs similar to those in urban areas at home. Except for the gentle undulating hills in the Ardennees, much of Belgium is fairly flat and crisscrossed with leafy tree-lined canals. Towns are bike-friendly and many are picturesque, making Belgium a wonderful country to cycle in. If you haven't brought your own bike, there is always a place to rent one; check with the tourist office in town. The friendly locals, who usually speak some English, are happy you are visiting their country and will go out of their way to help with directions.

Lovely recreational areas have been built just outside major metropolitan areas, providing scenic and relaxing places for people to enjoy being together. Besides well-run camping areas, these parks have tennis courts, children's playgrounds, cycle paths, and separate fishing and wind surfing lakes. All the camping places listed have good maintenance. Camping for two persons, a car, and a tent will cost just under 20 euros.

BRUGGE

Secluded and unimportant industrially, historic Brugge has scarcely changed since the Middle Ages, when it was one of the most important cities in Northern Europe. Merchants then were given favorable tax exemptions and flocked here. Russian furs and Spanish fruit were traded for Flemish tapestries and lace. Brugge became an emporium, hosting grand trade fairs in her beloved festive manner. But the relentless silting of the river and England's refusal to sell her wool brought the city's demise. Today's visitor crosses quiet canals over miniscule medieval bridges and is treated to venerable church spires and quaintly gabled houses, feeling as if time has stood still.

Sparkling with luminous color, harmony, and meticulous detail, the early Flemish paintings of van Eyck, van der Weyden, Memling, and Bosch gleam more life-like than real life. Stately portraits laden with symbolic detail gaze from glittering frames, and sardonic observations of everyday life are spiced with burlesque effects. The best are in the Groeninge Museum; open daily. Amazing in detail, the lace collection in the Arentshuis Museum's Kant collection attests to the love of elaborate dress by both men and women; open daily. A tiny park between the museums is the perfect spot to eat a picnic lunch, listen to a concert from the Belfort's carillon, and reflect upon history. Directions: Walk south of Belfort on Wollestraat. Cross the bridge to Dijver, busy with flea market stalls, and turn west to walk along the canal to the complex of museums.

One of the holiest relics of medieval Europe is the phial purported to contain the blood of Jesus that is kept in a magnificent silver tabernacle in the upper chapel of the Heilig Bloed basilica; open daily. Next to the basilica, enjoy the elegant façade and elaborate ceiling work of the Stadius; open daily. Directions: From the northeast corner of the Belfort walk along Breidelstraat to the Burg.

Before the sun sets, climb up the belfry staircase of the Belfort Tower to look out over the rosy-hued town. Then watch the town gently illuminate while you drift down the lazy canal in an excursion boat. Boats are boarded south of the Burg.

In mid-July, Brugge hosts an exciting array of music including blue-grass, blues, reggae, and rock in a three-day open-air festival called Cactusfestival.

▲Camping: • 15km west of Brugge in Jabbeke. Exit A10 at Exit 6 and follow signposting. Recreatiepark Klein Strand (50-81 1440); lovely location in a large, peaceful recreational area with small lake; cabins; bus to Brugge; Feb-Oct; $$. • Southwest of Brugge in the suburb of St Michiel. Exit A10/E40 at Exit 7 Brugge-Centrum, and drive towards the Ring Road N31. Camping St. Michiel (50 38 0819); doable on bicycle to the historic area; older; traffic noise; open year round; $$.

Gent

The ability to quietly discover the inner personality of his subjects was painter Jan van Eyck's gift. Looking with an objective eye, he recorded his findings with infinite detail, revealing secrets that were perhaps otherwise unknown. His most famous masterpiece, the Adoration of the Lamb in St. Bavo's Cathedral, is rich in symbolism and glows with brilliant color. Directions: Follow signage to centrum, St. Bavo's, and parking. Historic Gent's medieval gabled guild houses drip with a kaleidoscope of flowers and are delightful examples of the Flemish Golden Age. The Castle of the Counts still looks unfriendly, just as it does in Bosch's paintings. A circular wall curtained the castle, protecting the feudal counts from the unruly citizens. Today, visitors pass through these massive walls for a self-guided tour of the castle's labyrinth. Directions: Walk northwest of St. Bavo's, cross the river and follow signage for Het Gravensteen. Bored with the idealized subjects popular during his day, Hieronymus Bosch painted imaginative, and often humorous, pictures of daily life. A good collection of his work is housed along with Bruegel the Younger's wedding pictures in the Museum of Fine Arts; closed Mondays. Around the corner, the Museum of Contemporary Art has an impressive international collection. Directions: South of the historic area, just east of the train station. Follow signs to Citadelpark and parking. The museum is on the northeast corner of the park.

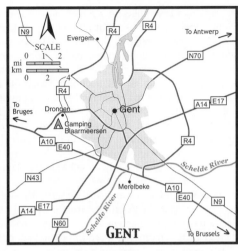

The whole town is very lively in the last week in July during the Gentse Feesten. A wide variety of music, theater, street food, and fireworks goes on for nine days. Use public transportation from your campground, and where you'll need to reserve a place ahead.

▲Camping: • West of Gent in the suburb of Drongen. Exit off A10/E40 at exit 13 for Gent-West/Drongen. Drive five kilometers in the direction of Gent following signposting. Camping Blaarmeersen (92 21-5399); lovely location on a tiny lake next to a recreational area; close to public transportation to Gent; $$.

BRUSSELS

The center for the European Union, Brussels now bristles with international energy, diversity and creativity. North African delis are next-door neighbors to avant-garde art galleries. Men in djellabas and woman in long skirts and veils pass by windows displaying trendy clothing and accessories. There's a cacophony of languages: Flemish, Russian, Spanish, English, Arabic, German, and French. Brussels is in a new and colorful bloom.

I like to begin enjoying the city at the plaza in front of St. Catherine's cathedral. It's located in a working class neighborhood and the old market in front of the cathedral is steeped in old Belgium flavor, with local fish-mongers selling the day's catch. You can treat yourself to sitting down on a public bench and enjoying a plate of succulent moules, or mussels, while you watch people on their morning errands. From here, I turn into rue Dansaert, which runs through the city's oldest immigrant neighborhood. It brims with exotic colors. I continue down to St-Gery and turn into its narrow cobblestone streets, which once housed the city's wholesale food and textile trade. The buildings now house the studios of successful architects and designers who give venerable old Brussels a new look. Les Halles St-Gery, once the city's food market, hosts exhibits of local artists, so pop in for a look. Directions: Metro St. Catherine.

Gazing upon pictures that either oozed with discreet charm or were secretive or exuberantly witty, yet still simple to understand was a great delight to the wealthy burghers. The powerful works of the notable artists of this Golden Age, particularly Ruben and Bruegel, are still captivating, and a large collections hangs in the Musee d'Art Ancien on blue and brown color-coded routes. Images of dreams both thought provoking and perplexing form the core of the Musee d'Art Moderne surrealist collection, with Delvaux and Magritte being important contributors. In addition to the exciting permenent collection, the museum hosts outstanding temporary exhibits. Both museums are part of Musee Royaux des Beaux Arts. The collections are extensive, so be selective; closed Mondays. Directions: Metro 1 to Parc, then walk south on Rue Royale for half a kilometer to Place Royale and the Museum Complex.

Never using a straight line when he could use a curved one, Belgian architect, Victor Horta invented art nouveau. His designs swirled sensously, encompassing magnificent wood, wrought iron, and stone. He loved light, and his designs allowed sunlight to filter through stained glass, skylights, and spacious window glass. His home and studio are now enshrined as the Musee Horta; open afternoons only, closed Monday. Directions: Metro 1 to Louise, then tram 91 or 94 to the museum on Avenue Amerique.

Haunting and savage sounds of tom-toms, scary masks, and a huge dugout canoe are your exotic greeting at the Royal Museum for Central Africa. In the late 19th and early 20th-centuries Belgium controlled the Republic of Congo. The source of much of Belgium's worth can be traced there. During a recent renovation, one wing was curated with the ambiance, artifacts, and archives of 19th-century explorers and a second wing chronicles the brutalities of the Belgian dominance. The contrast is poignant and honest; closed Monday. Directions: In the suburb of Tervuren at the edge of Foret de Soignes. Directions: Metro 1 to Montgomery, then tram 44 to the tram terminal. It's a short walk on the main road to the museum.

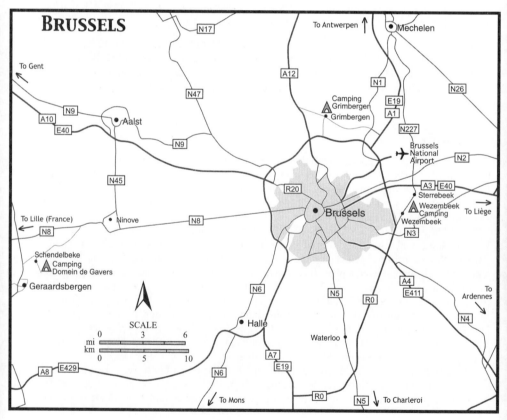

The city's famous flamboyant square, the Grand Place-richly edged with Baroque guildhalls-is extra special in the evening when all its grandeur is illuminated. It's an awesome reminder that Brussels' past brimmed with mercantile wealth. Afterwards, walk north of the square to experience the fairy lit quarter of rue des Bouchers, where the elaborate window displays of fish restaurants hope to lure customers. Don't even think of missing the experience of standing in front of, and also being inside of, the brightly lit up L'Utime Atom-the "building" in the shape of a giant atom. It's Brussels's version of the Eiffel Tower. Directions: Metro to Central Station then walk west half a kilometer.

▲Camping: • 30km west of Brussels and 30 km south of Gent, in Geraardsbergen. Exit N8 onto N42, and drive south 7km to Geraardsbergen, Follow signposting north in the direction of Schendelbeke. Camping Domein de Gavers (54 41 6324); lovely location along a small river in a large scenic recreational area; popular with families; cabins; open all year; $$$. • Just north of Brussels in the suburb of Grimbergen. Exit the ring road/RO at exit 7 onto N202. Then follow signposting for Vilviurde on N211. Turn left at second traffic signal and drive one mile to local pool and campground. Camping Grimbergen (02 270 9597); bike rental; strict rules; traffic noise, bus to Brussels; open May-Sept; $$. • East of Brussels in the suburb of Wezembeek. Exit ring road/RO at exit 2. Drive into Wezembeek and follow signposting. Wezembeek Camping (02782-1009); convenient for metro to Brussels; airport and road noise; open Apr--Sept; $$.

ARDENNES

Nestled between France and Luxembourg, the Ardennes make a restful stop. Forests of beech riddled with footpaths hide eerie rock grottos. Rivers wind and twist through gorges providing fun for canoeists, and campers relax along riverside settings next to picturesque villages.

La Roche-en-Ardenne

Beloved by the Belgians, who come to enjoy the fresh air and tranquility, this friendly little village is a favorite. Canoe and mountain bike rentals are available on the main street, where you can also purchase maps for hiking and biking into the forests and river valley.

▲Camping: • South of Liege exit E25 at exit 50. Drive west on N89 for 17km in the direction of La Roche-en-Ardene. From Namur drive 34km southeast on N4, exiting at Marche. Drive east 20km on N888 to La Roche-en-Ardenne. Drive north of the village along the river towards Hotel Liege. Camping de l'Ourthe (56 41 2323); beautiful location; popular swimming area; open May-Sept; $$.

The Lesse River Valley

The Lesse River is a safe and a relatively easy river on which to paddle a canoe. Call the day before to reserve your canoe with the canoeing company in Anseremme. They will arrange a shuttle. The river is peaceful and scenic, particularly early in the morning. Directions: Anseremme is south of Dinant off the ring road at exit 3.

▲Camping: • In Houyet. Drive south 13km from Anseremme on N95. Exit east onto N929 and drive 13km to the village. Camping Les Hirondelles (82 66 6954); nice, peaceful location; open May-Sept; $$.

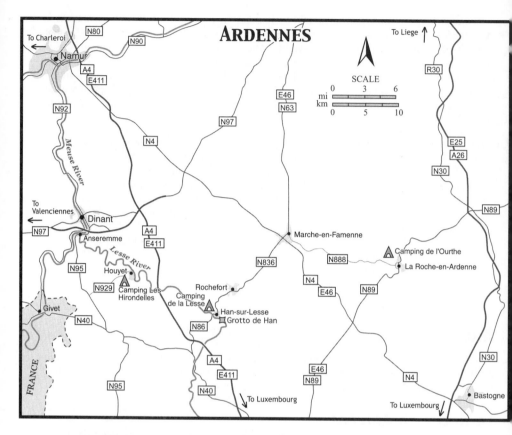

Han-sur-Lesse

The Lesse River forced its way through a large dome-shaped mountain, creating huge mystical grottos, then emerged miles later to join the Meuse River. Known as the Grotto de Han, it is one of the largest caves in Northern Europe and a popular excursion. The largest grotto, The Salle de Dome, is immense and very impressive, measuring 430 meters high. Echoing voices add to the mystique. At the end of the tour, visitors board boats to cross a tiny lake and then float out through a tunnel into the sunlit world. Directions: South of Namur. Exit A4 at exit 23 and drive northeast 5km to the Grotto de Han.

▲Camping: • In Han-ur-Lesse. Camping de la Lesse (84 37 7290); nice location on the river; canoeing; popular with families; open May-Sept; $$.

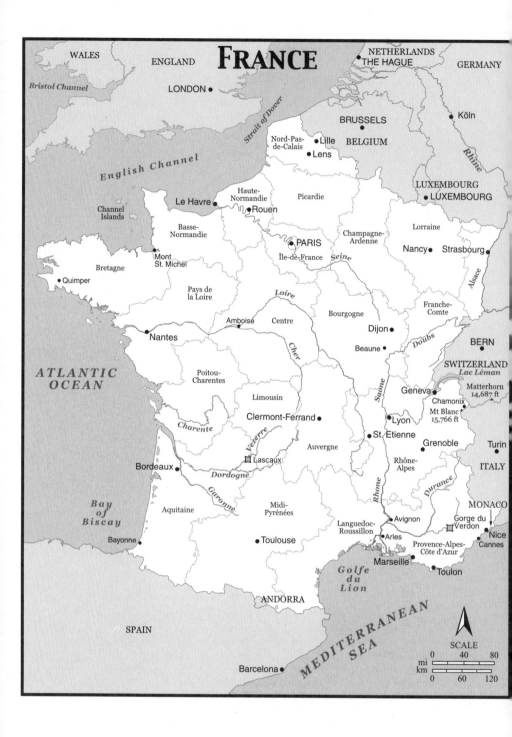

FRANCE

www.franceguide.com

The moment you set foot in France, you sense it's appealing uniqueness. Like its fabulous cuisine, France is a country of great individuality, spontaneity, color, aroma, and taste. Whether elegant or simple, the French always have style. Quality of life is top on their list.

Shopping is an authentic thread in the fabric of the French. Merchants are an intensely proud group of people with a fine set of aesthetics. Their goods are painstakingly arranged-with special attention paid to shape, color, and texture-making a vibrant and lovely mosaic. Lively street markets are moveable feasts with a symphony of aromas and sounds. The marketeers include songsters, comedians, tutors, and culinary advisors. Prices are chalked on a board, and haggling isn't appreciated. Formal politeness is central to all transactions in France. It is considered rude if you don't say hello, good bye and thank you in their language; "bonjour madame" or "monseir, "and "au revoir madame or monseir," and "merci beaucoup and s'il vous plait."

France is one of the most popular countrysides in Europe to cycle. Rolling hillsides aromatic with lavender, thyme, and grapes are embroidered with small roads leading to farms and quiet villages. Major highways leave these small roads relatively free of traffic. I always bring my bike to France.

Scenic rivers large and small lace the country. Paddling a canoe or kayak is a popular sport and a satisfying way to take in the scene. Rentals are available in areas where the sport is popular. I love to float down a river in an innertube so I always include a couple when I pack my bags for a trip to France. After filling them with air from a nearby service station, my partner and I check out the river for the best put-in and take-out. Then we lock one bike to a tree downstream at the take-out. We mark the take-out with a scarf tied to a tree which can seen from the river, and we visually memorize the surroundings, perhaps a rock or cliff. We then drive back to the put-in to park and lock the car. Slipping into the river in our tubes, we begin a fun float. At the end of the float, one person stays with the tubes while the other person takes the car keys and bikes back to get the car.

The French like to get from here to there quickly. Ultra-modern toll roadways satisfy this. You are expected to drive with assertion. Being overly cautious or timid can cause a collision. Speed limits are similar to those at home. Fines are heavy for speeding and must be paid immediately. Credit cards accepted. Blue signs with a white "P" indicate a parking area. After parking, look for a ticket dispenser. If you notice that all the cars are parked on one side of the street but not the other, follow suit. If you get a parking violation, buy a fee stamp at a magazine stand, affix it to the ticket, then stamp and mail it.

Camping in France is a joy. Long ago municipal authorities appreciated the need for an inexpensive way for citizens to enjoy their beautiful country and built plenty of campgrounds. Some are rustic and old-fashioned. Newer ones can be resort-like. There are many more than those listed. Listed opening and closing times are conservative. Camping for 2 persons, a car, and tent will cost about 20 euros noted here as $$, resort-like places will be cost more than 25 euros and are noted here as $$$.

PARIS

Paris is a theatre where actors and actresses, instead of being on stage, are in the audience. Watch the show from a park bench, cafe chair, or museum bench. Stroll through food markets, peek into tiny gardens, window-shop enjoying the artistic detail of patisseries, charcuteries, boulangeries, boutiques, and antique shops. Like its complex wines, Paris needs slow and thoughtful sipping.

Intoxicating with hundreds of museums, don't miss seeing the most famous, but see smaller ones too. Museums are expensive to staff and maintain, so admissions are pricey. Select carefully, then savor your choice like exquisite cuisine. Most museums are closed on Monday or Tuesdays. Substantial discounts are given to children, students, teachers, and seniors; bring identification.

Parisian love of innovation enables artists, musicians, and writers to work in a stimulating environment. Today you can visit the neighborhoods where famous residents once lived and the cafes where they hung out. You can stand before their original works in museums and visit their gravesites.

Shopping in food markets is intensely important to Parisians. It's here, perhaps more vividly than anywhere else in the city, that you're able to see the authentic soul of the city. Here are my favorites: On Tuesday, Thursday, and Saturday: Open-air Marche Maubert; popular because of its convivial merchants; one of the oldest in Paris; Metro Maubert Mutualite. On Sunday and Thursday: Open-air Marche Lenoir; immense and glorious with a large selection of mouth-watering ready-to-eat foodstuffs; Metro Bastille. These open-air markets open at 8 AM and close at 1 PM. Street markets are held everyday but Monday at the same location and are open all day, closing for lunch from 1 PM to 4 PM, reopening from 4 PM to 7 PM. These are my favorites:

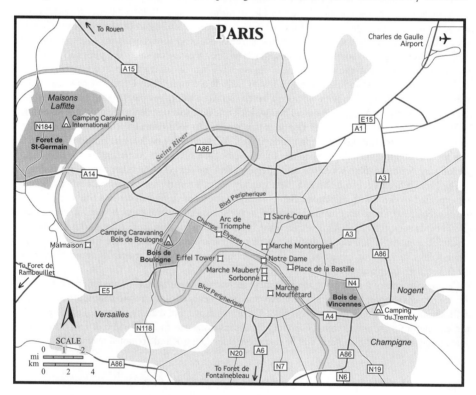

Street market Rue Montorgueil, beginning at Rue Ramuteau; authentic and fun; Metro: Les Halles. Street market Rue Mouffetard, beginning at Rue de L'Epee-de-Bois; popular with tourists because of the lively hawking and jostling. If you walk a little farther, off Rue de l'Arbalete you can enjoy the intrigue of the African market; Metro:Monge. Street market Rue du Poteau, begins at Place Jules-Joffrin, above Sacre-Coeur; one of the prettiest and most elegant; Metro: Jules-Joffrin.

Before you enter the city, purchase Michelin's "Paris Plan 10/12." You'll need it to get to your first camping place. This excellent road map includes metro stations, parking areas, major sights, and gas stations. The free maps aren't detailed enough.

Paris's public transportation system is one of the most advanced in the world. Use the route finder system found by the ticket booth in the Metro to determine the route for your desired destination. Press where you want to go, and your route will be displayed. Jot down transfer stations. When you get off the train, look at the wall map by the tracks, it helps you to determine what exit to use. Taking the bus is a nice way to see the local scene inexpensively. Bus stops display routes and corresponding bus numbers. Each stop's name is clearly marked at the stop itself. Always validate your ticket in the machine, or show your "Carte-Orange" or "Formula-One" card to the driver.

Many visitors buy a "Paris-Visite" or "Formula-One" ticket for traveling on public transport. The ticket is valid for two to three days, beginning when you start using it. It is good for discounts at some tourist attractions and can be used on metro, bus, and RER (train). It can be purchased at the airport and large Metro/RER stations. But the "Carte-Orange" ticket is more economical if you arrive at the beginning of the week and plan to spend more than three days. It is also valid on the metro, bus, and RER. Meant for locals, it is valid Monday through Sunday of the week of purchase and requires a photo. Bring a passport-size photo from home or have one taken in a photo booth in one of the larger stations so you can purchase your Carte-Orange on arrival. Try to speak French when you buy it. Here's how: At metro ticket booth ask for a Carte-Orange for zone one and two. (If you are staying farther out than Camping Bois de Boulogne, you may need one for zone three and four). " Bonjour madame (or monsieur) une carte-orange pour zone une et deux, s'il vous plait." Then pass your photo to the agent. The agent will tell you how much it costs. If you don't understand ask the agent to write it down by saying,"Notez, s'il vous plait. Merci beaucoup." You'll be more relaxed if you avoid buying it during the rush hours at the beginning of the week. Then each time you come to a metro turnstile, insert the magnetic ticket in the ticket slot. When you enter a bus with either the Carte-Orange or Formula-One, show it to the driver. Don't put the magnetic ticket into the bus validator. You can also buy tickets in groups of ten. A regular ticket doesn't allow for transfers from metro to bus or vice-versa. The metro stop for Camping du Bois de Boulogne is Pont Maillot Metro/RER station, within a zone 1-2 ticket.

▲Camping: • On the northwest edge of the city at the west end of the large park, Bois de Boulogne. Off the Blvd. Peripherique, ring road, exit Porte Maillot. Start driving through the park at Restaurant l'Oree du Bois on Av. Mahatma Gandhi, in a westerly direction. Stay on this road as it winds through the park to the Seine River. Then turn south and take the river road, Allee du Bord de L'Eau, to the camping place. It's on the east side of the Seine River, just north of the Pont Suresnes. Camping Caravaning du Bois de Boulogne, Allee du Bord de l'Eau (0145-24-3000); convenient and very popular; shuttle bus to the metro station; bungalows; open all year; $$$$. • 15km southeast of the city, in the suburb of Champigny-sur-Marne. East of the Blvd. Peripherique, ring road, and Bois de Vincennes, exit A4 (the Paris-Metz road) at exit 5, Nogent Marne/Champigny. Drive south on Bd. De Stalingrad (D/45) to Av. General de Galle (N303) then turn west. At the second stoplight, turn north onto Bd. De Polangis and follow signposting under A4. Camping du Tremblay, (0143-97-4397); traffic noise; bungalows; open all year; $$$. • 18km northwest of Paris in the suburb Maisons-Laffitte, between A14 and A15. Off A13, exit Poissy and go in the direction of Maison-Lafffitte; good signposting. Camping Caravaning International, Rue Johnson (0139-12-2191); bungalows; cycle trail along the Seine;

close to public transport to city; open all year; $$$$. • In the Orly Airport area. 26km south of
Paris close to the town of Evry. Take exit 6 off A6 and follow signposting to Villiers-sar-Orge.
It's on the river close to the train station. Camping Beau Village (0160-16-1786); convenient to
trains; road and train noise; open all year; $$.

PARIS AREA
Versailles and Mamaison
Passionate to surpass artistic Italy, The Sun King, Louis XIV, transformed his father's hunting
lodge into a dazzling, gilded palace. Vast waterways, fountains, and sculpture center on Apollo,
the Greek sun god. Be in line for tickets by 8AM. Hameau de la Reine, Marie Antoinette's play
village and Temple of Love, and the smaller palaces Grand and Petit Trianon are at the north end
of the vast gardens. You can drive and park there, or get in a royal mood by sailing down the grand
canal. Directions: Southwest of Paris, exit the Peripherique onto N12 for Versailles. Signposting
to the palace and parking are excellent; closed Mondays.

Home of Napoleon's wife, Empress Josephine, this mansion is small and intimate with a lovely
rose garden. The original furnishings and personal possessions of Josephine bring warmth to the
famous couple's memory; closed Tuesday. Directions: West of Paris, exit off Peripherique onto E5

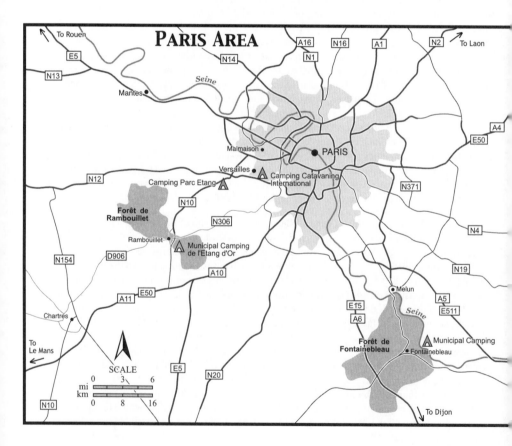

and drive 7km in the direction of St. Germain-en-Laye, exiting north at Reuil-Malmaison. The park and residence are on the southwest side of the village close to the river Seine.

▲Camping: • 3km east of Versailles. Drive east of the Chateau on Av. de Paris. At the 4th stop light, turn south following signposting. Camping Caravaning International; (0139-51-2361); large; close to train to Paris open Apr-Oct; $$. • 3km south of Versailles, in the suburb of Montigny-le-Bretonneux. At the netting of A12, N10, N12 take exit for Bois d'Arcy and follow signposting to the small lake and recreational park. Camping Parc Etang-de St Quentin-en-Yvelines (0130-58-5620); road and train noise, convenient for train to Paris; avoid low sites during rainy season; open year round; $$.

Chartres

Auguste Rodin wrote that cathedrals "offer man a spectacle of magnificence, both comforting and inspiring; the spectacle of ourselves, the image of our soul, elevated to eternity." Chartres, a queen of cathedrals, exemplifies this spirit. After a devastating fire in 1194, she was reconstructed using the original Gothic plans but benefiting from the new knowledge of flying buttresses. Of her original 186 pictorial stained-glass windows, 152 remain, filling the cathedral on sunny days or at sunset with unearthly light. Bring binoculars; open daily. Directions: About 80km southwest of Paris, exit A11 or N10 for Chartres. Cross over the river Eure, and the massive cathedral will be majestically before you.

▲Camping: • In the Foret de Rambouillet. Exit N120 for Rambouillet follow signposting east on D906. Municipal Camping de l'Etang D'Or (0130-41-0734); lovely setting; bike rental; large; popular with families; call ahead; open all year; $$.

Fontainebleau

Built with a passion to out-do, cause envy, and exude power, Fontainebleau was built and embellished as a lavish spectacle. A visit here bears witness to those desires. Nearby Foret de Fontainebleau makes an appealing, restful setting for walks and cycling; open daily. Directions: Exit south off the Peripherique onto E15. Avoiding the forks for Orly Airport, stay on E15/Autoroute du Soleil. The park/palace complex is well signposted

▲ Camping: 5km northeast of town on the east side of the river in the village of Samoreau. Drive east out of Fountainebleau on 210 in the direction of Provins and follow signposting. Municipal Camping (0164-23-7225); nice location by the river; close to the train to Paris; parking separate from camping; open Mar-Oct; $.

NORMANDY

This is off-the-beaten-track countryside with luscious green pastures, aromatic apple orchards, and black-and-white Norman cows. Roads meander peacefully through tiny villages and past isolated farms selling fruit, cheese, cider, and calvados at their gates. Cycling and long walks are particularly rewarding ways to enjoy its natural and unpretentious beauty-its most endearing charm. Tourist offices are well stocked with maps at all levels of difficulty for walking and cycling. Rentals are available in most towns.

Musee Claude Monet/Giverny

Monet's gardens burst with the exciting colors and textures seen in his paintings. His home and the water lilies, dripping wisteria, and Japanese bridge are as they were when he lived here. No advance ticket sales or picniking; free parking at the house; closed Mondays and from Nov-Mar. Directions: 76km northwest of Paris, half-way to Rouen, exit A/13/E5 for Vernon. Pass through the little town following signage for 7km to the Musee.

▲ Camping: • Drive north on the east side of the Seine on 313 for 22km to les Andelys. Then go west, crossing over the Seine to the village of Bernieres-sur-Seine. Caravaning Chateau-Gaillard (0232-54-1820); beautiful setting; popular; open Apr-Oct; $$$. • Near Louviers on the west side of the Seine, southeast of the village of St. Pierre du Vauvray. In a park by the chateau. Camping St. Pierre (0232-61-0155); small; nice location; open all year; $$. • In the same area. Camping Chateau de Bouafles (0232-54-0315); nice location; open all year; $$.

Rouen

Flamboyant pointed gables, pinnacles, clock towers, and cupolas embellish France's most famous Gothic cathedral. Bells chime throughout the day, filling the air with sweet melodies. Joan

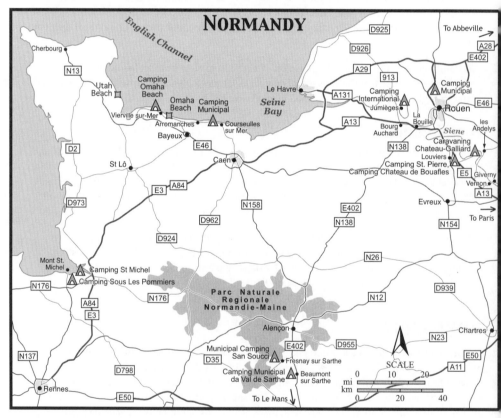

of Arc, heroine of France, was martyred in Rouen. Take the metro to Vieux Marche and pause in front of the immense cross and impressive modern church that mark the infamous spot where she was burned to death. Then walk east on Rue du Gros-Horloge, a narrow street lined with half-timbered houses, to the gilded clock, Gros-Horloge. Climb the stairs to the belfrey for a marvelous view of the old town's rich conglomeration of towers and spires. Continue east to see the cathedral for the first time from the west façade, Monet's favorite view. It is a mesmerizing spectacle. For a complete contrast to the bustle of Rouen, drive to La Bouille, ten kilometers southwest of the city on the southside of the Seine. It's a tiny village of half timbered houses and narrow twisting lanes that are inviting and gay with flowers. Directions: N138 then D64.

▲Camping: • 3km northwest of the city in the suburb of Deville-les-Rouen. Follow the signs for A150 out of town, and exit for the suburb. Camping Municipal (0235-74-0759); traffic noise; open all year; $$. • 26km west of Rouen in Jumieges. Exit A13 at Bourg Achard and drive north on 913 six kilometers to Jamieges and Regional Parc Brotonne. Camping International (0235-37-9343); close to a sports field; medium size; open Apr-Oct; $$.

Parc Naturel Regional Normandie-Maine

Forests of beech and oak crown hilltops and meadows are lush with pastureland here. Parisans come to relax in its timeless beauty. Canoeing and cycling are popular, and rentals are available. Ask at the tourist office in Alecon, pl La Magdelaine.

▲Camping: • Both of these are small with nice locations on the river; open Apr-Oct; • At the west end of Fresnay-sur-Sarthe off 310. Muncipal Camping San Souci (0243-97-3287); $ and in In Beaumont-sur-Sarthe; Camping Municpal da Val de Sarthe (0243-97-0193); $.

Bayeux and the D-Day Landing Beaches

Wars are never humorous, but finding comedy in them years later can be refreshing. A cartoon story of the Norman Invasion was painstaking embroidered nine centuries ago. You can almost hear the giggling embroiders as they stitched their homey, action-filled story. Viewing this at the Musee de la Tapisserie de Bayeux is a lighthearted way to bone up on medieval life. Directions: Follow signs for Centrum off the ring road. The museum is on Rue Nesmond, on the southern edge of the historic area; open daily. Coastal towns in the area have museums with touching memorials for individual troopers. For an overview, drive to Caen and visit Musee Memorial. Then drive or cycle the circuit linking the battle sites.

▲Camping: • On the beach in the village of Vierville-sur-Mer. Exit off E46, 15km northwest of Bayeux, for the village and beach. Camping Omaha Beach (0231-22-4173); pleasant location; open May-Aug; $$. • 21km northeast of Bayeaux in the sand dune area close to Courseulles-sur-Mer. Follow the coast road 14km east of Arromanches. Camping Muncipal (0231-37-4610); nicely tucked into the dunes; difficult for large caravans; open Apr-Sept; $.

BRITTANY

Wildly craggy cliffs, cloud-filled skies, and a tortuous sea give the Bretons a fierce and independent spirit. In tiny villages here, ancient stone houses line cobblestone streets and fish markets burst with fresh catch. Along the cliffs, birds soar, screech, and plunge into the spectacular sea, while inland, ancient stone megaliths testify to vigorous settlers. The flat terrain makes cycling popular. There are many camping places. I've listed a few nice but less expensive ones.

Quimper

At the Festival de Cornouaille, held the last week in July, Bretons regaled in traditional costumes, celebrate with folk music, dance, and food. On summer Thursday nights, traditional dance and music can be enjoyed behind the cathedral.

▲Camping: • Close to the town of Benodet, at the mouth of the river. Camping Poulquer (0298-57-0419); close to the ocean; medium size; open mid-May-Sept; $$. • 28km southwest of Quimper off 785 exit at Penmarch and drive 10km east on a small road exiting for Lesconil. At the beach road turn west and drive two kilometers. • Both of these are small and have nice locations on the beach; open May-Sept. Camping Karreg Skividen (0298-58-2278); $$ and Camping Les Ormes ((0298-58-2127); $$.

Parc Regional d'Amorique

Though relatively small in area, d'Amorique encompasses a wide variety of terrain and natural life. Ferries go to Iles d'Ouessant for bird watching. On the rocky headlands you can watch cormorants perched with their wings spread wide to dry. From the bluff you'll see loons and grebes elegant with their slender necks, floating gracefully over swelling waves. Monts d'Arree's walking

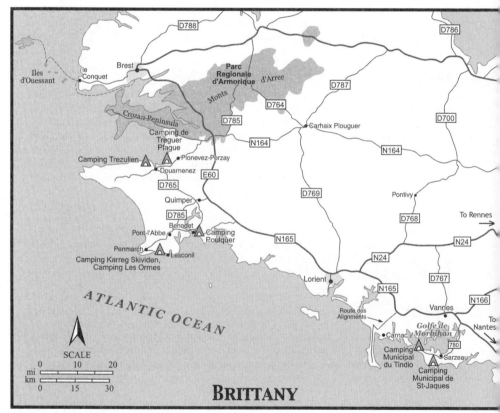

BRITTANY

paths through quiet forests are made mystical when you read the ancient legends. Pretend you're on the Sahara desert when you climb the immense sand dunes on the Crozan Peninsula.

▲Camping: • North of Quimper 24km, drive 12km east of Douarnenez to the village of Plonevez-Porzay then drive west on the coast road. Camping de Treguer-Plague (0298-92-5352); nice location by the water; open May-Sept; $$. • Just north of Douarnenez out on Pointe Treboul. Camping Trezulien (0298-74-1230); windy but scenic; medium size; terraced; open May-mid-Sept; $$.

Golfe de Morbihan

Arms of land embrace the sea here, creating a huge bay where prehistoric man settled. Musee de Prehistoire in Carnac Ville, the Routes des Alignements northeast of Carnac Ville, and the swirl-and-spiral-decorated megalithic stones on the Gavrinis Islands all testify to 4500 through 2000 BC settlements. Under starlit skies, a sound and light show adds to the mystique.

▲Camping: • On the southwestern tip of the bay, in the village of Sarzeau. 8km south of Vannes exit west onto 780, the bay road. Drive for about 19km to Sarzeau, then drive out to Pointe St. Jacque. Camping Municipal de St. Jacques (0297-41-7929); nice location; open May-Sept; $$. • In the same area but farther out on the point in the village Arzon. Camping Municipal du Tindio (0297-53-7559); on the ocean; large; open Apr-Oct; $$.

Loire Valley

In the16th century, Royal France was filled with satin, curled wigs, and intrigue. From the grandiose to the tiny, the chateaux tell the tale of the glamorous French Rennaissance. Looking like an over-crowded chessboard, Chambord is the dream palace of the era's most illustrious king, Francis I. Friend and co-planner, Leonardo de Vinci, helped make it a marvel of whimsy, ingenuity and design. Leafy plane trees stretch and arch to form Chenoceau's romantic canopy entryway. Spanning the river Cher, six women's taste, wit, and elegance embroidered the palace's history, creating one the Loire's most graceful architectural gems. Dressed in men's clothes, a zealous seventeen-year old village girl visited Charles VII at Chinon, pleading to lead French troops against the English. Persuaded, he gave her a suit of armor and a white charger. Her indomitable spirit awakened a sense of national pride that led to the final end of the Hundred Year War. Highly evocative sound and light shows, musical and dramatic performances, garden exhibitions, and costumed festivals fill the Loire's calendar adding to its allure. Visit the web before you arrive so you don't miss out: www.loirevalleytourism.com. The south side of the Loire River is most picturesque. Entrance fees to the castles are high, so be selective. Gardens and exteriors are often the best part. Enjoying books and films set in this era before you come will make the architecture, furnishings, and gardens come alive.

The region's fertile soil and temperate climate load the tables of the morning markets with irresistibly beautiful succulent fruit, crisp garden-grown vegetables, cave-cultivated mushrooms, and sweet-smelling home-grown roses. For diversion from castles, take a look at the exciting collections of racing cars in Le Mans.

The Loire Valley sweeps in a wide arc through central France. It's mostly flat terrain so cycling is a terrific way to take in the sights. Most towns have a bicycle rental shop, and the tourist office have colorful brochures describing picturesque cycle-routes. Paddling down the rivers is lots of fun and canoe rental is available. The rivers offer good birding, so bring binoculars and a bird guide.

▲Camping: There are many places. Here are a few favorites. • In the heart of the chateau area in Azay-le-Rideau, 27km west of Tours. Exit off A10 at Ste. Maure-de-Touraine and drive west 13km to St. Gilles, then turn north and drive 17km to Azay-le-Rideau. Camping Muncipal le

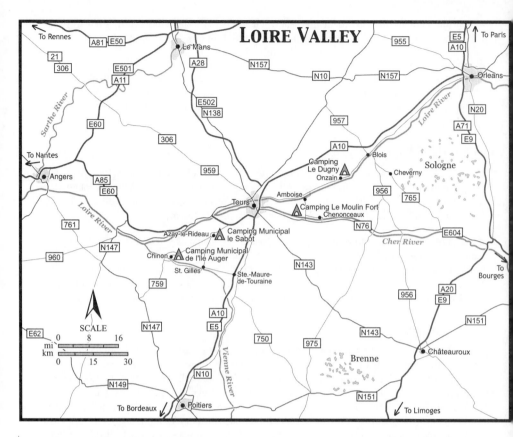

Sabot (0247-45-4272); lovely location; close to the sound and light show; pool; open Apr-Oct; $$. • In Chinon along the Rive Vienne. From A10 exit at Maure-de-Touraine and drive west 13km to St. Gilles, then continue west for 17km to Chinon. Camping Muncipal de l'Ile Auger (0247-93-0835); pleasant spot on the river with a nice view of the castle; open April-Oct; $$. • Along the Rive Cher, 12km south of Amboise off D40 by the bridge. Camping Le Moulin Fort (0247-23-8622); medium size; pool; open mid-June-mid-Sept; $$. • 18km west of Bois,on the north side of the Rive Cisse/Loire in the village of Onzain. Camping Le Dugny (0254-20-7066); medium size; close to the cycling path; open all year; $$.

ATLANTIC COAST
Arcahon
   Dunes, beaches, and sun attract the locals like bees to honey. Surfers love this area, where the waves and scene are the best in France. Dune du Pilat found eight kilometers south of Arcahon, is the highest dune in Europe and fun to climb. Take a canoe trip into the wetlands of Bassin d'Arcachon and Parc Ornithologique, where little streams twist and turn jungle-like amidst lush swamp-loving plants and water birds. Great Blue Herons, impressive in their four foot height, hold a stiff posture bending their head forward to sight prey. Smaller snowy egrets, always so

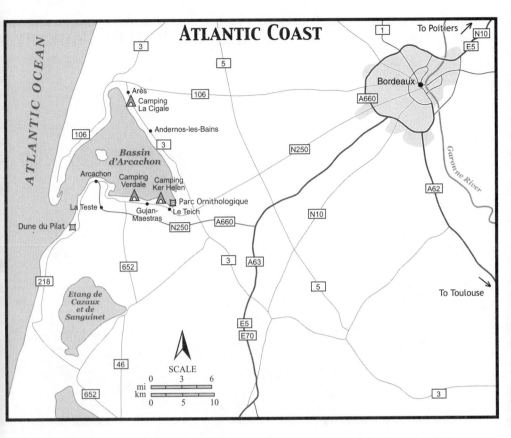

ATLANTIC COAST

lovely in their snow-white plumage, are often seen stirring the water a bit with one foot in hopes of bringing up a tasty morsel. Boats leave from Le Teich.

▲Camping: There are many places here are a few smaller ones. • On the north side of the Bassin near Arès. Camping La Cigale (0556-60-2259); smaller; nice location; shade trees; pool; open May-Sept; $$. • Near Parque Ornithologique. On the south side of the Bassin 2km east of Gujan-Maetras. Camping Ker Helen (0556-66-0379); medium size; pool; bungalows; open Mar-Nov; $$ • In the same area, west of Gujan-Maetras in the suburb of la Hume. Camping Verdalle (0556-66-1262); good location on the beach; open May-mid-Sept; $$.

FRENCH BASQUE COUNTRY
Bayonne

Devishly hansome men, attired in white except for red scarves around their necks, daringly chase bulls through town during the Fete de Bayonne. The five-day festival begins on the first Wednesday in August. Music, floats, and bullfights add up to a very lively scene.

▲Camping: • 4km from Bayonne off N117 in the direction of Pau. Camping La Cheneraie (0559-55-0131); large; terraced; shade trees; pool; open Apr-Sept; $$.

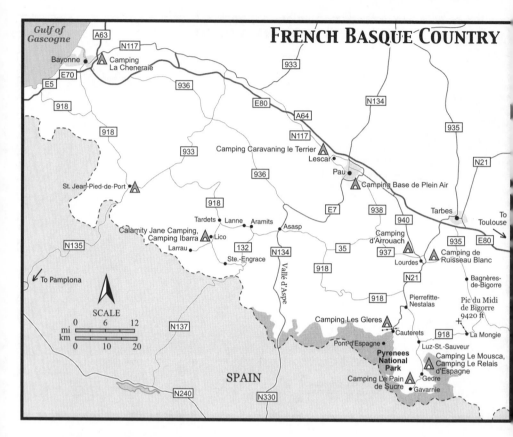

St Jean Pied de Port

Wide overhanging roofs line the narrow street climbing up to the ancient citadel here, an important stop on the pilgrimage route to Santiago de Compostela. Today day-trippers from Bayonne fill its streets. From the Vieux Bridge start your climb up the steeply cobbled rue de la Citadelle, keeping an eye out for the doors of houses with small brass-covered cockleshells-the badge of the pilgrims. Continue up the rough cobblestone to the massive Citadelle, where you can absorb the view of backyard gardens, the valley, and the Pyrenees. Enjoy warm evenings with locals at the sports field, beret-topped elders watch stony-faced, noticing every nuance of the younger men as they play pelota. Observe the subtleties between the farmers and buyers selling goats, pigs, and sheep at the Marche Couvert on Monday mornings. Walking paths take you up to meadows that carpet the low hills. White-washed farmhouses punctuate the rocky landscape, and the air is aromatic with oak and chestnuts. Sheep with puffball-like wool and black legs gaze up dreamily and their bells ring sweetly. Pick up a map at the tourist office. Directions: 50km southeast of Bayonne on 933.

▲Camping: • On the Spanish/French border along the river Nive by the sports field. Both of these are open May-Sept. Municipal Camping Plaza Berri (0559-37-1119); $$ and Camping Narbaitz (0559-37-1013); $$.

Gorges de Kakouetta

Sculpted during the ice age, the gorge now has a riverside trail. This is an easy two-three hour walk with dramatic cliffs lining an ever-narrowing passage into a fairyland of mosses, ferns, delicate orchids, waterfall, and rushing river; admission fee; open daily; Apr-Oct. The route leading here passes through lush scenic countryside. Stop at one of the farmhouses to buy their homemade cheese. Purchase supplies and gas and secure local currency at a cash machine before you leave the larger towns. Directions: Exit N134 two kilometers south of Asasp onto 1918 in the direction of Aramits and drive 12km. Continue 3km to Lanne and then 8km to Tardets. Follow signposting for Larrau for 5km to a fork. Take D113 for Larrau and St Engrace. The entrance to the gorge is just west out of the village of St. Engrace, very close to the Spanish border. Plan to spend the day so after your gorge walk you can walk along a stone walled road into little almost forgotten villages that cling to softly sculpted mountainsides. Your hike will be enhanced by the jangle of cow bells, waves to the villagers, and sights of meticulous vegetable gardens, and a look into a Roman church and cemetery.

▲Camping: • 5km past Tardets in the direction of the gorge in Lico. Calamity Jane Camping; simple but a wonderful location on the river; popular with cyclists; swimming grotto with deep pools and warm boulders; small café; open May-Sept; $. • In the same area, farther up the road to the gorge. Camping Ibarra (0559-28-7359) better for caravans, scenic setting on the river; open April-October; $$.

Parc National Pyrennes

Near the park, foothills are sweet-smelling with rolled hay. Whitewashed farmhouses, hunched under heavy stone roofs, and diminutive village churches with three-pointed belfries sparkle in the sunlight. The rushing rivers, grassy meadows, and tinkling streams tumbling from turbulent peaks and crevasses refresh hikers on the park's trails. Directions: Drive southwest from Pau on E7, then south on N134 to the Aspe River and Valley and the Parc National Pyrennes. From Lourdes drive 50km south on N21, then continue up the narrow gorge to the spa village of Cauterets on D920, and on up to the park entrance. South of Cauterets take the chairlift or trailhead up to Pont d'Espagne where three cataracts join in a spectacular convergence. From here walk up to Lac de Gaube, a serene deep lake surrounded by voluptuously shaped mountains. The most famous natural wonder in the park is the mountain amphitheatre, Cirque de Garvarnie, where waterfalls tumble grandly from one ledge to another. You can walk down to the bottom of the largest, the Grande Cascade. Hiking trails and donkey rides leave out of the village of Gavarnie up the Cirque. Directions: Take the smaller road off D921 at the village of Pierrefitte-Nestalas and go 18km to Luz St Sauveur. Continue another 20km through the deep gorge to Gavarnie. A spectacular new astronomical museum and observatories opened just above Pic du Midi de Bigorre at about 3000 meters. Directions: Take the very steep and winding D918 east of Luz St Sauvenur up 20km to La Mongie. Then board the cable car for the exciting ride up to the summit and the museum. Bring your binoculars in order to get a closer look at a magnificent griffon vulture wheeling in the sky.

▲Camping: • At the north end of Cauterets follow signposting on N920. Camping Les Gleres (0562-92-5534); small; close to the cable car; open all year except Nov; $$. • 18km south of the exit off N21 onto the road to Gavarnie in the village of Luz St. Sauveur. Camping International (0562-92-8202); beautiful location; well cared for; open June-Aug; $$$. • 20km further up the mountain in the village of Gedre. Camping Le Mousca (0562-92-4753); nice location on the river; small; pool; open July-Aug; $$. • Three kilometers north of Gedre. Camping Le Relais d'Espagne (0562-92-4770); small; pleasant; open Jan-Oct; $$. • 10km further up the mountain, 3km north of Gavarnie on the river. Camping Le Pain de Sucre (0562-92-4755); small; convenient to hiking trails; July-Aug; $.

Pau

Beloved by the English, this city gleams with elegant parks and apartments. In early morning, drive up the Blvd. Des Pyrenees to be dazzled by the light and shadow of the writhing peaks of the Pyrenees.

▲Camping: • Northwest of the city 9km, on the south side of A64/E80 in the suburb of Lescar. Exit A64/80 at exit 10 for Pau. Turn west onto 117 in the direction of Bayonne and drive to the bridge. Camping Caravaning le Terrier (0559-81-0182); convenient; open all year; $$$. • Two kilometers south of the city on 937, in the direction of Nay Bourdettes near a tennis park. Camping Base de Plein Air (0559-06-5737); convenient; open May-Sept; $$.

Lourdes

After seeing the famous Bascilica and Grotto, join the nightly torch-lit procession of singing pilgrims. It starts at 8:45 at the Grotto of Massabielle. If you are going into the Pyrenees, stop at the Musee Pyreneen. It's housed in a chateau perched high on a rocky bluff on the east side of the river by the sanctuaires on Rue Bourg. It houses a fascinating collection of maps, equipment, and photos from pioneer hikers; open daily.

▲Camping: • On the east side of the city. Exit off N21 east onto 937 in the direction of Bagneres de Bigorre. Camping Ruisseau Blanc (0562-42-9483); pleasant; shady; open March-mid Oct; $$. • One kilometer northwest of the city on 940 in the direction of Pau. Camping d'Arrouach (0562-94-2575); nice location; simple; open all year; $$.

DORDOGNE VALLEY

About 20,000 years ago, people lived here with amazing elegance and simplicity. Evidence of their Ice Age existence was found in the now world-famous Vezerre Valley caves. The immense dignity and power of the animals still soars from the paintings. Today, the most famous of the cave drawings from Lascaux are protected for scientific study. Painstaking care was given to the reconstruction of Lascaux II, a replica of the original cave. It is a brilliant reproduction; open daily in July and August otherwise closed Monday. Immensely popular and a premium tourist attraction, be sure to reserve tickets in advance on your credit card by calling up to seven days ahead. July-Aug (05-53-51-96-23); Sept-June (05-53-51-95-03) or arrive early to avoid a very long line. It is easier to book tickets for either the first morning tours or the lunch time tours. In summer, tickets are sold only in Montignac, in the kiosk next to the tourist office, close to Eglise St. George on the left bank of the Vezerre River.

At Font de Gaume, one kilometer east of Les Eyzies de Tayac, you can still enter a narrow fissure in the rock to see for yourself the authentic, excitingly fluid drawings, 18 to 10 thousand-year-old, of bison and deer. To preserve the cave drawings, the number of people allowed to enter the cave is limited. Tickets are at a premium. It is necessary to reserve on a credit card up to a week ahead (05-53-06-86-00); open daily. You'll find the new Musee National de Prehistoire in Les Eyzies a valuable source of information; closed Tuesdays except in July and August when it is open daily. Directions: The Vezerre Valley is about 100km east of Bordeaux and about 50km southeast of Perigueux. D706 runs through the valley, and there is good signposting for all the caves.

Floating down the Dordogne or Vezerre Rivers in a canoe or kayak or an inner-tube is a kick. Canoes and kayak rentals are readily available. There are plenty of places for put-ins and take-outs. If you've brought inner-tubes, blow them up at a local gas station and lock a bike to a tree at the take-out. After the float one person can stay with the tubes and the other can bike back to

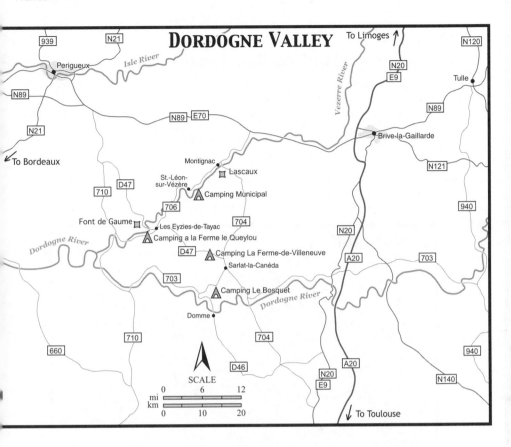

the car with the car keys. The Dordogne's quiet country roads traverse serene rolling hillsides and lead into small mellow villages with stone churches and ancient houses. Cycling is terrific way immerse yourself in its beauty. Rentals are available throughout the region. Pick up a map of the cycle routes-from easy to difficult-and information about rentals at any tourist office in the area.

Perhaps the most beautiful medieval towns in the Dordogne is Sarlet-la-Caneda. It's discreetly restored, with a labyrinthine of tiny alleyways and delightful courtyards. A large Saturday market bustles with activity under the shadow of the St. Marie church at the Place de la Liberte. Foie gras and walnut oil are specialties along with wild truffles, cepes, and morel mushrooms. Park on the ring-boulevard and walk or bike into the historic area. Still guarded by medieval gateways, the touristy and very pretty village of Domme enjoys a commanding view of the Dordogne River and the surrounding region.

▲Camping: Camping is expensive in this area. Here are a few less costly ones. • 3km west of Les Eyzies de Tayac off D706. Camping a la Ferme le Queylou (0553-06-9471); lovely hillside location; small; quiet; $$. • On the river in the village of St Leon sur Vezerre. Camping Muncipal (0553-50-7316); small and basic; $. • 3km north of Domme follow signposting off D46. Camping Le Bosquet (0553-28-3739); small sites; pleasant location; open mid-Apr-Oct; $$. • 6km west of Sarlet-la-Caneda off D47 in the direction of Eyzies-de-Tayac. Camping La Ferme-de-Villeneuve (0553-30-3090); beautiful location; terraced; open May-Oct; $$$.

LANGUEDOC
Parc Naturel Regional du Haut-Languedoc

Amid the mesmerizing drone of cicadas, the fragrance of wild thyme, the outcrops of rocks too steep for vegetation, and the red tile-roofed houses in tiny forgotten villages you might think you're in Greece. Spelunkers flock to the park, because many of the caves were first explored in modern times by their hero Edouard-Alfred Martel. Directions: 52km north of Carcassonne on 118, exit east onto N112 and drive 30km to St Pons de Thomieres. Exit north onto a small mountainous road in the direction of St Pons and the park headquarters.

▲Camping: • Exit N112 at St Pons-de-Thomieres, and drive north up the mountain on D907 for 31km, passing St. Pons to the mountain lake la Ravieg and the village of Rouquie. Camping Rouquie (0563-70-9806); beautiful location on the lake; small; terrassed; open Mar-Oct; $$.

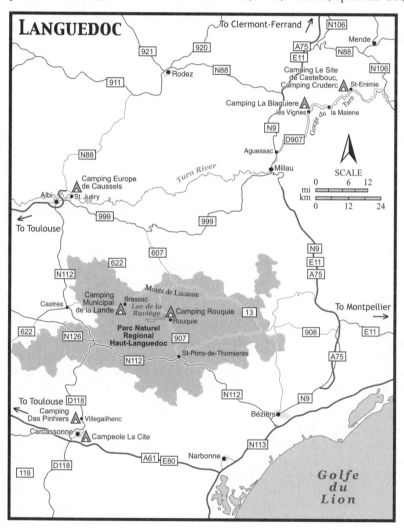

• On the western edge of the park, along the river in the village of Brassac. 58km east of Toulouse exit off N112 in the direction of Castres. Drive northeast for 13km. Continue east on a small road for 24km to Brassac. Camping Municipal de la Lande (0563-74-0911); small pleasant place along the river; shade trees; open Apr-Oct; $.

Carcassonne

As you walk across the drawbridge into this ancient, fully-restored, fairy tale-like walled city, it's easy to conjure up images of handsome knights in armor jousting while beautiful women dressed in embroidered silk watch admiringly. It has everything a medieval walled city should have: a moat, an exquisite church with glittering stained glass, and bastions from which brave men could pour molten tar on besiegers in times of assault. To get into a romantic mood, arrive late in the day and stay for the evening lighting of the ramparts. Park just outside the Cite in one of the car parks.

▲Camping: • Exit for Cite off A61/E80. There is signposting close to the river. Campeole La Cite (04-6825-1177); convenient; open Apr-Sept; $$. • Drive north out of the city on D118 to the suburb of Villemoutaussou. Camping Das Pinhiers (04-6847-8190); good for kids; swimming pool; nice location; open May-Sept; $$.

Gorge du Tarn

Floating down the Tarn River through this majestic verdant gorge is a delight. Absolutely vertical cliffs, 100 meters high, rise dramatically from the river. From the put-in at St. Enimie, it's 14km to the take-out at La Malene. Rent a kayak or canoe or use an innertube. A taxi can be arranged to bring you back to your car or if you've brought your bike, lock it to a tree at the take-out and bike back to your car with the car keys after the river float. Directions: The gorge starts 7km north of Millau, about 115km north of Montpellier on the Mediterranean coast. Exit east at Aguessac onto D907. The road follows the river so you can check out the water as you drive.

▲Camping: • In Ste. Enimie. Camping Le Site de Castelbouc (0466-48-5808); good location on the river; open Apr-Sept; $$. • In the same area, Camping Cruderc (0466-48-5053); on the river; pool; open Apr-Sept; $$. • 25km east of Aguessac on 907 in les Vignes. Camping La Blaquiere (0466-48-5493); on the river; terraced; open May-mid Sept; $$.

Albi

This was Toulouse-Lautrec's home town and the largest collection of his works are here. His pictures are hung at the Palais de la Berbie next to the Cathedrale St. Cecile. The Moulin Rouge and its neighborhood was his favorite subject. Many of his works are humorous, making the viewing amusing. Splurge on the excellent audio guide and take time to sit in the lovely garden and enjoy its quiet ambiance. Directions: Albi is 75km north east of Toulouse.

▲Camping: • East of town in the direction of the suburb St. Jury. Camping Europe de Caussels (0563-60-3706); convenient; open May-Oct; $$.

BURGUNDY

Blazing yellow fields of mustard spread across rolling hills of carefully manicured, centuries-old vineyards in Burgandy. Here and there small villages hug the scarred and crumbling ruins of an empire whose abbeys remain as testimonies to power and wealth.

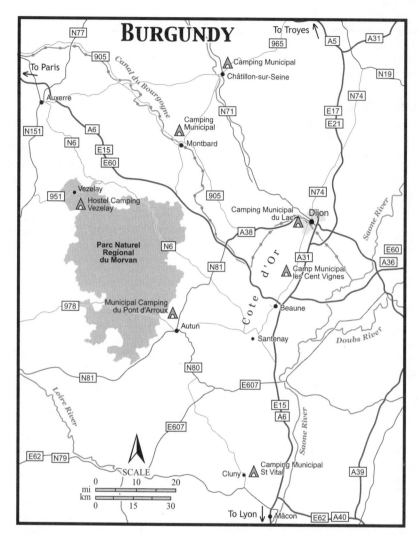

Beaune

Like a precious jewel in a lovely pin, rich and charming Beaune sits in the center of Burgandy. Hotel-Dieu, a 15th-century hospital with a deeply pitched, multicolored tiled roof is justifiably the town's prize attraction; open daily. The Musee du Vin tells the whole story of wine making, from planting the grapevines to uncorking the bottle; open daily. At Marche aux Vins wander through dusty cellars sodden with the smell of wine-soaked wooden vats and sample wine from upturned barrels; open daily.

Cote d'Or

To see the vines and visit the wineries that produce some of France's most famous wines, drive from Dijon to Beaune on N74. This route winds through the Cote d'Or and is a thrilling trip for any serious wine connoisseur. Stop halfway at Chateau du Clos de Vougeot, the center for the brotherhood of wine, and visit the museum and wine tasting room. Enjoy the musty vapors of aging wine in the 14th-century wine cellars at Chateau de Meursault, just south of Beaune on N74.

Dijon

Palais des Ducs, once the home to the powerful, now houses an outstanding collection of art. Don't miss the room where designer Sambin's woodwork is exhibited; then look for his work on the grand doorways of the hotels in the historic center; closed Tuesdays. Bring your shopping bag and allow yourself to indulge in some of the great mounds of mouthwatering foodstuffs at Dijon's covered market Les Halles; just off rue de la Liberte; open mornings; Tues, Fri and Sat. The International Fetes de la Vigne celebrating the grape harvest in early fall is wildly popular and great fun with music, food and of course, lots of wine tasting; www.ot-dijon.fr.

▲Camping in the Area: • One kilometer northeast of the city. Exit from the intersection of A6/A31 onto A6 and drive one kilometer west. Exit onto N74 in the direction of Beaune and follow signposting. Camping Municipal les Cent Vignes, close to Eglise St. Nicolas (0380-22-0391); lovely location close to the river; walking or cycling distance into Beaune; popular; open May-Sept; $$. • 3km northwest of Beaune at the northwest end of the suburb Savigny-les-Beaune. From Beaune's ring road exit on N74 in the direction of Dijon. Turn west almost immediately in the direction of Savigny and drive 3km. Muncipal Camping Les Premiers Pres (0380-26-1506); pleasant location with views of vineyards; open May-Sept; $$, • Northwest of Dijon in Chatillon-sur-Seine at the junction of N71 and 965. Follow signposting in the center of town by the fountain; part of a park with nice swimming pool. Camping Municipal Chatillon-sur-Seine (0380-91-0305); nice location; small; open May-Sept; $$. • On the west side of Dijon, signposted off A38, about one kilometer west of the train station. Camping Municipal du Lac, 3 Bld. Chanoine Kir (0380-43-5472); nice location along the river; walking/cycling path to Dijon; open Apr-mid-Oct; $$.

Abbey of Cluny

Quiet and majestic, this abbey was once an immensely powerful force in France. Today it is an evocative place.

▲Camping: • East of town off E15. Camping Municipal St. Vital (03-8559-0834); nice location; well cared for; open June-Sept; $$.

Parc Naturel Regional du Morvan

Hawks, buzzards, and falcons flap their wings slowly, then glide gracefully in the cool morning air. In the afternoon, they circle on outstretched wings making great arcs high in the sky above this wooded countryside clothed in green meadows and yellow vetch. Gem-like Vezelay, a medieval village, sits at the top of a hill. Follow in the steps of pilgrims by walking up the steep cobblestone main street to the soaring Basilique de St Madeleine.

▲Camping: • Down the hill from Vezelay. Drive south on a small road in the direction of L'Etang. Hostel Camping Vezelay (03-86-332-418); simple; open Jun-Aug; $$. • In Autun on the Ternin River just north of the Pont d'Arroux. Municipal Camping du Pont d'Arroux (03-8552-1082); nice location; open May-Sept; $$.

WESTERN PROVENCE

Aromatic with lavender, graceful with silver-green olive trees, and brilliant under blue skies, this coun-tryside was too splendid for the conquering Romans to leave. Instead, wealthy families moved to these lush agricultural lands to build luxurious mansions with originality and extravagance. They graced them with gardens, courtyards, thermal baths, intricate mosaic-tile floors, and plumbing systems. To entertain themselves they built grand amphitheaters, and to keep the city clean they built aqueducts. After visiting the impressive historical sights and museums, free your spirit in the countryside-where narrow panoramic roads wind their way into ravines, up wooded slopes to ancient castles, and into evocative stone villages where you'll be treated to secretive arched alleyways and playful fountains.

Orange

Orange still hosts grand music festivals in its magnificent Roman theatre. Known for its lively and fun-loving spirit, this town is easy to have a good time in. Take time to find out about its festivals before you arrive; www.choregies.ass.fr. Just outside of town, in the village of Seguret, cobblestone alleyways and steps wind their way through tightly grouped buildings to a jewel-like square and castle ruins. Directions: Drive south of Orange on N7 for 8km. Exit east onto 977 and continue for 19km.

▲Camping: • 10km southeast of Orange in Jonquier. Take exit 21 off A7 then exit almost immediately south onto N7 in the direction of Carpentras and drive 10km. Municipal Camping Les Peupliers (0490-70-6709); part of a recreational area; large; well run; popular;

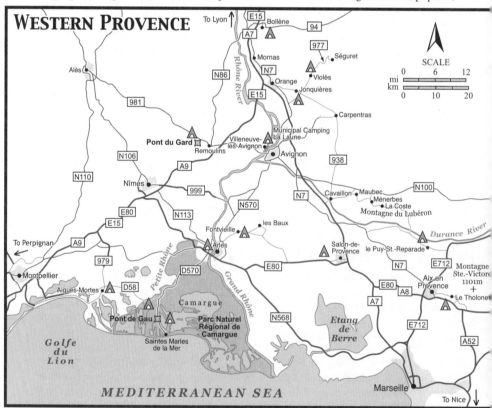

mid May-Sept; $$. • Follow the previous directions passing through Jonquier to 977 and the river. Turn north and drive 5km to Voiles and follow signposting. Camping du Domaine des Favardes (0490-70-9464); small; pool; popular; open May-Sept; $$. • 20km north of Orange, just east of Bollene. Take exit 19 off A7 and follow signposting. Camping La Simioune (0490-30-4462); convenient to the autostrata; open all year; $$.

Avignon

A wildly popular festival of theatre, dance, film, and music is held here during the last three weeks in July and the first week in August. The city becomes a stage, with streets teeming with clever mimes, hilarious clowns, and talented musicians. The main festival premieres theatre productions by living playwrights of international reputation. Avignon is a walled city and is dominated by the huge edifice of the Palais des Popes where the main productions take place. You'll need to plan several months in advance, buy tickets, and reserve camping; www.festival-avignon.fr

▲Camping: • Just north of the historic area, take the new bridge, Pont Daladier , then immediately exit east onto Chemin de la Barthelasse. Camping Municipal Pont-Saint-Benezet (0490-82-6350); beautiful location with great views of the Palais des Popes; well cared for; very popular; open Apr-Oct; $$$. • Closer to bridge, Camping and Hotel Bagatelle (0490-86-3039); popular with school groups; well used; convenient; open all year; $$. • Northwest of Avignon in Villeneuve-les-Avignon. Exit off N100 just west of the bridge and drive north on N580 following signposting 3km past the walled village. Municipal Camping Le Laune (0490-25-7606); part of a recreational area; bus to Avignon; popular; open Apr-mid-Oct; $$.

Pont du Gard

To enjoy the breathtaking achievement of this world-famous Roman aqueduct, rent a canoe and paddle up the gently flowing the river. Directions: 27km north of Nimes, exit A9 for Remoulins and drive northwest for 4km. Don't miss the terrific new visitor's center.

▲CampingCamping: • 2km northwest of Remoulins by the Pont du Gard. Camping La Sousta (0466-37-1280); great location for seeing the Pont; large; popular; shade trees; open Mar-Oct; $$. • In the same area but two kilometers farther from the Pont. Camping International Les Gorge du Gardon (0466-22-8181); large; popular; large pool; open mid-Mar-Oct; $$.

Aixe-en-Provence

Bursting with rosy-hued peaches, vibrant tomatoes, aromatic basil, and farm-fresh cheese as well as cookware and the bright fabrics of Provence, the morning market in Aixe-en-Provence is one of the area's best. Packed with ladies with shopping bags, it takes place on Pl. des Precheurs on Tuesday, Thursday and Saturday mornings. If you want to avoid the crowd, get there by 8:30 AM. Park at the large parking area close to the bus station, signposted off the circular one-way boulevard.

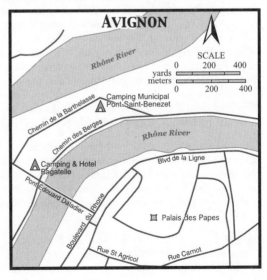

Cezanne loved this countryside. His last studio, Atelier Paul Cezanne, is a touching memory of his life; open daily. Directions: Walk north out the market area then up the hill on Ave Pasteur to 9 Ave Paul Cezanne. You can follow in his footsteps by heading east out of town on D17 towards Montagne Ste.-Victoire, whose beauty obsessed him. At the base of these mountains, in the village of Le Tholonet, trailheads varying from easy to difficult, lead farther up to the high ridges.

Pride of the town is Musee Granet and its fine collection of the art from the 16th to 20th-centuries. The museum also has fine pre-Roman archeological exhibits; open daily. How often do you have the chance to see dinosaur eggs? Don't miss the exhibit at the Museum of Natural History. The historic core of the city is a beauty with cobblestone streets winding around 17th and 18th-century mansions into delightful tiny squares with refreshing public fountains.

The International Festival of Lyric Art, one of the oldest and most prestigious musical festivals in France, takes place here in July. Usually highlighting Mozart, the festivals introduces young singers on their way up. Most of the operas are held outdoors in the palace courtyard. You need to purchase tickets and arrange for camping months in advance: www.aix-en-provence.com.

▲Camping: • 23km north then west of Aixe-en- Puy-Ste.-Reparade. Take exit 15 off A51/E712 and drive west 5km to Puy-Ste.-Reparade, passing through the town in the direction of Rognes for 2km. Camping Municipal le Logis (0442-61-8262); small; nice location with view of the Luberon mountains; open Apr-Sept; $. • 31km west of Aixe-en-Salon de Provence. Take exit 14 off A54/E80 onto D17 in the direction of Eyguiere and drive 6km. Turn west onto D72 and following signposting. Camping Nostradamus (04409-56-0836); nice location on the canal; train noise; small; open Mar-Nov; $$. • On the southeastern edge of Aixe. Exit A8 at Aix Est/Les 3 Sautets in the direction of Val Ste Andre and follow signposting. Camping Chantecler Airotel (0442-26-1298); large; beautiful location with view of Ste. Victoire; cabins; swimming pool; open all year; $$$.

The Camargue

As the Rhone passes into the Mediterranean, it flows into the open arms of the Camargue estuary. Birdsong fills the air as multitudes feed on the great abundance provided by farmlands and marsh. Flocks of pink flamingoes, their bills held upside-down and swinging from side to side, feast in the algae-rich waters. Herons stand statue-like then utter a deep croak and flap ponderously away. The park's entrance is at Pont de Gau. Start at the Musee Ornithologique. Bring your binoculars and insect repellent or face net and enjoy the 6km walk through the bird sanctuary; open daily. In the morning or evening light, the birdsong and marshland aroma, create an especially dramatic environment. Directions: Exit off 570 5km north of Les Sainte Marie for Pont de Gau. Don't miss the fascinating exhibits in the Musee Camarguais, which tell the story of traditional life in this haunting and unique landscape where black bulls and wild white horses once ran wild. Directions: Drive 12km south on Arles on N570. Gypsies from all over the world come to honor their patron saint Sarah on the May 24 and 25. It's an incredibly colorful scene, with impromptu dancing, music, bullfights, eating, and drinking. Designated cycling paths skirt the shoreline east of Les Sainte Marie, where rentals are available. The light is different here. Van Gogh loved it.

▲Camping: • Just west of Ste-Marie-de-la-Mer off D38 on the Petit Rhone. Camping Le Clos du Rhone (0490-97-8599); large; popular with families; cabins; open Mar-Sept; $$. • Northeast of town off D85A. Camping La Brise (0490-97-8467); large; popular with families; open Jan-Oct; $$. • West of the Camargue in Aigues-Mortes. Camping Le Petite Camargue (0466-53-9898); resort-like; popular with families; all amenities; open May-mid-Sept; $$$.

Arles

Arles was the Roman's first settlement in France. Loving the warm, star-filled summer nights, they built a beautiful stone arena. It is well preserved and is France's premier location for both

Spanish and French versions of bullfighting. For a memorable evening sit under the canopy of stars and enjoy an open-air dance or musical performance at the Theatre Antique located just south of the Roman Arena. During the day, under pristine blue skies that dazzle the eyes, explore the vine-covered slopes and fields of sunflowers lazily turning their plump faces to the sun. Then wander down the narrow alleyways in town, and you'll understand why Van Gogh fell in love with Arles. In mid-summer enjoy the work of world-renowned photographers at the International Photography Festival. A fabulous permanent collection of photographs and works from Provence-inspired artists makes a stop at the Musee Reattu definitely worth while; open daily.

Standing atop a rocky mountain and bringing to mind a child's sandcastle, the half ruinous miniscule village of les Baux makes a perfect picnic place. Directions: Drive northeast of Arles on 17 for 9km in the direction of Fontvielle. Pass through the village continuing on 17 for 3km. Exit north on a small road for les Baux and drive 2km.

▲Camping: • 10km northeast of Erles in Fontvielle, near Baux. Exit east of Arles onto D17 in the direction of Fontvielle. Municipal Camping les Pins (0490-54-7869); pleasant location with shade trees; open Apr-mid-Oct; $$. • In Arles. Follow signposting for St Gilles west on N572, then turn north onto D37. Camping Crin Blanc (0466-87-4878); small; open April-Sept; $$.

Montagne du Luberon

The tranquil, slightly decayed charm of Provence villages recall images on its artists' canvases. Clusters of cypress, rows of ancient olive trees, shaded promenades, and small fountain-adorned squares are delightful places to lose yourself in a heady blend of earthiness and sophistication. Don't be in a hurry. Savor the little homey, uncomplicated moments and you'll be enchanted. Directions: East of Avignon take N100, exiting here and there on small roads to the villages. One of my favorites is Lacoste, with its rough-chaparral hilltop setting. I like to walk up to its haunting, castle ruins for a picnic. Directions: Drive 23 km east of the Avignon airport on N100. Exit south onto a small road in the direction of Menerbes and LaCoste and drive 7km.

▲Camping: • 9km east of Cavaillon in the village of Maubec. Muncipal Camping (0490-76-5034); small; terraced; pleasant setting with shade trees; open Apr-Oct; $.

PROVENCE

Steeped in sun and all that it brings, the Provence can be lovely. Seductive with color and aroma, street markets overflow with abundance-just like the beautiful people who stroll along the beach. Bougainvillea and mimosa drip off the decks of fine villas, and cafes line the beach. Inland a sea of lavender unfurls in purple waves. Market days transform little villages into a festive scene where there is a welcome that is warm and authentic. Besides food stuffs, the markets also have provencal soaps, lavender products, and olive-wood utensils. Pick from a huge variety of cured and seasoned olives, freshly-baked bread, and voluminous stands of sausage and artisanal cheeses, and then find a place under the shade of a plane tree for a gourmet picnic.

Massif des Maures

Enchanting hilltop towns, vineyards, chestnut trees, and pines wrap around the Massif, which stretches inland and east from Toulon. During the day shady squares with spring-fed fountains are wonderfully restful, and in the evening, when the cafes are evocatively lit, it feels like you're in an outdoor medieval museum. In the ancient village of Collobrieres, cork and chestnuts are prepared for market. In Grimaud, freshly-baked bread from the La Chartreuse de la Verne

Monastery's ovens is aromatic and delicious. Medieval La Garde-Freinet hosts street markets on Wednesday and Sunday. Cogolin has artisan studios that can be visited.

▲Camping: • In Grimaud. Exit N98 at Port Grimau and D559. Cross over bridge and almost immediately turn west onto D558. Camping La Pineda (0494-56-0436); medium size; open Apr-mid-Oct; $$. • In Coglin off D48 in the direction of St. Maur. Camping de l'Argentiere (04-9454-5786); nice location; pool; tennis; open May-Sept; $$.

Provence/Cote d"Azur

▲Camping in the Cote d' Azur: There are plenty of camp grounds, many are expensive. Here are a few that are a little less expensive. Call ahead for reservations. • 32km south of Cannes, just north of Agay near the viaduct and Antheor-Plage; follow signposting off N98. Camping du Viaduc (0494-44-8231); nice location; small; open Apr-Sept; $$. • In the same area. Camping Azur Rivage (0494-44-8312); small; terraced; shade trees; parking separate from camping; open mid-Apr-Sept; $$$. • South of Agay towards St. Raphael in the village of Le Dramont. Camping Royal (0494-82-0020); small; nice location by the beach; open Feb-Oct; $$$. • Six kilometers away from the beach in a nice wooded area close to Frejus. Exit A8/E80 at exit 38 and drive west of Frejus on N7. Exit almost immediately west onto D4. Drive one kilometer and then exit west onto Bagnols-en-Foret. Camping Malbousquet (0494-4087); small; pleasant; terraced location; pool; open Apr-Sept; $$.

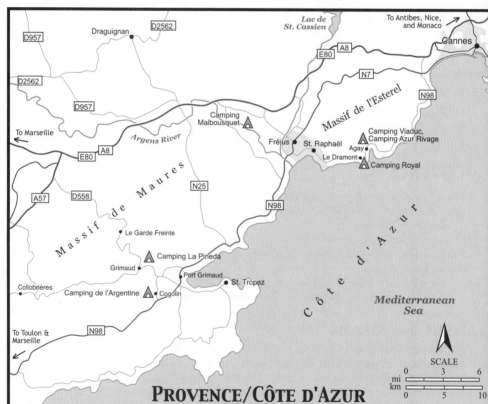

Picasso at Antibes and Vallauris

Ceramic art has been important to Vallauris since the Roman settlement. For six years Picasso lived and worked here. The work he created is fanciful and exuberant. His haunting panels of War and Peace cover the walls and ceiling in a little chapel at the top of the main street. Admission to the chapel includes seeing the abstract artwork of Picasso's friend Magnelli, as well as a nice collection of traditional and contemporary ceramic work from Provence; closed Tuesday. Directions: Drive 6km east of Cannes in the direction of Juan-les-Pins. Exit for Vallauris on the west side of Juan-les-Pins. Grateful for the studio within the Grimaldi chateau, whose spectacular views in every direction inspired him, Picasso donated to Musee Picasso much of the work he had done during this period. The collection includes paintings, ceramics, sculpture and tapestry; closed Monday. Directions: Take exit 44 off E80 in the direction of Antibes. Exit for Port-Vauban and follow signposting for Place du Chateau and Musee Picasso.

Vence, Matisse and the Foundation Maeght

The light, color, and sensuality of the Cote d'Azur were an irresistible allure to impressionist artists. In the tiny Chapelle du Rosaire in Vence, Matisse painted his final masterpiece as a present to the nuns who had nursed him through a long illness; open Tuesday and Thursday. Directions: North out of Vence on Route St Jeannet, 466 Av. Henri-Matisse.

One of Europe's most significant collection of modern art is housed in the gardens and galleries of the Foundation Maeght, an also architecturally-stunning museum. Works of Calder, Miro, Chagall, and Kandinsky blend harmoniously in a natural setting; open daily. Directions: West of Nice take exit 48 off E80/A8 in the direction of St Paul-de-Vence and drive 7km. The white arches of the museum rise almost pagoda-like outside the hilltop village. It is well sign-posted. Park in one of the large car parks outside the village on the road to Nice.

Provence/Cannes Area

▲Camping in the Cannes Area: • 4km southwest of Vence on D2210, the road to Grasse. Camping Domaine de la Bergerie (0493-58-0936); good location; large; popular; shade trees; open Apr-Sept; $$. • 6km west of Vence on the Rive Loup in the village of Tourrettes-sur-Loup. Follow signposting off D2210. Camping les Rive Loup (0493-24-1565); medium size; pleasant location on the river; popular with families; difficult entrance for large caravans; open Apr-Sept; $$. • 17km from Vence in the gorge of the Rive Loup. Exit Grasse northeast onto D2210 and drive one kilometer. Follow signposting for Le Bar-du-Loup. Camping Les Gorge du Loup (0493-42-4506); beautiful location in the gorge; small; difficult for larger caravans; terraced; open Apr-Oct; $$.

Grasse

Sniffing expensive perfume then breathing in fresh air at the ancient and colorful square, Place des Aires, makes a sensuous fusion. Go to where the real essence is produced, the Parfumerie Fragonard; open daily. Directions: Drive 3km outside of town toward Cannnes to Les Quatre Chemins.

▲Camping: • On the east side of town take D2085 in the direction of Nice then follow signposting onto D111. Municipal Camping (0493-36-2869); nice location in town; bus to the beach; small; open April-mid-Sept; $$. • 9km west of Grasse along the Siagne River on D2562 in the direction of Draguignan in the village of Auribeau-sur-Siagne. Camping Le Parc des Monges (0493-60-9171); nice location; small; open mid-May-Sept; $$.

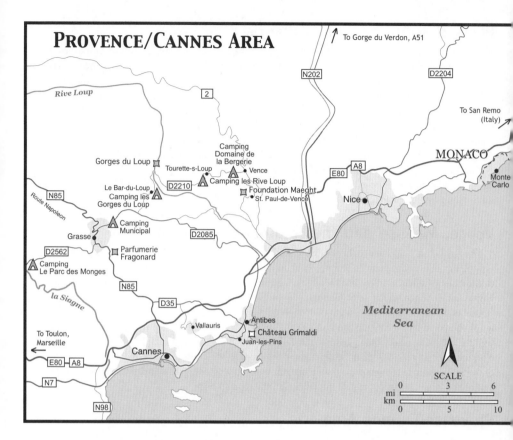

Gorge du Verdon

In this small, Grand Canyon-like gorge, craggy cliffs are softened and made aromatic with oak, conifer, and broom. Proud mountain villages, rich with history, cling to the wild and rugged landscape. Once a raging torrent, the Verdon River now runs at a more sedate pace because of upstream dams. At the Galetas Bridge it spills into the sparkling aquamarine waters of Lac de St Croix so radiant it seems to be an apparition. The hub of the vacation area centers in the village of Castellane where you can arrange for white water rafting, bungee-jumping, hang-gliding, parasailing, and cycling. Expert cyclists ride the whole route.

Two major hiking routes descend from the ridge of the gorge down to the river. The Martel Trail, which experienced hikers can do in seven hours, is steep and rugged. It leads down through the spectacular Samson Corridor, then through a pitch-dark 670 meter tunnel and on to the rushing Verdon River where a refreshing dip rewards you. The Imbut Trail is shorter. If you are prone to vertigo, be aware that there are several sections of the trail that are very narrow. Cables in the rock face have been installed here. The steep ascent back up the cliff, the Vidal Sortie, includes some ladders and areas prone to rockslides. Get advice, and maps and perhaps arrange for a guide at one of the sport shops in Castellane.

On the north side of the gorge, the D952 has a justifiable reputation as a white-knuckle driving route. The narrow road is devoid of guard rails and has startling precipices, that become even more hair-raising with on-coming campers and tour buses. The wonders of the gorge can be enjoyed more tranquilly on D957 and D71, where there are guardrails and viewing areas.

Moustiers, a picturesque village on the northeast end of the lake, was once an important center of the earthenware industry. Today, finely glazed pots, or faiences, are available in profusion in shops with gardens alive with the aroma of honeysuckle, rosemary, and lavender. Walk over to the two-room museum where the interesting story of the industry is told. Then sit under the shade of the plane trees in the central square and watch men wrangle over points as they play petanque.

To find the gorge on the map, look between Aix-en-Provence and Grasse and then a bit north. Several routes lead to the gorge. N85 is the most popular. From the west, exit A51 at exit 21 for Aubignosc and drive east in the direction of Digne-les-Bains on route de la Lavande. From the south, drive north out of Grasse on N85 taking the Route Napoleon. This is a popular camping area with many places to choose from. (call ahead for reservations) Here are a few less expensive ones.

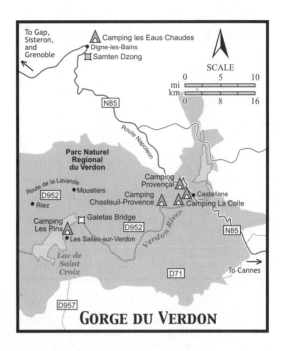

GORGE DU VERDON

▲Camping: • 8km west of Castellane on D952 on the river. Camping Chasteuil-Provence (0492-83-6121); good location; large; terraced with shade trees; open May-mid-Sept; $$. • Along a white-water part of the river. 2km west of Castellane exit north onto GR4, a small road. Camping La Colle (0492-83-6157); small; terraced with shade trees; open Apr-Oct; $. • North of Castellane, on the N85 in the direction of Digne. Camping Provencal (0492-83-6550); views of white-water; small; open Apr-Oct; $. • On the west side of the town of Castellane (0492-83-6302); small; convenient for walks to town; open Apr-mid-Oct; $. • On south side of Lac de Ste Croix close to the village of Le-Salles-du-Verdon. To avoid the narrow D952 or D71 drive to Lac Ste. Croix from the south on D957. Camping Les Pins (0494-70-2080); lovely views of the lake; open Apr-Oct; $$. • In the same area. Camping La Source (0494-70-2040); small; terraced; open April-mid-Oct; $.

Parc National Mercantour

Resting on your back here under a sweet-smelling pine, you might spot the living metaphor of wild country-the golden eagle. Watch for it soaring high in the air or launching from a rocky ledge with a flapping of wings that can span more than two meters. When prey is spotted they plummet at high speeds, grabbing the prize in their powerful talons. The park is the largest eagle-nesting area in France. Sunny and arid, the narrow reserve stretches to the Italian Alps. Archeology enthusiasts come to explore the Vallee des Merveilles and the Cirque de Fontanable. Over 100 thousand prehistoric open-air engravings have been found dating from 1800 to 1500 BC. They are not obvious. Consider hiring a guide in St. Dalmas-de-Tende for best viewing. Directions: South end of the park, close to the town of Tende on E74/N204. The park is north of Nice on the Italian border.

PARC NATIONAL MERCANTOUR

To Cuneo, Torino

Parc National du Mercantour
Tunnel de Tende
Valèe des Mervilles
Casterino
St. Sauveur-sur-Tineé
Maritime Alps
St.Martin-Vesubie
Tende
St. Dalmas-de-Tende
D2565
D2205
N204
E74
D2566
SCALE
mi 0   4   8
km 0   6   12
To Ventimiglia

▲Camping: • From Nice drive 24km north on N202 along the river. Exit for Pla-du-Var and 2205 and drive north 32km to St Sauveur-sur-Tinee. Camping Municipal (0493-02-0320); nice location on the river close to the village; small; simple; open mid-June-mid-Sept; $.

Alpes de Provence

Hidden in the limestone around Digne-les-Bains is the largest geological reserve in Europe. The Centre de Geologie's exhibits and videos make a good first stop; open daily. Directions: Leave Grenoble on N85 in the direction of Gap/Sisteron. Continue to the north end of Digne-les-Bains. Alexandra David-Neel's incognito and solo (except for her guide) travels to Tibet in 1924 made her famous. Her home, visited twice by the Dalai Lama, is open to the public. Directions: Drive one kilometer out of town on the road to Nice. Watch for signage for Samten Dzong. Great fields of lavender in a palette of purple sweep up and down the soft slopes of the plateau east of the Durance River, once an important Roman crossroads. Tucked in a narrow valley the cheery village of Riez boasts 1st-century Corinthian columns and medieval gates. Directions: Take exit 18 off E712 and drive east on A6 for 29km. Thermal bathing is popular.

▲Camping: • East end of Digne-les-Bains. From N85 follow signposting east onto D20 . Camping les Eaus Chaudes (04-9232-3104); thermal baths close by; pleasant location; open May-Sept; $$.

Parc Naturel Regional du Vercors

Mount Aiguille, or Needle Mountain, stands majestically over a sea of the finger-like protrusions of Vercors. Its natural labyrinthine of limestone tunnels protected resistance fighters during World War II. Spectacular scenery surrounds the drive through the park. Directions: Located between Valence and Grenoble, exit off A49/E713 at St. Nazaire-en-Royans onto D532. Drive east on D531. Gorge de la Bourne and Gorges du Meaudret are part of the loop drive.

▲Camping: • At the southeast corner of the loop drive in Vassieux-en-Vercors. Camping Naturalle les Pins (0475-48-2882); small pleasant spot; simpler; open mid-June-mid-Sept; $. • At the northwest corner of the loop drive in St Jean-en-Royans on the Rive Lyonne. Municipal Camping (0475-47-7460); medium size, simple; open mid-Apr-Sept; $.

Lyon

Many of France's best chefs have apprenticed in Lyon. It's a place of pilgrimage for people involved with food and wine. In the late afternoon, wandering around the old town, you'll sniff enticing aromas drifting out of the kitchens' back doors. Lyon was an important marketplace during the Renaissance. Wealthy silk merchants, many Italian, built magnificent mansions-each with

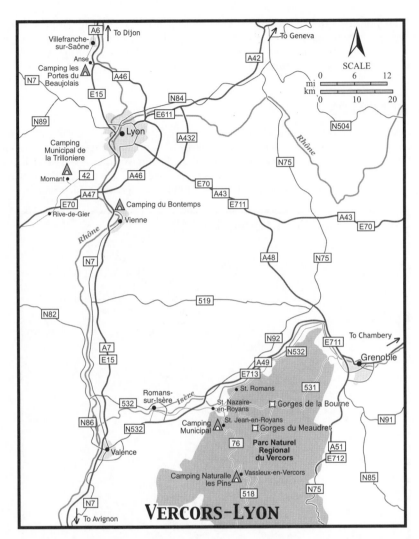

a private alley-way-like entryway. Called trabole, these passageways interconnect with the main streets and are secretive and elegant, with vaulted ceilings, stairways, and courtyards. To wander through them today, even getting a little lost, is fun. You can purchase a map and story of the traboles in a bookstore or at the tourist office. Directions: Metro: Hotel-de-Ville then walk north towards Jardin des Plantes and Les Traboles. Lyon is city where music reigns supreme. Attracting fine musicians from all over Europe, the streets sparkle with exciting street music throughout the summer. June 21st is France's National Day of Music when musicians pour into the city from all over France to fill the air of the historic area with exciting sounds. There is a wonderful sense of camaraderie among the musicians that spills over into the audiences.

▲Camping: • South of the city, exit A6 for Vienne-Nord in the suburb of Vernioz. Camping du Bontemps (0474-57-5852); nice location in a park; swimming pool; tennis; open May-September; $$$. • North of the city, exit off A6 for Anse. It's close to the junction of A6 and

A46. Camping Les Portes du Beaujolais (04-7467-1287); nice location on the river; open mid-Mar-Oct; $$. • 28km southwest of Lyon in Mornant. Exit A47/E70 at exit 11 onto 42 at Rive-de-Gier. Drive northeast 7km then exit onto a small road for Morant. Municipal Camping de la Trilloniere (0478-44-1647); small; basic; open May-Sept; $.

FRENCH ALPS

Massive peaks tower dramatically here above grassy meadows that are cheerful with a host of wild flowers. From the top of a mountain accessible by cable car, the light is remarkable and the distant peaks seem close. Alpine villages nestle in the luscious grass. From woods of larch, beech, and pine it is easy to spot a marmot; if alarmed they utter a loud shrill whistle. The famous Grande Randonnee Trail stretches the full length of the Alps, from the Jura to the Mediterranean.

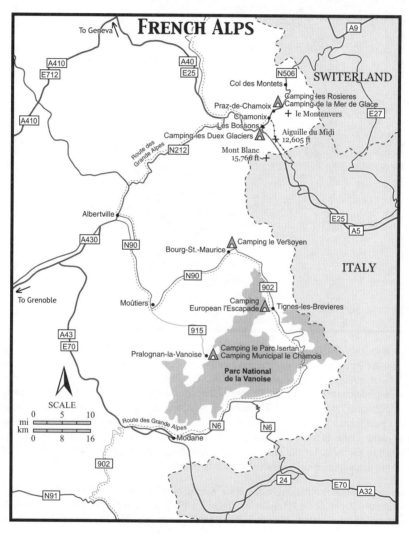

Parc National de la Vanoise

Now a refuge of the Alpine ibex, Vanoise was France's first national park. Its peaks are the biggest in the Alp range. The protected meadows glow with an overwhelming profusion of flowers. Because access to the park is on foot only, you'll experience an immense serenity once you are beyond the initial five or six kilometers of the more than five hundred kilometers of marked trails. Before you begin the trail, take the nature walk in the Tueda Reserve along the banks of the Doron River to learn about the alpine flowers and plants you'll see. Directions: The park is northeast of Grenoble. Drive 115km northeast of Grenoble on A41 then A43. Exit south onto N90/Route des Grandes Alps in the direction of Moutiers. Drive southeast out of Moutiers on 915 in the direction of Vanoise National Park for 28km.

▲Camping: • 28km southeast of Moutiers in Pralognan-la-Vanoise. Camping Le Parc Isertan (0479-08-7524); beautiful location along the river with views of the mountains; open all year; $$. • In the same area. Camping Municipal le Chamois (0479-08-7154); nice location; open June-mid-Sept; $. • At the north end of the park close to the Italian border at the intersection of D902 and N90, in Bourg-St. Maurice. Camping le Versoyen (04-7907-0345); nice location; open June-Sept; $$. • On the east side off D902, in Tignes-les-Brevieres. Camping Europeen L'Escapade (04-7906-4127); beautiful location; close to a chairlift; pool; open June-Aug; $$.

Mont Blanc/Chamonix

Europe's highest peak, Mount Blanc, has lured mountaineers for over a century. It's justly famous cable car, the Aiguille du Midi, from Chamonix is a spectacular ride. The first stage to Plan des Aiguille takes just nine minutes, climbing to an altitude of over 2000 meters. The second stage is the thriller. It jets 600 meters between two towers, and at the summit you are at almost 4000 meters elevation and very close to Mont Blanc's peak. Because the mountains often cloud over by noon, arrange to be at the top by 9 or 10 AM so you can take in the unforgettable view of the glacier and dazzling peaks. Roundtrip to the Aiguille du Midi is costly. Don't bother unless the weather is clear. Book tickets ahead (50-53-40), or arrive at the ticket booth by 7 AM. Even if it's hot in Chamonix, take a hat, warm jacket, sunglasses, and sunscreen. Remember you are at dizzying heights, so rest and adjust your body before taking off on hiking trails. If you have binoculars, bring them. You won't want to miss walking through the Galerie de la Vallee ice tunnel. To ride over the enormous glacier, book tickets from Chamonix to Helbronner. The ticket includes an additional 40-minute ride, in a small gondola, at the summit with stops for photos. Directions: The station for the cable cars, telepheriques, to Aiguille is on the south side of the river off Route des Pelerins.

The one and a half hour cog-railway train ride to Montenvers and the Mer de Glace has terrific views of the glacier. For a special treat purchase tickets for an additional cable-car ride and entrance to the Grotto de Glace ice cave. Every year, ice is worked by artists into beautiful sculptures that shine with a heavenly light. Hiking trails web the mountainside and are signposted for length and difficulty. Directions: Behind the train station in the center of town.

In between hikes and cable car rides, drive to the village of Col. Des Montes and wander along the nature trails at the Reserve des Aiguilles Rouges. It's a must for anyone even vaguely interested in alpine wildflowers and shrubs; open daily. Directions: Route des Nantes north out of town. In town be sure peruse the memorabilia of mountaineering in the Alpine Museum; daily 2-7 PM. Get a close look at chamois and ibex in a natural setting at the Alpine Animal Park. Directions: West of town follow signs on N506 for des Houches to Merlet. Directions: Chamonix is southeast of Geneva, close to the Italian border.

▲Camping: • 3km south of Chamonix near the village of les Bossons signposted off N205. Camping les Deux Glaciers (04-5053-1584); beautiful location; open all year; $$. • Along the

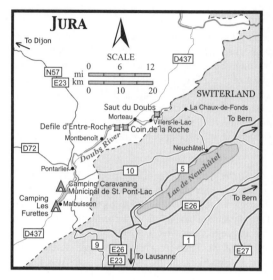

river just south of Praz de Chamoix. Camping les Rosieres (040-53-1042); beautiful views; simple; open Feb-mid-Oct; $$. • 3km north of Chamonix-Mont-Blanc in the suburb of Praz-de-Chamonix. Camping de la Mer de Glace (04-5053-0863); fabulous views of the Mt. Blanc; open mid-May-Aug; $$$.

Jura

Tucked behind a chain of bright green high pastures, dense forests of beech and pine, and craggy limestone mountains, the Jura has managed to escape the invasion of tourists. In the morning and evening you share the road with wide-eyed cows rhythmically moving to and from the day's pasture. Scenic cycling or driving routes take you past torrential waterfalls racing down rocky cliffs into clear streams and rivers decorated with chartreuse moss-covered boulders. In cool caves the famous comte cheeses age. The word for "forest" in the language of the Gauls is "Jura", and today timber and skillfully worked wood are still important sources of income. Because the limestone soil has revealed outstanding fish and dinosaur fossils, scientists named the Jurassic period after this region. For a scenic drive or cycling, follow the Doubs River on D437. Start at Pontarlier. Cross over the bridge and follow signposting for Montbenoit and then Morteau. The road narrows and darkens in the canyon, Defile d'Entre-Roches. Stop and walk into the mysterious ravine. At the grotto of La Chapelle, park again and cross the tiny bridge and look up at the caves in the rock. The river road then passes through the dramatic Coin de la Roche ravine and then spills out into the open, where lush pastureland surrounds the vacation town of Morteau. After the 31km ride stop here to sample the local specialties of smoked sausage and comte cheese. Then head east on 461 down the hill 14km through the charming village of Villers-le-Lac to the waterfall, Saut du Doubs, and the Swiss border. Directions: The Jura is southeast of Dijon close to the Swiss border.

▲Camping: • South of Pontarlier on the northwest side of the lake in St. Point Lac. Camping Caravaning Municipal de St. Point-Lac (0381-69-6164); small; nice location; popular with families; open June-Aug; $$. • On the southeast side of the lake in Malbusson. Camping Les Furettes (0381-69-3150); on the lake; large; popular with families; open Apr-Sept; $$.

ALSACE

Half-timbered houses laden with geranium-filled window boxes and a rolling countryside planted neatly with grapes make Alsace ideal for relaxing and cycling. Strasbourg is refined and graceful, with interesting museums and cathedrals. Colmar's cobblestone streets and miniscule bridges are perfect for photographs. And winding through it all is the wine route, with plenty of places to sample the product. Start your wine route tour from Colmar by cycling or driving west 4km on D417 to Wintzenheim. Cross the river taking the small road three kilometers to the village

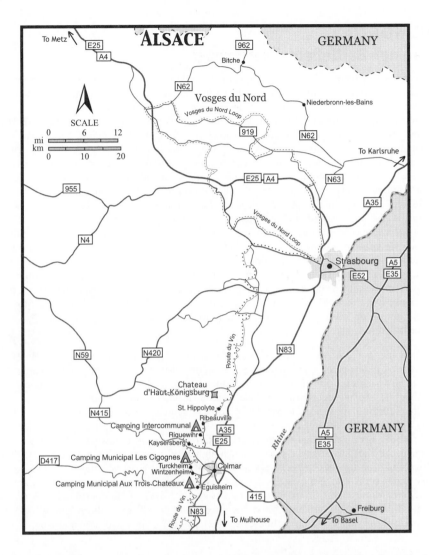

of Turckheim. Follow the Route du Vin signposts up the mountain road for 19km through vine-yards and charming villages. Pause at Kayserberg, where Albert Schweitzer was born. Turn east and then north to Riquewihr, a tiny, picturesque, walled village. Then continue north to medieval Ribeauville. St Hippolyte, six kilometers farther, has a terrific viewing area of the region from the terrace at the Chateau d'Haut-Koenigsbourg. All through the summer, wine festivals and street markets enliven the friendly ambiance; www.stratsbourg.com. Tagged a UNESCO biosphere, the Vosges du Nord's wooded hillsides, dotted with strangely-shaped rocks and bogs lush with pristine wild flowers, hide a wealth of protected fauna. Peregrine falcons, kingfishers, and great crested grebes nest here. Walking paths have well placed hides and posted interpretive information. Directions: A4 between Metz and Strasbourg runs along the southern border. Tourist centers are close to the German border at Bitche and Niederbronn-les-Bains on 962.

THE NORTH
Lorraine/ Battlefields/Northcoast

Lorraine's wide plains echo with memories of war and the troops of Julius Caesar, Charlemagne, Napoleon, and Hitler. Memorials and museums bring the battles alive. Start at the Musee Memorial de Fleury, where videos and photos make a lasting impression. Be sure to go downstairs to see the reconstruction of the once shell-torn village. Directions: Verdun is east of Reims. Take exit 31 off E50 and drive northeast out of Verdun following signposting for Douaumont. Visit the network of caves that sheltered wounded soldiers during World War I. Called Les Boves, they are beneath the Grand Place in Arras. Directions: Take exit 15 off A1. On the northwest coast, directly across from England, you can visit the sites of the important crossings as well as the Eperlecques Bunker- now the museum La Coupole-to see the Nazi liquid oxygen factory and launching pad aimed for London. Directions: Southwest of Dunkerque. Take exit 2 off E15 onto N43 and drive 20km to St Omar. Drive northwest of St Omar on 928 following signposting to Foret d'Eperlecques.

The grass-topped cliffs and sandy beaches on the northwest coastline at the Cote d'Opale and Baie de la Somme are suprisingly secluded considering that it is a busy channel-cossing spot. From here you can watch a pandemonium of gulls, terns, and razorbills wheeling in the air currents while gregarious clumps of cormorants hang out on rocky ledges. Bird enthusiasts shouldn't miss taking the nature trails into the private preserve, Parc du Marquenterre; open daily. Directions: Exit the A16/E402 south of Boulogne-sur-Mer at Abbeville. Follow signposting for Baie de Somme on 940 near Le Crotoy. Parc du Marquenterre is on the northwest edge of the Baie de la Somme.

▲Camping in the Area: • South of Verdun near D34. Camping les Breuils (03-2986-1531); convenient; pool; open May-September; $$. • On the north coast at the Baie de la Somme close to the bird sanctuary and the town of Le Crotoy. Exit A16/E402 south of Boulogne-sur-Mer at Abbeville. Follow signposting for Baie Somme and Le Crotoy on 940. Camping Les Trois Sablieres (0322-07-0133); small; wonderful views; difficult access for large caravans; pool; open Apr-Oct; $$. • In the same area and easier for large caravans. Camping la Ferme (0322-27-0675); basic; open Apr-Oct; $.• Convenient for ferries and tunnel crossings. Both of these are popular, call ahead to reserve a place. They both have nice ocean views and are busy with the arrival and departure of campers. • 5km west of Calais on the coast near the village of Sangatte. Take exit 14 off A16 for Sangatte. Follow signposting to the north side of the village. Camping Les Noires Mottes (0321-82-0475); open mid-Mar-mid-Nov; $. • 8km north of Calais in Oye-Plage. Take exit 20 off A16 onto 940 in the direction of Oye-Plage. Follow signposting to the west side of the village. Camping Bouscarel (0321-36-7637); open mid-Mar-mid-Nov; $.

Germany

www.germany-tourism.de

Passionate to learn, create, and excel, Germans strive to be a model of modern society. Their passion for the arts has filled their museums with fabulous, artistically-presented collections. Lovers of music and frivolity, their summer festivals, symphony halls, churches, cathedrals, and beer halls are all delightful. Their cities burst with a multi-cultural mix of exotic flavors and colors created by the job opportunities in their profitable industries. Proud of the best of their legacy, the country spends immense sums on restoration and exhibitions. Having a population that is avid about the outdoors, the country is laced with walking/hiking/cycling trails, and recreational equipment is readily available for rental. Intensely pretty towns with leafy promenades, cobbled market squares, and usually at least one impressive church hug the banks of ribbon-like rivers. Geraniums bloom in window boxes and overflow from hanging baskets on street lamps.

The Germans are trail-blazing campers. Campgrounds are easy to find, well maintained, beautifully located, and popular. Locals maintain large tent vacation homes on sites they lease from campground owners, spending time in them on weekends and during vacations. The owners of the campgrounds like the extra income from those of us who stay only a short time, but it's easy to feel like an intruder at a private club. I've found that if I compliment their gardens, children, and pet, in German, they smile and we can have a bit of conversation. Campground rules include being quiet in the morning and during the afternoon nap time. Being neat and tidy also earns a star of approval. I make an extra effort to clean the shower-toilet area after use and make sure my campsite is thoroughly clean before departing. Because camping is so popular, I recommend checking in by 2 or 3 PM. On Fridays, if you're close to a tourist area or popular recreation areas, check in by 11 AM. Reception areas in smaller campgrounds might be closed for a long lunch. About 20 euros will cover the cost for two persons, a car, and a tent in most places noted here as $$. Resort-like campgrounds and those located in popular areas will cost just over 25 euros and are noted here as $$$.

Because the Germans are leaders in the building of vast, efficient roadways, you won't find getting around difficult. Use the fast lanes with caution and only for passing. A car that seems a long way back is suddenly right behind you. Good navigation skills are important while driving in Germany. Study the map carefully, highlight your route, and list the roads you'll be exiting off and getting on. Even though signage is excellent, traffic moves quickly, leaving little time for indecision.

Be particularly cautious around trams, where the pedestrian has the right of way. Pedestrians also have the right of way at crosswalks, as do cyclists in cycle lanes. A fixed green arrow on a red traffic light allows you to turn in that direction after coming to a full stop. Germans are serious about their rules. Ticketing and on-the-spot fine paying keeps it this way. Your driver's license from home will be sufficient so don't bother getting an international one. Their comprehensive motorway network, called Autobahn, dominates the roadway system and takes most of the long-distance traffic off the smaller roadways. Autobahn signs are blue, and the number is preceded by A; there is no speed limit. International roadway signs are green with a preceding E; the speed limit is 130 kph or 80 mph. Secondary roads have a preceding B; speed limit is 64 kmp to 50 kph, depending on the weather. Gas stations abound; most open early and close late. Adjoining mini-markets and cafes provide modern conveniences. Emergency phones are placed along roadways with pictorial instructions. Your roadway insurance from home is respected. Roadway attendants probably won't speak English, but gestures and a phrase book or dictionary will probably suffice. Placing the warning triangle (included in every rental vehicle) on the roadway behind the vehicle is compulsory. Anyone driving so slowly that a line of cars has formed behind must pull over to let the other vehicles pass. Learn these terms because they are often not in international graphic symbols: einbahnstrasse-one-way street; links fahren-keep left; parken verboten-no parking; umleitung-detour.

Parking is handled efficiently. At tourist and market areas, parking payment is often made at a centrally located ticket dispenser. Keep change handy for them. The cost of parking is about the same as it is at home. Large car parks are found just outside the congested areas and public transportation is close by. Bringing your bike from home or renting one to pedal along with the locals through the historic areas and countryside is lots of fun.

BERLIN

Berlin's long-held passion for art and archeology has made its riveting museum collections some of the best in the world. The city and its outlying areas are a paradise for art and history lovers, no matter where ones interest lies. As if facing an elegant and immense table of delicious food, be selective or you'll be overwhelmed. Living and breathing culture, its opera companies, symphonic orchestras, theatres, and galleries are world-renowned. For ticketing use the web or call Fullhouse Service (030) 30 87 85 685 or Hekticket Theaterkassen (030) 230 99 30, or go directly to the box office.

Powerful architecture reconstructs the history of antisemitism towards German Jews in the Judisches museum, where uneven floors, weirdly canted walls and ceilings, and an empty cell lit only by a slit of light convey the terror of the camps; open daily; U-bahn Hallesches. Mount the stairs to a new dome in the Reichstag symbolizing a hope for transparency in a democratic government; open daily; S-bahn Unter den Linden. Wander up the spiraling and airy renovation at the German History Museum, the Zeughaus, a stimulating environment for special exhibits; closed Monday; S-bahn Hackescher Markt. Admire pieces from the most celebrated modern artists in the slick steel Neue Nationalgalerie; closed Monday; U-bahn Potsdamer Platz or Mendelssohn. Enjoy the reunion of the great Prussian, German, and Dutch masterpieces in the new Gemaldegalerie; closed Monday; U-Bahn Potsdamer Platz.

Highest priority, however, should be given to the Pergamonmuseum. Here reconstruction tries to evoke the original experience with a soaring staircase, altar and monumental freize excavated from Bergama, Turkey. The energy exuding from the freize, depicting a battle between gods and giants, is masterful. Walking down the Processional Way to the Ishtar Gate-huge Babylon piece from the 6th-century BC reconstructed around the original pieces-you'll be transported to the ancient world where civilization took root. Its original size and importance can be appreciated when you examine the intricate model. This immense museum is fascinating. Recorded English sound tracks and texts are great; closed Monday, S-bahn Friedrichstrasse or Hackescher or Bus100.

Tree-lined boulevards and brilliantly-colored flower beds soften the gargantuan monuments and buildings. Tiergarten Park, sitting right in the middle of all of this, is a whimsical place filled with raffish youngsters on skateboards, Turkish women in colorful scarves enjoying barbecues,

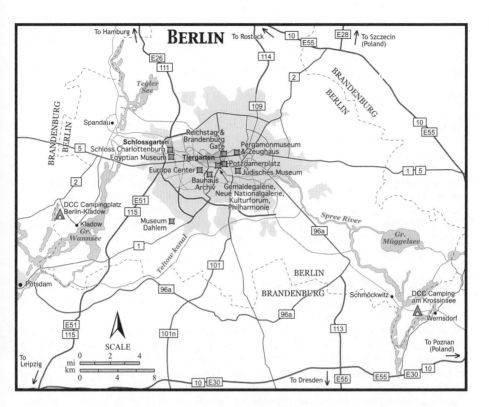

sunbathers stretched lazily on grassy meadows, mothers chatting as they push baby strollers, and kids trying to perfect their skill on bicycles.

On the south side of the Tiergarten, between the park and the canal, beautifully landscaped streets wind around the Kulturforum. At the Philharmonie you can listen to the Berlin Philharmonic, one of the world's best symphonic orchestras. Purchase tickets ahead; www.berlin. philharmonic.com. The Museum of musical instruments is next door. Streamlined and glass-paneled Bauhaus-Archiv is a pilgrimage site for modern applied-art enthusiasts. Here you can examine the collection of one of the most influential art institutions in the 20th century; closed Tuesday and free on Monday; U bahn-Nollendorf-patz.

Save some energy for a couple of the museums farther from the city. The breathtakingly beautiful, almost hypnotic 3000-year-old Bust of Nefertiti in the Egyptian Museum is one of the city's most glorious treasures, but the rest of the collection is amazing too; closed Monday; U-bahn Richard Waner Platz or Sopie-Charlotte-Platz. Driving directions: North side of the city across from the entrance to the Schloss Charlottenburg. Take exit 6 off 100. Enormous ancient boats from Oceana are just one of the highlights at the Dahlem Museum, whose enthnographic collection from around the world is outstanding. Kids love this museum; closed Monday; U-bahn Dahlem Dorf. Driving directions: Southwest of the city in the suburb of Dahlem. Exit 100 onto 1 south in the direction of Dahlem, then follow signposting for the museum.

Locals here go out of their way to help you with directions and it's easy to chat with them in a museum or café. Bring a good guidebook, and visit the excellent tourist information office-particularly the one at Europa Center; U & S bahn: Zoo Station, www.smb.spk-berlin.de. Purchasing a Berlin Welcome Card makes sense. The host of discounts and unlimited travel benefits will entice you to see and do more in this beautiful and stimulating city. Jump onto bus 100 or 200 for an inexpensive city tour. Berlin's bicycle-only lanes make pedaling a fun way to join the locals and a less tiring way to see the sights. Rentals are available at the Zoo Station and from other outfitters, check with the tourist office.

▲Camping: None are close to the city. • Southeast of the city, east of the Flughafen Berlin-Schonefeld, between E55 and 113. Exit E30/10 at exit 9 and drive north along the waterway to Wernsdorf. Then go west towards Schmockwitz. DDC Camping am Krossinsee (030 675 8687); my favorite for Berlin; nice location on the Krossinsee; cabins; recreational area; open all year; $$. • West of the city, off 5, exit south onto 2 for 18 km, then drive southeast in the direction of Kladow for 2km. DDC Campingplatz Berlin-Kladow, Krampnitzer Weg 111-117 (030 365 2797); popular with families; open all year; $$. • Southwest of Berlin. On the western edge of the suburb of Spandau, close to B2/B5. Take exit 7 off E51 and drive west one kilometer. At the fork follow signposting for Spandau and camping. Campingplatz Breitehorn (030 365 3408); nice shady location; open April-Sept; $$. In the same area. Off A1 exit Flughafen Tegel. Follow signposting for Saatwinkler Damn and camping on Gartenfelder Str. City-Camping Hettler and Lange (030 3350 3633); convenient; open all year; $$.

Potsdam and Park Sanssouci

When the cultural leadership of Germany passed from Dresden to Prussia in the middle of the 18th century, Prussia's great military commander Frederick the Great began building a fabulous palace and garden for himself. He named it Sanssouci, meaning "without care." Wanting to escape from the rigors of political life and spend time with a small circle of friends, he kept the palace small and intimate. He was an accomplished flautist and designed the rooms to promote an ambiance of music, dancing, and seduction. Seven vineyard terraces and arcades of trelliswork embellish the palace exterior. Of all the fun Frederick had in building Sanssouci, the Chinese Tea House excited him the most. He incorporated the fanciful visions of the Orient, which had been introduced to him by his grandfather. The teahouse has a conical roof supported by columns simulated as guilded palm trees. Casually spaced between the columns are groups of life-size figures; one group is in the midst of a tea ceremony, another is being enticed by pineapples and mangoes.

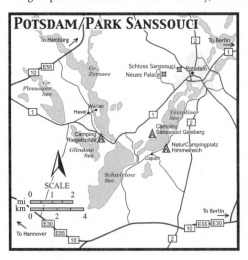

A mandarin sits playfully under a parasol on the roof's apex. Inside is an exquisite collection of Chinese porcelain. It is a marriage of oriental subject and western sculptural style that simply will take your breath away. Keeping in the playful mood, gay children rather than the usual solemn deities are models for sculpture in the larger gardens. The center fountain depicts the light-hearted story of a sea nymph. At the end of the Seven Years War, Frederick built the richly decorated Neues Palais to house his court and state visitors. The park is free, but admission is charged for the palaces and interior of the teahouse; open daily. Directions: Potsdam and Sanssouci are southwest of Berlin between E55 and E51. Follow signposting from either highway.

▲Camping: • Drive southwest of Potsdam on B1 for 5km and follow signposting from the highway. Camping Sanssouci-Gaisberg, An der Pirschheide (033 275 5680); lovely location on the Templiner See; open May-Sept; $$. • 6km farther west on the Glindower See. Off A10/E55 take exit 22 onto B1 in the direction of Werder. Drive east six kilometers to the village of Havel. Camping Riegelspitze (033-274-2397); nice location; cabins; open May-Sept; $$. • On the southeast side of the Templiner See near Caputh. Exit north off A10/E55 at exit 17 or 18, and drive north on B2 for 2km then west for Caputh. NaturCampingplatz Himmelreich (033209 70475); nice location on the lake; open all year; $$$.

SOUTHEASTERN GERMANY

Walking/cycling paths wind through the tree-shaded parkland of the World Biosphere Reserve called Spreewald, Built from marshland formed from the Spree River, it is used today by people paddling two-man kayaks or sitting back in little tourist boats pushed by boatman on the small rivers, canals, and tiny lakes. It good touristy fun. Purchase the map, Wanderkarte, because the waterways and walking/cycling paths meander through a large area and it is easy to get disoriented. Kayak rental is available in both Lubben and Lubbenau. Directions: Drive 54km south of Berlin on E36/55. Exit north onto 87 and drive 8km to Lubben and Speewald.

▲Camping: Just south of Lubben. Exit E36/E55 at exit 7 or 8 and following signposting. Spreewald Camping (03546 7053); pleasant location on the little river; smaller; open Apr-Oct; $$.

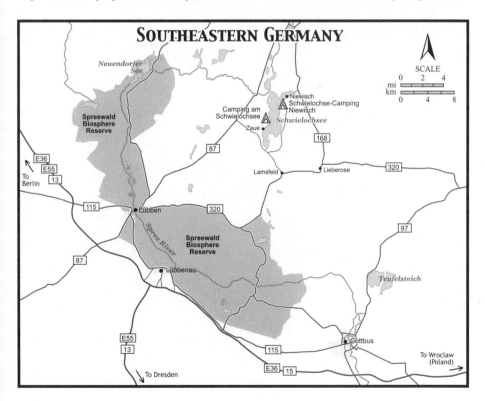

One of East Germany's most admired gardens, Muskau-Branitz, was created by draining the marshland along the banks of the Neisse River in Cottbus at the Polish border. Befriended by Goethe, Prince van Puckler-Muskau traveled to England, North Africa, and Asia gathering species and ideas. His influence on gardening became immense, particularly in regard to trees. The parkland is notable for its immense beeches and oaks. An earth pyramid was raised in an artificial lake as a gravesite for the prince and his wife; open daily. Directions: Drive 83km south of Berlin on E36/15 in the direction of Cottbus. Turn north at exit 5 and follow signposting for Schlosspark.

▲Camping: • Northeast of Lubben on the Schwielochsee. Exit E55/E36 at exit 8 for Lubben. Drive 8km then exit east onto 320 and drive 11km in the direction of Lieberose. Turn north at Lamsfeld and drive 4km to Schwielochsee. Camping Am Schwielochsee (0354 78 512); lovely location on the water; large; open Apr-Oct; $$. • Northeast end of the lake in Niewisch. Schwielochsee-Camping Niewisch (033676 5186); nice location on the water; boat launch; open April-mid-Oct; $$.

BODE RIVER VALLEY:
The Harz Mountains and Quedlinburg

More hilly than mountainous with beautiful serene lakes, pine-scented forests, and towns that seem plucked out of fairytale books, this is an excellent area to camp with kids. Nature preserves, vintage narrow gauge railways, mine and cave tours, hiking trails to waterfalls, and scenic loop cycling/driving routes are highlights. Campground offices have loads of brochures, and staff can help with additional details.

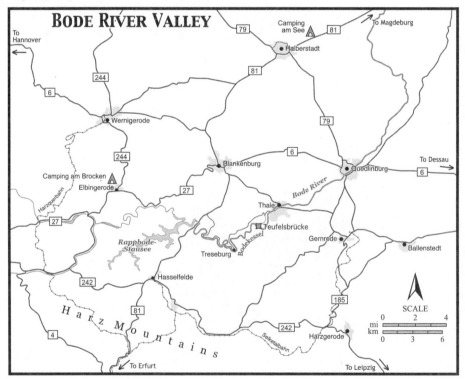

Spend a leisurely day taking the classic walk from Thale to the Teufelsbrucke, then up the Schurre trail for its grand view of the dramatic Bodekessel gorge. From here continue on to Treseburg where you can stop for a treat before heading back. Bring your wild flower guide because the area is noted for its springtime bloom of tiny orchids, daphnes, and lilies. It's a popular birding area too. Directions: Thale is 10km west of Quedlinburg. Follow signposting south of Thale along the Bode River in the direction of Rosstrappe.

Steam-train buffs come from all over the world to enjoy a ride on the Harzquerbahn, Germany's most scenic narrow-gauge rail line. It's hard to resist a ride when you hear the whistle blow and see the ancient locomotives start puffing their way up into the mountains. The train leaves from Wernigerode. Directions: Wernigerode is 30km west of Quedlinburg. At the north end of town follow signposting for Hauptbahnhof. Pick up a brochure with timetable at the campground. Wernigerode's marketplace is a medieval jewel, so pick up a self-guided walking tour map. Check ahead to time your visit for one of the town's lively festivities that take place throughout the summer.

▲Camping: • West of Thale in Elbingerode, northwest of town. Camping am Brocken, (0394-544-2589); nice location; open all year; $$.

In the early part of the 10th century, Quedlinburg was the headquarters of the German nation, home of the Saxon king, and site for several meeting of the Imperial Diet. Today the entire old town is UNESCO-listed because more than 1500 half-timbered houses. Refreshingly not restored but left as they are, the town's inner core will interest even bored kids. Some alleyways are so narrow you can touch the leaning houses on both sides. Use the village map so you don't miss any of the fascinating nooks and crannies. It's available at the camp office and tourist office.

▲Camping: • From Halberstadt, drive east on B81 for 3km, then exit north to Halberstadter See. Camping am See (039-41-60-9308); nice location; separate nude bathing area; open all year; $$$.

ERFURT/WEIMAR AREA

Cherished by Germans, this modest quiet town situated on the banks of the Ilm River was the home of the German Enlightenment. The list of residents who helped found German culture is astounding: Goethe, Schiller, Liszt, Herder, Richard Strauss, and artists and writers associated with the Bauhaus. Park at the south end then walk through the shady park along the river that Goethe, an avid gardener, helped to design. Visit both the Goethe's Gartenhaus and the Liszthaus. Then step inside Goethe's elegant mansion to visit the moving rooms in which he lived and worked. In adjoining rooms you can peer over cases that hold the original manuscripts of his work. The poems are written in his own hand. Take time to visit the Stadtmuseum. It will make your visit to Weimar more meaningful. The collections are devoted to the town's impressive history, plus there is an excellent natural history section which will enhance your time in Germany's natural areas. If you plan ahead, you can arrange to attend a performance in its national theatre where Wagner's Lohengrin premiered. Exciting pieces of modern art, particularly of Paul Maenz's, can be seen at the Neues Museum; closed Monday. Goethe and his patron, Duke Carl August, studied and worked together to develop the gardens at the duke's summer residence. Called Belvedere because of its rooftop terrace, the formal gardens with hedge-enclosed rooms and flower beds make a serene place to spend some time. Directions: Drive or cycle south of town 2km following signposting. Buchenwald, 8km north, was once a grim concentration camp but today it is a place of remembrance; closed Monday. Directions: Drive north of town crossing the railway line and 85. Continue for 3km then turn west continuing through the Buchwald parkland and follow signposting for Konzentrationslager.

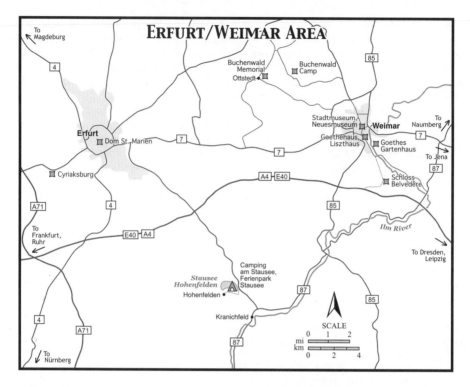

▲Camping: • 20km west of Weimar. exit E40 south at exit 47 in the direction of Kranichfeld and drive to Hohenfeldern. Camping am Stausee (0364-504-2081); peaceful location on a tiny lake; open all year; $$.

Erfurt

Garden enthusiasts come from all over the world to enjoy Erfurt's enormous spring garden show at the castle grounds of Cyriaksburg. At other times visitors can still see the greenhouse displays and the museum of gardening. Directions: Drive west of Erfurt on 7 in the direction of Gotha for 5km exiting for Cyriaksburg; closed Monday. Dom St Marien is one of Germany's many remarkable Gothic cathedrals. The light that falls from its 12 very high, slender stained glass windows-some dating from the 14th century-spreads a fluorescent radiance throughout the somber interior. Once Erfurt brimmed with clerics from every monastic order. It was here that Martin Luther shut himself away behind the door of the Augustine cloister.

▲Camping: • On a tiny lake 15km southeast of Erfurt. Exit E40/A4 at exit 47. Drive south 6km in the direction of Kranichfeld. Ferienpark Stausee (036450 42081); pleasant family park area; open all year; $$.

Naumberg

The twin towers of Naumberg's Dom dominate the city's skyline. Here for the first time, in an almost revolutionary style, secular personalities were presented within the spiritual context of the church. Displayed beneath sumptuous canopies, the founders of the church and their wives have sculpted features so realistic that their faces could be portraits from life. The great vitality of the figures is constrained by the dignity and calm of the perfect stonework of the cathedral itself. With binoculars, examine the carved leaf-work of the capitals and choir screen because even individual species of flowers and shrubs can be recognized. Very little is known about the artist who left such great art; closed Sunday. Directions: Drive east of Weimar on E40 for 24km. Turn north onto 88 and drive 37km to Naumberg.

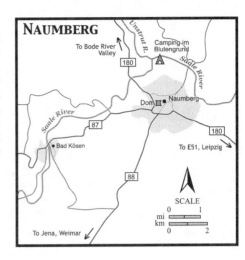

▲Camping: • On the river Saale. Drive north of town on 180 for two kilometers then follow signposting for camping. Camping im Blutengrund (03445 202711); nice location; popular with families; open all year; $$.

Worlitz

Proposing that an entire countryside-including a town, a forest, and farms be planted with an eye for beauty as if it were a park, Prince von Anhalt-Dessau greatly influenced country planning throughout the western world and eventually the development of the American metropolitan park system. The prince was inspired by Rosseau and the great liberal aristocrats of England, whose parks functioned as centers of enlightenment and helped to counterweight the conservative royal court. What he called his "Garden Kingdom" covered a huge area along the banks of the Elbe River. Throughout, little bridges of various design connect the charming islands. Staying for a summer evening boat concert, when both the orchestra and audience sit peacefully in the mirror-like lake, is especially memorable. Directions: South of Potsdam drive 60km south on E51 to 187. Continue on E51 for another 12km then take exit 9 and follow signposting for Worlitz Park.

▲Camping: In Lutherstadt Wittenburg, southeast of the junction of 187 and E51. Marina-Camp Elbe (03491 4540); smaller; nice location; open April-Oct; $$. South of the above on the small lake Bergwitzsee. Exit E51 at exit 10 and drive 14km to Bergwitz. Camping-und Wassersportpark Bergwitzsee (034921 28228); large; in a recreational area with water sport rentals; open all year; $$.

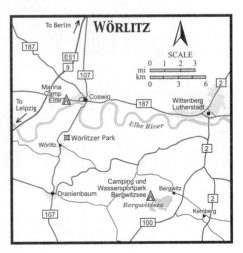

DRESDEN AREA

Once called Germany's Florence, Dresden has emerged remarkably beautiful after faithful and painstaking restoration of the horrendous destruction caused by the saturated bombings of Allied forces during World War II. Start immersing yourself in the glory of Baroque Dresden from the Bruhlsche Terrace.

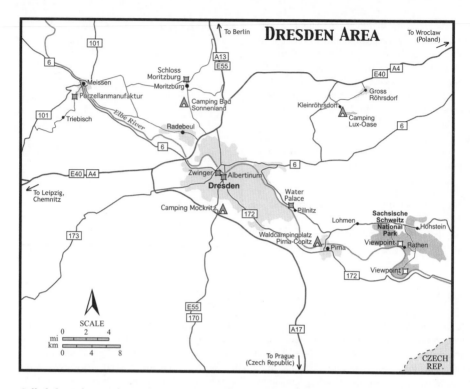

Called the Balcony of Europe, it has a splendid view of the Elbe River. Afterwards, walk over to the Albertinum, where Dresden's fabulous Grunes Gewolbe Collection, a fantasy of royal jewels, crowns, ivory, and porcelain, is kept. The priceless pieces are beyond belief. Save some time to visit the second gallery, Neue Meister, to see haunting landscapes and work from the Expressionist art group Die Brucke; closed Thursday.

The palace quarter, or Zwinger, was built for extravagant entertainment. It's a Baroque show-piece of grandiose fountains, pavilions, and elaborate gateways. It was built by the residing King of Poland, whose significant wealth was accrued from extensive deposits of silver ore. His love of fine antique Chinese porcelain led him to encourage his own craftsmen. Dresden's porcelain artists became the finest porcelain makers in the western world. Visiting Porzellansammlung and seeing both the 2,000-year-old Chinese porcelain collection and the finest of the Dresden works makes for thoughtful comparison; closed Monday. Crossing the courtyard, don't miss visiting the Gemaldegalerie Alte Meister. It's holds one of Europe's finest collections of masterful works by Rubens, Rembrandt, Raphael, Van Dyck, and Titian as well as many other renowned artists; closed Monday.

With remarkable skill, the very latest in computer technology, and an international fund-rais-ing campaign, Dresden's Frauenkirche has been lovingly restored with its original stones being remarkably placed in their original location. Only ten percent of the masonry is new. Take the tour; open daily. Dresden has excellent large parking areas close to all the main tourist areas. Keep change for the ticket dispensers.

▲Camping: • South of the city in the suburb of Modkritz, signposted off B172. Camping Mockritz, Boderitzer Str. 30 (035-471-8226); quiet, surburban atmosphere; open most of the year; $$. • Northeast of the city, close to Gross-Rohrdorf. Exit E40 at exit 85, and drive south just over 2km then east for 2km to the small lake at Kleinrohrsdorf. Camping Lux-Oase (035-9525-6666); nice location by a small lake; resort-like; popular with families; Mar-Oct; $$.

Impressively restored Schloss Moritzburg, a Baroque hunting lodge, makes a nice place for a picnic lunch and photographs. Directions: 14km north of Dresden exit E40 west at exit 81B, and then drive about 12km farther. Dresden porcelain fans wouldn't think of missing Meissen, the site of Europe's first-and one its finest-porcelain factories. Staatliche Porzellan-Manufaktur Meissen is southwest of town 2km in the direction of Triebisch. Schauhalle is another porcelain factory in the vicinity and makes a good alternative if lines at the former are too long. Both have interesting tours of porcelain production and showrooms; open daily. Directions: Drive 30km north of Dresden on E40.

▲Camping: In Moritzburg. Take exit 80 off E40/A4 and follow signposting for Moritzburg and camping. Camping Bad Sonnenland (0351 830 5495); nice location on a pond; open Apr-Oct; $$.

Fantastic, craggy rock formations have made Sachsische Schweitz National Park a mecca for rock-climbing enthusiasts, hikers, and birders. There is a superb view of the Elbe River's bend from a high plateau in the Lillenstein mountains close to a medieval fortress. Directions: Drive southeast of Dresden on 172 for 12km in the direction of Pirna. Exit east before Pirna following signposting for Lohmen for 8km. Continue east for 4km to Hohstein. Exit south taking the small mountainous road in the direction of Rathen and beyond to the Bastei for 8km.

The giant colonnade of the Water Palace at Pillnitz provides a rhythmical backdrop to its serene garden along the banks of the Elbe River about 12km south of Dresden. Designed for the wild parties Augustus the Strong loved to host, a monumental curving, sphinx-guarded flight of stairs led party-goers to the river. Today the pagoda-like roofline is edged with magnificent rhododendrons, and there is a lilac garden next to the new palace.

▲Camping: • On the Elbe River, on the west side of Pirna-Copitz (03501 523773); nice family camping place; open Apr-Oct; $$.

Leipzig

Bach lived and worked in this city of musical traditions as did Mendelssohn, Schumann, and Wagner. It is easy to enjoy one of the many summer performances by touring choir groups or the renowned Thomanerchoir-which Bach once directed-at the Thomaskirche. Directions: Walk southwest of Markt on Thomaskirchof. Just south of the church, stop in at the Bach house to view its large collection of mementos from his life's work plus some of the musical instruments used during the era; open daily.

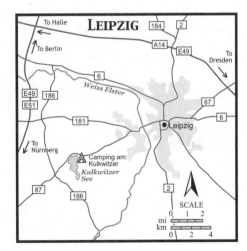

▲Camping: • On the west side of Leipzig on a small lake. Off E49/E51/A9 take exit 18 in the direction of Leipez and drive 4km. Turn south and drive 6km following signposting for Kulkwitzer See and camping. Camping Am Kulkwitzer See (0341 9411514); tranquil location on the lake; popular with families; open Apr-Oct; $$.

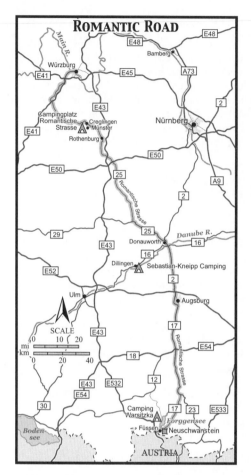

The Romantic Road/ Romantische Strasse

Prim old villages filled with houses decorated with brown timbers, red geraniums, and lace curtains dot this idyllic rural setting. A woodsy landscape of old farms is quilted in shades of green pastures and fringed by orchards of gnarled trees. Turrets from castles and cathedrals rise like chess pieces from the forest. In quiet, sunny castle courtyards you can rest on benches set atop cobblestones worn smooth from horses hooves and wagon wheels. In larger cities, once Roman, now casually sophisticated, you can examine a host of cultural relics. A popular walking/cycling path called the Radroute Romantische is one of the best ways to experience the idyllic rural scenery that inspired the 18th-century movement of artists, composers, and writers whose era is now called the Romantic Age. Directions: The Romantische Strasse runs between the Bavarian Alps in Fussen to the Main River's vineyard country around Wurzburg. All tourist bureaus have maps of the route.

▲Camping: At the north end of the route close to Creglingen, which is 20km north of Rothenburg. Off 290 exit south in the direction of Munster and drive 3km. Campingplatz Romantische Strasse (07933 20289); good place to meet other travelers "doin' The Road"; open mid-Mar-mid-Oct; $$$. Mid-way along the route, on the Danube River in Dillingen. Off E43/7 take exit 117 and drive east on 19 in the direction of Hermaringen for 4km. Continue for 21km going south and then east along the river to Dillingen. Follow signposting for camping by the bridge over the Danube. Sebastian-Kneipp-Camping (09071 503655); nice location on the river; new; open all year; $$. In the Bavarian Alps near Fussen at lake Forggensee. Drive north of Fussen on 16 for 12km in the direction of Rieden and Rosshaupten.. Exit east to the lake following signposting for camping. Campingplatz Warsitzka (08367 406); lovely location; smaller; open all year; $$.

BAVARIA
Munchen

Munchen's free-spirited, fun-loving, and easy-going approach to life is infectious. It is a metropolis with a village heart where high-tech innovation blends easily with old-world charm. The city pulses with life and gemutlichkeit, or good feeling, which may stem from their passion for beer. The lust is not hard to understand when you consider the deliciousness and pureness of the beer manufactured here.

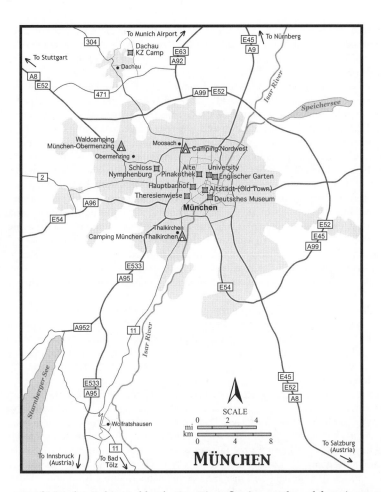

The center of Munchen is bisected by the Isar River, flowing northward from its source in the Bavarian Alps. Most of the city's sights are on the left bank. Start your exploration at Marienplatz, the center of the Altstadt. It is named after the guilded statue of the Virgin Mary who has stood on her column gracefully guarding the city for over three centuries. Look up at the 85-meter Neues Rathaus' tower to see the fourth largest glockenspiel in Europe. Twice a day, at 11 AM and 5 PM, the chimes peal and people gather to watch 32 brightly-colored figures enact both a jousting tournament honoring a wedding and a dance marking the end of the plague. Bring your binoculars. Climb the stairs of the Gothic St Peterskirche on the eastside of the square for a superb view and orientation. Note the twin onion domes of Frauenkirche, the city's landmark. Lush gardens and green parklands tie together the marriage of Munchen's Gothic, Baroque, and Neoclassical architectural styles. The University, north of Marienplatz in Schwabing, is bordered by the largest garden in Europe The Englischer Garden. The Nymphenburg, with its beautiful pavilions and fountains of the royal Bavarian court, is farther north. Looking down at the south edge of Marienplatz you'll see Viktualienmarkt, where the quality and presentation of foodstuffs is mouthwatering and hard to resist. The boisterous, smoky, fun-loving establishments of the pub quarter, are just east of Marienplatz. To the west beyond the Hauptbahnhof is Theresienwiese where for 16 days, (beginning in mid-September and ending on the first Sunday in October) oompah-pah music keep merry-making throngs happy while they guzzle beer, munch on juicy sausage and spit-roasted chicken, and sing and dance on the tables. The party originated to celebrate the engagement of Princess Therese and Crown Prince Ludwig and was so much fun it has been an annual event ever since.

Munchen is rich in interesting museums, churches, and historic sights. The new Pinakothek der Moderne completes one of the world's most remarkable museum complexes. The Alte Pinakothek's world-renowned collection of the German masterpieces includes Durer's self portrait. Brueghel, Rubens, Van Dyck, Titian and El Greco masterpieces round out the collection. Across the courtyard, in the Neue Pinakothek, there is a nice collection of the Impressionists. Completing the ensemble, in what is meant to be an "invisible" building on the outside, is the new Moderne. Inside this bland shoe-box of a building is a dream of shadowless, sugar-white galleries that branch off from an airy three-story rotunda. Here the colors from the German Expressionists simply combust under the luminous intensity of the all-skylight ceiling. Its collection of drawings, designs, and architectural models is superb; open daily. Directions: Ubahn-Konigsplatz. Covering everything from mining to astrophysics and from first automobile to the equipment of air traffic control, the huge Deutsch Museum is the world's best museum of technology. Learning how things work becomes fascinating with the help of staff-led demonstrations and experiments. Museum docents help you with interactive exhibits and there is a terrific kids' wing. Use the map and schedule of demonstrations to select what interests you most; open daily. Directions: S-bahn Isartor.

The Englischer Garden, one of the largest parks in Europe, stretches from the center of town for miles along the Isar River in a northeasterly direction. Walking and cycling paths and a beer garden at the Chinesicher Turm make it a perfect place to take a break from museums and sightseeing. Buy a tourist card at the campground and use the public transportation, called the MVV. It has closeby access from the campgrounds and is easy to use. Just stamp your ticket as you enter a station and hop on board.

For side trips from historic Munchen, castle-lovers will enjoy Schloss Nymphenburg located northwest of the city. The complex includes a porcelain museum, royal coaches, lovely gardens, and intriguing pavilions; closed Mondays. Dachau was Hitler's first concentration camp. Today it is only slightly softened by grass. An explicit exhibit of photographs documents the horror. See the film; you don't need wait for the English version to understand. Small chapels of various religions are in the complex. Locals like to float down the Isar River on warm summer days. You can join them if you've brought an inner tube or inflatable mattress from home. Most people start their float from Wolfratshausen or Bad Tolz, south of Munchen. Directions: Drive south of Munchen on 111, the road that hugs the west side of the Isar River, in the direction of Wolfratshsn for 25km. Bad Tolz is an additional 25km south.

▲Camping: • 4km south of the city in a park in the suburb of Thalkirchen, along the western bank of the Isar River. From A95/533 take exit 2. From E54/A99 take exit 1. Follow signposting for Thalkirchen then Zoo and camping. Camping Munchen-Thalkirchen, Zentallandstr 49 (089-723-1707); best location for the city and very popular; great place to meet fellow travelers; popular with school groups; fun and friendly but often noisy; open April-Oct; $$$. • Northwest of the city in the suburb of Obermenzing. Off the Stuttgart-Munchen autobahn, E52/A8, follow signposting southeast for Munchen centrum, avoiding the ring. Take exit 82 and follow signposting for Obermenzing and camping. Waldcamping Munchen-Obermenzing (089 8112235); part of a forest park; convenient to the autobahn; traffic noise; open mid-March-Oct; $$. • Northwest of the city in the suburb of Moosach; close to the intersection of E52/99 (the ring road) and 304/Dachauer Str; not far from Olympiapark. Exit south off E52/99 onto 304, and drive in the direction of Munchen centrum, then exit south for Moosach. Camping Nordwest, Auf den Schrederwiesen 3 (089-150-6936); noisy with trains and traffic; open year round; $$.

Chiemsee

The most fascinating part of the Schloss Herrenchiemee-a Ludwig II extravaganza-is the fascinating exhibit of his memorabilia in the museum. Boats to Herreninsel, where the palace museum is, depart from Prien. The sparkling lake has many tourist-oriented activities. Directions: 90km southeast of Munchen on E52, in the direction of Salzburg. Exit north at exit 106 for Prien and Lake Chiemsee.

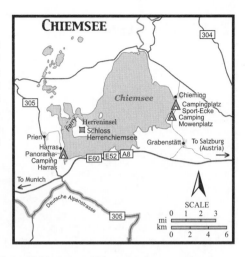

▲Camping: All camping places mentioned are close to the lake, popular with families and open Mid-April-Sept. • 2km south of Prien on the lake. Off E52/E60/A8 take exit 106 and drive 3km in the direction of Prien then an additional 2km to Harras. Panorama-Camping Harras (080-51 90460); beautiful location; $$$. • On the east side of the lake, exit E52 north at exit 109, and drive 13km to Chieming, then one kilometer south of town on the lake road. Campingplatz Sport-Ecke (086-64-500); beautiful location; $$$. In the same area. Camping Mowenplatz (08664 361); smaller; car parking separate from tent site; nice location on the lake; $$$.

BAVARIAN ALPS

Towering mountains, exciting cable cars, frescoed houses, more of Ludwig's castles, scenic drives, and well-marked hiking trails draw plenty of holiday visitors to this area. The Deutsches Alpenstrasse was built in the 1930s to facilitate scenic drives through the German Alps. The road meanders through pretty villages, along pleasant rivers, and up to meadows sweet with summer vetch. There is also a gorgeous route from Oberammergau, over the Ammer-sattel, and then down to the Plansee to Reutte. It is long and winding but breathtakingly beautiful and little trails lead out for pleasant walks when you want to take a break from driving. Check with the tourist office to verify whether the whole route is open before setting out.

Germans have a passion for reaching the top, so the area is riddled with exciting but expensive cable cars and narrow-gauge railways. The one up to the Zugspitze, the highest peak in Germany, is particularly popular. Check with the tourist office in Garmisch-Partenkirchen for full descriptions. For a classic hike, take the High Alpine Walk to the Gorge of Hollental. The trail hugs a tiny cleft in a narrow rock gorge carved by a still-powerful waterfall. Members of the German Alpine Club constructed the Hollentalklamm in the early 1900s. Sometimes it seems more like a mining tunnel than a trail as you traverse the slippery path through tunnels lit only dimly with an electric light bulb or window carved out of the rock wall. Throughout the narrow gorge the cascade plunges with pounding force over immense mossy boulders. At one point the trail is a cantilevered bridge over the torrent. Gradually the power subsides and what was once a great torrent becomes a gentle stream bordered with grass and colorful wild flowers leading into the beautiful glacial basin of Hollental. A very pleasant terrace-café and picnic tables welcome you. You can sit and eat your made at the campground-picnic lunch while sipping a well-earned cold beer. Chatting with fellow hikers about the beauty of the scenery makes the break even more fun. There is trailhead parking in Hammersbach, just south of Grainau. The trail leads up from a creek and then climbs through a forest of pine and birch. At entrance to the gorge a small admission fee is collected.

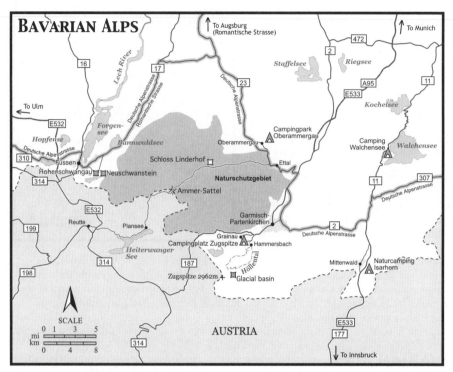

The only castle King Ludwig finished and lived in was Schloss Linderhof. Here he dressed like a sultan and smoked a hookah in his Moorish pavilion. Guests lingered leisurely in the cavernous Venus Grotto decorated with "before-Disney" stalactites garlands. While the king sat in a conch shell floating in the middle of a tiny illuminated lake, favorite arias by Wagner were sung; open daily. Directions: 11km west of Ettal.

Berchtesgaden National Park

Geographically an enclave of Austria, Berchtesgaden National Park has a fjord-like setting with cable cars and excursion boats. High up in the mountains at the eastern end of the park, Hitler established his famous Eagle's Nest-a foreboding granite structure. The final ascent is torturously steep with hairpin curves that bend over the gorge. Views defy description. You must go by excursion bus or take the hiking trail. It is popular to take the bus up then hike down. Directions: Eagle's Nest is reached through the village of Obersalzberg about 50km south of Salzburg. From E55 south of Salzburg contine south on 160, then 305, then 319. No motorized traffic is allowed around the Konigssee. It is surrounded by steep mountains and laced with mountain trails. To miss the crowds exit B305 west of Berchtesgaden at Ramsau and drive to Hindersee to the trailhead for the lakeshore walk. The drive between Berchesgaden and Ruhpolding on B305 is especially scenic. The road passes through lush valleys and between steep mountains sometimes seeming perilously close to the river. From Ruhpolding to the delightful alpine village of Reit im Winkl, the Alpen Strasse road that runs between two beautiful rivers.

▲Camping: • In Graineau, three kilometers west of Garmisch-Parkirchen. Campingplatz Zugspitze (088-21-3180); close to the hiking trails for Zugspitz; close to the road but not overly noisy; open all year; $$. • In Mittenwald, off E533/2. Naturcamping Isarhorn (08823

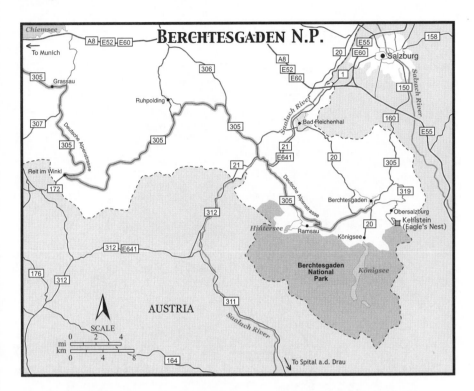

5216); beautiful location in the pines; open all year; $$$. • On the southwest end of the Walchensee, northeast of Garmisch-Parkirchen. Exit off 11 and follow signposting for Walchensee and camping. Camping Walchensee (088-58-237); lovely location; open May-Sept; $$. Just east of Oberammergau. Campingpark Oberammergau (08822 94105); nice location; all amenities; car parking separate from tent site; open all year; $$$.

Altmuhltal Naturpark

Dipping your paddle into the charming Altmuhltal River for a leisurely ride through some of Bavaria's loveliest little valleys is a great way to enjoy Germany's largest nature park. Rentals and shuttle services are readily available. Look for lady's slipper and dark red-helleborine orchids in the meadows in late spring. In summer, butcher's bloom and mezereon are in full bloom. Bring your wild flower field guide. Watch closely while you're walking quietly into the pine and birch forests because you are likely to hear spotted woodpeckers and see tiny nuthatches and creepers as they feed on the insect rich trees. Directions: Located south of Nuremburg and north of Ingolstadt. All the camping places are nicely located and cared for.

▲Camping: • On the river close to the town of Beilngries. Exit off E/45 at exit 58 and drive east along the river to town, then go south to the river. Camping An der Altmuhl (084 61 8406); open all year; $$. • Off the same exit on E/45 but drive farther south, passing under the roadway to Kipfenberg. AZUR Camping Altmuhtal (084 65 90 5167); open all year; $$$$. • Farther west along the river, west of Eichstatt in the town of Dollnstein. Campingplatz Dollnstein (084 22846); smaller; $$.

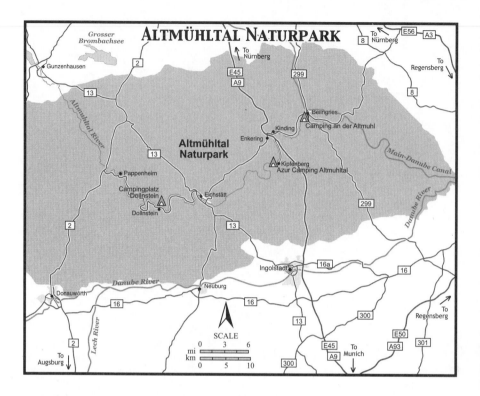

Nurnberg

Alive with street music, artists, and the remnants of a rich past as a 16th-century merchant town, Nuremberg is a picturesque blend of pink sandstone and half-timbered buildings. The absorbing and honest museum Faszination und Gewalt (fascination and force) tells the story of the Nazi period from the perspective of the Nuremberg citizens. It does not gloss over the glamour of Nazism to the Germans,

nor does it seek to hide the hysterical Fuhrer worship. It's the small details of the memorabilia that is most telling. You'll be emotionally stunned; closed Monday. Directions: Southeast of the city, not far from the campground, in a glass structure adjoining the Kongressbau, in the large park Luitpoldhain. German composers such as Beethoven, Bach, Mendelssohn, Wagner, Hayden, and Richard Strauss have made an enormous contribution to world culture. In the Germanisches Nationalmuseum you can examine some of the instruments they used. The fine collection of Durer's Renaissance paintings includes the famous portrait of his master. Nuremburg's goldsmiths were superbly talented during the Rennaissance; don't miss the incredible silver-gold sailing vessel; closed Monday. Directions: U-bahn Opernhaus.

▲Camping: • 4km southeast of the historic area, exit off E45/E51 at exit 52. Off E50/A6 take exit 59. Follow signposting for Stadion, then camping. KNAUS-Campingpark Nurnberg (0911 981 2717); pleasant location close to walking/cycling paths; by the famous stadium; open all year; $$$. Northwest of Nurnberg in the suburb of Zirndorf. Off A73 exit for Nurnberg-Furth and follow signposting for Zirndorf-Grosshabersdorf, then camping. Campingplatz Zur Muhle (0911 693801); convenient to the road; open all year; $$.

Bayreuth

The most famous artists, composers, and writers of the 17th century were invited by a lively princess to spend time here, creating one of the most elegant and sophisticated courts of the times. The lavish opera house, Markgrafliches Opernhaus, has a glittery and glamorous interior that is made entirely of wood. Wagner buffs will want to visit Festspielhaus, set on a tiny hill north of town, where only Wagner operas are performed.

▲Camping: • In Frankische Schweiz nature reserve, between Beyreuth and Nuremberg. Exit E51 west at exit 44/Pegnitz onto 470, then drive about 10km to Pottenstein. Camping Barenschlucht, Weidmannsgesees 12 (092 43 206); lovely location; open all year; $$. • 3km farther on 470. Campingplatz Jurahohe (092 439 173); better for caravans; lovely location; $$.

Bamberg

Strolling through Bamberg is like walking through pages of beautiful photographs in an art or architecture book. The elaborately carved stucco, colorful frescoes, entrancing sculptures, and soothing waterways remain untouched by war. The city impresses even the most jaded traveler. Try to get tickets to the town's renowned Bamberger Symphoniker. When concerts are held outdoors under a canopy of stars, the setting and music make for a very memorable evening. The tourist office sells tickets; reserve ahead (0951 980 8220). Leafy beer gardens are sprinkled throughout the city and hills. Beer-makers, lured by the beautiful surroundings, produce 200 varieties of brew.

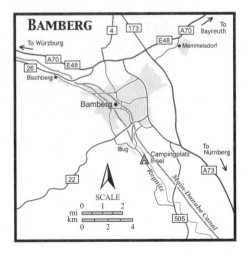

▲Camping: • 5km south of town in the suburb of Bug, on the west side of the Regnitz River just south of B22. Off E48/A70 take exit 16. Campingplatz Insel (0951 563 21); lovely location; open all year; $$.

Wurzburg

When Tiepolo, the Italian fresco master, and Neuman, the master German builder, joined forces, the grandiose Wurzburg Residenz became one of the finest palaces in Germany. Heavily influenced by the French, it is reminiscent of Versailles.

▲Camping: • Close to the palace, at the intersection of 19 and E43 in the suburb of Heidingsfeld. Off E43/A3 take exit 70. Camping Kalte Quelle (093 165 598); nice location; open April-Oct; $$.

Need more text to fill out space here

WESTERN GERMANY
Stuttgart

Hi-tech, prosperous, and surrounded by vineyards, Stuttgart is home to both the Mercedes Benz and Porsche automobile plants and museums. In gleeming mint condition, 70 historic vehicles-including the world's two oldest cars, a luxury car handmade for Japan's emperor, and the first automobile built especially for the Pope-are enclosed in the Mercedes museum; closed Monday. Directions: East of town in Oberturkheim, just south of the suburb Bad Cannstatt. Stuttgart has beautiful parks, an outstanding zoo, a botanical garden, an excellent modern art museum, and Roman ruins. Join the locals cycling along the banks of the Neckar. During August, the town is even more vibrant with street music and wine, beer, and food booths as locals take a break from work and celebrate Sommerfest and Weindorf.

▲Camping: • East of the city center, in the suburb of Bad Cannstatt on the east side of the Neckar River, sandwiched between B14 and B29. Campingplatz Cannstatter Wasen, Mercedesstrasse 40 (071 155 6696); close to the Mercedes museum; open all year; $$.

Heidelberg

Mark Twain's hilarious descriptions, visions of magically lit landscapes painted by Turner, and sweet nostalgia for military life felt by those in the army who were formerly based here are reasons Heidelberg is a popular destination with vacationing Americans. On the first Saturday night in June and the second Saturday night in July, fun-loving mobs throng to see the fireworks in front of the Schloss. Historic pageants, open-air concerts, and opera performances keep the town jumping with visitors throughout the summer. The centerpiece for all of this is the Schloss.

Start your city exploration by boarding the funicular at the lower Kornmarkt Station, which takes you to the ramparts of the castle. Or vividly relive medieval times by walking up the steep cobblestone lane. Spend some time in the touristy, but fun, student taverns filled with a jumble of faded artifacts. In the Kurpfalzisches Museum, housed in the Palace Morass on Hauptstrasse, the bones from the 500,000-year-old Heildelberg Man are safely tucked away, but you can see a copy of his jaw-bone and an amazing lime-wood Altar of the Twelve Disciples; closed Monday. Well-marked underground garages make parking fairly easy in Heidelberg. Pick up a free city map from a hotel as you proceed into town.

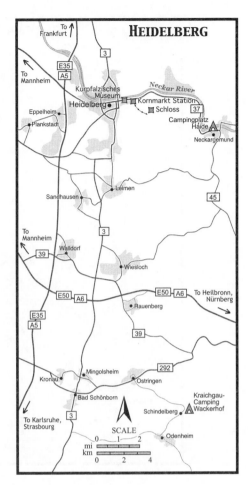

▲Camping. • 8km east of Heidelberg in the suburb of Neckargemund. Drive east from the city on 37 (the road hugging the south bank of the river) for 8km in the direction of Neckargemund. Campingplatz Haide (062 232 2111); on the river; bus to the centrum; open Apr-Oct; $$. • 20km south of Heidelberg. Off E35/A5 take exit 41 onto 292 and drive 11km to Ostringen. Turn south in the direction of Odenheim and drive 8km to the village of Schindelberg. Kraichgau-Camping Wackerhof (07259 361); picturesque setting in a tiny village; tranquil; open April-mid-Oct; $$.

Schwarzwald

Once the forest here was so densely packed with trees that it was dark, even during the day. Today light filters down on well-marked gravel paths. It is a popular tourist destination. Scenic drives can include the old-fashioned open-air museum in Gutach. Directions: Drive northeast of Freiburg on 294 in the direction of Waldkirch for 11km. Cross over the river and drive north on the road that hugs the west bank of the river for 6km to Gutach. Readers of Hermann Hesse novels will want to detour for his museum in the Nagold Valley at Calw. Directions: Off E41/81 take exit 28 onto 296 in the direction of Herrenberg and drive northwest for 20km. For a more scenic drive through the Schwarzwald on 463, exit off E52/8 at exit 45 for Pforzhem and drive south. You won't forget being mesmerized by hundreds of clocks ticking and cuckoos chirping from intricately made timepieces in the clock museum in Furtwangen. Directions: Drive south east of Freiburg on 31 for 30km. Turn north on 500 and drive up the mountain for another 30km. For indulging in spa bathing in Baden-Baden, the Friedrichsbad or Caracalla-Therme spas are good choices.

▲Camping: There are many camping places in this area. Some are full-scale resorts. Here

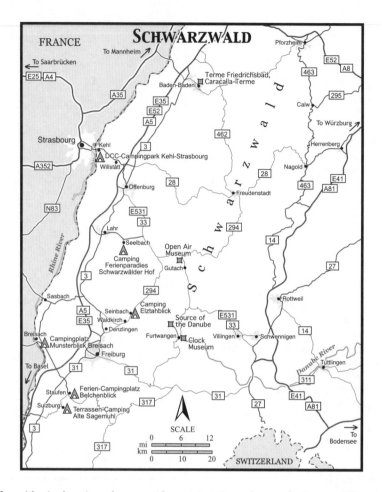

are a few with nice locations that are mid-range in price and a couple that would be splurges. In the mountains 10km south of Freiburg. Exit E35/A5 at exit 64a and drive southeast in the direction of Staufen for 11km. Follow signposting south of the town to the railroad tracks and the river. Ferien-Campingplatz Belchenblick (07633 7045); beautiful location close to walking/cycling trails; sauna; open all year; $$$. In the same area. Continue south of Stauben for 6km then turn east and drive one kilometer to the village of Sulzburg. Terrassen-Camping Alte Sagemuhl (07634 51181); nice location; smaller; open all year; $$. • Close to the Schwald Panoramic Road. Off E35/A5 take exit 61 onto 294 and drive east 3km. Continue on driving northeast 14km on 294 through Denzlingen, Waldkirch, to the village of Siensbach and camping. Camping Elztahblick (07681 4212); beautiful location; open mid-Mar-Oct; $$. • Close to the Rhein (Rhine) River, west of Freiburg. Off E35/A5 take exit 59 and drive west 13km to Sasbach. Turn south onto B31 in the direction of Breisach and drive 15km. Then follow signposting for camping. Campingplatz Munsterblick Breisach (07667 93930); close to the walking/cycling route along the Rhein; open Apr-Oct; $$. • Across the river from Strasburg, close to the town of Kehl. Off E35/E52/A5 take exit 54 onto E52 in the direction of Willstatt. Drive 12km then follow signposting south for camping. DDC-Campingpark Kehl-Strasburg (07851 2603); pleasant and convenient spot on the river; close to the walking/cycling route along the Rhein; open mid-March-Oct; $$. • East of Lahr exit E35 at exit 56, and drive east for 12km to the village of Seelbach, then south to the river. Camping Ferienparadies Schwarzwalder Hof (07823 960950); beautiful location; resort-like; open all year; $$$.

The Rhine River Gorge

The Rhine is Europe's heartbeat. With a grand and powerful air, it has been a source of myths and legends for centuries, a conduit for trade, a focus for industry, a link and boundary between nations and cultures, and an object of pleasure. Hundreds of romantically gloomy castles, many built by medieval princes who carefully guarded them and charged for the right to pass on their stretch of the river, are perched on impossible crags. Some have been restored in a symphony of spires and turrets while others are in ruins. Storybook villages stand along the river's edge, squeezed in between the river and vineyards that ripple off the hillsides. Dipping into side streets reveals photogenic secret corners, tempting wine bars, tiny cobblestone squares, and century-old homes. In between, shady woodlands mix lazily with sunny wheat fields. Enjoying the excellent cycling/walking path that hugs the riverside most of the way is a great way to admire the scenery and avoid the motorized tourist traffic. Bridges and inexpensive car-ferries link both sides. From Mainz, the cycle/walking path hugs the bank of the river gorge on the side opposite from the motorized traffic. You'll likely meet fellow

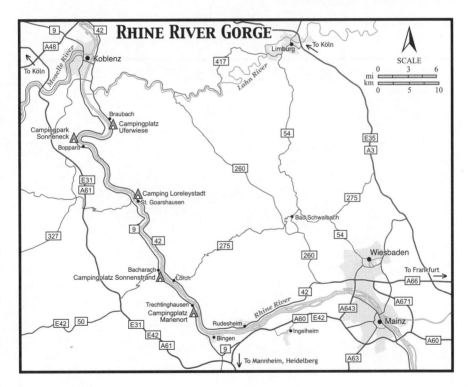

walkers and cyclists from all of the world. Koblenz, sitting almost in the center of the gorge where the Mosel and Rhine rivers meet, is a good place to rent a bike and pick up a map of the route. Check with the tourist office in the centrum/Deutsches Eck, where's there are some large parking garages.

▲Camping: All of the following have nice locations close to the Rhine River and are not overly large. Two-lane highways run on either side of the river B9 on the west side and B42 on the east. Trains also zoom along on both sides, so train noise is unavoidable. 15km south of Koblenz, on the east side of the river, off B42 in the town of Braubach. Campingplatz Uferwiese (026 27 1422); smaller; open mid-Apr-Oct; $$. Farther south, just north of the town of Boppard, on the west side of the river, signposted off B9. Campingpark Sonneneck (06742 2121); open Apr-mid-Oct; $$. Farther south in St. Goarshausen, on the east side of the river, signposted off B42. Camping Loreleystadt (06771 2592); Apr-mid-Oct; $$. In Bacharach on the west side of the river, signposted off B9 south of town. Campingplatz Sonnenstrand (06743 1752); open Apr-Oct; $$. In Trechtingshausen, 10km north ofRudesheim. Campingplatz Marienort (06721 6133); open all year; $$.

Bodensee/Lake Constance
Water-loving vacationers fill these shorelines. It's not hard to find a camping place.

FRANKFURT AM MAIN
Besides having one of the busiest airports in the world, Frankfurt has some very good museums, an excellent zoo, and a beautifully restored old town. The Altstadt and most of Frankfurt's best

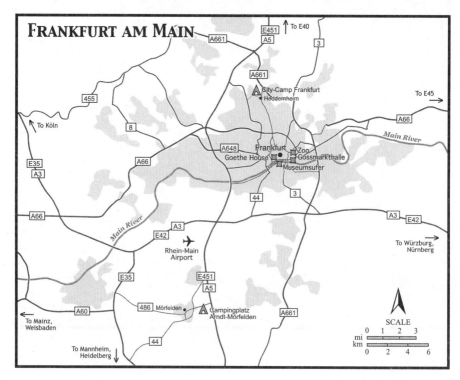

museums hug the River Main within a walkable area from each other so it is a very easy city to enjoy. Directions: U-Bahn Willy Brandt. Glassless interior windows frame incredible objects of art from around the world in the Museum fur Angewandte Kunst, one of Germany's most impressive applied arts museums. Giggling over the film industry's enormous collection of memorbilia in Germany's best film museum and then taking in a movie at the museum's cinema is a light-hearted way to spend an afternoon. Both of these museums are in an area called the Museumsufer, on the south side of the river. Just walk over the bridge from the Altstadt. Both the Historisches and Judisches Museums in the Altsadt area are excellent. Frankfurt is Goethe's birthplace so you can visit a reconstruction of his home and get goosebumps when you gaze over his original writing desk and handwritten notes. All these museums are closed Monday. I love to visit Frankfurt's excellent and well-cared for zoo. If you have a long layover at the airport, have jet-lag, or just love animals be sure to avail yourself of this treat. It's on the east side of the centrum, just north of the huge Grossmarkthalle off Hanauer Land and Am Tiergarten. There's good parking or take the U-bahn to Zoo station.

▲Camping: • North of the city, in the suburb of Heddernheim. Exit A661 at exit 7, Eschersheim/Heddernheim. Alternatively take A66 into centrum and then take exit # 21. Drive north staying right, following signposting. City-Camp Frankfurt, An der Sandelmuhle 35 (069 57 0332); convenient; very popular; reserve ahead or arrive early; open all year; $$. • Close to the airport. Drive east out of the airport and turn south almost immediately onto E451/5. Drive south for 8km. Take exit 24 in the direction of Morfelden and follow signposting. Campingplatz Arndt-Morfelden (06105 22289); convenient for the airport; traffic and jet noise; open all year; $$.

NORTHERN GERMANY
Koln

Koln's enormous cathedral, built on the site of a Roman temple, is breathtaking. Mysterious light from the magnificent stained-glass windows and finely etched spires give a weightless look to the elaborate stone edifice. The Cross of Oak carved in 976 and the bigger-than-life-size figure of Jesus were masterpieces of art in their time. Use a guidebook for more details. Right next to the Cathedral, in striking ultra-modern buildings, are two of Germany's most important museums. The Wallraf-Richartz houses an enormous and important collection of 15th-to 19th-century art. In stark contrast the Ludwig displays 20t--century art, including many famous surrealist pieces. In the Romisch-Germanisches Museum, Bacchus/Dionysos stars in a huge excavated Roman floor mosaic. Created with over a million pieces of tile and glass, its state of preservation is impressive. This museum's collection of glass is said to be the best in the world. Medieval Koln was an imperial city, and today it is home to a masterful group of Romanesque churches.

▲Camping: • South of the historic area about 6km, along the west side of the Rhine in the suburb of Rodernkirchen. Exit E40 at the intersection of E/40 and B555, and drive east towards the river and park. Campingplatz Berger, Uferstrasse 71 (040 392 211); in a park area with a cycle/walking path to the cathedral and also through the park; open all year; $$. • On the other side of the river, cross the Rodenkirchener Brucke, take the first exit, 13. Drive back to the river. Camping Stadtischer Familienzelplatz, Weidenweg (040 831 966); open May-Sept; $$. • Northeast of the city in the suburb of Dunnwald. From E37/1 take exit 98 onto E35/A3 and drive south 10km. Take exit 26 onto B51 to Dunnwald and follow signposting. Camping Waldbad (022 603315); close to the Wild Park; tranquil; open all year; $$.

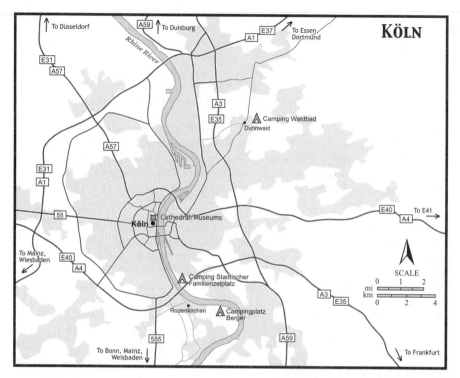

Hamburg

Awarded the title of the greenest city in Germany, Hamburg's wonderfully clean air and lovely parks that wind along the shores of its two huge lakes make it a perfect place to wind down. The best way to begin enjoying and understanding this grand city of commerce and finance is on a harbor cruise. Choose a small ferry rather than a large one. Relaxing on this harbor cruise you'll see quays with warehouses and docks, as well as ancient restored ships moored alongside the gargantuan hulls of container ships. The small ferry also turns into the canals to Speicherstadt for wonderful old town views. Directions: Purchase tickets and board at Pier 2. Hamburg is one of the wealthiest cities in Germany and has art galleries filled with fine collections. Vibrant markets offer goods from around the world and its exceptional zoo was the first in world to display animals in their natural environment. As in all seaports, the bars and brothels make their colorful contribution, but the city has a low crime rate. You can safely wander about enjoying the eclectic environment, made even more famous by the Beatles' presence in 1960. Directions: S-bahn to Reepebahn. Hamburg is justifiably proud of the Kunsthalle and its important collections. The large display of Friedrich paintings, with their haunting landscapes of mountains and the Baltic coast, is outstanding. By wandering around in the Museum fur Kunst und Gewerbe, an applied arts museum, you can transport yourself through the centuries; the Art Nouveau section, or Jugendsil, is extraordinary. Directions: Both are north of the Hauptbahnhof. If you are in town on Sunday, get up early and be at the Fischmarkt by Landungsbrucken by 8 AM. It's wildly noisy with hawkers calling out the virtues of their wide range of fish. It opens at 5 AM. and starts slowing down by 10 AM. Directions: U or S-bahn to St. Pauli Landungsbrucken. Afterwards join the locals in the parks and colorful gardens framing Alster Lake. Line skaters gracefully glide along the lake-side path accompanied by cyclists and walkers, while sailboats joyfully scoot across the beautiful water. Rentals are available.

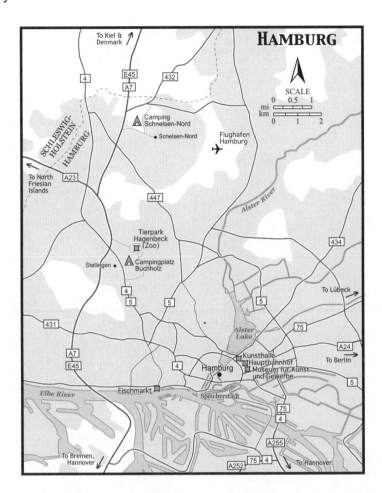

▲Camping: • 8km north of the city in the suburb of Stellingen. On E45, exit at 26 for Stellingen. It's on the eastside of the highway and convenient to the zoo and volkspark. Campingplatz Buchholz Kieler Str. 374 (040 540 4532); close to U-bahn to city; open all year; $$. • 16 km north of the city, exit off E45 at exit 24 Schnelsen-Nord, then drive west towards the IKEA market. Camping Schnelsn-Nord Wunderbrunnen 2 (040 559 4225); bus to city; open Apr-Oct; $$.

Enroute to Ostsee

▲Camping: Exit E28 west at exit 12, then go north on B198 to the village of Eichhorst. Drive north on a smaller road for 3km to Werbellinsee. All of the following have nice locations on the water and are popular with families. • Camping am Spring (033 363 4232); open all year; $$. • Close to E28, take exit 12 to Finowfurt, then drive west to the water. Ferienpark Udersee (033-35-218); open May-Sept; $$. • Exit E28 west at exit 7, then go for 6km to the village of Warnitz and the Oberuckerseee. Camping Oberuckersee, south of the village on the water (039 963 459); open May-Sept; $$.

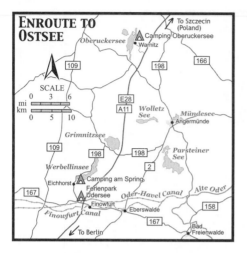

ENROUTE TO OSTSEE

OSTSEE AND RUGEN ISLAND

Dazzling white beaches and steep cliffs stretch out over this northern island, a favorite destination for beach-lovers since the 19th century. At Nationalpark Jasmund hikers enjoy the coastal bluff trail to the famous Stubbenkammer chalk cliffs. Tiny fishing villages with weathered thatched cottages still seem authentic. Ferries cross over to the miniscule island Hiddensee where cycling/ walking paths web alongside sand dunes to the villages. Rentals are available.

▲Camping: On Rugen Island. There's lots of camping places; some are quite large. Here are a few smaller ones.
• On the northwest coast across from

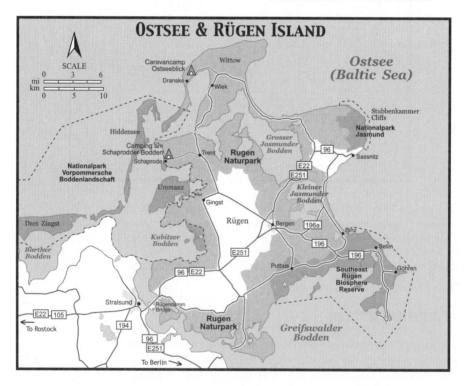

Hiddensee. After crossing the Rugendamn Bridge to Rugen Island drive east 16km on E22. Turn north in the direction of Gingst and Trent and drive 22 km. Turn west and drive 7km following signposting for Schaprode and camping. Camping am Schaproder Bodden (038309 1234); beautiful location; smaller; close to walking/cycling route; open Apr-Oct; $$. • Further north. Follow the same directions as above but from Trent continue on the main road north for 18km in the direction of Wiek. • On the west side of Wiek, exit onto a smaller road and drive 6km following signposting for Dranske and camping. Caravancamp Ostseeblick (038391 8196); lovely location; smaller; open all year; $$.

Muritz National Park Area

If you have a yen for wilderness and water sports, this area has hundreds of lakes with connecting waterways. All kinds of boating equipment can be rented. Bird enthusiasts will enjoy the bogs and marshes. Directions: Drive 80km south of Rostock. Exit E55/19 east onto 192 and drive 19km.

▲Camping: • Southwest edge of Lake Muritz, 3km north of Robel. Campingplatz Pappelbucht (039931 59113); smaller; nice location on the lake; open Apr-Sept; $$. • At the north end of the lake on the west side of the town of Waren. Campingpark Ecktannen (03991 668513); large; nice location on the water; open Apr-Oct; $$.

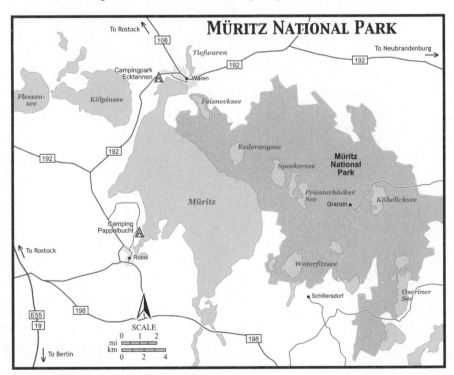

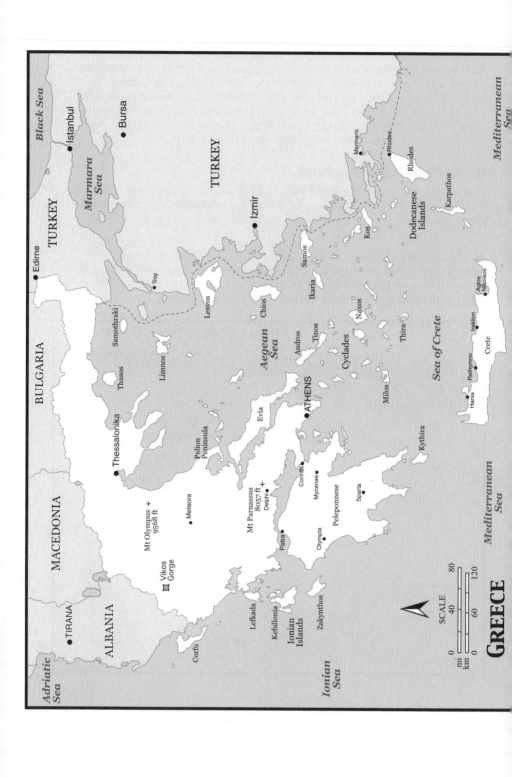

Greece

Greece beckons with legacies so powerful that the flames are still not quenched. Its mysticism seduces vivid imaginations. Geographically and culturally, it lies on a fault line between east and west. Rugged mountains divide its valleys and plains, encouraging an individualistic spirit that produces vigorous and enterprising individuals. A map of the country is a jigsaw puzzle of land and sea.

Greece is the perfect place to visit when the rest of Europe is cool and rainy. May and September are prime for tent camping. The weather then is warm enough for swimming but not overly hot, and evenings are pleasantly warm.

Local vegetables and fruits, fresh meats and fish, yogurts and cheeses all spill from stalls in the town's morning market, or agora. In large towns the market is open every morning. I bring a small, collapsible insulated bag from home when I visit Greece. The fish at the open markets is delicious and not overly expensive. Ask for some ice when you make your purchase. Bakeries and stores with other grocery items and household goods are usually nearby. Ice chests are readily available in larger grocery stores but finding ice for them is not always easy. Perhaps the campground will have it. Otherwise, watch for ice freezers outside of gas stations, or ask for ice, pronounced *payghoss*, at the meat market inside the supermarket.

Bring a backgammon board from home so you can sit outside at the café, or *kapheneia*, and play alongside the locals. Make a list of basic Greek words and phrases with their pronunciations and keep it handy in a pocket. Pull it out now and then and practice. Then while you're at the *kapheneia* say a couple of Greek pleasantries such as: good morning, pronounced kahlee**meh**rah; or good afternoon, pronounced kahlee**speh**rah; or how's life?, pronounced tee **kah**nehteh; or what a lovely day, tee ee**peh**rokhee **meh**rah. These are all easy to pronounce. Locals don't expect you to speak Greek, so when you do they are appreciative and you get a big smile.

Driving on mainland Greece isn't overly difficult, but you need to be alert for aggressive drivers and you need to drive aggressively yourself to avoid an unsafe line of cars behind you. On two-lane roads, hug the edge a bit if you don't want to pass the vehicle ahead of you. This enables faster vehicles to pass without going too far into the on-coming lane. Passing doesn't seem to have much to do with the lines painted on the highway. Cars pass if the drivers feel they have enough clearance. Truck drivers pull over to the right hand side to let you know it is safe to pass. At a stop sign on the mainland, most drivers just slow down and look around a bit. They'll expect you to do the same. Uphill drivers have the right of way. Blinking headlights mean "I'm coming, watch out." Roadways have dramatically improved in the last few years. Even in remote areas, where they are only one-and-one-half lanes wide, the roads are usually covered with asphalt. Rest areas are indicated 500 meters ahead on newer roads, and highway signs often have enough space in front of them for drivers to pull off to examine maps. Cars are fuel-efficient and distances between sights aren't great, so even though gas is expensive it usually isn't burdensome. But do fill up with gas before traveling to remote areas. Before you leave home or before you leave the airport in Greece, purchase a map with an expansion of at least 1:650.000, or better yet 1:300.000. The money spent will make your life on the road easier. You'll note that there is often a slight difference in the spellings between signs, maps, and guidebooks. You'll get used to looking for similarities. Signs are usually posted in both the Cyrillic and Roman alphabets, Cyrillic first. Away from the tourist areas, directions may be only in Greek. Greek highways are usually not numbered but rather named for where they go. The new autostradas charge a toll of about 2 euros.

Unless you are traveling in July and August, ticketing for car ferries can be done the day of departure. Stop at the tourist office (EOT) in Athens and pick up the weekly departure schedule, or check online before you leave for your trip. Check the travel time to your destination carefully, as routes vary dramatically. Ferries traveling from one island group to another sometimes have only one or two departures a week. The cost of transporting a car on the ferry will be about three times the deck class fee for one passenger. But a car enables you to camp, prepare seaside meals, and get to out-of-the-way sights. You won't be able to access your car during passage, so take up on deck: collapsible ground chairs (some also unbuckle to make a small mattress), a blanket, blow-up pillows, food and beverage, and games and books to occupy time. These items make inexpensive deck passage more pleasant and yet aren't too burdensome to cart around as you move from one spot or another on the boat.

In addition to what is listed in *Camping Equipment* at the beginning of the book, when I travel to Greece in July and August I also bring waterproof shoes so I can swim and snorkel close to rocky shores and hike in gorges with rivers. If I plan to do some serious snorkeling, I also add fins, mask, and a rubber float mat to my gear. For sleeping during the hotter months I forgo a sleeping bag, which I find too hot, and instead bring a sheet "pillowcase" for the thermal mattress, another for a cover, and a lightweight thermal blanket for early morning coolness.

Moderately-priced campgrounds will usually have a small store, a common area for relaxing and meeting fellow travelers, a simple café and taverna, a common area for cooking and washing dishes, and hot-to-warm showers that are often solar heated. Shade from tamarisk, pine, and oleander is supplemented by shade frames. Some campgrounds have swimming pools. Campground offices often observe a lunch /rest time and can be closed between 3 PM and 5:30 PM. Generally the gates remain open, so you can set up and go back later to register. Showers are included in the camping fee. Staff will speak fairly fluent English, even in the remoter areas. Discounts are often given to International Camping Club members (see appendix).

I've listed the opening times of major sights for the months of May through September. Check the closing times of museums and archeological sites. Some close in the early afternoon, while others stay open through early evening. Many are closed on Monday and have shorter hours on Sunday. There are sizable discounts for seniors and students whose country belongs to the European Union, so show your identification at the ticket booth if you qualify. Getting an early start on the day makes your stay in Greece more rewarding. Ancient sites are more mystical in the early morning and late afternoon. Midday is a good time for a pouring over the fascinating artifacts in air-conditioned museums, traveling to your next destination, or having a picnic lunch and snooze.

ATHENS

Isolated from the city hubbub by the steep-sided Acropolis, the Parthenon is still dazzling and radiant-a tribute to the beauty of clarity and harmony of lines. It was built to honor the goddess Athena, whom they believed had helped them win victory over the Persians at Salamis. The Parthenon, begun in 480 BC, was of secondary importance to a giant forty-foot statue of Athena. She was carved from ivory and decorated with gold by Phidias-Athens' favorite sculptor-then placed in a sacred chamber. Reproductions of the goddess wearing her helmet crested with sphinx and grif-

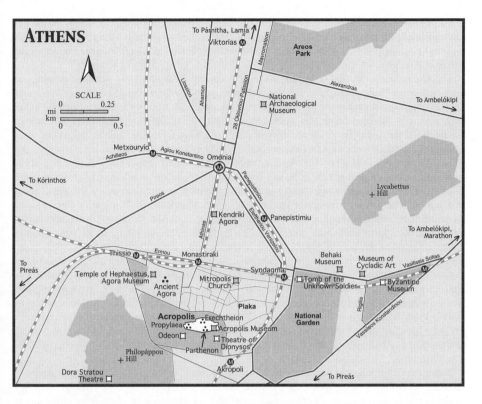

fins are on view in the Acropolis Museum. The masterpiece of sculpture, however, is the Ionic frieze. Measuring about one meter high and almost 160 meters long, it depicted the Panathenaic Procession and ran under the peristyle and along the entire length of the temple. A small portion can still be seen on the west side. Other portions are on view in the Acropolis Museum, but the best sections are in the British Museum in London. Delightful in their womanhood and grace, the six lovely maidens of the Caryatids support the roof of the Erechtheion, adding noble and youthful vigor to the site. The Panathenaic Way extends from the terrace above the Agora along a gradual, zigzagging route to the Beule Gate. Imagine the actual beauty, noise, and excitement of the Panathenaic Procession-handsome young cavalrymen in uniforms, dramatic four-horse chariots, richly dressed musicians, and beautiful young offering-bearers. Much of the Parthenon was destroyed in 1686 when a Venetian shell landed on Turkish gunpowder stored in the temple during their occupation. After absorbing the architecture, turn to gaze over the Acropolis walls for a terrific panoramic view of the lively city, bare mountains, and conical Mount Lycabettus.

Allow time to visit the Acropolis Museum, where the masterful freize of the battle of gods and giants is truly powerful. You'll smile as you gaze at joyous votive statues of young women with engaging mocking smiles and elaborate hair designs. The famous calf-bearer, a charming archaic statue, exudes a warmth and sweetness that is hard to forget. Directions: The main entrance to the Acropolis is through the Propylaea, a monumental ancient gate on the west side; open daily. Wear rubber-soled shoes, as the ancient pathways are slippery from so many footsteps. Try to experience the Acropolis in the early morning light right when it opens or in late afternoon.

On entering and exiting the Acropolis, you'll pass the restored marble half-bowl of the Odeion theatre built in 160 AD by Herodes Atticus. Attending one of the summer starlight performances of music, dance, or drama during the Athens Festival is a highlight of any stay in Athens. You'll feel like an ancient Athenian as you sit on the same marble stones that have echoed drama and music for a millennium. It's best to book ahead; www.henllenicfestival.gr. Directions for the acropolis: Metro to Akropoli.

The Dora Stratou troupe performs, sings, and dances throughout the summer evenings at their theater on Philopappus Hill. Here, in a simple outdoor theatre perfumed by eucalyptus and cypress trees, you can enjoy the exciting music of the bouzouki while virile men in tight breeches and radiant women in elaborately-embroidered traditional attire stamp and twirl. Directions: Southwest of the Acropolis on the southwestern side of Philopappu Hill. Call for tickets and time schedule (210 92 14 650). You can usually book that day; closed Monday.

The Ancient Agora is a good choice for peaceful strolls. Once noisy with chatter and argument, the ancient streets are now quiet and fragrant with roses and laurel. Pericles, Aristophanes, Thucydides, and Plato all strolled here, arguing over the principals of democracy and the concept of freedom. The Temple of Hephaestus and the Agora Museum help bring alive this heart of ancient Athens, where our concept of democracy originated; closed Monday. Directions: Metro to Monastiraki. Then walk south on Areos following signage. The labyrinth of tiny stepped lanes hugging the northern side of the Acropolis is reminiscent of the Cycladic Islands. Still quiet, they are a nice reprieve from tourist-baiting Plaka just beyond. Directions: Metro Monastiraki. Walk south on Areos following signage for Ancient Agora. From Panos walk east on Tholou. For another pleasant walk, wander over to the leafy National Garden just east of Syntagma Square. Rest on a park bench and absorb the local scene. Then wander over to the Tomb of the Unknown Soldier to smile at the impressive Evzones. These tall military sentries are in very fancy dress, indeed. The changing of the guard takes place daily at 20 minutes before the hour. On Sunday mornings at 11 AM an elaborate full-dress parade occurs with a lively band and goose-step marching. Directions: Metro to Syntagma.

Besides the Acropolis, the National Archeological Museum is Athen's most important treasure. Housing one of the world's most important collections of Greek art, it reveals the full splendor of the Grecian's intense love of beauty. And now, after refurbishment it is considered one of the ten finest museums in the world. The dazzling treasures found in the royal tombs of Mycenae, a city once rich in gold, greet you in the first room. The world-renowned golden death masks, the famous golden bull-carved goblets, and the superb golden-horned bull's head all take your breath away. Throughout the spacious, well-lit museum sculptural pieces attest to the culture's intense appreciation of natural beauty. Take a break and have a snack in the leafy open-air atrium; open daily, with shortened hours on Monday. Directions: Metro to Omonia and then walk north up to Oklovriou-Patission 44.

The Museum of Cycladic Art brings together the best artifacts from the Greek island archeological excavations. The collection is exquisite and beautifully curated, and inspired many artists-including Picasso; closed Sunday and Tuesday. An extravagant collection of dazzling embroidered regional clothing, accompanying rich body ornaments and carefully reconstructed sitting rooms from Asia Minor are highlights at the elegant Benaki museum; closed Tuesday. Directions: These two museums are in the same area. The Benaki is across from the northeastern corner of the National Garden on Vassilissis Sofias. The Cycladic is two blocks farther east off the same street. Metro to Evangelismo.

For earthy fun visit the Kendriki Agora, where Athenians haggle over fresh slabs of meat, symmetrical octopus, and piles of chickens. Lively cafes dot the area dispensing inexpensive, tasty Greek fare. Directions: North of the Ancient Agora and west of Syntagma Square. Metro to Monastiraki. Then walk north to Ermou. Cross over Ermou and continue walking north on Athinas. The carnival spirit of the Plaka is a comedy of locals, tourists, and vendors. You haven't really experienced Athens if you don't come here. Directions: From Syntagma Square, walk southwest using the dome of Mitropolis Church as a point of reference. The Sunday flea market in Monastiraki is a good place to shop for quirky mementoes while munching on a tasty snack. Directions: Metro to Monastiraki.

Athen's most daunting archeological excavation was its metro dig, which took ten years to finish. It was dug by hand in the heart of Old Athens. Over 50 archeologists and 200 labors participated in the dig, which went more than 20 meters deep. Besides vases, amphorae, and coins, they found intriguing water-supply lines designed with sealed-lip joints and coded in alphabetical sequence with sophisticated removable lids for cleaning. The two most prized relics are a small statue of a graceful youth carved in 100 AD and a bronze head of what must have been a dramatic large statue created in 480 BC. Today the finished metro stations in the center of Athens shimmer with marble and hold intriguing exhibits with informative descriptions. The pride of the Athenians, the stations are busy but surprisingly quiet, efficiently run, and very clean.

The columns of Poseidon's Temple at Cape Sounion stand on a high cliff at the farthest tip of the Greek mainland. Battered by wind and sea and eroded by iodine, the regal columns are dazzling white-like salt. They are especially evocative when the rising or setting sun reddens the slopes of nearby islands; open daily. There are many nice beaches in the area so pack a picnic. Directions: 71km south of Athens on the scenic coastal road 91, Athens-Sounio, follow signposting.

▲**Camping:** •Best for Athens. North of Athens in the shady, upscale suburb of Nea Kifissia. Exit Athens airport onto the autostrata in the direction of Athens. There's a toll station just after you enter the autostrata. You'll need euros or a charge card for payment. Drive north for 9km. At the intersection of the autostrata and 54 continue north and then west on the autostrata for another 9km in the direction of Thessaloniki, passing through a tunnel. Take exit 8 onto the National Road Athens-Thessaloniki. Drive north 5km exiting for Nea Kifissia. (This exit is easy to miss; watch closely.) Drive east into town. Go almost completely around the round-about with fountain, turning back west towards the National Road. Go under the overpass. Continue west into the residential area for 5 blocks, following signposting to Dimitsanas. Turn north and drive 2 blocks. Camping Nea Kifissia (210 807 5579); excellent location; shady large terraces appropriate for both tents and caravans; lovely swimming pool overlooking the mountains; close to bus for metro to Athens; open all year; $$. Shopping note: At the round-about in Nea Kifissia there is an upscale supermarket. Upstairs you'll find camping gas and other supplies to start your trip. Across the street is a Starbucks and nearby an excellent patisserie. Getting to Athens note: Leave your car at the campground. Walk 2 blocks to the bus stop on Messinias. Take local bus 75 to the metro station Aghios Antonios (Red Line #2). From the metro station Aghios Antonios back to campground take bus 522 or 523, getting off where you got on. There is a cash machine at a nearby bank. Directions: From the campgrounds drive east on Messinias to the road that parallels the west side of the National Road. Drive 3 blocks to Bank Pireus. •Closer to Athens but on the very busy and noisy old National Athens-Korinth road. From the intersection of the National Athens-Thessaloniki and the old Athens-Korinth road 8/94, drive west on the old Athens-Korinth highway for 4 kilometers. Watch closely for signposting on the north side of the road. It's easy to miss because the road is very hectic in this area. If you

are coming from Korinth, you'll need to pass the campgrounds, make a U-turn, and go back less than one kilometer. To get to the bus stop to go into Athens, you must walk or rather run, across this highway. Camping Athens, 198-200 Athinon Av (210 581 4114); restaurant; modern showers and toilets; noisy; open all year; $$$. •At the tip of the Athenian pennisula, 4km northeast of the Poseidon/Sounias Temple. Really too far away to go into Athens for the day, but a great place when you want to spend some time at the beach, visit the temple at a romantic time, or recover from jet-lag. From the airport drive south in the direction of Sounio for 32 km on 89. Camping is located at the western edge of the village of Kato Posidonia. Camping Bacchus (22920 39572); lovely tranquil and shady setting; small; terraced; simple café; open all year; $$. •Just north of Rafina, on the bluff overlooking the sea, east of Athens. This area is not as nice as the beaches farther south, but it could be a convenient overnight. Exit 54 for Rafina. Drive into town. Turn north in the direction of Kollino Limanaki and drive one kilometer. Turns towards the beach and drive 500 meters. Camping Kokkino Limanaki (22940 316034); small; close to a restaurant; open May-Sept; $$.

THE PELOPONNESE
Corinth

A crossroads between the mainland and Peloponnesus-the Aegean and Ionion seas-ancient Corinth's control of the main routes since the Mycenaeans provided an important income for city. Today tourists stop to look down the 90-meter-deep, steep-sided cleft stretching six kilometers to the sea in a line as straight as a ruler.

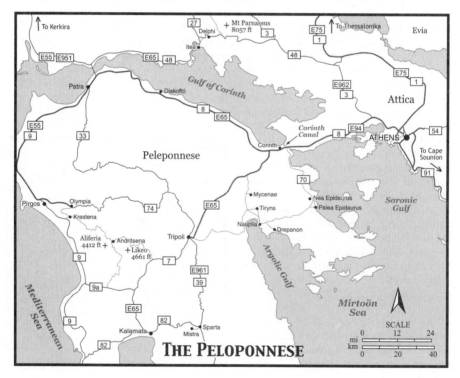

▲**Camping**: From the Corinth Canal drive south on 70 for 10km in the direction of Epidavrus. Exit for Isthmis Beach and drive 4km. Camping Isthmia Beach (2741 037720); convenient, pleasant location; open May-Oct; $$.

Mycenae Area

Almost as fascinating as the ancient story of Homer's hero Agamemnon is the story of Heinrich Schliemann, who in 1874 came to Mycenae following his passion to excavate the riches he hoped had been left by Agamemnon. What he found instead was an entire civilization. Today, curving cyclopean walls, a beehive tomb, and plethora of fascinating artifacts reveal what the Mycenaean civilization created by itself and what it had learned from the Minoans in Crete. In ancient Mycenae, you'll walk under Europe's oldest monumental sculpture the Lion's Gate and see the ruins of the Royal Circle of tombs. Be mindful that you are looking at the archeological site where-the world-famous gold masks, the exquisite Warrior Vase, and the golden cups depicting the taming of the bulls-were found. These treasures along with many more are now beautifully exhibited in Athens's National Archeological Museum. The enormous and harmonious beehive tomb is tucked discreetly into the other side of the hill. Standing in front of and inside it you can't help being in awe and silence. Before you start your walk through the archeological site, study the exhibits in its excellent museum; open daily. Directions: 15km west of Corinth, exit E65 for Mycenae and drive 2km to the village.

▲**Camping:** •West of the town. Camping Atreus (0751-76221); nice views of the hills; swimming pool; open all year; $$. •Just west of the archeological site. Camping Mykines (0751-76121); small; nice walk to the archeological area; open all year; $$.

Tiryns

The Cyclopean stones that make up the defensive wall of this fortress, located very close to Mycenae, attest to the power the Mycenaeans welded in the 14th and 15th-centuries BC. They fortified their cities, built castles, and observed a military style. Aggressive and skillful at warfare, they built colonies in Asia Minor-most notably at Troy so they could control the entrance to the Black Sea. Raids against Egypt and Crete soon replaced the supremacy of the Minoans in the Mediterranean. Note the entrance ramp to Tiryns. It was wide enough for their formidable war chariots; open daily. Directions: On the Argos-Nafplio road, just north of Nafplio.

Epidavrus

Greeks came to this splendid setting in hopes of being cured of their ailments. Shrewd and enterprising priests, wanting to distract their patients from their woes and also separate them from their money, entertained them with great theater. Climb to the top of this remarkable theater, passing 55 rows of crescent-shaped seats, so you can view its perfect symmetry. The acoustics are extraordinary, and it is considered the most beautiful and best preserved of all Greek theaters; open daily. Stop in the museum to view the remnants of its lovely architectural ornaments. Highlights

MYCENAE AREA

are the exquisitely carved acanthus leaves and rosettes artistically decorating column capitals and the portions of a coffered ceiling from the marble rotunda that were painted with lilies. In July and August during the Festival of Epidaurus, starlit performances of plays written by the ancient Greek playwrights are performed. Directions: From Corinth exit south on the coast road 70 for 46km to Nea Epidaurus, continuing one kilometer to Palea Epidaurus and the archeological site.

▲Camping: •In Palea Epidaurus on the beach road at km 2. Both have: nice locations; well maintained facilities; open April-Oct. Camping Verdelis (0753-41322); $$. Camping Bek as Beach (0753-41524); close to a recreational area; $$.

Nafplio

One of the prettiest towns on mainland Greece, Nafplio sits at the edge of the often turquoise waters of the Argolic Gulf. Old Venetian houses drip with bougainvillea, and narrow streets lead to Turkish fountains, galleries and boutiques. Walking along the promontory, you'll pass canopied cafes, yachts, and the ferry out to the tiny fort Bourtzi. Drive up the mountain before sunset, passing the Akronafplia Fortress to a large car park at the end. Here romantics watch the setting sun paint the blue lagoon-like sea with reflections of crimson and golden mountains. There's a real feeling of accomplishment after you've climbed up the 990 steps that cling tenaciously straight up the cliff to the Palamedes Fortress, named after a very brave hero who is said to have invented the game of dice. Embroidery is one of Greece's most varied and prolific handicrafts. The Folk Art Museum's collection is outstanding. Displays of spinning, weaving, dying techniques, fabulous traditional costumes, dioramas, and life-size photographs of village life make it memorable stop; closed Tuesday. Directions: From Corinth drive west 15km on E65. Exit south onto 70 and drive 33km to Nauplia.

▲Camping: This is a popular area for vacationing Greek families with many campgrounds to choose from. •My favorites: Follow the main coast road heading east out of Nafplio for 2km passing through Aria. Exit for Lefkalia and drive south towards Assini Beach. Assini Beach Camping (27520 61587); smaller; nice location in a citrus grove; close to the beach; very pleasant common areas; open May-Oct; $$. In the same area. Xeni Beach Camping (27520 59338); small; short walk to the beach; cute touches in the campground; Greek dancing lessons in the evening; restaurant and taverna; open May-Oct; $.

Olympia Area

Shaded by pines and cypresses in a gently undulating countryside, the ruins of Olympia are more dreamy than dramatic. Not so two thousand years ago though, when chariot races, javelin and discus throws, and wrestling filled the daily calendar. It was dominated by an elevated Temple of Zeus, containing what some consider Phidias' masterpiece-the great statue of Zeus sitting on his throne. Carved in marble with gold and ivory overlay and set with precious stones, it was 12 meters tall and counted as one of the Seven Wonders of the Ancient World. Athletes trained for nine months at Olympia to compete during three main days of the games. Olympia was a man's world; married women were prohibited. During the games, musicians, storytellers, acrobats, virile men, and seductive women provided an eclectic atmosphere, with both noble and common distractions available. On the last day of the games, the ceremonial distribution of laurel wreaths took place. Winners brought great honor to their families and hometowns. The decorative elements of the Temple of Zeus are exhibited in their original arrangement in the museum; open daily. Directions: Northwest side of the Peloponnese pennisula, 18km east of Piyrgos on 74.

▲Camping: •Up the hill from Ancient Olympia, on the northwest side of the village. Camping Diana (26240 22314); small; shady; swimming pool; closed in Dec; $$. •In the same area but with especially fine views of the hills and sunsets. Camping Alphios (2624 22951); larger; more resort-like with restaurant; open Apr-mid-Oct; $$$.

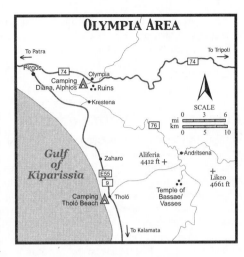

Temple of Bassae/Vasses

Isolated and surrounded by some of the highest peaks in Peloponnesus, the Temple of Bassae/Vasses was built in thanksgiving for deliverance from the plague. From its sublime location, you look out across a superb panorama of wild ravines and misty mountains. In June the profusion of wild flowers is stunning. Today a giant tent protects it during its restoration. Directions: Located on the western edge of central Peloponnesus. At the intersection of E55 and 76, 18km south of Pirgos, drive 50km in the direction of Andritsena. The road is winding but two-laned and well paved all the way to the site. The vistas are beautiful much of the way. Stop to take in the beauty and fragrance of the profusion of golden scotch broom and purple vetch that cascades down the mountainside. Goats graze, slate-roofed houses hug the mountainsides, and at the temple you may only hear the sweet tinkle of goat bells and the rustling of the leaves in the ancient olive trees.

▲Camping: Off E55, at the beach 37km south of Pirgos. 5km south of Zacharo, turn onto a small road towards the beach following signposting for Tholo Beach. Camping Tholo Beach (26250 61345); low-key and simple; grassy with shade trees; simple café; close to the beach where fisherman put out to sea; open Apr-Oct; $.

Sparta/Mistra

The ruins of the powerful military encampment of Sparta lie tucked in between meadows and orchards in the valley of the Eurotas River. In its heyday, seven-year-old boys and girls were selected for the highly disciplined and rigorous life. Taught early never to murmur a complaint, they lived a "spartan" and communal life and were the supreme commanders in the Persian War with Xerxes. They fought furiously and died with valor. Little remains of the former totalitarian society that scorned art and architecture and lived in simple dwellings

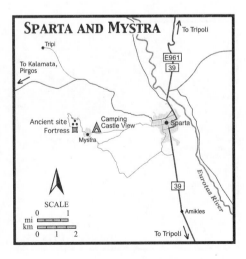

Reminiscent of stories from *The Thousand and One Nights*, the domes of churches and monasteries peek through cypress and orange trees around Mistra. When it was the metropolis of Peloponnesus, the town was very successful in the breeding of silkworms. A Frankish medieval fortress crowns the hill. As you walk up the stony path, you are treated to the red-tiled, bonnet-like domes of the churches and glorious views of the Eurotas

Valley. Restored frescoes glow with color and bring to mind the work of Crete-born El Greco. Directions: Sparta and Mistra are located in the southeastern section of the Peloponnese. From Tripoli, exit off E65/7 south onto E961 and drive south 60km.

▲Camping: •2km from Mystra. Camping Castle View (0731-83303); lovely views of the ancient ruins; small pool; open Apr-Oct.; $$

Peloponnese North Coast

In a crazy feat of Italian engineering, railroad workers wrestled with stone and rock to set rail up a steep gradient through the dramatic Vouraikos Gorge. Finished in 1896, it was used to transport minerals from the mines. A ride on this unique rack-and-pinion railway is a treat and very popular with young and old alike. It's easy to become child-like and pretend that you're on a fancy miniature train with tracks running through tunnels, over bridges, and along steep-sided cliffs. The scenery is idyllic, with little pastures, small villages, and the cheerful Vouraikos River. In season you'll need to buy your ticket at least a full day ahead. For an additional cost you can reserve a front seat. Directions: From the magnificent, full-sail-like Patra Bridge drive southeast on E65 for 50km. Exit for Diakopto. Turn under the highway overpass, and then turn back west towards the peninsula and Diakofto. In town, turn right at the first street, following signposting for the train station. There is a large car park just north of the train station.

▲Camping: At the north edge of Akrata. Exit E65 for Akrata. Pass through town following the main road to a small bridge. Cross the bridge and immediately turn east onto the small road and drive towards the beach for one kilometer. Camping Akrata Beach (26930 31988); nice location on the beach; popular; arrive early for a good site; simple restaurant; open Apr-Oct; $$.

THESSALY
Delphi

It's the setting, rugged and grand, hugging the gaunt gray cliffs of Mount Parnassus that makes this "navel of the earth" hard to forget. The florid chiseling of the Ionic capitals have weathered over two millenniums. The dark superstition attending the underground temple of the sibyl, the haunting beauty of the Sacred Way, and the leafy walk up through hundred-year-old olive trees to the stadium are all poetically beautiful when experienced in the crowd-free, just-opening morning time or in late afternoon. Use midday to peruse the sumptuous sculpture found in the temple now displayed in the museum. The works are a tribute to beauty, strength, and mind; open daily. In the early evening, when the crowds have left, wander down the hillside and enjoy some quiet time as sun sets over the evocative Temple of Athena.

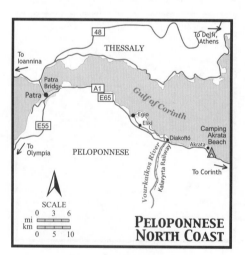

The serpentine drive up to Delphi is dramatically beautiful. Waterfalls of wild mustard cascade down the rocky slopes, and acacias in full summer bloom wave in the breeze outside villages that cling tenaciously to the mountainside. Delphi is one of the most evocative places to camp in all of mainland Greece. From your campgrounds, you'll view a sea of the silvery-green foliage of olive trees and the deep-blue of the Gulf of Corinth. Directions: Located 170km west of Athens, on the north side of the Bay of Corinth, on the hillside above Itea. Drive north out of Athens and Camping Kifissia on A/1 E/75 in the direction of Larisa. Exit west onto 44 for Thiva. Continue driving through the beautiful farmlands of wheat and vine, then up the mountainside for 90km.

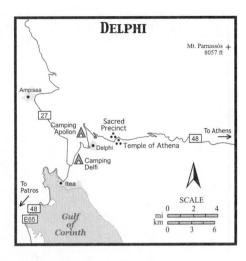

▲ **Camping:** •Closest to the archeological area. Located 2km west of the village, on the main road. Camping Apollon (0265-82750); gorgeous views; swimming pool; nice walk to the archeological area; popular; open all year; $$. •4km west and down the hill from the village. Camping Delfi (0265-82363); wonderful views of the Bay of Corinth; swimming pool; open all year; $$.

THE PELION PENINSULA

This peninsula is so lush that it confounds your image of Greece. It feels like a Greek version of Tuscany with an added touch of sea. The air is heady with the fragrance of broom and wild geraniums. Sea foam dusts the hills in a soft glow of ivory, and pink rock-roses bloom without restraint. The abundance of wild flowers makes beekeeping and honey production an important local commodity, and you'll see beehives placed strategically in meadows of lavender. Lush apple, pear and almonds orchards enable the production of delicious preserves. Both honey and home-made preserves are sold along the roads and in village shops. In the area's traditional villages multi-shades of roses are carefully tended and chickens still run across the road from schist-stone homes that cling to the hillsides. Walking paths, called *kalderimia*, link some villages and have become popular hiking routes. Large forests of leafy oak, plane, and chestnut trees bring welcome shade. Fed by springs and snowmelt, creeks run down the hillsides like miniature waterfalls to eventually flow into sea. Here tiny secluded coves and sandy beaches are perfect. Regional cuisine, traditional architecture, and folk customs are all cherished, and each village is unique.

Two-laned mountain roads snake through shady ravines and along mountain contours. Getting from one place time to another is time consuming, but the vistas are grand, roadside wildflowers fragrant, and birdsong sweet. Park outside the smaller villages and walk in. Streets that start out fairly wide become so narrow you can end up having to back out. Don't try to drive from one miniscule village to the next without parking outside the first one and checking the road farther on by foot. Show a local your map and ask if it is possible for you to drive to your desired destination. Directions: Located on the Aegan 57km south of Larisa. Exit E75 onto E92 and drive 18km east in the direction of Volos to where roads branch off to the coastal or mountain villages. Stop in Volos and stock up on supplies and gas. Both are limited in the villages.

The cobbled, winding streets that meander up and down the steep hillside in Makrinitsa make this village a good introduction to the area. Visit their homey folk museum. A well-marked, steep trail traverses farther up the mountain to the deserted monastery Sourvias. The trailhead is off tiny plaza Branis. Directions: From the center of Volvos drive north in the direction of Anakassia and Portaria for 6km. At Portaria turn northwest onto the smaller road signposted for Makrinitsa

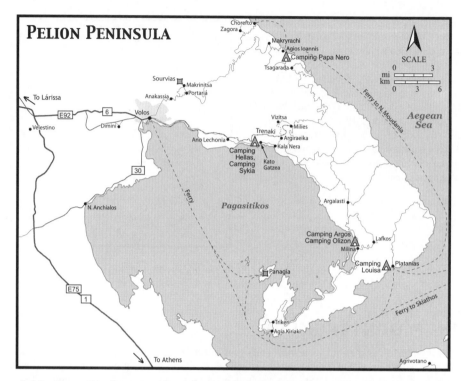

and drive 3km. Gurgling water from the marble fountain at the town's square in picturesque Zagora invites a rest. The center of cottage-craft industries and apple orchards, it is a good place to shop for souvenirs and pick up some delicious jam and honey for camp breakfasts. There's great hike from Tsagarada through a steep ravine to a beach. At the mouth of the ravine a stairway was built for managing the final steep descent. Ask at the travel agency in Agios Ioannis for the local hiking map and information about kayak rentals and horseback riding.

▲Camping: On the beach on the northeast side of the peninsula in Agios Ioannis. From the village of Makryrachi drive south 3km to Anilio. Turn to descend down the steep narrow winding road for 9km following signposting for Agios Ioannis. Camping Papa Nero (24260 49238); rustic natural setting; large, flat, grassy area with shade trees; simple facilities; popular with families; open June-Aug; $$.

Multiple-span stone viaducts, tunnels, deep ravines, and an exciting iron-trestle bridge make a ride on the narrow-gauge steam engine, named Trenaki especially enjoyable. It chugs its way from the restored train station in Ano Lechonia to Milies where it arrives 90 minutes later. Cobbled streets, a plane tree-shaded square, and a museum of local culture just off the square provide some interesting things to explore in Milies before riding back. There are only a few carriage cars so call several days ahead to arrange tickets. (24210 24056). The Ano Lechonia ticket office opens at 9 AM. Directions: Drive 9km south of Volos on the coast road to Ano Lechonia. Follow signposting for the train station.

There are some great loop hikes in this area. One starts at the chapel in the little mountain village of Vizitsa and winds its way down to Kala Nera and the coast via Argyraeika. Legends of wild half-human and half-horse Centaurs residing in caves and trotting along the sandy beaches and into the gorges here make hiking even more interesting on Pelion. For kayak and wind-surfing rentals and guides for longer hikes, check with the travel agency on the beach front street in Kela Nera.

▲**Camping**: •On the west coast 10km east of Agria in Kala Gatzea. Both of these upscale campgrounds have flowery landscaping, modern facilities; lovely terraces and nice restaurants; open Apr-Oct. Camping Hellas (24230 22267); $$$ and Camping Sykia (24230 22279); $$$.

At the peninsula's southeastern end, the little port village of Platanias has a nice sandy beach, colorful fishing boats, gardens colorful with roses, pleasant water's-edge cafes and an excursion boat to Skiathos. It's a peaceful place to hang out for a while. The campground is beautifully landscaped and restful and a small store in the village sells groceries and camping supplies. Directions: From Volos drive south on 34, the main road, for 40km to Argalasti. Continue for another 9km. Follow signposting towards Lafkos up the mountainside and along the plateau for 5km. Turn south following signposting for Platanias for 10km.

▲**Camping**: •On the road into the village of Platanias. Camping Louisa (24230 71260); peaceful location under the pines; short walking distance to the beach and small port; open June-Aug; $$ •On the southwestern Pagasitic Coast close to Milina. From the mountain top village of Argalasti follow signposting down the mountain for 10km towards Milina. Watch for campground signposting on the bluff one kilometer north of Milina. Exit the main road and drive one kilometer down the small, rough, winding road. Camping Argos (24230 54144); lovely location on a pebble beach under olive trees; simple facilities; small terraced sites; café; spectacular sunsets; open May-Sept; $. •In Milina. Camping Olizon (24230 65236); better for larger caravans; nice shady location on the beach; convenient for walks to town; beautiful sunsets; café; open May-Sept; $$.

Meteora

Perched on seemingly inaccessible, massive rock pedestals situated among a wonderous rank of pinnacles, steeples, and spires, the monasteries of Meteora are one of Greece's great sights and included in the list of World Heritage Sites. They have a unique mystique and for me as enigmatic as Cappadocia in Turkey. In both places devotees sought inaccessibility by the outside world. Initially, expert rock climbers from the village probably assisted the monks. They climbed up the high, almost sheer-sided rock pedestals-perhaps using removable ladders. Later, cranks wound with rope pulled up supplies as well as monks. These windlasses, or cranks, can still be seen. Superb 16th-century frescoes, intricately carved altar screens and crosses, and elaborately painted icons were eventually funded by the wealthy.

Today you can drive up the mountain on a winding asphalt road or take a bus up to the highest monastery and hike down. If you'd like to hike, take the bus from either Kastraki or Kalambaka in the morning. Make your first stop the grandest and highest of the monasteries-Megalou Meteorou. Then walk down the trails and dirt roads that pass by the monasteries. Staff at the campgrounds will provide a map. Steep stairways ascend into all the monasteries. There is a small but excellent museum at Meggalou Meteorou, and the frescoes are particularly fascinating at Ayiou Anapavsa. You will be asked to use one of their wraps if you're wearing shorts. Directions: At Larissa exit A1/E75 west onto

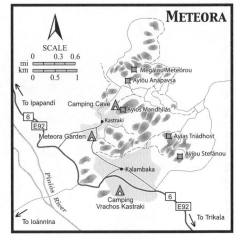

METEORA

SCALE
0   0.3 0.6
mi
km
0   0.5   1

To Ipapandí   Camping Cave   Ayíos Mandhilás
                               Kastraki
Meteora Garden   Ayías Triádhost
                                      Ayíou Stefánou
              Kalambaka
              Camping
              Vrachos Kastraki
To Ioánnina   To Trikala

Megálou Meteórou
Ayíou Anápavsa

Piniós River

E92 in the direction of Trikala and drive 62 km. Stay on E62 and drive another 9km to Kalambaka. Drive through town on the main street to the western end. Follow signposting up the mountain for Kastraki and Meteorou.

▲**Camping:** •Closest to the monasteries and my favorite campground in north mainland Greece. From Kalambaka, drive north up the mountain in the direction of the monasteries to the northern edge of the village of Kastraki. Camping Cave (24320 24802); incredible location beneath the cave shrine Ayios Mandhilas; beautiful swimming pool; small; possible noise from motorcycles racing along the road at night; open April-Sept; $$. •At the southern edge of Kastraki. Meteora Garden (0432 22727); larger; nice swimming pool; popular with groups; better for larger caravans; open April-Sept; $$ •In Kalambaka follow signposting on the main road. Camping Vrachos Kastraki (2432 022293); large; pool; convenient to the main road; open all year; $$.

Mount Olympus

It's a thrill to stand in the warm Aegean in the early morning or evening, the waves gently lapping against your legs. First you enjoy the expanse of eggshell-blue sea brushed with pink and gold-trimmed clouds. Then, just by turning around, you see Mount Olympus! Home of the gods, it stands royally draped in snow while you stand bathed in the warm Aegean. This sacred mountain was the home of the twelve gods of ancient Greece. Pilgrims climbed the mountain and northern invaders of southern Greece came through the passes. Ancient settlements grew up along the routes.

A plethora of well-marked, easy-to-follow trails wind around the mountains, into canyons, and ravines. The wild flower display in May and early June is remarkable. Enthusiasts should bring a wild flower identification book from home. An excellent guide, *Flowers of Greece*, by Maria Tani, is

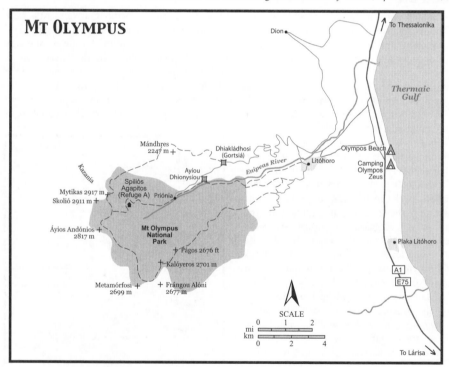

translated in several languages. You might find it. Directions: From Larissa drive 58km north to Litohoro. This lovely drive passes through the Vale of Tembi and along the Ossa coast. If you are tired and want to camp enroute, the municipal campground at the north end of the Valle of Tembi in the village of Stomio is quite pleasant. The reeds behind the beach make for some fine birding.

To enter Olymbos National Park, exit A1/E75 for Litohoro and drive west for one kilometer. Turn north just before the main square, cross over the bridge, and then turn west following signposting for Olympos. Drive 3km to the park kiosk where you'll be given a park brochure. Continue up the mountain. The most popular trail up Mount Olympus begins at Prionia, 18km from Litohoro. At the parking area, enjoy the crystal clear waterfall of the Enipeas River tumbling down over boulders through a lush river ravine. Next to the trailhead gate is a small hut selling beverages and snacks. The trail climbs through the beautiful Enipeas River Gorge and it's woods of mostly beech and pine. Incredible views of the towering Olympus peaks are seen all the way up. The trail starts steep but becomes less daunting after one kilometer. You'll appreciate hiking sticks, however. On the lower stretches, you're treated to wildflowers such as of lilies of the valley, fairybells, and shooting stars. You'll meet fellow hikers from all over the world. It takes most people three to four hours to hike to Shelter A-Spillios Agapitos where for a small fee you can use the terrace if you've brought your own lunch. Beverages and tasty homemade food are available for purchase. If you'd like to climb to the top, plan to lodge at Refuge A-Spillios Agapitos, for a night or two. It's important to get an early start from here for the three-to-four-hour ascent to the highest peak-Mytikas-before it clouds up in the afternoon. The trail is steep from Shelter A up to the summit. It passes through a sparse forest of Balkan pines, then zig-zags up through scree for a good hour before reaching the ridge and the 500 meter chasm, *Kazania*. Along one side is the *Kaki Skala* or evil stairway-an hour-long rock scramble beside the deep chasm just before the summit of Mytikas at 2917 meters. If you decide not to attempt this difficult and dangerous climb you can instead take the much easier trail leading to Skolio-the second-highest peak, at 2911 meters.

Refuge A is extra special. Efficiently run by generations of one family who have grown up loving the mountains it can accommodate up to 120 persons but is still cozy. It's hard to beat a night spent here beside a crackling fire and under a brilliant canopy of star light. Tasty meals, snacks, picnic lunches and even cappuccino are for sale. Due to the effort involved in bringing up supplies, they aren't inexpensive. Call ahead for reservations (23520 82300 English speaking staff).

Olympus National Park boasts 800 different kinds of wildflowers, some quite rare. The meadow Barba, about an hour's walk from the Dhiakladhosi (Gortsi) Trail parking area, is a mass of color in the later spring and early summer. This easy trail leads through a lovely forest where tiny blue, yellow, and purple violets peek out from behind rocks and dappled light streams through a canopy of chartreuse leaves. The trail goes much farther and gets more strenuous, skimming the base of the peaks and looping with the trail from Prionia. Directions: 13 km from the park entrance note a park information sign on the main road. Turn onto a short dirt road here and drive up to a small car park next to a mule corral. Take the trail beside a wooden railing.

The old Monastery of Agios Dionysios, built in the 16th century just above the Enipeas River, was blown up by Turks in 1828 and then again by the Nazis in 1943. Both believed that the monks were sheltering resistance fighters. The ruins are poignant and photogenic. In a miniscule hut, a monk sells mementos. Directions: Located one kilometer before the end of the road at Prionia, follow signposting for the monastery down a narrow mountain side road.

Both Phillip II and his son Alexander the Great worshipped in ancient Dion, just north of Litohoro. An earthquake and mudslide safely buried the area's ancient treasures. Excavations begun in 1990 found public baths, city walls, a mosaic floor, and sanctuaries where the votive statues were still intact. The museum in this leafy, shady place carefully houses the finds, including a 1st-century pipe organ; open daily. Directions: Exit A1/E75 2km north of Litohoro.

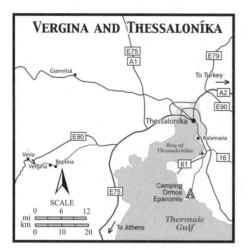

▲Camping: On the beach at Plaka Litohoro. This likable little resort town has several wonderful bakeries where you can buy delicious goodies warm from the oven, good supermarkets with camping supplies, and inexpensive terrace cafes. Directions: Exit E/75 for Plaka, cross the railway tracks and drive along the coast road connecting the beach villages. • These are both right at the beach with good facilities and cabins. Camping Olympos Zeus (23520 22115); open Apr 15-Oct 15; $$. Olympos Beach; open May-mid-Sept; $$. There are others in the area..

Vergina and Thessaloniki

Small ivory heads representing both Phillip II and Alexander the Great plus a skull with a disfiguring facial wound that Phillip was known to have sustained give undisputed proof that the tomb unearthed here in 1977 by Manolis Andronikos was that of Phillip II the Macedonian king and father of Alexander the Great. Finds from the site and its tomb are the richest trove since the discovery of Mycenae and Knossos. Visitors descend a long ramp to underground-recreated tombs. It is an evocative and mysterious setting. Treasures include delicate gold-leaf head-wreaths and a gold *larnax*, or ossuary casket, where Phillip II's bones were found. An especially lively frieze of Phillip and Alexander on a lion hunt with their entourage was found remarkably intact behind rubble from another tomb. The King's bones were given reburial in Vergina; closed Monday. Directions: Exit A1/E75 west onto E90 33km south of Thessaloniki, and drive 37km in the direction of Veria. On the east side of Veria, exit south towards the reservoir and drive one kilometer. Cross the bridge and following signposting 5km for Vergina/Beptina. Follow signposting for parking.

Thessaloniki is an exciting cacophony of Balkan, Anatolian, and Sephardic cultures born from its position on Via Egnatia-the ancient roadway between Constantinople and Rome. In the evening, a colorful mix of strollers walks along the waterfront promenade. The Turkish quarter called Kastra is especially exotic, with lots of steps and overhanging upper balconies. Directions: Take bus 22 or 28 from Plateia Eleftherias. The pride of the city is its Archeological Museum, whose startlingly beautiful collection "Gold of Macedon" features exquisitely crafted ornamental along with practical objects; open daily. Directions: Walk inland towards Platia H.A.N.T.H from the White Tower on the waterfront. Take bus 69 from the campground or if you prefer to drive, park in the large parking garage close to Plateia Eleftherias.

▲Camping: • 33km from Thessaloniki, on the east side of the gulf. Exit A2 for Kalamaria and airport. Continue south for 10km. Exit west onto 61 and then almost immediately exit for Ormos Epanomis. Drive 15km to the beach and camping. Camping Ormos Epanomis (23920 41378); close to the beach; popular with families; open May-Oct; $$

Vikos Gorge

Wildly rugged mountains, miles of forest, river-slashed gorges, and tiny stone villages make this one of Greece's most beguiling regions for hikers. The Vikos Gorge is justly popular. As you descend down the gorge, canyon walls tower above you-some yawning with secret caves. The whole gorge is lush with wild flowers, ferns, shrubs, trees, and butterflies. At the bottom, a refreshing river forms inviting pools between boulders that are perfect for secluded swims and sunning. Don't rush. Stop and take time to absorb the magnificence. Perhaps go only part way into the gorge, enjoy some solitude among perfectly clear boulder-shrouded pools, and then retrace your footsteps back to your car. Waterproof shoes will

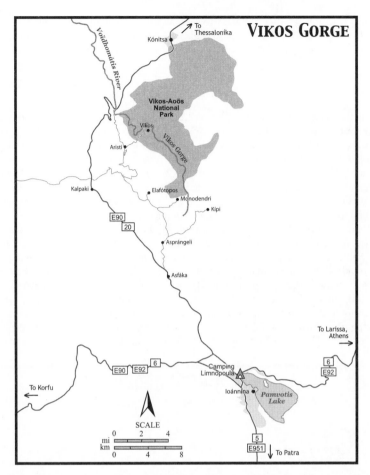

make wading through the river and its boulder edges more enjoyable. Hiking from one end of the gorge to the other is popular and definitely doable in a day. You'll meet other international fellow hikers. The trail is well marked and not overly hard if you are moderately fit and used to climbs with some elevation. A walking stick is appreciated in steep areas and in sections where the trail is narrow, steep-sided, and scree-laden. If you'd like to hike through the entire gorge, make reservations ahead for staying in the village where you plan to ascend out. Then either retrace your route through the gorge to your car or make arrangements with a local to drive you back. Monodhendhri, at the south end of the gorge, is a popular and easy place to start. Directions: From the intersection of E92 and E951 (close to the campground in Ioannina) drive north 17km in the direction of Konitsa. Exit east just past the village of Asfaka onto a two-lane road for Asprangeli and drive 10km. At the fork follow signposting for Monodhendhri, wind farther up the mountain for 9km. The views are breathtaking. The last kilometer of road is one lane and the final 500 meters is cobblestone. Park outside the village of Monodhendhri and walk up the cobblestone path. At the first fork turn right. Continue past the 17th-century church on to the newly constructed stone amphitheatre and the trailhead.

The mountain village of Vikos, at the north end of the gorge, is the closest to Monodhendhri and less expensive to stay in than the Papingo villages that are patronized by wealthy Greeks. Call Ioannis Dinoulis Rooms for reservations (2653 042 112). Directions: Drive north of Ioanina on E951 in the direction of Konitsa for 33km to the village of Kalpaki. Exit east onto a smaller road for Aristi and drive 12km continue through the village and up the mountain for another 5km to Vikos.

▲**Camping:** At Pamvotis Lake at the northwest end of Ioannina, next to a nautical club. Camping Limnopoula (26510 25265); lovely grassy setting with shade trees on the lake; popular; arrive early; walking distance from the historic area and market; open May-Sept; $$.

CRETE

Separating the Aegean and Mediterranean seas, this large, fertile island cradled one of the most brilliant civilizations of the Western Bronze Age. Today, olive trees gnarled with age shade the haunting ruins. In 2500 BC Minoans used sail, oar, and probably the keel to brave the open seas and transformed themselves from hunters and gatherers into farmers, craftsmen, and traders. This sea trade brought not only new ideas but also tin from Asia Minor (now Turkey), copper from Cyprus, and luxury goods from Egypt. High up on mountain plateaus, fertile valleys are still filled with orchards of apples, figs, and pears. In rocky gorges, trails cooled by pleasant streams and perfumed with pine lead from mountaintops to the sea.

The campground owners in Crete decided it would be good for business if they had plastic tables and chairs for their customers to use at their campsites. This is a wonderful treat for car-campers. If you don't see any, ask at the office. They might be stacked somewhere, or maybe you can borrow from the campground's café. Your camping space will be shaded with tamarisk and olive trees, but don't expect much grass and landscaping except around the common terrace area because watering is expensive. Most campgrounds have at least a simple café, taverna, and store. Several have nice restaurants. Almost all are located in scenic locations close to the beach. A few have very nice swimming pools.

Zig-zagging from north side of the island to the south side is the only way you'll see the whole island, because the rocky and mountainous south shore doesn't have a road that hugs the coastline

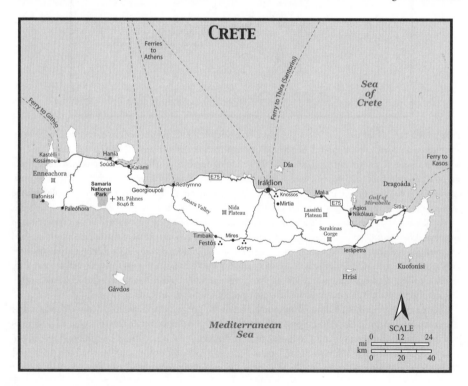

from east to west like the north shore does. Throughout the island, main roads linking the larger towns are well-maintained asphalt with two marked lanes. Side roads are also well-maintained asphalt but are often only one and one half lanes wide. Except on weekends, these scenic side roads have little traffic. If you suffer from vertigo they might not be a good choice for you. The National Highway E/75 is a fast moving divided highway. It links the north side of the island east to west. When crossing the island from north to south, take time to pull over and breath in the fragrant blend of thyme and rosemary and to stand in awe of the dramatic mountain scenery. And stopping to join the locals playing backgammon under a leafy grape arbor in one of the hilltop villages could count as some of your most memorable times in Greece.

Most archeological sites are open daily 8 AM to 7 PM. If you arrive right as the ticket booth opens at 8 AM or after 5 PM, they'll be more peaceful and mystical. Knowing the evocative stories that excited the archeologists will make your visits to the sites more fascinating. Read ahead at your library and about the mysterious Minoans whose contribution to art in 1900 BC was exceptional.

Iraklion

The Archeological Museum at Iraklion carefully houses the now world-famous treasures found at Knossos and other excavations on Crete. Tiny seals cut from stone are so finely carved that a magnifying glass is necessary to appreciate their beauty, both natural and poetic. Vases carved from rock are expertly shaped, smoothed, and decorated with drawings that testify to a vigorous Minoan life. Ritual vessels with great bull horns, statuettes of the Snake Goddess, double-edged axes, gaming boards, a circular plaque of clay stamped with hieroglyphic signs, and the astonishing Bee Pendant reveal the startling freshness, spontaneity, and exquisite taste of the Minoan artists. This creative liveliness and movement of their art remains their most spectacular legacy. The fact that they built their towns without fortification and on only slightly elevated ground gives the overwhelming impression that the Minoans enjoyed a life free from war and that sensuous and natural pleasures prevailed. Directions: On the east side of old Ikalion, on the northeast corner of the roundabout at Platia Eleftherias. From the car park on Dikeossinis walk west two blocks, following signposting for the museum; open daily.

Don't miss the daily market, where mounds of tomatoes still smell of the sun, vats of a mind-boggling array of olives glisten in oil, and stacks of purple eggplant gleam as if polished. The fish is excellent, so bring an insulated bag with some ice. Saffron, expensive in other countries, is inexpensive here. The threads are best and it will store for a long time at home, arousing fragrant memories of your experiences in Greece. Take a few minutes to sit down at one of the tables by the old Turkish pumphouse at Platia Kornarou, at the north end of the market. Men talking with their friends under the shady trees are quintessential Greece and its memorable to sit alongside such an ambiance. The Winged Lion Fountain on Platia Venizelou, just south of El Greco Park, is one of Iraklion's Venetian landmarks. Enjoy its cool and refreshing splashes. Inexpensive cafes and closeby Greek snack or *souvlaki,* stands make it a good spot to rest and watch the local scene.

Memorabilia of Zorba the Greek author Nikos Kazantzakis, a painting by Ikaklion's hometown artist El Greco, and photographs of Cretan Tsoudero who became prime minister of Greece in 1941 are highlights in the Iraklion's Historical Museum. Directions: Follow signposting off the waterfront road at

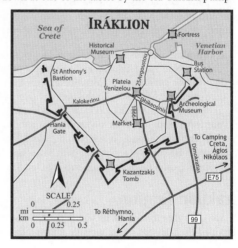

the west end of the historic area; closed Sunday. From the simple tomb site of Kazantzakis on the Martinenga Bastion on the south edge of the walled town, you can enjoy a poignant view out over the red roofs of the city. Kazantzakis would approve of the usual lizard sunbathing on his tomb as you read his epitaph: "I believe in nothing, I hope for nothing, I am free." Directions: Martinengo Bastion is located in the middle of the south side of the ancient city walls. For the best view of the city and its romantic setting on the Mediterranean, walk from the causeway leading out to the 16th-century fortress at the end of the Old Harbor jetty. It's extra special in the evening when the fortress is flooded with light. During the day, visit the eerie storage rooms and passages inside the thick-walled fortress; closed Monday. Directions for the historic area in Iraklion: Exit off the National Highway onto Dimokratias. Follow the road north, then west into the historic area where there is signposting for a large carpark on Dikeossinis.

In 1900 BC, a sprawling, multi-storied complex with as many as 1500 rooms spilled from the fertile hillside here without fortification. Located just beyond today's Irakleion, it was called Knossos, and was once the center of Minoan power. In 1900 AD, Sir Arthur Evans-a brilliant and rich Englishman with a passion for archeology unearthed its palace. He then worked for more than 25 years to restoring it. Frescos, vessel paintings, and a carved seals brought reality to what once was thought to be a fairytale-the cult of the bull, where death defying-athletes somersaulted over a charging bull in heart-stopping spectacles. The astonishing beauty of the palace remains. Columned balconies look out into a lovely inner courtyard. A labyrinth of long corridors that once sang with spirited frescoes can still be traversed. A grand staircase built around a light well leads down to apartments graced with dolphin frescoes. Resurrected from the rubble, storage jars as tall as a man provide proof that Minoans used a hand-turned wheel around 1900 BC. Other artifacts include a fresco fragment of a lady so chic she was dubbed "the Parisienne" and a gypsum seat that might have been Europe's earliest throne. Their ingeniously contrived plumbing and drainage systems were a technical achievement of high order and not surpassed until Roman times. Tantalizing mystery still marks the Minoans of Crete, but the magnificence of their culture is evident; open daily 8 AM to 7 PM. If you get there when it opens or within the last couple hours before it closes you have it almost to yourself. Directions to Knossos: Take the mid-Iraklion exit off the National Highway E/75 onto 90 and drive south in the direction of Knossos for 5km; open daily.

Afficionadoes of Kazantzakis will want to continue farther south from Knossos to visit his home. Sculptural works significant to his writings decorate the central square next to his fine home/museum. Ask to see the video on his life first, then pour over the photos, manuscripts, and mementos. Purchasing the musical sound track from *Zorba the Greek* adds extra fun to your trip; open daily. Directions: From Knossos continue south for one kilometer. At the fork stay east in the direction of Spillia and Skalani. Continue climbing up the hill for 8km to Mirtia. The village streets are narrow. You might find it easier to park outside and walk in.

▲**Camping**: •18km east of Iraklion, just west of the touristy beach-village of Kato Gouves. From the National Highway, exit 11km east of the airport at the exit for Gouves (watch closely, it's a small road). Continue east on the road paralleling the highway for 500 meters. Turn north and drive under the highway overpass. Stay right. Drive 500 meters to the Elco gas station. At the fork turn west towards the beach. Continue, staying west as you wind your way through the narrow streets of the beach town. At the beach road turn west and go to the end of the road. It's next to the old Allied Forces base. Camping Creta (0897-41400); closest to Iraklion; nice walking path along beach to other resort towns; airplane noise; simple terrace café; shade trees; open May-Oct; $$.

Iraklion Region

Heady fragrances of citrus will enhance your drives and walks through the prosperous farmlands of the Messara Plain, a fertile lowland that has provided agricultural wealth for centuries.

Alongside a patchwork of alternating neat squares of orange, apple, and olive trees are rich fields exploding with watermelon, cucumbers, and beans. So when archeologists began excavation and found remains that gave proof to an ancient culture of great power and wealth, it wasn't really a surprise. It is this remarkably early production of olives and grapes-two of the great staples of later Mediterranean agriculture-that might have allowed the Minoans their leap forward. It is likely, too, that they raised sheep and goats. Exporting to Egypt, Asia Minor, and the Greek mainland permitted the Minoans a larger and more complex culture in response to demands for crop regulation, handling of produce, and government.

Many of the treasures discovered at Gortys, Festos and Ayia Triadha are remarkable. The most dramatic and important discovery at Gortys is a law code inscribed in 500 BC. The code indicates a rigid hierarchy and systemized administration that is more elaborate than anything conceived by later Greeks. Written between 1450 and 1375 BC, the script is named Linear B. Fragments of it are in the Odeion, a covered theatre beyond the apse of the early church. Written in Doric script, it reads from left to right and then right to left, or *boutrophedon* style. The laws reveal immense differences between the rights of free citizens and the rights of serfs and slaves. Here Minoans served under the harsh rule of the Dorians. Later, under Roman rule, the city became the seat of government for Crete and the place Christianity made its first impact on the Cretans. After the Saracen invasion, the city was abandoned.

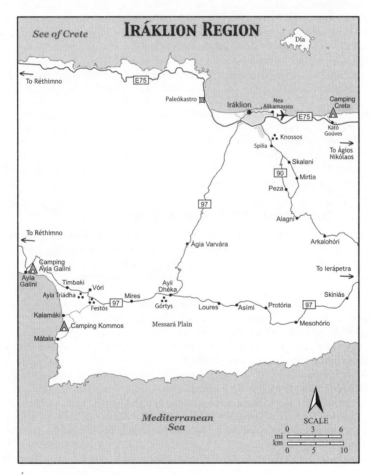

The Festos Disc, now carefully secured and on exhibit in Iraklion's museum of Archeology, is considered by many experts to be the earliest known example of printing. Hieroglyphic characters were pressed into the wet clay of the circular slab before it was fired. The script called Linear A was probably written as early as 1700 BC but remains undeciphered. In the bare ruins of the site, only blocks of massive stone luxuriate on the ground populated in spring by plum-colored clover and yellow-flowering caper plants. Ruins of a majestic sweep of stairs stand almost insolent in a contrived swelling designed so Minoan royalty could look down on their subjects as well as out over a grand view. Beyond the stairway lie the ruined walls of an immense complex of buildings. There are no fluted columns or lion's gates here; only the naked power still stands.

A delightful floor fresco with octopus and fish, the famous Harvester, Boxer, and Chieftain Cup vases of carved steatite, and exceptionally fine seal-stones were unearthed at the villa named Agia Triada after the church nearby. These fabulous artifacts, some of the most creative and artistic found on Crete, are safe and on exhibit in the Archeological Museum in Iraklion. The small and elegant ruins sit on a small hill overlooking the sea suggesting wealth rather than royalty. Mild sea breezes tinged with the fragrance of pine and fruit perfume the air. Locals call it paradise. Because all these sites are still under excavation, you can feel the same excitement that archeologists experience as they look at columns, stairways, and foundations peeking through the earth. Once they are more fully excavated, the sites will become well known and heavily visited. Conserve energy and time to see all three.

In 1992 the Cretan Ethnological Museum in the town of Vori, very close to Festos, won special commendation by the EU. Its lively exhibits tell about island life from its music to its olive oil and raki production. World War II left vivid memories for the islanders. Examining the collection of photos here will help you appreciate the struggle. Directions: From the western edge of Iraklion, exit the National Highway south onto 97 in the direction of Agil Deka and Matala. Drive 41km to Gortys. For Festos, continue west on 90/97 for 17km to the fork following sign-posting south for Festos. For Agia Triada return to 97 and continue west for one kilometer following signposting. For Vori, exit 97 north at the fork for Festos. The museum is behind the church. All are open daily.

▲Camping: •Close to the beach in Agia Galini, 16 km northwest of Festos, signposted one kilometer north of Agia Galini on 97. Camping Agia Galini (2832 91386); an extra-nice campground; beautiful pool; nice walk to a sandy beach and some beach-fronted terrace cafes; good place to meet other international travelers; well-run restaurant and bar; open May-Oct; $$. •6km east of Matala on 97. Camping Kommos (28920 45596); on a hilltop close to the archeological site; can be windy; bus to town and beach; road noise; open May-Sept; $$.

Lassithi Plateau and the Dikteon Cave

Hugged as if by an adoring mother enfolding her precious child, a fertile soil that boasts luxuri-ous fields of artichokes, lettuce, and fava beans, the Lassithi Plain is protected by rugged surround-ing mountains. Well-kept orchards are sweet smelling with oranges, apples and pears. Once noted for its festoon of windmills pumping spring water to the fields, today these same windmills relics provide evocative memories and great photos. A quiet road encircles the farmlands, passing tran-quil villages with inviting shops and cafes so lovely you would never suspect the terrific bloodshed that took place here when the Cretans rose up against the occupying Turks.

It's an easy walk up to Trapeza Cave, where there are fine views of the farmlands. If you bring a flashlight, you can climb inside to imagine Stone Age people-from whom the Minoans descended-living inside. Relics found here testify to the Minoans use of the cave. Directions: On the circle road heading east, exit north after passing the first road into the plateau's largest town, Tzermiadho. Then follow signposting for Trapeza Cave.

Clinging to the shoulder of the jagged mountainside, in the village of Psihro, is the plateau's big-gest tourist attraction. The Dikteon Cave, where legend claims Zeus was born, is cathedral-sized and finished with gnarled stalagmites, shelf altars, and a small lake. It provides an errie setting that encourages retelling the ancient story. Figurines, tools, and an altar inscribed with Linear A have been unearthed. The Mediterranean ear bat inhabits the inner cave found on the right as you enter. The climb up and the descent are both fairly steep and slippery from so many footsteps, so wear rubber-soled shoes. Directions: Psihro is on the southwest corner of the plateau. Follow signposting off the circle road to paid car park and the cave trailhead; open daily.

If time permits, stop and wander through the untouristy and especially photogenic village of Ayios Yeoryios. Be sure to walk up the hill to examine the artifacts in the pleasant folk museum. Directions: Ayios Yeoryios is in the middle of the southern villages.

It's an almost mystical walk to Karfi, a very dramatic 12th-century Minonan sanctuary site. Bring your binoculars, because you might be able to add the griffon vulture to your life-list of birds. They are often seen using the updraft thermals here while hunting. Directions: Drive into the town of Tzermiadho. Follow the most western street up the hill, passing the health center. Continue up, following signposting for the Nissimos plateau. Drive to the small chapel to the west and park. Close to the chapel, follow the trail marked Karfi. It's an easy hike up. Directions to Lasithi Plateau: Exit the National Highway E/75 6km east of Hersonissou and drive up the excellent winding, scenic mountain road in the direction of Mohos, then Tzermiado, for 22km. There are some nice pull offs for views and photos.

▲**Camping**: •34km east of Iraklion and six kilometers east of the exit for Malia, exit the National Highway in the direction of Sissi and drive towards the beach. At the fork stay right. Sisi Camping (0841-71247); lovely location on the bluff overlooking the sea; large tamarisk forest area; grounds are a bit rustic, but secluded atmosphere is very nice; pool; open May-Oct.; $$. •On the eastern edge of Hersonisos. Although listed as a campground this is really a very pleasant place with tiny cabins right at the edge of the sea. The cabin guests use the communal toilet/ shower and cooking areas. There's a small area designated for tents in a center section between the cabins. Exit E/75 north for Hersonisos and Stalida and drive 300 meters east on a road running parallel to E/75. Follow signposting for Lychnostatis museum. Then follow camp signposting next to the entrance to the museum. Caravan Camping ((0897 22025); beautiful location; small tent sites; simple but nice cabins; taverna; older toilet/shower facilities; open May-Oct.; $$.

Gulf of Mirabelle

It's no wonder that Crete's highest-priced resorts overlook the Gulf of Mirabelle where the sea shimmers turquoise and deep blue below dramatic limestone cliffs. From the campground's pool area, you can immerse yourself in the starry night and view the twinkling village lights across the bay. You'll want to extend your stay.

High up the mountain from Agios Nikolaos, just before the tourist village Kritsa, stop to examine the 14th-century Byzantine frescoes in Panayia Kira. Though not in good condition the frescos are evocative and have been restored with discretion. They are considered Crete's best. The film based on Kazantzakis' novel, *He Who Must Die*, was shot here. Directions: At the south end of Agios Nikolaos, exit the National Highway for Krista. Drive up the mountain road for 8km. The church is one kilometer before Krista, signposted on the road; open daily. A large carpark in Krista makes it convenient to stop and look at the local wares. It's a regular stop for tourist buses.

Ancient Gournia enjoyed a lovely view of the Gulf of Mirabelle from its setting in the saddle of two hills just one kilometer from the sea. Today Lombardy pine, pink oleander blossoms, flowering dill, and fragrant thyme quietly decorate what was once a lively and noisy Minoan town. In 1901 an American woman, Harriet Boyd-Hawes, began the excavation that unearthed crafts-people's shops, many one-room houses centering around a central square, and a small palace with courtyard. Gournia is the most well-preserved of all Minoan towns. A couple of good pull-offs along the coast here make it a great place to snorkel in the crystal-clear water. Tiny sedums of lavender and pink peek out between the rocks. A refreshing fragrance of thyme mingled with seawater encourage walking farther out on the lava-like reefs. Here and there are small salt-encrusted basins. Some look man-made, perhaps by Minoeans who might have collected salt from them. Directions: Exit the National Highway E/75 18 kilometers southeast of Ayios Nikolaos following signposting for Gournia. Then drive south one kilometer.

Sitting in the tiny taverna in minisule Monastiraki, overlooking the olive and grape covered hillside across from ancient Vasslliki, is a Tuscany-like experience. From the terrace tables you can watch the sun set in a red sky over an arc of mountains. Take a peek inside to see the immaculate little kitchen where delicious *mezedhes* or appetizers of handmade stuffed grape leaves and delicate cabbage stuffed pastries are carefully prepared by the woman owner/chef/server. On your way to the village, you can't help but exclaim when you catch a glimpse the Ha Gorge. Its drama is reminiscent of an Inca ruin. Only the expert can climb up into it and over to the lake beyond. But those with less skill can clamor up the rocky ridge and at least look up into it. On your way, do pause at the tiny Byzantine chapel. Directions: At the fork on the E/75 for Sitia and Ierapetra turn south in the direction Ierapetra and drive 3km. Exit east onto the small road for signposted Monastiraki. Follow signposting first east and then south to the village. For the gorge, make the same turn onto the small road but continue straight. Park near the chapel and walk 500 meters to the gorge.

For a real Cretan experience drive up six kilometers to Moni Faneromeni. Most of the road is winding, vertiginous, and narrow but it is asphalted. At the end it beecomes gravel. If you get nervous, pull off and park and hike up the rest of the way. The view of the Gulf of Mirabelle from here is unbeatable. Sheep and goat bells tinkle sweetly, and if you go in the morning or late afternoon or morning you can watch them being hand-milked. They are corralled, then called through a corridor one by one. You'll be impressed by the strength and skill of the shepherd. There are photo opportunities galore. The monastery itself looks deserted and forlorn. Directions: From the campground drive west on the old national road for 2km. Exit onto the small road signposted for the monastery and drive up the mountain for 6km.

▲**Camping:** •This campground is so lovely you'll want to stay for awhile. 20km southeast of Agios Nikolaos exit the National Highwy E/75 north and follow the road west to the beach. Gournia Moon Camping (0842-93243); wonderful remote location on a bluff above the Bay of Mirabelle; located next to what was once a smuggler's cove beach, now with diving rocks and crystal-clear water great for snorkling; shady sites; nice swimming pool with adjoining restaurant and bar; open May-Oct; $$.

Southeast Coast

Long stretches of almost deserted sandy beaches are very appealing if you're aching for some time away from it all. This part of the south coast is warmer than the north coast so, it's particularly appealing in the spring and fall. Little towns dot the coastline east and west of Ierapetra, doing what small towns do without tourism in mind. When shopping for supplies here, you'll pay just what the locals do. There are some good walks around Mirtos located 15 kilometers west of Ierapetra. The most dramatic and fun is the walk into the Sarakinas Gorge. Wear waterproof shoes, because sometimes you are walking in a creek. It is 2km to the top. Plan to relax and kick back afterwards at the Taverna Farangi, where the trailhead begins. On Friday evenings, in summer, it's extra-special when the fine music of the lyra and bouzouki are played. Directions: From Mirtos drive 4km northwest on the main road to Mournies. Exit onto the smaller road for Mithi and drive north 2km. Follow signposting for Taverna Farangi. For a seacoast-hugging walk, head west from Mirtos and walk some or all of the 6km to the village of Tertsa. There are ample sandy cove beaches and some great diving rocks for invigorating plunges into the crystal-clear water.

▲**Camping:** •7km east of Ierapetra. Koutsounari Camping (0842-61213); on the beach; shady and protected from the wind; laundry; traverna; open May-Oct.; $$.

Rethymno Region

Mixed like a deck of cards, Rethymno is at once old Ottoman, 16th-century Venetian, and modern Crete. The Venetian Gate leads to the old quarter's labyrinth of tiny streets, where ancient minarets, wooden balconies, domed mosques, and a Venetian fountain make an exotic mix. From the ramparts of the old fortress, you can breathe in the sea air and look out over the town. At the Historical and Folk Art Museum, vintage photos, old-fashioned farming and household implements, and traditional costumes help you envision the rural life of not-too-long ago. In the evening, musicians sing and play the lyre while people dance in an all-around convivial atmosphere. On Thursday mornings, stock up on supplies along with the locals at the open-market next to the car park. If you're here in mid-July, don't miss the lively wine festival enhanced by local folk dancing. In August, buy tickets at the tourist office for one of the concerts held in the fortress during the Renaissance Festival. Directions: Exit the National Highway E75 at Rethimno in the direction of Dimitrikaki. Follow signposting to the large car park by the park. Walk north towards the harbor.

International sympathy went out to Crete at the end of their fight for independence from the Turks. The monastery, Moni Arkadiou, is still a place of pilgrimage for Cretans today. In 1866, rather than surrender to the conquering Turks, hundreds of courageous Cretans took their own lives here in a huge explosion of ammunition. During World War II, the monks gratefully received supplies by parachute from the British to pass on to the guerrilla fighters defending the country against the Germans. Visit the moving museum. Directions: 13 km east of Rethimno exit the National Highway E/75 south onto 90 in the direction of Hamalevri. Drive south 3km, then exit

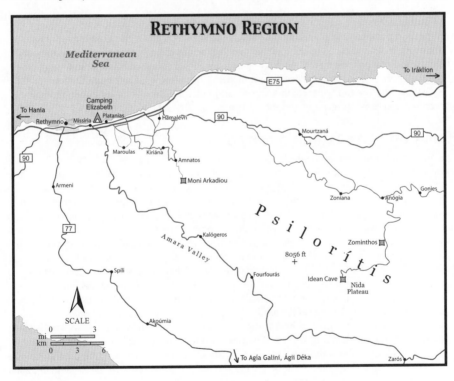

onto a smaller road in the direction of Krianna and Amnatos and continue south on this road for 7km. At the fork, stay south following signposting up to the monastery for 2km.

A profound stillness hovers over the huge, almost empty grassland crater on the Nida Plateau. It is so still that only the hum of bees diligently collecting nectar from the tiny "goldfields" wild flower that carpets the lower mountainside and the faint tinkle of bells and bleating of sheep from the crater floor can be heard. Scattered here and there are sturdy stone huts built with adjoining corrals, where shepherds bring their flocks to be milked each day. Most people come to walk up to the Idean Cave, visited by both Plato and Pythagoras. Like the Dhikti cave, it vies as the birthplace of Zeus. Archeologists have unearthed artifacts from 3000 BC. Bring your binoculars, because the rock faces are popular perching ledges for raptors. It's not uncommon to sight a golden eagle or even a bearded or Egyptian vulture. Black kites, hooded crows and ravens are all common. Enjoy your picnic lunch on the terrace overlooking the crater of the half-finished visitor center. Directions: From Rethimno, drive east 13km on the National Highway. Exit south onto 90 for Hamalevri, and then drive east 23km to Mourtzania. Follow signposting south up the mountain in the direction of Zoniana and Anogia. (From Iraklion, drive west on National Highway E/75 2km to Gazi. Exit south onto 90 and drive 4km to the fork. Stay south and then west in the direction of Gonies, then Anogia for 21km.) After passing through Anogia, follow signposting for Zomintos and drive up the mountain for 16km. Continue across the Nida plateau for another 5km to the visitor center and parking. On either leg of the journey, wander around the narrow alleyway-like streets of Anogia, appreciate the fine textiles in the tiny shops, then join the men at the street-side *kafenia* to watch the world go by.

▲Camping: •5km east of Rethymno exit the National Highway for Maroulas. Drive east on the road paralleling the highway for one kilometer. Drive under the highway overpass in the direction of the beach. At the fork stay west in the direction of Platanias. Cross the small bridge and drive one kilometer. At this eastern edge of the village of Missiria, note signposting for camping. Turn towards beach, and then east to camping. Camping Elizabeth (0831-28694); shady; close to the beach; nice shower and toilet facilities; good birding in the open space between the campground and the village; open May-Oct.; $$.

Hania and the Samaria Gorge

Seductive and romantic in the evening, when lights twinkle from harbor-side tavernas, Hania is probably the most loved of Crete's cities. In late afternoon, walk out on the scythe-shaped harbor jetty to enjoy fresh sea breezes, the sunset, and a lovely view back on the old town. Several museums, a maze of tiny streets, and an old defensive wall will enhance you meanderings. At the morning market, peaches smell like roses and piles of pump purple grapes give off a musky aroma. You'll see rough chunks of chalky-white feta stacked alongside deep-green Cretan avocados. It's an exciting celebration of summer and sings out to be relished. Directions: From the National Highway exit north onto Apokoronou. Drive north and follow signposting for parking on Kidonias. Walk north 4 blocks to the Agora Markthalle in a large cruciform building across from Platia Venizelou. The Naval museum is a nice change from archeological museums. The collection includes interesting model ships, old maps, and photos from 1941 when the Germans bombed Hania; open daily. The Mosque of the Janissaries, located picturesquely on the edge of the harbor, is the oldest Ottman building on Crete.

Ayia Triadha monastery, out on the Akrotiri peninsula, was built in Venetian style. Well-tended fields and olive groves pleasantly front it. Purchasing some of their aromatic olive oil can enhance your camp cooking. After wandering around the almost-deserted cloisters, climb the stairs by the campanile for a wonderful view of the peninsula and the sea. Directions: At the east end of Hania exit off the National Highway for the airport and highway 90. Drive 24km to the airport, then follow signposting north 4km more to the monastery; open daily.

Towering cliffs hide a steeply descending riverbed in a narrow box canyon of the Samaria Gorge. In late spring the river is still fast moving, and pale wildflowers peek out from rocky ledges. Raucous ravens and silent circling vultures patrol the sky. After paying an admission to park staff in Omalos, you'll join other enthusiastic hikers descending the steep wooden staircase or *xyloskalo*, for the 18km hike. Keep your date-stamped ticket to show to park staff at the end. Most people take five to six hours to walk through the gorge, allowing for rests and a picnic. Directions: To assure availability, buy tickets a day ahead for a sunrise public bus ride up to Omalos from Hania, with a return bus ticket from Hora Sfakion (where the boat leaves you off) back to Hania. The bus station is directly west of the carpark in Hania. Emerging from the gorge in the afternoon, it's another 20-to-30 minute walk to the village of Agia Roumeli and the Libyan Sea. It's a good idea to purchase tickets for the boat ride from Agia Roumeli to Hora Sfakion when you arrive at the village. The ticket booth is at the beach. Until departure, enjoy a rest beside the beautiful sea. Bring a picnic lunch, bathing suit, energy snacks, and plenty of water. Wear rubber-soled shoes or hiking boots. You'll need local currency for the entrance fee, boat ride, and a cool drink in Agia Roumeli. Spring water is available to fill your water bottle as you hike.

▲**Camping:** •4km west of Hania in Kato Daratso. Exit the National Highway for Daratsos. Stay north heading straight for the beach (avoiding the turn west into Daratsos). Several blocks from the beach, watch for campground signage near a playground. Drive east through an attractive new apartment complex to the campground. Camping Hania (0821 31138); shady; close to a very nice sandy cove beach; nice children's playground; popular with groups; older toilet and shower facilities; taverna; simple café; open May-Oct.

WESTERN CRETE

Located on the northwest coast, Kastelli Kissamou is Crete's most western town of any size. Little attention is paid to tourism, which is part of its charm. Two nice campgrounds on the Gulf of Kissamou make it worth the drive.

▲**Camping:** •Exit the National Highway 3km east of Kastelli Kissamou for Drapanias, and drive towards the beach. Turn east on the beach road and drive one kilometer to Nopigia. Camping Nopigia (0822 31111); beautifully landscaped; lovely pool; excellent facilities, including restaurant and taverna; very shady; open May-Oct; $$. •Follow the same directions but turn west at the beach road and go one kilometer. Camping Mythimna (0822 31444); nice facilities; close to the beach-bluff walking trail; open May-Oct; $$.

The drives to the south coast from here are dramatic and interesting. Ancient olive trees gnarled, twisted, and blackened with age cling tenaciously to the steep mountainsides. Red poppies and sweet fennel grow profusely. Enticing villages, where roses spill seductively over white washed walls also cling to near-vertical mountain cliffs. The roads curl through narrow, neatly swept streets, and locals look to see who is coming. They'll return your smile and wave.

On the road going to Paleohora and Elafonisi, you can take a break in your journey by stopping midway across to visit a group of interesting villages strung along a country road. They call themselves Enneachora. Directions: Drive south 12km to Koutsamatados. Just before town, there is a curved, one-car wide, tunnel with stoplight at each end of the entrance. After passing through the tunnel, pull over for a climb up to the cave of Ayia Sofia. The activity will help you regain your calm, especially if you have a treat in the enticing cliff-hanging café. Then continue your drive for another four kilometers to Vlatos. At the fork you have a choice. You can drive up to Milia, an upscale remote eco-village located up a steep and narrow road. Or you can stay west at the fork

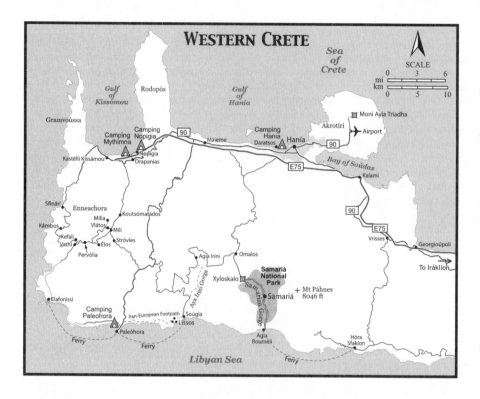

and drive through the larger, easier-to-get-to, very charming villages of Enneachora: Perivolia, Elos, Kafali and Vathi. Park outside the villages because the streets are very narrow. Enjoy the shady squares, refreshing little fountains, bubbling streams, and tiny Byzantine churches. Once deserted, Milia's ancient stone houses have been carefully and artistically restored. Magnificent old plane and chestnut trees shade the whole village. Appealing to those who want serenity, the village's loudest sound is probably the trill of birdsong. Directions: Follow the signposting west up the mountain road just north of Vlatos. It begins as a two-laned asphalt road and later becomes a well-maintained one and one-half lane gravel road for 2.7km. Park outside the village and tiptoe in.

Elfonisi's white sand and turquoise waters are idyllic and like no other beach in Crete. What makes this national park so unique is the miniscule island with a shallow sandbar that is in between it and a long sandy beach. The shallow, warm, aquamarine water is fun to splash across and perfect for toddlers. At one end of the sandbar the water is deeper, making it more fun and challenging for older children. The island has natural coves with wind protection and a rocky seaside with crashing waves. There are lounge chairs to rent and a snack stand. Directions: Exit E/75 at Kasttelli Kissamou and drive south 50km in the direction of Elfonisi.

Paleohora's lovely setting on Crete's southwestern coast and its laid-back, not-overly-touristy atmosphere attracts international travelers, making it a good place to make some new friends. Open-air evening cinemas and lively tavernas add gaiety to warm summer nights. A ferry goes to and from Elafonisi each day. The E-4 Pan-European footpath starts right at the campground and follows the coastline east to the villages of Lissos and Souyia, an 18km hike. A late afternoon boat returns to Paleohora from Souyia. Get some advice on the route, however, because it leaves the coast and goes up the mountain and then through a gorge. Though not as dramatic as the

Samarian Gorge, the Ayia Irini Gorge (12 kilometer hike of 4-5 hours with time to rest), west of the Samarian Gorge and part of the same national park, sees far fewer hikers so you'll have the trail to yourself. If you're camping in Paleohora, you can take the early morning bus to Omalos. Tell the driver you want off at Ayia Irini. Hike down and catch the afternoon ferry from Souyia back to Paleohora. The trailhead is at the KriKri Café, which serves breakfast. You can also hike the Samarian Gorge by taking the morning bus to Omalos and then the ferry from Agia Roumeli back to Paleohora. Directions: 18km east of Kastelli Kissamou exit the National Highway at Maleme and drive south 55km in the direction of Paleohora.

▲**Camping:** •At the north end of Paleohora turn east following signposting for camping for 2km on the road closest to the beach heading east. Camping Paleohora (0823 41120); simple rustic facilities; good place to meet other travelers; some shade; close to the beach; open May-Sept.; $.

RHODES

The massive walls of the fortress in the city of Rhodes speak of the savage, uncompromising power of the Middle Ages. The island was sought by Suleyman the Magnificent, Mehemt II, and the Knights of Saint John. The wealthy trading port proved unconquerable except from within. Today, beguiling bougainvillea and hibiscus soften the huge fortress walls, palace, and archways. At sunset the ramparts shine like burnished gold. Coats of arms still guard doorways along the steep Street of the Knights leading to the Grand Master's palace. Under an arch, the lion of Venice listens indifferently to the call of the muezzin and the tolling of church bells.

The fortress is like a tiny medieval town. Stop at the information office outside the main gate to gather materials to make your meanderings more interesting. Get squeeky clean in the 18th-century Turkish Bath; closed Sunday. Reflect on novelist Lawrence Durrell's idol, the Marine Venus, in the archaeological museum. Visit the old synagogue to pay homage to the Jews of Rhodes and Kos who were sent to death camps. Experience the techno magic of the Sound and Light Show; nightly except Sunday. Take Greek dancing lessons or just enjoy the show at the Folk Dance Theatre. The museums and palace are closed Monday.

The spectacle of the Temple of Athena at Lindos is unique in the world. Perched on a rough ocher acropolis, above an endless royal-blue sea, the columns stand proud and invincible like the goddess herself. She was venerated for her power to still tempests. For protecting the long, slender boats that traded with Phoenicia and Egypt, she was bestowed with gifts from Alexander the Great, King Amasis of Egypt, and King Minos of Crete; open daily. As you the walk up reflect on the great and famous who have tread the same path.

The best and most popular beaches are on the east coast, where weather is better. Rural villages in the interior are untouristy and provide a refreshing change from seaside scenery. Surrounded by cultivated fields, the little towns have nice leafy parks with deciduous trees. Pack a picnic lunch and stop along the way. Petaloudes, the Valley of the Butterflies, is the only tourist attraction. The resin from liquidamber trees attracts thousands of moths to roost on their trunks. Well camouflaged, the moths rest quietly with folded wings, conserving their energy for the final phase of their life. Western Rhodes is prone to gusty winds and rough seas. Here and there are ruins that make a scenic destination for walk or picnic.

▲**Camping:** 16km south of Rhodes City. Exit the city on 95 and drive south in the direction of Kallithies, pass through the village, and drive to the beach. Faliraki Camping (2241 085358); one kilometer from a sandy beach; shady; pool; children's playground; open June-Sept; $$.

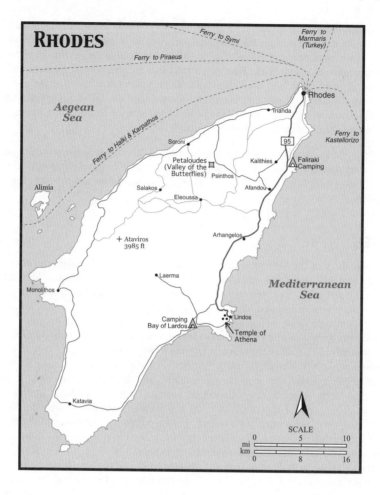

Italy

www.italiantourism.com

Like its food, Italy is a full-bodied and generous country. Some areas are simple, with rich flavors and aromas; others are more graceful and elegant. It is a country where love, food, art, and business are joined in near perfection. An easy-going ambiance pervades in a happy, sometimes haphazard way. Here there is no need to fret over the imperfections of life. Perhaps it's this-true-to-nature simplicity that is Italy's most important charm and lure.

With its hundreds of campgrounds, Italy is an extremely popular camping destination. If you play tennis, bring your racket, as many of the campgrounds have tennis courts. The registration office and gate are often closed for a long lunch and rest. Ask about the cost of showers when you register, and get change or tokens. The opening and closing dates listed here are conservative but reliable. Depending on the weather, you might find them opening earlier or closing later. Most campgrounds charge about 18-22 euros per night for two persons, a car, and a small tent indicated here as $$. Simple campgrounds cost less. Resort-like campgrounds or those close to popular tourist areas can cost over 25 euros indicated here as $$$.

If you are used to driving on fast freeways and in big cities, you'll adapt easier to driving in Italy. Keep commute times in mind when you are coming in or out of a big city. The lightest traffic occurs early on Sunday morning. Expect tolls, and carry change. Major toll roads take charge cards. Renting or leasing a car in Italy is more expensive than in most other countries, so consider renting in a neighboring country.

Admission to major museums and historic sites is expensive. Be selective and then allow time to thoroughly enjoy the ones you chose. Use a guidebook to understand them more completely. If you study Italian history and art before your trip, your visit will be more meaningful. You can now book ahead at the tourist office for some of the major museums. Some open only for a long morning, and most are closed on Mondays. Check the current opening hours with the tourist office. Bring binoculars to get a closer look at the glorious mosaics, the details in frescoes, and the extraordinary carvings in stone and wood.

Italians put eating and relaxing high on their priority list. Long midday closing periods are common. Keep in mind the saying "When in Rome, do as the Romans do". Join the locals and do your sightseeing and shopping in the morning or later in the afternoon.

Italy is a festive place in summer. Some events feature well-known performers. When you first start making plans, contact the Italian Government Tourist Office and visit their website for a current schedule of events, exhibitions, and ticketing information. You'll need to purchase tickets in advance for the most popular ones, but do go to a few, as they are exciting and memorable. Book the campground ahead, and arrive early if a special event is in town.

ROME

Historically one of the most important places in the world, Rome's history crowds in and over every corner of its twisting cobblestone streets, grand piazzas, cathedrals, and ancient ruins. It's a city that is best savored when you've immersed yourself in its history before the trip. Some say there is more to see here than any other place in the world.

Start early each day. Most of the major museums close at 2 PM. Afternoons can be spent leisurely absorbing its incredible atmosphere. Some ticketing for museums can be done ahead at the tourist office or on the internet. A good city map is essential, and a compass can be helpful. I find riding around on my bicycle most enjoyable, and getting a little lost is part of the fun. Enjoy the simple pleasures of everyday life in Rome. Pick a few major sites that are important to you, and savor them slowly, as you would a delicious meal.

Line up for the Vatican Museums early in the morning at the entrance on the north side of the Vatican City wall. Purchase a *Guide to the Vatican Museum and City* here, and read it while you wait in line. The line moves fairly quickly, so don't be disheartened if it is lengthy. The self-guided tours are color-coded. Choose the one that suits your interest, and follow the color. The richness of the treasures you'll see is incredible. Be sure to allow time and energy to fully enjoy Raphael's *"Stanze"*; the harmony, colors and sensitivity of the artist's work are breathtaking. The Sistene Chapel and Michelangelo's overwhelming ceiling frescoes of *"The Creation"* and *"The Last Judgement"* will probably be the most fabulous large-scale painting you'll ever see. Bring binoculars; closed Sunday, except the last Sunday of the month when it is open for a long morning and admission is free. Seeing all this brilliant work is just the cream on the top of a very rich cauldron. Saint Peter's Piazza and the Basilica-with Michelangelo's *"Pieta"*, the glorious dome, and the views from the roof won't disappoint; closed Sunday, except the last Sunday in the month when admission is free. Directions: Bus 64 or Metro Ottaviano.

Try to make history come alive as you wander. In your mind, recreate the sounds, smells, and life of the Romans as you view the Colosseum, Pantheon, Palatine Hill, Roman Forum, Piazza Venezia, Pantheon, and Piazza del Campidoglio; all open daily. Directions: Metro Colosseo. Taking the hop-on-hop-off city bus tour is a good way to orient yourself. You can buy tickets and then get on or off for as long as you like at any of the nine main tourist stops. Look for the "I" bus. The Piazza Navona, Campo de' Flori, Piazza di Spagna, and Fontane di Trevi are touristy but fun to explore. Take a break in the restful gardens of the Villa Borghese or at one of the cafes in the tiny squares in Trastevere. Use your guidebook to select from the multitude of other fascinating sights. Pick up a free *This Week in Rome* for the current happenings in concerts and exhibitions.

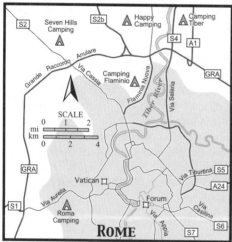

Public transportation is readily available at all the camping places, so leave your car behind. You can buy tickets and get information at the camp office. Reread "Using Public Transportation" and "Traveling Safe and Smart" in this book's first section.

For a break from city life, pack a picnic and drive 40 kilometers east of the city to Tivoli. Immerse yourself here in the old elegance of the gardens at the Villa d'Este or Villa Adriana.

▲Camping: • Closest to the historic area. West side of the GRA (ring road). Close to S1 take exit 1 in the direction of San Pietro/Centrum. Drive east on Via Aurelia for just over one kilometer. Watch for the pedestrian walkway over the Via Aurelia.

Then look for the camping sign on the south side. Roma Camping, Via Aurelia 831 (06-664-18147); minutes from the Vatican by bus close to campground; doable bicycle ride to the historic area; good place to meet fellow international travelers; close to an excellent covered market; cabins; open all year; $$$. • On the north side of town, close to S2 and S3, take exit 6 off the GRA. Drive south onto Via Flaminia Nuova, staying left. Camping Flaminio, Via Flaminia 821 (06-336-26401); close to public transport; close to Tiber River walking/cycling trail; pool; open all year; $$. • In the same area but a bit north. Exit off the GRA at exit 5 and drive north on S2 bis and Via Cassia Veientana. It's close to the intersection of Via Cassia Veientana and Via Prato della Corte. Happy Camping, Via Prato della Corte 1915 (06-336-26401); swimming pool; camp shuttle bus to metro; open April-Oct; $$$. • In the same area just west of A1 exit off the GRA at exit 6. Drive north just over one kilometer to S3/Via Flaminia. Drive east onto Via Tiberina. Camping Tiber, Via Tiberina at km 1400 (06-336-12314); next to the Tiber River; camp shuttle bus to metro; cabins; swimming pool open April-Oct; $$$. • In the same area. Exit the GRA at exit 3 onto S2/Via Cassia. Seven Hills Camping, Via Cassita 1216 (06-303-10039); swimming pool; cabins; cafe; shuttle bus to metro; open year-round; $$$.

LAZIO

Vibrant fields of sunflowers turn their faces in unison to the sun, giving your eyes a feast as you travel on tree-lined back roads. In summer, the fields are edged prettily with the lavender and pink of wild sweetpea. Here and there, perched high atop a hill seemingly in the middle of nowhere, medieval walled villages sculpt the skyline. Farmlands roll out like colored quilts. The air is fresh, driving is a pleasure, and summer festivities abound. Ask the Italian Tourist Office in your country to send you a current events calendar, and visit the internet to get ticketing information. Book ahead for the most famous. This is a good area for a camping experience at an *agriturist*-a small farm that has a few rooms and campsites. You'll share food and homemade wine with the owner's family. These places can be difficult to find, so get directions from the local tourist office before setting out

Orvieto

Located halfway between Florence and Rome, Orvieto is an ideal stopping place. Masterfully perched on top of a volcanic plug, the ancient town looks down peacefully on the farms below. The drive to the top ends at Piazza Popolo, where parking is easy; or park at the train station and take the funicular up. Walk or bike through the narrow streets to the Duomo. Sit in the shade with the locals and just gaze on this fantasy of stunning mosaics, sculptures and spires. The cathedral is one of Italy's best, so bring your binoculars. Delicate tendrils of vines link the scenes of the creation to the judgment in the extraordinary carving on the marble piers. The intricate detail of the colossal bronze doors is exceptional. Interior walls are banded with horizontal Moorish stripes that create a sense of height and spaciousness, a welcoming and handsome change from the exterior. Bring change to illuminate the chapels, especially Cappella di Brizio.

▲Camping: • In Rossa Ripasena, a small hill of tiny farms just west of historic Orvieto. After descending the hilltop from Piazza Popolo, cross the bridge over the river and stay left on the small road. Agricampeggio Sossogna, Rocca Ripasena 6190 (07-63-343141); lovingly restored farmhouse; extremely peaceful and comfortable; tents only; $$$. • 11km southeast of Orvieto, at the southern tip of Lago di Corbara. Drive south 7km on 205 in the direction of Narni. Turn east on 448 and drive 4km in the direction of Todi. Entrance is on a steep, blind curve. Camping Orvieto (0744-950-240); close to the lake; swimming pool open June-

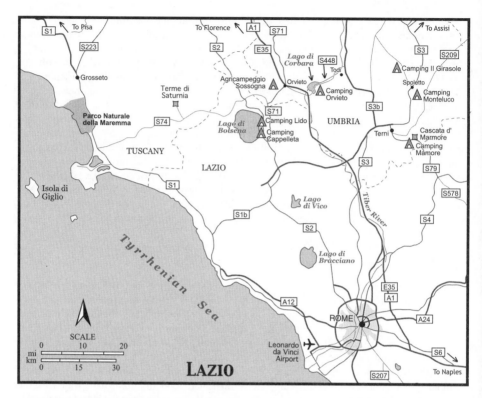

Sept; $$. • 22km west of Orieto on Lake Bolzeno. Drive southwest on S71 for 12km. At the fork stay south, following signposting for Bolsena for 8km. These both have good locations on the lake south of town; sandy beach; open May-Sept; $$. Camping Lido (0761-799258) and Camping Cappelletta (0761-799543).

Spoleto

This graceful and sophisticated town is a beautiful setting for summer of musical, cinematic, and cultural events. Purchase tickets ahead www.spoletofestival.it Spoleto has a history of many layers that includes prehistoric walls, the remains of a Roman amphitheatre, and the gates from which Hannibal was supposedly turned away. As you wander through the churches note the works of Lombard artists. Some of the frescoes are humorous with savage beasts struggling with man.

There's a very good brochure/map for the pretty woodland, old mule tracks, and dirt road walks that connect most of the little villages. The brave and adventurous will want to take the "Railway Walk". It follows the railway route that once ran through the Valnerina Valley and over the mountains into Spoleto. Featuring some spectacular viaducts and tunnels (one is two kilometers long) the walk is not for those who suffer from vertigo or are frightened by long periods of walking in complete darkness. It is a Club Alpino (CIA) trail. Wear sturdy boots and bring a flashlight with new batteries, energy food, and water. The long tunnel, Galleria di Caprareccia, is on the San Anatolia side. If you park and start in San Anatolia di Narco, the trail begins off the main road on a small road signposted for Scheggino. If you park and start the trail in Spoleto, the trail begins at the viaduct Ponte delle Torri, then climbs steeply up to the tower and from there to the mountains. San Anatolia di Narco is due east of Spoleto on S209.

▲**Camping:** • Before climbing the hill and just after you've crossed the bridge, exit S3/Terni-Rome road east, passing the Chiesa di San Pietro. Turn south on Monteluco. Camping Monteluco (07-43-22-03-58); tiny and crowded; close to the special events; open May-Sept; $$. • Exit off S3 in the direction of Montefalco. Take the small road north 10km. It's outside the village of Petrognano. Camping II Girasole (0743-51335); swimming pool; tennis courts; cabins; open all year; $$.

Cascate delle Marmore

In the pleasant warmth of a summer evening people come to enjoy the sound and light show at one of the largest waterfalls in Europe, Cascate delle Marmore-initially created by the Romans to protect the area from flooding. The show starts in the early evening, usually between 5:30 and 6 PM. Check at a tourist office for the current time schedule. You can view the falls from the top in the village of Marmore or from the bottom on S209. A steep walking path connects the two viewing areas. If you're in the area during the day when the water flow is turned down, it's fun to soak in the swimming pools at the bottom of the cascade. Look for parked cars, and follow the path. Directions: Southeast of Terne, between S209 and S79 in the village of Marmore.

▲**Camping:** • In the village of Marmore. Camping Mamore (074-467198); basic amenities; open June-Aug; $.

Todi

Men have probably lived on Todi's windy hilltop overlooking the Tiber Valley for at least 3,000 years. Spearheads, axes, and daggers of polished stone, give evidence that Umbrian tribal people lived here before the Etruscans. The famous bronze sculpture of Mars is now displayed in the Vatican, and fine goldwork, earrings, and necklaces uncovered here are now in museums in Florence and Rome. Todi is off the tourist trail, so it's easy to imagine yourself in medieval Europe while you sit peacefully in the perfectly preserved Piazza del Popolo. It's in this setting, grand opera-like, that summer art and music festivals take place.

UMBRIA
Assisi

The spirit of St. Francis-a monk who renounced wealth and lived a life of charity and poverty-still hovers in the tranquil air of the beautiful Basilica, Duomo, and Santa Chiara tucked up into Mount Subasio. However, Eremo delle Carceri, the caves where he lived and prayed, are more in keeping with the monk himself. Good parking is available outside the walls of the cathedral area at both the north and south ends. The Basilica has an upper and lower church. Plan to see both. Bring euros so you can light up the walls to see Giotto's famous frescoes of St. Francis's life. Note his use of light and shadow, but most of all look for characterization in his figures. Binoculars help. A guidebook makes this a more meaningful experience. Shorts and sleeveless shirts aren't allowed. The hiking trail and road up to the Eremo, St Francis's forest retreat, are just outside the gate of Rocca Maggiore near the Porta Cappiccini. It's an uphill climb of four kilometers, but not terribly steep. It's here that he would meditate as he wandered through the forest. Visitors walk silently by his humble bed and a tiny chapel hollowed out of rock. The views are magnificent. Directions: Drive east of Perugia on S75. Exit onto S147 in the direction of Assisi and drive 15km.

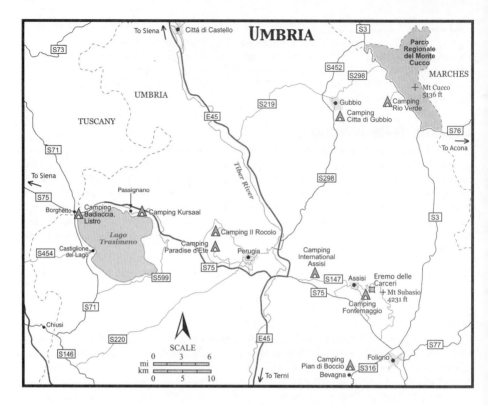

▲**Camping:** • Follow signposting up the hill to Porta Nova. Turn right and follow sign-posting to the Eremo Delle Carceri. After passing under the arch, continue up the fairly steep hill for one kilometer. Camping Fontemaggio (07-581-3636); fabulous views; tranquil; basic amenities; open May-September; $$. • 3km west of Assisi, on S147. Camping International Assisi, (07-581-3710); easier for caravans; good facilities; shuttle to the Basilica; open all year; $$. • In between Assisi and Spoleto, close to Foligno, exit S75 west onto S316 in the direction of Bevagna. Camping Pian di Boccio, in Bevagna (07-423-60391); cabins; disco; swimming pool; open May-Sept; $$.

Pergugia

A university city and the regional capitol, this bustling city exudes style. Arches, passageways, parks, and stairways intertwine making the historic area, which is closed to traffic, feel like a castle village. To get a real sense of the place, join the locals in their evening stroll on Corso Vannucci. Well-known international musicians fill the air with exciting sounds throughout summer; particularly excellent is the Umbria Jazz Festival in July. Buy tickets ahead www.umbriajazz.com. A large car park is on the main road, Via Lorenzo, at the bottom of the hill, and an escalator takes you up the hill. The tourist office at Piazza IV November will fill you in on events and provide a map.

▲**Camping:** • West of the city on S75 at km 13 exit north onto a small road. Climb the hill for 4km to the village of Colle della Trinita. Camping Paradise d'Ete (07-517-2117); nice location; small; cabins; open June-Aug; $. • On the same road. Camping II Rocolo (075-517-8550); better for caravans; open June-Aug; $$.

Lago Trasimeno

This placid and shallow, mirror-like lake, where water lilies float and dabbling ducks assiduously feed along the reed beds has a subtle charm. It's popular with locals who come to relax and have fun. Wind surfing, waterslides, paddle boats, cycling, and horseback riding keep kids and the young at heart entertained.

▲**Camping**: The lake has plenty of large campgrounds to choose from; some are resort-like with swimming pools. All of these have nice locations on the lake. Follow signposting for Val di Chiana, then circle road around the lake. • On the north side of the lake close to Passignano. Camping Kursaal (828-085); pool; some shade; small café; open Apr-Oct; $$$. • On the west side of the lake close to Castiglione del Lago in Borghetto. Camping Badiaccia (596-59097); some shade; pool; parking separate from tent; tennis; open April-Oct; $$. • In the same area. Camping Listro (595-1193); smaller; open Apr-Sept; $$.

Gubbio

Gubbio has a splendor all its own. Set on the windy slopes of the Umbrian Appenines, it has a history of stoic independence that survives today. It's foundations are pre-Etruscan. In the Museo Civico you can examine the–Eugubian Tables-bronze tablets dating from 200 to100 BC. They are the earliest record of Umbrian language and thought to describe certain priestly duties; open daily. Medieval traditions survive in the town's crossbow competition, the Palio della Balestra, when locals dress with pride in traditional costumes. It is held on the last Sunday in May. During the festival of Ceri held earlier in the month, men race through the streets and up a very steep path to the Basilica carrying large ornate constructions topped by a wax saint. The forested Apennines Mountains and their cascading waterfalls are seen right in town, and as in Siena, the buildings and narrow cobblestone streets have a rosy hue. High pastures studded with wild flowers and old farmhouses provide an exceptionally beautiful walk. Start by taking the funicula up to the Basilica, then follow the paths skirting the fields. Directions: Exit E45 east of Perugia and drive northeast on S298 for 30km to Gubbio. Park at the base of the hill in the large car park and walk up.

▲Camping: • Exit town on S298 in the direction of Perugia and drive just over one kilometer. Camping Citta di Gubbio, in Ortoguidone (075-927-2037); nice location; swimming pool; bike rental; cycle/walking paths; open May-Sept; $$.

Parco Regionale del Monte Cucco

At over 900 meters deep, the 20-kilometer-long Grotte di Monte Cucco tunnels through Monte Cucco. One entrance is reached via a long iron stairway. Park guides are from the Centro Nationale di Speleologia in Costacciaro. Naturally, the park is a haven for cave lovers from all over Europe. Hang gliding is also popular in the area. Directions: East of Gubbio (as the crow flies) exit S3 for Costacciaro.

▲Camping: • Drive east up the mountain road to the village of Fornace. Camping Rio Verde (075-917-0307); lovely location; basic amenities; open May-Sept; $.

TUSCANY

Quintessentially Italian, Tuscany boasts fabulous art, mouth-watering cuisine, and fertile rolling hillsides that are meticulously lined with ancient grapevines, silver-leafed olive trees, and sunflowers. Entering this area is like encountering an enormous buffet of delicious food knowing, unfortunately, that you can only eat a small amount of what is offered before you will be full.

WESTERN TUSCANY
Florence

Florence, like Rome, is best savored if you have read about the main characters in its history before you arrive. So several months ahead of your trip, use your library to enjoy the stories of the lives and works of the major artists of the Italian Renaissance. Doing so will enhance your experience immeasurably. The major museums are expensive. Choose just a few, and spend your time leisurely enjoying them. Use a guidebook in the museums, and don't feel guilty for skipping parts. Main sights are closed on Monday. You can confirm museum hours, purchase advance tickets for major museums, and peruse the city's current offerings at the main tourist office north of the Duomo at Via Cavour 1. For a small booking fee, you can call Firenze Musei at 055-2948 and reserve tickets. When you arrive at the museum, follow signs for the pre-booked ticket booth where you can pay for your tickets without waiting in line. Or you can use the web; www.weekendafirenze.com. You'll need to book at least three days in advance, have an e-mail address, and pay a six euro booking fee. Binoculars will help you appreciate the intricate detail of artistic works.

Piazza Duomo is the traditional place to begin an exploration. Use a guidebook to help you appreciate the masterful work of the most important artistic geniuses of the Renaissance, whose

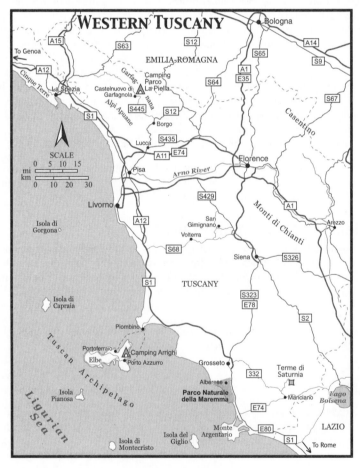

works you'll see here. Brunelleschi's brilliant Duomo, Florence's landmark, reflects the surrounding hillsides in color and form. It represents the confidence and high aspirations of the Renaissance. A network of stairways between the inner and outer domes give insight to the architect's thorough planning and design. Look for them on the left aisle near the Dante fresco. Up in the dome gallery you'll be able to get a closer view of the impressive stained-glass windows. Your visit to the Duomo will mean more if you read its fascinating and touching story in advance; open daily. Over-shadowed by the Duomo, Giotto's lovely pastel-colored Campanile seems small. It is most famous for its sculptural reliefs, which tell how the medieval popu-

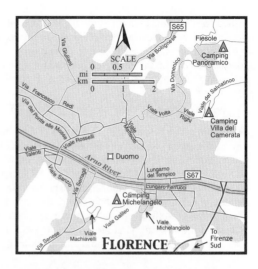

lation viewed the world and religion; open daily. The awesome drama of Ghiberti's Baptistery doors, particularly the East Doors, give reason for them to be considered the most beautiful bronze doors in the world. Relics from construction of the Duomo and some of its original sculptural works can be enjoyed in Museo dell'Opera del Duomo. Michelangelo's "*Pieta*", carved for his own tomb, is displayed on a landing of the stairway. Donatello's and della Robbia's delightful bas-reliefs, found on the remnants of marble choir balconies seen in the first room, are ranked as some of the best work of the Renaissance; open daily. Directions: From Camping Michelangelo, walk or bike down to the Arno River. Go west on the south side of the river. Cross over the Pont Vecchio bridge. Continue straight ahead to Via Calimala and the Duomo.

Take a break to walk over to Market Centrale, an immense, colorful cornucopia where people chat, whistle, swear, sing, or call to each other over proscuitto hanging like Japanese lanterns, pillars of parmesan cheese, entangled octopus, and mounds of tiny green beans decorated with fresh herbs. There is a sense of drama and artistic disorder. Stand back to watch, and you'll see the prideful Tuscan personality emerge as merchant and customer negotiate. Directions: Walk/bike north from the Piazza Duomo/Giovanni on Borgo San Lorenzo located on the northwest corner of the Piazza San Lorenzo. Turn west on Via Canto de Nelli, continuing west on Via dell Ariento. Market Centrale is housed in an old two-story warehouse and closes at 1 PM. A flea market operates outside the entrance. Charming, inexpensive trattorias are tucked in around the area.

The Bargello and Uffizi museums are similar in scale to the Louvre in Paris. If time is short, choose one. Once inside, with guidebook in hand, plan a route to see your favorites while your senses are still fresh. The Uffizi's extraordinary art collection will leave you breathless. Botticelli's sublime mythological paintings "La Primavera" and "The Birth of Venus", Da Vinci's "Adoration of the Magi", Raphael's "Leo X with Two Cardinals", and Titian's "Venus of Urbino" are just a few of the most treasured pieces in Italy's most important art gallery; closed Monday. Directions: Just off the south side of Piazza Signoria on Degli Uffizi. The Bargello houses the best sculptural works of the Italian Renaissance. The Michelangelo, Cellini, Donatello, and Giambologna creations are daringly innovative. Expressive movements, emotion, and depth of character carved from stone explore the erotic and mysterious psyche of the Florentines; closed Monday. Directions: From the southeast corner of Piazza Duomo, go south on Via del Proconsolo. It's located on the northeast corner of Piazza S. Frirenza. From a monstrous block of marble, Michelangelo carved "David" as a symbol of the artistic and intellectual aspirations of the Renaissance. It excites a strong emotional reaction with its enormity and perfect beauty. It is displayed alone in one room of the Galleria dell'Academia; closed Monday. Directions: From Piazza San Marco, walk southwest on Via Ricasoli.

Save time for watching children feed the pigeons on Piazza della Signoria, for checking out the goods being sold on the Ponte Vecchio, and for draping yourself over the Arno River wall to watch canoeists as the sun turns the water golden. It is easy to cycle in historic Florence.

Florence Area

▲**Camping**: The best for the city. • South of Florence, exit A1 at Firenze/Certosa. Drive north toward the center of Florence on the Siena/Firenze road/S2. Go up through the park on Viale Galileo, following signs to Piazzale Michelangelo. Camping is just past the monument and viewing area. Camping Michelangelo, Viale Michelangelo 80 (055-681-1977); very popular; good place to meet fellow international travelers; book ahead or arrive early; fabulous views of the Duomo and Arno River; easy bike ride to the historic area; bike rental; bus close-by; stairway down to the Arno River; covered common terrace area overlooking the city; open all year; $$$.
• South of the city, exit A1 at Firenze Sud. Drive north 3km to the Arno Bridge Verrazzano. Turn west onto S67 and drive about 2km. Follow signposting north in the direction of Fiesole.

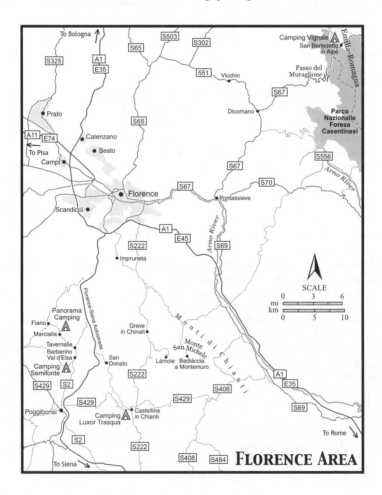

FLORENCE AREA

Signposted at the roundabout for Viale Augusto Righi. Camping Villa di Camerata, Viale Righi 2 (055-601451); on the grounds of a hostel; popular; arrive early; close to a large supermarket and public transport; open year-round; $$. • In the same area. Follow the same directions, but continue farther up the hill to the historic village of Fiesole. It's just north of the village on a steep narrow road. Camping Panoramico, Via Peramonda 1(055-59186); wonderful views; shady with trees; cabins; bus service from the piazza in Fiesole to Florence; open all year; $$S. • Near A1 and S2, south of Florence. Exit A1 at Firenze/Certosa. Follow signposting up hill. Camping International Firenze, Bottai, (05-5237-4704); swimming pool; convenient to the autostrata; bus to Florence; cabins; open May-Sept; $$$.

FLORENCE AREA
Hiking in the Casentino

To escape the bustle of the cities and towns, head up to the mountains for walks beside lively creeks and tumbling waterfalls through lush green meadows, and on high, breezy ridges. The northern Apennines, where the Arno has its source, is a region known as the Casentino. It is the border between Tuscany and the Emilia Romagna. Here the hillside woods are a variety of turkey oak, maple, elm, and chestnut. Farther up, white fir, mountain ash, and beech trees dominate. You'll see woodpeckers busily gathering acorns and hear them tapping holes in the trees to store them. Kites hunt in the open meadows, hovering over their prey like helicopters. Anemones, primroses, and violets hide in the woods while gentians and poppies grow lustily in the meadows and the courageous saxifrage peeks out on windy, rocky, higher slopes.

From the little mountain village of San Benedetto in Alpe there is an exceptionally scenic walk. The highlight is the Acquacheta waterfall, whose wide veil of water shimmers in the sunlight as it crashes over the high rocks deep in the wooded valley. Dante spent part of his exile here. There are beautiful wild flower meadows close to the falls. The trail continues past the falls to the rugged Passo del Muraglione and into the village of Il Muraglione. Go midweek as the area is popular. Directions: Exit Florence east on 67 in the direction of Pontassieve and drive 37km to Dicomano. At the fork stay east on 67, and continue for another 25km to San Benedetto de Alpe.

▲**Camping:** In San Benedetto in Alpe. • Camping Vignale (0543-965245); lovely location, basic; open June-Aug; $.

Monte de Chianti Region

South of Florence, in the Monte de Chianti region, meticulous vineyards and silvery olive groves sweep over warm fertile hillsides. Old farmhouses surrounded by kitchen gardens and sweet-smelling fruit trees look down from hilltops studded with stately cypresses. Beautiful walking and cycling paths meander through the woods and farmland into peaceful forgotten valleys. Little-used roads often link charming 12th-century villages, where refreshing fountains, café-strewn plazas, and sometimes mazes of stone passageways provide the ambiance one hopes for in Tuscany. You can walk or cycle along tractor paths, the peripheries of fields, and the edges of olive groves. Old stone walls, laden with blackberry vines, beg you to taste. Romanesque churches with handsome bell towers, ancient stone houses with colorful gardens, old farm buildings, and perhaps a crumbling castle or monastery all add to the fine views of the Chianti countryside. Marked walking paths designed by the Club Alpino Italiano (CAI) web the region. Check with the tourist office for a map.

The loop route from Lamole to San Michele is a particularly pretty one. The route starts at the intersection at the south end of Lamole. It climbs up stone roads that edge vineyards to the top of the hill, where there are fine views. Then it returns through San Michele along blackberry-edged paths through classically Tuscan landscape back to Lamole. Directions: South of Firenze take 222 in the direction of Impruneta. Drive 22km to Greve in Chianti. Continue through town for 2km then take the small road east for Lamole.

Tyrrhenian Sea

GROSSETO AREA

▲**Camping:** South of Florence close to Poggibonsi. Drive south of Florence on the Firenze-Siena autostrada for 15km. Exit west in the direction of Tavernelle, then drive south 9km to Barberino Val d'Elsa and follow signposting. • Camping Semifonte (055-8075454); peaceful; bike rental; pool; open April-Oct; $$. Exit Firenze-Siena autrostrada for Tavernelle. Drive 6km to Tavernelle. Turn west on a small road and drive 3km in the direction of Marcialla. Continue up the hill one kilometer in the direction of Fiano. • Panorama Camping (0571-669334); beautiful location; bike rental; open April-Sept; $$. East of Paggibonsi. Drive south of the Firenze-Siena autostrada 20km. Exit east at the San Donato exit. Drive south on the road parallel to the autostrata for 12km to Castellina in Chianti and follow signposting up the winding dirt road. • Camping Luxor Trasqua (0577-743047); pool; quiet; open June-Aug; $$.

GROSSETO AREA
Terme di Saturnia

This is definitely an off-the-beaten-track kind of adventure. Cascading down the hillside, the sulphur springs of Terme di Saturnia form natural rock pools that are divine to soak in. Directions: The springs are west of Lago di Bolsena. From S74 at Manciano turn north on S322, and drive 2km. Follow signage for Saturnia. Before entering the town, exit for Terme di Saturnia. Look beyond the spa hotel for a small road with parked cars. Park, then follow the path to the cascade.

▲**Camping:** In Marina di Grosseto. From Grosetto take S322 in the direction of Marina di Grosetto and follow signposting. Camping Rosmarina (0564-36319); close to a sand beach; separate car parking from tent; open June-mid Sept; $$. In the same area. Camping La Marze (0564-35501); large; close to the beach; all the amenities; bike rental; car parking separate from tent; open May-Sept; $$.

Parco Naturale della Maremma

On the coast south of Grosseta, in a protected coastal reserve, umbrella pines, birds, and long stretches of unspoiled coastline make for a tranquil outing. Directions: Park in the main square at Alberese. Visit the park headquarters to enhance your knowledge of the area, and pick up a trail map. Entrance is by park bus only.

▲**Camping:** In Marina di Grosseto. See Terme di Saturnia.

Pisa Area

The Leaning Tower of Pisa is once again open for visitors after expenditures of over 30 million euros. Armies of dreamers and dabblers made proposals. Finally, realizing that it could collapse at any time, a panel of structural and geotechnical engineers, architects, art historians, and archaelogists worked to formalize a plan to stablize it. Part of the solution was soil extraction, coaxing the leaning south to rotate a bit to the north and tilt almost 16 inches less. The south edge of the top still leans out more than 15 feet beyond the base. The climb up to the bell tower is fun but scary. On the south side you weave about as you try to negotiate the slanted steps and hang on for dear life to the railings, while on the north side you feel as if you are going uphill although the stairs go down. Below you stretches the Piazza Miracoli with its marvelous assemblage of Romanesque architecture–a quartet of masterpieces. Rising from the emerald green lawn, the cathedral features an Islamic dome and gray-and-white striped marble and bristles with columns and arches. The Baptistry, Duomo, and Camposanto are also delights, and the Musee dell'Opera de Duomo is excellent. Use your guidebook to help you choose

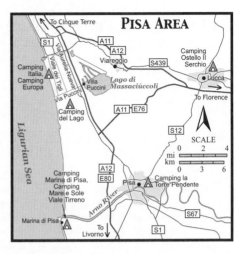

what you want to see, and purchase a combo ticket for those sights. This university town hosts many summer festivals. Plenty of parking is available outside the Campo walls. It's an easy place to visit.

▲**Camping:** • Off A1, drive into Pisa on S1. North of the Arno Bridge, take Viale delle Cascine east for half a kilometer. Camping la Torre Pendente (050-561704); convenient, cabins; bike rental; open May-Sept; $$. • On the beach at Marina di Pisa. Camping Marina di Pisa, Via Litoranea (050-32038) or Camping Mare e Sole Viale Tirreno (050-327-57); both are popular with local families; open May-Sept; $$.

Island of Elbe

The clear water and sandy beaches of Elbe are warm and inviting. Camping is resort-style and expensive. Board the car ferry from the mainland at Plombino.

▲**Camping:** Lots! • A less expensive area is Porto Azzurro. Camping Arrighi, at km 12 (05-6595-7822); on the beach; open May-Sept; $$$.

Lucca

A classy city that seems to do things right, Lucca is the capitol and heart of Tuscany's rich agricultural region. Visit the bustling morning market on Wednesday and Saturday at Piazza Anfiteatro, where the aroma of basil, vine-ripened tomatoes, and sweet peaches wafts through the air. The array of mouth-watering foodstuffs will tempt you to buy too much. The city's ancient walls are still intact; in fact, you can take a 4km walk along the top of them. Opera buffs wouldn't think of missing the small museum and birth home of Puccini.

▲**Camping:** In Viareggio close to Villa Puccini. Exit A12 for Viareggio and then turn immediately onto Via Aurelia Nueva in the direction of Livorno. Drive 3km to Torre del Lago. Follow signposting on Via Puccini. Camping del Lago (0584-359702); large; all amenities; pool; bike rental; open April-Sept; $$$. In the same area but on Viale dei Tigli. Camping Italia (0584-359828); $$$ or Camping Europa (0584-350707); $$; both are large; all amenities; close to the beach; disco on weekends; open April-Sept. • On the north side of the walled historic area, at Piazzale Martiri della Liberta. Drive northeast on Via Batoni, then turn right at Viale Civitali and then right on Via del Brennero. Camping Ostello Il Serchio, Via del Brennero 673 (0583-341811); a hostel and campground; basic amenities; open May-Sept; $.

North of Lucca/Parco dell'Orecchiella

In the high altitude Garfagnana region, mild terrain and grand views of the jagged peaks of the Alpi Apuane make for very pleasant casual walks. Marked walking paths weave between Corfino and the park's visitor center and botanical garden, which has an excellent exhibit of animal feces that can add fun and insight to your walks. Directions: From Lucca drive north on 12 in the direction of Borgo for 20km. 4km farther exit onto 445 and drive northwest for 24km to Castelnuovo di Grafagnana. Then take the smaller 324 north 8km up the winding road to Castiglione di Garfagnana and park.

▲Camping: North of Castelnuovo di Garfagnana. Follow signposting on a rough dirt road to Pieve Fosciana.. Camping Parco La Piella (0583-62916); small; peaceful; open June-Aug; $$.

Cinque Terre

Clinging to rocky cliffs like limpets and spilling into narrow ravines like scattered petals, five towns that were once inaccessible except by donkey or boat now host visitors who hike along narrow trails connecting the villages. Called the Via dell'Amore, the route follows the stepped alleyways of the villages and winds up and down paths cut from rocky cliffs with views of the turquoise Mediterranean. Pristine white spume curls onto the sand and rocks, lace-like. Stone houses are painted the brilliant yellow and rose of wildflowers..

Now part of a national park, the seven kilometer walking path between the villages requires an inexpensive ticket. Purchase the ticket and a map at the train station. Get an early start to relish the best light on the sea and village. Pack or wear your swimsuit, wear waterproof shoes for walking on the rocky beaches, and then tuck lunch, water, perhaps goggles, snorkel, and a small blow-up beach cushion into your pack. Plan to spend the entire day enjoying the hike and the beaches.

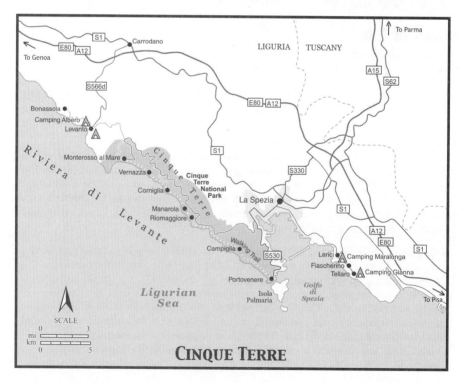

CINQUE TERRE

A local train runs between the villages. A one-way ticket allows you to stop at any one of the villages in one direction. Tickets are validated before boarding. The stops at the villages are short so be ready to get off. If the train is long, you might have to open the door and get out in the tunnel itself. Colorful little boats ply the waters transporting folks between the villages. A Cinque Terre Card also is sold that entitles you to both the hike and local train/bus transport. Directions: The Cinque Terre is close to La Spezia, between Genova and Livorno. From camping drive to La Spezia's train station where are car parks are nearby.

▲Camping: • South of the villages on the Bay of Lerici. Camping Maralunga (0187-966-589); tents only; terraced; close to the water; open June-August; $$. • Farther south in Tellaro. Camping Gianna, on the Lerici-Tellaro road (0187-653-49); good for caravans; nice location; open June-Aug; $$$. • North Cinque Terre on the beach in the village of Levanto. From S1 (the road paralleling A12) exit 28km north of La Spezia for the village of Carrodano. Drive south on the narrow and winding S566d for 12km to Levanto and the beach and following signposting for camping. Camping Albero (0187-800400); small; pleasant; April-Oct; $$. The next three are in the same area but have small terraced sites where access is difficult for caravans, parking is separate from tents; open from April-Oct; $$. Camping Aqua (0187 808465); Camping Pian di Picche (0187 800597); Camping Cinque Terre (0187 801252).

EASTERN TUSCANY
Siena Area

Whatever the Sienese do, they do it with dash and style. Siena hosts the most famous festival in Italy, the Palio. It is a thrilling spectacle of bareback horse-racing held in the historic square, the Campo. Resembling

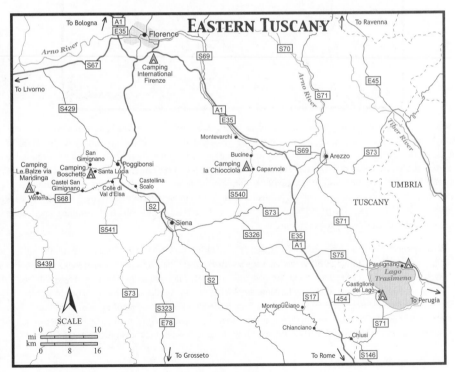

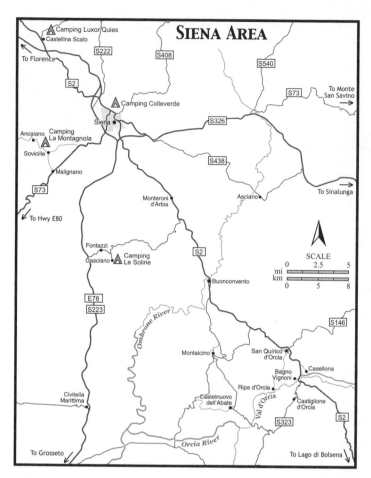

a shallow amphitheatre, the Campo is a great place to linger, be lazy, eat a sandwich, or read a book on non-festival days. As you rest, you can gaze up at the fine palaces and at the slender, graceful tower-the emblem of the city's magnificence. It's worth working up the energy to climb the tower's stairway for the unbeatable panoramic view of Siena's countryside. Be sure to walk up the hill to the cathedral, Siena's highest point. The interior is boldly decorated with striped pilasters, Gothic vaulting, and a blue firmament ceiling painted with gold stars. Its unique marble flooring was created over several hundred years by artists who designed 56 scenes with sgraffito. There's good parking outside the walls, but be careful to note which of the many gates of the walled city you enter–it's easy to get confused.

▲Camping: • Northeast of town, exit S2 at Siena Nord. Drive south back toward Siena to climb the hill. Follow signposting. Camping Colleverde, Via Scacciapensieri (0577-280-044); lovely views; swimming pool; bus to Siena; open April-Sept; $$. • Exit Siena southwest on 73. Stay west in the direction of Sovicille following signposting for 5km. Camping La Montagnola (0577-314473); nice shady location; bus to Siena; car parking separate from tent; quiet; open May-Sept; $$. • 8km north of Siena off S2. Exit north for Castellina Scalo. Drive 3km crossing railway tracks. Drive up a steep winding road following signposting. Camping Luxor Quies (05-7774-3047); pleasant location; convenient to the autostrata; open June-Aug; $$.

South of Siena/Walking and Cycling

Fairly gentle terrain through rolling farmland where sunflowers and grain crops give way to well-tended vineyards make cycling from Buonconvento to Montalcino a nice journey. The area produces one of Italy's finest wines, Brunello. Montalcino sits high on a hilltop with stunning views. Its 16th-century fortress was the last refuge for Charles V. An affluent, quiet town, its plazas are flower-filled. Directions: Drive south out of Siena on 2 in the direction of Monteroni for 23km to Buonconvento.

Since Etruscan times the waters of Bagno Vignoni have been enjoyed both by the rich and famous and by those not so. You can ask to use the pool at one of the hotels or, for more adventure, hike down to the river itself. Look for the small dirt road on the north side of the river. You'll see parked cars. Take the cliff path. Directions: Drive south out of Siena on 2 in the direction of Monteroni for 47km to Bagno Vignoni.

The colors and contours of the Val d'Orcia make for splendid walks and cycling. As you begin your journey in the direction of Ripa d'Orcia park in Castelnuovo dell'Abate and take in the view of the refined abbey, sitting atop a terraced hillside. If you are walking or have a mountain bike, you'll enjoy taking the gravel route to Podere La Fornace and the River Orcia and then the footpath on to Ripa d'Orcia. Directions: Drive south of Siena on 2 in the direction of Monteroni for 43km to San Quirico d'Orcia. Continue through town for 4km. Exit onto 323 in the direction of Castiglione and drive 12km. At the fork stay northwest and continue up the winding mountain road to Castelnuovo dell Abate.

▲Camping: • Exit Siena south on E78/223 in the direction of Civitella Marittima and drive 17km. Exit east at Fontazzi and drive 4km to Casciano. Camping Le Soline (0577-817410); lovely location; terraced; pool; open May-Sept; $$.

San Gimignano

Lofty towers, fortress walls, and hard-to-beat panoramic views of Tuscany make this tiny village a very photogenic and popular stop for travelers. Time your visit for late in the day so you can join the locals in their evening walk through their perfectly preserved village to watch the sun set over the hills and fields-perhaps a patchwork of brilliant yellow formed from rape, scarlet from poppies, and chartreuse from barley. In summer, outdoor movies are shown up on top of the hill at the old fortress Rocca. Good parking is provided just outside the walls. Directions: Drive south of Florence in the direction of Siena for 40km. Take the exit onto 68 for Colle Val d'Elsa Sud and drive 13km to Castel San Gimignano. Turn north and drive 13km up to San Gimignano.

▲Camping: • 2km south of the town on the road to Volterra, in the village of Santa Lucia. Camping Boschetto (0577-940352); small; very popular arrive early; pool; open May-Sept; $$.

Volterra

From a distance, the Volterra hilltop silhouette appears errie. Its empty landscape has few trees, vineyards, or olive orchards. The soil layer here is thin clay that doesn't support trees or grapevines but is rich in minerals. It produced one of the largest and most powerful cities in the 8th and 9th-centuries–the Etruscan city of *Velathri*. Italy's best collection of artifacts from Etruscan settlers can be examined in Volterra's Museo Guarnacci, whose collection of cinerary urns is outstanding. Looking for individual artistry and humor makes viewing the collection even more enjoyable; open daily. Today the town is full of small alabaster workshops; some designing valuable art pieces, others producing attractive and inexpensive gifts. Directions: Close to the bus terminal at Piazza XX. After viewing, take a walk into the mysterious Balze ravine, where bits of the ruins of Etruscan Volterra are exposed. From one of the steep cliffs you can see the remains of Badia, an 11th-century abbey. A Crossbow Contest is one of the town's more colorful summer events.

▲**Camping**: • Northwest of the historic area, follow signage to Borgo San Giusto and Balze. Continue northwest to Via Mandringa. Camping Le Balze Via Mandringa (0588-87880); lovely location; tennis courts; pool; open May-Sept; $$.

Montepulciano

The highest of Italy's hilltop towns, Montepulciano has panoramic views of mountains and countryside as well as a warren of cobblestone alleyways, evocative churches, and vine-covered stone walls-all combining to make it one of Tuscany's prettiest hilltop towns. In tiny atmospheric wine cellars travelers are invited to imbibe the area's delicious Chianti wines. Gift shops sell a driving itinerary of the Tuscan wine region that makes it easy to thread your way through the softly undulating land growing olives, grapes, and wheat. A Thursday morning market is held outside the Porta al Prato, and low-key summer festivals provide local color and fun. Directions: Montepuliciano is directly west of Lago Trasimeno. Off A1 take the exit for Chiusi-Chianciano onto 146 in the direction of Chianciano and drive 18km. Then take the smaller road up the hill to Montepulciano.

▲**Camping**: See Lago di Trasimeno.

Lago di Trasimeno

This is a popular vacation destination for locals who come to relax and have fun. Wind surfing, waterslides, paddle boats, and horseback riding keep kids and the young at heart entertained.

▲**Camping**: • On the west side of Lago Trasimeno in Castiglione del Lago. All of these are large and adjacent to the lake; popular with families; watersport and bike rentals in the area; open April-Sept; $$. Camping Listro (075-951193); Camping Lido Trasimeno (075-9659350); Camping Punta Navaccia (075-826357). • On the north side of the lake in Passignano, on the lake road Val di Chiana. Camping Kursaal (075-827-182) or Camping Europa (075-82405) all the amenities; bike and boat rental in the area; cabins; open April-Sept; $$.

Arezzo

Arezzo's star attraction is the sensitive masterpiece frescoes of Piero della Francesca found in a nondescript Franciscan church, the Chiesa San Francesco. Ten monumental pieces create the cycle of "*The Legend of the True Cross*". A master mathematician, his paintings are organized according to geometric principals and symbolic significance. Today we know that they guided the representation of three-dimensional to two-dimensional surfaces right up to the time of the Impressionists. Scholars have found that Cezanne was greatly impressed by Piero and that he used Piero's same rising composition of geometric solids in some of his best work, which later became the bridge to the Cubist landscapes; open daily. Directions: Follow signposting for the train station and car park at the south end of town. Pick up a free city map at the tourist office in front of the train station. Walk northeast up Via Monaco to Via Cavor. Turn east and walk one block.

Once one of the richest Etruscan cities, today Arrezzo is noted for jewelry and fine furniture making. On the first weekend of the month, when antique collectors gather to sell and buy, the Piazza Grande becomes a mind–boggling spectacle of goods. Everything from Renaissance ceramics to 50's junk is displayed. Sunday is the biggest day. Directions: From Chiesa San Francisco continue down Via Cavour to Corso Italia. Turn north and walk to Via Fioraia, then east one block to Piazza Grande. For a picnic and rest from the market, walk northwest up the narrow streets to Passeggio del Prato-an enormous English-style park.

▲**Camping**: • About 30km southwest of the city on the west side of A1. Go south of Montevarchi on S69, then farther south on the small road in the direction of Capannole.

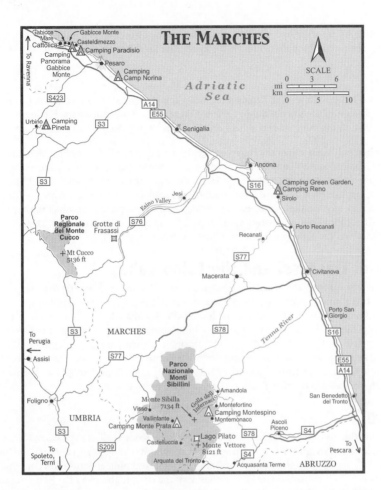

Camping la Chiocciola, in Capannole (055-995776); on the river; tennis; swimming pool; open May-Sept; $$.

THE MARCHES

Located between the Apennines and the Adriatic, this region is popular with sun-seeking locals and tourists boarding the ferries at Ancona. Well-versed travelers know there is more. The region boasts: Urbino–a classy university hill town with beautiful art and architecture, medieval Ascoli Piceno, and Monti Sibillin's Gorge of Hell.

Urbino

Urbino was a prestigious city during the 15th century. Montelfeltro, a ruler of outstanding intelligence, incorporated a fine fusion of aesthetics and practicality into the city. Today the Palazzo Ducale still sculpts the skyline. Fortress-like on the outside, it sparkles inside with the splendid architectural touches of Bramante and the elegant masterpieces of della Francesca. The Studiolo is a grand triumph in illusory perspective; open daily. Urbino is lively with summer events. Be sure to stop at the tourist office to find out what's happening.

▲Camping: • East of Urbino on S73b, drive 5km in the direction of St. Bernardino. Camping Pineta, San Donato (0722-4710); small, nice location; open May-Sept; $$.

Pesaro

Pesaro was famous during the Renaissance for its ceramics, and a good collection of these early works can be seen in the town's Museo Civico. Opera buffs enjoy visiting the home of Rossini at Via Rossini 34. A morning market is held off the main square, Piazza dei Popolo.

▲**Camping:** • 17km north of the Pesaro on the coast road. Exit S16 for Gabbice Mare, and drive south to Gabbice Monte. Camping Panorama (0721-208145); beautiful views of the sea; steps down to a secluded beach; open May-Sept; $$. In the same area between Cattolica and Pesaro exit off S16 for Gabbice Mare and drive south on the coast road to Casteldimezzo. Camping Paradiso (0721-208579); nice location; terraced; some shade; open May-Sept; $$. • South of the city 5km. Exit off S16 for the village of Fossoseiore. Camping Camp Norina, Fossoseiore (0721-55792); on the beach; cabins; car parking separate from tent; open May-Sept; $$$.

Grotto di Frassassi and the Esino Valley

For a nice change from the beach, explore the Esino Valley and its dramatic narrow gorge, Gola di Rossa. Then continue on to Grotto di Frasassi-one of the largest caverns in Europe-for a very interesting hour-long tour of five caves including the Ancona Abyss. Cave enthusiasts should make arrangements ahead and take the three-hour tour into little seen-chasms. Participants don appropriate outfits and are led by guides through narrow passages sometimes even crawling through tunnels-into amazing chasms for a spectacular show of stalactites and stalagmites. Call ahead to Consorzio Grotto di Frasassi (0732-90080). Directions: Exit A14 at Ancona. Drive north, then west on S76 for about 50km. The caves are well signposted.

Recanti

Examining the costumes and memorabilia of the famous tenor Gigli, at the Palazzo Communale, makes a nice change from the beach. After you can walk over to Palazzo Leopardi, the home of one of the 19th-century's finest poets-Gianomo Leopardi, and ponder some of his original work; it's just down from the main square. Directions: Exit the coast highway A14 at Porto Recanti and drive west on S77 for 11km.

Ancona

This is the largest port for ferries, with routes to Greece, Turkey, and Croatia. Aong the waterfront the port is well signposted and tickets are sold here at Stazione Marittima. Follow signs for the mercato if you want to stock up on food. It's a short walk from the waterfront to Corso Mazzini 130, where outside tables at inexpensive cafes make nice places to rest and soak up the atmosphere.

▲**Camping:** • 18km south of the city on the beach road to Sirolo. Camping Green Garden (071-9331317); close to the beach; open May-Sept; $$. • Closeby, Camping Reno (071-7360315); close to the beach; quiet; open May-Sept; $s.

Monti Sibillini, Piano Grande, and Gola dell'Infernaccio

Located in the southwestern region of the Marches bordering Umbria, Mount Sibillini, is popular with outdoor enthusiasts. Walking trails, hang gliding, mountain biking, and horseback riding enhance a stay. Information on rentals is available in Castelluccia. Buttercups, poppies, and daisies fill this upland meadow of the Piano Grande in a passion of color that is best in June. Bring your wildflower book and search for narcissi, fritillaries, wild peonies, alpine stars, and greenish-yellow lentil flowers. Park in Castelluccia. The trail begins on a small road that is off the main road from Castelluccia heading north towards Valle Canatra. Pick up a map at the Sibilla Hotel. For a more strenuous hike, begin the trail from the Refugio degli Alpini. It climbs up the side of Mount Vettore before descending to the brilliant Lago di Pilato, known for its spiritual qualities. Rare marine life has been found in the lake, so swimming isn't permitted. Trails continue up around the Mount Sibillini area. Directions: To find Monte Sibillini on the map, look at the area east of Spoleto. From A14 exit onto S4 between Ancona and Pesaro and drive west in the direction of the medieval village of Ascoli Piceno. Pass the town and continue on S4 for 19km to the village of Acquasanta Terme. Continue west on S2 for another 10km. Exit onto the tiny road for Arquata del Tonto and follow the winding mountain road for 40km to Castelluccia. There are wonderful views of the Piano Grande the whole way up. The Gola dell'Infernaccio, or Gorge of Hell, on the northeastern side of the mountain is a popular and dramatic but also easy hike. Directions: Exit S2 8km west of Asoli Piceno onto S78 and drive 34km up the mountain to Amandola. Then turn onto the small road up to the mountain village of Monteforte. The trailhead begins on the way up the mountain to Montemonaco.

▲Camping: • 14km north of Castelluccia in the direction of Visso in Vallinfante. Camping Monte Prata (0737-98124); lovely location; basic; open June-Aug; $. • Just south of Montefortino. Camping Montespino (0736-859238); large; beautiful setting; all the amenities; $$.

Gran Sasso

This massif is the highest of the Apennines peaks. The cable car in Fonte Cerreto outside of L'Aquila ascends 2117 meters to Campo Imperatore, where there are panoramic views and trails down the mountainside. Directions: 10km northeast of L'Aquila on A24 in the village of Fonte Cerreto.

▲**Camping:** • In Fonte Cerreto. Camping Funivia del Gran Sasso (606-06163); scenic and tranquil; close to hiking trails; open June-Aug; $.

Abruzzo National Park

The mountain setting, old-fashioned villages, and walking/cycling trails make this park a popular family vacation spot. If you've brought children to visit Rome, this park makes a nice nature break in the trip. The visitor center in Pascasseroli has a museum, a small zoo, and trail maps. The village also has a grocery store and a bike rental outlet. Directions: Exit A1 67km south of Rome at Frosinone. Drive east on S156 through lots of tunnels for 37km to Sora. Continue up the winding mountain road S509 for 46km to Opi and the park entrance.

▲**Camping:** • In Pascasseroli, close to the main visitor center. Campeggi dell'Orso (41-919-55); large; nice location; open June-Aug; $$. Farther into the park in Civitella Alfedena. Camping Wolf (0864-890306); large; pretty location; open June-Aug; $$.

Emilia-Romagna

The rich farmland of Emilia-Romagna has fostered a cuisine that is one of the most delicious in Italy. Markets here bulge with mouth-watering foodstuffs. Great composers and operatic virtuosos also gave it a sophisticated musical palate, and racing cars-the toys of the rich-have a home here.

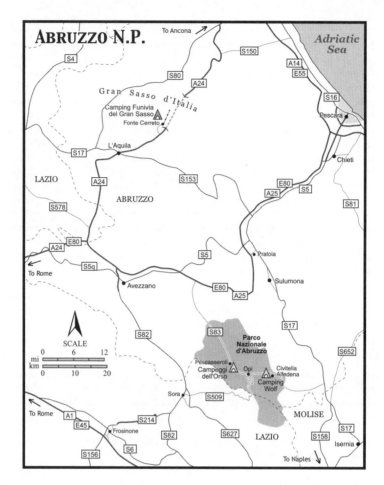

ABRUZZO N.P.

Adriatic Sea

To Ancona

S4
S150
S80
A24
A14
E55

Gran Sasso d'Italia

Camping Funivia del Gran Sasso
Fonte Cerreto

S16
Pescara

S17
L'Aquila
Chieti

LAZIO
A24
S153
E80
A25
S5

ABRUZZO
S81
S578

E80
A24
S5q
S5
Pratola

To Rome
Avezzano
E80
A25
Sulumona

SCALE
0   6   12
mi
km
0   10   20

S82
S83
Parco Nazionale d'Abruzzo
S17
S652

Pescasseroli
Campeggi dell'Orso
Opi
Civitella Alfedena
Camping Wolf

Sora
S509

To Rome
A1
S214
MOLISE
S17
E45
Frosinone
S82
S627
LAZIO
S158
Isernia
S156
S6
To Naples

Ravenna

After the Goths sacked Rome, Ravenna became the capitol of the Western Roman Empire. The Byzantine rulers, anxious to outdo their rival cities in magnificence, developed a crowning expertise in mosaic art. By placing glass at different angles, the artists achieved an unusual intensity. The Basilica di San Vitale holds the most breathtaking and oldest array of mosaics. Have euros ready so you can illuminate them, and bring binoculars to see the exquisite detail. Maxamillian's exquisitely carved ivory throne is on view at the Duomo. Dante wrote much of the *Divine Comedy* in Ravenna and his tomb is next to the Chiesa di Francesco. Musical events fill the city's calendar. You'll find a good morning market in the Piazza Andrea, north of the Piazza Popolo. A large car-park is near the Basilica.

▲**Camping:** • In a dune area just southeast of the city center, Lido de Dante. Exit S16 at km 157 onto Fiumi Uniti, and drive to the beach. Camping Ramazzotti, Lido di Dante (0544-772-768); olive trees; close to the beach and dunes; open May-Sept; $$. • Just north of the city center close to the ferry landing at Marina di Ravenna. On S16 south of the city stay right, exiting onto S67 for Porto Fuori, then follow signposting for Marina di Ravenna. International Camping Piomboni, Viale della Pace 42 (0544-530230); close to the beach;

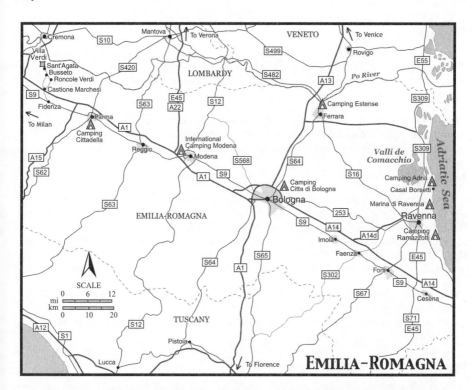

trees; disco; tennis; open May-Sept; $$. • 18km from Ravenna's ring road exit onto S309 for Casal Borsetti. Camping Adria (0544-445217); beautiful beach; large; all the amenities; disco; bus to the city; open May-Sept; $$. This is a popular beach camping area with more choices all the way up the coast.

Bologna

Bologna's famous university gives this city a dynamic atmosphere easily felt in the central squares of Piazza Maggiore and Piazza del Nettuno, where street theater and music are continuous. Large parking garages are located off the ring road at Piazza 10 Septtembre, near the bus station. Park and take a bus or ride your bicycle south down the Via dell'Indipendenza to the squares. The enormous Gothic Basilica di San Petronio has impressive door carvings by della Quercia. Across from the Basilica, ask about local events at the tourist office; many are free. To see the Leaning Towers, walk or bike east along Via Zamboni into the university area. The Pinacoteca Nazionale has a terrific collection of works by Giotto, Raphael, El Greco, and Titian; look for it beyond the Palzzo Poggi. Bologna is proud of its cuisine. Shopping is a mouth-watering experience both at the huge indoor Mercato Ugo Bassi at Via Ugo Bassi 27 and at the outdoor morning market close to Piazza Maggiore on Via Pescherie Vecchie.

▲**Camping:** • North of the city take exit 8/Fiera di Bologna off the ring road. Drive north following signposting to Via Romita. Camping Citta di Bologna, Via Romita 12/4a (05-132-5016); convenient location; close to the fairgrounds; cabins; open year-round; $$.

Ferrara

Castello Estense, this town's main monument, was once the glittering home of the eccentric Este dynasty. Now its fascination lies in knowing the family story so you can conjure up images of how it once was. Stock up on foodstuffs at Mercato Communale on Via Mercato, next to the Duomo on Via Garibaldi.

▲Camping: • On the northern edge of the city, exit A13 at Porotto-Cassana and drive south 3km. Take exit 4. Follow signposting to Via Gramicia, close to the ancient city walls. Camping Estense (0532-752396); convenient location; April-mid-Oct; $$.

Modena

Not only is Modena the hometown of the famous contemporary operatic tenor Pavarotti, it is also the birthplace of the exciting Ferrari and Maserati cars. Go to Galleria Ferrari to drool over a fascinating display of antique, modern, and Formula One Racing automobiles. Directions: Take S12 southwest of town for 23km. Exit for Maranello just south of the intersection of S12 and S467. Signposting leads to Via Dino Ferrari 43. The gallery is located in a flashy glass-and-steel building; open daily. While here, visit the Duomo one of Italy's best-preserved Romanesque cathedrals.

▲**Camping**: • Just west of the city in the suburb of Brucita. Exit A1 at Modena-Nord. Turn right at first traffic light and follow signposting to Via Cave Ramo. International Camping, Via Cave Ramo 111 (059-980-065); convenient to the autostrata; traffic noise; open May-Sept; $$.

Parma

Music is a passion in this charming city straddling the Po River. Here music flows constantly to packed, discriminating, and appreciative audiences. Giuseppe Verdi was born in the nearby country village of Roncole. His operas filled the handsome local opera house, Teatro Regio, as well as the opera houses of the world. Verdi loved his hometown, and his presence made Parma a center for music. Both tenor Luciano Pavarotti and conductor Arturo Toscanini were also born in the area. Today young musicians are trained at the prestigious Arrigo Boito Conservatory where concerts are frequent and often free. Opera buffs will be touched visiting Verdi's humble birthplace in Roncole Verdi; closed Monday. Directions: Drive west from Parma on S9 for 23km to Fidenza. Turn northwest onto the small road S588, crossing under A1. Continue for 6km. Exit at Castione Marchesi and drive 10km to Roncole Verdi. Rising from the plain, the land-locked island of Sant'Agata, north of Busseto, became Verdi's place of work and refuge. It was here, surrounded by dogs and horses, that he composed *La Traviata*. Part of the villa can be visited. Directions: Drive 5km from Roncole Verdi northwest to Busseto. Pass through town and continue north 4km on S588 to Sant'Agata and Villa Verdi.

Elaborate and grand frescoes from fine 17th-century fresco artists, including Parmigianino and Correggio, still sing with color in Parma's Duomo, the Baptistry, and the San Giovanni Evangelista; open daily. Bring euros to illuminate the frescoes, and binoculars to see the incredible detail. Directions: From Piazza Garibaldi, the center of the historic area, walk northeast on Strada Cavour to Piazza Duomo. The San Giovanni Evangelista is behind the Duomo on the eastern side.

Parma produces Italy's famous cured ham, or proscuitto and also its famous and widely-copied parmigiano and reggiano cheeses. Both are so skillfully tended here that they are now sought by gourmets throughout the world.

▲**Camping**: • Inside the old fortress, on the youth hostel grounds, in a recreational area. On the eastside of the Po River, south of the main historic area. On S9/Via Emilia East, drive west crossing under the railway bridge following signposting. Camping Cittadella, Parco Cittadella (0521-961434); good location for the Po River and historic area; good maintenance; open May-September; $$.

VENETO

Aristocratic, proud, and shamelessly self-satisfied, Veneto is brilliant in her dress of gilded treasures. The entire scene shimmers with dreams of moonlight ecstasies. But the city can also feel like a very large, crowded museum. Approach and discover it like a cat seeking prey. Museums are closed on Monday.

When you've caught your breath after arriving at Piazza San Marco, visit the tourist office to purchase a good detailed map of the historic area and to check the events happening while you're here. Don't depend on discovering Veneto's treasures with a free map; they won't have the detail you need. The public WC is through the passageway at the south end of the square. To get to the tourist office, walk from the Piazza to the waterfront–and then head west. It is by the vaporetti (boat-buses) boarding and ticketing area. Wander through Veneto's maze of waterways, over its ancient bridges, and into its tiny squares. Enjoy the labyrinth.

Take the vaporetti to the Accademia. Before entering this big museum wander over to Palazzo Venier and the Peggy Guggenheim Collection, which houses an eclectic display of excellent modern work plus a whimiscal garden. Reboard the vaporetti back at the Accademia, from the same side you disembarked, and ride up the Grand Canal to the Rialto Bridge. Cross over the bridge and, using your map, wander over to the Campo San Polo, where you can rest with the locals and watch children play. Then visit Frai, a massive Gothic cathedral holding masterpieces by Titian

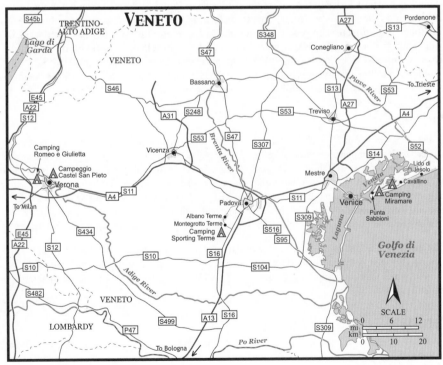

and Bellini. Behind the cathedral is the Scuola Grande di San Rocco with its unrivaled collection of Tintorettos. You'll find cafes and trattorias nearby at prices the locals can afford. Wait to visit Piazza San Marco in the evening, when the crowds have left. Then dance for free under the stars while orchestras play from the sidelines. Take the ferry back to your campground, enjoying warm breezes as you ponder the starlit sky and the fading silhouette of this most magical place.

On your second day, get an early start and take the ferry back to Veneto. Wander over to the open market at the Rialto, where you'll see gondolas unloading their fruits and vegetables. Joke with the fish merchants while you examine their vast selection, noting especially the cuttlefish–Veneto's specialty. Have a picnic lunch on the steps of the Accademia while watching the gondolas slide by. With guidebook in hand, you are ready to tackle the bigger stuff. The Accademia's fabulous collection documents the history of Venetian painting from the 14th to 18th-century. The treasures in the Palazzo Ducale vividly portray the self-aggrandizement of the founding statesmen, and Basilica di San Marco is a rich and exotic jewel case. Binoculars will enable you to see the intricate details in the brilliantly colored story-telling mosaics and the brush strokes on the dramatic, glowing paintings.

▲**Camping**: Camping is wonderful on the peninsula that reaches like an arm down to the Veneto Lagoon. You can take the ferry to Veneto from the campground, by far the most romantic and historic way to approach. All the camping places are close to the beach so early morning or sunset walks, bike riding, picnics, sunbathing and swimming can all be incorporated into a stay. A bus to the ferry landing goes up and down the peninsula but there is also a large car park at the ferry landing. Directions: Exit A4 north of the Veneto lagoon area onto P52 in the direction of Lido di Jesolo. Drive 20km. Turn south onto P42 and drive 5km to Jesolo, then another 11km to Cavallino and another 11km to Punta Sabbioni. There are plenty of campgrounds and markets. Many are full-scale resorts. These are less expensive than the resorts. • Drive to the end of the peninsula to Punta Sabbioni. Turn left at the ferry landing and follow the beach road. This is my favorite. Camping Miramare, Lungomare D. (041-966-150); private sand beach; within walking distance to the ferry but has shuttle; small store and café; popular; $$$. Almost to the end of the peninsula in Ca'Savio on the beach road. Camping Ca''Savio (041-966-017); large; all amenities; bike rental; popular; $$$. • South of Cavallino. Camping Guiliana (041-968039); small; close to the beach; $$. • Nearby. Camping Italy (041-968090); pool; close to the beach; $$. All are open May-Sept.

Padova

Giotto's masterpiece of 36 extremely well-preserved fresco panels illustrating the life of Jesus and Mary are cherished in this charming town. His skill with light and shadow, vivid coloration, and brilliant characterization made him an artist well ahead of his time. A beautiful park surrounds the Cappella degli Scovegni in which they are housed. Shopping at the bustling morning market at Piazza della Fruita amongst the coming and going of hand-held baskets and old-world commerce is a delight. Directions: Exit A4 north of town for Centrum/Train Station/Cappella. Park in the car park across from the train station, and cycle, bus, or walk south on Corso del Popolo. The grounds of the Cappella degli Scovegni are just south of the train tracks.

▲**Camping**: • South of the city, exit A4 at Padova Ouest and drive 21km south exiting for Abano Terme. Continue through town following signposting for Montegrotto Terme and sports center. Camping Sporting Terme (049-793400); tennis; swimming pool; thermal baths; open April-Oct; $$.

Verona

With rosy-hued historic buildings, lovely bridges across the Adige River, and world-famous opera and theater, this romantic, un-touristy walled town is beautifully restored and one of my favorites. It's easy to walk or cycle into the historic area, explore the side streets, and smile at the unexpected. You won't soon forget experiencing a famous opera performance at the historic Arena; book ahead with Ente Lirico Arena di Verona at Piazza Bra 28, 045-800-5151 or www.area.it. For theatre performances at the ancient Teatro Romano, inquire at the tourist office; 045-592-828, close to Arena and Piazza Bra at Via Leoncino 61 or use the same online address as for the Arena. Get calendar and ticketing information from the Italian tourist office before your trip or use the web.

▲**Camping:** • Exit A4 south of Verona onto S12 in the direction of Centrum. Staying just outside the ancient walls, drive east on Via Franco. Cross the Ponte Francesco, driving north on the east side of the Adige River on Via Lungadige. Just past the Ponte Peitra-the pedestrian bridge-take the main road Via Nievo east and wind your way up the hill. Campeggio Castel San Pieto, Via Castel San Pietro 2 (04-5592-037); tents or small caravans only; charming; fabulous location on a hillside within walking distance of the historic area; can be crowded, but it's a fun and easy place to meet fellow travelers; open May-Sept; $$. • West of town exit A22 at Verona-Nord, driving north on S12 then east on S11 towards Verona/Bresciana to km 295. Camping Romeo e Giulietta, via Bresciana 54, (04-5851-0243); good for caravans; large; bus to historic area; swimming pool; books tickets and provides shuttle bus to opera; open May-Sept; $$.

ALTO ADIGE/DOLOMITES

The relatively remote location of the Dolomites has protected them from vast numbers of visitors drawn to other parts of the Alps. Their sheer-sided pale-rock crags, sculpted in bizarre fantastic shapes, make for some of the most spectacular scenery in the Alps. The bright limestone reflects the changing skylight so at sunset the walls can change from yellow, to orange and then deepening red. If you are lucky the Dolomite peaks will shine with an Alpenglow after the sun has

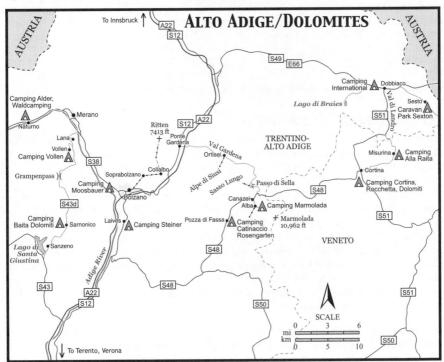

set. Exploring them will take you through undulating farmlands, deciduous forests, and rugged rockscapes. All grades of walking/hiking paths are mapped. Some stretches crossing scree strewn rock faces are aided with cable.

July is the best time for wild flowers. Throughout the grasslands, intensely blue gentians and orange lilies vie with each other in showy display. Alpenrose, similar to an azalea, masses along rocky ledges. Under the shade of beech and pine, lady's slipper orchids shyly peek through the grass. Farther up, bright clumps of yellow poppies are dazzling. The villages have a peaceful Tirolean charm that is relaxed and easy. Because of the area's Austrian heritage signage is in both Italian and German.

Lago de Braies, with its deep emerald-green water is like a picture postcard. An easy walking path around it begins at Hotel Lago di Braies where canoes can also be rented. Between Cortina and Dobbiaco is an area known as Valle di Landro. From here, trails lead up to dramatic summits. The trail to the summit, Mount Specie, is easier than most.

▲**Camping:** Around Dobbiaco: • Both of these are located in scenic locations with resort-like amenities including pool and disco; open May-Oct; $$$. 2km west of Dobbiaco on E66/S49. Camping International (0474-972-147). 11km southeast of Dobbiaco in Sesto/Sexton. Caravan Park Sexton (0474-710-444). • Around Cortina: All of these have scenic locations; popular with families; open June-Sept; $$$. 9km northeast of Cortina in the village of Misurina. Camping Alla Baita (0435-39039); close to a chair lift to mountain trails. Just south of Cortina on S51: Camping Cortina (0436-867-575) and Camping Rocchetta (0436-5063) and Camping Dolomiti (0436-2485).

Like Siamese twins joined together at the midriff, the Sassopiatto-Sassolungo peaks are the centerpiece for walks. The trailhead begins in the south from Canazei. A cable car from Passo Sella to Forcella Sassolungo operates from mid-June through August. The trail is brilliant with wild flowers, has several huts for snacks and light meals, and offers more difficult trails to higher elevations. A breathtaking ten-minute cable car to Ciampac from the village of Alba takes hikers up to the trailhead for Sella Brunec and Sass d'Adam where the panoramic views are extraordinary.

▲**Camping:** • 2km east of Canazei. Camping Marmolada (0462-601-660); scenic location close to the cable-car; open June-Sept; $$. • 9km southwest of Canazei in Pozza di Fassa. Camping Catinaccio Rosengarten (0462-763-305); scenic location; open June-Sept; $$.

Bolzano/Bozen and Around

Being on the southern side of the Dolomite Alps has blessed Bolzano with more sunshine than her northern neighbor, however afternoon showers are not uncommon. Walking paths web through pretty valleys splashed with a wide variety of wildflowers. Bringing a wildflower field guide adds to the pleasure of discovering them. High altitudes, accessed by chair lifts enable out of this world views of the rugged and austere beauty of the Dolomite peaks. The Oberbozen lift boards close to the railroad station taking passengers to the tiny picturesque village of Klobenstein/Collabo. From here, walking/hiking trails fan out; some lead to mountain huts and inns. Strong hikers might want to take another lift from here to reach the trailhead for a hike to Ritten Summit at 2260 meters. Directions: Bolzano is 140km north of Verona on A22.

The little town of Ortisi/St Ulrich in the pretty Val Gardena has an old-world charm and still produces handcrafted wooden toys and statues. From here, chair lifts take hikers to the Alpe di Siusi. Directions: Drive 25km northeast of Bozano on A22 to Ponte Gardena/Waibruck. Turn east onto S242 and drive 13km to Ortisei.

▲**Camping:** Closest to town. Exit A22 for Bolzano Sud and follow signposting 2km for Merano to km 224. Camping Moosbauer (0471-918492); pleasant location; pool; some traffic noise; open May-Sept; $$. • 6km south of Bolzano in the village of Laives/Leifers. Exit A22 at

Bolzano Sud and drive south on S12 for 6km following signposting for Laives/Leifers and camping. Camping Steiner (0471-950105); nice location; pool; some traffic noise; open April-Oct; $$. • More remote. 15km north of Trento exit A22 onto S43 and drive 36km. At the fork at the south end of the lake on S43d stay east and drive 13km to Sarnonico. Camping Baita Dolomiti (0463-830109); beautiful location close to hiking/walking trails; pool; open June-Sept; $$$.

Merano

Perhaps it's the massages, thermal baths, and saunas offered at Terme di Merano that give this town such an easy and relaxed air. Visit and indulge in some pampering. Directions: Merano is 28km north of Bolzano.

▲**Camping:** • 12km west of Merano exit S38 for Naturno/Naturns and follow signposting. Camping Alder (0473-667242) and Waldcamping (0473-667298). Both have lovely locations; pool; open April-October; $$. More remote. • Five kilometers south of Merano exit S38 for Lana. Follow signposting for Gampenpass driving up the steep mountain for 5km to Vollen. Camping Vollen (0473-568056); great scenic location; pool; open May-Sept; $$$.

LOMBARDY AND THE LAKES

Once ruled by both France and Austria this crossroads of Western Europe is the richest and most developed region of Italy. Lucky local workers take holiday breaks at nearby lakes.

Milan

Energized by work, money, and style, this city is the fashion and corporate capital of Italy. Shopping is a passion, and people show off their most recently purchased goods at the cinema, the theatre, and musical performances. The city tirelessly occupies itself with what communicates beauty in a subtle, understated, and discreet style. Hunting for bargains in second-hand shops and warehouses selling last year's fashions is reason enough for visiting Milan.

The heart of the city centers around the Duomo, which has been embellished for five centuries and is now the largest Gothic cathedral in the world. On the northern corner of the Piazza del Duomo is the almost as famous Galleria Vittorio Emanuele-with an opulent glass-dome, expensive shops, and trendy cafes. Pass through to reach Piazza della Scala. Il Teatro alla Scala is the world's most famous and perhaps most majestic opera house. Such legendary operas as Puccini's "Madame Butterfly" opened at this highest temple of the art. Don't miss its small but fascinating museum, where you can peek into the huge C-shaped auditorium from one of the red velvet-covered box seats; open daily; Metro 1 or 3: Duomo. The tourist office, at Via Marconi 1 on the southeast corner of Piazza Duomo, bulges with maps and brochures. It is an important stop. Their bilingual, yellow pages-like directory is very useful. A convenient tourist tram operates daily, taking visitors past all the main sights with off and on privileges that allow flexible sightseeing time. Most museums are closed on Monday.

Milan holds some of da Vinci's most famous works. His "The Last Supper", is housed in a former dining hall-the Cenacolo Vinciano-of the Chiesa di Santa Maria delle Grazie. Capturing the moment before the traitor is revealed, Leonardo portrays an extraordinary psychological depth unknown in previous paintings of the same drama. Freeing himself from the limitations of fresco painting, Leonardo freshly plastered the wall and painted at his own pace with the colors he chose. (In traditional fresco painting the paint is applied directly to wet plaster so that the color and plaster become one, requiring the artist to work quickly with a limited choice of color.) Leonardo's new technique failed. The plaster began to flake in his own lifetime. Restorers who added their own embellishments, darkened

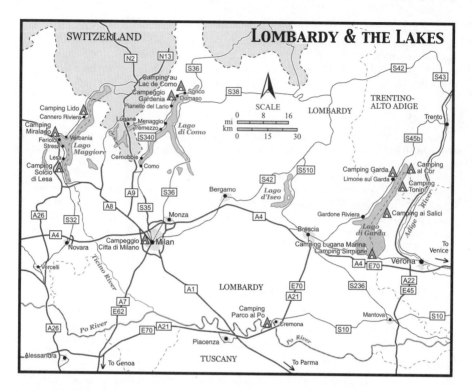

the bold and brilliant colors, changed the lines of the Apostles' features, and obliterated much detail further damaging the mural. Over 20 years of painstaking work has restored the mural to what is left of the original painted surface. Seeing it is a thrill. Only small groups are allowed into the carefully controlled atmosphere. Bring your binoculars. Ticketing must be done by phone at least 3-4 days before arrival; call: 02 894 21 146. Have your credit card and pencil and paper ready to write down your reservation time and confirmation number. Arrive at least 30 minutes before your reservation time to confirm your presence or your reservation will be sold to someone else. Audioguides are available at the Cenacolo Vinciano; closed Monday. Directions: Metro 1 or 2: Cadorna. Wooden models and drawings of Da Vinci's scientific work are cleverly displayed in one of the world's largest technology museums, Museo Nazionale della Scienza e della Tecnica; Metro 2: Sant' Ambrogio.

An extravagant collection of masterpieces from the 14th through 19th-centuries can be seen at the Pinacotecca di Brera; closed Monday. Directions: Metro 1 or 3 Duomo, Metro 2 Lanza. Just restored, the Museo d'Arte Contemporanea (CIMAC) in the Palazzo Reale houses an exciting collection of work from the 20th-century; open daily. Directions: Metro 1 or 3 Duomo.

Avoid Milan in August, when it is hot and many businesses close for vacation. During the first 10 days of June, you can enjoy the lively parades, street food, music, and theatre of Festa del Naviglio. Use the metro into and around the city; get directions from the campgrounds.

▲Camping: • West of the city, exit the ring road west at San Siro-Via Novara. Follow sign-posting for San Siro and then Via Novara and Parco Aquatico. Campeggio Citta di Milano Via G. Airaghi 61 (024-820-0134); close to the sports center; near the autostrata and metro to the city; traffic noise; cabins; open year round; $$.

Cremona

The delicate Stradivarius violin was created in Cremona. Fascinating musical displays are seen in the tiny Museo Stadivatiano at Via Palestro 17. Around the corner, in the Museo Civico, an entire room is dedicated to violins; closed Mondays. Parking is easy close to the train station on Via Mantova. From here it is an easy walk or bike ride into the historic area and the museums.

▲**Camping**: • Southwest of the city cross the river on Via del Sale then drive south in the direction of Piacenza following signposting for camping and sports center. Camping Parco al Po (0372-21268); shady location; bike rental; open May-Sept; $$.

The Lake Area

Stretching towards the Veneto like loosely beaded lapis lazuli, Italy's Lake District is lovely. Popular and tourist-oriented, it is a good place both to rest and watch the world go by and to take part in an active sport. Excursion boats ply the lakes, cable cars climb up to the Alps, and wind surfing, paddling, and cycling are all popular pursuits. Rentals are available. A well-marked network of hiking trails link lakeside and mountain villages; some are leisurely strolls and others are strenuous mountain climbs. The local tourist offices burst with glossy brochures. Many of the camping places are full service resorts. I've listed some smaller ones.

Lago di Garda

Sirmione, on the southern end, is a popular tourist stop. Walk across the surrounding moat and up through the almost Disneyland-like village to the northern end of town for a tranquil view of the lake. Working every shape of stone and wood into his bizarre garden, the poet-nationalist d'Annunzio il Vittoriale converted his house and garden into a monument to himself and the Italian people. Called the Gardone Riviera, it's on the west side of the lake and is worth a stop; closed Monday. Riva del Garda, an elegant area on the north edge of the lake is fun to wander through. Wind surfing, rock climbing, and mountain biking are all popular activities, and you'll find stores where friendly staff rent equipment, provide advice, and can arrange lessons. Limone sul Garda, on the west side of the lake, is a particularly good base for hikes and mountain-bike rides into the mountains. The network of trails is well marked throughout and leads into picturesque valleys and up to limestone crags. Trail maps are at the tourist office.

▲**Camping**: • At the south end of the lake in Sirmione. 2km east of the intersection to the castle-village. Camping Lugana Marina (030 919173); small; pleasant location; $$. • In the same area. Camping Sirmione (030-9904665); large; pool; $$. • In Torbole, at the northeast tip of the lake. Camping al Cor (04-6450-5222); cabins; $$. • In Limone, on the northwest end of the lake. Camping Garda, off S45 at km 101.5 (03-6595-4550); close to a boat launch; $$. • On the east side of the lake in Malcesine, halfway up the lake. Camping Tonini, on S249 at km 72 (04-5740-1341); close to boat launch and cable car; $$. • At southeast end of the lake in Pai and north of Torri del Benaco close to a ferry launch. Camping ai Salici, off S249 at km 55.5 (04-5726-0196); nice location; $$. At the southeast end of the lake in Bardolino are several more. They are all large and popular with families; $$. All the campgrounds listed are open May-Sept.

Lago Como

It's fun to relax on a ferry while enjoying the beauty of the lake and a view of the famous palatial gardens of Villa d'Este, Cernobbio and Villa Carlotta near Termezzo. Or get an eagle's view of the lake on the 750-meter cable car ride to Brunate and then take a gentle walk back down the mountainside. Directions: Both are boarded at the waterfront in Como.

▲**Camping:** • At the north end of the lake in Sorico, at the mouth of the River Mera off S340 at km 25. Camping au Lac de Como (0344-84035); pretty location; open all year; $$. • Ten kilometers south in Domaso. Camping Gardenia, off S340 at km 20 (03-4496-262); cabins; good location; open May-Sept; $$. • 10km north of Menaggio, midway on the west side of the lake in Pianello del Lario, Camping Laguna Beach (03-4486-315); small; popular; naturist bathing allowed on beach; May-Sep; $$.

Lago Maggiore

Located at the base of the Swiss Alps, Lago Maggiore has a well established place in the heart of vacationing Italians. The garden and zoo at Villa Pallavicino are restful picnic spots, and taking a ferry out to one of the islands is a popular outing. A particularly nice walking path runs between the two lakeside towns of Cannobina and Cannero, with bus transportation providing a shuttle back to your car. From Stresa, you can drive or take the cable car up to Monte Mottarone for views, hikes, and bike rides. A twenty-five kilometer mountain bike descent route is particularly popular. Shops rent bikes and helmets and sell maps. Halfway up, stop at Giardino Alpinia to examine close-up the interesting plant species found on the mountain. The tourist office in Cannero has good walking and road maps, plus plenty of glossy brochures on things to do.

▲**Camping:** • On the northwest end of the lake in the town of Cannero. Camping Lido (0323-788-176); on the lake; $$. • On the southwest end of the lake in the town of Solcio di Lesa, south of Lesa. Camping Solcio di Lesa (0323-27497); lovely location in a pretty village; close to the railway tracks; cabins; $$. • Halfway up the lake on the west side 20km west of Verbania in the village of Feriolo. Camping Miralago (0323-28-226); scenic location; bike rental; popular; close to railway tracks; sandy beach; $$. All listed are open May-Sept.

VALLE D'AOSTA

Dramatically beautiful and crisscrossed with hiking trails, this area has been carefully protected by locals. Tourism is well organized and low key. Val di Cogne, a narrow gorge sculpted by the wildly beautiful Eyvia River, is one of the highlights. The lush green meadowlands in Cogne are wonderfulwith colorful wildflowers, and there are magnificent views of the mountains. In Valnontey, a breathtakingly beautiful trail follows the rushing river. Locals offer guided walks, and walking maps are readily available at the tourist office in each town. Directions: Val d'Aosta is in the northwest corner of Italy, close to the French and Swiss borders. Drive 6km west of Aosta on in the direction of Sarre, exit south for Aymavilles onto S507. Then drive south on S507 for 21km to Cogne. Follow signposting for 3km on a narrow mountain road southwest of Cogne to Valnontey. One tunnel follows another so pay close attention to the exit signs. Large car parks are provided outside both of the charming villages.

▲**Camping:** • In Sarre, 6km west of Aosta. Camping Monte Bianco (0165-257523); small; lovely setting in an orchard; convenient to Aosta; $$. In the same area. Camping International Touring (0165-257061); large; pool; June-August; $$. • 6km west of Aosta, take S26 in the direction of Sarre. Exit onto S507 and drive south 21km to Cogne. Follow signposting south up the narrow mountain road to Valnontey. Camping Lo Stambecco, in Valnontey (0165-74152); gorgeous views; close to an Alpine botanical garden; open June-Sept; $$. • In the same area but better for caravans. Continue west past Cogne for 4km on a narrow road to the village of Lillaz Camping Les Salasses (0165-74252); beautiful location;

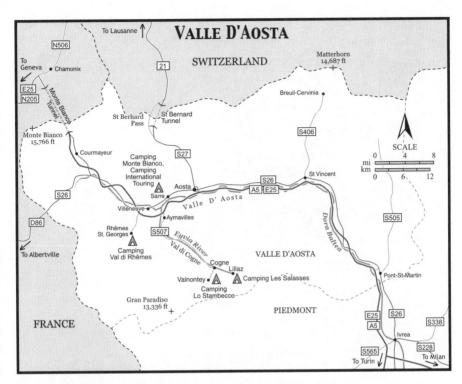

close to a chairlift for hiking; open June-Aug; $$. • Drive west of Aosta following signpost-ing for Villeneuve. Continue through town following signposting south along the river to Rhemes St George. The road to the camping place is steep and winding. Camping Val di Rhemes (0165-907648); beautiful location; open June through Aug; $$.

NAPLES AREA
Herculaneum and Pompeii

On a summer afternoon in 79AD, Mount Vesuvius suddenly erupted and literally buried the cities of Pompeii and Herculaneum under a layer of lapilli (small pieces of pumice) to a depth of 20 feet. Few escaped. People died of suffocation in the streets, in houses, and underground-where they thought they might escape the poisonous fumes. Victims are preserved almost intact, providing a silent, eloquent testimony to their way of life. In the late 1800s archeologists began the dig and gradually revealed a city that had been settled as early as the 5th and 6th centuries BC. They poured liquid plaster in spaces left by bodies and furniture to obtain the plaster ghosts we see today. At the tourist office at the entrance, the Porta Marina, buy a guidebook and map. The archeological site is huge and can be confusing. Don't succumb to touts who want to be your guide. Use a guidebook. Throughout the archeological site there are beautiful and imposing columns, exquisite doorways, colorful frescoes, spacious courtyards, niche-adorned baths, and grandiose atriums with graceful fountains and mosaics. It is not hard to imagine life as it was because the rooms are still alive with frescoes depicting their lives and loves. Pretend to jump back away from a clattering chariot, to smell the fresh baked bread from an open oven, and to look on enviously as men and women luxuriate at the baths. Casa dei Vettii, with its fabulous frescoes, has

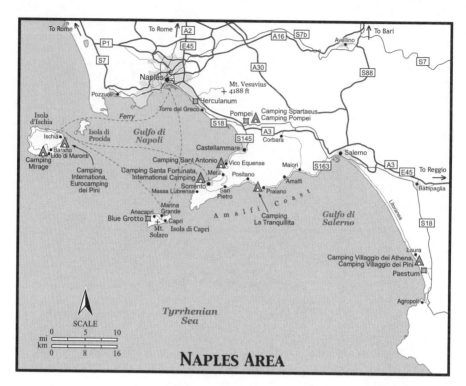

NAPLES AREA

been impressively reconstructed so allow extra time for it. Don't leave the site without visiting the Villa dei Misteri and its Dionysiac Freize, one of the greatest masterpieces from the ancient world. It's an evocative scene depicting brides being initiated into the cult of Dionysius, a forbidden Bacchic rite. The villa is outside the walls on the northwest edge of the ancient town; open daily. Directions: Drive 25km south of Naples on A3 exiting for Pompeii. Follow signposting for Scavi and parking.

Herculaneum, smaller and more intimate than Pompeii, was once a residential enclave for wealthy Romans. The mosaics alone are worth a visit. Don't miss it; open daily. Directions: Exit A3 at Ercolano Portico and follow signs for parking and Piazza Scavi.

The best artifacts from Pompeii and Herculaneum are in the Museo Archeologico in Naples, one of the most important collections of archeological artifacts in the world; closed Tuesday. To visit the Museo Archeologico, it is easiest to leave your car at the campground and take the Circumvesuviana train to Naples. Directions: The train station is within walking distance of the campground. After arriving at Stazione Centrale in Naples, follow signs downstairs for Metropolitano. When you buy your round-trip ticket to Piazza Cavour, ask the agent which track or *binario* it leaves from. Go through the solo metropolitano turnstile. Piazza Cavour is the first stop. Walk out of the metro through the exit on your right. Walk through the park to its west edge where the museum is located. Petty crime is clever and professional in Naples. Don't start out for a trip to Naples without rereading the tips in "Smart and Safe" in this book.

Mount Vesuvius looms over the entire area. You can drive or hike up to the summit and walk around the edge of the crater. It's fun to peer into the enormous cauldron and get a good whiff of the sulphurous aroma. Directions: Exit A3 at Ercolano Portico and follow signposting for Parco Nazionale Vesuvio. Stop at the Museo dell'Osservatorio on the way up if you have time. From the car park at the top, it is one and a half kilometer walk up to the summit area. Wear good walking shoes, bring a sweater or jacket even in the summer, and have euros for parking and admission for the summit walk. The six kilometer hike's trailhead begins at Quota 1000 car park. With only a 310 meter ascent it's not a difficult climb. The visas and solitude are restoring.

▲**Camping:** • Exit A3 for Pompeii. Follow signposting just after the toll area off A3. They are both close to the entrance of the archeological site. They are a bit scruffy but okay for a short stay. There is some noise from traffic; railway; and partying school kids; fair maintenance; $$. Avoid arriving at night. • Camping Spartacus (081-536-9519); Camping Pompeii (081-862-2882); Camping Zeus (081-861-5320).

Sorrento and the Amalfi Coast

Picturesque villages and towns spill down the cliff-sides here to the water's edge. There are no great monuments to see, but the fun is two-fold. First are the breathtakingly beautiful walks up alleyways and stairways decorated with brilliant yellow mimosa, where you can peek into open archways and gardens of oleander, palms, and citrus trees. On these grand flights of stairs, stone benches invite resting to view terraces clinging to precipitous cliffs above a brilliant sea. Second is simply relaxing in such a beautiful, admittedly touristy, place. Some beaches are covered with chairs and umbrellas that must be rented, but a few beaches are free. Pick up a map of suggested walks at a tourist office (the one in Positano is best). Then choose a route that suits your interests. The Sentiero degli Dei is particularly spectacular, though precipitous route along a nearly vertical mountainside. Walking sticks are essential. Adventurous hikers love it, however those with vertigo should not attempt it. For lengthy walks, use the bus to return to your start. Bus tickets must be purchased ahead. Buy them at the camping place or at sidewalk kiosk. There is good bus service between Sorrento and Amalfi, with stops at local villages that include beautiful Positano. Leave your car at the campsite and take the bus.

Driving on the narrow roads that twist and turn along this breathtaking coastline takes courage. Buses coming from the opposite direction can cause your knuckles to whiten and your heart to pound along narrow stretches. Get an early start, watch the sun rise, and enjoy the view. Don't try to drive in on a summer weekend when it becomes an enormous traffic jam. Directions: Drive south of Pompeii on A3 for about one kilometer where the road forks. Follow signposting for Castellammare for 6km. Then take the coast road S145 signposted for Sorrento for 22km. The road is narrow and winding after Castellammare.

To shorten the drive to Amalfi, follow signposting on A3 at the fork south of Pompeii for Salerno. Continue on A3 for 10km exiting south at Cobara stay east at the fork following signposting for Maiori and the coast road. For Amalfi, turn west and drive 5km. To shorten the drive to Positano, drive south of Castellammare 8km. Exit the coast road for Meta and follow signposting over the beautiful hills on S163 for 10km to San Pietro. Turn east on the coast road towards Positano, and continue 8km farther.

▲**Camping:** • On the Capo di Sorrento: 2km southwest of Sorrento in the direction of Massa Lubrense. Camping Santa Fortunata at Villaggio Turistico (081-807-3579); fabulous views; car park separate from tent; steep descent to the beach; disco; cabins; open May-Sept; $$$. • Off the same road but entrance is a little better for caravans. International Camping, Nube d'Argento, Via Capo 21 (081-8781344); steep descent to beach; pool; cabins; nice location; open all year; $$$. • Closer to Castellamare, near the village of Vico Equense. Follow signposting for Seiano-Spaggia, staying left at the fork in the tunnel. Then drive down a narrow and winding road for one kilometer. Camping Sant Antonio (081-8028570); spectacular views; difficult for large caravans; open Apr-Oct; $$. On the Amalfi coast 5km east of Positano, at the east end of the village of Praiano. Camping La Tranquillita (089-87-4084); small; lovely location; close to hiking trails; open May-Sept; $$$.

Capri

When you are this close to the famous island of the Blue Grotto it is hard to resist taking a day (camping is not allowed) to visit this very touristy spot. The cobalt-blue water created by the refracted light onto the sandy sea bottom is breathtakingly beautiful. Avoid: weekends when tourists are even more plentiful; foggy days, when the light in the grotto is poor; and windy days, when the grotto is closed because the sea is too rough. Boats leave for the Blue Grotto from Marina Grande in Capri; open daily. After seeing the grotto, take the bus or funicular to Capri Town, and walk out Via Tiberio to the ruins of Emperor Tiberius's villa, Villa Jovis. Then climb down the cliff-sided stairway, Salto di Tiberio, from which Tiberius supposedly had dissidents thrown out to sea. Anacapri, on the west side of the island, might be less crowded for café sitting, and if it's a clear day you might want to take the funicular from here to the top of Monte Solaro for an excellent view. Buses leave for Anacapri from Marina Grande and Capri Town. Directions to Capri: 15-minute ferries depart from Sorrento. In Sorrento follow signage for Marina Piccola. A large parking garage is close to the train station, or take the bus from your campground.

Ischia

If you yearn for an island camping experience, or perhaps want to do some snorkeling or scuba diving in beautiful waters, Ischia is a good destination. The island's outstanding garden, La Mortella, was carefully planted by British composer Walton and his wife, who together collected over 300 hundred species of flora from around the world. Thermal and mud baths are popular. Ferries leave from Sorrento and Naples. Directions: From Naples: Follow signposting for Statzione Marittima, then turn south following signposting for Parco Castello. Car-ferries leave several times daily from Naples and Sorrento. Buy tickets at the ferry. From Sorrento: Follow signposting to Marina Piccola.

▲Camping: From the ferry landing follow signposting south 4km in the direction of Barano. Continue farther south, following signposting off the main road to Lido dei Maronti. All of the following are large; popular with families; close to the beach; $$.
• Camping Mirage (99-051); open all year. South of the ferry landing drive south, following signposting for Ischia Ponte. • Camping International (99-1449); open May-Sept. In the same area • Eurocamping dei Pini (98-2069); open all year.

Paestum

Three well-preserved temples still stand silent and eloquent in grassy fields here, where long ago a great city founded in the 6th-century BC was chaotic with the bustle of markets. The temples lay hidden for centuries in a marshy sub-tropical forest. An adjoining museum holds original bas-relief friezes and a nice collection of still-colorful tomb paintings and urns; open daily. Directions: Exit A3 at Battipaglia for S18 and drive 23km in the direction of Paestum and Agropoli. The coast road, Litoranea, is much more scenic and can be accessed off S18.

▲Camping: 5km north of Paestum in the direction of Laura. Both of these are large; nice locations on the beach; pools; $$. Camping Villaggio dei Athena (0828-85-1105); open Apr-Oct; and Camping Villaggio dei Pini (0828-81-1030); open all year.

THE BOOT OF ITALY

In the mid-1900s, over half of the adult male population left southern Italy to find work in other places. Their families here farmed foreign-owned local estates at a subsistence level and so encouraged the emigration. Children necessarily assisted in farm work in order for the family to survive, so low literacy and education persisted for generations. Education was an unaffordable luxury. Families sent off their young men in hopes that they would find work that would bring a positive change to their lives so they could help those left behind.

Within one generation these Italian immigrants produced famous movie directors, film stars, musicians, politicians, and athletes–an amazing feat. Although educationally impoverished they were rich in stunning insight and instinct. When they saw an opportunity, they were not reluctant to jump at it. Now, later generations of these Italians return to the south in hopes of maintaining their Italian identity and finding their roots. You'll meet them in the tourist areas. If you spend some time chatting, they might share memories of grandmother's cooking and tell you that they are relieved to find that the same dishes she made are still being painstakingly prepared. The traditional dishes they remember were created ingeniously from the necessity of using what could be produced in the hot, dry region.

Stopping at the markets and roadside stands will give you an insider's view of the culture and daily life of the locals. Buy some fruits and vegetables-all picked when they are ripe and succulent. Take a break and watch the sometimes amusing interaction between merchant and customer. In the countryside, you'll see lots of prickly pear growing wild. At the market, you can buy it preserved as jam-a wonderful treat spread over warm, freshly-baked bread. Orecchiette-little ear pasta-is also a specialty. Purchase some for an easy-to-make delicious dinner: prepare it like any other pasta and top it with some flavor-filled sauteed vegetables and grated local cheese.

Shop, visit tourist offices and museums, and check into campgrounds either in the morning or after 4:30 PM because closing for a long lunch and rest is a beloved Italian custom that is still observed here. Towns and roads are deserted then so it's good time to take a drive. Stop to enjoy the tiny, picturesque villages clinging to hillsides. As you approach the coast, the views of the sea are painted blue, turquoise, and green all at the same time. Once fishing villages, many of the towns are now inexpensive travel destinations. Streets are lined with refreshment stands, souvenir shops, apartments, and pizza cafes-all hoping to profit from the summer business. In season, you'll be amazed to watch so many people passionately exchanging ideas at the same time. Cell-phones begin to look like a part of the human anatomy, and cars, motorcycles, and mopeds are everywhere. In early summer and fall, things are quieter.

Along the coast, vacationing southern Italians settle into a camping place-often with friends and family–and staying for several weeks. Campgrounds often have a bar where music plays late. Bicycles, surfboards, and paddleboats are rentable. Many beaches are privately owned and carefully maintained with colorful umbrellas, and lounge chairs for rent. It's easy to have fun in such a convivial atmosphere.

Apulia

Twisted and torn by time, ancient olive trees flicker their tiny gray-green leaves-sometimes exposing the undersides like twinkling sequins on the dry, grassy slopes overlooking a lapis lazuli sea in Apulia. Sparkling white in the sun, tiny white-washed square cottages are topped by conical domed roofs and decorated with slender round finials. Called *truilli* they are built with layers and layers of thin gray stone and in villages seem to merge one into another.

Villages are placid and peaceful. Along the coast, you can sit at a café table and watch fishermen push out in boats piled high with hand-mended nets, and wander aimlessly through narrow, twisting, serpent-like alleyways that open into shadowy piazzas. Loving an opportunity for a festival, towns and villages celebrate a saint's day with enthusiasm. Portable arches are installed over main passageways and thousands of small colored lights are strung to illuminate the way from the church to the main piazza. A small brass band provides music, and vendors set up food stalls where tasty snacks are sold. The whole town turns out to greet their neighbors and pay homage to the saint who's effigy is carried along the parade route. The atmosphere is friendly and inviting.

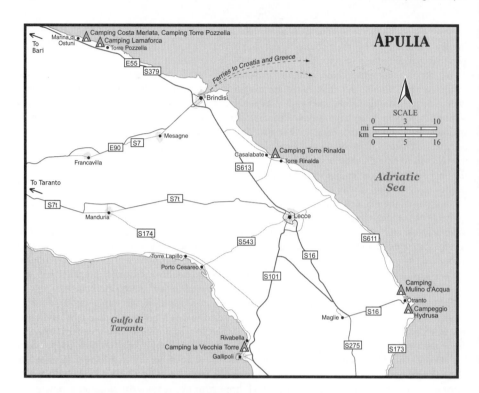

PROMONTORIO DEL GARGANO

Ancient forests of beech and oak cover the limestone mountains in Parco Nazionale del Gargano. Tranquil, well-marked walking and cycling trails lead through the shady groves. Directions: 13km west of Vieste at Villaggio Umbra. "The Route of the Angels", a pilgrimage route in the Middle Ages which began in Normandy, passed through Rome and culminated at Promontori de Gargano. Visiting the Santuario di San Michel here, makes an interesting day away from the beach. Directions: Drive 13km north of Manfredonia, then exit onto S98B in the direction of Monte Sant' Angelo. The Gargano is a popular area for vacationing Italians. Resort-like camping places are beautifully located on the beach, rent wind-surfing and cycling equipment, and have lively bars/discos that are good places to have fun with fellow campers. You won't be able to keep your car next to your tent. Although this policy is inconvenient for car-campers, it keeps the camping surroundings more scenic and quiet. Time is allowed for short trips with your car to your site to set up and break down.

▲**Camping**: These are a little smaller and less expensive. • On the coast road between Peschici and Vieste at Baia di Sfinale. Villaggio Turistico Grotta dell' Acqua (0884-91-1136); open May-Sept; $$. • In the same area at Santa Maria di Merino (088470-6174); $$.

Brindisi and Ferry Crossings

Ferries have cross the Adriatic from this natural harbor here to ports in Greece and Croatia since Roman times. Traffic jams and petty theft are rampant in the summer. Deal directly with the ferry company, rather than with a local travel agent, to confirm your reservation (two hours ahead of departure) or to purchase tickets. Hellenic Mediterranean is the largest and most reliable company 0831 52 8531 or www.hml.it/. Be cautious with your car and the things in it, and bring a good book to read while waiting. Arrange ahead everything you are taking up on deck so it is easy to grab once you are parked on the ferry. The cars are parked tightly and quickly and cannot be accessed during the crossing. Bring food, beverages, books, games, and collapsible ground chairs to make the trip more comfortable and fun. Directions: Follow signposting from main roadways for Costa Morena, the new port, from which most ferries depart.

PROMONTORIO DEL GARGANO

▲Camping: • 25km north of Brindisi, off the coast road S279/E55 at Torre Pozzella. Camping Lamaforca (0831-96-8496); nice location on the beach; popular with families; open June-Sept; $$. • Just north at Marina di Ostuni. Camping Costa Merlata (0831-30-4064) and Camping Torre Pozzelle (0831-30-8505); both are large; nice locations on the beach; open May-October; $$. • On the coast 25km south of Brindisi. Drive south on S613 for 25km. Exit east in the direction of Casalabate and drive 9km to the coast road. Turn south and drive 2km to Torre Rinalda. Camping Torre Rinalda (0832-38-2161); large; resort-like; open June-August; $$.

Castel del Monte

Castel del Monte, an eccentric octagonal 13th-century fortress often appears bright white against a perfect blue sky–rising triumphantly like a crown. It is UNESCO listed and completely restored; open daily. Directions: From Barletta drive 9km south on S170 in the direction of Andria. Pass through Andria and continue south on S170 for 18km to the Castel.

Itria Valley

Emerging from olive groves like sprouting mushrooms or nomadic tents, the dome-shaped tiny homes called *trulli* were built stone by stone without mortar when farmers cleared their tiny plots of land for planting. In the town of Alberobello a tight cluster of a thousand or more trulli rise up a steep hillside. Visitors hike up stepped streets and are invited into some of the tiny, cool, white-washed living rooms with stone-slab floors. Directions: From Bari drive south on S100 for 33km to Gioia. Turn east on S604 and drive 29km to Alberobello.

▲Camping: • In Alberobello. Follow signposting off S172 on the east side of town. Camping Bosco Selva (0804-32-3462); small; convenient; open April-Sept; $$.

Lecce

The cream-colored exterior of Lecce stone is soft and mallable when it is first cut. In the 17th century, imaginative and good-humored local artisans carved it with Baroque extravagance. When the stone was exposed to the elements, it hardened and maintained its richness then slowly faded to a delicate shade of honey-gold shade. Today the city glows with Baroque architecture. The façade of Santa Croce is particular magnificent and shouldn't be missed. It literally blazes with Baroque detail that finally explodes in a rose window. Directions: Santa Croce is northwest of the castle off the west side of the large public park. Binoculars will help you enjoy the skill, imagination, and good humor of Lecce's 17th-century craftsmen. Directions: Lecce is 38km south of Brindisi.

▲**Camping:** • On the beach 20km north of Lecce. Drive north of Lecce 20km on S613. Turn east for the coast in the direction of Casalabate and drive 9km to the coast road. Turn south and drive 2km to Torre Rinalda. Camping Torre Rinalda (0832-38-2165); large; resort-like; nice location in a dune area; open Apr-Sept; $$.

Otranto

Two great elephants support the roots and trunk of a tree depicted in the enormous 12th-century mosaic floors in Otranto's cathedral. Off-shooting branches enclose an array of monsters, mythical creatures, prophets, conqueror Alexander the Great, biblical character Jonah (whose leg is protruding from the whale's mouth), and even King Arthur on his horse. Called *The Tree of Life*, it is wild with enthusiasm and vitality. Behind the cathedral, a tiny 8th-century Byzantine church is filled with the remnants of frescoes that once covered every inch of paintable surface. Directions: Drive 29km south of Lecce on S16 to Maglie. Turn west and continue on S16 for 16km to Otranto.

▲**Camping:** • South of town by the port. Campeggio Hydrusa (0836-80-2389); small; basic; open June-mid Sept; $$. • On the coast road S611 north of Otranto. Camping Mulino d'Acqua (0836-80-2191); nice location on the beach; resort-like; open June-August; $$$.

Gallipoli

Enormous mounds of sea urchins-a specialty at Gallipoli's colorful fish market-beg to be sampled. Locals lustily gouge out the succulent morsels, munching on them raw, and might call out for you to join in. Bring your camera. Directions: On the east coast of the Gulf of Taranto. Drive southwest of Lecce on S101 for 39km.

▲**Camping:** On the coast road 3km north of Gallipoli in the village of Rivabella. Camping la Vecchia Torre (0833-20-9083); on the beach in a dune area; large; resort-like; car parking separate from camping; shade trees; open June-Sept; $$$.

BASILICATA

Mile after mile of almost-deserted beaches edge the Caribbean–blue water of the Gulf of Taranto on the Ionian Sea. Inland, golden hills of wheat stretch to the horizon while golden eagles soar overhead with long, broad wings. Vegetable stands, shaded with violet blooms of the morning glory vines, are piled high with sun-dried tomatoes, shiny red peppers, and braided plump garlic. Cut off from the rest of Italy, the poor lived in the cool and protective caves that honeycombed the hillsides well into the 20th-century. Today the troglodyte area in Matera is UNESCO listed. The cave-homes, built of tufa stone, are called *sassi* and reach part way out from the canyon walls. Some of these grottos have been refurbished, and colorful Byzantine frescoes still decorate the walls of several churches. A musical cacophony, echoing off the narrow corridors and uneven walls in the evening when dinners are being prepared and children are playing, adds to the uniqueness of the place. Directions: 40km southwest of Taranto, exit the coast road at Metaponto onto S407, then drive northeast on S7. Following signposting for Matera continue east for 64km. Park at the train station in Matera. The tourist office is one block north of the train station and sells good informational maps of the *sassi*. From here, walk east to Piazza Vittorio Veneto and the entrances to the two *sassi* ravines, Barisano and Caveoso; open daily.

Once Hannibal's headquarters and later Pythagoras's home and school, Metaponto was founded in the 7th-century by the Greeks-who introduced wheat, olives, and grapes to the coastal land. Stop at the Museo Archeologico in the park close to the train station; open daily. 18km farther south in Porticoro, take a break in the journey to examine the fascinating funerary artifacts found in the area's excavations; closed Tuesday. Directions: Metaponto is on the coast road 40km southwest of Taranto.

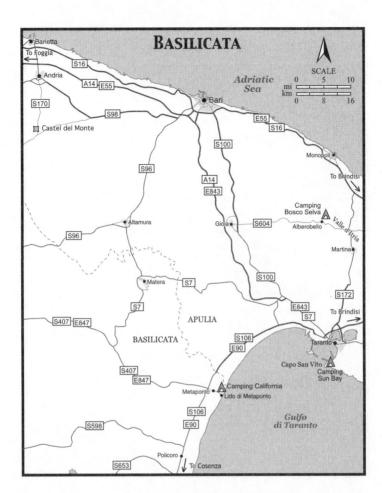

The weather along the Gulf of Taranto is reliably sunny and cloudless. Coastal pines provide shade, the beaches stretch out with miles of white sand, people are relaxed and unpretentious, and everything costs less than in the north. It can seem like a little paradise of languid days of sea and sand, particularly in early summer and fall.

▲**Camping:** • At Lido di Metaponto. Camping California (0835-74-1842); large; disco; bike rental; shuttle to the beach; open June-Sept; $$. • Just south of Taranto, beyond the break-water of the harbor. Follow signposting south of Taranto for Capo San Vito. Camping Sun Bay (0997-33-5133); small; lovely views of the sea; shaded with pines; open all year; $$.

CALABRIA

Two shining seas, the Ionian and the Tyrrhenian, splash on the cliffs and beaches of the toe of Italy's "boot". The water looks like liquid turquoise. Massive rocky cliffs plunging dramatically to the sea break stretches of sandy beaches. The coastline, named hopefully the Calabrian Riviera, is strung with inexpensive tourist resorts and campgrounds. Instead of fishing boats, suntanned

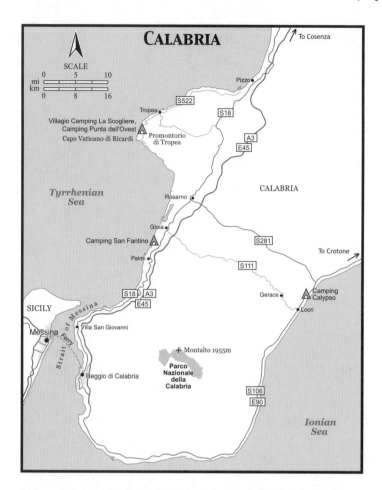

vacationers bob up and down in the gentle surf. In late spring and early fall the air is crisp and the sea shimmers brightly on a brilliant gold beach. Inland, on high rolling hills of relative desolation, tiny cobblestone villages remain locked in time past. Relics of the Moorish and Norman fortresses, now mostly piles of ancient stone, can be seen on hillsides.

La Sila Highlands

Remote and relatively untouched by tourism villages and towns here cascade down hillsides. As you explore the warren of old passageways that are hardly more than slots, you'll see whitewashed buildings with outside staircases and hear an ancient dialect of Albanian. In the Parco Nazionale Calabria, ancient beech and chestnut trees shade the walking paths that climb up craggy peaks to excellent views of the wild landscape. Directions: From the east coast drive west of Crotone on S107 for 49km to San Giovanni in Flore. Pass through town and drive 6km more to S108b-a narrow, winding mountain road signposted for Lago Arvo. Continue 12km farther.

▲Camping: • On Lago Arvo in Lorica. Camping Lorica (0984-53-7018); remote lovely spot on the lake; shady with pines; small; basic; open mid May-mid-Sept; $.

Gerace

The lovely 10th-century village of Gerace sits high on an impregnatable crag. Founded by refugees from coastal Locri, who fled to escape the attacking Saraceans, it is full of little medieval churches and houses. Wild flowers poke up between the cobblestones, and goats wander about. Take off your shoes and rest at a café in front of the cathedral. Afterwards enter the coolness of the sanctuary, paying particular attention to the columns that are believed to be from an ancient temple in Locri. Ceramic vases spilling out from the shops bear the designs of Magna Graecia, which the region was called when it was one of the Greek colonies. Directions: Drive 8km south of Sidermo, where the east coast road S106 and the inland road S281 linking both seas intersect. Turn northwest onto the narrow mountain road S111 and drive 9km.

▲**Camping**: 8km north of Locri. Camping Calypso (096-48-2028); smaller; nice location on a beautiful sandy beach; open May-Sept; $$.

Reggio di Calabria

Standing proud and defiant, the rare bronze Riace statues are perfect in the physique of the Classical period. They were only recently found buried in the seafloor off the Calabrian shore and just to see them is worth the drive to Reggio. Carefully displayed in Il Museo Nazionale, which was designed to protect them against earthquakes, they are breathtaking. *Il Vecchio* or "The Old One" scans the horizon for possible attack through glass eyes, while *Il Giovane*, "The Young One" stands ready to face imminent danger. The museum is at the end of Reggio's lovely mile-long seafront promenade lined with gracious statues, fountains, and palm trees. Directions: From A3/S106 follow signposting for the ferries and port. Drive south along the seafront following signposting for Stazione Lido and the museum. Ferries leave from here for Sicily and the Aeolian islands. In Reggio following signposting off A3/S106 at the north end of town.

▲**Camping**: • 50km north of Reggio on Lido di Palmi. Off A3 exit for Palmi on the north side of the tunnel. Off S18 exit for Gioia and drive south 6km. Camping San Fantino (0966-47-9430); nice location on a cliff with a path to the beach; convenient to the autostrata to Reggio; open March-Oct; $$.

Promontorio di Tropea and the Tyrrhenian Coast

Stretches of long, sandy beaches make the Promontorio di Tropea Calabria's prettiest Tyrrhenian coastal area. Clamped to a cliff above the sea is the very pretty town of Tropea, where startling views of the sea meet your eyes at every turn. Directions: Exit A3 18km south of the intersection of A3 and S280, and drive towards the beach on the narrow but scenic S522 for 31km in the direction of Tropea. Farther down the coast on scenic S18 from Rosarno to Scilla, the views out to sea and over to Sicily are exceptionally beautiful, particularly at sunset.

▲**Camping:** • South of Tropea on the undeveloped beach road in Capo Vaticano di Ricadi. Both of these are beautifully situated; large; resort-like; open all year. Villaggio Camping La Scogliere (0963-66-3020); $$ and Camping Costa Verde (0963-66-3090); $$$. In same area. Camping Punta dell'Ovest (0963-66-3489); small; on an unshaded sandy beach; basic; open July-Sept; $.

Sicily

There is something hauntingly alluring about Sicily. Perhaps it's the gnarled olive trees and warning agave spears, or maybe its the gray mountain villages carved from rock. Maybe it's the historic players, mythical and real: Aeschylus and his heart-rending tragedies; Dionysius prophesizing from his cave; Aeneas stopping on his way to Rome; Ulysses lured by the sirens. The whole of Sicily is like an island museum–Europe's most important one. Almost every conquering nation has left its mark here. Visitors are treated to engaging mountain towns with exceptional Roman mosaics, a Greek theatre still presenting the ancient tragedies, dramatically rugged coastlines (some boasting Greek temples), long stretches of sandy beaches, and more sunny, warm days than the rest of Europe.

With such fabulous scenery and good weather in early fall and late spring (summer can be overly hot) camping in Sicily has been popular with Europeans for years. Many campgrounds are resort-like. A long lunchtime is *derigueur*, so arrive to check-in before noon or after 4 PM. Ask about showers when you do, and get appropriate change or tokens.

There is good bus transportation from the campgrounds close to Palermo and other large towns, so it is best to leave your vehicle at the campground and take the bus. Invest in a good map that has an expansion for the larger towns. Don't rely on free maps or maps from guide books

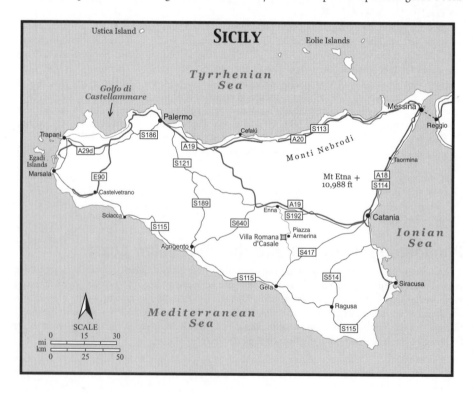

for driving. Both driver and navigator need to study the map and make notes about mileage and signage before driving into or leaving a larger town or city in Sicily. You won't have time to look at a map in the midst of traffic. The driver needs to be alert to the traffic and drive with assertion. Both the driver and the navigator need to stay calm. Don't let angry drivers or honking bother you; it is part of everyday life in Sicily.

The Mafia exerts its power here and theft is a problem. Reread and then follow carefully the suggestions in" Traveling Smart and Safe" in this book. The advice might make you think that it is dangerous to drive in Sicily. It's not. These are good safety precautions for any big city. Heed them and then don't worry.

Water sandals and a beach air mattress or collapsible ground chairs make the rocky beaches and coastal waters easier to enjoy. I take my snorkel and mask so I can snorkel in the beautiful coves, but rentals are available.

At Sicily's colorful markets, mounds of glistening tomatoes, freshly made linguine, sweet strawberries, spicy salami, and tasty cheeses all beg to be bought and enjoyed under colorful tarps. Take extra precautions, particularly in Palermo and other touristy towns where pickpockets and bag snatchers operate. When I go to the market, I leave my daypack in the car trunk and carry my purchases in a shopping bag I buy locally for this purpose. I loop the straps over my head and shoulders and hold the bag in front of my body and fill it with purchases. I keep my shopping money in the bottom of this bag under my beautiful bounty of groceries.

Palermo

Glowing Byzantine mosaics in Palermo's Capella Palantina testify to the golden age of Arab and Norman domination in Palermo, when the city rivaled Cordoba and Cairo in beauty. Although the city was badly damaged by the Allied Forces' massive bombings in 1943, you can still see the influence, however decaying, in the architecture of the churches, alleyways, and markets. Piazza Marina, once part of the harbor, is now shaded by immense ficus trees and makes a good place to start an exploration. Puppet theatres provided entertainment for thousands of Sicilians in the 1880s. Elaborately dressed puppets and marionettes acted out stories of good guys fighting bad guys and of heroes romancing beautiful women in front of intricately decorated stages. One of the world's most important international collections of marionettes and puppets is housed in the Museo Internazionale delle Marionette, just east of the northeast corner of the Piazza; closed Sunday. Walk through the elegant doorway of the Palazzo Abetellis and up the stairs to Galleris Regionale, where Sicily's most important collection of art-including Messina's best-known work, the exquisite

The Annunciation, is housed; closed Sunday. Directions: Walk south from the southeast corner of the Piazza Marina to Via Alloro. West of Marina Piazza on Via Emanuele, you'll come to Palermo's most intriguing square, Piazza Pretoria. Here you can rest among statues of mythological creatures and sirens that surround the beautiful Fontana Pretoria. Spend some time in the tourist office across the street from the fountain gathering maps and information for the rest of your trip. Before you leave the city and venture out to the archeological sites, examine the mosaics, frescoes, metopes (stone-carved frescoes), and other highlights from Selinunte now preserved in the Museo Archeological Regionale; open daily. Directions: Walk north on Via Roma

from Via Emanuele, passing Piazza Domenico. The museum is just south of Via Cavour on Via Roma. Across from the lush palms and manicured gardens of Piazza Vittoria is the Palazzo dei Normanni and the extraordinary Capella Palantina. The intricately-carved wooden ceiling, brilliant mosaics, and exquisite marble candelabrum and pulpit are a masterful harmony of Arabic-Norman artistry; open daily; free. Directions: Entrance to the Capella is on the south end of the Palazzo, across the courtyard and up a large stairway. Reasonably-priced concerts and exhibitions are held throughout summer. Spasimo, once a church now a cultural center, has information and sells tickets. Directions: Walk south from the southwest corner of Piazza Marina along Via Vetreria to Via Spasimo. Leave your car at the campground, and take the bus to Palermo. Buses to Palermo pass by both campgrounds. Bus tickets must be purchased ahead. Buy them at the camp office.

▲Camping: • 11km northwest of Palermo in Sferracavallo on the southwest side of Cape Gallo. Follow signposting off A29. Camping Degli Ulivi (091-533021); nice location close to a rocky beach; smaller; separate car parking from tent area; quiet; open April-Oct; $S. • In the same area but farther west in Isola delle Femmine. Follow signposting off A29. Camping La Playa (091-8677001); large; popular; close to a sandy beach; open April-Oct; $$.

Montreale Cathedral

Ablaze with glittering golden Byzantine mosaics, columns and arches intricately-carved with Arabic geometric motifs, and carved marble Biblical scenes, Montreale Cathedral is a masterpiece of Arab-Norman artistic achievement. Don't leave Sicily without seeing it. Bring your binoculars and have euros to illuminate the mosaics; open daily. Directions: 8km west of the city in the hilltop town of Montreale, signposted off S186.

WESTERN SICILY
Segesta and Erice

Thought to be originally founded by the exiles of Troy called Elymians, Segesta's 5th-century BC Greek temple stands solemn and majestic on a hill above the ancient town. The temple is barely scathed by the ravages of time and war. Walk up the hill or take the shuttle bus to the theatre, carved into the hillside for dreamy views of the sea and countryside; open daily. Directions: 32km east of Trapani. Exit for Segesta off A29 on the west side of the tunnel and follow signposting. The Elymians built Erice on top of what seems to be an inaccessible mountain. Virgil wrote the *Aneid* here. Climb the street beside the cliff edge to reach the Norman castle and the Temple of Venus. As you walk up the narrow medieval walkways, note the varying Baroque detail over portals and the square paving stones with smaller stones laid carefully in one direction. Directions: 8km northeast of Trapani.

▲Camping: • On the coast north of Erice in the village of Tonnara Bonagia. Camping Lido Valderice (0923-573086); popular; close to the beach; open June-Sept; $$.

Reserva dello Zingaro

Completely free of motorized traffic and webbed with trails to mysterious grottos and pristine beaches, Zingaro is a perfect place to spend a couple of days hiking and swimming. Birders should add binoculars to their daypack, because a wide variety of raptors make their home here. Horseback riding and diving excursions are also available. The delightful, ridge-perched, miniscule village of Scopello has a commanding view. Directions: Exit S187 or A29 for Castellammare

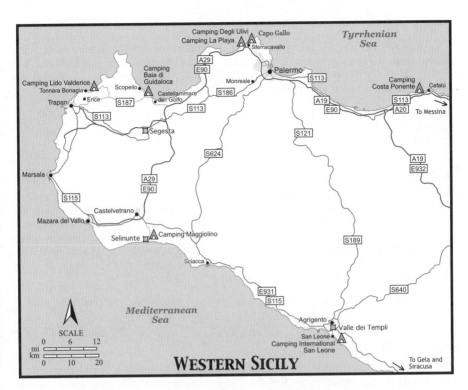

del Golfo and drive up the coast road for 10km to Scopello. Pass through the village and drive 2km to the park entrance and car park.

▲**Camping:** • 2km north of Castellammare in Calabianca. Camping Baia di Guidaloca (0924-541265); attractive location; open June-Sept; $$.

Villa del Casale

Many experts consider the mosaic floorings in the Valla del Casale, to be some of the most exceptional in the world. Protected for centuries by a covering of mud, They are now UNESCO-listed and protected by a roof and raised walkways. Imaginative and gay, they make you smile as you imagine the playful goings-on in such a grand palace during the 3rd and 4th centuries. The palace had elaborate baths, a gymnasium, an immense courtyard garden, latrines and aqua ducts, and a dining hall–all once elaborately decorated with mosaics. Two floorings are extraordinary. One tells of exciting, lively hunting scenes with ferocious lions. Another depicts beautiful maidens in bikinis that would be in fashion today; open daily. Directions: Villa del Casale is in the middle of Sicily, 31km south of Enna, just west of Piazza Armerina. Exit S192 or A19 for Enna. Drive south on S117b, passing through the village of Pergusa and by-passing Piazza Armerina. South of Piazza Armerina turn west on S191, following signposting to Villa del Casale.

▲**Camping:** • Drive south to the coast on S117b. Turn west at Gela and continue 19km on SS115 to the village of Falconara. Eurocamping Due Rocche (0934-349006); popular with families; close to the beach; open May-Sept; $$.

Cefalu

Travelers enjoy the sun and the vaguely Arabic atmosphere of this little seaside town, where cafes and shops line the waterfront. For some exercise, hike up to the rocky crag La Rocca. The trail begins alongside the Banco di Sicilia at Piazza Garibaldi. The ramparts on Capo Marchiafava, close to the cathedral makes a scenic picnic spot. Parking can be a problem in high season.

▲Camping: • 3km west of town. Camping Costa Ponente (0921-420085); very popular with families; call ahead; sandy beach; separate parking from tent area; bus to Cefalu; open May-Sept; $$$.

Selinunte

Dramatically set at the edge of the sea, Selinunte was a powerful market city in 580 BC and successfully blended the Phoenician and Greek cultures. Eight temples with colossal Doric columns have emerged from excavations. For the most dramatic effect time your visit so that your last sight is the setting sun silhouetting the graceful columns. The reds and golds that tinge the clouds over the deep-blue sea is unforgettable. Allow several hours to view this huge area; open daily. Directions: 35km east of Marsala, exit A29/E90 east of Castelvetrano onto S115 in the direction of Sciacca. Continue for 11km, following signposting for Selinunte on S115d.

▲Camping: • On S115d, 3km from Selinunte. Camping Maggiolino (0924-46044); wonderful location for seeing Selinunte; small; bike rental; open April-Oct; $$.

Valle de Templi

This UNESCO-listed ancient Greek city is one of Sicily's most important historical sites. It sits amid cypress trees and meadow grass that stretch over an escarpment of volcanic rock. The temples here are most magnificent when they are painted with the gold of the setting sun, so time your visit accordingly. Starting at the archeological museum, makes an exploration more meaningful, but it has limited hours. The archeological complex is divided into two sections. Start at the east end, where the Temple of Concord–considered to be one of the best preserved Doric temples in the world-and the Temple of Heracles are located; open daily. Directions: On the southwest coast, east of Agrigento. Follow signposting off S115/E931.

▲Camping: • Close to the beach just south of Valle dei Templi and east of the village of San Leone. Follow signposting, which leads away from the beach. Camping International San Leone (0922-416121); large; popular; open June-Sept; $$.

SOUTHEAST SICILY
Siracusa

Sitting on the enduring stone of Siracusa's Greek theatre, it's easy to let thoughts drift to Greece's golden-century tragedians–Aeschylus, Sophocles, and Euripides-whose plays premiered here in the 3rd-century. Their messages remain apt. They were echoed by Shakespeare, Goethe, and Schiller; closed Monday. The plays are staged again on even numbered years. For tickets, call 0931-67415 or use www.apt-siracusa.it. Still eerie are the once-subterranean stone quarries, the Latomies, where prisoners carved out slabs of limestone used for building the monuments. Some quarries are being restored. Cross over from the Latomies and climb up into the Roman amphitheatre. Imagine the sounds of the lusty and raucous crowd that once reveled in the violent gladiator spectacles; closed Sunday and Monday. Directions: Follow S115 east along the

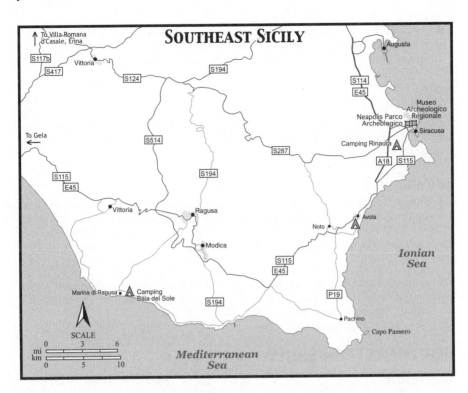

coast, passing the harbor. Turn inland, following signposting for Gelone then *Parco* and car park. Excavations throughout the island have yielded many important discoveries, and the rich material is now beautifully curated in the airy Museo Archeologico Regionale Paolo Orsi; closed Monday. Directions: Within walking distance of the Parco Archeologico.

Ortygia

Traveling from the mainland over the bridge to Ortygia, you pass the 6th-century Temple of Apollo-giving notice that Ortygia was once the heart of Siracusa. The tiny island's exciting history weaves in Roman, Greek, Norman, and European cultures. You'll see evidence in courtyards, wrought-iron gates, and intricately-carved columns. Around the Piazza del Duomo are some particularly impressive Baroque facades. In the evening, join the locals as they pause in their stroll at Fontana Aretusa. Directions: Follow S115 east along the coast. After passing the harbor, turn east onto via Bengasi, following it as it winds its way over the bridge. There is a large car park on the northwest end of the island.

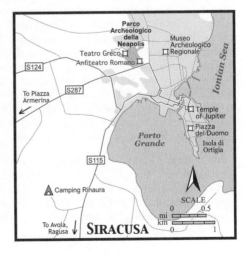

▲**Camping:** • 4km southwest of Siracusa, in the orchard of a large farm. Drive south of the city on S115 in the direction of Avola. Follow signposting, crossing the railroad tracks. Camping Rinaura (0931-721224); large; quiet; popular; bike rental; open May-Sept; $$.

Noto

Flower petals are used as paint by the artists who decorate Via Corrada Nicolaci for the flower festival *Infioraci*, held on the third Sunday of each May. But everyday visitors can always see the extravagant flourishes of the newly-restored Baroque buildings. Directions: 32km south of Siracusa on S115.

Ragusa

Exuberant façades give Ragusa and its old town, Ibla, a delightful ambiance. Park in the lower town by Piazza Liberta. Walk north along the Via Roma to Corso Italia, following it up to the stairs that lead to Ilba and the ornate Duomo and piazza. Meander eastward through the narrow streets to a very pleasant park for a rest or snooze. Directions: 87km southwest of Siracusa on S115.

▲**Camping:** • 24km south of town, on the coast. Follow signposting for Marina di Ragusa. Camping Baia del Sole (0932-239844); nice location; swimming pool; bike rental; separate car parking from tent; quiet; open May-Sept; $$.

NORTHEASTERN SICILY
Taormina

Squeezed into terraces above the Ionian Sea and Mount Tauro, Taormina drips with lush bougainvillea in lavender shades. It has been a favorite holiday spot for the rich and famous since the 5th-century. Well loved and cared for, it retains much of its medieval character even though inundated with visitors from Easter through October. Standing at it's Greek theatre, which has stunning view of the sea and Mount Etna, allows viewing the colossal work of both man and nature. Ancient dramas are performed during an international arts festival in July and August; open daily; Ticket ahead www.taromina-arte.com. After visiting the theatre, stop at Trevelyan Garden. A unique bee-shaped aviary is set amid its flowering subtropical plants and shade trees. The garden is a great place for a rest and picnic. In town, visitors wander up and down stepped alleyways and narrow streets, enjoying stylish displays in elegant shops, mouth-watering arrays in the pastry shops, and enticing menus of fine restaurants with terrace dining. For an adventurous five kilometers drive and incredible view of the sea and surrounding countryside, head up the twisting, sometimes precipitous, mountain road, to Castelmola. Cars are not allowed in the center of the tiny town, so use the car park by the bus station. Directions: 50km south of Messina on the coast. Follow signposting for the large Lumbi Car Park 500 meters north of town off any highway. A shuttle bus runs from the car park to the center of town.

▲**Camping:** • 10km north of Taormina, in the village of Alessio Siculo on the north side of the A18 tunnel. Camping La Focetta Sicula (0942-751657); nice location close to the beach; quiet; popular; bike rental; car parking separate from tent; open May-Sept; $$. • 4km north of Taormina, on the coast in the village of Letojanni. Camping Paradise (0942-36306); large; popular with families; bike rental; open May-Sept; $$. Buses run between the coastal towns with stops in Taormina.

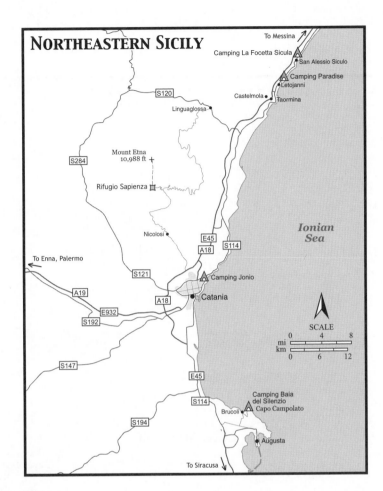

NORTHEASTERN SICILY

To Messina
Camping La Focetta Sicula
San Alessio Siculo
Camping Paradise
Letojanni
Castelmola
Taormina
Linguaglossa
S120
Mount Etna
10,988 ft
S284
Rifugio Sapienza
Nicolosi
E45
S114
A18
Ionian Sea
To Enna, Palermo
S121
Camping Jonio
A19
A18
Catania
E932
S192
SCALE
0   4   8
mi
km
0   6   12
S147
E45
Camping Baia
del Silenzio
S114
Capo Campolato
Brucoli
S194
Augusta
To Siracusa

Mount Etna

Eruptions and lava flows keep islanders wary of their beloved landmark. Getting a close-up view of the hot lava is a little scary, but fascinating. On the north side of the volcano, guided trips leave for the crater in four-wheel-drive vehicles from the tourist office in Linguaglossa–where there is also an exhibit of the flora, fauna, and geology of Mount Etna. On the south side, the guided trips leave in jeeps from Nicholosi. Strong hikers start from Rifugio Sapienza north of Nicolosi, following the trail on the west side of the volcano. Directions: On the south side, exit A18 north of Catania and drive north 20km in the direction of Nicolosi. From the north, exit A18 12km south of Taormina onto S120 and drive 9km to Linguaglossa.

▲**Camping**: • At the north end of Catania, close to the railway and rocky beach. Camping Jonio (095-491139); convenient for visiting Mt Etna; separate car parking from tent; open May-Sept; $$. • 44km south of Catania, exit S114 for the coast and Augusta. After 8km instead of turning south for Augusta follow signposting north 8km to Bucoli. Camping Baia del Silenzio (0931-981881); close to a small somewhat sandy beach; popular with families; open May-September; $$.

LUXEMBOURG

www.etat.lu/tourusm

Like a delicious tidbit left over from a grand feast, Luxembourg is often overlooked by tourists, making it even more delectable. Charming, isolated villages are set picturesquely here along swift-moving rivers, and tiny lakes nestle into valleys held by forested hills. Summer festivals add an enjoyable laid-back ambiance. Luxembourg celebrates its national day on June 23rd with fireworks and parades, and citizens enjoy a day off from work.

Vacationers from the Lowland countries come to Luxembourg to enjoy the peaceful atmosphere of the surrounding mountains and rivers. The tradition of camping is well established. Well-cared-for campgrounds, lovely settings, and amenities that appeal to adults and children alike make it a popular family vacation destination. Camping for two persons, a car, and a tent will cost about 20 euros and is noted as $$.

The country is a cyclist's paradise. Cycling is easy along its river valleys and challenging over inclines in the mountains of the north. To encourage cyclists, the country created over 600 kilometers of dedicated cycle paths, a goodly portion of it over old railway lines. They lead through forests, along bubbling rivers and creeks, and into idyllic villages. Luxembourg's population is concentrated in the capital, leaving the countryside basically rural and the backroads and even the highways relatively quiet. It is a perfect country to enjoy cycling with the family. One of the most popular routes is along the River Sure. This almost level route twists with the river between Vianden, Reisdorf, Echternach, and Moerdorf, passing through woodlands and by ancient bridges and monuments. It's easy to park in one of the little villages and pedal to the river and cycle path. The tourist office has a colorful brochure describing the cycling paths for the country.

Vianden and Environs

The tiny medieval village of Vianden is the quintessential fairy-tale village. Cobblestone streets wind alongside the river, leading to an elegant castle that was once home to wealthy counts who ruled the region. Take the cable car up 450 meters for a panoramic view of the strikingly beautiful countryside, then walk down the path to the castle. The chapel, with its colorful frescoes, and the Count's Hall tapestries are highlights; open daily. Victor Hugo sought refuge here in 1870. At the house where he lived in exile, you can examine drawings he made of the village and pore over copies of his original writings. It serves also as the tourist office. If you're with children, be sure to visit the Folklore Museum, where dolls and toys are part of the collection; open daily. Directions: Drive 30km north of Luxembourg City on N7, then 3km east to Diekirch, passing through the town. Exit north on N17 and drive 15km farther to the village of Vianden.

Located due west of Vianden, Bourscheid's castle has a spectacular view. During July's medieval days or Schlassfest you can join the locals at barbeques, music events, and jousting contests. The

203

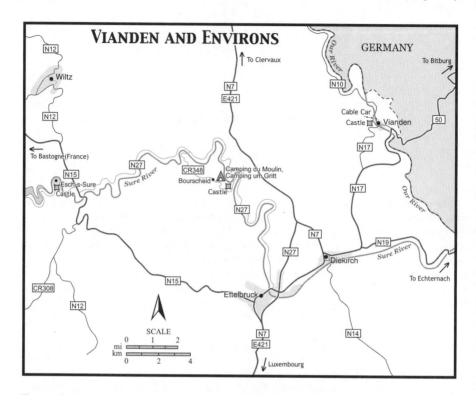

village and castle of Esch-Sur-Sure are tucked into the elbow of the river which makes a stunning almost-full circle. The little road between Bourscheid and Esch-Sur-Sure, follows the river and is particularly scenic for picnics and cycling. Directions: To reach Esch-Sur-Sure drive 30km north of Luxembourg City on N7 to Ettelbruck. Then drive northwest on N15 for 15km. Bourscheid is 10km east, on the Sure River.

The Battle of the Bulge, one of World War II's most bitter confrontations, took place in Diekirch. In its Museum of Military History life-size dioramas, painstakingly created from photographs, make a vivid impression of the hardships the soldiers on both sides endured during the freezing cold winter of 1944. Exhibitions on the resistance movement and internment camps pay tribute to local heroes. Directions: Drive 30km north of Luxembourg City on N7 to Ettelbruck then continue 5km farther to Diekirch. The Museum of Military History is just off the main square, on Place Guillaume; open daily.

▲Camping: • On the Sure River in Bourscheid. Camping du Moulin (99 0331) or Camping um Gritt (99 0449); both have nice river side settings; popular with families; open May-Oct; $$.

Moselle Wine Region

To see how sparkling wine is in produced the old-fashioned manner, take the tour at Caves St. Martin in Remich. Then drive to the adjoining village of Bech-Kleinmacher and wander through a tiny vintner's home, now the Musee A Possen. To expand your knowledge of wine making, take the Promenade Viticole. On it you'll walk through real grapevines peeking up through the leaves to catch a whiff of the heady perfume from the luscious fruit. Directions: Drive 22 km north of Remich along the Moselle River to the village of Wormeldange. Pass through the village to the Caves Cooperative, where the self-guided tour through the vines begins. Starting in late August, festivals celebrating the grape harvest are a happy mingling of the farmer-vintner, the hobbyist-vintner, and the enthusiastic tasters. Directions: Off ring road A-1 in Luxembourg City, exit east on N2 and drive 18km to Remich.

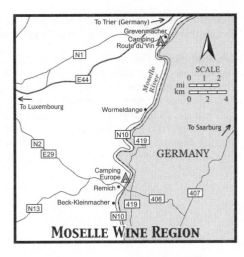

▲**Camping:** • At the north end of the wine route in Grevenmacher. 20km east of Luxembourg City on E44, take exit 13 and drive 2km more to Grevenmacher. Follow signposting to the Moselle River and camping. Camping Route du Vin (75 0234); lovely setting on the river; swimming pool; tennis; popular with families; open April-September; $$$. • At the southern end of the route in Remich. 20km southeast of Luxembourg City on E29, exit for Remich and follow signposting for the Moselle River and camping. Camping Europe (69 8018); nice setting on the river; popular with families; swimming pool; mini-golf; tennis; open April-mid Sept; $$.

Luxembourg City

The most stunning feature of Luxembourg City is it's setting. To enjoy its full impact, start your tour by gazing over its ancient ramparts, towers, and royal palace from the Kirchberg Plateau. The historic area is now UNESCO listed. Directions: Exit the ring road A1 on the east side of the city at exit 7. Before crossing over the Alzette River on the Charlotte Bridge, exit Avenue Kennedy and wind your way up the hill to the Kirchberg Plateau. On the way, you'll pass modern European Union buildings.

To get a sense of the defensive position the city historically held, wander through the musky tunnels that were carved out of the hill to form the Bock casemates, or artillery enclosures; open daily. Directions: On the east side of the river, just off the Monte de Clausen bridge. As you walk or cycle along the Alzette River notice the slit-windowed towers of the ramparts and the Renaissance façade of the Grand Duke's Palace. Then rest in the main square, Place Guillaume. Directions: Walk west of the Palace 100 meters. The Palace is open for tours on weekday afternoons and Saturday morning. Tickets are sold at the tourist office on the square. On Wednesday and Saturday the square is a lively market place. The interesting high-tech City Museum keeps you abreast of the newest inventions; closed Monday. Directions: Walk east of the Palace on Rue Marche aux Herbes. A particularly jolly time to visit the city is during its Schoeberfoer, or Market Fair. Opened by royalty in the last week of August, the fair

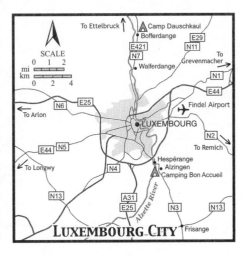

continues through the beginning of September. One of the largest and oldest of its kind in Europe, this fair is easy to enjoy and definitely worth a detour.

▲**Camping:** • 10km north of the city on N7, exit 4km north of Walferdange for Bofferdange. Camp Dauschkaul (33 2434); lovely hillside setting with tranquil views; terraced; very small; open May-Sept; $. • 5km south of the city, along the Alzette River in the suburb of Alzingen. 10km south of the city exit A31/E25 onto N13 in the direction of Frisange. At Frisange, exit north on N3 in the direction of Hesperange. Just south of Hesperange, follow signposting to Alzingen and the Alzette River. Camping Bon Accueil 2 rue du camping (36 7069); convenient; public transport to the city; close to a recreational park; open April-Sept; $$

PORTUGAL

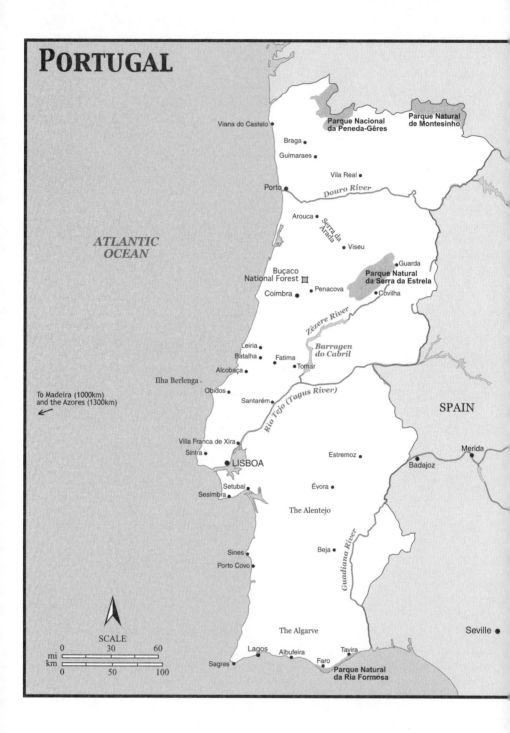

Viana do Castelo ●

Parque Nacional
da Peneda-Gêres

Parque Natural
de Montesinho

Braga ●

Guimaraes ●

Vila Real ●

Porto ●

Douro River

Arouca ●

*Serra da
Arada*

Viseu ●

● Guarda

*ATLANTIC
OCEAN*

Buçaco
National Forest ⊞

Parque Natural
da Serra da Estrela

Coimbra ●   ● Penacova   ● Covilha

Zezere River

Leiria ●

*Barragen
do Cabril*

Batalha ●   Fatima ●

Alcobaça ●   ● Tomar

Ilha Berlenga ▸   Obidos ●

To Madeira (1000km)
and the Azores (1300km)
←   Santarém ●   *Rio Tejo (Tagus River)*

SPAIN

Villa Franca de Xira ●

Sintra ●   Estremoz ●   Merida ●

● LISBOA   Badajoz ●

Setubal ●   Évora ●

Sesimbra ●

The Alentejo

Sines ●   Beja ●   *Guadiana River*

Porto Covo ●

The Algarve   Seville ●

SCALE

| 0 | 30 | 60 |
mi
km
| 0 | 50 | 100 |

Lagos ●   Albufeira ●   Tavira ●

Sagres ●   Faro ●

Parque Natural
da Ria Formosa

Portugal

www.visitportual.com

When the exploration of outer space was launched scientists knew that the moon was there and that they could develop technology to reach it. In the 15th-century, without concrete knowledge, or instruments, Portuguese navigators launched explorations more speculative than trips into outer space. They sailed into the unknown, where they were taught they would fall off the edge of the earth. All great achievements need inspiration and leadership, and Prince Henry, though not a navigator in the narrow sense, filled this role for Portugal. With a passion to know what lay beyond, he organized and financed the building of ships, the schooling of navigators, and of many exploratory voyages. Portuguese navigators were the first to measure and find a relationship between the world's oceans and land. They tied this information together with maps and produced instruments that led the Old World to the New World. It was a geographical revolution. Epic voyages led them to the islands of Madeira and the Azores–still part of the country today. They continued down the coast of Africa from Guinea to the Cape of Good Hope. Portuguese Vasco da Gama opened the sea routes to India, then Cabral landed in Brazil, and other caravels (light sailing ships) continued east to Malacca and China. Portuguese ships returned with new ideas, spices, precious stones, and woods. By the end of the 17th-century, when Spain had been successfully pushed back over the border, gold and precious stones flowed from the mines of Brazil, then a Portuguese colony. The citizens celebrated their wealth with buoyancy and optimism in a delirious, theatrical fashion. Great swashes of gilded wood covered the altars of cathedrals in a complex ornamentation of sinuous lines, cherubs, and flowers. The Manueline style, named after Manuel I who reigned from 1495 to 1521, was born. This lively artistic expression reflected their maritime expansion with intricately carved wood resembling twisted rope, nautical ties, and coral all gilded gorgeously with gold. The Moors had taught them the technique of firing painted tiles or azulejos. The tiles became a hallmark Portuguese decorative style in which the color of the ocean prevailed through the 19th-century. The Portuguese today regard their navigational history with pride but don't care to do it again. They never intended to rule the world. They just wanted to enjoy the riches of buying low and selling high. Cathedrals and museums throughout Portugal a requiem to this remarkable age. Bring binoculars so you can see the incredible details found throughout.

Today's architectural designs are geometric and majestic, with a swooping minimalist global style. Once almost frozen in the 19th-century, the country is now in harmony with the rest of Europe. The new architecture, six-lane highways, sports stadiums, railway stations, and 3-dimensional art are indelible characteristics of present-day Portugal. Fortunately the past has not been lost in the process. Portugal is still essentially a rural country, with small-scale towns and villages that retain a strong sense of regional identity.

Loving to be with family and friends, the Portuguese often take time out from their usual routine of hard work to participate in grand, colorful processions featuring exquisitely embroidered capes, elaborate dresses, meticulous suits, flower-bedecked floats, and marching bands. Fond of sharing food, the fiestas include a huge communal meal, where traditional foods of the region are proudly prepared by locals and generously shared with family, neighbors, and visitors. It's worth planning your itinerary to include one.

The country is almost outlined by the sea. On the mainland's western Atlantic side, blissfully empty beaches–popular with surfers and naturalists–alternate with high dramatic cliffs. The south boasts spectacular sunny weather, so the Algave's idyllic beaches particularly those west of Lagos, are now backed with burgeoning development. Lying closer to Morocco than Portugal, the verdant volcanic island of Madeira's blackrock shoreline provides crystal clear water for snorkeling and scuba diving. For glorious sandy beaches, Madeirans take the ferry to the island of Porto Santo. In the Azores, the views of the sea are retained in a natural purity that is rarely seen today's world.

Roadways have been vastly improved in the last few years. Scenic six-lane divided roads connect major cities. Secondary roads connecting small towns and villages are well surfaced, and traffic is generally light. Drivers are courteous. Locals will go out of their way to help you. Driving regulations and speed limits are what you are used to at home. Standardized international pictorial signs are used. As in the rest of Europe, your membership in a nationally approved roadside emergency club will be honored. Gas costs are similar to the rest of Europe. Be sure the map you use is current, because many new roadways have replaced older ones.

The Portuguese love to barbecue, so campgrounds have plenty of grills. You can expect covered cooking and dishwashing areas. Showers have warm water and are spacious. Information about the local sights, public transport, and tourist cards are usually available at the campground office. Two persons, a car, and a tent will rarely cost over 20 euros. Those that charge about 20 euros are indicated here as $$ and those that charge 18 euros or less are indicated as $. A Camping Card International is required and must be left in the office until you check out. (See Appendix.) Obitur Campgrounds are privately owned and provide discounts to members. info@orbitur.pt

Food costs are less than in most European countries. In small towns, trucks loaded with fruits and vegetables sell good quality foodstuffs at a reasonable price. Join the locals and shop from them, too. Twenty-four-hour ATMs are popular and easy to find outside banks. Before leaving a larger town, get local currency, fill up with gas, and purchase supplies. Museum entry fees are reasonable, and most are closed on Mondays.

Travelers are surprised to find northern Portugal so mountainous, the Azores so beautiful and untouched by tourism, and a culture so content with itself. The Portuguese are unpretentious and a bit reserved. So keep your list of Portuguese phrases handy in your pocket and use them to start a conversation. Faces will light up and beam with pleasure, and the locals will go out of their way to help you.

LISBOA

Built in tiers on seven hills, this beautiful city has a grand setting on the Tagus River. Though large, it feels like a town. It has an engaging, low-key sophistication that is at the same time brazenly modern and sweetly old-fashioned. A severe earthquake in 1755 caused the almost complete destruction of the city. No strangers to seemingly insurmountable problems, the Portuguese faced the devastation with focused practicality. They emerged with a new city featuring lovely 18th-century-style tree-lined boulevards, cobblestone streets, and mosaic sidewalks.

With her back to the rest of Europe, Portugal has always looked out to the sea and been lured to explore–almost as if by the siren call of mermaids. Daring and courageous sailors left the comfort of their 16th-century homes to set sail into this unknown. It is this courage that is commemorated in the Belem quarter, a good place to start your exploration of the city. Begin with the magnificent Mosteiro dos Jeronimos, built soon after Vasco de Gama returned from his historic voyage with monies from the lucrative spice trade. Its decorations exalt both the secular and sacred with joyful exuberance. Note the delicate, almost porcelain-like, tracery of the cloister, where slender

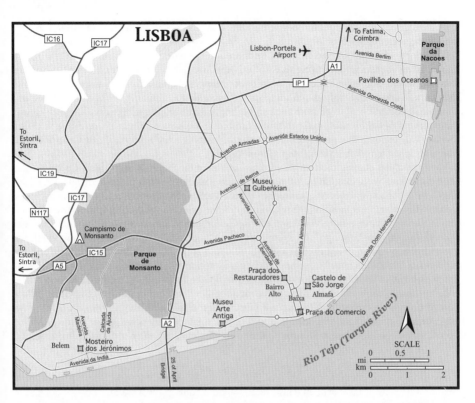

octagonal pillars rise like palm trees in exotic lands to a spectacular vaulted ceiling. Throughout, sea motifs of shells, ropes, and anchors give testimony to the glories of this Golden Age. With binoculars you'll be able to admire the details more distinctly, particularly the extravagantly sculpted south portal. Climb the stairs to the choir loft for a lovely overview of the church. Pay tribute to Vasco de Gama at his tomb, located just inside the entrance and marked with a caravel. Then turn to admire the monument to Portugal's most revered poet, Luis Camoes, marked with a lyre and quill; closed Monday.

The Museu da Marinha, in the west wing of the monastery, houses a fascinating collection of miniature boat replicas showing the transition from bark-built boats to the faster square-rigged caravels. Also on display are 16th-century navigational instruments and maps plus artifacts from trading in India and China. Real boats on view in the museum's extension, include an 18th-century royal galley, a rabelo from the Duoro, and fishing boats from the Algarve; closed Monday.

Emerging from the museum, cross over towards the waterfront to the Monument to the Discoveries fronted by a statue of Prince Henry the Navigator. It is a tribute to explorers famous and not so famous, the poet Camoes, and the painter Goncalves. On the north side of the monument is a huge paving-mosaic compass decorated with galleons and mermaids plus a map showing the sailing route of the 15th and 16th-century explorers. Just beyond, an elevator tower provides views of Belem and the Tagus River. The Torre de Belem is a confection of carved rope, openwork balconies, and battlements and resembles a gigantic Moorish-inspired chess piece. It once sat in the middle of the Tagus River, welcoming homesick sailors and at the same time guarding the city, Climb to its roof for a fine view; closed Monday. Stop by the Centro Cultural de Belem, a stark modern building located west of the monument, to see its current exhibition and calendar of performing arts; open daily. Directions to Belem: From the waterfront, tram 15; from the campgrounds, bus 50.

Fascinated with fine art and treasures from around the world and grateful to the Portuguese people for giving him refuge during World War II, the Armenian oil magnate Calouste Gulbenkian founded Museu Gulbenkian. Set in a lovely park, the airy galleries artistically display the remarkable work of artists and craftsmen from around the world. Breathtaking works of Islamic art and a beguiling collection of work from the flamboyant Art Nouveau jewelry artist Lalique, who was a close friend of the founder, make this museum one of Lisbon's highlights. Don't miss it; closed Monday. Directions: Northeast of the city: Metro Palhava or Sao Sebastiao. The Centro de Arte Moderna is just across from its garden; closed Monday.

The Parque das Nacoes, built on the eastern waterfront for Expo '98, starts with the spectacular Gare do Oriente metro station by Calatrava. Its centerpiece is the dramatically designed Pavilhao dos Oceanos, whose enormous and diverse collection imaginatively recreates all the ecosystems of the world's oceans. Emphasizing the relationship of one ocean to another, this innovative oceanarium is one of the largest in the world and is designed for international visitors with informative text and videos in several languages. It's another don't miss; open daily. Interactive exhibits on science and technology appeal to all ages and make learning fun at the Pavilhao do Conhecimento and the Pavilhao da Realidade Virtual. They are a highlight for teenagers. Directions: On the Tagus River at the eastern end of the city at Parque da Nacoes. Metro Gare do Oriente or drive and park.

In the Museu de Arte Antiga, Portugal's national gallery, you can examine a fascinating collection of Chinese porcelain and Portuguese faience (decorated earthenware), the country's most important paintings, and treasures that reflect the country's relationship with Brazil, Africa, China, and the Indies; closed Monday. Directions: Southwest corner of Barrio Alto; buses 27, 40, 49, or 70.

In the late afternoon go up to Castelo de Sao Jorge, a former Moorish castle. Elegant peacocks stroll through the gardens, and swans float gracefully in the ponds. From its ramparts, you'll have a panoramic view of Lisboa; open daily. After, walk downhill to the Miradouro de Santa Luzia, a tiny park-like terrace where you can watch the broad expanse of the Tagus River turn golden in the sunset. Then continue down through the Alfama's narrow streets, where songbird cages hang outside on balconies and old women in black gossip in doorways. You'll become part of a friendly mix of children playing ball and storekeepers chatting beside their sidewalk hugging displays of strawberries, melons, and eggplants. This is authentic old Portugal. Directions: Take tram 28 or bus 37 to the top. After walking down, take a waterfront tram to Praca do Comericio and then bus 43 back to the campground.

A traveler doesn't experience all that Portugal has to offer without hearing fado, the emotionally powered, poignant music of sorrow and love, or saudade, that is nurtured on the earthy back streets. Women sing with beautiful sultry voices that are haunting. Patrons follow along, often with tears in their eyes. Unique to the music is the guitarra, a mandolin-shaped instrument whose echoing sound enhances the singer's voice. Run by the artists themselves, fado houses are popular with locals as well as tourists. Brazilian and African ties have produced some of the most exciting music and food you'll find in Europe. The music will make you want to cry, laugh, and dance sometimes simultaneously. Some say that to understand saudade is to understand Portugal itself. Ask the English-speaking staff at the tourist office to help you pick a musical venue or use your guidebook.

In the morning, grab your camera to photograph the Mercado da Ribeira. The city's main market is housed in an imposing domed building. It's a lively scene, with fish-mongers hawking the day's catch and women grinding kale for the traditional soup caldo verde. You'll want to purchase some queijo fresco (fresh sheep's cheese) for picnics.

Leave your car at the campground and use Lisboa's efficient and fun transportation system. One of most delightful ways to experience the city is to ride the trams. They wind up and down the hills past aging elegant buildings, through picturesque old neighborhoods, and through a downtown that feels arrested in time. Buses connecting with trams and metros stop at the campground. Buy transportation and museum tourist cards when you check in.

These are only highlights. Lisboa offers much more for the traveler. Stop by the main tourist office at Praca dos Restauradores, a beautiful tree-lined square at the northwest end of the Baixa quarter; open daily. Directions: Metro to Restauradores.

▲Camping: • On the southwestern edge of Monsanto Park. From 1C19 or A5 exit for IC17 and follow signposting. Municipal Campismo de Monsanto (01-760-2061); extra nice; in a pine forest setting; pool; cabins; nearby public transport; office sells public transport tickets and tourist cards, cafe has live music and is a good place to meet fellow international travelers; open all year; $$.

LISBOA REGION
Sintra

Lovely wooded hills and natural springs lured the Moors to this enchanting setting. Since then, the royal, rich, and eccentric have indulged their fantasies with exotic gardens and elaborate palaces. UNESCO-listed, this magical little hill town is very popular. The Royal Palace in the main square is built on Moorish foundations and is an amalgamation of the many styles of the royals who have occupied it. Colorful stories about the inhabitants add to its intrigue; closed Wednesday. Romance must have been foremost in King Ferdinand's mind when he built his elaborate palace on Sintra's highest peak. Called Palacio da Pena, it exudes kitsch charm with an arabesque entryway, life-size torchbearers holding giant candelabras, and eclectic furnishings from all over the world. Trails through a wild garden lead to secret ravines, gazebos, fountains, and a romantic chalet; open daily. Directions: From the Lisbon road, follow signposting at the bottom of the hill besdie Sao Pedro church. Similar garden intrigues can be enjoyed at UNESCO-listed Quinta da Regaleira; open daily. Directions: Walk half a kilometer beyond the tourist office in the direction of Monserrate. The exotic Monserrate gardens spilling down the steep hillside are only partially maintained, but it's easy to imagine the romance and fantasy the setting once provided. Directions: Follow the signposting 4km up the hill behind the tourist office. Desiring to be removed from the world, 14th-century monks carved retreats into the rocky hillside west of Sintra. Hidden among the pines and oaks, the hermitage of dwarf-like cells–called the Convento dos Capuchos–provided simple seclusion for 300 years. Directions: Follow signposting up the hill for Palacio de Pena. At the fork continue on EN247-3 in the direction of Capuchos and Peninha. At the second fork, take the small road north to the convent.

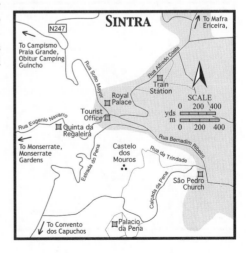

▲Camping: • In Praia Grande. Follow signposting from Sintra for 11km to Colares then one kilometer to Praia Grande. Campismo Praia Grande (01 29-0581); older; pool; popular with families; open all year; $. • On the beach between Sintra and Lisboa, six kilometers northwest of Cascais. From Lisboa exit A5 at exit 12. Drive west to the coast on N247 and follow signposting. Obitur Camping Guincho (214 87 0450);

nice location in a dune area behind the beach; large, shady with pines; open all year; $$ • 24km north of Sintra just north of Ericeira. Drive north of Sintra on N247 for 24km and follow signposting to the beach. Camp Municipal Mil Regos (261 86 2706); nice location close to the beach; popular with families; open May-Sept; $.

Ilha Berlenga

Thousands of gulls, puffins, and cormorants find the calm summer waters and rocky shores of this preserve perfect for nesting and raising their young. Comical and sweet, the young birds are fun to watch. As soon as you get off the ferry, arrange for the exciting and popular boat trip through the 75-meter tunnel, Furado Grande, and on to the beautiful Covo do Sonho. Ferry tickets must be bought at least a day ahead in July and August. from offices on the jetty below the fort in Peniche. Snorkeling, diving, and fishing trips can be arranged ahead with Turpesca (262-789-960) or Berlenga Praia (262-782-636). Take a walk on the narrow causeway beyond the lighthouse that leads to Forte de Sao Joao Baptista, now a hostel. If you want to spend the night, both the hostel and campgrounds require advance booking at the tourist office in Peniche. Directions: 25km west of Obidos. Exit IC1 at exit 14 and drive 25km west on IP6, then follow signposting on N114 for Peniche.

▲Camping: • 2km northeast of Peniche in Baleal. Campismo Baleal (262-769-333); beautiful setting; small; $$. • On Ilha Berlenga. Campismo Natural Preserve Ilha Berlinga basic; open June-Aug; $. (To camp on the Ilha arrangements must be made ahead with the tourist office on the river at the east end of Peniche.) • In Peniche. Just out of town on the beach road. Campismo Peniche Praia (262-78 3460); nice location in the dunes; little shade; large; open May-Sept; $. Similar campground in the same area. Municipal Campismo de Peniche (262 78 9529); tent sites separate from parking; open all year; $.

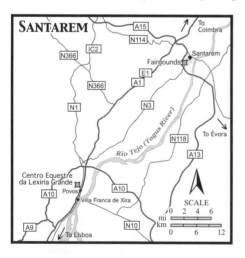

Santarem

In the Portuguese tourada, the bull's horns are capped and he is not killed. Elegant, long-legged horses dance in graceful circles while horsemen tease the bull. Fans are thrilled to watch the star matador leap onto the bull and grab its horns. The most skilled and traditional touradas take place in Santarem's enormous agricultural fair during the first ten days in June. You can purchase tickets ahead: www.cm-santarem.pt. Directions: Drive 56km north of Lisboa on A1/E1, exiting for Santarem and the Tagus River. In early July the gaudy, fun-filled Vila Franca de Xira Festival features bull running and bullfights, folk dancing, boat races on the Tagus, and delicious food grilled over smoky barbecues. Directions: 24km north of Lisboa on A1/E1. Portugal's national horse breed, the Luistano, can be enjoyed in stylish displays of dressage at the Centro Equestre da Leziria Grande located three kilometers south of Vila Franca de Xira near the village of Povos; closed Monday.

▲Camping: See Tomar.

Obidos

If you climb up the steep stairway to this charming, picture postcard-pretty town's rampart walls, you can look down on red-tiled roofs, white-washed houses, and a pleasantly simple Renaissance church. Deep color from lemon trees, bougainvillea, and pelagoniums brighten the narrow cobbled streets lined with little shops selling handicrafts and art. For an extra thrill continue walking the ramparts, which at times are very narrow and without handrails. Directions: From Praca de Santa Maria follow sigposting for Ingreja de Sao Tiago and the street that leads to the wall. Take time to admire the lovely azulejos panels in the interior of the Porta da Vila–the southern 18th-century gate into the historic area.

▲Camping: • At the beach in Sao Martinho do Porto. Drive north of Obidos for 20km on IC1. Exit west onto 242 and drive west 4km to Sao Martinho do Porto. Turn north in the direction of Nazare and drive one kilometer. Campismo Colina do Sol (262 98 9588); nice wind protected location in dune area; large; little shade; pool; popular with families; open all year; $.

Alcobaca Area

The monastery at Alcobaca commemorates and gives thanks for the Portuguese victory over the Moors in 1147–the event that founded their nation. The magnificent Cistercian monastery is one of Portugal's most impressive monuments. Gothic in design and with pure and simple lines, its enormous soaring columns lift a vaulted roof of grandiosity and harmony in its immense central nave. In an adjoining nave attentive carved angels sweetly guard the beautifully sculpted tombs of Pedro I and Ines de Castro, whose romance ended in disaster. For over six centuries the monastery had enormous regional power and owed no allegiance to even the king; open daily.

▲Camping: • Follow signs from the main square for the sports field and camping. Muncipal Campismo (262-42 2265); pleasant terraced setting next to a playground and tennis courts; smaller; open June-Sept; $$.
• At the beach in Nazare. From Alcobaca drive northwest on N8 for ten kilometers to Nazare. Stay east of the centrum following signage for N242 and Marinha Grande for 2km. Campismo Vale Paraiso (262 56 1800); resort-like in a lovely dune area with pines; very large and popular; 2 pools; parking separate from campsite; bike rental; open all year; $$. • In the same area. Camping Orbitur-Valado (262 56 1111); less resort like; open March-Oct; $.

Batalha

Undaunted by hopeless odds against the Spanish and with a genius for strategic planning, Nuno Alvares Pereira led his men with such great courage he has been compared to Alexander the Great. Spanish Juan I was married to Portugal's legitimate heir and was so confident of his success on the battlefield that for the Battle of Aljubarrota he brought his falcons along so he could enjoy a hunting expedition after what he thought would be a brief foray. Some Portuguese supported the Spanish king, making this a civil war with brothers fighting brothers. Today in a profusion of rampant joy, the Dominican Abbey at Batalha celebrates and gives thanks for the glorious Portuguese victory and independence from Spain. Walk the length of the naves, then move on to the royal cloister and its showy virtuosity of arches, columns, and a huge Gothic Lavabo. Embellished with an orgy of Manueline flourishes blended into Gothic severity, the abbey is one of Portugal's most significant monuments. Workman and nobles worried about the unsupported star-vaulting in the chapter house, but the architect Domingues was not concerned and stood directly underneath the ceiling to prove the correctness of his calculations. You can stand there, too. The dramatic impact of the beautiful columns reaching out to pure sky in the Unfinished Chapels–a mausoleum for King Duarte that is just outside the chapter house–is unforgettable. Prince Henry the Navigator's elevated tomb is set into a wall niche in the Founder's Chapel. The Abbey is open daily.

Fatima

Prayerful devotees approach the devotional shrine to Fatima with intense emotion. Completed in 1953, the enormous Basilica has stained-glass windows depicting scenes of the appearances of the Virgin to two peasant children. Pope Paul II visited Fatima three times and beatified the dead peasant children. Similar to Santiago de Composetela in Spain and Lourdes in France, this shrine is approached by some penitents on their knees. There is a candlelight service at night; open daily.

Tomar

Crowned by the stone walls of a massive Knights of Templars' castle, Tomar's interesting history, pleasant river park, sidewalk cafes, and country roads that are nice for cycling–making it good place to take a break in your journey. Drive up to castle and park. After visiting the garden, climb up the stairs to the Convento de Cristo. Turn west after entering the nave and examine the fascinating window at the end. Masses of laurel leaves, poppies, and acorns twist around armillary spheres, knotted ropes and anchors. It's a tribute to Portugal's seafaring men and a fine example of Manueline ornamental style. From here, climb the spiral staircase up to a terrace overlooking over the friars' garden and chapter house ruins. Every four years a famous week-long fiesta draws Portuguese from all over the country to this usually quiet little town. The Fiesta dos Tabuleiros is celebrated with a bullfight, fireworks, barbecues, dancing, and a culminating procession of white-clad women balancing four-to-five-feet-high trays of bread and flowers.

▲Camping: • In town next to the stadium. Cross over the River Nabao on the old, second bridge. Turn towards the stadium and follow signposting along to the end of the stadium. Municipal Campismo de Tomar (249 32 9824); convenient and popular; well managed; traffic noise; open May-Sept; $. • Southeast of town on the reservoir lake. Drive south of Tomar on N110 for 7km exit east onto N358 and drive 6km to Castelo do Bode. Campismo Castelo do Bode (249 84 9262); nice lakeside location under the pines; tent sites separate from camping; open May-Sept; $. • 7km north of town on N110. Campismo Rural (249-301-814); peaceful countryside setting; popular with cyclists; bike rental; open May-Sept; $.

CENTRAL PORTUGAL
Coimbra Area

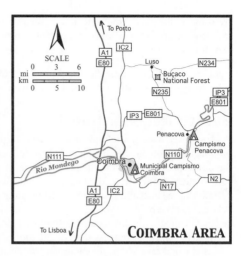

COIMBRA AREA

Perched on a hillside with views grand enough to broaden the perspective of its students, Coimbra University not only gives the town an upbeat rhythm, it also enhances the town with Portugal's grass roots fado music, a raw and powerful yet delicate musical incantation. Don't miss visiting one of the darkened taverns after 10 PM, when you'll hear women wrapped in black-shawls wail mournful songs telling tales of unrequited love, the death of a hero, or of a sailor yearning to be home.

Begin your exploration of the city by walking up through a tangle of narrow streets and stairs to the old quarter, and then farther up to the massive university gate and courtyard. Once a royal palace, the university has fine panoramic views and a library sumptuous with precious wood and Baroque gild. Purchase time-allotted tickets by the clock tower. Directions: Walk up the stairs, named Quebra-Costas, from Rua San Pedro through the old Moorish gateway on the southeast end of the old quarter. Just a short walk downhill takes you to Se Velha (Old Cathedral). Built on the remains of a mosque the cathedral is one of the loveliest Romanesque buildings in Portugal. Its triforium–a gallery of columns that run above the lateral naves–have solid enormity, and its logical, geometric design gives it elegant dignity. During summer, it's a tradition to sing fado on the cathedrals stairway.

One of Portugal's prime archeological sites, Conimbriga is just south of Coimbra. Although only a small portion has been excavated, a Roman forum with covered portico and temple, public baths, and aqueducts can be admired. Most impressive are the remnants of the mansions and their gardens. Examining the scale model in the museum first will help you to understand the excavation. Directions: Drive south of Coimbra on IC2 for 10km.

The Mondego River plunges from Portugal's highest peak before reaching Coimbra, where it passes gracefully through the town. Along the river's banks, people gather for a bus shuttle up to Penacova to kayak. For kayaking on weekdays, call one day ahead, in the evening, to the English-speaking staff at O Pioneiro Mondego; 239-478-385. For weekends, reserve one week ahead. Shuttling is best from Coimbra, not Penacova.

▲**Camping:** • On the east side of the municipal stadium and pool. Drive into the stadium entrance and make a sharp right turn just before the gate into the grandstands. Municipal Campismo Coimbra (039-71-2937); popular with international tourists; shady and pleasant; traffic noise; open all year; $.

Penacova

This is one my favorite areas of mainland Portugal. The Rio Mondego's glistening waters inspire musings from poets and artists and whoops of joy from cyclists, paddlers, and fishermen. It's an easy scenic 20 kilometer paddle to the first take-out, or 25 kilometers to Coimbra. Along the way, you can jump into the river from large boulders and you'll see morning glories shrouding stone walls, scarecrows trying to ward off hungry birds from tiny terraced vineyards, and spectacular black and white-plumed hoopoe birds swooping down for fish and then riding the current. Cycling along the river roads into villages that cascade down hillsides–with stops for a dip in the river–makes for a very enjoyable day. In town, park in the main square and shop in the small but excellent bakery, butcher shop, and produce market. Directions: Drive south of Coimbra on the east side of the riverside road. Turn east on N110 and drive 18km to Penacova.

▲Camping: • Cross over the bridge just south of Penacova and turn north. Campismo Penacova (039-477-946); wonderful location on the river; bike rental; peaceful; open all year; $.

Bucaco National Forest

Moss-covered stone walls, giant ferns, and steep steps up to cascading spring water are among the magical sights in this arboretum-like woodland, which is particularly pleasant mid-week. In the 6th-century, Benedictine monks sought sanctuary here under the hermitage of trees. In the 15th-century, monies from the overseas expansion built a Carmelite monastery on the site of the present Palace Hotel and provided for the planting of a wide variety of exotic trees and plants. The Palace Hotel was built as a royal hunting lodge and is a bizarre pastiche of the Manueline style. In its arcades are tiled scenes from Camoes' great epic, Lusiads. Marked paths lead through the woods, passing cork-lined hermitages used by the monks. Don't miss the path to Cold Fountain, whose waters rise in a cave within the mountain and then cascade down 144 steps into a lively pool lined with magnolias and hydrangeas. Nearby is delightful Fern Valley Lake. Either drive or hike up to Cruz Alta for a panoramic view that includes Mondego Valley and the Serra da Estrela. Directions: Northeast of Coimbra on N235, follow signposting for ticket gates into the walled forest.

Viseu

Vasco Fernandes, known as the Great Vasco, was born in Viseu and helped found a school of painting that thrived here in the 16th-century. Inspired by the Flemish painters, particularly Van Eyck, Vasco's paintings exude the intricacy and richness of his mentor's work. The Museu de Grao Vasco's collection includes one of his best pieces, St. Peter on His Throne; closed Monday. Directions: On the north side of the Se (cathedral) housed in a bishop's palace. Viseu's fine 12t- century cathedral square is graced by the elegant baroque façade of the beautifully propor-tioned Church of Misericordia. The highlight of the church's interior is the Renaissance cloister. Directions: Follow signposting from major roadways for Se.

▲Camping: • In Viseu follow signposting off IP5 for Viseu Este. Drive 2km following sign-posting for Parque do Fontelo. Campismo Orbitur-Viseu (232 43 6120); nice location in the lovely countryside; popular with international campers; some shade; open April-Sept; $$.

Parque Natural da Serra da Estrela

In glacier-formed valleys, likable little villages with narrow schist-paved alleyways sit quietly beneath the peaks of Estrela. Here, a centuries-old way of life is still undisturbed. At the praca, or square, you can savor a treat at an outside table of a tasca, or cafe, and look out across the valley. In these mountain villages the economy is based on sheep and goats, and fine smoked sausages and exceptional hand-made cheese are produced. With their generations of acquired knowledge and discipline, the people live close to the land and learn early not to waste anything. Around the houses which appear almost to have grown out of the rocky hillsides–hens cluck and pigs grunt, and on the hour you'll be treated to a concert of church bells bonging, cocks crowing, and dogs barking. On the slopes, where modern machinery is unsuitable, heavy burdens are still carried on harvesters' heads. Narrow, steep roads cut into forests of pine and eucalyptus and are scented with golden broom, rosemary, and lavender. As you drive or walk along them, you'll notice fountains fed by mountain streams built especially for the burden-carrying villagers. Stop here and raise your cup of water in a toast of gratitude, as they do. As you watch the herds of sheep or goats

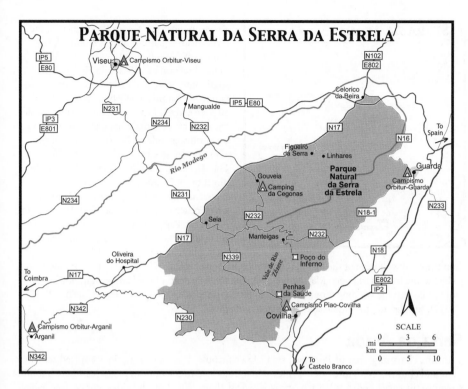

pass by, note the extraordinary sheepdogs. They look like athletic Saint Bernards. Left with the responsibility of the flock, they are authoritative, with a powerful stride and sharp bark, and you can't help but admire their skill in keeping the herd in tow.

The park preserves antiquities, and along walking paths connecting the villages you'll see ancient stone huts and enclosures built painstakingly from brown-orange slate. Alongside rushing streams, vintage water wheels still stand under leafy chestnut and oak trees. In cultivated green valleys, rivers flow beneath scree-covered slopes where pink and white forget-me-nots peek from the chinks in rocks.

The trailhead for Poco do Inferno and Valle de Rio Zezere begins in the spa village of Manteigas. The trails have blissful views of the mountains, streams are sweet-smelling with anise, and old granite bridges remind you how ancient the path is. You'll hear flocks of goats crying like children as they follow the music from the nanny's brass and steel bells. It's fun to watch them trotting down the hillside's invisible trails, hopping from rock to rock, only occasionally stopping for a rub of the head or a nibble of grass. Midway between Manteigas and Gouveia you'll see strangely shaped rocks on a hillside rugged with gorse and bracken. This region is a landscape of sharp contrasts. Stop at the national park office on the main street in Manteigas to talk to English-speaking staff, examine the topographical map, and purchase a guidebook. Don't pass up buying some of the region's famous serra cheese, tasty sausage, and crusty bread for a picnic.

Penhas da Saude is the starting point for serious hiking. Desolate looking in the summer, it is close to the highest peaks. The park office in Seia on Praca de Republica is a good source for maps and guidebooks. Linahares, 20 kilometers southwest of Celorico da Beira, is a miniscule living-museum style-village. In the ancient church, you can see paintings by Grao Vasco. Then follow the little road near the schoolhouse in the direction of Figueiro da Serra, where you'll walk on heavy slabs of rock that were once a Roman road.

▲Camping: • On the southwest edge of the serras near Arganil. North of Coimbra, take exit 13 off A1/E80 onto IP3 and drive 46km in the direction of Oliveira do Hospital. Exit south onto N342 and drive 4km up the mountain road. Campismo Orbitur-Arganil (235 20 5706); lovely location along the river; small; terraced; canoe rentals; open all year; $. • On the northwest side of the park near Gouveia. 12km north of Seia on N17, exit at kilometer 114. Drive through the village of Melo in the direction of Gouveia to the historic manor house. Camping da Cegonas (238 74 5886); small; peaceful; open all year; $. • At the north end of the Parque near Portugal's highest city, Guarda. Exit IP5/E80 at exit 27 and drive up the mountain to Guarda. Follow signposting on the southwest edge of the town. Campismo Orbitur-Guarda (271 21 1406); pleasant location close to the town park; open Mar-Nov; $. • At the southeast end of the Parque, 5km northwest of Covilha up the winding mountain road to Penhas de Saude. Campismo Piao-Covilha (275 31 4312); simple; nice mountain setting; open May-Sept; $.

Serra da Arada

In this charming area of Portugal, small towns ripple down steep hillsides covered with oak, pine, and chestnut trees into river ravines. Goat trails lead to the bottom of gorges where bubbling streams still carve bedrock. Narrow roads worm their way along hillsides, connecting villages populated with modest, frugal people. As you walk through villages, you'll breath in the fragrant aroma of grasses, nod to the occasional resident who will usually nod back, and peek into walled gardens where kids play two-man soccer and women tend vegetable gardens. In the evening, blackbirds sing out with pleasure to the setting sun in a melody that ripples across the valley.

Arouca is the hub of the area. Get information on early summer white-water rafting, hiking, and interesting drives at the tourist office on the main square. Bring your map and confirm your routes there. Directions: Between Aveiro and Porto exit IC2 at Oliveira and drive east on N224 for 12km in the direction of Vale de Cambra. Drive through town following signposting for Arouca continuing for another 20km on N224.

▲Camping: • In the Serra da Ferita at Merjal, 18km southeast of Arouca, close to the Seven Crosses. Exit Arouca at the roundabout on N326, west of the main square, and drive south up the mountain following signposting for Firiz and Figueiredo. The narrow road winds up the mountain and through the villages. At the fork to Granja, stay west following signposting for Vale da Raiz. There are panoramic views at the top of the mountain. Descend the mountain in the direction of Merujal, passing the Seven Crosses. Muncipal Campismo Serra da Freita (256 94 7723); nice setting under the pines; covered cooking area; open May-Sept; $.

NORTHERN PORTUGAL
Porto

A famous wine, the country's language, and the country's name all stem from this important Portuguese city. Located on the estuary of the Duoro River, it has long been attractive to merchants. The Romans settled here in the 3rd-century, but the Phoenicians were here even before them. It is here that Prince Henry the Navigator built the ships that lead to discoveries of new lands and their wealth.

Start by taking a rattling tram ride along the riverside and up through the narrow, twisting streets, where houses seemingly stacked one upon another are decorated with the morning wash, bird cages, and bicycles. Directions: Tram 18 from Hospital Santa Antonio on Rua do Carmo. Take time to view the historic Sao Benito train station's mecca of azulejos. Use your binoculars to examine the detail in scenes of rural festivities and historic events. Then walk north to Praca da Liberdada, then west on Rua dos Clerigos for two blocks to Jardim Chagas. Turn south and you'll come to what was once Porto's prison but is now the moving Centro Portugues de Fotografia. Afterwards, walk east on Rua dos Caldeireiros and follow signposting down the alleyways that plunge into Porto's atmospheric, medieval, quay-side Ribeira quarter, which is UNESCO-listed. You'll see reddish and yellow ochre-colored buildings, "banners" of washing strung between eaves, and a lively street scene. Have your camera when you visit the two-tiered old Mercado Bolhao. It resembles a Moroccan souk, with garden fresh produce mixing colorfully with live rabbits and chickens, flavorful cheeses, crusty loaves of bread, and household supplies. Directions: Walk north up from the Sao Benito train station, passing the Praca da Liberdade to Pacos do Concelho. In late afternoon, take a walk over the Ponte Luis bridge from Cais de Ribeira. Stop midway for beautiful views of Oporto's tiered Old Town then continue over the bridge to Vila Nova de Gaia–a patchwork of terracotta roofed warehouses on cobblestone streets. It's a mecca for port wine aficionados. Dozens of tours and tastings are offered. You'll learn that port is the product of over 30 varieties of grapes, grown on the steep terraced slopes of the Duoro River Valley. The smaller ones have an intimate feel, but don't miss the larger Sandman's sitting directly on the riverbank. Housed in remnants of an 18th-century monastery, it has an excellent museum. Afterwards, walk back across the bridge catching the magic of the cafes along Cais da Ribeira illuminated with strings of tiny lights. Rest at one of the outside cafe tables and watch handsome port-carrying rabelo boats bob up and down on the river and savor the views of the across-the-river port wine treasures. The waterfront market stalls are a great place to look for souvenirs.

The sprouting genealogies of The Tree of Jesse, dressed in polychrome and gilded wood, are so excessive in decoration that clergy of Igreja de Sao Francisco refused to hold services. The famous theatrical, high-relief altarpiece is reminiscent of an opera chorus, so bring binoculars; open daily. Directions:

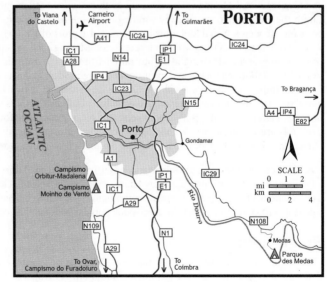

West of Ribeira on Rua do Infante Henrique. The Casa-Museu Guerra Junqueiro is located in the charming former home of the poet and holds gems from his lifetime collection of art. The Islamic pieces are particularly intriguing; closed Monday. Directions: Walk down from the southeast corner of the Archbishop's Palace and the Cathedral.

Don't miss the Fundacao de Serralves de Arte Contemporanea and its excellent collection. It's one of Oporto's cultural highlights. The museum is set on a hillside in a beautiful residential area on the western outskirts of town; closed Monday. Plan to picnic in its outstanding modernist sculpture garden and take in the view from its graceful teahouse. Directions: Take tram 18 to the top of Avenida Gomes da Costa or bus 78 from Praca da Liberdade.

▲Camping: • On the River Duoro 16km southeast of Porto. Off A1 exit for Gondomar. After first roundabout exit onto N108 in to the direction of Entre os Rios and drive 18km to Medas. Parque des Medas (224 76 0161); lovely location on the river; steep descent; terraced; pool; boat rental; popular with families; open April-Oct; $$. • 4km south of Porto close to the beach town of Madalena. Off the ring-road ICI, exit south for Espinho and N109. Drive south 3km to Madalena. Take small road to the beach. Campismo Orbitur-Madalena (227 12 2520); large; pool; popular with families; shady with pines; some airport noise; bus to Porto; open all year; $$. • In the same area. Campismo Moinho de Vento (227 13 5948); smaller; basic; open all year; $. Further south near Ovar. Exit ICI for Espinho and N109. Drive 24km. Exit for Ovar. Pass through town and drive west on a small road for 6km to Furadouro. Campismo do Furadoiuro (256 59 6010); part of a camping club; nice location on the beach; convenient train to Porto; open all year; $$.

Guimaraes

Grand with a sense of history, Guimaras was Portugal's first capital and is one of the most attractive places in the country. Gold, silver, and linen work are still high prized and you'll find artisans working in shops down tiny alleyways. From the main square, Largo da Oliveira, walk up the Rua de Santa Maria to the heart of the old town, where iron grillwork and granite arches decorate the superbly restored old buildings. An exceptionally fine collection of Portugal's finest silverwork is in the Museu Alberto Sampaio, housed in the lovely cloister of Nossa Senhora da Oliveira; closed Monday. Continue up to the massive battlements of Castelo de Sao Miguel. Climb the ancient narrow stairway winding up to the tiny tower, and then stroll along the ramparts for the views. You'll look down on feudal-size plots of land where the famous vinho-verde vines climb like snakes onto wooden frameworks. Making a living here is hard and success doesn't come from grand and daring ideas but rather from simple, relentless work. There are no long siestas and elaborate lunches and evening meals are modest and eaten early.

At the impressive archeological site Citania de Briteiro, a network of paths leads visitors past paved streets, subterranean cisterns, and aqueducts built by the Celts in the Iron Age. Two replicas of ancient circular dwellings have been recreated on original stone foundations. The most evocative finds are in Guimaraes' archeological museum, Museu Martins Sarmento; closed Monday. Directions: Exit N101 5km north of Guimares and follow signposting east for 8km.

▲Camping: • 7km north of Guimaraes on N101 to Caldas das Taipas. Follow signposting for Piscina (pool). Campismo Caldas das Taipas (053 57 6274); pleasant location in a pretty town; open June-Sept; $. • Up the mountain south of town in Parque da Penha. Municipal Campismo da Penha (053 51 5912); lovely location; pool; popular with families; open June-Sept; $.

Braga Area

Catholicism is part of being Portuguese. The nation's history can't be separated from it. Believing that good fortune is a gift not a triumph, the Portuguese give thanks for their blessings

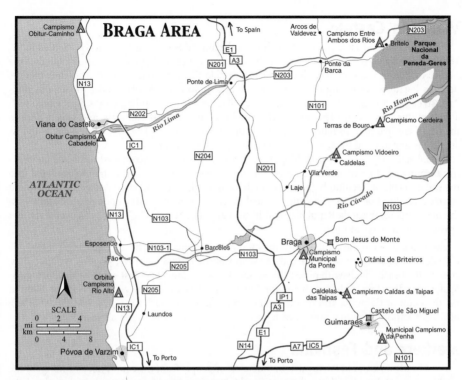

by hosting some unique and colorful religious processions. In sumptuous church interiors, priests lead congregations in prayers of thanks. Tearful woman and stoic men kneel and pray, and a heavy scent of incense fills the air. After, a solemn procession leaves the church to the death-march beat of drums and the funeral music of brass bands. The Virgin, dressed in her finest garments, is carried high for all to see. Black-cloaked penitents march slowly together followed by solemn-faced dignitaries. Afterwards, everyone relaxes and has fun at a lively communal meal prepared by buxom women vigorously rubbing chickens with a mixture of finely chopped red peppers and garlic before slapping them over red-hot coals. The mouth-watering aroma will entice you to join a smiling group of locals who will welcome you at a long table overflowing with platters of chicken, baskets of chewy bread, bowls of salad sprinkled generously with radishes, and pitchers of local wine. All of this is relished along with much laughter and toasts to neighbors and family.

Climbing for spiritual solace is one of the world's most widespread traditions. At Bom Jesus do Monte, the climb is up the ornamental stairway that cascades down a lush green hillside. Here Jesus' last journey to Golgotha is symbolized in fountains built into the walls of the staircase and in tiny chapels featuring tableaus of life-size terracotta figures. Ultimately you reach the summit, the church, and the three crosses on the rocky crest of Golgotha. If you don't feel like climbing, you can ride the creaky funicular. Directions: Drive east out of Braga on N103 and follow signposting.

▲Camping: • 28km west of Braga, near the beach. Drive west of Braga on N103 in the direction of Barcelo for 13km. Exit west onto smaller N205 and continue west for 13km. Pass under ICI and drive towards the beach. Turn south onto N13 and drive 2km following signposting for a golf course. Obitur Campismo Rio Alto (252 61 5599); recreational area; very large; no shade; cabins; open all year; $$.

Viana do Castelo

Baroque facades flecked pleasingly with moss decorate this popular beach town. Settled in the 18th-century by merchants made wealthy by Brazilian gold and diamonds, it is the capital of the Minho folk culture and holds rich examples of azulejo tile work. These painted ceramic tiles are perhaps Portugal's most impressive traditional art. If you are anywhere near the area in mid-August, be sure to visit for the romaria. Every village in the surrounding area is represented with a float in this procession. The fiesta includes a blessing of the fishing boats, and streets close to the wharf are "painted" in religious themes with colored sawdust. The whole three-day festival is an old-fashioned good time, with barbecues, fireworks, and dancing.

Feudal-size strips of land stretching inland from the sea have encouraged mini-size cooperative farming. Iodine-rich seaweed dries on frames and fences, waiting to be incorporated into the soil as fertilizer. Behind high granite walls, farm equipment and vegetable gardens surround square monolith homes topped with red-tiled roofs. On Fridays, a large open market operates in the main square, Praca da Republica, and it's fun any time to take the small passenger ferry that crosses over the river to town.

▲Camping: • On the south side of the mouth of the Lima River, by the old bridge, at Praia de Cabedelo. Obitur Campismo Viana do Castelo-Cabedelo (058 32 2167); popular with families; close to the beach; shady with pines; closed mid-Nov-mid-Jan; $$. • Just south of the Portugal-Spanish border, close to the beach and the Rio Minho. Drive north of Viana on N13 for 24km in the direction of Caminha and follow signposting. Campismo Orbitur-Caminha (258 92 1295); pleasant location; close to a sandy beach on the river; railway noise; open all year; $$.

Markets and Festivals

For a heady dose of old Portugal, join the bustle of people from the countryside heading for the weekly open market. You'll breathe in an earthy fragrance from huge mounds of potatoes, kale, apples, and fava beans, see racks drip with hand-stuffed linguica smoked carefully over chestnut wood, bowls of olives glisten with flecks of garlic and chilis. And tables piled with Portuguese sweet bread golden with egg. Ample-figured women in black will squeeze past looking for bargains. Sharp-eyed shoppers carefully watch the scales and penciled calculations and when merchants return your greeting, it is in a shy and reticent manner. The largest and busiest markets are:

Thursdays at Barcelos' Campo da Republica–a real extravaganza from dawn until late afternoon.

Bi-monthly on Mondays in Ponte de Lima along the riverbank.

Every other week on Wednesday evening in Ponte da Braca at the15th-century bridge. Every other Wednesday night alternating with Ponte da Barca in Arcos de Valdevez at the main square.

Directions: Barcelos is 20km west of Braca on N103. Ponte de Lima is 35km north of Braca on A3/E1. Ponte da Braca is 18km east of Ponte de Lima on N203.

At the end of summer the usually taciturn Portuguese let down their hair at festivals that become going-away parties for family and friends who are returning to their homes and work abroad. The celebrants parade in oversize carnival-like costumes called gigantones, brass bands march, and fireworks explode. Special markets are held for linens and other folk arts. The longest and liveliest festival is Ponte da Braca's Feira de Sao Bartolomeu during the third week of August. In Ponte de Lima the celebration is on the second and fourth weekend in September, and in Arcos de Valdevaz on the second weekend in August.

▲Camping: • See Braga.

Parque National da Peneda-Geres

Walks in this beautiful national park are scented with the fragrances of yesteryear. You'll pass columns of hay drying on ropes hung from the limbs of chestnut trees, walled patches of corn, and ancient stone espiqueriros (granaries) decorated with crosses. Stop in one of the villages huddled next to a stream, and pass through the beaded curtain of a tiny grocery store to buy some local mountain cheese and smoked linguica and choose a bottle of vino verde–a young refreshing wine–from a shelf of dusty bottles. The narrow roads here twist through lush fertile valleys and up to wild ridges, where they leave the rest of the world behind.

The best interpretative center is at the park office in Ponte da Barca. Here you can talk to English-speaking staff, examine a large-scale map, and view photographs of the unusual flora, fauna, and agriculture. The trails threading through the mountains to ancient villages are the same that generations of herders and villagers used, and marking is poor. Consider hiring a guide if you want to take a long hike; you'll be contributing to the local economy and will gain a trouble-free, enlightening experience; call a day ahead to the park office in Ponte da Barca; 258-452-450. Directions: Exit A3/E1 35km north of Braga at Ponte de Lima. Drive east 18km on N203 in the direction of Ponte de Barca. Stop at the interpretative center. Directions: From the old bridge follow Rua Conselheiro Rocha Peixoto east to Largo da Misericordia.

▲Camping: • 10km east of Ponte da Barca on N103, on the river just outside the entrance to the park in the village of Britelo. Campismo Entre Ambos os Rios (258 68 361); close to the villages; simple; open June-Sept; $. • In the mountain spa town Caldas do Geres. Drive east of Braga on N103 in the direction of Chaves for 27km. Turn north just past the village of Cerdeirinhas onto N304. Pass through Caldas do Geres and continue west up the steep winding road crossing the bridge over the reservoir. Campismo Vidoeiro (253 39 1289); beautiful setting on the river; close to thermal pools; terraced; some shade; open mid-May-mid-Oct.; $. • In the same area. Follow the directions above except at the bridge stay left and continue on N304 for 15kms up the steep winding road to Camp do Geres. Campismo Cerdeira Camp do Geres (253 35 1005); large; shady with pines; parking separate from campsite; bike path; close to lake; open May-Sept; $.

▲Enroute Camping: 22km south of the Spanish autostrata A52 in Chaves. Exit N103 at Chaves and follow signposting to the river and bridge. Campismo Municipal Sao Roque (076-227-33); simple but pleasant; quiet; open May-Sept; $.

Parque Natural de Montesinho

Softly rolling plains, painted ochre in summer, stretch out lazily in the sun and then ascend steeply to a succession of stony ramparts. Poplars and willows shade the banks of rivers. In evening sheep and goats return home and wait patiently outside their own stable gate. Decisions affecting the community are made at chamados, or town meetings, rather than in the region's capital building. In remote villages hidden in the hillsides, villagers have learned to share equipment, labor, and ideas in order to survive.There is no pressure need here to be anything other than what you are. Walkers and cyclists are enticed by the calm beauty of this isolated region and the quietness that is broken only by the twittering of birds, the humming of insects, the rustling of leaves.

▲Camping: • From the ring road IP4 exit onto N103 in the direction of Pedralba. Follow signposting up the steep hill. Campismo Cepo Verde (273-999-371); pleasant tranquil location; pool; open April-Sept; $.

SOUTHERN PORTUGAL
The Alentejo

Founded by the Romans, who valued the land for the production of grain, this sun-baked region occupies one-third of Portugal–from the Tagus River in the north to the Algave in the south. Today the plains of Alentejo stretch out like a vast golden ocean, with only the occasional sprinkling of stunning unspoiled whitewashed villages featuring doors and windows edged Moorish-style in blue or yellow. A strange and secret beauty lurks in this emptiness of big skies and rolling countryside clad in cork oaks, olive trees, and vineyards.

Evora

Evora rises from the plains, surreal-like, with parts of her walls still intact. Colonized by Julius Caesar in 60 BC, Evora is described in Pliny the Elder's natural history book as Ebora Cerealis. The town grew steadily in importance in the Middle Ages and became the headquarters of the Knights of Avis, who ruled the region. Luckily, its elegant 16th-century mansions were tapped by UNESCO, making restoration possible.

In the heart of the old walled city stand 14 elegant Corinthian columns that are reminiscent of the city's Roman rule. Across from the Temple Romano, guests pay well to sleep in the cells and dine in the cloisters of the ancient Convento dos Loios. Walk from here down the hill to the severe, fortress-like cathedral, where soldiers fought and residents took refuge against Spanish and French intruders. After passing through its Gothic interior, climb the stairway to the coro alto (terrace), for a perfect view of the two unusual towers. Don't leave before viewing the high-

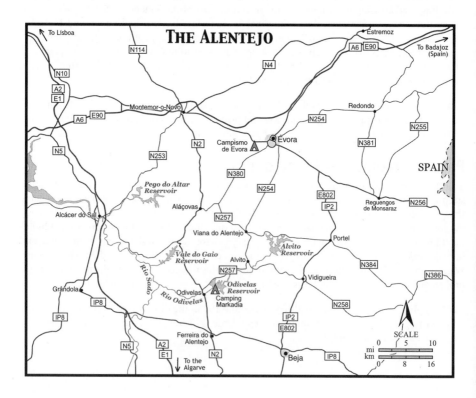

light of the museum's treasures–an exquisite ivory statue of the Madonna whose midriff reveals a tiny triptych of scenes from her life. Directions: Follow signposting for parking on Estrada da Circunvalacao, then walk up the hill to the main square, Praca do Giraldo. The tourist office is on the southwest corner. Pack picnic lunch and cycle out along the flat, quiet roads to see the megalithic sights–the mysterious stones here date from 4000 BC–and pass a pleasant day in the Portuguese countryside. The tourist office has a map and information on bike rentals. On the second Tuesday artisans and merchants come from throughout the region for the monthly market. Traditional arts and crafts are still very much alive in the Alentejo region, expect a good selections of carpets, ceramics, laces, linens, and leathers.

▲Camping: • 2km southwest of town off N380. Off the ring road take exit 4 for Alcacovas and N380 follow signposting. Campismo de Evora (266 70 5190); very popular arrive early or call ahead; pool; popular with families; café; tennis; open all year; $$.

▲Enroute Camping between Evora and the Algave: On a reservoir lake between Evora and Beja. 13km north of Ferreira do Alentejo at Odivelas exit N2 east onto N257 and drive 7km. Camping Markadia (284 76 3141); beautiful tranquil location; sandy lakeside beach; boat rental; tennis; pool nearby; some shade; open all year; $$.

Estremoz

Prized marble is quarried in elephantine blocks near Estremoz. With a Tuscan-like hilltop setting, it is one of Alentejo's most evocative fortified towns. Sunset paints the massive Vauban-style walls and gateways in soft hues of pink and lavender. Plan to pick up supplies just outside the old walled town at the main square and social hub, Rossio. Such a vast farm region produces a great open-air market, particularly on Saturday. You'll also find a plethora of interesting ceramics as well as sheep and goatskin products that can make memorable gifts.

Alentejo's Atlantic Coast

Unspoiled and still wild, Alentejo's Atlantic coastline boasts low-key villages and idyllic sandy beaches snuggled secretively between dramatically wind-chiseled cliffs. Surfers, birders, and naturalists find pleasure here. Whitewashed houses trimmed colorfully in blue and red line the streets of Porto Covo, a tiny village situated 14km south of Sines. Relics of an old fort sit high on a bluff above its cove beach. Colorful fishing boats transport people to the offshore Ilha do Pessegueiro for beach picnics and swimming. Vila Nova de Milfontes hugs a tiny bay where Rio Mira meets the sea. It's a pretty, little, low-key resort town with sandy beaches and the waves surfers adore. Direction: 38km south of Sines off N390. Farther south, the pleasant village of Zambujeira do Mar has stunningly white sandy beaches backed by dramatic black cliffs. A trail along the bluff gives hikers who don't mind scrambling down rocky cliffs access to more remote beaches. Directions: Exit N120 west at Sao Teotonio and drive 6km. North of Sines, bird enthusiasts and fisherman enjoy the lagoons and estuaries around Melides. Directions: Exit N5 for Grandola and drive west on N261 for 18km.

▲Camping: • In Porto Covo: Exit IC4 8km south of Sines and follow signposting south in the direction of Porto Covo for 6km. Campismo de Porto Covo (069-951-36); beautiful location on the beach; open all year; $. • In Vila de Milfontes: Drive 26km south of Sines on IC4 to Cercel. Turn onto N390 and drive southwest 12km to the Rio Mira. Campismo Campiferias (283 99 6409); on the river, shady, close to beach and village; open all year; $. North of the Vila de Milfontes. Campismo Sitava Turismo (283 89 9343); tennis; café and store; open all year; $. • In Praia da Zambujeira.. From Odemira drive south on N120 for

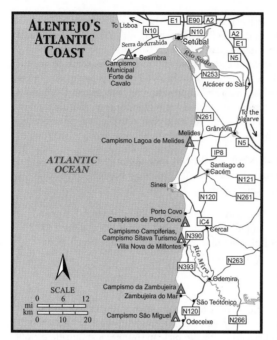

ALENTEJO'S ATLANTIC COAST

To Lisboa · E1 · E90 · A2 · N10 · N10 · A2 · E1

Serra da Arrabida · Setúbal

Sesimbra · N5

Campismo Municipal Forte de Cavalo · N253

Alcácer do Sal

To the Algarve · N261

Melides · Grândola

Campismo Lagoa de Melides

IP8 · N5

ATLANTIC OCEAN

Santiago do Cacém · N121

Sines · N120 · N261

Porto Covo

Campismo de Porto Covo · IC4

Campismo Campiferias, Campismo Sitava Turismo · N390 · Cercal

Villa Nova de Milfontes

Rio Mira · N263

N393

Odemira

SCALE

Campismo da Zambujeira

Zambujeira do Mar

São Teotónico

mi · 0 · 6 · 12

km · 0 · 10 · 20

Campismo São Miguel · N120 · Odeceixe · N266

11km to Sao Teotonio. Turn west and drive 6km to Zambujeira. Campismo da Zamabujeira (283 96 1172); lovely setting with great views; terraced; eucalyptus shade; close to the village; open all year; $$. • In the same area but 2km farther south. • North of the village of Odecixe. Campismo Sao Miguel (282 94 7145); scenic location; cabins; resort-like; open all-year; $$. • At the Melides Lagoon. From Grandola drive west 18km on N261. Campismo Lagoa de Melides (269 90 7151); large; older; security guards; popular with families; convenient for early morning birding on lagoon; open Apr-Sept; $$.

Sesimbra

Close to Lisboa and located in a sheltered south-facing bay, Seimbra is protected from the cold north winds by the Serra da Arrabida. Its fishing-village character has been replaced by sidewalk cafes, beach resorts, and second homes. Climb up to the Moorish castle for panoramas of sea and countryside.

▲Camping: • Close to the lighthouse, waterfront, and old fort. Campismo Municipal Forte do Cavalo (212 23 3694); nice views of the village; terraced; steep hill approach; popular with families; open Apr-Oct; $.

The Algarve

A finger of the Atlantic leads through the Strait of Gibraltar to the Mediterranean Sea. The area is lined with beautiful sandy beaches and has summers that last a little longer. Long attracting sun seekers from northern Europe, the Algarve's Mediterranean-style resorts now vie for space between whitewashed villages tucked into harbors. Dramatic golden cliffs and seawater lagoons are interspersed with half-moon beaches and stretches of fine, soft sand that seem to go on forever.

Tavira and Parque Natural da Ria Formosa

This town's Rio Gilao is graced by houses with filigreed balconies and still has a Roman bridge crossing it. The Moors occupied the Algarve longer than anywhere else in the country and if you climb up to the Moorish castle at the top of the hill you will have a spectacular view of the peaked red-tiled roofs, the lagoon, and the sea that separates Portugal from Morocco. At the harbor side morning market, you can purchase some of the luscious oranges and densely sweet figs that were exported by ancient fleets traveling to far away places. After, wander down to the port to breathe in the aroma of the sea and the morning's catch as you pass the piles of fishing nets and salt-encrusted boxes. Tuna is the star on the menu, and it's difficult to pass up a tasty snack or a fresh piece for cooking later.

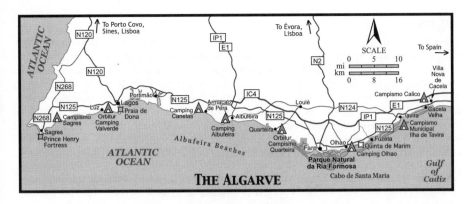

THE ALGARVE

In a labyrinth of lagoons, channels, and wetlands, birds stop enroute between Africa and Europe to breed and raise their young. The rare purple gallinule resides here all year. Resembling a chicken, except for a brilliant red beak and feet, they are fast runners but poor fliers. Originally from Eastern Europe, the red-crested pochard ducks swim side by side then suddenly rise straight up and literally run across the water. Fiddler crabs scuttle in between tides searching for tasty morsels. Take binoculars in the early morning and evening to watch the vast number of birds and crustaceans feeding on these only recently protected sand dune islands. Directions: 3km east of Olhao exit off N125 for Quinta de Marim, the interpretative center for the region as well as the lagoon fauna and flora. Beautiful sand dunes and beaches stretch for miles on the park Ilha Tavira. A passenger ferry goes to the island from Quatro Aguas located 2 kilometers southeast of Tavira, convenient for picnics on the beach and early morning or evening bird watching.

▲Camping: • 12km east of Tavira on a hillside overlooking the sea just north of Cacela Velha. Exit N125 at Cacela Velha and drive north to Vila Nova de Cacela. Campismo Calico (281 95 1195); lovely location in a very pretty village; terraced; open April-Nov; $$. • On the island. Campismo Municipal da Ilha de Tavira (281 23 3505); beautiful location; simple and pleasant; small store; open May-Sept; $. • 16km east of Faro in Olhao. Exit IP1 for Faro. Drive south 6km on N2. Turn south onto N125 and drive 8km following signposting. Camping Olhao (289 70 0390); large; café; store; tennis; bike rental; pool; bus to Faro; car parking separate from campsite; open all year; $$.

Albufeira

Although this fishing town has become the hub of activity for the Algave, you can still see colorful fishing boats beached on the sandy shores. Both Romans and Arabs loved the area and prospered with trade. Today most of the historic area is pedestrianized, and some of the buildings still have Moorish touches.

▲Camping: • 24km east of Albufeira exit IP1 for Loule-Quarteira, then drive south on N396 for 8km to Quarteira. Orbitur Campismo Quarteira (289 30 2826); nice location close to the beach; large; pool; tennis; resort-like; popular; open all year; $$. • In a recreational area close to the beach in Albufeira. Exit IP1/E1 for Albufeira. Follow signposting of N125 for one kilometer. Camping Albufeira (289 58 7629); resort-like; bike rental; especially nice pools; open all year; $$. • In the same area but a few kilometers north in Armacao de Pera signposted on N125. Camping Canelas (282 31 2612); large; resort-like; pool; popular; tennis; open all year; $$. • In the same area. Campismo Armacao de Pero (282 31 2260); large; resort-like; pool; open all year; $$.

Lagos

Swimming through the tunnels and caves at Praia de Dona at sunset or in the morning might become one of your most memorable times in the Algarve. Between swims you can rest in tiny coves sheltered by towering cliffs of purplish-tinted rock. Directions: West of town on waterfront road leading over the hill to the promontory. This town was Prince Henry's base for the deplorable slave market. It is marked today only by a plaque on the arcades, where trading took place next to the Customs House on Rua da Senhora da Graca off Praca da Republica. Directions: East of the hospital off the waterfront road Avenida dos Descobrimentos. Although the 1775 earthquake and subsequent tsunami waves caused extensive damage to the town, some Moorish archways of the old walls survived. Directions: Walk from Praca Republica west on Rua do Castelo dos Governadores.

▲Camping: • Just west of Largos. Exit N125 3km west of Largos for Praia da Luz and follow signposting for 2km. Orbitur Campismo Valverde (282 78 9213); resort-like; pool; open all-year; $$.

Sagres

Out on this windswept promontory, Prince Henry's students looked down on the enormous rock-made rose compass studying the strengths and directions of the prevailing winds. By visiting the fortress he used as a navigation school, you can imagine what early navigators must have felt before they sailed out to Brazil, Angola, the Cape of Good Hope, Goa, and Macao. ▲Camping: • Signposted off N268 in the direction of Cabo de Sao Vincente. Orbitur Campismo Sagres (282 62 4445); good location with nice views; can be windy; shady with pines; medium size; bike rental; open all year; $$.

THE AZORE ISLANDS

Carpets of lush green grass, serenely embroidered with the blue and pink of hydrangeas, spill from mountainsides to the endless blue sea surrounding these mid-Atlantic islands located 1,300 kilometers west of mainland Portugal but only four hours of flight time from Boston. Pristine crater lakes, some warmed by hot springs, reflect the passing clouds. Cows herded by youngsters, horse-drawn carts loaded with milk cans, and walking villagers share with just a few cars and pickups, the winding two-laned roads banked with more hydrangeas and ginger lilies. Walking-paths lead up and into once-active volcanic craters, to waterfalls lined lushly with ferns and azaleas, and to isolated, rustic stone villages. Rare birds, particularly the Azorean bullfinch, make the islands a birding destination for both the committed and the occasional enthusiast.

Throughout the Azores' beautiful cove settings are used to construct natural swimming areas that the whole family can enjoy. Breakwaters are built to form lagoons where snorkeling is possible. Openings in the walls allow seawater to come in as breakers for bodysurfing. Adjoining swimming pool with diving board and toddlers' wading pool completes the swimming area. Eco-tourism is catching on in the Azores. Check with the tourist office in the larger towns to book guides and rent equipment for fishing, hiking, scuba diving, and boating. In small towns and villages, a carefully tended bandstand is the center of town celebrations. Hilltop churches are outlined affectionately with strings of lights. As you wander down the streets, you'll smile at homey scenes and your greeting will be returned by people who seem at peace with themselves. In today's world it is hard to find a place so naturally beautiful and yet relatively unaffected by tourism.

Trucks loaded with fruit and vegetables pass through the villages, providing quality goods for a reasonable price. Join the locals and shop from them, too. Meat in the market is frozen, so buy it in the morning so that it is ready to cook in the evening. Barbecuing is popular, and parks and campgrounds have grills. Include charcoal on your shopping list. Each island listed has at least

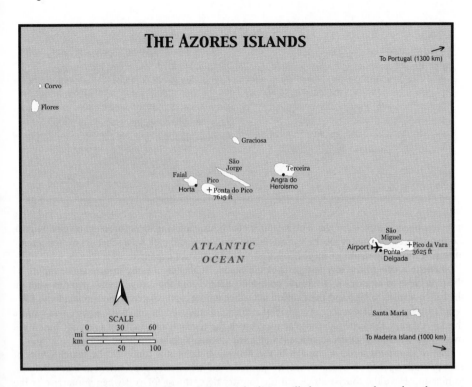

THE AZORES ISLANDS

→ To Portugal (1300 km)

Corvo

Flores

Graciosa

São Jorge

Faial

Terceira

Pico

Angra do Heroismo

Horta

+ Ponta do Pico 7615 ft

ATLANTIC

OCEAN

São Miguel

Airport +̖⋅ + Pico da Vara
Ponta 3625 ft
Delgada

SCALE

| 0 | 30 | 60 |

mi

km

| 0 | 50 | 100 |

Santa Maria

To Madeira Island (1000 km)

→

one campground. Sometimes toilet and shower facilities will show wear and age, but they cost next to nothing and the beauty of the scenery makes up for it. The basalt rock of the volcanic islands can be slippery on some of the cobblestone paths so always wear rubber-soled shoes when hiking. Sometimes the walking paths pass through private gates; be sure to leave them as you found them.

The Azoreans love festivals and fill their summer with them. Emigrants return from abroad for vacation to the warm welcome of family and friends. Streets are decorated with flower petals in extravagant designs. Processions of proud parents and family follow youths draped in exquisitely embroidered capes. From hay-filled carts, pretty girls in scarves pass out loaves of crusty bread. Afterwards, visitors are welcomed to feasts of Sopas do Espirito Santo (a hearty soup), and Alcatra, (a tasty type of barbecued beef). Bands play, girls flirt, boys wink, and there is much laughter and dancing.

The two-lane roads that skirt the islands' coastline meander through or by all the villages. Always fill up with gas in the larger towns. Only one or two roads actually cross the island. You won't zip from one place to another on the Azores. It's a leisurely pace in a leisurely place.

Sao Miguel

The largest of the nine islands, Sao Miguel is still only 65 kilometers long. International flights to the Azores arrive and depart from its capital Ponta Delgada. Three 18th-century arches grace the waterfront, where pedestrian walkways are in elaborate patterns made of tiny tiles placed with exacting thoroughness. Visit the Museu Carlos Machedo to see the large relief model of the island, paintings of Azorean life by Rebelo, and exhibits reflecting life on the islands; closed Monday.

Before you leave the airport, stop and talk with the friendly English-speaking staff at the tourist office. They have the driving and hiking maps you'll need for all of the islands. Have them

help you make the pre-arrangements necessary for hiking into the forest preserve on Sao Miguel. Confirm the current dates for the various island festivities, and pick up a schedule for the ferries. Traveling from one island to another on a ferry is fun and not expensive.

Nordeste is one of the loveliest parts of the island. It shelters a campground at the mouth of the river close to an extra nice natural swimming area. From the campground, you can walk up the hill to a small village and then continue farther up the luscious green mountainside. A 19th-century seven-arch bridge forms a graceful entrance to the village. Sit in the square and admire the 15th-century Igreja de Sao Jorge as you absorb the tranquil simplicity of everyday life. Walk over to the traditional crafts school and watch the women weaving on hand looms.

One of the rarest birds in the world, the Azorean bullfinch, is found in the laurel forests of Pico de Vara. Special permission must be granted from the forestry department in Ponte Delgada to hike in. Have the tourist office call the forestry department for you when you arrive at the airport. Serious birders should ask them to arrange a local birder as a guide. A trail leads up through Planalto dos Graminhais to Pico da Vara. At its 1,105-meter summit is a great view of the northeastern side of the island and the sea. Directions: Drive west from Nordeste on R1-1. After passing Feriera Grande, watch for signage for Planalto dos Graminhais. Drive up the hill to Espigao dos Bois, where the trail begins.

Magnificent Lago do Fogo shouldn't be missed. An eruption in the 16th-century formed the crater-lake whose crystal-clear blue water shimmers in the sunlight. Directions: Coming from Ponte Delgado, drive 11km east on the coast road to the town of Lagoa. At the fork, on the eastern outskirts of town, turn north following signposting for Lagoa do Fogo. Drive northeast up the winding road for 10km. Coming from Ribeira Grande, turn south at the fork at the eastern outskirts of town. Following signposting for Lagoa do Fogo, drive 12km up the mountain road. For a more remote experience to Lagoa do Fogo, take the road to Lombadas. Directions: East of Riberia Grande turn inland, following signposting for Caldeiras da Ribeira and Lombadas. At the fork, continue following signposting for Lombadas. Park at the Lombadas water-bottling factory then walk behind the factory where the trail begins. Follow the stream on the left side. At the crossing sign the trail begins to climb steeply, but you are rewarded with magnificent views of the lush valley below. At the top, the trail levels out and has fine views of an exquisite turquoise lake, Lagoa do Fogo.

On the south side of the island, Lago do Congro, a smaller crater lake, makes a nice short-hike destination. The somewhat steep trail is lushly lined with wild hydrangeas and deciduous trees. Directions: Drive east of Villa Franca do Campo for 5km. Turn north at signposting for Lagoa do Congro and drive 5km. On the southeastern end of the island, the tiny jewel of a beach, Lombo Gordo, is a favorite with locals, but driving down to it is not for the faint of heart. If you choose to walk be mindful of the steep return. Directions: From Nordeste drive south on the coast road for 15km. Watch closely for a narrow, steep stone road just past the Miradouro da Madrugada. It's 2 kilometers down. The coast drive south of Nordeste is exceptionally beautiful. The spectacular sheer cliffs and the endless azure sea are breathtaking; allow plenty of time to stop at the miradouros, (view points). Continue south and then west to Furnas, where dramatic terraces of rock steam with hot, bubbling springs. Hibiscus, camellias, and azaleas add color under a stunning collection of century-old trees that shade the stream and ponds in the park behind the Terra Nostra hotel. Enjoy a rest along the grassy banks of the lovely Lagoa as Furnas, a popular lunch/nap stop. A walking path on the west end of the lake goes up to Pico do Ferro, where you'll have an excellent view of the whole Furnas valley. Directions: From Furnas take the Ponta Delgada road for 3km. The seawater of Praia do Fogo is warmed by underwater volcanic activity, making it a perfect place for swimming and some lazy time. The scenic road from Furnas to Ribeira Quente has several miradouros that have picnic tables and barbeques. On the road to the small town, you'll pass a large grocery store that is convenient for picking up supplies. Directions: From Furnas, drive south 8km to Ribeira Quente.

▲Camping: • At the northeastern tip of the island in Nordeste. At the north end of town follow signposting to the bottom of a steep stone road. Campismo do Nordeste (296-488-185); lovely location at the mouth of the Guillerme River; close to the natural swimming pool; parking separate from camping; simple; open May-Sept; $.

Like two sisters dressed in silk, the emerald-green and sapphire-blue lakes sit pristine and quiet in their crater bowls of verdant green. Caldeira das Sete Cidades, seen on the cover of many Azorean tourist brochures, is on the northwest end of the island. Start your exploration from the top of the caldeira at Vista do Rei, where the rim walking path begins. Directions: From Varzea follow signposting up the mountain for Sete Cidades, stopping at Vista do Rei before you descend to the pristine lakes and the toy-like little village of Sete Cidades with its square-towered chapel set at the end of an alley of pines. It's a very tranquil place, you'll hear only the song of birds and the whisper of wind in the trees as you walk around its of twelve kilometer circumference.

▲Camping: On the lake. This is not an official campground, so be discreet and set up the tent in the evening and take it down in the morning.

Faial/Pico/Sao Jorge

Oceanic depth falls off almost immediately from these islands, so there is a rich abundance of cetacean life. Great sperm, blue, sei, orca, and pilot whales prompted the Azoreans into historic supremacy in whaling. They were expert at harpooning and were sought by whale boat captains from other countries. The ghosts of the whalers, known as "sea wolves", remain in Pico, once the center of the Azorean whaling tradition. The waters now teem with protected whale and dolphin species and today people go out on the ocean in exciting inflatable rafts to see the baleeiros (whales) swish by and the dolphins whoop it up. To appreciate the courage of the whalers and also make your own trip more meaningful, before going out examine the fascinating whaling canoe, exquisitely carved whale bones, tackle, and memorbilia at Museu do Baleeiros in Lajes on the south side of the island. Expert guides at Espaco Talassa in Lajes are led by radio messages from staff who scan the sea from the former vigias (lookouts); 092-67-2010.

For the last week of August you can join hundreds of Azoreans in a gleeful celebration of the whales. During the rest of summer, you can whoop it up with the locals at the Emigrant Festival in July when the locals welcome back their family and friends who work abroad and in the first week of September when they celebrate the harvest of the grapes that make their fine Verdelho wine.

Mount Pico rises astonishingly in the center of the island, daring the adventurous to climb its 2,351meter peak. At the top, hikers climb into the 30-meter deep crater or walk around its 700-

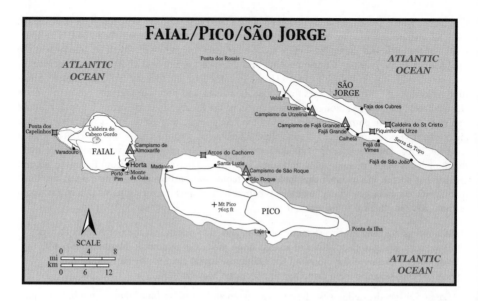

FAIAL/PICO/SÃO JORGE

meter circumference. Fumaroles still steam from its base, an errie reminder that the volcano is not dormant. It's popular to start the hike several hours before dawn in order to reach the summit in time to watch the sun rise. Because of early morning fog, hiring a well-informed guide for a predawn hike not only helps the eco-tourist economy but it makes the seven-plus hour hike troublefree and interesting; make arrangements several days ahead at any of the island's tourist offices. The trail is well marked and easy to follow during the day. Hiking boots are essential and walking sticks are appreciated, as the trail is rough with volcanic rocks. Carry water and energy food. For a less strenuous experience walk through the dramatic Arcos do Cachorro, where the ocean thunders through tunnels and grottos of lava. Directions: Follow signposting on the north side at Santa Lucia, east of Madalena.

Take a ferry over the narrow ocean canal to tiny Faial, an island popular with international yachtsmen crossing the Atlantic. Intricate carvings in fig wood are an island craft and are the highlights in the Museu da Horta collection of nautical memorabilia. Don't miss it; closed Monday. Drive up to the Caldeira do Cabeco Gordo to peer down into the mystical, silent steep-walled crater. A path winds around its rim. Directions: Drive west of Horta on the coast road, following signposting to Varadouro. Just before the town, follow signposting up the mountain for Caldeira. At Vulcao dos Capelinhos, it's easy to imagine what a holocaust looks like. In 1957 and 1958 the area was devastated when a volcano erupted and buried a lighthouse and homes with its molten lava. Directions: Drive west of Horta to the promontory Ponta dos Capelinhos. Drive or hike up to Mount Guia for spectacular views of Faial and Pico then descend to relax on the sandy beach at Porto Paim. In the first week in August Semana do Mar (Sea Week) draws a generous sprinkling of international enthusiasts for an all-around good time highlighted by sailing and kayaking regattas.

▲Camping: • On Pico in Sao Roque. Campismo de Sao Roque do Pico (292-642-422); wonderful setting; basic; open May-Sept; $. • On Faial north of Horta at Praia do Almoxarife. Campismo de Almoxarife (292-292-131); beautiful location on the beach; open May-Sept; $$.

Sao Jorge

Sao Jorge is a quiet haven just waiting to be discovered. Here hikers are richly rewarded with grandiose vistas of billowing grassy pastures that drop sharply to sheer cliffs about which waves thud and collapse. The Serra do Topo trail stretches down from steep mountain slopes to tropical fajas (slopes), where the climate is so tropical passion fruit grows. Parts of the trail are old cobblestone paths along streams that once turned the tiny water mills now hidden in the lush vegetation. It descends into a crater to the remote and beautiful Calderia do St. Cristo lake. From the crater the trail descends down to Faja dos Cubres, a tiny harbor where fishing boats launch. Directions: For a very reasonable fare, friendly taxi cab drivers will pick up passengers from the campground, take them to the trail head, and then pick them up at Faja dos Cubres. By letting a local show you what he is proud of and fill your day with the best the island has to offer you are contributing to eco-tourism. The trail begins northeast of Calheta at Piquinho da Urze and ends at Faja dos Cubres on the north side of the island. For a steep hike with spectacular views, start at the old road at Faja dos Vimes. The trail crosses the Cavalete river, climbing up steeply at first, then moderately before descending to Faja de Sao Jorge, where there are exhilarating views of waterfalls. Then it crosses the Sao Jorge river and continues into the village of Faja de Sao Jorge, where a taxi can be called. Sao Jorge's cheese is savored in fine European markets, so be sure to make it part of your picnics while here.

▲Camping: • North of Calheta at the beach in Faja Grande. Campismo da Faja Grande (295-412-214); beautiful location on a seaside bluff; open June-Sept; $$. • South of Velas at the beach in Urzelina. Campismo da Urzelina (295-414-401); scenic terrace above a rocky shoreline; pool; $$.

Santa Maria

At Santa Maria's Mare do Agosto (August Tide Festival), it's music that counts. The festival takes place during the second week in August at one of the Azores' longest sandy beaches, Praia Formosa. You'll mingle with camping guitarists and vocalists and hear music mixed with the surf's crash under a romantic canopy of stars. Sao Lourenco Bay is considered to be one of the most beautiful bays in the Azorean archipelago. Vineyards here are carefully divided by basalt walls that give a lush checkerboard effect to a half-crater hillside before it reaches the sea.

Santa Maria is the closest island to mainland Portugal and was the first to be settled. The pioneers brought their chimney designs with them from the Algarve and the fine cylindrical forms still rise from pyramidal-bases on whitewashed houses. Fine examples can be seen in the village of Malbusca. Members of Christopher Columbus' West Indies crew landed here and grateful to be home gave thanks in the tiny 15th-century church in Anjosprobably the oldest church on the islands. With only indigenous materials to work with, the islanders have carefully carved the native basalt into lovely designs to decorate their churches. Particularly impressive is the Baroque façade of Nossa Senhora da Purificacao in the village of Santo Espirito. Santa Maria is a small island, so enjoy a few countryside walks between villages.

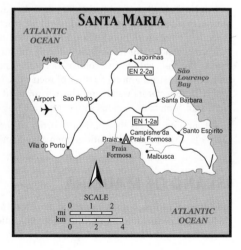

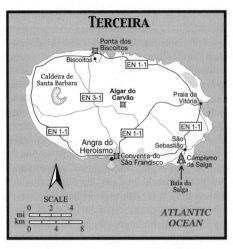

Map labels:
TERCEIRA
Ponta dos Biscoitos
Biscoitos • | EN 1-1
Caldeira de Santa Barbara
EN 3-1 | Algar do Carvão | Praia da Vitória
EN 1-1 | EN 1-1 | EN 1-1
Angra do Heroismo | São Sebastião
Convento do São Francisco | Campismo da Salga
Baía da Salga
SCALE
mi 0 2 4
km 0 4 8
ATLANTIC OCEAN

▲Camping: • At Praia Formosa. Campismo da Praia Formosa (296-882-213); wonderful location at the beach; open May-September; $.

Terceira

Terrorized by an invading force of 16th–century Spaniards, the weaponless islanders here cleverly gathered what they had an enormous herd of cattleand released the mooing creatures on the beach, preventing the Spaniards from landing. Seemingly never tired of being courageous, the islanders have played vital roles in Portugal's civil war and in World War II and today are honored by UNESCO for heroism. Angra do Heroismo's historic area shows off the wealth it once knew when the galleons, heavy with gold from South America, landed for supplies and repairs. After a devastating earthquake in 1980, the UNESCO listing gave the city the support it needed for restoration. Exhibits in the Museu de Angra do Heroismo, housed in the lovely Convento de Sao Francisco, reflect these events; closed Monday. After visiting, step inside the church next door and remember Vasco da Gama's sorrow after his return from his first trip to India, when he laid to rest his brother Paulo.

A huge lava flow on the north side of the island, now only slightly covered by the sea, makes a fun and popular place for a swim. Called Biscoitos (biscuits) because of the pools created by the lava. Wine makers of the fine Biscoitos wine have long felt that foot-pressed grapes produce a finer wine than machine-pressed grapes. In their interesting wine museum you can see the big vats where people danced knee-high in grapes (not an easy task) while the fiddler played.

You won't want to miss stepping inside the dramatic volcanic origins of Terceira at Algar do Carvao. After walking through a long tunnel, you'll peer into a 45 meter–high, moss-covered light well, then walk down into an enormous 100 meter–deep volcanic blast hole. Huge arches of black-and-ochre obsidian decorate the walls and reflect mystically in the pool; open daily. Directions: Midway in the island. Take ER2 out of Angrado Heroism in the direction of Praia da Vitoria and follow signposting for Algar do Carvao. Fumaroles, red-encrusted rocks, and sulphur-scented air compose a surreal world for storytelling and photographs at Furnas do Enxofre. Directions: Follow signposting on ER5 just west of Algar do Carvao.

Terceira is noted for its bulls, and during the summer some of village festivals host a touradas a corda. The bull, with festive colorful decorations on its horns and a long rope around its neck, is set free in the street among a crowd of men. The bravest is left to taunt the bull with a long black umbrella. Spectators watch and cheer from rooftops and sidelines. At the bullring in Angra do Heroismo, a matador and his supporters ride fine horses in a more elegant challenge.

▲Camping: • On the southeast corner of the island at Baia da Salga. Campismo da Salga (295-905-451); beautiful location; open May-Sept; $$.

ISLAND OF MADEIRA

Closer to Morocco than mainland Portugal, Madeira is a jumble of high mountains, steep ravines, and coastal lowlands created from volcanic action. In a voyage financed by Prince Henry the Navigator, the Portuguese explorer Joao Zarco found a warm island abundant in water and heavy with forest that was perfect for growing "white gold," or sugar cane. Slaves were brought from nearby Africa to terrace the hillsides and create the irrigation channels that are still keys to Madeira's prosperity.

Though lacking the sandy beaches and peaceful remoteness of the Azores, Madeira has a charm of its own. Often shrouded by rain forest-like foliage, Madeira's levadas (irrigation channels) have trails alongside them that provide exhilarating walks of great beauty. Directions: Drive west from Funchal on 101, passing through the long coastal tunnel following signposting to Ribeira Brava. If you don't mind driving on a narrow road clinging precipitously above the ocean and through dark, one-way tunnels, turn north onto 104 and climb up the terraced mountainside. Bougainvillea drips prettily from whitewashed villas, and banana trees grow wild here. Stop at the vista point at the top for a terrific panoramic view then descend down the winding forested road to Sao Vicente and the sea. Turn west onto 101, where the narrow rock-hewn road clings just above the sea. Continue for 53 kilometers out to Porto Moniz, where the island's campground is located and where there are trailheads for levada walks. If you prefer to avoid the narrow coastal road to the campground drive west from Riberia Brava on 101 for 12 kilometers to 209. Turn north onto 209, and climb up the mountain for eleven kilometers to 110. Turn west and follow the high plateau road for 23 kilometers through the Paul da Serra and Parque Natural da Madeira, and then descend down the mountain to 101. Turn north and drive seven kilometers on 101 to Porto Moniz.

▲Camping: • In Porto Moniz. Camara Municipal de Porto Moniz (091-85-3447); excellent location close to natural rock swimming pools; small; popular with international travelers; open May-Sept; $$.

One of the most popular walks is from Rabacal on the Paul da Serra plateau to the waterfalls of Risco and 25 Fontes, a less than 2-hour round-trip hike. From the harsh plateau, the trail descends to a rain forest-like habitat of mosses, ferns, and streams. Directions: From camping in Porto Moniz, drive south on 101 for 7km to the fork for 110. Turn onto 110 and drive 17km to Rabacal. Park in the lot at the viewing and picnic area. Follow the signposted trail to Levada do Risco and

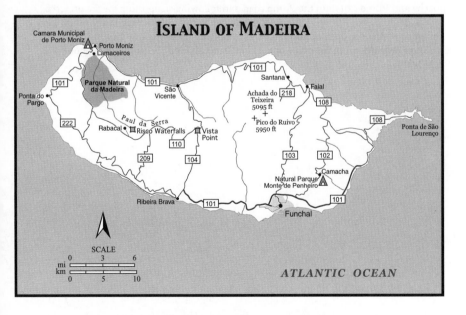

descend 100 meters. Enjoy the cascade originating from the tiny Lagoa do Vento, then return on the same trail. Then before you reach the parking lot, follow signposting north for Levada das 25 Fontes. When you come to the levada, walk in the opposite direction of the flow of water to a pond and the cascades of 25 Fontes.

Waterfalls, maiden-hair ferns, and miniature begonias shroud the rocky cliffs, forests whisper with laurel and oak leaves, and dark tunnels smell musty on the Fonte do Galhano levada walk. Most people can stand up straight in the tunnels and don't feel nervous after the first one. The tunnels are wide and the levada wall is knee-high. A flashlight or headlamp are essential. Many of the tunnels are short, less than 100 meters; two are 200 meters. At times you'll be in complete darkness except for your flashlight. The tunnels are clean and free of flora and fauna. Round trip the hike takes four to six-hours. Bring a waterproof jacket for changeable weather, energy food, and water. Directions: From camping in Porto Moniz, drive one kilometer up the hill to the village square, mercado, and bank. Continue up the hill for three kilometers more, following signposting for Lamaceiros. At the flower-planted divider strip, turn east continuing to following signposting for Lamaceiros. Drive through the village. At the fork and signposting for Porto Moniz, turn away from Porto Moniz and drive to the reservoir station in the forest and park. The trailhead is across the road from the station's office building.

Hiking in central Madeira is highlighted by the ascent to Pico do Ruivo, where the views over the rugged rocky landscape and down into the narrow river gorge are superb. Ethereal clouds and the rising sun make for heavenly scenes at sunrise. Directions: From Funchal, drive north on 103 for 28km to Faial. Turn north on 108 and drive 6km to Santana. Turn inland and drive up the mountain on R218 for 7km to Achada do Teixeira. Park at the trailhead. Include a waterproof jacket for changeable weather, water, and energy food in you daypack, and wear rubber-soled shoes. Follow the well-marked trailhead 3km to Pico do Ruivo. To extend the hike continue along the backbone of the mountain, where you'll have a choice of trails descending and then ascending in several directions.

▲Camping: • South of Camacha at the preserve at Monte de Penheiro. Directions: East of Funchal exit 101 north onto 102 following signposting for Camacha. At the fork for Camacha and Pismo exit onto the Pismo road and following signposting for the preserve at Monte de Penheiro. Natural Parque Monte de Penheiro; lovely setting in the pines; used for outdoor education; open all year; $$. • • (Important note: To camp here you must have permission procured from the office of parks in Funchal: fax 351-291-203-803 phone 351-291-232-014.)

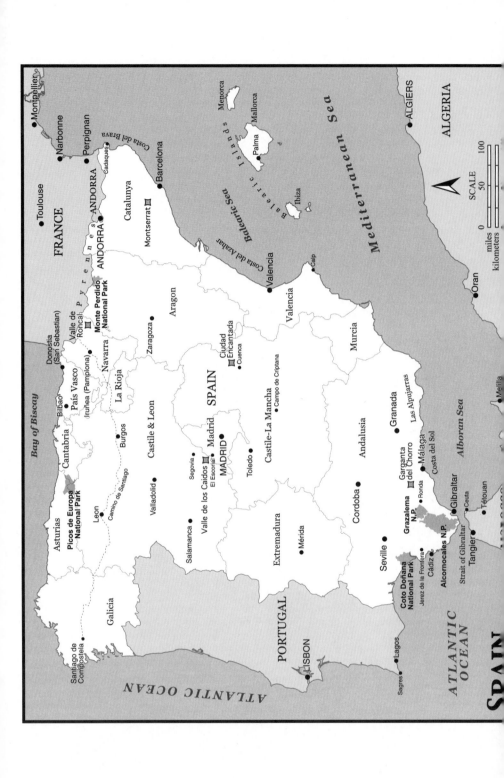

SPAIN

Spain

www.visitspain.com

Nothing is more important to a Spaniard than his roots and native region. It is this regionalism that gives Spain its unique character. To experience it, you must get off the beaten track. Every town is a center of intense social and political life, with the plaza mayor as heart and core. Cool, leafy, and delectable with plenty of benches these plazas are where you go to enjoy the human rhythm of the locals. Spend some time in them. Every evening, people take a *paseo* (stroll) around their town's most beautiful area. It's a ritual not to be missed. In the morning and evening church bells clang with purpose, rousing and summoning rather then chiming for pleasure. At dusk in the villages, lambs and goats bleat, dogs bark, and children's voices ring out in play. To Spaniards, the pleasures of eating, drinking, and conversation are foremost. *Tapas* (appetizers) are an integral part of the Spanish cuisine. In the evening bars proudly display these specialties, often so prized that they are almost an art form. The custom is to move from one bar to another, sampling them. It's easy to make a meal of them. Spain is a romantic, erotic country, where poetry speaking of tragedy, desperation, and betrayal are prized. Music has a subtle rhythm and beat provided by clapping hands and stamping feet and dancers lock eyes and theatrically move in rhythmical courtship.

Spain is experiencing a cultural renaissance. The country is being transformed with cutting-edge museums and innovative performing arts spaces. As a country, it has shifted from isolation to a place on the world's main stage. Its warm weather, beautiful beaches, savage mountain terrain, dramatic architecture, exciting art, fabulous cuisine, and lively street life, have made it one of the world's most popular vacation destinations. Europeans longing for sun have packed their camping gear and headed south to Spain for many years. Campgrounds abound. Some are resort-like, while others are simple grassy areas with a few shade trees. Often a swimming pool, small store, simple cafe, common terrace, and hot showers are part of the well-maintained campgrounds listed. A tent, car, and two persons will usually cost around 20 euros and are indicated in this guide by $$. Resort-like campgrounds or ones that are close to major tourist sights will be closer to 25 euros.

Every town and village has a patron saint to honor, a date to celebrate, or a tradition to maintain. Spaniards love a party and like to invent new ways to enhance the older traditions. There always is a parade, fireworks, guitar music, dancing, and copious amounts of eating and drinking. Sleepy villages awake with vigor. It's exhilarating to have a journey coincide with such enthusiastic celebrations. Finding the obscure and unexpected ones can be just as much fun as the more well known and organized.

Driving in Spain is not difficult. Massive expansion has added over 3,000 autostrata kilometers. Many autostratas are toll-free and have pleasant rest areas with gas stations and cafes. International signage is used and signs are well posted. In tourist towns, reasonably priced parking is often provided underground. Look near the shopping area. Mountain roads are in good condition but are usually two-lane and winding. A continuous white line on the right side of the road indicates a lane intended primarily for pedestrians and cyclists. It also indicates no stopping for vehicles except for emergencies. The police are diligent, and visitors must pay fines immediately. Charge cards are acceptable for on the spot payment. In major cities, leave your car at the campground and take public transport to the city. Your best source of information about this will be your fellow campers, who know the important details that campground staff sometimes forgets to mention.

Except in remote areas, cash machines are easy to find and use. Gas cost is similar to the rest of Europe, and supplies cost what you are used to paying at home. Some major museums and sights no longer close for the traditional long lunch and rest. But most still do, allowing you to enjoy them in the early evening. Spaniards are friendly, easy to be around, and want to make your stay and visit as pleasurable as possible. They enjoy a good time and want you to have one, too. However remember the old Spanish proverb, "It's beautiful to do nothing and then rest afterwards." They have mastered the art of waiting.

MADRID

Buzzing, vibrant, and alluring Madrid is now firmly a 21st-century city without sacrificing its past. Some like to start their visit at the Puerto del Sol because it is the city's absolute center, with a *kilometro cero* plaque in the sidewalk. It's as well a meeting place and the location of Madrid's famous bear, and symbol, within a lovely fountain. Directions: Metro Sol. Others begin at Plaza Mayor, a masterpiece of Renaissance architecture built by the Hapsburgs when Spain was at its height of power. Painted in glorious Baroque vermilion, the plaza has witnessed practically every imaginable human spectacle from public executions and Inquisition trials to royal weddings and ballet performances. Now it is surprisingly quiet and restful. Directions: Metro Sol, then walk west on Calle Mayor. But I like to start at Retiro Park, where I can join the promenade of *Madrilenos* (locals) along its tree-lined walkways, laugh with kids at a puppet show, and drop some coins in the "living" statue's box so the gold-glazed figure will turn slowly to bow and wink. Directions: Metro Reterio. After absorbing the ambiance here, I am ready to tackle the bigger stuff and make a stop at the tourist office on the southwest corner of the Plaza Mayor.

Madrid is a royal city with refined tastes. The golden triangle of art–the Prado, the Thyssen-Bornemisza, and the Reina Sofia–has undergone extensive renovation. The museums are now connected by the Paseo del Arte, similar to Washington DC.'s Mall, and it's a ten minute walk from one end to the other. Reina Sofia's stunning new public atrium, by French architect Jean Nouvel, is all steel and glass with walls covered in what looks like scarlet patent leather. Its single most important work is Picasso's stupefying mural-size *Guernica*, considered to be one of the most powerful antiwar statements ever made. The Reina Sofia is a museum/cultural center whose collection concentrates on 20th-century art; closed Tuesday. Directions: Metro Atocha.

At the Prado, Madrid's most famous museum, Goya's powerful and famous black paintings are startling. Heavy with symbolism, they are considered to be among his finest and most enigmatic. View them, but then seek out the more evocative ones he painted in France. His portraits are free of fawning flattery and treat beauty with sensitivity, respect, and psychological insight. Spend some time scrutinizing Velazquez's powerful portraits of weavers and blacksmiths as well as his complex masterpiece *Las Meninas*. Don't leave the museum without smiling at the eccentric pleasures seen in Hieronymus Bosch's *Garden of Delights*. The museum boasts not only the largest collection of Titians, but important works by Raphael, Correggio, and van der Weyden. Don't try to see the entire museum. Use a guidebook to seek out what interests you most; closed Monday. Directions: Metro Banco de Espana, then walk south along the Paseo del Prado.

The stunning Museo Thyssen-Bornemisza Collection, which Madrid acquired in 1993, has completed an addition of six new graceful galleries filled with their remarkable collection spanning art his-

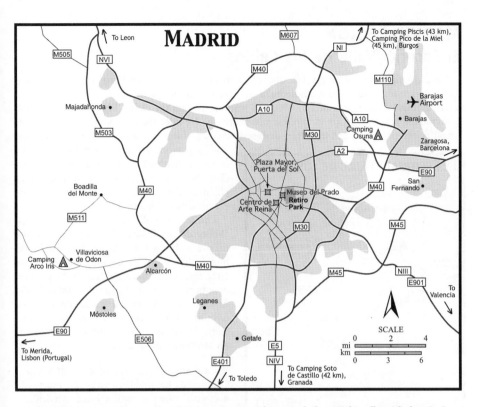

tory from Renaissance giants to French Impressionists. It's particularly user-friendly, with descriptions in English; closed Monday. Directions: Across the plaza from the Prado, on the northwest corner.

In the evening, nibble tapas with *Madrilenos* at a sidewalk table around the Plaza Ana and it's spiderweb-like neighborhood. You'll imbibe a Madrid distillation watching apartment dwellers walk their dogs, intense university students in excited debates, and old and young walking slowly hand in hand. Directions: Metro Sol, then walk south on Calle Carretas, then east on Calle de la Bolsa.

▲**Camping**: • Close to the airport. 8km east of the city, exit off N-11 at km. 8.3 in the direction of Barajas and follow signposting west of the railroad tracks. Camping Osuna (917 41-05); older; little grass or shade; noisy; metro to city center; open all year; $$$. • 20km southwest of the Madrid. Exit Madrid's ring road M40 at exit 36, and drive west on 511 in the direction of Boadilla del Monte to km 7.8. Follow the road south in the direction Villaviciosa de Odon to km 12. Camping Arco Iris (916 16 0387); resort-like; parking separate from tent; pool; tennis; some shade; bus or train to Madrid nearby; open all year; $$$. • 43km north of Madrid in Navalafuente. Exit N1/E5 at exit#50 for Guadalix de la Sierra and follow signposting for the village of Navalafuente. Camping Piscis (918 43 2253); scenic views; bus to Madrid nearby; pool; popular with families; June-mid-Sept; $$. • In the same area but on the east side of N1/E5 in the town of La Cabrera. Exit N1/E5 at exit#57 La Cabrera, and follow signposting. Camping Pico de la Miel (918 68 8082); resort-like; cabins; close to a lake; popular with families; open all year; $$$. • 42km south of Madrid along the Rio Tajo in Aranjuez. From NIV exit onto M305 in the direction of Aranjuez. In town drive east along the south side of the river. Camping Soto del Castillo (918 91 1395); shady; pool; bike rental; train to Madrid; cabins; open all year; $$.

MADRID REGION
El Escorial/Valle de los Caidos

Built as a place to bury the royal families of Spain, El Escorial is a forbidding, lonely monument to royal excesses. The royal mausoleum, a monastery, and an enormous church were finished after 22 years of labor provided by 300 men working around the clock. Phillip II watched the construction from chair carved into the mountainside. He filled the great library with priceless manuscripts, paintings, and tapestries designed by Goya. Later, sick and dying, he spent hours watching services from a tiny room off the choir, his diseased leg propped up on a specially built chair; closed Monday. Directions: 60km northwest of Madrid. Follow signposting off either M505 or NVI.

The best part of visiting *Valle de los Caidos* (Valley of the Fallen) Franco's monumental tribute to himself and those that fought for him–is the view of the countryside. The giant cross and church were constructed by political prisoners who died blasting the vast cave-like basilica out of the granite mountain and then erecting an impossibly tall stone cross; open daily. Directions: 9km north east of Escorial on M600 just off NVI.

▲Camping: • 3km south of town off M600. Camping El Escorial (918 90 2412) resort-like; shade canopies; cabins; bus to Madrid; open all year; $$$.

Segovia

Viewed in front of the orange and gold explosion of a Spanish sunset, the giant, double-decker, unmortared stone arches of Segovia's 1st-century Roman acqueduct are breathtakingly, dramatic. Towering 30 meters above the Plaza de Azoguejo and reaching an expanse of 800 meters are 123 arches, the acquaduct brought water from 15 kilometers away. It was an incredible engineering feat for its day. Directions: Southeast corner of the town; follow signposting from major roadways. In Spain, dazzling altarpieces fanning out joyfully in an orgy of gold often offsets somber Romanesque cathedral exteriors. Sometimes the Mudejar elements are firmly embedded in the architecture, with finely carved geometric patterns interlaced with figures of saints and plant motifs. In Segovia, you'll see this florid and fanciful construction in both the Alcazar and Cathedral; open daily. Directions: At the northwest end of town; follow signposting inside the ancient walls.

▲Camping: • Southeast of the city. At the intersection of N603 and CL601 drive east in the direction of La Granja/San Ildefonso for 3km. Camping Acueducto (921 42 5000); shady; pool; small; bike rental; bus to town nearby; open April-September; $$.

Salamanca

Graceful and harmonious like San Marco's in Venice, the Plaza Mayor in Salamanca is etched with shady *paseos* (arcades), along buildings that glow with amber beauty in the setting sun. Take time to study the intricacies of the plaza's accents, balconies, and facades. Along with the universities in Bologna, Paris, and Oxford, the university in Salamanca was one of the finest in the medieval world. When you walk through the library and cloisters, it's easy to imagine scholars long ago discussing revolutionary new ideas; open daily until 1 PM. For panoramic views of the countryside climb the Torre Mocha to its outside platform.

▲Camping: • Just east of the city in the suburb of Santa Marta de Tormes. Exit east from Salamanca on N501 in the direction of Avila for 4km. At round-about exit for Santa Marta de Tormes and following signposting for Hotel Regio. Camping Regio (923-130-888); part of a Hotel Regio; shady; pool; open all year; $$.
• 23km south of the city on C510 in the town of Alba de Tormes follow signposting one kilometer south of town. Camping Tormes (923-160-998); pleasant setting close to the river; little shade; open all year; $$.
• 3km northwest of Salamanca in the suburb of Villamayor. At the interestion of N620 and SA300 drive northwest one kilometer in the direction of Ledesma to Villamayor and follow signposting. Camping Ruta de la Plata (923 28 9574); small; pool; pleasant; open all year; $$.

Leon

From mammoth stained-glass windows, a kaleiscope of brillant red and gold hues dance on the somber stone walls in Leon's Gothic cathedral. You'll swear there is more glass than stone; open daily. Directions: East end of the historic area; follow signposting from all major roadways.

▲Camping: • 5km southeast of Leon in the village of Golpejar o Sobarriba. On N601 exit southeast of Leon in the direction of Valladolid and drive 5km following signposting east for Golpejar o Sobarriba. Camping Ciudad de Leon (987 68 0233); small; pleasant; bike rental; pool; open June-Sept; $$. • 25km southeast of Leon in the village of Mansilla de las Mulas. Drive southeast of Leon on N601. Exit west onto N625 at km 310 in the direction of Mansilla de las Mulas and follow signposting. Camping Esla (987 31 0089); small; pleasant; open July-Sept; $$. • 34km south of Leon on N630 exit east onto 621 and drive 8km towards Valencia de Don Juan. Camping Pico Verde (987-750-525); pleasant; some shade; open June-September; $$.

▲Enroute Camping
Between Burgos and Leon • 45km southeast of Leon on N120 in Sahagun follow signposting. Camping Pedro Ponce (987 78 1112); pool close by; some shade; open April-Sept; $$.
Between Burgos and Madrid • In Aranda de Duero. Follow signposting north of the city off N1 at km. 162. Camping Costajan (947 50 2070); nice natural setting with pool and shade trees; open all year; $$.

Burgos

Burgos provides a nice stopping place between more famous destinations. Its gigantic Gothic cathedral boasts two immense spires decorated richly in a florid fantasy; open daily. The pedestrian plaza in front of the cathedral is a good place to relax in the sun or shade.

▲**Camping:** • 2km southeast of town on the river. At the intersection of N120 and N623
exit southeast for Caballeria and Cartuja Miraflores. Follow signposting on the south side of
the river. Camping Municipal Fuentes Blancas (947 48 6016); pleasant setting on the river;
pool; large; open April-Sept; $$.

Toledo

As you approach Toledo, the town walls, rooftops, imposing Moorish Alcazar, and 100-meter
spire of its Gothic Cathedral rise sharply above the bridge over the Tagus River. It is famous as El
Greco's home. Born in Crete in the mid-1500s, El Greco traveled to Italy and studied the works
of the great Renaissance masters with Titian. He came to Toledo in his mid-30s in hopes of large
commissions from Phillip II that didn't materialize. Having rejected the Renaissance concepts of
perspective and proportion, he was unencumbered by patronage and free to develop his own style
of loose brushstrokes and sharp contrasts of light and shadow. In Santo Tome Church you can
view his masterpiece, *Burial of the Count of Orgaz*, open daily. Though his best works are in the
collections of museums throughout Europe and the USA, a large collection of his work is at Casa
del Greco; closed Tuesday. His real home, where he lived with his mistress and mother of his son,
was a large apartment in a friend's mansion once located in the Juderia where the park, Paseo del
Transito is today.

Across from the park, visit the Synagogoa del Transito. Built with the town's Moorish heritage
in mind, Hebrew inscriptions decorate the walls, and artifacts of Jewish life in Spain are displayed;
closed Monday. A few steps away in the Santa Maria La Blanc, which was once the city's oldest
synagogue and later became a church, you'll see to mosque-like rows of columns in a quiet cor-
ridor.

In the Cathedral off the Plaza Mayor, examine the carved choir stalls telling the story of the
Christian conquest of Granada from the Moors. Then look at the Cathedral's high altar, which
soars in such a great fantasy that you are left dazed by the orgy of gold; closed Sunday morning.
The windows of the Alcazar provide fine views of town, and photos from the two-month siege in
1936, when the Nationals occupied the Alcazar, are displayed; closed Monday.

In the late afternoon, when day-tripping tourists have left, locals come out for some convivial-
ity with their neighbors at Plaza de Zocodover–making it a great place to see a little of the real
Toledo. The Museum de Santa Cruz, down from the eastern side of the square, houses several El
Greco masterpieces, works by Goya and Riberia, and a large collection of rugs and tapestries; open
daily. In the early evening, drive up the hill high above the gorge of the Tagus to view tiny Toledo,
suspended on a rock above the river and glowing in the fiery orange light of sunset. It could be
your most lasting memory of the town.

▲**Camping:** • On the west side of Toledo. Drive west of town in the direction of Pueblo de
Montalban on 502. Cross the bridge over the Tagus, and follow signposting for less than a
kilometer. Camping El Greco (925 22 0090); lovely setting; pool; bus to historic area; small
store and café; open all year; $$$. • Exit 401 8km north of Toledo for the town of Olias
del Rey, and follow signposting up the hill. Camping Toledo (925 35 3013); use if El Greco
camping is full; convenient to 401; bus to Toledo; open May-Sept; $$.

Cuenca

High up from the plains on a broad, flat plateau perched above two rivers, Old Cuenca still
clings to the edge of almost vertical cliffs. The famous Hanging Houses, an intriguing complex of
buildings that cantilever precariously out over the river valley, now are home to the well-known
Museum of Abstract Art and its collection of the best of Spanish abstract artists; closed Monday.
Narrow streets lead through tunneled passageways to treacherous flights of stairs. Not far from the

Hanging Houses, the Archeological Museum displays a collection of Roman statuary plus paintings of the people who once lived in Old Cuenca. You'll find parking close to the cathedral and square. Directions: 70km southeast of Madrid on E901, exit east onto N400 at Tarancon and drive 84km.

▲**Camping:** • Exit north of town into the Jucar Gorge and the limestone park Cuidad Encantada on CU921, and drive 6km. Camping Cuenca (969 23 1656); pleasant; pool; some shade; cabins; mid-March-Sept; $$.

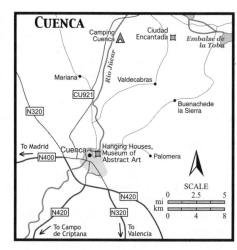

La Mancha and the Windmills of Don Quixote

A few white windmills made famous by Cervantes' romantic hero, the indomitable Don Quixote, still stand like flailing giants in the village of Campo de la Criptana in the La Mancha region southeast of Toledo. Once an area devoid of shade and water, today it is a vast flat land of fields filled with wheat, corn, and vines. Stop in the nondescript little town's park to eat your picnic lunch. As you rest, you'll see a classic Spanish scene: old men intense in a game of *boule*, women dutifully sweeping the sidewalk, and dogs sleeping in the shade. Directions: 68km southeast of Toledo on 400, at the junction of 400 and E05 at Madridejos, drive east 30km on 400 to Alcazar. Outside of town exit east onto 420 and drive 7km to Campo de Criptana.

Cordoba

With great Moslem zeal, Emir Abderrahman I began in 785 the construction of what he hoped would be a mosque rivaling any in Arabia. Today the Mezquita still stands as one of the greatest Moorish monuments in the world. A crew of skilled craftsmen and 16 tons of small pieces of glass for the mosaics were provided by the Christian Emperor in Constantinople. Columns were brought from the ruins of Roman and Visigoth buildings. Varying in height, some columns had to be placed deeper in the ground and others raised. Resting on the top of each row of pillars, a tier of horseshoe arches was built and atop this a second tier, forming an intertwining of branches as in a forest. As the population of the city grew, the mosque was expanded, and 200 years later it was double the original size. The many doors of the mosque opened out into a large patio, letting light filter into the vast space. Among the few ornaments in the patio were oranges trees whose blossoms perfumed the air, a slender *minaret* (prayer tower) where devotees were called to prayer, and a lovely fountain where they cleansed themselves before praying. The

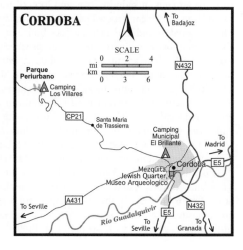

mihrab (prayer niche) was octagonally covered by a domecarved from a huge block of marble and is resplendent with intricate carvings. Once, an enormous bejeweled Koran lay on an altar of ivory and precious wood. Perfumed oil was lit in 300 candelabras, some of whose lamps were made from bells stolen from the Santiago shrine in 997. When the Christians conquered Cordoba in 1236, most of the doorways were filled in, and in the 16th-century, to the protest of local citizenry, a large choir was built in the center; open daily. Directions: On the west side of Rio Guadalquivir. Follow signposting from E/5 for Central Cuidad. Park on the east side of the river, by the small Arab fortress, and walk across the bridge to the Mezquita.

After visiting the Mezquita walk west into the *Juderia* (Jewish quarter) where whitewashed houses line quiet back streets. Seek out the small statue of Maimonides, considered by many to be one of the foremost Jewish thinkers. Born in Cordoba, he lived close to where the statue is tucked. Peek into tiny courtyards, where patio floors are paved with pebbles in pleasing designs and flower pots drip with the tendrils of sweet-smelling jasmine vines. At 12 Judios Street, stop at the Cordoban House Museum to get a sense of the 12th-century charm evident in its tranquil patio, fountain, and furniture. Next to the *Zoco* (craft center) you can look at bullfighting memoribilia in Museo Taurino. Outside the Puerta de Almodovar stands a statue of the philosopher Seneca. Born in Cordoba in 4 BC, his philosophy has been an important influence in Spanish thought. Directions: North end of the Juderia. The Museo Arqueologico houses its collection of artifacts from Iberian, Roman, Islamic, and early Christian eras amid the ferns and shady courtyards of a Renaissance mansion; closed Monday. Directions: Walk northeast out of the Mezquita.

▲**Camping:** • In Cordoba. Exit E5 for Mezquita. Cross the river passing the Mezquita and old town on the south side. Drive north on the main boulevard following signposting for Parador. The road changes its name as it threads its way through town. At the Plaza de Colon turn north onto Brillante and drive one kilometer. Camping Municipal El Brillante (957-282-165); popular with international travelers; pool, small store; bus to the historic area; open all year; $$. • In Parque Periurbano, a nature center. Follow the directions for El Brillante, but continue 500 meters farther. Turn east onto San Jose de Calasanz, following signposting for Los Villares. Continue up the hill for 8km. Camping Los Villares (957-453-211); natural setting under the pines; spacious sites; interpretive center; covered terrace; open May-Sept; $$.

Seville

Under starlit skies, warm breezes mingle with the notes of a quavering guitar and a voice deep with the laments of sadness, love, and loss–all poignant reminders of ancient Seville when the Moors from Africa constructed palaces, dykes, quays, and towers that were marvels of engineering. They repaired the old Roman acqueduct, built a bridge over the Guadalquivir, walled the river, and constructed towers to guard the city. Ships traveled up the river, and Seville became the emporium of the Mediterranean. Their fabulous *alcazar* (palace) and mosque vied in splendor with the mosque in Cordoba. On the imperial tower Giralda, four immense spheres proclaimed greatness. The city's intellectual pursuits gave it unquestioned leadership in the medieval world.

Reminiscent of the Levant the Mediterranean climate, dry mountain terrain, and olive tree groves attracted Jews. They flourished under the Moorish rule, holding important positions as emissaries and ambassadors among the various Moorish kingdoms. Many of the caliphs had Jewish physicians, and Jewish scholars refined the courts. Seville was noble and rich, replete with every comfort and luxury, and a rendezvous for scholars and artists

This was the city that Ferdinand III, the Saint, surrounded with his immense army in 1247. They burned houses, destroyed orchards, trampled harvests, and tore out vineyards. The siege lasted for 16 months. In the end, hunger and despair caused the inhabitants to surrender. The great mosque of Seville was torn down, but the Giralda was left standing because it was so beautiful. Inside, you can walk up the ramp built to allow mounted passage to the bell tower for great views; open daily. On the site of the mosque, an enormous cathedral was built with a special chapel for Ferdinand III. He lies enshrined there in a massive silver casket, near his son, Alfonso X the Learned, one of the great rulers of medieval times. The cathedral is the third largest in Europe; open daily. Only a small portion of the original *alcazar*, next to the cathedral, remains. Various rulers have added and changed the palace to suit their taste, but the *Mudejar* art remains highly colored and imaginative. In apartments used by the navigators there is a model of the Santa Maria, the ship used by Columbus, and the famous painting *Virgin of the Navigators*; closed Monday. Grand, well-planned gardens adjoin the palace, and a small passageway leads to the shady miniscule squares and streets of the Santa Cruz district.

An outstanding collection of the sensitive paintings by Zubaran and El Greco's portrait of his son can both be viewed at the Museo de Bellas Artes; closed Monday. Directions: North of the historic area, east of the river and the Plaza de Armes bus station. Community celebrations are at the heart of Spanish culture and, whether they celebrate a saint or a season, are immersed in ritual. With almost everyone participating, the shared experience binds the community together. Around Easter, Seville celebrates Semana Santa and Feris de Abril with an Andalucian brilliance. Experiencing even a part of either of them brings lasting memories. Because of the extraordinary color of the sand and the proportions of the ring itself, the *Maestranza*, Seville's *Plaza de Toros* (bullring), is probably the most handsome in Spain. Some of the most famous events in bullfighting have taken place here. Arranging for tickets for an event is difficult and expensive, but it's easy to tour the museum; closed Sunday. Directions: West of the cathedral, along the Guadalquivir.

Italicia, a 3rd-century Roman town, was the birthplace of three emperors: Trajan, Hadrian, and Theodosius. At this archeological site, use your imagination to see 40,000 people in the grand amphitheater and take note of the fanciful birds in the mosaics. Directions: Exit the northwest corner of the Seville onto E803, and drive north for 8km through the village of Santiponce following signposting.

▲**Camping:** These two in the suburb of Dos Hermanas are nicer for visiting Seville than those closer to the city. Consider leaving your car at the campground and take the bus ride the city. 12km south of the city in the suburb of Dos Hermanas. Exit A4/E5 at km 555 and drive east 3km. • Just before the bridge. Camping Villsom (954 72 0828); large; pool; open all year; $$. • Across from the roundabout in the center of town. Camping Club de Camp (954 72 0205); large pool; close to the bus for Seville; older; open all year; $$.

CADIZ AND AROUND
Coto Donana National Park

This mobile sand desert of marshes, dunes, and shallow waterways close to Africa, is one of Europe's most important nesting areas for migrating birds. Seasonal flooding during late autumn and winter provides extensive *marismas* (areas of shallow water) where almost half a million birds can be present. These *marismas* gradually dry out during spring and summer, leaving pools and

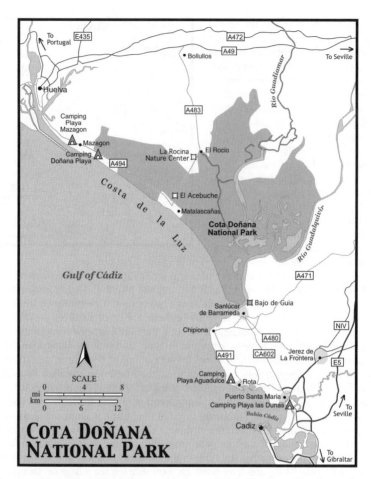

COTA DOÑANA
NATIONAL PARK

mud that are rich source of food. Warm weather and rich-silted marshlands continue to make a paradise for the masses of migrating birds. Fragile flamingoes bow their long necks, relishing the algae-rich soup. Herons and egrets watch silently for a passing fish and launch, as if from a spring-board, when disturbed. Long-billed stilts bow and preen in courtship rituals. Spoonbills nest in cork oaks. Visitor centers and obligatory guided tours enhance your study of this UNESCO World Heritage biosphere.

Serious birders will want to spend their time around the visitor center at El Acebuche, 5 kilometers north of Matalascanas. Consider a guided tour 959-448-711. The visitor center also has daily overland tours by Land Rover and horseback. The birding is excellent and free from the bridge on C435 in El Rocio and at Coto del Rey. A nature trail begins at the La Rocina nature center. Directions: From Seville drive west on A49 for 50km to Bollullos. Take exit 10 onto 493 and drive south 34km in the direction of Matalascanas and the beach. The visitor center is signposted El Acebuche 5km north of Matalascanas on 493.

▲Camping: • 23km north of Matalascanas on the beach road in Torre del Oro. Camping Donana Playa (959 53 6281); large; some shade; pool; store; café; tennis; open all year; $$$.
• 6km farther north in Mazagon. • Camping Playa Mazagon (959 37 6208); large; popular with families; pool; store; café; open all year; $$.

A four-hour boat ride up into the park's marshland, with several stops for bird-and-animal watching and a look into the simple fishermen homes constructed from indigenous materials, makes a nice outing. Binoculars can be rented on board. The boat launches from the Bajo de Guia quay at the southwest end of the park in Sanlucar, across from the interpretive center. It operates daily in the morning and afternoon. Directions: From Seville drive south on A/4 for 85 kilometers. Take exit 4 off A4 and drive west 4km to Jerez de la Frontera. Follow signposting through town for Sanlucar/480, continuing for 24km. At the football field in Sanlucar drive north on the main road, staying north until reaching the Bajo de Guia.

Jerez de la Frontera/Flamenco

The art of flamenco flowered and bloomed best in the towns with a large population of gypsies. Eccentric, bohemian, and heartrending, the music in its purest form is elusive to the outsider. Visit the Centro Andaluz de Flamenco, which preserves and promotes the rich literary-musical background of flamenco with archives of recordings, books, videos, and photographs. Staff can recommend *penas flamencas* where you can experience good *cante* (song); open weekdays 9 AM to 2 PM; free. Directions: In Jerez de la Frontera at Plaza de San Juan in the elegant Palacio Pemartin. Take exit 4 off A4 onto 382 and drive east towards the centrum.

Cadiz

Zurbaran's essays of light, color, and texture are particularly powerful in his paintings of the Carthusian monks. Calling himself the painter of imagination, his textural work is masterful. The Museo de Belle Artes houses an exceptional collection of his work; closed Monday. Directions: Northwest end of the town at Plaza de Mina. Take exit 6 off A4 and drive west following signposting for the port, then continue north passing the Plaza de Espana. Turn south at the waterfront and follow signposting for tourist information. Park, and walk to Plaza de Mina. Beautiful parkways line the water at Bahia Cadiz, so take a leisurely stroll and indulge in freshly fried fish from one of the stands.

▲**Camping in the Area:** • On the beach west of Jerez de la Frontera in Rota at Punta Candor. Drive north of Rota of El Puerto on 491, following signposting for Rota. Turn onto beach road 604, following signposting for Punta Candor. Camping Playa Aguadulce (956 84 7078); by the beach; popular; open April-Sept; $$. • In the same area. Camping Punta Candor (956 81 3303); large; sunshades; close to the beach; cabins; open all year; $$. In Puerto de Santa Maria, two kilometers south of the marina and Puerto Sherry resort. Camping Playa las Dunas (956-87 2210); large; popular; next to a park with playground and pool; close to beach; open April-Oct; $$.

Ronda/Parques Natural de los Alcornocales and Grazalema

It is the extraordinary high, angular limestone setting of the isolated, *puebloes blanco* that is so captivating in this region. Once Moorish the homes were painted white to reflect the hot sun. Cherry orchards and long rows of grape vines embellish their wild mountain beauty. Sitting atop a narrow gorge whose sheer walls drop down 130 meters on three sides, Ronda is probably the most dramatic and memorable of the villages. Here a path from the Plaza Maria Auxiliadora leads down to the bottom and the Guadalevin River. Take your camera, because the view of the immense arched 18th-century bridge, the Puente Nuevo, is especially photogenic here. Bring binoculars too because from either the bridge or from along the walking trail you'll have a chance to see lesser kestrels, a small colorful falcon, as well as alpine and pallid swifts and purple martins

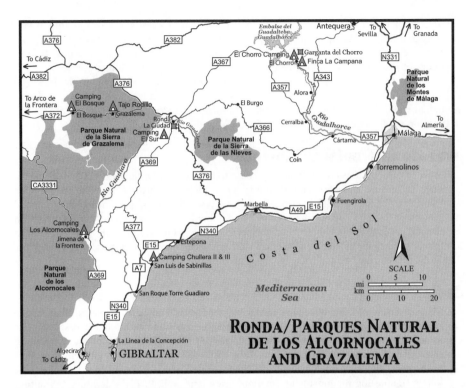

RONDA/PARQUES NATURAL
DE LOS ALCORNOCALES
AND GRAZALEMA

that nest in the small cavities of the cliff-face. The best tourist office for the whole region is nearby at the Plaza de Espana. Stop by for maps and advice on the great walks in the area–including in Parque Natural de los Alcornocabes and Grazalema–and news on local festivals. During the second half of July a week long international music festival of note takes place in nearby Jimena de la Frontera. It features classical, folk, jazz and flamenco music. www.jimenafestival.com On the south side of the bridge, La Ciudad is a maze of little alleyways some with wonderful views. At the north end is the stately Palacio del Marques de Salvatierra and to the east of it is a path down the hillside to the beautifully preserved cupolas and intricate glass windows of *Banos Arabes* (public baths); closed Monday.

Over several generations, the highly talented Romero family developed classic bullfighting traditions. Francisco Romero started using the cape in the 17th-century. His son, Juan, introduced the use of a matador support team. His grandson, Pedro Romero, perfected the classic technique and became one of Spain's all-time great matadors. Looking at Pedro's original bullfighting attire in the Museo Taurino and seeing the historic bullring where they all fought is a thrill for aficionados. Photos of Ernest Hemingway and Orson Wells intently watching the spectacle are also in the museum's collection; open daily. Directions: The Plaza de Toros is well signposted from all roadways. Directions: Exit E5/E340 10km north of Algerciras onto A369 and drive north 90km.

▲**Camping:** • Exit Ronda from A369 on the southwest side, following signposting for 2km. Camping El Sur (952 87-59-39); nice shady location; pool; popular with international travelers; small store; open all year; $$. • 31km north of Algeciras just outside of tiny village of Jimena de la Frontera. Follow signposting from A369 on the north side of town. Camping Los Alcornocales (956 64 00 60); on a small hill with views; terraced; restaurant; bike rental; open April-Sept; $$. • On the western side of Parque Grazalema, 31km from Arcos de la

Frontera in El Bosque. Up the hill behind Hotel Las Truchas. Camping El Bosque (956 71 62 12); part of a hostel; good place to meet fellow hikers; extra nice pool; open May-Sept; $$.
• In Grazalema on the hill above the village. Tajo Rodillo (956 13 20 63); nice location close to the trailheads; bike rental; open May-Sept; $$.

Garganta del Chorro

Over the years, Rio Guadalhorce, located just south of placid lake Embalse de Guadalhorce, has slowly threaded its way through a 400-meter high-sheer limestone wall and created a dramatic narrow gorge called Garganta del Chorro. In the 1920s, a precarious catwalk was built halfway up the face and along the entire length of the gorge. On opening day King Alfonso XIII bravely walked its entire length in order to bring notoriety to the hydroelectrical scheme. Only remnants remain today, but they entice rock climbers and daredevils. Though not recommended for independent climbers who are less than expert, a guided trip can provide a safe thrill. The owners of nearby Finca la Campana have developed a farm with simple lodging, camping space, and pool. Experienced Swiss climbers, they lead guided trips through the gorge; www.el-chorro.com. Without a guide, you can take a trail that gives you a good view of the catwalk and then continue on up to the mountaintop for a view of the lake. Directions: From El Chorro Campground, walk along the lakeside path leading up the hillside past the old stone bridge. When you are almost at the top, you'll see the treacherous El Camino across from the railroad bridge. Continue up the hillside, following paths that lead farther into the valley and then up to the mountaintop. Directions: Drive west out of Malaga for 19km on A357 in the direction of Cartama. Continue driving on the west side of the river for 14km. Cross over the bridge 3km beyond Cerralba and drive 6km to Alora. Staying on the west side of the river, continue 17km to El Chorro. Cross over the dam to the east side of the reservoir, and follow signposting for camping.

▲Camping: • At the reservoir and mouth of the gorge. El Chorro Camping (952 49-5197); natural setting; extra nice pool; friendly staff; cafe; open May-Oct; $$. • 2km from the train station. Follow signposting from the train station onto a small road. Finca la Campana (626 963 942); scenic location; good place to hang-out with other sports-minded people; open May- Oct; $$.

The South Coast Beaches

Enticing sunny days, warm evenings, sandy beaches, and a beautiful blue sea bring tourists to the Costa del Sol in droves. These are just a few of the many pleasant campgrounds along this coast.

▲**Camping:** • Southwest of Estepona. Exit N340 at km 142 for San Luis de Sabinillas. Camping Chullera II & III (952 89-0196); nice location on the beach; open all year; $$. • 33km east of Malaga exit N340 for Torre del Mar. Drive southwest of town on the coast road. Camping Laguna Playa (952 54-0631); close to the beach; cabins; pool; some shade; open all year; $$. • South of Granada on the beach in Motril. Exit N340 for Puerto de Motril and follow signposting. Camping Playa de Poniente de Motril (958 82 0303); large; on the beach; pool; bike rental; open April-Oct; $$. • 45km west of Almeria exit N340/E15 at Adra. Turn west onto the beach road N340, and drive to km384. Camping Las Gaviotas (950 40 0660); terraced setting; close to the beach; bike rental; open all year; $$. • 30km east of Almeria exit N344/E15 in the direction of Campohermosa, and drive 21km in the direction of La Negra and the beach. • Camping Nautico La Caleta (950-52 5237); on the beach; small; pool; open all year; $$.

Granada

On a low, fertile hillside, within sight of tall Sierra Nevada mountain peaks, Granada hides her treasure, the Alhambra. Here, Moorish palaces unfold in a series of delicately beautiful rooms. Start at the somber fortress walls (*Alcazaba*) where the view over the city and the surrounding countryside is splendid. It is from here that the Moors kept in touch with their outposts in the mountains. As you meander along the paths lined with tall cypress trees, boxwood, and ponds, you soon realize that this is a very large complex of woodlands, water, gardens, and buildings. Inside palace rooms are stalactite traceries, delicate geometric patterns, and inscriptions of Arabic poems that intertwine with artistic motifs, arches, and slender cushioned columns. Cool courtyards are scented with citrus and calmed by pooled and running water. Take time to sit in the verdant gardens outlined by delicately enscripted walls silently extolling the Koran. If you arrange your time so that you are here in the early evening, when it is quieter, the lacy chain of rooms become more mystical and the sound of water resembles the poetry it was meant to be. For detailed study, spend time in the Museo de Arte Hispano-Arabe examining their outstanding collection of Islamic artifacts; open 10 AM-2:30 PM; closed Monday. Many consider the Alhambra the most impressive Moorish monument in the world; open daily.

Ticketing for the Alhambra must be done, at a minimum, by noon a day ahead. If you plan to visit in August, arrange tickets before you leave home. 958-210-584. Tickets aren't available at the Alhambra; they are sold at the Granada bank in town. Some of the campgrounds are computer-linked to ticketing making it convenient to purchase tickets when registering. Directions to the Alhambra: For inexpensive, unlimited parking, use underground parking at Neptune Shopping Center. Exit N323 at exit 132; the shopping center is just off the roadway. Park, then walk up Calle de los Recogidas to Plaza Nueva. Take the Alhambra shuttle bus up the wooded hillside to the entrance.

To enlarge your study of Moorish, Roman, and Visigoth settlements in the area, visit the Archeological Museum housed in the richly decorated Casa de Castil; closed all day Monday and Tuesday morning. Directions: From Plaza Nueva walk north along the river road Carrera del Darro to number 43. Close by at Carrera del Darro 31, three water spigots –one warm, one cold, and one perfumed–filled the baths for the Moors at the *Banos Arabes*; closed Monday and afternoons. After, wander around the neighborhood, which still exudes a Moorish ambiance. Once a silk market, the narrow streets of the Alacaiceria are now filled with interesting shops and cafes. The Plaza Bib-Rambia is a good place to rest and absorb the scene. The fanastic marble royal mausoleums of Ferdinand and Isabella in the Capilla Real of the Cathedral were made more elaborate than

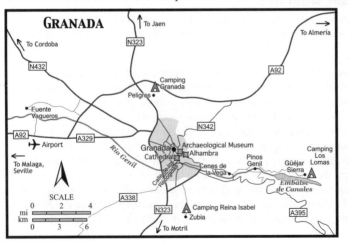

they wished; open daily. Directions: The Cathedral is in the center of the Alacaiceria area; follow signposting from main street leading up to the Alhambra.

The home of Garcia Lorca, one of Spain's most beloved poets and dramatists, is sweet with memories; closed Monday; guided tours are on the hour 10 AM-1 PM and 6 PM -7 PM.

Directions: Northwest of the Granada in Fuente Vaqueras. Exit N323 onto A92 and drive 8km west. Exit for Fuente Vaqueras. Follow signposting north on a small road for 11km, passing fields of tobacco and their drying sheds. Drive to the center of the village to the roundabout. Follow signposting north for 500 meters. The almost unnoticed house-museum is across from the theater on a small side street at Calle Garcia Lorca 4.

▲Camping: • 4km north of the city in the suburb of Peligros. Exit A92 at exit 241A onto N323 for Peligros. Drive south one kilometer. Take exit 123 for Peligros. Drive east over the overpass into the village. Follow signposting and drive north up the small paved hillside road for one kilometer. Camping Granada (958-340-548); on a hillside with views of Granada and the Alhambra; tranquil, small; open all year; $$$. • In the mountains 16km southeast of Granada in the village of Guejar Sierra. Southwest of Granada exit off N323 at exit #132 for Rondo Sur, and drive 11km passing through the town of Cenes and the village of Pinos Genil. Follow signposting for Guejar Sierra. Camping Los Lomas (9 58 48 4742); very popular arrive early or call ahead; views of the mountains; some shade; close to a small lake; terraced; pool; cabins; open all year; $$. • 14 km south of Granada in village of Zubia. Exit N323 at exit 132 for Rondo Sur. Drive 2km. Exit south of Zubia and drive 6km. Camping Reina Isabel (9 58 59 0041); popular arrive early or call ahead; restaurant; cabins; pool; open all year; $$$.

The Alpujarras

Bound on the north by the Sierras and on the south by the Mediterranean coast, the Alpujarras were once a hideout for bandits and Moorish rebels. Boabdil, Granada's famous *caliph* (Muslim ruler), sought sanctuary here after he was forced to turn over the keys of the Alhambra to

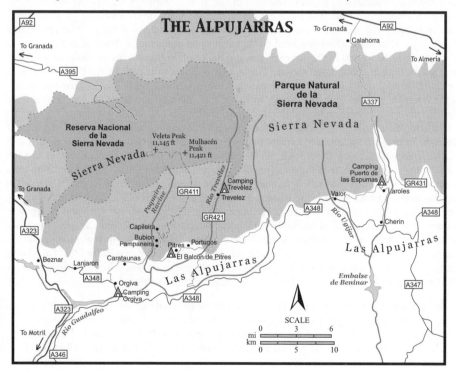

Ferdinand and Isabella. Embracing the cultures of Arab-Andalusia, the areas tidy whitewashed villages are perky with geraniums and bougainvillea drips from wrought-iron-railed balconies. Narrow, twisting streets lead to charming shops where resident weavers, ceramists, and painters work. An international mix of travelers relaxes in miniscule town squares. You can join *romerias* (summer pilgrimage walks from a village church into the mountains), watch reenactments of the battle between the Christians and the Moors, and take hikes on trails with sweeping views of the terraced mountainsides and high peaks. The Alpujarra paths thread down to rushing rivers and alongside levees watering the fertile terraced farmlands, where poppies and daisies decorate fields of fava beans, wheat, and potatoes. Some continue into wooded areas that are shady with chestnut, walnut, and oak trees. Distinctive circular chimneys top the stout, stone slab-roofed houses. Donkeys still carry loads of hay and grandmothers dressed in black knit in the sun.

Orgiva, the capital and commercial hub for the area, has a sizable group of international residents. Inside the 16th-century Moorish palace on the main street, New-Age marketers sell wholegrain bread and other natural food products along with jewelry and incense. Fill up with gas, purchase supplies, and get local currency here. The road heading into the Poqueira Ravine, whose terraced walls rise to Veleta Peak, is just west of Orgiva. On your way up through the villages, stop in Pampaneira and visit the information center for the Sierra Nevada, called Nevadensis. A good topography model of the Alpujarras, a large posted map, hiking-route maps and booklets, and a friendly English-speaking staff person will all assist you in planning walks, hikes, and horseback rides in the area; open daily. Directions: In the northwest corner of the small square. In the villages, woven rugs with Alpujarran designs dating from Moorish times drape over wrought-iron rails of small weaving shops. A tiny Tibetan monastery, renowned because its foremost monk is a prominent disciple of the Dalai Lama, offers lectures and retreats. The monks welcome visitors from 3-6 PM daily in their stone monastery with *stupa* (shrine) and stunning views. Visitors can also attend daily lectures or spend retreat time in one of the cabins; 958 343 134. All day or several day guided horseback rides into the gorge are offered at Dallas Ranch, located 2 kilometers outside of Bubion; 958-763-135. From Bubion, a pleasant 6 kilometer walking path leads to Pitres. Directions: The trailhead is signposted on the main street down the hill from Teide cafe.

Capileira is the highest of the three villages, and trailheads begin here for the peaks of Mulhacen and Veleta, both at about 3,400 meters. For an easy walk, take the path by the Pueblo Alpujarra complex leading down to the river. It passes through terraced fields and by farmhouses tidy with vegetable gardens and fruit trees. In the village museum in Capileira, you can examine handicrafts, tools, photographs and the traditional clothing of Old World Alpujarra. To join in a *romeria* to Veleta Peak, be in Capileira in the first week in August or in Pitres in the second week of August. In mid-September, reenactment battles between the Christians and the Moors are especially memorable in Valor. Directions: 38km south of Granada on N323/E902 exit east onto A348 close to the town of Beznar in the direction of Lanjaron, and drive 15km. Then turn north onto a small road in the direction of Carataunas just before entering the town of Orgiva. Drive 14km up the mountain road towards the village of Pampaneira. 2km east of Pampaneira is a fork; stay left and drive 4km more for Capileira. Farther east, the Trevelez Ravine is stark and savage with villages that are less prettified and touristy than those in the Poqueira Ravine. Trevelez is considered by many to be Spain's highest village at 1,476 meters. The trails to the high sierra peaks are marked better from here, so serious hikers climbing the peaks usually start in Trevelez. Directions: At the fork to Bubion/Capileira stay right instead of left, and drive 4km following signposting for Portugos. From Portugos, it is a14km steep, winding drive to Trevelez.

▲**Camping:** • Just west of Pitres. El Balcon de Pitres; terraced hillside; pool; open all year, $$. • In Trevelez. Camping Trevelez; basic; $. • In Orgiva. In town take the road south along the Rio Guadalfeo and drive 2km. Camping Orgiva (958-784-307); small; pool; simple café; some shade; all-year; $$. • Further east In Laroles. On C332 exit north at Cherin and drive 7km to Laroles then continue north another kilometer in the direction of Lacalahorra. Camping Puerto de las Espumas (958-760-231); convenient for Valor festivities; views of the mountains; some shade; open all year; $$.

Southeast Coast

Here and there along the coast, hidden between highly developed coastal resort towns, are some very pleasant places to spend time. Stop in Calp and climb 332 meters to the top of the monolith-like rocky outcrop Penon de Ifach, made more fun by a tunnel trail near the top. The view is stunning all the way up and even better on the other side of the tunnel. Directions: Exit A7 at exit 64 and drive east in the direction of Altea. Turn north and drive 11km to Calph continuing out to the spit where there is parking for the hike. The tiny village of Moraira, tucked into a beautiful cove, has made a concerted effort to keep a quiet, sedate atmosphere.

▲**Camping**: • In Moraira. Exit A7 at exit 63 for Benissa. Drive north of Benissa 4km and follow signposting east in the direction of Teulada. Continue east, then turn south for Moraira. Drive south of the village. Camping Moraira (96-574-5249); terraced hillside; extra nice amenities; pool; close to the beach;

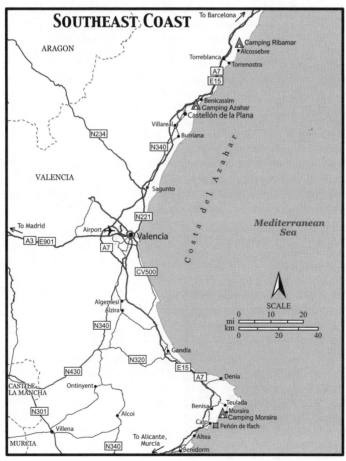

open all year; $$$. • Between Valencia and Tarragona. Exit off A7 at exit 44 onto N340 for Torreblanca. Turn south and follow signposting for Torrenostra and the beach. Turn north on the coast road and drive 11km to Alcossebre. Camping Ribamar (96-441-4165); close to the beach; some shade; pool; open April-Sept; $$. • 60km north of Valencia in Benicassim. Exit off A7 at exit 45 onto N340 and follow signposting for Benicassim and Castellon de la Plana and Hotel Voramar. Camping Azahar (964 30 3196); large; terraced; pool; popular with families; open all year; $$.

Valencia

Once one of the quieter corners on Spain's coast, this historic, 2,000-year-old city is on the rise. Sparing no expense, it has made way for the modern. Where the Turia River once flowed and flooded, now sits Valencia's outstanding City of Arts and Sciences (CAC). This massive bone-white structure arcs over shallow, cloud-reflecting fountains. Plunked right down in the middle of the city center, it was built to promote knowledge, science, art, and respect for nature. Exhibits are interactive and signs remind visitors that it is forbidden *not* to touch, think, or feel. The ancient river banks are now grassy, inviting a snooze or people watching. A walking, skating and biking path now meanders down the middle, and rentals are available. Through a series of tunnels and caves, you can get very close to a huge selection of sea-life collected from the seven seas. Walruses, dolphins, turtles, penguins, and sharks are all exciting and dramatic, but the real prize goes to the native wetlands exhibit featuring a mangrove swamp and tunnel cave. Under a glass and metal helmet-like dome, the Palace of Art hosts an exciting venue of opera, theatre, and dance. Treat yourself to a performance.

Valencians smile readily and are proud of their city and its surroundings. The small town atmosphere is appealing, naïve, and cosmopolitan all at the same time. Locals love a good time, and festivals are ongoing. The most famous festival, Las Fallas de San Jose, occurs in March. Its highlight is a procession of elaborate and hilarious papier mache depictions of famous people and events. At the end of the week, the floats go up in flame in an exciting ceremony. The week long festival is elaborate kids' play with adult style and includes fireworks, bonfires, and parades. The best floats and a large collection of photos are displayed in the Museu Falles; closed Monday. Directions: South of the historic area at the north end of the river-bed park. Take bus 13 from Plaza del Ayuntamiento. To see how these elaborate floats are made, go to the Museo del Artista Fallero; closed Sunday. Directions: Take bus 27 from Plaza del Ayuntamiento. Throughout

the summer, the festival-loving Valencians celebrate. You can dance in the street, watch battles between Moors and Christians, be part of a tomato-throwing free-for-all, or gorge on rice and seafood dishes at the national paella contest; www.communitt-valcencian. com. The tourist office is on the south side of Plaza Ayuntamiento. For fine art, don't miss the outstanding Museo de Bellas Artes. It is considered Spain's third-best fine art museum after the Prado and Bilbao; closed Monday. Directions: In the Jardin del Real on the north side of the river-bed park. Take Bus 11 from the Plaza Ayuntamiento. Da Vinci fans will want to visit the cathedral to pay homage to the alleged Holy Grail, a dark red chalice worn by Jesus in the Last Supper. Some say it was hidden in a small chapel deep in the Pyrenees during the Spanish Civil War. Bring binoculars because it is small and difficult to see from the viewing area. The silk market, La Lonja, is in a vast Art Nouveau building. Mouth-wateringly delicious foodstuffs are artistically displayed and hard to resist. Food art in miniature adorns most bars in the evening. You can assemble dinner from a multitude of these *tapas* (small dishes) but save the toothpicks because these are counted for payment when you decide its time to move on for more at the next bar. The Barro del Carmen district has a particularly laid-back, refuge-like atmosphere with winding back streets and young gypsies performing flamenco guitar solos.

In the late afternoon, drive south of the campground to board a small, flat-bottom boat and drift one of Europe's largest fresh-water lagoons, La Albufera. White herons stand quietly waiting to stab a passing fish or frog, gracefully launching into flight with their long neck tucked in when disturbed. Chattering kingfishers call in flight; watch for their shaggy, big-headed blue-and-white bodies perched in the waterside reeds. Choose a small, family-run boat trip rather then the large one for a closer view of the wild life. Directions: 4km south of the campgrounds at El Saler, on the coast road. Drive through the park entrance gate for the best boat trips. Legend says that it was in La Albufera that *paella* (a famous seafood and rice dish) was invented. The story goes that over campfires beside the lagoon, hungry fisherman cooked rice from the surrounding rice paddies adding freshly caught crayfish and shrimp, then some sausage, tomatoes, and onions for extra flavor. Valencia celebrates paella with a festival.

▲**Camping**: 7km south of Valencia in El Saler. Exit A7/E15 at exit 59 and drive east 5km to Cullera. Pass through town and take the coast road north in the direction of El Saler and Parque Albufera. It's across from the pedestrian walkway to El Saler Beach. • Camping DeVesa Gardens (961 61 1136); shady; pool; popular with families; bus to city center; open June-mid –Sept; $$. • In the same area. Camping Coll-Vert (961 83 0036); pool; shady; close to bus to city center; open April-Oct; $$.

EASTERN COAST
Barcelona

By its very nature exhilarating, Barcelona's rhythm must be slowly absorbed. Like a younger sibling envying all that an older one does, Barcelona keeps a ready eye on France. She looks out to sea, getting ideas from her neighbors and gaining a kaleidoscopic sophistication that is never stagnant. Begin experiencing the city at Los Ramblesa unique pedestrian boulevard that is a world of its own and the city's heartbeat. Wander randomly, letting its rhythm flow over you. Living "statues" turn slowly, bow, raise a hat, or wink when an admiring pedestrian contributes to their fund. An old man sings the same song again and again as he mournfully strums his guitar, while close by a vigorous middle-aged woman stamps her feet and clicks her castanets to the accompaniment of rhythmic clapping. A cacophony of birdsong draws you to myriad colorfully feathered creatures ready for admiration and sale. You can't help but smile. Without noticing you can

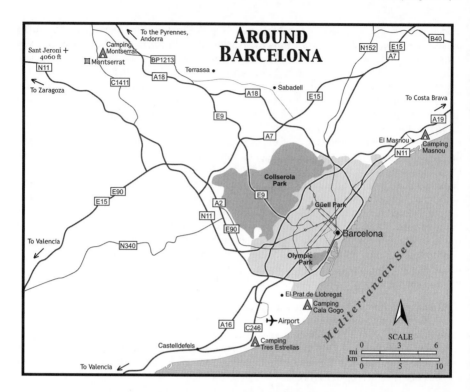

pass one of the world's best opera houses, the Liceu, and the elegant Rococo Palau de la Virreina, where you can purchase tickets special entertainment. Look for the doors of the Mercat de La Boqueria, a vast emporium with overwhelming piles of foodstuffs. Select a snack from a hundred varieties of olives, flavorful cheeses, and crusty bread. At the end of Los Rambles, the tall column dominating the harbor area is a monument to Christopher Columbus. Crossover here to breathe in the salty air and admire the sea flecked with sailboats. Directions: Los Rambles begins off the southeast corner of Placa de Catalunya.

Tucked into narrow streets, that are shadowy even on a sunny day, the ancient Barrio Gothic is still vital. Walk to the Placa de Sant Jaume, the spacious square where Romans once held forums and where people still gather for music and lively conversation. On the weekend, musicians play and you can watch or join in the *sardana* (Catalunya's heartfelt folk dance). If you watch carefully, you'll notice that quietly, without anyone giving a signal, a woman will carefully put her purse on the ground. Another will join her, then a man will carefully fold his jacket and place it on the pile, too. Soon a large circle forms of people of all ages, who dance silently. At first their steps are slow, turning left and right while holding their arms closely to their sides. Then the beat picks up and, with faster steps, they raise their arms slightly. Finally, with even faster steps and hands held high above their heads, their bodies sway beautifully to the tempo of the music, mesmerizing everyone who watches in the *placa*. Franco once forbid the dance in fear of an uprising.

Challenged by new ideas from their neighbors, Barcelona's architects developed an intense desire to avoid the ordinary. Casting aside balance and austerity they devised new pillars and capitals that looked like turbans, mushrooms, and spikes. They spread softly tinted cement onto uneven surfaces, then pressed in brilliantly colored tiles. They put together florid, giant, sculptural groups. When you visit these unique sites of early modern architecture, allow time for the harmony of the place to assert itself. You won't want to miss either the Palau and Parc Guell or La

Pedrera, but the highlight is the fabulous Sagranda Familia, where Gaudi worked ceaselessly on the plans and construction of this now very famous church. You can take an exciting elevator ride up to a high balcony, then climb stairs to even higher levels where you are almost eye-level with some of the spires. Before, take time to examine the models, sketches and photographs in the museum to better understand what you are seeing.

Drawings by Picasso when he was young, colorful paintings and tapestries by Miro, and fascinating collages by Tapies are just the highlights in the unique museums devoted to each of these artists. In the new Museu d'Art Contemporani, viewers have exciting encounters with what is happening in the contemporary art world. Escalators take you part way up to the magnificent Palau Nacional, where works by Velazquez, El Greco, and Zurbaran, and a notable collection of photographic work, are just part of the Museu de Art Catalunya's huge collection.

In 2005, Barcelona transformed at 74-acre complex in the industrial riverside district of Saint Adria de Besos into a huge convention space for southern Europe. The dramatic Forum building rests on a nearly 40-acre open plaza with breathtaking views of the ocean. Above it, a roof composed of photovoltaic panels converts sunlight into nominal amounts of electricity for the city. Here, alongside a riverside esplanade, people from all over the world come together to eat, drink, swim, sunbathe, and during a convention, learn something about global issues. Directions: Metro L4 to El Maresme Forum. To learn more about Barcelona's rich and varied offerings, stop by the tourist office to inquire about special events, pick up a map, and get information about the easy-to-use metro and buses. The best tourist office is on the main boulevard northeast of the Placa de Cataluya at Orts Calalanes 658.

▲**Camping:** These three are all in the same area. They are under the pines in a natural setting with a nice beach nearby. A bus to city center leaves every half hour. Leave your car at the campground. Public transportation in Barcelona is excellent. 18km south of the city exit A16 at exit 14 for Castelldefels and C246. • On C246 at km 13.2. Camping Tres Estrellas (936 33 0637); pool; open May-Sept; $$. • On C246 at km11. Camping El Toro Bravo (936 37 3462); pool; open May-Sept; $$. • On C246 at km12.5. Camping La Ballena Alegre (902 50 0526); large; resort-like; pool; open April-Sept; $$$. • 6km northeast of the city exit off A19 at exit 8 for Masnou and drive to km 633 on N11. Camping Masnou (935-551-503); close to the beach; pool; bus to city center; open all year; $$.

Montserrat

One of Cataluna's most important pilgrimage sites, Montserrat is wedged into crevices below rocky spires reminiscent of the great Tibetan monasteries in the Himalayas. It is said that religious hermits, who once lived in the caves, hid from the Muslims a beautiful wooden statue of the Virgin. When found much later, the Catholic Church confirmed it to be the last statue carved by St. Luke. Since then, the royal, the famous, and the poor have climbed the steep mountain trail in hope of finding solace; open daily. A web of trails–from easy to strenuous–leads to the ruins of hermitages, past wind-sculpted rock outcrops, and on to high peaks. To shorten the hike, take the funicular Sant Joan up the first 250 meters; operates daily. Parking is on the hillside on the way up. Payment for parking is made at the tollbooth on the way down. Directions: 25km northwest of the Barcelona follow signposting off A9 or N11.

▲**Camping:** • Below the Sant Joan funicular. No cars are allowed beyond the parking area so carry in camping gear. Camping Montserrat (835-0251); small; basic; open May-Sept; $.

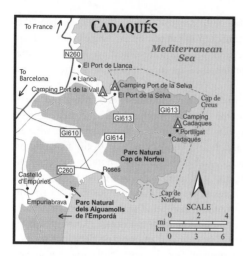

Cadaques

Hidden behind hills and accessed only by a small road, beautiful Cadaques was made famous when Salvador Dali built an eccentric home here on the edge of the sea. Strongly influenced by Freud, Dali painted his dreams and paranoia. It's fun to wander through his house and studio, imagining it alive with the artist, his adored wife, and their famous artistic and literary friends. Directions: Cadaques is directly west of Figueres, out on the edge of the pennisula. Exit A7/E15 either north or south of Figueres onto N11. Exit onto C260 and drive 16km in the direction of Roses. At the fork stay north and drive 15 kilometers more to Cadques. Dali's home is just north of town in the tiny harbor village Port Lligat; open daily. Visiting the art galleries and small art museums adds interest to walks in the town and harbor area.

▲**Camping**: In Port Lligat. Turn north just as you enter Cadques and follow the small steep road for one kilometer. Camping Cadaques (972 25 8126); large; nice location; pool; café; store; open April-Sept; $$$. • Northwest of Cadaques in Port de la Selva. Exit A9/E15 at exit 3 for Llanca and N260. Drive south for 2km then northeast on N260 for 15km to Llanca. Turn south on the coast road and drive south 4km to Port de la Selva. These are both in the same area and fairly close to the beach. Camping Port de la Selva (972 38 7287); May-Sept; $$. Camping Port de la Vall (972 38 7186); small sites; open April-Sept; $$.

The Pyrennes

Unlike the lush green French Pyrennes, the Spanish Pyrennes have a savage, rock-strewn beauty. Trails lead from grassy meadows up through chaparral-covered hillsides smelling of rosemary and broom, and on into shadowy gorges where boulder-strewn riverbeds lead to refreshing waterfalls. Scattered lightly

through the foothills are villages where you can attend summer celebrations and small-town sports events. Fill up with gas, purchase supplies, and get local currency before driving in.

Valle de Roncal

Extravagant travel posters depicting blue sky and crisp outlines of villages seem overdone, but in the Val de Roncal they are real. Lose yourself in the leisurely pace of the regions villages. You'll find ancient, modest churches that have remained much the same as when they were built. In the village square, locals chat, kids play ball, and parents beam as neighbors exclaim over babies. Under shady beech trees, old men watch people passing by and are happy to help with directions. In the morning, follow the delicious aroma of fresh bread along cobbled alleyways to tiny bakeries. In the evening, watch the sunset burst gloriously in bronze and gold. Hiking trails lead over tiny humpback bridges meant for shepherds and bleating herds of sheep and goats, on into gorges deep with shadows, past waterfalls and explosions of wild iris, and up to summits with views of pyramidal shaped mountains. There's a refreshing clear quality to the air and a blissful silence.

Stop at the tourist office in Roncal to examine the large map of the area and find out what summer festivities are on the calendar during your stay. If you are here in May and June, when the water level is high, you can make arrangements to rent a kayak or be part of a white-water rafting group. Directions: Exit north onto 137 at the eastern tip of the Yesa reservoir and drive 31km to Roncal. After getting information at the tourist office, continue to the smaller, more picturesque village of Isaba.

▲Camping: • North of Isaba at km 6 on 137. Camping Asolaze (948-89-3034); nice pine scented location; cabins; popular with hikers and cyclists; sunny meadows; store with a large topographical map and hiking maps; open May-Sept; $$.

Monte Perdido National Park

Directions: 13km east of Jaca exit N330 north onto N260 and drive 12km to Biesca. Turn east, following signposting for the park.

Valle de Broto

This wide glacier-formed valley southwest of the park opens up to grassy meadows edged with nicely forested hills. Country roads wind through pleasant villages where there are trailheads for easy walks and bicycle rides. At summer festivals in Frajen in late July and in Oto in mid-August, the locals will welcome you at the town square for music, fireworks, and dancing.

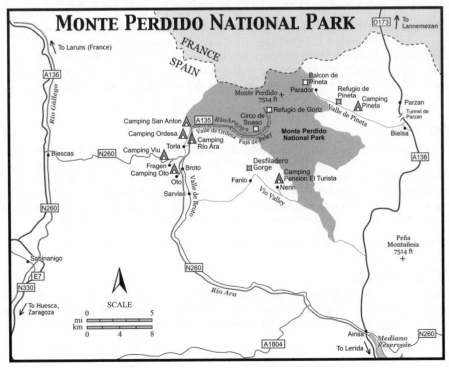

▲**Camping:** • In Viu at km. 484 on N260. Camping Viu (974-486-301); popular with cyclists; on a hillside with scenic views; open May-Sept; $$. • In Oto. At the north end of Broto on the westside of the river, take the road south one kilometer to Oto. Camping Oto (974-486-075); picturesque location; close to hiking route GR15; open May-Oct; $$.

Valle de Ordesa

Torla is the tourist center for the national park. Rentals can be arranged at the campground or tourist office for kayaking, mountain biking, rock climbing, and canyoning. In July and August, when the area is heavily visited, try to arrange a mid-week visit. Private cars are no longer allowed in the park. Park in the large car park just south of Torla's tunnel, and take the shuttle bus. The shuttle operates from early morning to early evening and stops first at the interpretive center, then at the old parking lot and trailheads, and then returns to Torla. Hikes range from easy to difficult. Always carry energy food, water, and a waterproof jacket.

If you want to spend several days inside the park, make advanced reservations for a stay in a *refugio* (hiker's hostel) so you don't have to pack in a tent and cooking equipment. Just take enough energy food for the time on the trails and enough water for the hike to the first *refugio*. Once there, your bed and simple food are provided. Refugio Goriz has a good location at the base of Mt. Perdido, 2km from the Circo de Soaso at 2,200 meters. 974-341-201

Traversing Ordesa Valley by way of the Circo de Soaso is a popular full day hike. The trailhead begins at the Azaras River footbridge and climbs to Los Cazadoes, where there are panoramic views, then continues along the Faja de Pelay to the Circo de Soaso. The route passes through a shady beech forest. In May and June the waterfalls along the trail are powerful. For an easy scenic walk from Camping Rio Ara, follow the road north along the eastside of the river for one kilometer to the trailhead. From here the trail continues north for a little more than one kilometer, then turns east into the park. 4km farther brings you to the old car park and the shuttle bus back to Torla.

▲**Camping:** • Half a kilometer north of Torla exit east off A135 onto a small road crossing over the medieval bridge. Camping Rio Ara (974-486-248); grassy lawns and shade trees; close to the river; very popular; cafe; open May-October; $$. • One kilometer north of Torla. Camping Ordesa (974-486-146); pool; popular with caravans; open May-Oct; $$$. • Just over 2km north of Torla at km 96. Camping San Anton (974-486-063); hillside setting; small; closest to park entrance; open May-Oct; $$.

Vio Valley

Drier and more savage than the Ordesa Valley, the Vio Valley's big attraction is the Desfiladero Gorge. It is popular with international travelers interested in canyoning and is a good place for beginners. Arrange in advance for guides and equipment with the tourist office in Fanlo; 974-486-184. Views of the grand and massive summit of Pena Moutanesa are outstanding in Nerin, and if you're here in mid-August you can join the fun at their summer festival. Directions: Exit N260 at Sarvise, 3km south of Broto, and drive west for 12km on a small, paved winding road in the direction of Fanlo.

▲**Camping:** • In Nerin by the Pension El Turista (974-486-138); basic; open May-October; $.

Val de Pineta

Balcon de Pineta, a shelf hanging 1,200 meters above the valley floor at the top of Circo de Pineta, attracts expert climbers and energetic hikers. Directions: Exit A138 north of Bielsa just south of the Tunnel de Parzan and drive 15km west on a small paved road in the direction of Parador.

▲**Camping**: • 7km west of the Tunnel de Parzan on the Parador road. Camping Pineta (974-501-089); basic; open May-Sept; $. • 11km west of the Tunnel de Parzan. Refugio de Pineta (974-501-203); newer; close to the Parador road; open all year; $$.

Euzkadi (Basque) Country

In Spain, the four provinces of Vizcaya, Guipuzcoa, Alva, and Navarra make up what is called Basque or Euzkadi country. It is a small, neat geographical unit that fits tidily into the right angle of the Bay of Biscay. The largest cities are Bilbao and San Sabastian along the stunning, rugged coast, Alava on the south plain, and Guernicaits symbolic capitalin the green Mundaca River Valley. Abrupt savage mountains have given it natural fortifications and inaccessibility. When the Basques speak of their homeland, they are referring to land that is on both sides of the Pyreneesin France and in Spain. Their language, which is quite unlike any other in Western Europe, still ties them together and more young people speak it today than 100 years ago. It is their national treasure so road signs are in both Euzkera and Spanish. Basques are energetic, adventurous, physical people who vie with one another at festivals to see who can lift the heaviest stone, sever a log with an ax, and row old fishing boats in open sea. The most famous contest is the bull-running in Irunea. The countryside is punctuated with whitewashed stout stone farmhouses houses with gently sloping red-tiled roofs and brightly colored balconies. The houses sit solid in isolation among green fields of maize crops. At sunset in the villages, you can look across to the soft round forested hills and watch them turn blue with fading light. Here old men wear the navy-blue Basque beret, known as *chapela*, rakishly at a tilt or pancake style on the full crown of the head.

Irunea (Pamplona)

The capital of Navarra, Irunea rests at the base of the Pyrennes and except for the frenetic week of the Fiesta de San Fermin, it is a pleasant university town. The running of the bulls is the famous highlight of the fiesta but throughout that week it's a round-the-clock celebration with bands, parades, fireworks, fairs, and thousands of tourists and locals out to have an enormously good time. The fiesta begins July 6 and ends on July 14.

▲**Camping**: • North of town. Follow signposting for Villava/N121A. Pass through the town of Villava, following signposting for camping on the west side of N121A in the village of Eusa. Camping Ezcaba (948-330-315); shady hillside; pool; bus to city center; open all year; $$$. Note For the fiesta: Make reservations well in advance, expect noise throughout the night from partying folks, and little space between tents or caravans.

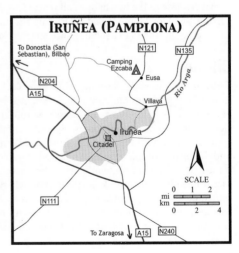

Donostia (San Sebastian)

Wedding cake-like pink and white buildings, brass street lamps, and graceful bridges give Donostia's Belle Epoque flavor a festive twist. In the evening the hansome new Kursaal Performing Arts Center designed by Rafael Moneo glows like Japanese lanterns through thick opaque glass sheathing. This is where the world-famous jazz festival and film festival take place. The *Parte Vieja* (older city) wraps

DONOSTIA (SAN SEBASTIÁN)

itself around La Concha Bay, a shell-shaped protected waterfront set into the base of Mt Urgull, a substantial rock promontory at the harbor. In the evening, musicians, mimes, jugglers and magicians perform along the waterfront.

At the far end of the Bay of Biscay Eduardo Chillid's monumental sculpture, *Comb of the Wind*, rises from the rocks. More than forty rusty monoliths stud the hillside. In the mountain town of Hernani, the sculptor displays his smaller pieces of delicate alabaster, hanging "gravitations", inside his redesigned farmhouse. Describing his airy studio as a cathedral, the artist encourages visitors to do something mostly unheard of in an art museum, touch the sculptures. Watch the video first; closed Tuesday. Directions: Drive 7km south of Donastia on 131.

▲Camping: These are just a few of the many excellent campgrounds. • 14km west of Donostia in Zarautz. Exit A8/E70 for Zarautz. In town drive east following signposting. Gran Camping Zarautz (943 831-238); on the beach; resort-like; cabins; open all year; $$$. • 27km west of Donostia on the coast road 638, between the towns of Lekeitio and Ondarroa in the village of Mendexa. Leagi Camping (946 84-2352); good location; little shade; open all year; $$. • East of Ondarroa in the village of Mutriku. Camping Aitzeta (943 60-3356); smaller; close to the beach; open all year; $$. • West of Donostia in the suburb of Igeldo. Exit A8/E70 for Monte Iguedo. Drive up the hill for 5km following signposting. Garoa-Camping Igueldo (943 21-4502); nice terraced location; shade; open all year; $$$.

Bilbao

Resembling smooth, gleaming white chocolate swirls, the undulating curves of titanium and stone of Guggenheim Museum Bilbao, designed by Frank Gehry, are as exciting as the collection of art that they hold. Works by Picasso, Miro, Tapies, Kandinsky, and DeKooning grace the spacious, pillow-white interior spaces. Special exhibits that can include sculpture, photography, and applied arts are from the very best of the world's modern artists. Spend time outside watching the undulating play of changing light reflected in water from its titanium shell. The building is a milestone in the history of contemporary architecture; open 10 AM-8 PM; closed Monday. Directions: Metro to Moyua, then walk north on Alameda de Recalde to the river and the museum. The Museo de Belle Artes holds important works by El Greco, Zurbaran, Goya, and the best of the Basque artists and is considered one of Spain's most important art museums; closed Monday. Directions: On the river west of the Guggenheim, across from the Plaza de Museo.

Walking is a pastime full of rewards in Bilbao. Midway along the Grand Via, at the Plaza Moyua, you'll come to a slinky glass-and-steel construction that resembles caterpillars burrowing into the pavement. It is the new subway designed by Norman Foster. Locals call the brightly lit tubes with spare, high-tech platforms and staircases hung in space–Fosteritos. There, design embodies motion. Take a ride to Casco Viejo, the old town, where trestlework lanterns hang from balcony corners, and second-story bowed windows paneled in dark wood

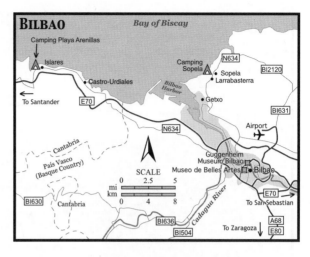

are ornamented with weathervanes, scrolls, and the coat of arms of famous writers and artists who once lived within. Wander without a plan through alleyways that spill into tiny squares or onto the riverfront. Fine buildings with flowerboxes ring the airy Plaza Nueva, and gentle sounds often fill the air from lone musicians or the hundreds of canaries for sell. Twice a year, in Plaza San Vicente, a songbird contest is held. After the bird handlers speak soothingly to their feathered pets, cages are hung on numbered stakes and judges lean their heads towards them to hear their remarkable trills.

▲**Camping**: • Close to the beach north of Bilboa in Sopelana. From major roadways drive north of the city, following signposting for Getxo, then Larrabasterra, and then Sopelana. Follow signposting towards the beach and camping. Camping Sopelana (946 76-2120); on a hillside close to the beach; cabins; pool; cafe; metro nearby; open all year; $$$. Between Santander and Bilbao. Exit N634/E70 7km west of Castro-Urdiales at exit 159 for the village of Islares and drive to the beach. Camping Playa Arenillas (942 86-3152);on the beach; some shade; open April-Sept; $$$.

Picos de Europa

Very green and often damp, Asturia is incongruous with the rest of Spain. It is sprinkled with red-tile roofed farmhouses, crystalline rivers, and steep sided mountains and there is little in the way of great architectural works or museums. In the small villages the Celtic origins are remembered by bagpipe bands playing on Saturday nights, when both young and old dance. Many of the beaches lie in narrow coves, where the sea has carved vast caves and tunnels. When the tide is out, the walks are terrific.

Three towering massifs, separated from each other by steep gorges, make up the Picos of Europa. These gorges are so sheltered from climatic extremes that the flora is Mediterranean. In the spring, flower enthusiasts can find many rare species of wild and exotic orchidsas well as Pyrenean lilies, yellow hoop-petticoat daffodils and deep-pink dog's tooth violets growing in the meadows where rare and endangered butterflies flutter. The chamois, now present in large numbers, can be seen precariously balanced on high ledges. Golden eagles, both griffon and Egyptian, soar in the thermals of the gorges, and tree pipits and nuthatches twitter in the trees. Receiving most of its weather from the Atlantic, Picos de Europa's climate is cool and moist. The valleys are lush, and a mist frequently shrouds the pale limestone peaks. Glaciers during the Ice Age created lunar landscapes on the mountain plateaus, and underground water created huge caverns decorated with stalagmites and stalactites.

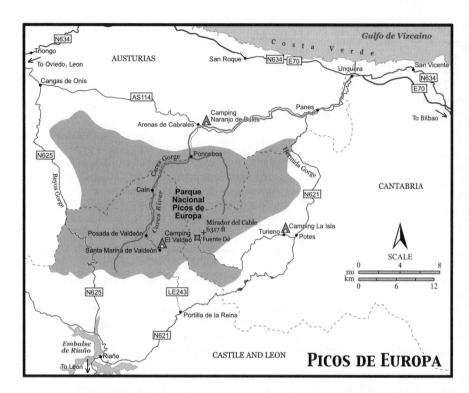

Narrow, steep, winding roads pass through villages clinging to the mountains that soar in every direction. New houses are latched onto old ones. Cars yield to goats and cows. Old men wear berets and play *boule*. Bells ring out from churches dwarfed by the rock faces. The area is hugely popular with walkers and hikers of all levels. The classic and most famous walk in Picos de Europa is through the sheer limestone Cares Gorge. The trail was hewn out of the rock for hydroelectric purposes and is high above the thundering Cares River. It is a 24 kilometer round-trip starting from either Cain or Poncebos. Many people just hike part of the way and turn back. But the full hike is easy to do in a day. The trail passes from one side of the almost sheer cliff walls to the other via little bridges, and sometimes you are inside the mountain itself. In places the walls are more than 2,000 meters high. Bird enthusiasts should take binoculars because the tiny and elusive wallcreepers commonly feed off the cliff walls.

Roads lead into the Picos and the Cares Gorge from the north coast, and from the south through Riano and Leon. Directions from the south: From Leon, drive north on N630 for 25km to La Robla. Exit east onto C626 in the direction of Bonar for 30km. Continue east in the direction of Olaja de la Varga for 20km. Turn north on 621 and drive 30km in the direction of Riano and the Embalse de Riano reservoir. Drive east through town in the direction of Portilla de la Reina for 18km. Turn north and drive up the steep and narrow mountain road LE 243 to Posada de Valdeon. Many hikers start from here, but if you're pressed for time or energy or feel you car isn't capable of the steep ascent a 4WD bus takes hikers up 3km farther to Cain.

▲**Camping:** At the south end of the Cares Gorge. • 4km south of Posada in the tiny Santa Marina de Valdeon. Camping El Cares (742 676) scenic location; terraced; narrow bridge to campground; open June-Sept; $$. Just outside Posada. Camping El Valdeon (742 605); convenient for the trailheads and tourist center; good views; open June-Sept; $$.

Directions from the north coast to the north end of the Cares Gorge: Exit N634 12km west of San Vicente for Unquera and N621. Drive south and then west up the mountain for 35km on AS114 to Arenas de Cabrales. Turn south and continue up the mountain for 8km to Poncebos.

▲**Camping** at the north end of the Cares Gorge: Just east of Arenas de Cabrales. Camping Naranjo de Bules; popular; open April-Sept; $$

An exciting three-minute *teleferico* ride from Fuente De takes you up 900 meters to the top, where the views are stunning. Plan to go up early to miss a long line. Take a picnic lunch and a short hike if you want more solitude. Directions: Exit N634 12km west of San Vicente for Unquera and N621. Drive 12km. At the fork stay south on N621 and continue up the mountain road (Desfiladero de la Hermida) for another 27km to Potes. In town, exit N621 and following signposting west for Fuente Di. Drive up the mountain road for 25km. The little towns here cater to vacationers.

▲**Camping**: 3km west of Potes, in Turieno. Camping La Isla (730 896); nice setting; pool; open June-Sept; $$.

Galicia

The delicious aroma of freshly baked bread, octopus tentacles dripping from salt-encrusted boxes, brown hams lightly fringed with mold hanging alongside garlic-scented sausages, black-shrouded women with sharp, dark eyes busily negotiating with merchants his is the melange you're treated to in Galicia's morning markets. On its waterfronts, weary fisherman chat as they laboriously mend nets. From the coastline bluffs at Cabo Finisterre, dramatic ocean vistas that were once thought show the end of the world now offer a lusty beauty. Through this high and desolate headland roads follow rugged cliffs with startling views and harrowing precipices. In estuaries little villages with miniscule plazas and houses with traditional balcony facades cascade down from the hillsides, and in secluded coves nature lovers breathe in the salt air, watch sea gulls feed at the tide's edge, and revel in the surf.

▲**Camping**: These are just a few of the many nice campgrounds with lovely locations. • On the west coast at Cabo Finisterre. Follow signposting from C550 or C552 to Cocubion, then continue southwest to the tip of the pennisula. Camping Ruta Finisterre (981-746-302); sce-nic view; terraced; pine shaded; open June-mid Sept; $$$. • 17km east of Coruna in the sub-

urb of Bergondo. Exit off N651/A9 at exit 3F for Bergondo and follow signposting. Camping Santa Maria (981-795-826); 2km from the beach; open May- Sept; $$. • North of Ferrol in the village of Meiras. 11km north of Ferrol exit C464 for Meiras and the beach. Camping Valdovino (981-487-076); small; open June- Sept; $$. • On the north coast. 35km west Aviles in Luarca. Drive 12km west of Luarca to the village of Otur. Camping Playa de Otur (98-564-0117); close to the beach; parking separate from camping; open May-Sept; $$. • 40km west of Santander. Exit E70/N634 at Cabezon de la Sal and drive north 5km following signposting for Comillas. Camping Comillas (942-720-074);on the beach; little shade; open June-Sept; $$.

Santiago de Compostela

A grand statue of a zealous St James, shrouded in a huge cape, proclaiming his news greets travelers to Santiago de Compostela. His upturned hat is embellished with scalloped shells, his feet are shod in rough sandals, and his huge hand clutches a massive walking stave. Standing in the immense space formed by the four plazas of the Cathedral at Santiago de Compostela and looking up its two tall, flame-like towers and incredible facade is awe-inspiring. But the real glory is inside at the Great Portico de la Gloria, the 12th-century masterpiece of Maestro Mateo. Mateo worked on the Portico for 20 years, creating a sensitive and harmonious arrangement of hundreds of figures. Using three arches, the work represents the new Church rising from what was believed to be the false dogmas of Islam, the evils of greed and pride, and the Old Testament. The natural figures display individual characteristics and moods and were initially rich in color and laced with gold. Partake slowly of the squares, cathedral, museum, and cloisters savoring the details; open daily. Directions: Follow signposting from all major roadways.

In the 11th century the shrine was rebuilt, the road improved, and monasteries, convents, hospitals, and hostels were built to accommodate and protect the pilgrims. The *camino* (road) became an international route called the Camino de Santiago. The full name of the route included the word *Compostela* (field of star) in reference to the star that directed the devout to St James' missing remains. A scallop shell became the insignia of pilgrims, reminiscent of St James' use of the shell in baptism. The route is clearly marked today, and many still walk, cycle, or drive part or all of it as it threads its way through once forbidding landscape now softened by dry farmlands. As you pass through the old villages, you can admire the workmanship of Roman bridges and the clean lines of simple churches. The *Camino* leads right through the towns, rather then avoiding them as new roads do. Walking down the main street enables you to absorb the ambiance of the

town's daily life and perhaps, pick up bits of conversation between the local people. If you smile and greet people; they will return your greeting. Some walkers join up with others for parts of the walk, while others choose to do it alone. Walkers stop and listen to *Camino* veterans tell of what lays ahead, to compare blisters, to make friends, and build unforgettable memories. Directions: For a map of the route and list of accompanying campgrounds, stop by the tourist offices in Pamplona or Estrella.

Santiago's relative isolation from Madrid is reinforced by the mountains and local dialect and has fueled a fierce local pride. With centuries of visiting pilgrims from all over Europe, they view themselves as separate and distinct from Madrid. A City of Culture project sprang up from this combination of local pride and European outlook. Counting on the world to pay attention to major architecture, the medieval city funded a massive performing arts complex City of Culture of Galicia. Peter Eisenman, known for his love of oblique lines, was the chosen as the architect. His design of gently undulating forms clad in glass and stone pours down the mountainside. It includes a library, a landscaped forest, and a theatre for ballet, opera, and symphonies.

▲**Camping**: • Northeast of the city in the suburb of Lazaro. Take exit 67 off E01/A9 and follow signposting west back towards the city and camping. Camping As Canelas (981-580-266); pool; cabins; some shade; open all year; $$.

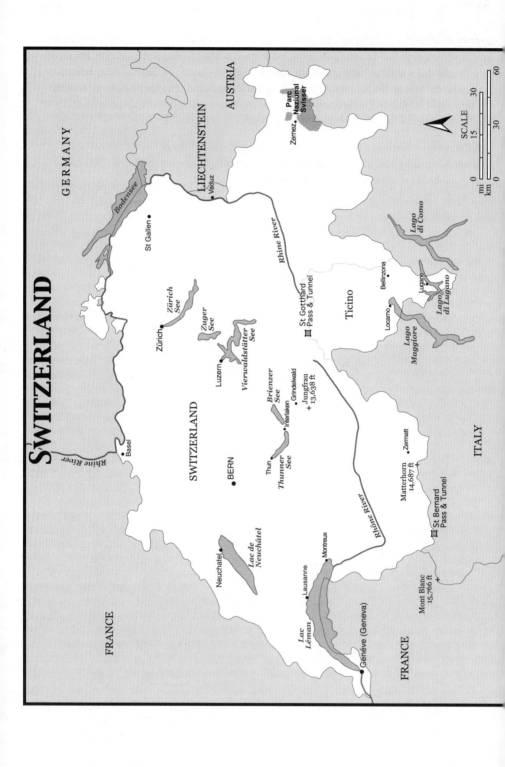

Switzerland

www.myswitzerland.com

In Switzerland's alpine meadows, pale lavender foxgloves wave in the breeze and violet-red etch sweeps across like swaths of paint. Pockets of edelweiss peek like soft stars from steep crags. Sparrows sing gaily, and air-borne hawks display elegance in movement. There is a timeless beauty to the countryside and an ancient, deep-rooted bond to the earth.

Switzerland's rural areas are a paradise for active relaxation. Experts at making sports doable for persons at a beginning or advanced skill level, the Swiss provide equipment, clothing rentals, shuttles, guides, and classes. Their cog railways, tramcars, cable cars and trains make getting to the upper meadows fun and easy. Carefully planned trails run the gamut of ability levels so that all hikers can appreciate the glorious scenery, gain a satisfaction from the experience, and accomplish it without being overstrained. Trail markers indicate ability level and approximate time it takes to get from one place to another. Maps give geological and flora information.

The bold and rugged beauty of sculpted rock massifs lures rock climbers. Guides, schools, equipment, and clothing are available for those who want the thrill of surmounting the pinnacles and crevices. If you'd rather drift bird-like over the spectacular Alpine scenery, try tandem or solo hang gliding or ballooning. To encourage pedaling down old pass roads or along Alpine trails, the Swiss Rail System rents and transports bikes. Water enthusiasts can paddle down an untamed river, wind surf across a pristine lake, or kayak into fjord-like coves. If you're traveling with kids, or just feel like being one, you can take a bobsled ride that barrels down a winding mountain track, plunge down immense water chutes at a waterpark, or climb high up into the treetops on a rope ladder. For a more tranquil adventure board a steamer that plys the mirror-smooth lakes.

Switzerland is particularly proud of its fascinating Transport Museum in Lucerne, it's fabulous art collections in Zurich, Berne, and Basel, and its world-famous Abbey Library in St. Gallen. All will stretch your imagination and knowledge. Switzerland was initially abundant only in stones and water. In the battle for survival in such a hostile environment, the Swiss produced an Alpine character that was suspicious, independent, frugal, and contentious. They defeated Austrian armies in three battles and even Napoleon realized that their belligerence would never allow them to be turned into French subjects. You can only admire the conscientious hard work, frugality, and mechanical genius in this highly successful country that have produced an abundance of international patents and a genius for financial management. Fast superhighways link the major cities. An annual *vignette* (highway stamp) costing just over 20 euros must be attached to the windshield of all vehicles using the superhighways. If you don't rent your car in Switzerland, buy one at a border crossing or gas station. They seem excessively expensive to the traveler who is just passing through the country for a day or two, but they are cost-efficient for the country as a whole. Toll stations are expensive to operate and are gradually being eliminated and replaced by stamp-tariffs throughout Europe. Tunnels through the Alps can be quite lengthy and should be avoided during commute times. Though costly in time and gas, the smaller roads are stunningly beautiful and often twist up through pine-scented forests, past medieval villages, and across meadows embroidered with gaily-colored flowers, cascading rivers, and crashing waterfalls. You'll probably want to use both. International pictograph sign-posting is excellent: Triangular signs with red borders warn of dangers; round signs with red borders indicate prohibitions. Public buses have the right of way, and you must obey any signals they give. Switzerland's car rental rates are some of the lowest in Europe.

To encourage bicycling, the Swiss Rail System does not require returning a rented bicycle to the same station you rented it from unless the rental is only for half a day. Pick up the free Rail-Bike brochure at a train station, and make reservations for the most popular routes. Cycling routes lead through vineyards, along lakes and rivers, through small towns, and to historic sites. Purchase the excellent Bicycling Map of Switzerland at a railway station or airport bookstore. It includes scenic routes for all ability levels and notes interesting stops along the way. Postal buses pass daily through even the smallest villages, delivering and picking up mail. Check the local schedule and use them as shuttles for walks or cycle rides. The postal bus does not have room for bikes. If you have brought your own bike, park and lock it after your ride. Take the postal bus back to your car, returning with your car to pick up the bike. Lake steamboats allow a limited number of bikes onboard.

Walking or hiking is an important national pastime. Paths are clearly marked and pass through dappled green and shadowy mountain gorges, along pristine avocado-green lakes, through tiny quaint villages, and up or down the awe-inspiring Alps. Beech forests provide a canopy of lacy light-green leaves covering a carpet of ferns. In the early morning mist they are magical. Deep-red alpenrose, a type of rhododendron, can cover acres with a saturation of luscious color, while spikes of purple-hooded monkshood spring from lush damp meadows. Wild flowers are protected and must not be picked. And although wildlife can be scarce, the winsome clang of cowbells and the tinkle of sheep bells are omnipresent, and on trails with rocky crevices the marmots shrill warning cry is heard. Easy-to-read detailed maps and guidebooks are readily available in all of the tourist offices. Many walks begin by parking at the train station and then taking a cable car, cog-rail train, or postal bus to the trailhead. Trails are classified as *wandererweg* (low altitude trail marked with yellow signs) and *berweg* (rough, high-altitude trail marked with red/white/red postings). The trail markers are seen on rocks and trees as well as on regular posted signs. Double signage indicates that the trail has a change of direction. A blue dot indicates a hiking trail, while a red dot indicates a cross-country ski trail. The weather in the Alps can change quickly and dramatically, producing a sudden rainstorm in the middle of a sunny day. Bring a daypack, comfortable walking shoes, a lightweight waterproof jacket with hood or a poncho, a warm but lightweight sweater, and a water bottle. Pack energy food, water, a hiking map, emergency whistle, and a compass into your daypack before each hike.

Swiss campgrounds are usually in scenic locations close to a lake or stream. Campers get grassy meadows, covered common areas, warm showers, good maintenance, and fresh bread in the morning. Resort-like campgrounds are abundant. They have exceptional facilities but are expensive. I've searched for less expensive campgrounds that have a pleasant location and two persons, a car, and a tent cost around 20-22 euros. These are indicated here as $$. Those over 25 euros are indicated here as $$$. The office is usually closed for lunch between noon and 2 PM. The Swiss acknowledge the International Camping Card so bring it to use for a security deposit instead of your passport.

Museum hours are typically from 10 AM to 5 PM. Smaller ones close for lunch; many are closed on Monday. Stores in small villages are sometimes closed on Sunday and Monday. You'll find parking close to train stations.

BERN

Switzerland's capital is a city with a secret smile and giggle, so it's a good place to begin an exploration of the country. Wandering through the tiny streets of the old town, you'll smile at the whimsical fountains; delight in the parade of mechanical dancing bears and clowns in the clock tower, and laugh at the real bears cavorting in the bear pits. Start by picking up the colorful walking map for the historic area at the train station tourist office. Then climb the tower in the Gothic Munster Cathedral. From here you can gaze down on a huddle of reddish-brown roofs resembling the hats of shoppers in a marketplace. Lift your gaze and you are treated to mountain peaks rising up through a sea of mist. This panoramic view provokes reflection on the striking achievements of this small country. Bern's outstanding botanical garden is a great stop for a picnic lunch. Directions: Cross the Kornhausbrucke from the old town, and then continue north along the quay for 200 meters.

Works by Bern's homeboy and Switzerland's most famous artist, Paul Klee, are displayed in Bern's exciting new Paul Klee-Zentrtum museum designed by Renzo Piano. They include dream-like works of fantasy and comedy in a colorful distortion of reality. Directions: Tram 5 to Ostring. The city's Kunstmuseum has an exceptional collection by the 15th-century Swiss artist Hodler, as well as by contemporaries of Klee such as Kandinsky, Modigliani, and Picasso; closed Monday. Directions: Close to the Lorrainebrucke, on the old town side; Holderstrasse 8-12. Before heading to the Alps visit the Swiss Alpine Museum. An incredibly detailed relief map, stories of heroism and everyday life, and excellent flora and fauna displays will add immensely to your experience in the mountains; closed Monday. Directions: Cross the Kirchenfeldbrucke from the old town to Helvetiaplatz, where Bern's major museums are clustered. The Alpine Museum is at Helvetiaplatz 4. If you are here on a Tuesday or Saturday morning, stock up on supplies at the lively open market on Bundesplatz. Directions: On the north side of the Parliament Building. Walk south from the train station to Bundesgasse, then east to the square. It's easy to take public transportation from the campgrounds, and good underground parking is available at the train station.

▲**Camping:** 3km southeast of the city in the suburb of Waburn. Off 6 exit Ostring. Follow signposting to Waburn and camping on the west side of the River Aare. Camping Eichholz (03 1961 2602); closest to the city; large; cabins; public transport to city; open May-September; $$. • 6km northwest of the city on a lake. Exit A1 for Bethlehem. Follow signposting for Wohlen and the lake. TCS Kappelenbrucke (03 1901 1007); popular with families; bike rental; open all year; $$$.

Around Bern

Just south of Bern, pre-Alpine hills and rolling plateaus are laden with fruit orchards and dairy farms. Clanging cowbells, chiming church bells, and birdsong fill the air with a "Heidi" ambiance. Called the Emmental Region, cheese museums, ancient walking paths, and flag waving towns lie beneath the towering mountains. Weekly morning markets bustle with local shoppers, buying high quality food at a reasonable price, so plan to stop and stock up on supplies. On Thursdays a morning market is held in Burgdorf at the Old Town Square, and on Friday mornings one is held in Konolfingen on Viehmarktplatz. For touristy fun, join the throngs watching cheese being made at the Show Dairy. It's free and open daily. Directions: Drive northeast of Burgdorf up the mountain to the village of Affoltern, then follow signposting for Schaukserei. In Fribourg, an easy-going non-touristy town, medieval wooden bridges cross the River Sarine onto cobblestone streets lined with picturesque homes that are lit outside at night with wrought-iron lanterns. The town's especially colorful on Wednesday and Saturday mornings when stalls in the Place Python, located in the center of the modern part of town, are loaded with flowers and vegetables. If you are in the area on the last Saturday of the month you can purchase memorable souvenirs and gifts from artisans at the crafts market held on the cobblestone street down from Place Python, Rue de Lausanne.

▲**Camping**: 16km north of Bern on A1/E25, exit east onto 23 for Burgdorf and drive 4km. Follow signposting for pool and camping. CampingWaldegg (07 8871 8780); small; view of the castle; open May-Sept; $$. On the Schiffenensee, northeast of Fribourg. Exit west off E27 at Dudlingen. Follow signposting in the direction of Murten. Camping Schiffensensee (37 433 4860); nice location on the lake; large; popular with families; tennis courts; mini-golf; open April-Oct; $$

Jungfrau Region

This region is quintessential travel-poster Switzerland, with superb views of giant peaks, narrow forested gorges, pristine lakes, tumultuous waterfalls, cog railways, a profusion of Alpine trails, and picturesque villages and towns that welcome visitors. Tourist-oriented, the region's goal is to provide oases of quiet beauty and adventure for everyone. Interlaken, located between the two lakes Brienzer See and Thuner See, is the hub. Extreme sports are a specialty in this region. If you are ready for some thrills, peruse the racks of colorful brochures at tourist office, train station, and campground. You'll find excellent outfitters for para-gliding, bungee-jumping, white-water rafting, canyoning, and kayaking.

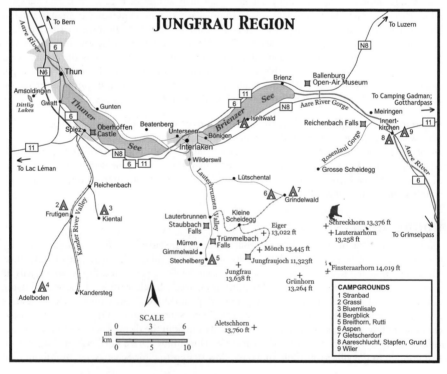

JUNGFRAU REGION

CAMPGROUNDS
1 Stranbad
2 Grassi
3 Bluemlisalp
4 Bergblick
5 Breithorn, Rutti
6 Aspen
7 Gletscherdorf
8 Aareschlucht, Stapfen, Grund
9 Wiler

The town hosts a highly spirited stage production of Schiller's beloved story about William Tell and the Swiss fight for independence from the Hapsburgs. Performed in a huge outdoor theatre, the production is lively with flower-garlanded cows, galloping horses, and barking dogs; performed Thursday through Sunday night; get tickets at the campground or tourist office. Directions: Follow the centrum signs from N8 to the railroad station. The historically accurate open-air museum in Ballenberg recreates country living from every region in Switzerland. Wooden chalets, stone farmhouses, vegetable gardens, and fields where farm animals graze are all tucked into the property's woods. Check the schedule at the entrance for demonstrations of life on the farm; open daily. Directions: Located at the northeast end of Brienzer See, 3km east of Brienz. It is well signposted; from highways 6/11 or 4. Sidewalk cafes and flowers spill from the two-level shopping street of Hauptgasse in Thun, whose old-style ambiance is enhanced by a turreted castle standing guard on top of the hill. Perched prettily on the edge of the lake at Spietz, elegant Oberhofen Castle has massive flower gardens and a maze of luxuriously decorated rooms. To see the lakeside sights, take a seagull escorted steamer and enjoy a graceful glide across the lakes of Brienzer See and Thuner See.

Cycle routes in the area include an almost level 23 kilometer loop that goes south along the westside of Thuner See, looping to the tiny Amsoldingen and Dittlig lakes. A downhill route of 30 kilometer on the south side of Thuner See follows the River Kander through a snowcapped mountain gorge bright with flower-filled meadows. Park at the train station in Spietz, and take your bike on the train up to Kanderstag. On the east side of the Brienzersee, from Brienz to Interlaken, an almost level bike route passes good bathing beaches and the picturesque fishing village of Iselwald. At the southeast end, the route turns inland at Boigen and gradually climbs up to the waterfalls in the Lauterbrunnen Valley. At the northeast end it is more level, passing through the Aare river gorge to Meiringen. It becomes a challenging route from Meiringen, ascending 1,400 meters for a 17 kilometer ride up through the magnificent mountain scenery of the Rosenlaui Gorge and on to the Reichenbach falls. This could become a downhill ride by taking a train up through the gorge to Grosse Scheidegg. Walkers take this same route. To find the cycle paths, use the Bicycling Map of Switzerland.

Walking trails lace the entire area, passing the celebrated brown-and-white cows whose jangling bells lend a lighthearted rhythm to your step through the meadows. Routes pass waterfalls that plunge wildly from sheer cliffs where chamois graze. Songbirds twitter sweetly in pine-scented woodlands, and wispy clouds float around the sharp-edged massifs, including the famous Eiger, Monch, and Jungfrau. Trains, buses, and cablecars allow for easy downhill walks, and cozy mountain inns provide rest and refreshment. Nestled in a tiny glacier bowl, Grindelwald serves as a picturesque town for cablecar lifts to the mountain meadows, tundra summits, and to trailheads for routes into the Lauterbrunnen Valley, Staubbach, and Trummelbach Falls. In July, "lul-lul-lahee-o-o-o" echoes joyfully across the stupendous precipices during the town's yodeling festival. Directions: Drive south out of Interlaken for 8km in the direction of Lauterbrunnen and Grindelwald. At the fork, it's 12km to Grindelwald and 4km to Lauterbrunnen. High above the Lauterbrunnen Valley, both Gimmelwald and Murren perch prettily on cliffs with classic vistas of the Jungfrau. Scenic trails wind like lengths of yarn through the entire area. Only if the weather is predicted to be clear should you get up early and take the train to Jungfraujoch, which at 3,452 meters is the highest railway station in Europe. The fare is expensive, but early riders get a discount. Dress warmly, bring sunglasses and a picnic lunch, and be ready for lines. The steep ride begins at Kleine Scheideggthe plateau halfway between Grindelwald and Gimmelwald and picks up passengers at Interlaken, Grimwald, and Lauterbrunnen.

▲**Camping in the area:** There is an abundance of campgrounds throughout the whole region. Many are resort-like and expensive. I've searched for less expensive but still scenic ones that are close to hiking trails or points of interest.

East of Interlaken on the lake. • On the east side of the Brienzer Sea at Iseltwald, close to the tunnel. Strandbad Camping (33 845 1201); terraced; lovely location; popular with families; open May-Sept; $$.

Close to Gimmelwald and Murren. • Follow signposting from Interlaken south in the direction of Murren for 17km. Pass through Murren to the village of Stechelberg. Breitorn Camping (33 855 1225) and Rutti Camping (33 855 2611). They both have lovely locations with view of the mountains; close to hiking lifts to the trailheads; open all year; $$.

Close to Grindelwald. • At the end Grindelwald in the direction of Gletscherdorf/Schlucht (glacier) down a steep descent towards river. Gletscherdorf (33 853 1429); close to Eiger glacier; open May-Sept; $$. • 6km southwest of Grindelwald. Before town center exit west downhill towards train station. Follow signposting up hill. Aspen (33 853 1124); small; nice views of Eiger; open May-Sept; $$

In Innertkirchen close to the Aareschlucht Gorge hiking trail. These all have lovely views of the mountains. • Aareschlucht (33 971 5332) open July-August; $$; • Stapfen (33 971 1348); open all year; $$ and Grund (33 971 4767); open all year; $$. • Closeby in the village of Wyler. Wyler(33 971 8451); open April-Oct; $$.

9km east of Innertkirchen in Gadmen. Gadman (33 975 1280); close to hiking and rock climbing area; "tipi" cabins; open mid-May-mid-Sept; $$.

South of Spiez. 13km south in Frutigen. • At the south end of town on the east side of the river. Grassi (33 671 1149); caravan rental; nice location on the river; open year round; $$. • 30km south of Spiez in Abelboden. Bergblick (33 673 1454); close to lifts to the mountains; caravan rental; open all year; $$. • 13km south of Spiez in Kiental. 7km south of Spiez at Reichenback exit for Kiental and drive 6km to Kiental. Bluemlisalp (33 676 1235) close to lift for hiking; open all year; $$.

Luzern

Luzern makes an easy and interesting stopping place on your way to or from the mountains. The Transport Museum alone is worth a detour to the city, particularly for kids. It's a hands-on place filled with trains, airplanes, and boats that they can inspect and actually climb on. Informative films stimulate the senses while letting you rest your feet; open daily. Directions: On the north side of the lake, close to Camping Lido at Lidostrasse 5. Parking is available or take the bus. Luzern is an easy town for a stroll. Starting at Kapellplatz, walk across the famous covered bridge, Kapellbruke. Then walk west on Furrengasse to see the brightly painted facades of the 15th-century buildings as you wander towards Kornmakt. Stop for a "close-friend peek" of Picasso in his namesake museum on Furrengasse. An immense collection of photos taken by a close family friend, David Douglas, hang on its walls; open daily. Pick up a snack from the quayside stalls along the Reuss River, then drive or take a bus to see Luzern's famous Lion Monument. The melancholy rock-hewn lion gazes sadly over his fountain, contemplating the professional Swiss soldiers who died trying to protect Marie Antoinette from the furies of revolutionary Paris. Directions: At the northwest end of the lake, follow the main street, Alpenstrasse, to Zurichstrasse and Glacier Park. Mark Twain visited both Luzern and nearby Mt. Rigi. In *A Tramp Abroad,* he spins a hilarious yarn about how he journeyed to Mt. Rigi to see the sunrise. It's a very popular hike and destination for tourists and locals alike. Directions: Take the train from Kussnacht, on the northern tip of Lake Luzern, to Seeboldenalp, where there is a nice walking path and a cog-rail train to the summit. Across the lake from Mt. Rigi, a cog-rail train, that advertises itself as the steepest of its kind in the world, whisks riders to the top of Mt. Pilatus.

If you have kids with you, the Goldau Nature Park is a good outing. Tame forest animals wander about in the wooded park and allow petting, while others are viewed in natural enclosures. An adjoining adventure playground has a rope ladder leading up into the pine trees. Bring food and charcoal for a barbecue in the picnic area; open daily. Directions: Goldau is off N4, southeast of Luzern. Drive east of Luzern towards the Zuger See, then exit onto N4 and drive about 16km. The Swiss Walking Trail along the Urner See opened in 1991 to commemorate the 700th anniversary of the Swiss nation. The route's northeast corner is at Brunnen. It follows the lake south to Flugen, then

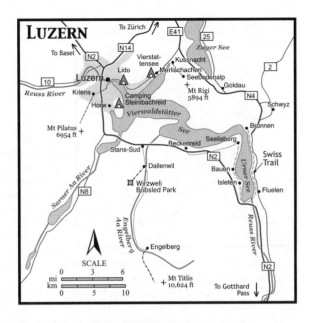

over on the west side to Isleten, Bauen, and Seelisberg. Directions: N4 ends at Brunnen at the northeast corner of the Urner See, southeast of Luzern. To begin on the west side, exit N2 at Beckenried and take the small road that twists 14km through beautiful scenery and out to the promontory and Seelisberg.

For a summer bobsled ride, take the aerial cable ride from Dallenwil up to Wirzweli Bobsled Park; open daily. Directions: From the Stans-Sud exit off N3 it's 4km to Dallenwil. Wednesday river-rafting trips on the Engelberg Aa River can be booked with the tourist office in Engelberg. If the weather is clear, take a cablecar ride up to Mt. Titlis. The Engelberg Aa River recreational area is south of Lucerne, off N2. Directions: Drive 9km south of Lucerne on N2 exiting at Stans-Sud, continue south in the direction of Engelberg.

▲Camping: • On the lake 9km east of Luzern off roadway 2, before the village of Meggan in Merlischachen. Vierwaldstattersee (41 377 4044); walking/bike lakeside path to Luzern; open April-Sept; $$. • Close to the Transport Museum signposted Lido. Lido (41 370 2146); popular; large; adjacent to lakeside walking/biking path; open April-Oct; $$. • South of Luzern, close to the lake in the suburb of Horw. Camping Steinibachried (41 340 3558); close to the lake; large; cars separate from tents; large; bus to Lucerne; open April-Sept; $$$.

ZURICH

Switzerland's inexpensive car rental rates make Zurich a good arrival city. The airport is small and easy to get in and out of for a first-time European traveler and driver. A terrific lakeside campground is relatively easy to find, and such a tranquil setting makes a good place to rest from jetlag. The Kuntsthaus is home to Switzerland's most impressive collection of fine art, ranging from 15th-century to contemporary. It has a sizable collection of Hodler's oils and Giacometti's sculpture, and a whole room is dedicated to Marc Chagall; closed Monday. Directions: From the closest bridge to the lake crossing the Limmat River, walk east on Ramistrasse to Hirschengraben One. On a sunny day, the luminous color streaming in through the stained-glass window

crafted by Chagall in the Fraumunster Church is awe-inspiring. From here, walk across the Munster Bridge to examine Giacometti's stained-glass windows in the Grossmunster Cathedral, where Zwingli once preached stern "work and pray" sermons. Directions: The Munster Bridge is the second bridge from the lake. The churches face each other across the river. Visiting a zoo is the perfect change of pace, and Zurich has an excellent one. Directions: In the Zurichberg woods, on the east side of the Limmat River, north of the city center. Nice walking paths follow the shoreline of Lake Zurich, which you can enjoy as James Joyce did when he wrote *Ulysses.* Joyce is buried in Zurich. Kids love Alpamare, an enormous water park with wave pools, exciting slides, and flumes; open daily. Directions: Drive south of Zurich on N3 or Seestrasse for 32km along the west side of Lake Lucerne to Pfaffikon.

Radiant in theatrical beauty, St Gallen's Abbey is world-renowned because of its stunning library's Baroque interior and enormous collection of medieval books and manuscripts. Visitors shuffle across the gorgeous inlaid floors in felt slippers, gasping at the breathtaking ceiling frescoes and the incredible floor to ceiling rare book collection.; open daily. Directions: 70km from Zurich, close to the Bodensee.

The Gotthard Pass separates Swiss-Italian Ticino from central Switzerland. To cycle or walk the scenic old Gotthard Road on the north side, drive up to Goschenen and the north portal of the Gotthard Tunnel, then cycle or walk down to Wassen. Bicycle rental and transport is available at Goschenen; reserve ahead.

▲**Camping:** • 8km southwest of the city in the suburb of Wollishofen. Drive out of the city on 3 in the direction of Thalwil. At Wollishofen, take exit 3 and drive south on the lakeside road, Seestrasse. Camping Seebucht (01-482-1612); lovely location on the lake; bus to Zurich; popular; car separate from tent; open May-Sept; $$$. • East of Zurich on the Greifensee. Drive southeast of Zurich on 52 for 10km. Exit for Maur and the lake. Rausenbach (019 80 0959) and Maurholtz (019 80 0266). They are both popular with families; noise from airplanes (in Zurich flight path); cars separate from tent; open April-Oct; $$. • Near St Gallen. Drive northeast of St Gallen to Wittenbach then take the smaller road west to Bernhardzell. Camping Leebrucke (071 298 4969); close to the river; small; open May-September; $$.

Engadine Valley and Parc Nazuiunal Svisser

Alluring little villages with creamy-white houses studiously etched with sgraffiti–intricate curlicued designs and pictures–line the cobblestone streets and squares in the Engadine Valley, Switzerland's southeastern corner. Here alpine meadows are ablaze with high alpine wildflower color. Views of snowy mountains, pine-scented forests, and glittering lakes become almost ho-hum. Pristine and vigorously protected Parc Naziunal Svisser is Switzerland's only national park and is perfect for bird and wildflower enthusiasts. Stringent rules even protect noise levels, so sightings of chamois, deer, and ibex are common. Golden eagles, white-winged snowfinch, and citril finch are just some of the species often sighted. The elusive tiny wallcreeper climbs the rocks at the bottom of the Clemgia Gorge, in the northeastern end of the park, making life-list-

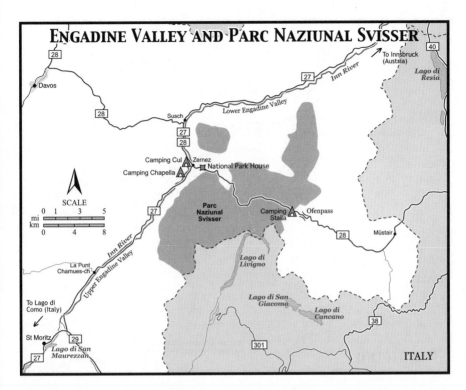

ENGADINE VALLEY AND PARC NAZIUNAL SVISSER

ing birders very happy. Marmots peek up through moss campion and mountain heather. With patience, hikers find the beloved edelweiss and fairyslipper orchids. Bring guidebooks from home or purchase one. Post buses run frequently throughout the park, making it easy for shuttles to and from hiking trails. The staff at National Park House, located one kilometer east of Zernez, has information about what sightings were made and where that week in this pristine and unique park. Directions: Zernez is 32 km east of Davos or 30 km northeast of St. Moritz.

▲Camping: • Follow signposting out of town in the direction of St Moritz. Cul Camping(81 856 1462); beautiful location; easy walk into town; open May-Sept; $$. • On the same road. From the railway station drive one kilometer, crossing over the high bridge. Chapella Camping (81 854 1206); small; basic; pretty location on the river; open May-Oct; $$. • 20km southeast in the direction of Mustair at the foot of the Ofenpass. Staila Camping (81 858 5628); great location for hiking in the park; pool; tennis; open May-Oct; $$.

The Ticino
High up in the mountains, not far from the Rhone and Rhine rivers, the Ticino River bursts from its snowbound source to make its way down through granite and gneiss to Lago Maggiore. Linking Italy with Switzerland, the Ticino is more Italian than Swiss in cultural heritage and way of life. Swiss wooden chalets give way to split-slab granite roofs covering stone houses in tiny hillside villages. In the sunny valley floor and on the terraced hillsides, a Mediterranean ambiance prevails. The lakeshore of Lago Maggiore is heavily indented, separating the towns with tranquil, flower-filled lakeside parks. Narrow river gorges, dappled with sunlight from chestnut and pine trees, hide tiny villages with stone staircases, medieval bridges, and friendly wine grottos.

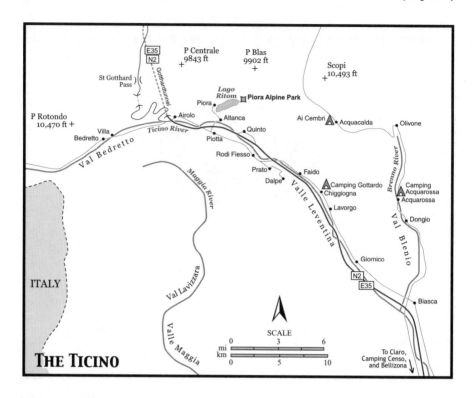

Valle Leventina

Those hurrying to Lago Maggiore and Italy often bypass this scenic area. It begins at the top and south side of the Gotthard Pass. At Airolo, a small road leads west into Val Bedretto, passing the picturesque riverside villages of Villa and Bedretto. On the east side, you can walk or bike along Lake Ritom to Piora Alpine Park. Directions: In Airolo drive south on the old road to Piotta, then take the small road up through Altanca to the power station at Piora and park. Piora Alpine Park is just beyond the northeast end of the lake. Beyond tranquil Quinto, between the villages of Rodi-Fiesso and Giornico, the old Gotthard Road thunders with tumultuous waterfalls. On the south side of the river at Rodi-Fiesso, a tiny road leads up through the villages of Prato nd Dalpe to high pastures. Post buses can provide shuttles between the little villages for cycle rides or walks. However, they don't have room to transport bikes, so if you have your own bike drive up to your starting point and park your car. At the end of your descent, lock your bike to a bike stand and take the post bus back to your car. Return with your car to pick up your bike. It's popular to ride down the old canton road from Airolo to Biasca, and bicycle rentals are available at the Airolo station. Besides the incredible beauty of the scenery along this route, little villages make great places for snacks and rest. Rented bikes are returned to the Biasca rail station at the bottom. Use information from the Bike-Rent brochure to make reservations ahead.

▲Camping: • Exit N2/E35 for Faido, and drive to the village of Chiggiogna. Camping Gottardo (091-866-1562); beautiful location close to the waterfalls; small; popular; pool; open all year; $$$. • Exit N2/E35 for Biasca. Continue south on the smaller road in the direction of Bellinzona for 10 kilometers to Claro. Censo Camping (091 863 1753); lovely location; pool; sauna; some road noise; open April-Sept; $$.

Valle Blenio

Just east of the Valle Leventina, the Valle Blenio is lush with orchards, vineyards, and wine grottos. Years ago the grottos became the favorite spot for the men of the village to meet on Sunday. They'd play a game of bocce, and then sit under a shade tree and talk things over while drinking a glass of local wine. Often someone brought a special snack from home. Over the years the grottos attracted the town residents and later people from the city. Now in these shady, rustic settings, usually close to a bocce court, people still relax over glasses of local wine and simple food. Directions: Exit highway 2 at Biasca, and drive north to Dongio. The villages between Dongio and Olivone are particularly picturesque. Romanesque stone churches with free-standing bell towers overlook the villages from the hillsides. The dramatic, pyramid-shaped Sosto peak looms over the north end of the valley.

▲**Camping:** • Exit N2/E35 at Biansca, and drive 13km north to the village of Acquaross, just north of Dongio. Camping Acquarossa (091 871 1603); restful location; barbecue; popular with families; open all year; $$. • 18km farther, north of Acquaross in Acquacalda. Ai Cembri Camping (09 1872 2610); small; beautiful location close to the river; open March-Oct; $$$.

Bellinzona

Charming piazzas, shaded arcades, and three castles make this market town a nice stop. Often overlooked by vacationers on their way to the lakes, it retains a small town ambiance. The Saturday morning market in Piazza Nosetto, the town's heart, is superb. The stairs of the narrow alley next to the San Pietro church in Piazza Collegiata lead up to Castello Montebello. From the ancient walls of the Castello, there is a grand panorama of the town, the Ticino valley, and Lago Maggiore. A fine archaeological museum is housed in Castello Grande, noted for its two 13th-century towers.

▲**Camping:** • Southwest of Bellinzona, 5km west of the town of Sementina in the village of Guido. Camping La Serta (091 859 1155); small and simple; pleasant location on the river; open April-Sept.; $$. • 11km northeast of Bellinzona. Exit N2/E35 at Bellinzona nord onto 13 and drive east 7km to Roveredo. Vera Camping (91 827 1857); great location on the river; popular with kayakers; open April-Oct; $$.

Valle Verzasca

Secluded and quiet, the road into this shaded valley climbs up past vineyards and through moss-covered tunnels to the tiny cliff-clinging village of Corippo, once noted for its weavers. Built long before cars came along, its streets are for pedestrians only and you must park below. Stone steps lead past a gurgling fountain, eaves drip with bougainvillea, and under shady grape arbors families gather to eat and relax by their miniscule vegetable gardens. The highlight of the valley, however, is the medieval double-arched bridge, Ponte dei Salti at Lavertezzo. In the summer, swimmers dive into the tumbling green waters of the Verzasca River from smooth boulders that line its banks, or from the bridge itself. Directions: Drive west of Bellinzona on 13 for 15km to Gordola. Exit onto the small road heading north into the valley in the direction of Brione and Sonogno. The bridge is 10km from Gordola.

Valle Maggia

A favorite with walkers, the villages of Maggia Valley are set amid meadows and vineyards. Sixteenth-century painted-wood ceilings and frescoes grace the lovely little chapel of St. Maria della Grazia, near the bridge in the village of Maggia. Five kilometers farther, the Soladino Falls thunder down from their 90-meter height. At the village of Cevio, another five kilometers on, a narrow corkscrew road winds up through the spectacular countryside, through the village of Cerentino, to Ticino's highest village at 1,503 meters, Bosco Gurins. Directions: Leave Locarno driving west then northwest, staying on the east bank of the Maggia River. At the Brolla Bridge continue on the east side of the river, passing the village of Avegno di Fuori. It's 9km from the bridge to the village of Maggia.

▲**Camping**: • In Gordevio, 5km south of Maggia. Da Renato Camping (91 753 1364); close to the river; tennis; playground; open April-Oct; $$.

The Lakes and their Towns

Lively Locarno's summer guests enjoy themselves in an al fresco setting. Considered one of the sunniest spots in Switzerland, lakeside beaches and sidewalk cafes are gay with people soaking up the rays. In August, it's jammed for the International Film Festival. Though Ascona's narrow streets are lined with tasteful art galleries, exquisite jewelry stores, and stylish boutiques, a stroll through town with a stop at Chiesa St. Pietro e Paollo to admire the interior 16th-century frescoes is free. The Museo Comunale d'Arte Moderna has a terrific collection; closed Monday. In July, jazz and gospel music fill the warm evening air as the town hosts a New Orleans Music Festival. Lugano's beautifully landscaped lakeside parks come alive under starry skies with music festivals and outdoor movies. While away some time on a boat ride or walk to Gandria, an old fishing village that is now popular with tourists.

▲**Camping**: Lake Locarno is dotted with large, very expensive, resort-like camping places. Here's a couple that are more reasonable. At the north end of the lake close to Vira. Exit 13 at Locarno and drive east in the direction of Vira and the lake. Vira-Bellavista Camping (91 795 1477); small; simple; open May-Oct; $$. Off the northeast end of the lake in the village of

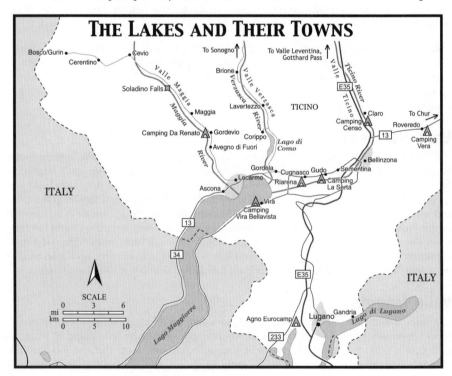

Cugnasco. Riarena Camping (91 859 1688); large; nice pool and playground; open April-Oct; $$$. Just north of Lugano. Exit A2/E35 for Lugano Nord and drive east one kilometer to the suburb of Agno. Eurocamp (09 1605 2114); good location; large; popular with families; open April-Oct; $$.

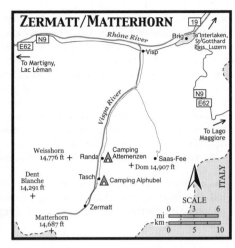

Zermatt/Matterhorn

There is something magical about the Matterhorn. Its colossal overhang, a powerful optical illusion, makes you feel that you are looking up at an enormous, masterfully crafted sculptural piece. Although it is a magnet for serious mountain climbers from all over the world, plenty of lower trails allow gentle meanders. Take a cable car or chairlift to trails above the timberline for the best views. It's often cloudy, so wear warm clothes. Fascinating stories of early attempts at climbing the Matterhorn and the tragedy of the eventual conquest, are told in the Alpine Museum.

Zermatt has no cars. You'll need to leave yours behind and stay at one of the inexpensive hostelries. Use your guidebook to reserve ahead or check the list in the train station upon arrival. To reach Zermatt, you must take the train. Drive to Tash, six kilometers from Zermatt, and park at the railway station. Directions: Zermatt is almost due east from Geneve. 70km east of Martigny exit N9 at Visp and drive south on the small road following the rail tracks for 30km up to Tash.

▲**Camping**: • In Tash. Camping Alphubel (27-967-3635). • Just before Tash, outside of Randa. Camping Attemenzen (27 967 2555). Both have lovely locations; are large; parking is separate from tent; open May-Sept; $$. There are numerous campgrounds along E62 coming into the area.

GENEVE

When you walk or bike ride along the quay of Lake Geneve, known as Lac Leman in this French-speaking city, your eyes are drawn to Geneve's symbol–Jet d'Eau, the enormous geyser of water that gushes up 140 meters. Gazing farther out onto the lake, your eyes feast on the perky sails of sleek yachts, fine old schooners, and flag-waving steamers. If you turn from the lake at Jardin Anglais, you can see the city's other symbol the carefully planted flower clock. From here, amble into the Old Town, Vielle Ville, and lose yourself in its twisting alleyways. Stop in one of the neighborhood parks and join in the contemplation of a game of chess being played on a giant board. Meander farther up the hill to the Cathedrale St. Pierre, where

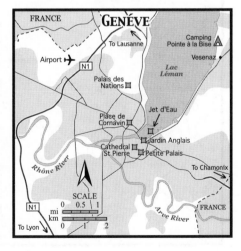

John Calvin preached his fierce sermons turning Geneve into the Protestant Rome. The famous Reformation monument is nearby. Then take a restful steamer ride, watching the mountains that nestle the lake pass by. On a clear day, Mont Blanc will be visible, probably swathed in a tulle of cloud. Boats leave from Pont du Mont Blanc. You enter the compelling Musee International de la Croix-Rouge through a trench that feeds into a mirrored courtyard where you see only the reflected images of yourself beside bound and blindfolded stone figures. Rent the audio-guide to learn the astonishing details of prison life, natural disasters, and war. The museum should not be missed; closed Tuesday. Directions: Take bus 8 from the train station at Place de Cornavin. More than just a grand collection of art, the Petite-Palais's encyclopedic collection is housed in a lovely mansion and is curated to help the viewer understand the various schools of art from 1880 to 1930; open daily. Directions: Take bus #1 or #3 to Blvd. Helvetique.

▲**Camping:** • 7km north of Geneve on the east side of the lake. Exit N5 for Vesenaz, and follow signposting to the lake. Camping Pointe a la Bise (22 752-1296); lovely location; large; popular with families; cycle path to the city along the lake; public transportation close by; open April-Sept; $$.

Along Lac Leman

Lausanne is Europe's rollerblading and skateboarding capital. It litterly "hisses' from the spinning of tiny wheels and the clack of boards. Its large multi-ethnic populace gives it a youthful almost sexy (for Switzerland) ambiance. In tune with this is the eccentric collection in the Musee de l'Art Brut, a bizarre and fun collection of works by unknown and self-trained artists; closed Monday. Directions: North of the lake, just south of the suburb of Prilly, follow signage for Palais de Beaulieu. The gallery is at 11 Av. De Bergieres. Banks of videos replay the crowning moment

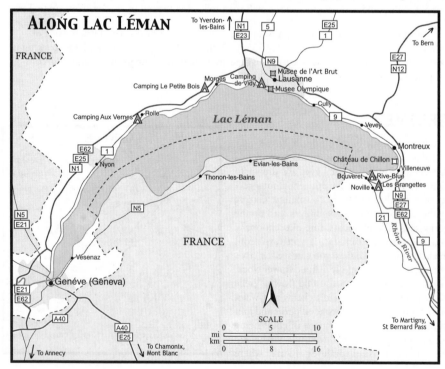

of some of the most famous Olympic events in the Musee Olympique; open daily. Up the hill from it, the Musee de l'Elysee presents a remarkable, continuously changing cycle of photographic work. Directions: On the lake at Ouchy, Lausanne's resort town. Montreux's brooding Chateau de Chillon is situated on the lovely swan-dotted shoreline. Its stony, pillared dungeon was Bryon's inspiration for *The Prisoner of Chillon*; open daily. Directions: • Off N9, 3km south of town, on the lake. Lively all summer long with music festivals, Montreux's most well known is the two-week-long Montreux Jazz Festival in mid-July.

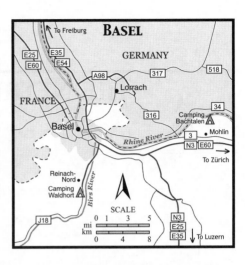

▲**Camping:** • On the west side of Lac Leman off E25/N1. On the lake at Rolle. Aux Vernes Camping (21 825 1239); beautiful location; popular with families; open April-Sept; $$. • In Lausanne. Exit N1 at Lausanne-Sud/La Maladiere, and follow signposting. Camping de Vidy (021-624-2031); in a recreational area; large; bike rental; bus to the city; popular with families; open all year; $$. • On the southeast end of Lac Leman not far from Montreux. Exit E27/E62 for Villeneuve and drive west in the direction of Evian for 2km to the east side of Bouveret. Rive-Blue Camping (24 481 2161); good location on the lake; large; popular with families; parking separate from tent; open April-Sept; $$. • In the same area but south of Bouveret in the village of Noville. Les Grangettess Camping (21 960 2030); great location; popular with families; parking separate from tent; open April-Sept; $$.

Basel

Exceptionally high quality collections of art in Basel's many top-rated museums make this a must-stop for art enthusiasts. The city's electorate has voted to spend millions to acquire some of the best 20th-century works. Masterfully designed buildings by the likes of Renzo Piano, Mario Botta, and Frank Gehry house these incredible collections. Fondation Beyeler, the Kunstmuseum, Jean Tingley, and Vita Design are all known internationally. Art Basel, the largest contemporary art show in the world, is held in nearby Messe in mid-June.

▲**Camping:** • On the Rhein River, about 30km east of Basel. Off E60/3 exit for Rheinfelden following signposting to the end of the village Rhein for 4km. Camping Bachtalen (06 1851-5095); small and restful; near the Rhine; open April-Sept; $$. • 5km south of the city in the suburb town of Reinach. Exit off J18 at Reinach-Nord, and follow signposting for just over a kilometer where road curves at the tram station. Camping Waldhort (06 1711 6429); tram to city center; pool; popular with families large; open Mar-Oct; $$.

THE NETHERLANDS

SCALE

| mi | 0 | 15 | 30 |
| km | 0 | 25 | 50 |

West Frisian Islands

Ameland

Waddenzee

Afsluitdijk

Leeuwarden

Groningen

Friesland

IJssel Meer

Edam

NORTH SEA

Haarlem

AMSTERDAM

Apeldoorn

De Hoge Veluwe National Park

DEN HAAG

Utrecht

Arnhem

Europort

Rotterdam

GERMANY

Rhine

Delta Expo

NETHERLANDS

Essen

Eindhoven

Duisburg

Düsseldorf

Antwerpen

Gent

Köln

Schelde

BRUSSELS

Maastricht

Bonn

FRANCE

BELGIUM

Maas River

Liege

THE NETHERLANDS

www.visitholland.com

Picture a young woman, her bicycle basket overflowing with a riot of brilliant blooms, pedaling steadily along a leafy canal lined with perfectly symmetrical gabled houses. This is quintessential Holland. Throughout the country, back roads and cycle paths fringe patchwork fields of brilliant flowers and apple-green meadows where skylarks sing. They cross canals over wooden bridges and wind through cheerful towns. Bridges lift, holding back traffic while a small boat floats by. Carillon bells ring from tall church steeples with favorite hymns, folk songs, and waltzes. Town halls take the place of palaces with pinnacles, finials, and lace-like arches. Cozy cafes are fragrant with fresh-brewed coffee and apple tarts, and they hum with music and folks immersed in quiet conversations.

Bicycles are dearly loved and revered. Even the queen mingles with her subjects by riding her bicycle to market. With seeming ease, pets, flowers, groceries, and children are all carted happily on one bike. Stores, office buildings, parking facilities, and public transportation are all designed to accommodate them, and most major roads have a wide, separate bike lane. Make sure your set of wheels has a bell. Paths get crowded, particularly during commute time and lunch break. It's best to avoid cycling then. Bike rental shops are plentiful. Many campgrounds are close to excellent cycle paths and often rent bikes. Train stations also have rentals.

Cyclists are obligated to use the separate cycle lanes or *fietspad* (indicated by round blue signs with a white bike), when available. These lanes have their own traffic lights. White-dotted lines on a paved road indicate a cycle lane that can be used by motorists if not being used by cyclists. A lane with a continuous white line may not be used by motorists. Almost the same rules that apply to motorists, apply to cyclists. Where there are no traffic lights, cyclists must give way to traffic from the right. Remember this before you go out into a roundabout. Use a good bike lock, and attach it to the front wheel and frame and then to something solid. If you bring an expensive model from home, don't take it into major cities where expert bike thieves work. Instead, either rent one for the day or use public transportation. Always lock your bike.

You might want to join some other travelers on a cycling tour with guide. There are over 16,000 kilometers of separate cycle-paths in the country! So it's a safe and easy country to cycle as a family. The campground brochure rack or tourist office can provide you with local and country cycle path maps. Cycling through the picturesque towns and villages of Monnickendam, Volendam, Marken, and Edam, takes you across canals with hand-operated drawbridges, and past fish-smoking houses, and colorfully painted homes on stilts. Cycling paths wind around old harbors with weekend skippers and past Gothic churches and swimming beaches. Trains are bike friendly except for commute times: 6:30-9:00 AM and 4:30-6:00 PM. Your bike needs a train ticket, too. Lift yourself and your bike onto a car with a bike decal, then seat yourself beside your bike or put it in the luggage area. For more information: www.visitholland.com, then "click" active then "cycle".

Roadways are in excellent condition and well signposted. Except for Amsterdam and Rotterdam, cities are easy to drive into and park. But parking outside city centers is encouraged in the form of large parking garages and nearby public transportation that is efficient, modern, and comfortable. To cut down traffic into the country's larger cities, motorists must pay a toll to enter. Kind, polite, and helpful, the Dutch love to talk about their country and will go out of their way to give directions and information.

Masters of innovation and experimentation, the Dutch have applied their knowledge to social issues, agriculture, and industry. Experts in waterways, bridges, and hydraulic dams, they now export their knowledge of water technology. Though on the globe, the Netherlands is but a speck, in world history the Dutch have played a part way out of proportion to their country's size. Leaders in banking, shipping, and trade since the 17th-century, they established an empire on the other side of the world, set an example of democratic social order, and opened a new school of art with an astonishing group of excellent painters. Their open minds, unshakable good cheer, and ability to do a lot with a little has tuned not just their sea wall, but their culture as a whole.

Their museum collections are world-famous and older museums have been drastically restyled to keep up with the times. Many museums are closed on Monday. The variety of classical and innovative music and arts festivals is extensive. The Holland Festival in June is a month of theatre and dance throughout the larger cities. Book ahead: www.visitholland.com.

Camping is popular with vacationing Dutch families. Campgrounds are modern and well maintained, with family toilet/shower rooms, cafes, and small stores. Many campground stores bake their own bread fresh daily. What a wonderful treat to get bread still warm from the oven in the morning. Many are located close to nature reserves, tourist areas, recreational areas, sandy beaches, and some even have a pool with waterslide. They usually have a cycle path. The friendly staff are generous with help and fluent in English. Most campgrounds lease large vacation tents, which encompass a good portion of the campground. These areas are usually separate from campers who stay for a few days or overnight. Camping for two persons, a car, and tent will usually cost about 20 euros and is indicated as $$. Resort-like campgrounds will cost over 25 EU indicated as $$$.

AMSTERDAM

Wild and watery, picturesque and sophisticated, Amsterdam is probably Europe's grooviest canal town. People come to live it up, light up, inhale culture, cruise the canals, pedal around, and exclaim over flowers. In the 13th-century, Amsterdam wasn't much more than a dam across the Amstel River. Its fortunes were stimulated in 1602 by the Dutch West India Company, whose ships and sailors brought back exotic riches from the Far East. The square-riggers were unloading cargoes of silk, spices, and porcelain in the huge port. Amsterdam became the first center of bourgeois capitalism in Europe. Its location in the middle of Holland provided a protected harbor and access to both the Baltic and Rhine. Persecuted merchants, who were driven out of other countries found refuge here, giving the country the advantage of their centuries-old mercantile expertise.

Today, drifting down Amsterdam's leafy canals lined with dignified and harmonious houses, one can imagine how the markets were swamped in color and carnival and how the delectable smell of baking bread and smoking pork mingled with the aroma of fresh leather and exotic spices. Dressed like birds of paradise and strolling like peacocks, the wealthy members of the mercantile and craft guilds were highly conscious of their personal dignity and fine attire.

Along the banks of most of the canals stand rows of trim, narrow canal houses patterned with gleaming windows. They are capped with gables festooned with scrolls and fruits and flower-painted confectionary-white and looking remarkably like the whipped cream heaped on the city's hot chocolate. It's a watery web of canals—160 of them spanned by 1,281 bridges! The tangle would be extremely confusing if the three major canals weren't laid out in a handy U that wraps around the city center. Amsterdam is largely below sea level. Without the dunes and dikes on the North Sea coast, it would be underwater. A system of sluices and pumps renews the network with fresh seawater.

Stop at the main tourist office, VVV, outside Central Station on arrival. It overflows with glossy brochures and information about current events, museums, and galleries in Amsterdam and all of the Netherlands. An array of impressive events occurs in summer. Many are free. Fit a few into your visit. Amsterdam has a large number of famous museums. Buying a museum card at the VVV saves considerable money if you plan to see more than just a couple.

The Metro and trams are efficient, convenient, and easy to use. Employees speak fluent English. Buy a *strippenkaart* voucher for ten rides from the campground, a metro station, a magazine shop, or Central Station. Ask for the free transport map and English guide of the transport system. Each time you travel, validate the ticket for the number of persons using it and the number of zones you are traveling. Take the circle tram first. It makes a wide loop that passes close to most of the major sights. In summer, one departs and returns to Central Station every few minutes.

The grassy wedge of parkland edged by Amsterdam's most famous museums is called Museumplein. Here you'll find the Rijksmuseum, the Van Gogh, and the Stedelijk. Fascinating books have been written about the most famous Dutch painters; reading some before your trip will make visits to these museums more meaningful. There's no more solid bastion in Amsterdam than the Rijksmuseum. Featuring slate roofs and brick towers, this repository also has high-ceilinged galleries displaying millions of works of art: paintings, sculptures, porcelain, silver, dollhouses, tapestries, and more. To most casual visitors the museum is synonymous with Rembrandt, particularly his gargantuan portrait of a militia company, *The Nightwatch*. Rembrandt was a master with the play of light. The figures appear remarkably true to life, right down to a different shine on boots and ribbon. With the museum map in hand go directly to the galleries that interest you most. Featuring a keen interest in human psychology, the best of the pictures are thoughtful introspection of character with a powerful handling of light and shade. Rembrandts are mingled with Hals, Steens, and Vermeers and the museum has a lovely garden in back; open daily.

The Theo Van Gogh Museum houses not only the riveting pictures by his brother Vincent, but a chronological collection of the Post-Impressionists: Gauguin, Monet, Bernard, Pissarro, Signac, and Seurat. All are curated to help you understand the artistic influences they had on one another. Each room is painted in the vibrant, radiant, and emotional colors they loved. Theo's son, V.W. Van Gogh, agreed to sell his enormous private collection if the new museum was built. The Kroller-Muller Museum also added many of their important works to the new museum. The sensational Post-Impressionist collection that resulted is one of the most important in the world; open daily.

Afterwards, climb the former skateboard ramp in the adjoining park and rest with locals as you gaze down at the Concertgebouw, the colorful trams, and the gable work and facades of the neighborhood buildings. The Stedelijk Museum of Modern Art houses permanent and temporary art exhibits extending into photography, ceramics, glass, and sculpture. Simplicity and clarity are hallmarks of Dutch design. You see the designers' hand in everyday objects from stamps to garage bins. In the Stedelijk you are impressed by the bold patterns, just handfuls of color, and designs that feed into one another. The Dutch have a long and famous tradition of photography committed to social issues, don't miss the thought-provoking section the museum as dedicated to this; open daily. The Concertgebouw, known throughout the world for its wonderful acoustics and outstanding performances, sells reasonably priced tickets from 10 AM to 5 PM daily and after 7 PM for that evening's performance. Every Wednesday, they kindly provide a free lunchtime concert.

Vondel Park, just a few minutes' walk west of Museumsplein, has walking paths that wind around leafy thickets and a swath of greenery that includes an extravagant rose garden. Here children feed the ducks that waddle around the ponds. Workers and tired tourists take short naps on its grassy meadows. Mothers admire babies in prams. And joggers keep in shape. A large collection of film memorabilia and screenings from its outstanding archive can be viewed in the old Vondelpark Pavilion, now the Filmmuseum. On Sunday afternoon the park is particularly colorful and fun with a humorous, almost anything-goes atmosphere. Wander over to the park's stage, where something is usually going on. Becoming a part of the communal spirit, laughing, and clapping with locals, is a delightful way to enjoy the Dutch.

At the Anne Frank House–immortalized by the diary the young girl wrote while hidden from the Nazis–the walls of her miniscule room are still decorated with pictures she cut from magazines. It's a popular pilgrimage. Go after 6 PM to avoid long lines; open daily until 9 PM. Directions: Walk west of Dam Square on Raadhuis to Prinsengracht. Turn north and walk 2 blocks. It's on the north side of Westerkerk, whose icon cathedral tower rewards with a panoramic and orienting view of the area after a strenuous hike up its stairs. The west edge of the canal ring, the Jordaan district, is named after the French word for garden. It has picturesque little shops, many devoted to a narrow interest. Amsterdam's brown cafés are named after their wood furnishings and wood-paneled walls that are mellowed by centuries of tobacco smoke. They are congenial places to meet locals. More like living rooms than bars, they have a cozy atmosphere created by good food, good drink, and good company. At the flower market on the Singel canal, docked barges overflow with botanical beauty–fragrant lilies, every hue of tulip, even bonsai trees. Directions: Just northwest of Dam Square. The Saturday morning market, along Cuypstraat, stretches over a kilometer and merchants in stalls sell most everything. It's multiculturism at its best, with goods of every description. Plan to buy some of the mouth-watering food for a picnic or snack, and don't forget your camera. Directions: Trams 16, 24, or 25. For many, no trip to Amsterdam is complete without visiting the Red Light District–a maze of alleys with rose-lit windows and a girl on display in each. The ambiance is laid-back and not threatening. Directions: Just northeast of Dam Square. Walk north on Warmoesstraat. Consult your guidebook to make selections from the over-flowing and imaginative cup of Amsterdam's offerings.

▲Camping: • 10km south of Amsterdam. From the airport exit onto 1/A2 and drive east, then south, for 8km. Exit onto A9 and drive east in the direction of Amersfoot. for 4km. Exit for Gaasperplas and follow signposting under the overpass. Gaasper Camping (20 696 7326); close to the Metro; strict rules keep the grassy areas nice; car park separate from campsite; very popular; security gate with deposit for key; open Apr-Dec; $$. • On the east side of the city on an island in the Usselmeer. Exit A10 onto S114 in the direction of Zeeburg. Drive south 10km then follow signposting. Camping Zeeburg (20 694 4430) popular with partying people; good place to meet fellow travelers; open all year; $$. • On its northeast corner of the city. From the ring road A-10, take exit onto N116, Amsterdam Nord. Follow signposting for centrum, and then follow signposting for camping. Camping Viliegenbos (20 636 8855); popular with young international campers; great place to meet fellow travelers; car parking separate from campsite; cycle path to city center; can be noisy at night; open Apr-Sept; $$. • In Amstelveen, east of the airport. At the airport and the junction of A4 and A9 exit east onto A9 in the direction of Amstelveen. Take exit 6 onto N231 and drive south for one kilometer. Turn left over the canal bridge and drive 2km following signposting for camping. Camping het Amsterdamse Bos (20 641 6868); airport noise; bus to city; car parking separate from campsite; open April-Oct; $$.

WEST OF AMSTERDAM
Haarlem

Robust painter Frans Hals was admired by both Van Gogh and Manet for his frank, full-bodied colors, and bold-moving strokes. He is remembered in the 17th-century almshouse where he lived out his final years with a collection that illustrates his evolution as a painter. The gargantuan picture, *Banquet of the Officers of St. George* bursts with colorful figures wearing immense sashes and established his reputation; open daily. Directions: Off A9 or A208, follow signs for centrum. Use the dome of St. Bravo's to guide you. The museum is just south of it at Groot Heiligand 62.

At the Grote Markt, step into St. Bravo and examine the famous Baroque organ boasting 5,000 pipes. Just outside the church, look up at the elaborate and capricious stepped gables of the Meat Market. From behind the church, it's a short walk to the canal and the Teylers Museum, which is the oldest museum in the country and houses a interesting collection of drawings and artifacts.

Just west of town, an elegant residential area gives way to Kennemerduinen National Park–an appealing dune and beach area. The route is popular for cycling. Directions: Off A208 exit onto 200 for Bloemendaal Aan-Zee.

If you are here in April or May, when the tulips are blooming, don't miss seeing the Keukenhof Gardens. It is perhaps the most fabulous flower garden in the world. The ephemeral tulips and other gorgeous blooms are a rainbow of colors painted with artful precision; open daily. Opening and closing dates vary according to the weather: www.keukenhof.nl. Directions: South of Haarlem on 208 in Lisse.

Kennemerduinen Nature Reserve

The wild, windswept beauty of the beach and dunes invites spending some solitary time. The inland lake, Vogelmeer, provides a resting area for migrating birds, and a bird-watching platform is available on the south shore. Check with the visitor's center at Parnassia to learn about what to look for on your walks. Directions: From Haarlem drive east on N200 in the direction of Bloemendaal aan Zee for 5km. Turn north and drive 2km to the park entrance at Parnassia.

Beverwijk Bazaar

Exotic and fun, this ethnic, weekend covered bazaar is one of Europe's largest. Its carnival-like atmosphere provides a change of pace. Bring your camera, and plan to enjoy some live music as you indulge in delicious snacks. Directions: 13km north of Haarlem, take exit 2 off A9 on the north side of the Noordzeekanal bridge and follow signposting for Beverwijkse.

▲**Camping in the area:** • In the dune area by the park. Off A9 exit onto 200 for Bloemendaal Aan Zee, and drive to the beach. Camping De Lakens (0900 384 6226); close to the beach and parklands; open April-Sept; $$$. • Due west of Keukenhof Gardens in Noordwijk, take the road north along the dune to Noordwijkerhout. Camping Jan de Wit (252 372 485); in a dune area; large; popular with families; car parking separate from campsite; open April through Sept; $$.

NORTHEAST OF AMSTERDAM
Cheese Markets

Touristy, but also fun and delicious, the cheese market porters in in Alkmaar don colorful hats and put on a show of tasting and weighing; Fridays between 10 AM and 12 Noon. Directions: Drive north of Amsterdam on A9 for 27km to Alkmaar. Exit for centrum and follow signosting for Waagplein. Use one of the large car parks then walk towards the main square, Waagplein. If you're still in a market mood, head north a couple of kilometers to see a fruit and vegetable market on a barge in Broek op Langedijk. At one time the tiny islands' rich soil and meticulous farmers grew a huge quantity of produce for Amsterdam. Farmers would load up and sell their produce on barges, a practice reenacted today; open daily. Directions: From Alkmaar, drive north on N245 in the direction of Langedijk for 3km exiting for Broek op Langdijk and follow signposting for Broeker Veiling.

Waterland

Gabled houses here are decorated like wedding cakes, with arched doorways rich in fanciful designs. Tiny gardens overflow with marigolds and hollyhocks, and narrow cobblestone streets wind like pieces of a medieval jigsaw puzzle through the little towns of Waterland. In the Rococo interiors of the Town Halls, it's easy to picture the Burgomaster in his enormous wig staring intently at a humiliated prisoner, in baggy pants and clumsy shoes while an audience of "bigwigs", extravagant in ruffs of rich starched lace and plumed high black hats, looked on. Canoeing, biking, and wind surfing are popular sports, and rentals are available in Monnickendam and at the Het Twiske nature reserve in Landsmeer. Directions: Cross over the waterway on the north side of Amsterdam on A10, and drive north on scenic N247.

Zuiderzeemuseum

One of the country's best open-air museums, Zuiderzeemueum recaptures life as it was in the harbor town from 1882 to 1932. Craftsmen, shopkeepers, and men and women tending the home and farm dress in traditional clothing and demonstrate how things were done in the "olden days"; open daily. Directions: Exit A7 east at exit 9 and 15km to Enkhuizen.

▲**Camping in the Area:** • In Edam. Exit N247 on the north side of town, and drive towards the harbor. Camping Strandbad (299 37 1994); on the water; popular with wind surfers; small; cabins; bike rental; reserve ahead; open April-Sept; $$. • On the Markermeer Sea close to Monickendam. Exit N247 for Marken/Monickendam. Drive 5km following signposting. Camping-Jachthaven (204 03 1433); nice location with sandy beach; bike rental; bus to Amsterdam; open Mar-Oct; $$. • 8km from Enkhuizen in Wijdenes. Camping Het Hof (229 50 1435); popular with windsurfers; parking separate from campsite; cycle paths; pool; open April-Sept; $$.

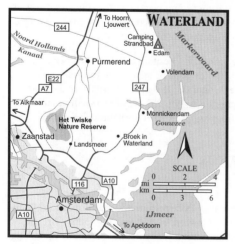

EAST OF AMSTERDAM
Hoge Veluwe National Park

Located only an hour from Amsterdam, this park is a precious spot of pine-scented tranquilly and beauty. It provides a perfect setting for the Kroller-Muller Museum's famous collection of 19th and 20th-century art. Noted for its Van Gogh collection, it also boasts works by Seurat, Picasso, and Modrian. A large sculpture garden includes pieces by Rodin, Moore, and Hepworth along with many others; closed Monday. Hundreds of bicycles are available for visitors for free to use on the lacework of cycle/walking paths. The highlight at the Visitor

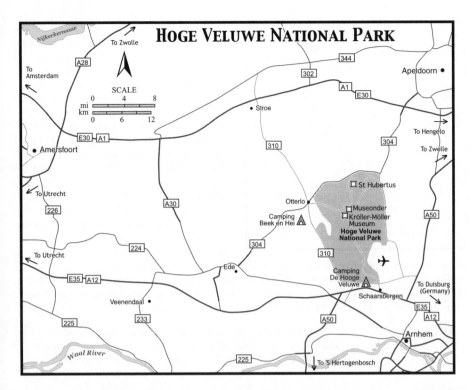

Centre is the Museonder Museum, the first underground museum in the world. Its mystical and fascinating scientific exhibits are geared to both young and old; open daily. If you want to see the impressive Art Deco hunting lodge, St. Hubertus, stop at visitor center on the day you want to visit the lodge. Reservations to see the hunting lodge can be made only at the visitor center and only on the day of your visit; open daily. Directions: From Amsterdam drive east on A1 for about 60km. Pass the exit for A30 and Ede, and drive 15km further on A1, exiting for N310 and Stroe. Drive south on N310, following signposting for 11km farther for Otterlo and Hoge Veluwe.

▲Camping: • Close to the Otterlo entrance to the park. Follow the directions to the park and Otterlo. Continue south through the village on N310 and follow signposting. Camping Beek en Hei (318 591 483); smaller; lovely location; close to the main park sights; open all year; $$. In Otterloo. Follow the directions above to Otterlo. Vakantiepark de Zanding (318 59 6111); very large; resort-like; cabins; pool; popular with families; open Apr-Oct; $$$. At the Arnhem park entrance in Schaarsbergen. North of Arnhem exit A12/E35 at exit 25 onto N310 in the direction of Arnhem. Then drive east on N311 to the park entrance. Camping de Hooge Veluwe (26 443-2272); very large; resort-like; popular with families; cabins; open April-Sept; $$$.

SOUTHWESTERN NETHERLANDS
Den Haag

The Mauritshuis, Den Haag's brightest jewel, houses a renowned collection of the Dutch master painters whose works exemplify a high degree of technical competence. Galleries are filled with evocative landscapes in which light makes the muted colors glow, as well as pieces depicting

lively music and raucous drinking. Several of Vermeer's most famous pieces, including *Girl with A Pearl Earring*, are here along with several of the intriguing Rembrandt self-portraits. Almost every work in the museum is a masterpiece. Directions: From A12/E30 drive west, exiting for Binnenhof and Den Haag CS train station. The museum is in a mansion on the east side of the Binnenhof; closed Monday. For a complete change of pace, walk across the Binnenhof to the Gevengenpoort and take a tour of the prison and its Chamber of Horrors. Then board either tram 7 or 8 to the Peace Palace and Court of International Justice. Tours include viewing the valuable gifts given to the Peace Palace by countries around the globe. From here it's a short walk to Panorama Mesdag to see the life-size circular picture of the fishing port in the late 1880s. Thirty million dollars bought Mondriaan's unfinished *Victory Boggie Woogie* for the Gemeentemuseum, so it's a highlight along with the museum's photography section; closed Sunday and Monday. Directions: 5km north of the campground in the suburb of Statenkwartier; follow signposting.

▲**Camping:** • Drive south of the Den Haag along the coast road in the direction of Kijkduin. Vakantiecentr. Kijkduinpark (70 448 2100); close to the beach and acquarium; large and resort-like; popular with families; open all year; $$$.

Delft

A pleasant but touristy canal town with old-world charm, Delft's fame comes from the blue-and-white tiles produced in the 17th-century. Originally copied from pieces of Ming dynasty China, the tile were so skillfully made that the Dutch were able to sell them to the Chinese! A nice collection is displayed in Museum Lambert van Meerten, but the best pieces made are in the Rijksmueum in Amsterdam.

▲**Camping:** • On the east edge of town, in the city recreational parkland Delfse Hout. Exit A13 for Pijnacker, and drive east following signposting. Delftse Hout Camping (213-0040); pleasant location; cabins; café and bar; cycle paths; open all year; $$. • In the same area but in the village of Delfgauw. Camping Uylenburg (214 3732); smaller; quiet; cycle paths; pen April-Sept; $.

Rotterdam

The wave of artistic energy and institutional creativity in Rotterdam is rapidly becoming the envy of Europe. With a bland ranks of postwar apartment buildings and hodgepodge of cranes that edge one of the world's largest harbors, it is a seemingly unlikely setting. Yet Rotterdam is developing a cultural model that straightforwardly acknowledges, and even embraces, its transition from an almost exclusively Dutch city to one whose non-Western, predominately Muslim immigrants, account for one-third of the metropolitan area's population. The city has a vision of integrating non-Western, predominantly Islamic art, as a cornerstone of their cultural policy. With European Union funding, the De Doelen, Rotterdam's major concert and conference hall and Rotterdamse Schouwburg, the city's major theatre, are bending over backwards to make Moroccans and Turks part of the their multiculturalism.

The Kop van Zuid dockland's renovation has earned it the nickname "Manhattan on the Maas". It reflects the vitality of a city that rose from the ashes of 1940 bombardments. The elegant Erasmus Bridge, nicknamed "The Swan", has a 456-foot-tall, asymmetric concrete pylon glowing silvery-white, and is the city's icon. Celebrity architects have given the city a dynamic, Berlin-like "almost anything goes attitude". Alluding to the tower of Pisa, Renzio Piano's KPN Telecom Tower has one façade that leans forward at a six-degree angle. Directions: Metro Wilhelminaplein. The Netherlands Architecture Institute in Museumpark is housed in a stunning building with reflecting moat, and is a must see. Architecture buffs won't want to miss taking the special architectural tour. Directions: Tram #5 or Metro Eendrachsplein. One of The Netherlands's best museums, Museum Boijmans Van Beuningen, is just across the way. It holds some of the best of the Dutch masterpieces plus an impressive array of work from Renaissance Italy and European Impressionists. The sculpture garden makes a perfect place to enjoy a break and snack; closed Monday. Directions: Tram 5 or Metro Eendrachtsplein Looking up at the immense container ships and oil tankers from the water is both a humbling and an exciting experience. Spido Cruises has harbor tours departing daily from the pier near Erasmusbrug: Metro-Leuvehaven.

One of the most actively multicultural art and music festivals in Europe is Rotterdam's Dunya Festival. *Dunya* means "world" in both Arabic and Turkish. The festival has grown into a five-day event where Arabs, Africans, Gypsies; and the usually stolid Dutch transcend ethnic, national, and religious differences by dancing, singing, and laughing together. Other festivals include the hugely successful Poetry Festival, which makes a point of featuring poets from the far corners of the world, and the Film Festival, which has become one of Europe's best. With a population that represents most of the cultures of the world, it's no wonder that Rotterdam's festivals are especially exotic. The DeParade in June is a nation-wide traveling inverse-circus extravaganza. On the last weekend in July the Zomer-Carnaval and Zomerpodnin summer stage are both hugely popular featuring decorated trucks and big beat music. Try to attend at least one.

Kinderdijk

Perhaps no other sight in The Netherlands focuses more on the Dutch attempt to reclaim land from water than the 19 ancient windmills that rise above an empty marsh in Kinderdijk. Kept in operating condition since the 18th-century, their creaks and groans are ghost-like. There's a four-kilometer walking path along the dykes and on Saturday in July and August all operate between 2 and 5PM; closed Sunday. Directions: Kinderdijk is at Albasserdam, southeast of Rotterdam and signposted off A16 just over the waterway.

▲**Camping in the area:** • On the Oude Maas river in Barendrecht, just south of Rotterdam. From A15 or A29, exit east to Barendrecht and follow signposting to Ijsselmonde, a recreational parkland and campground. Camping de Oude Maas (677-2445); pleasant setting in the marina area of a recreational park; road noise; open all year; $$. • Closer to Rotterdam. At the junction of A13 and A20 follow signposting for Rotterdam centrum and camping. Stadscamping Rotterdam (10 415 3440); convenient; road noise; cabins; open all year; $$.

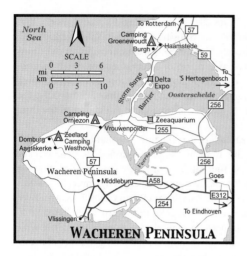

WACHEREN PENINSULA

Wacheren Peninsula

In response to the 1953 devastation caused by high tides and flooding in Zeeland–a cluster of islands and peninsulas south of Rotterdam–the Dutch embarked on a project that spanned 30 years and resulted in the most complex engineering project the world has ever seen. True to the country's heritage of making group decisions, the Storm Surge Barrier was a compromise between environmentalists, fishermen, and farmers. Waterland Neeltje Jans adjoins the Expo and provides a hands-on experience with water. It cleverly appeals to both young and old, has a dolphin rescue center, and should not to be missed; open daily. Directions: For the coastal route, use 57; otherwise take A58 to Middleburg, and then go north on 57. A sand dune park with woods and hiking/cycling paths is nearby in Westerschouwen.

The Wacheren peninsula, located southwest of the Storm Surge Barrier, is a low-key and popular vacation area for the Dutch. Stunning fields of brilliantly colored flowers, picturesque villages with inviting sidewalk cafes, softly-shaped sand dunes, and sunny beaches make you want to stay awhile. There's a terrific paved cycling/walking path through the sand dunes and another that fringes the flower fields and then passes through some villages.

▲Camping: • On the north side of the Storm Surge Barrier in Burgh-Haamstede. Camping Groenewoudt (3111-165-1410); pool; open April-Sept; $$. • On the south side of the Barrier in Vrouwenpolder. Camping Ornjezon (3111-859-1549); large; pool; small cafe; close to the dunes and beach; open May-Oct; $$$. • Close to Domburg on the Walcheren Pennisula. Drive south off the Barrier on 57 for 9km in the direction of Middleburg. Exit for Domburg and drive another 9km, following signposting for Aagtekerke. Zeeland Camping Westhove (0118-58-1809); close to the flower fields; villages; and beach; open April-Oct; $$. There are lots of campgrounds in this area. Some are expensive and resort-like.

NORTH HOLLAND
Groningen

In a dramatic decision to cut down traffic congestion, Groningen voted to remove a large downtown roadway and allocated a considerable amount of money for cycling paths. It's a joy to pedal here along with the friendly locals who fill the streets. Carillon bells ring out sweet melodies and flower stalls spill out glorious color, making you wish your hometown had voted likewise. Whimiscal and colorful, the Groninger Museum hangs over a canal inviting you to smile and enter. Start upstairs with the entrancing Dutch silver masters and

Chinese ceramic collections. The museum is noted for its avant-garde acquisitions and temporary shows; closed Monday. Directions: Follow the canal south. The museum is across from the restored Art Nouveau train station. Much of Holland's wealth still comes from shipping. Imaginatively presented exhibits in the Noordelijk Scheepvaart Museum make it easy to understand the lure of the sea; closed Monday. Directions: North of the train station across from the canal.

▲**Camping:** • 13km east of Groningen on A7/E22 in the direction of Winschoten exit for Foxhol, and drive south to Kropswolde. Then follow signposting through the Zuidlaardermeer parkland. Camping Meerwijck (59 832 3659); beautiful lakeside setting in a large parkland; children's indoor pool; popular with families; open April-Oct; $$.

Friesland/Ameland/Texel

The emerald-green dairy fields of Friesland, carefully reclaimed from the sea by hard-working peasants and farmers, stretch out like a prairie. Flocks of geese waddle around the great farmsteads, where house and farm buildings are under one roof. Well-fed black-and-white cows chew contentedly and magnificent black horses swish their manes and tails. This pastoral country of cream and butter was a land apart until the causeway over the great dyke was built. Dreams of exotic, faraway lands inspired the extraordinary development of elaborate designs in headdress, fabric, furniture, silver, and tile work. An extensive collection is displayed in the Fries Museum in Leeuwarden; closed Monday. Directions: Follow signs to centre and large car park. Using the steeple of the Grote Kerk as a guide, continue east. The museum is east of Grote Kerk, on the east side of a narrow canal on Turfmarkt. Once an important port supplying Londoners with huge quantities of butter and cheese, Harlingen is a pleasant place to enjoy some fresh fish and small-town ambiance. During the 17th-century the residents of Hindeloopen, a tiny village tied to fishing rather than farming, devised ornate and fanciful designs for

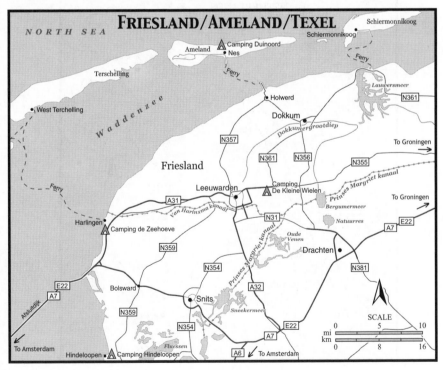

their clothing and furniture. Today the still colorful village makes a nice stop. On the weekends, the Ijsselmeer is covered with the sails of hundreds of boats and wind surfers prettily resembling a swarm of butterflies. Directions: Off A7/E22 exit 21km from the north side of the great dyke at Bolsward onto N359. Drive 14km south. Exit for Hindeloopen.

▲**Camping in the area:** • In Leeuwarden. Exit N355, five kilometers east of the city for the parkland Kleine Wielen and follow signposting. Camping De Kleine Wielen (0511-431-660); large family camp with separate lakeside setting for tents and caravans; convenient; open Apr-Sept; $$. • In Harlingen. South of town, on N31 follow signposting. Camping de Zeehoeve (517 41 3465); nice location on the water; open April-Sept; $. • In Hindeloopen. Camping Hindeloopen (514 52 1452); close to the water; tennis; wind-surfing school; open April-Sept; $.

The island of Ameland is popular with cyclists, bird watchers, and mud-flat walkers. It's a tranquil place even in high season. Plenty of bicycles stand ready to be rented at the island's ferry landing. Without peaks, canyons, or white water, adventurous Dutch go instead to the gigantic mud field exposed at low tide at the Wadden Sea for mud-walking or wadlopen. For this unique and very strenuous activity, participants are told to "Step lightly and keep moving." Each step sounds

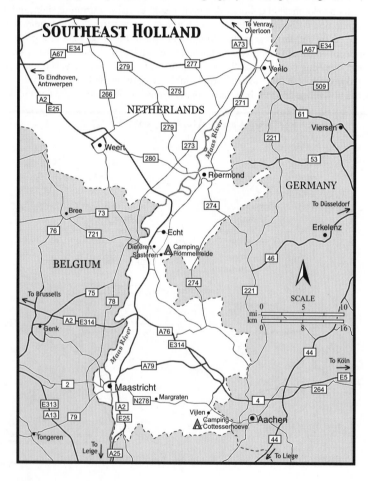

like plunging a drain and laughing gulls hoot at your attempts not to topple over. Afterwards, you'll never again see adventure or the Dutch in the same light. A guide is essential, and pre-booking is recommended. Beginners start with a 3 ½-hour circuit to a sand bar, but the hardier and more experienced go for more. Directions: Pick up a brochure at the campground or book with the tourist office in Leeuwarden or Dokkum. Fishing and whaling were prosperous industries in these islands, and the sailors and ship-pilots who learned to navigate the perilously shallow waters were sought after by the shipping industry throughout Europe. Ferries leave twice each morning and afternoon. Directions: Drive 13km west of Dokkum or 26km northeast of Leeuwarden to Holwerd, and then 4km farther to the ferry dock and car park area.

▲Camping: • On Ameland island north of the village of Nes follow signposting for Strand Duinoord. Camping Duinoord (519-54 2070); picturesque location close to the sea; can be windy; parking separate from campsite; cycle paths; open Apr-Oct; $$. • Close to the airport, west of Ballum. Camping de Roosdunen (519 55 4134); indoor swimming pool; parking separate from campsite; can be windy; open April-Nov; $$.

Because Duinen Van Texel National Park on Texel Island, is just an hour drive north of Amsterdam, the Dutch hop on a ferry to take some time off on the southern most Friesland Island, Texel. They tuck themselves into dunes to soak up sun, pedal through little villages, hike over mud flats and through pine forests, and then giggle over the antics of seals regaining health at Ecomare. Binoculars dangle from the necks of birders enjoying the vast wetland reserves–where thousands of Eurasian spoonbills perched on long spindly legs brush their long spoon-shaped bills like brooms through the sand. They are among the large variety of shorebirds who nest here. Directions: Catch the hourly car-ferry at Den Helder for the 20-minute ride. Drive north on N501 to the park and camping.

▲Camping: • Close to the nature reserve near De Koog. Camping Om de Noord (222 31 7208); smaller; nice location adjacent to the park; 2km from beach; car parking separate from campsite; open Apr-Oct; $$. • In the same area. Dune Camping Kogerstand (222 31 72080): large and resort-like; car parking separate from campsite; open Apr-Oct; $$$.

Southeast Holland

Tucked in between Belgium and Germany southern Holland's rolling hills, river valleys, pine forests, and pleasant villages are a pleasant change for the Dutch who spend most of the time on flat land. Its checkered history of repeatedly being besieged by foreign powers has given it a pan-European atmosphere, where festivals are celebrated with extra vigor. An excellent morning market is held every Wednesday and Friday at the Stadhuis in Maastricht. Directions: Off N278 follow signs for centre and parking. Use the steeple of St. Servaaskerk to guide you. Stadhuis is on the west side of the river, north of the cathedral and historic town square. Many fierce battles occurred during World War II east of Maastricht. Pause at the American War Memorial in Margarten. It is a peaceful resting place for more than 8,000 soldiers who died here. Directions: Drive 13km east of Maastricht on N278 to Margraten. For a vivid impression of war and its machinery, stop at the National War and Resistance Museum in Overloon; open daily. Directions: 4km west of Venlo and the German-Netherlands border exit A67/S34 for Venray. Drive north 18km to Venray on A73. Pass through the village, and drive 7km north of town to the village of Overloon.

▲Camping: • East of Maastricht. Off N278 exit 20km west of Aachen for Viljlen. Drive southwest following signposting. Camping Cottesserhoeve (434 55-1352); lovely location in the hills; open April-Sept; $$. • North of Maastricht 30km. Exit A2/E25 3km south of Echt, at the village of Dieteren, and follow signposting to Susteren. Camping Hommelheide (464 49 2900); nice location on the river; open all year; $$.

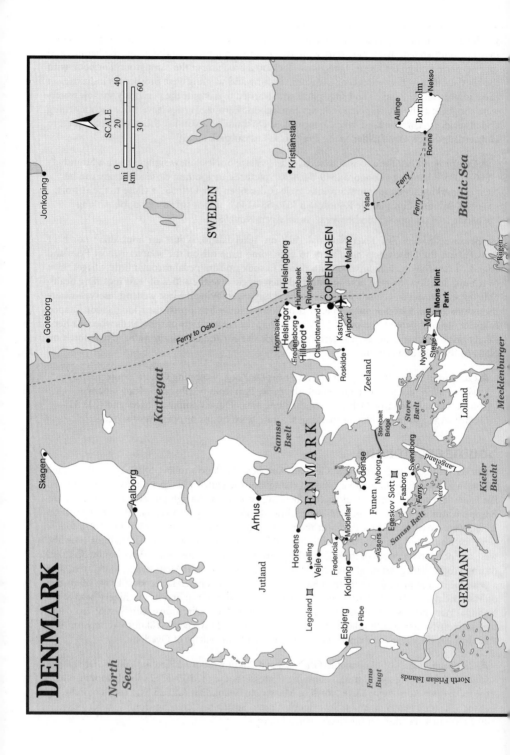

Denmark

www.visitdenmark.dk

Everywhere you go in Denmark, the sea brings movement and life. Nowhere in the entire country are you more than 70 kilometers from one marine indentation or another. The sea dominates their favorite hide-away, their summer, and their lives. The Danes pride themselves on smallness, social homogeneity, and intimacy. They think of themselves as relaxed and humor loving. They have a knack for enjoying themselves. They are an indulgent people who love to prolong the joys of childhood into middle age. One of the pleasures of visiting Denmark is watching the locals at their leisure. There is something effortless and graceful about it. They are not frantic or competitive. Families go bicycling, sailing, or walking on the beach. One of their favorite words is *hygge* which means a state of bliss without worry or bother. Danes love to tease and are fond of telling jokes, often about themselves.

The Danes like to say, "But we are only a little country." But for a little country, they have done some big things. Their efficient agriculture produces some of the finest cheese, butter, bacon, and beer. Its engineers are world famous. Their passionate egalitarianism—a peasant nation's response to memories of royal absolutism and a harsh German aristocracy—has given them a strong taste for education and self-improvement. They planted the roots of folk high schools and cooperatives earlier than other European countries, with visible beneficial results that justify envy. They've organized and shared. Denmark is a serene and pleasant country, almost a Shangri-La without mountains.

Denmark's position across the mouth of the "river of the Baltic" has given her the means and will to maintain her own identity. Her story is one of long struggle to control the narrows, to keep the Baltic open or closed, and to profit from the fact that maritime trade between east and west through the Baltic passes through Danish waters. Their history is, in a sense, the story of an unending struggle to control maritime entrances. Once their empire was huge, but as time went by countries claimed their independence. The Danes accepted it. This endurance of the unheroic, the stamina to accept what comes, has been an essential element in the Danish psyche.

Driving through Denmark, you are impressed by the harmony of landscape and people. A rural tranquility pervades. Fine horses and premium cattle luxuriate in verdant green pastures. An endless sky plays with colors and light over golden fields of wheat. White church steeples peek out through tree-shaded towns, where secluded courtyards and quiet gardens exude a love of privacy and peace. Miles and miles of tranquil beaches are fragrant with heather, dune grasses, and sea air.

Camping places are well established, well cared for, and convenient to public transportation, historic areas, and beaches. A common area housing toilets, pay-showers, a laundry room, and a covered cooking/eating quarter is centrally located and close to a large children's playground. Camping for two persons, a tent, and a car will cost about 20 euros per night indicated as $$. Most campgrounds also have cabins. A simple cabin costs about three times the price of tent camping and will include a stovetop, table and chairs, two sets of bunk-beds, and a small porch.

You provide your own bedding and cooking equipment, use the common toilet/shower area, and clean the cabin on leaving. Call ahead to reserve a cabin. A small store on the premise stocks some produce, fresh bread, snacks, and basics. The office staff speaks fluent English, has loads of glossy brochures and maps, and often sells the local tourist card. They are knowledgeable about the local sights and transportation and are happy to help. Denmark is popular with international travelers, and it's easy to meet them at the common cooking and eating area.

Roads are excellent, well signposted, and often named for where they go. E45 runs north and south on Jutland, connecting to E20 for east-west transport across Funen and the new suspension bridge to Zeeland and Copenhagen. Islands are usually connected to the mainland by bridges. Gas is not overly expensive, stations take charge cards, have small stores, and free toilets. One or two-hour ticket-dispensed parking and free parking is common. Cycling in Denmark's relatively flat countryside is popular. Their good cycle maps point out museums, castles, and interesting little villages. Pedaling through the beautiful countryside is a great way to spend the day.

Like Sweden and Norway, Denmark did not join the European money system. It instead continued with their *kronor* system. Cash machines are hassle-free ways of obtaining local currency. They are found in shopping areas, town squares, and outside banks and are user-friendly for people from many parts of the world.

COPENHAGEN

The Danes have a wonderful sense of harmony and style. You'll see it as you stroll through the city's most famous jewel, Tivoli Gardens, now more than 150 years old. Flowerbeds, always in glorious color, curve and wind luxuriantly. Flower baskets drip with brilliantly purple lobelia and softly pink begonias. In the evening, tiny lights twinkle and reflect in mirror-like ponds, and fountains gush playfully. Everywhere in this green oasis, right in the center of Copenhagen, is *joie de vivre*, frivolous and carnival-like. Old World fixtures, gardens, terrace cafes, and performance stages give only a slight nod to modern crazes. Visit during the day when gardens sparkle with color, and return at night, when millions of tiny lights twinkle and fireworks explode. Directions: The entrance is across from the train station; open daily.

This ancient waterside city has managed to integrate cutting edge modern design with past glories in a delightful harmony. It oozes with style but has a small-town feel. Danish artisans must import almost all the materials they work with. These talented craftsmen create designs that are colorful, graceful, imaginative, strong in texture, and rich in natural materials. A joy shines through all the art and applied art–whether it is old masterpieces, cool functionalism, or daring expressionism. The architecture of their distinguished art museums is remarkable; so do spend some time in them.

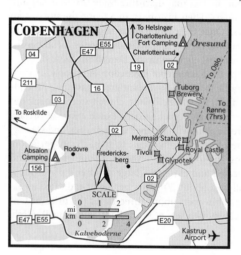

With capital from trade and shipping, Copenhagen built a royal city that bursts with beauty and vitality. Merchants from Venice, London, India, and the Baltic could sail right into the heart of the city. Board a riverboat and see first hand that the canals probe through the city all the way to the Royal Theatre, reflecting gaunt warehouses, an ancient wooden crane in the naval dockyard, 18th-century houses, and visiting yachts. On the water you'll see the stunning new Black Diamond complex– one of the city's most visual master-pieces at its most perfect angle. Built in 1999 of glass, steel and black granite, as an extension to the Royal library, it's a beautiful link to the 16th-century building. The complex's cultural section has a high-tech concert hall and a lovely hidden garden. Many of the splendid buildings were supervised by Denmark's Renaissance king Christian IV, and bear testimony to his taste. Watch how the water brings reflected light and color into the heart of the city. It even laps close to the garden wall of the Queen's palace. Listen for the bells of bicycles, ships, and churches. They seem to play a love song to this red-brick city bright with green copper roofs and blue trolleys.

Its most noteworthy businessman, Carl Jacobsen, a brewer of fine beer, gave superb collec-tions of art to the city. Profits from the famous Carlsberg beer provided him the funds to amass one of the largest private art collections of his time. He named it *Glypototek*, meaning a collec-tion of sculpture. The Ny Carlsburg Glyptotek Museum combines a daring inventiveness with refinement that is mindful of tradition. Begun in the late 1800s, its additions are linked by a monumental dome of cast iron and glass beneath which tropical palms and creepers flourish in a Mediterranean garden. Inside this treasure chest is a warren of rooms, each superbly comple-menting its works of art. The visual experience reflects the ideas of its founder: to educate the viewer. The development of ancient sculpture is carefully followed from its beginnings in Egypt. To view mummies in the Egyptian galleries, you step inside a tunnel evoking the claustrophobic experience of entering a real burial chamber. Take a break in the garden, and then move on to the impressive new wing. Its fabulous collection includes a complete set of Degas bronzes, outstand-ing pieces from all the major Impressionists and Post-Impressionists, and fine collections from the Classical French and the Barbizon Schools. Paul Gauguin is honored in a gloriously golden room painted with the exact coloration that bursts from his tropical paradises and Polynesian madon-nas. It's a wonderful climax to the magnificent collection; closed Monday.

Hop on a bike to pedal along the water's edge where you'll pass sidewalk cafes then cruise into leafy neighborhoods. Continue out past the royal castle, with its fairy tale guard outside. Afterwards pass Denmark's most famous landmark–Hans Andersen's almost self-consciously small, *Little Mermaid*, on the rocks at the water's edge. Cycling maps are available at the camp-ground and tourist office. You'll be joining stylish cyclists going to and from work, shoppers with a basket of groceries, and other tourists with whom you can share a wave and a giggle. Cycling is taken seriously though, so avoid the commute and lunch times on the cycle paths. One ring of a bell (not more or you are considered rude) means to pull over to the right so the bicyclist behind you can pass. Holding up a right hand means the cyclist is going to stop. Cyclists must come to a full stop alongside where passengers are embarking or disembarking from a bus or trolley. If you didn't bring your own bike, renting one is easy. Probably the most convenient place is Kobenhavns Cykler at Central Station, on Reventlowsgade; open everday. Use a good bicycle lock and never leave your bike unattended unless it is locked. For short little rides, use the "smiling face" free bikes with solid wheels and coaster breaks. You'll find them in stands throughout the city. Used like a shopping cart, you put a deposit 20 DKK coin in the slot, remove the bike, and get you coin back when you return the bike to any stand.

Stroll down Stroget Street, a Danish cornucopia of silver, mink, toys, porcelain, books, art, and furniture. Admire the beauty of Georg Jensen's fine silver jewelry and of the elegantly designed objects for the home in the four-story haven Illums Bolighus. This pedestrian street begins or ends at the city hall. Walk down the narrow winding streets to Nytorv, a huge open square lined with elegant buildings that include the Royal Theatre, home to the famous Royal Danish Ballet. Just around the corner from the Royal Theatre canal-lined Nyhavn, is colorful with gaudily painted 18th-century merchant houses. It has a honky-tonk atmosphere and its dives have names like Shanghai and Safari but though it tries hard to keep its bawdy reputation it is simply too Danish to really be dangerous.

The Danish Royal guard, decked out in royal blue with white stripes and in tall black bear-skin hats, is accompanied by a small band as it marches from the Amalienborg Palace through part of the old town every day at noon. The outstanding three-story Children's Art Museum was designed to encourage young minds to appreciate the work of the world's most brilliant artists past and present. Containing hands-on workshops as well as art galleries displaying pieces from other museums, it's a must stop if you've got kids along and an interesting photo stop even if you don't. You'll drool over the famous national snack, *smorrebrod,* that is seen beautifully displayed in shop windows. Butter is liberally laid on flavorful bread, then delicious pieces of cheese, meat, fish, and garnishes are added with artful flair. These open-face sandwiches are so pretty you hesitate to bite in. Take the waterbus to Christianshaven, an interesting community built in the old Danish ramparts and the setting for Peter Hoeg's novel, *Smilla's Sense of Snow.* Here, if you don't suffer from vertigo or claustrophobia, you can enjoy Denmark's most panoramic view by climbing up the bell tower of the tallest church in Copenhagen–the chocolate colored vor Freslserkirke. The wooden steps pass the giant bells, then continue to a trap from where you climb on up an outside spiral stairway that wraps around the copper and golden spire. You're 90 meters up. Copenhagen is Scandinavia's largest city and is hugely out of proportion to Denmark, but I still find it tranquil and serenely beautiful.

▲**Camping:** • North of the city in the suburb of Charlottenlund. Follow the coastal road 02 north of Tuborg Brewery for 2km. Charlottenlund Fort Camping, Strandvejen 144B (013 62 3688); very small; reserve ahead; wonderful location adjoining seaside park; covered cooking and eating area; cycle path to city; close to public transportation; open mid-May-September; $$$. • West of the city in the suburb of Rodovre. Take exit #24 off E47/55 in the direction of Frederiksborg and follow signposting. Absalon Camping, Korsdalsvej 132 (3641-0600); large; cabins; convenient; close to public transportation; covered cooking and eating area; open all year; $$.

NORTH OF COPENHAGEN
Karen Blixen Museum/Rungsted

Fans of the film *Out of Africa* stop here to absorb the spirit and story of the deceased author, on whose life the film is based. Adventurous and rather heroic, she wrote of her challenges, loneliness, and love. Letters, photos, and videos open to your eyes like pages in an old scrapbook; open daily. Directions: Drive 20km north of Copenhagen on 02. The museum is across from the yacht harbor.

Louisana Museum of Modern Art/Humlebaek

The museum and collection here are important and the art evokes a response. Powerful, strange, funny, playful, and sometimes haunting your need for reflection after viewing it is met in a grassy park thick with exotic trees and sculptural works swept by sea breezes. The elegant white villa sits on a bluff high above the sea. It was built by a Danish nobleman who married three women who were all named Louisa, hence the name Louisana. Children in tow will be lured into an artist's studio where they can experiment with paint; open daily. Directions: Drive 10km north of Rungsted on 02.

Kronborg Slot/Helsingor

Mysterious and powerful rather than graceful and elegant, this immense castle commands the narrows between Sweden and Denmark. Built to extract taxes from ships passing through the narrowest point of the Oresund, it was one of the great fortresses of Europe in the 16th-century. Shakespeare made it immortal as Hamlet's Elsinore and so it is often the setting for productions of *Hamlet.* It is fun to transport yourself back to that time, crossing the moat and winding your way down into the dimly lit, musty corridors of the cellars or up into the ornate royal chapel, chambers, and great halls; open daily. Directions: 5km north of Humlebaek. Now Helsingor's harbor is crowded only with ferries, nuzzling in and out between the bulk of the great castle, to make the short crossing to Sweden.

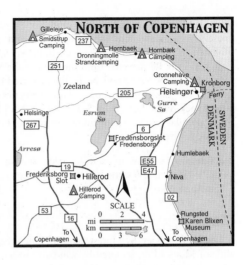

Hornbaek Coast

Snuggling in soft sand, hidden by dune grasses, with a brilliant blue sea a few steps away is pure heaven. Breathing in the mixed fragrances of scotch broom, pines, and salty sea air while pedaling down a coastal cycle path is heavenly too. Both are popular pastimes here.

▲**Camping in the area:** This is a popular vacation area. There are more camping places than listed below. Most offices are closed for a lunch and rest. Call ahead during August. • 5km northwest of Hornbaek on 237. Dronningmolle Srandcamping (49 71 9290); nice location on the beach; close to train to Copenhagen; very popular; sauna; open May-August; $$. • On the beach in Helsingor, north of Kronborg Slot on 237. Gronnehave Camping (49-28 1212); popular; cabins; open all year; $$$. • In Hornbaek, in the direction of Saunte. Hornbaek Camping (49-70-0223); fairly close to the beach; open all year. • 4km west of Gilleleje on 237. Smidstrup Camping (48 31 8448); close to the beach; cabins; swimming pool; open all year; $$.

Fredensborg Slott/Fredensborg

With a sweeping park-like setting that encompasses three islands, Fredensborg Slott is imposing. Leafy deciduous trees form canopies over pathways and luscious lawns that are embroidered with immense rhododendrons and hydrangeas. A sculpture garden honors its peasantry; open daily. Directions: Off 6, southwest of Helsingor and east of Hillerod on Lake Esrum.

Frederiksborg Slott/Hillerod

Inside this once royal residence, sunlight illuminates marble columns filigreed in gold and lavish vaulted ceilings. Dramatic tones from a Compenius organ resonate through the coronation chapel on Thursdays at 1:30 PM. The castle, now the Museum of National History, glows splendidly red at sunset; open daily. Directions: 30km northwest of Copenhagen in Hillerod, off 53 in the center of Hillerod.

▲**Camping:** • South of Hillerod off 53. Hillerod Camping (48-26-4854); convenient; open May-August; $$.

Roskilde

Steeples rise here proudly announcing the royal burial place, Roskilde Domkirke. The dynasties rest–some simply, some elaborately–beneath Gothic arches in adjoining chapels. Sonorous music from a Baroque pipe organ rings out during free summer concerts on Thursday evenings;

open daily except during services and weddings. Powerful armored warriors astride mighty horses once galloped across this countryside, and immense long boats, richly carved with fanciful monsters, silently skimmed the water. In the villages, craftsmen pounded out weapons of bronze, flint, and iron. Resurrected from the mud of the Roskilde fjord, five Viking ships, each built for a different purpose, are now brilliantly displayed behind huge glass windows facing out into the fjord. Vikingeskibshallen is open daily. Directions: At the harbor, on the east side. One of the largest rock music festivals in Scandinavia takes place here in late June featuring top stars, The wildly popular four-day happening is similar to the legendary Woodstock event in the USA. www. roskilde-festival.dk

▲**Camping:** • Drive north of Roskilde 4km on 6, exiting for Veddelev. Roskilde Camping (46 75-7996); lovely setting on the fjord; simple café; cycle path; popular; reserve ahead; open mid-April-mid-Sept; $$.

Mon

Hidden from view by a forest rich with lime-green foliage and dappled light, the gleaming white cliffs of Mons Klint, sculpted by wind and water, rise sharply above a turquoise sea. The sight of this remarkable play of colors is stunning and will be treasured in your memories. Orchids, primroses, and heliotropes hide in forests along with the domed mounds of Bronze Age tombs. In Nyord, one of Scandinavia's best bird preserves, avocets and godwits probe in the mud while terns peer down and then dive. The quiet little island has a sweetness and simplicity that is the essence of Denmark. Scarcely more than a string of small towns dot the island, each with a simple church. Some are joyfully lit up with gay, unsophisticated, 13th-century frescoes that tell Bible stories in simple lines and cool colors. Because the area is laced with tiny secondary roads that crisscross the farmlands, cycling is popular. Now joined to the mainland by bridges, it is easy to reach.

▲**Camping:** • After crossing the small bridge in Stege, drive north 7km along the bay in the direction of Ulvshale. Ulvshale Camping (5581-5325); wonderful location on a sandy beach; close to the bird sanctuary Nyord; covered cooking and eating area; bike rental; cabins; open April-mid-October; $$. • Outside the entrance to Mons Klint park. Mons Klint Camping (5581-2025); nice location close to the forest; large; swimming pool; tennis; bike rental; open April-October; $$$. • On the beach at the southwest end of the island close to Harbolle. After crossing the small bridge to Stege turn west on 287 in the direction of Bogo and drive 15km. Exit 287 onto a small road following signposting south for Harbolle for 5km. Camping Vestmon (5581 7595); lovely location in the dune area; small; open May-mid-Sept; $$.

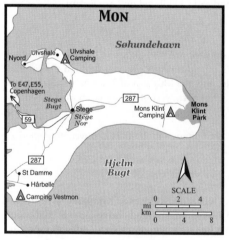

Bornholm

Along Bornholm's northern coast, the tide rushes in thick with brine. High on a cliff, the ruins of the fortress/castle Hammershus guard the narrow passageway to the Baltic. Beaches of fine sand stretch along the southern coast, where the shallow water is placid, warm, and clean. Parts of the film, *Pelee the Conqueror*, were shot in the fishing village of Gudhjem. Smoked herring is a specialty, and enticing little fish stores dot the island.

Diminutive fortified churches, whitewashed and cone-capped, are shaded by beech and hemlock trees. Rapeseed paints the landscape in burnished gold. Directions: Bornholm is off the southern coast of Sweden. Ferries ply the waters between Ronne on Bornholm and Ysted in Sweden in 2 1/2 hours. From Copenhagen it's a 7-hour ferry ride.

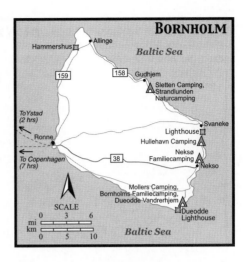

▲**Camping:** All of these have nice locations on the beach; are shaded by trees; have all the amenities; popular with families; and open May-mid-Sept. All are on the east side of the island. From the ferry landing at Ronne, drive 30km east on 38. • South of Gudhjem. At the intersection of 38 and the east coast road drive 28km north in the direction of Gudhjem. Sletten Camping (5648-5071); parking is separate from camping; cabins $$ or Strandlunden Camping (5648-5245); cabins $$$. • At the intersection of 38 and the east coast road at Nekso, drive north 8km in the direction of Svaneke. • It is south of Svaneke and lighthouse. Hullehavn Camping (5649-6363); $$. • At the intersection of 38 and the east coast road at Nekso drive north one kilometer. Nexo Familiecamping (5649 2721); bike rental; sauna; cabins; $$$. • At the white sand beach, Dueodde, south of Nekso 10km. Dueodde Vandrerhjem (5648-8119); cabin; bike rental; sauna; tent camping separate from caravans; $$. Bornholms Familiecamping (5648-8150); cabins; parking separate from camping; tennis; sauna; bike rental; $$$ or Mollers Dueodde Camping (5648 8149); cabins; pool; bike rental; tennis; $$.

FUNEN

Funen is Denmark at its most idyllic. It serves the nation as a lovingly cultivated front garden, with soil and climate permitting almost anything to grow. It shows off in an artist's palette of colorfully painted cottages, flowers in the most unexpected places, and flags flying as if everyday is a holiday. Larks sing and premium reddish-brown and black-and-white cattle munch contently in lush green pastures. Masses of wildflowers grow fragrant and colorful, berry bushes drip with fruit, and locals smile as they pedal by. This is Denmark's heartland. The world's largest suspension bridge gracefully spans the18 kilometers of water between the islands of Funen and Zeeland–the toll and thrill of crossing are both high.

Odense

Thousand-year-old Odense is Hans Christian Andersen's birthplace. Anderson, whose stories are elementary and universal in their picture of life, touches hearts around the world. Loving his fanciful characters and plots, readers also appreciate their deeper meanings. Today via a headset he can accompany you on a walking route around Odense to places of significance in his life. In the HC Andersens Hus you can examine original notes and manuscripts, look at intriguing memorabilia, and listen to his touching stories read by Lawrence Olivier and Michael Redgrave; closed Monday. Directions: On the east side of the old town. Park at the concert hall then walk down the cobblestone pedestrian street. In Funen's open-air museum, Den Fynske Landsby, tiny vegetable gardens, thatched-roofed farmhouses, and crowing roosters greet you. Directions: South of the old town, near the campground.

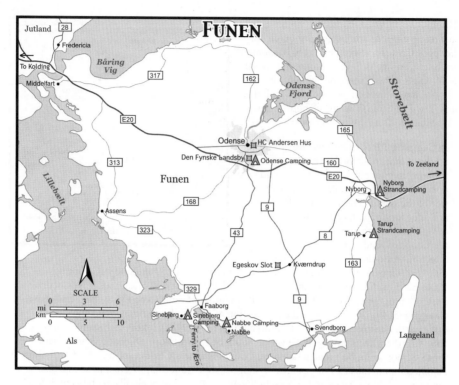

▲Camping: • Off E20 take exit 50 in the direction of Odense. Follow signposting south of the centrum. Odense Camping, Odensevej 102 (6611-4702); swimming pool; cabins; bike rental; open all year; $$.

Egeskov Slott

Fairy tales about beautiful princesses come alive at this intimate Renaissance castle. You can play hide-and-seek in a large maze formed by a three-meter high hedge and then pretend to drive off in an antique Jaguar sports car or on a restored Harley-Davidson motorcycle. It's also a romantic setting for a picnic lunch. Directions: From the Faaborg-Nyborg road 8, drive 2km west of Kvaendrup.

Nyborg

Consider a stop in the journey here before or after crossing Denmark's magnificent suspension bridge to Zeeland.

▲**Camping:** • On the beach, just north of the entrance to the bridge. Take exit 45 off E20. Nyborg Strandcamping, Hjelevej 99 (6531-0256); nice location at the beach; cabins; traffic noise; open April-Sept; $$. • South of Nyborg on a quiet grassy hillside over looking the sea with stairs to the beach. Take exit 46 south off E20 onto 8. Drive south 10km to Orbaek. Turn east on 163 for Tarup and drive 6km. These both have lovely peaceful locations with stairs to the beach; cabins; open April-Aug; $$. Tarup Strandcamping (6537-1199) or Kongshoj Strandcamping (6537 1288).

Faaborg

Cobblestone streets, half-timbered houses, and a pleasant little harbor make a stop here a nice break in a journey. Ferries run to the tiny island of Aero and to the Jutland pennisula.

▲**Camping:** • From Faaborg drive west on 8 for 5km. Turn south in the direction of Bjerne and drive 2km. Sinebjerg Camping (6260-1440); nice view of the sea close to a sandy beach; bike rental; open mid-April-mid-Sept; $$. From Faaborg drive east 6km on 44 in the direction of Svenborg. Turn south in the direction of Nab. Nab Camping (6261 6779); lovely location close to the beach; bike rental; cabins; open May-August; $$.

JUTLAND

Jutland is the Wild West of Denmark. Dunes, lagoons, salt marshes, moors, and long stretches of sandy beaches characterize much of the western coastline. In the summer, it is a fine place to get away from it all. The less wild eastern coast is more settled with farms and towns. The overall atmosphere is of a prosperous and well-organized community that makes intelligent use of its physical and human resources.

Jelling

The stones on which the mighty Viking King Gorm and his son Harald Bluetooth carved loving words are impressive in their simplicity. They represent a tenderness not often told in tales of seafaring adventurers. Carved in the 1st-century, the runic stones honor a wife and parents. They

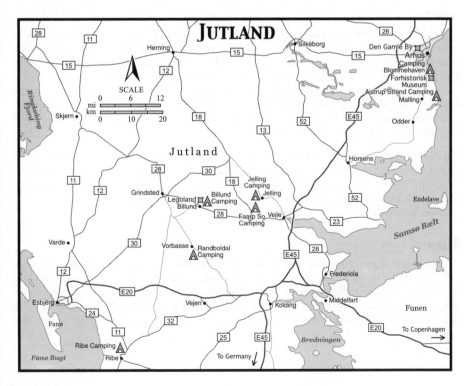

sit in dignity, without pretention, outside the doors of a small-whitewashed church. Directions: From the intersection of E20 and E45, drive north on E45 for 19km to Vejle. Follow signposting northwest of the Vejle 11km to Jelling.

▲**Camping:** West of town. Jelling Camping (7587 1653); cabins; pool; bike rental; simple café; open April-Aug; $$. On a small lake southwest of town. Faarp So Camping (7587-1344); nice setting; pool; open May-Aug; $$.

Legoland

How do you inspire ingenuity, teach patience and perseverance, and still keep a child entertained? For a parent, grandparent, caregiver, or teacher this is an enormous challenge. In the 1940s, Ole Kirk Christensen had an idea. He developed wooden toys that he named "lego" from the Danish phrase *leg godt* or play well. Today his toys spill out on floors all over the world. Legoland is a major Danish tourist attraction, inviting guests to discover, appreciate, play, and create with Lego blocks. You'll be amazed at the intricate facsimiles built with thousands of pieces. Girls will thrill over the non-Lego Titania's Palace, an extravagant 18-room dollhouse, and all kids will enjoy the driving school and western town; open daily. Directions: Exit E45 at Vejle, and drive west on 28 for 30km in the direction of Grindsted to Billund and Legoland.

▲**Camping:** • In Randbol, a wooded area 10km south of Billund. Off 469 exit at Vorbasse. Randboldal Camping (7588-3575); on a tiny lake; popular with families; open all year; $$. • Next to Legoland airport. Billund Camping (7533-1521); huge; simple cafe; cabins; open all year; $$$.

Arhus

Arhus's open-air museum, Den Gamle By, is one of Scandinavia's best Good Ole Days, restored 17th-18th-century market towns. Traditionally-dressed staff tell fascinating stories, bake pastries, forge tools, and weave. You can wander down the cobblestone streets after-hours for extra special photo shots. Directions: Exit the ring road on the west side of town for Vesterbrogade. The Forhistorisk Museum in Moesgard houses the Graubelle Man. Over 2000 years old, the remains were preserved amazingly well by the tannic acids and iron in a peat bog. From the museum, a path leads through wildflower graced woods and meadows to the beach. Directions: Drive south of Arhus on 451 for 8km in the direction of Odder.

▲**Camping:** • Drive south of the city on the coast road for 7km to Hojberrg. Camping Blommehaven (8627-0207); on the beach; large; bike rental; sauna; simple café; open April-mid-Oct; $$. • Drive south of Arhus for 22km in the direction of Malling. Exit east for the beach and Ajstrup Strand. Ajstrand Strand Camping (8693 3535); not far from the beach; cabins; bike rental; open mid-April-mid-Sept; $$.

Ribe

Cobblestone streets wind past canals, outdoor cafes, half-timbered stone houses, and small parks. From the top of Ribe Cathedral's 52-meter tower, you can gaze out over red roofs to the marshlands. At Vikingecenter, falcons swoop suddenly from the air to land on an outstretched arm, aromatic Viking soup simmers over an open fire, and in a tiny cabin glowing coals soften iron before being pounded by a craftsman. Directions: Exit E20 onto 47 and drive west 50km to Ribe.

▲**Camping:** • Exit 11 just north of the historic area in the direction of Farup. Ribe Camping (7541-0777); cabins; open mid-April-mid-Oct; $$.

Skagen

Though the most northerly place in Denmark, Skagen claims to enjoy more sunshine than anywhere else in the country. Just steps back from the water's edge, color-washed cottages line up in tidy rows in miniscule villages. Painters have been attracted for centuries by its extraordinary light that is different than anywhere else in the Baltic. The land here scarcely rises above the sea, making its vast beaches ideal for solitary walks and secluded picnics. Spend some time chatting with locals in their museums of odds and ends, art galleries and friendly pubs.

▲**Camping:** • In a dune area north of Skagen on 40 in the direction of Grenen. Grenen Camping (9844 2546); lovely location; large; cabins; parking separate from camping; bike rental; open May-Aug; $$. • In the same area. Poul Eeg Camping (9844 1470); large; bike rental; cabins; open mid-May-Aug; $$.

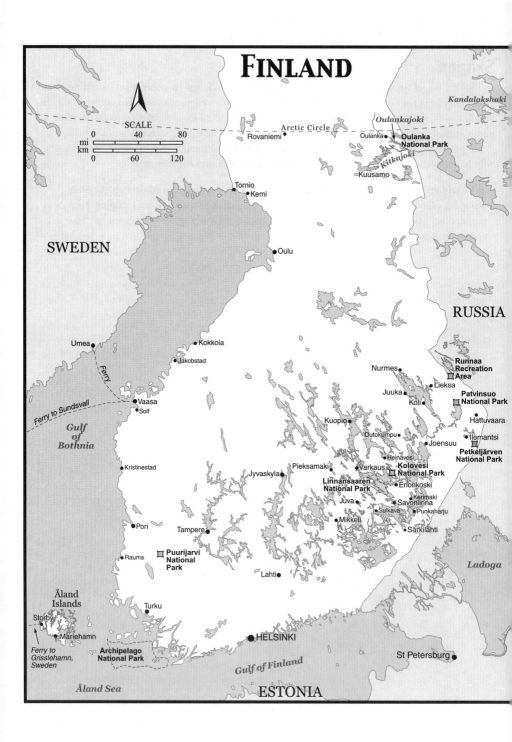

FINLAND

SCALE

mi
0   40   80

km
0   60   120

Arctic Circle

Kandalakshaki

Oulankajoki

Rovaniemi

Oulanka • ▼ Oulanka
National Park

Kitkajoki

Kuusamo

Tornio
• Kemi

SWEDEN

Oulu

RUSSIA

Umea •

Kokkola

Jakobstad

Nurmes •

Runnaa
Recreation
Area

Juuka •

Lieksa

Patvinsuo
National Park

Vaasa
Solf

Koli •

Ferry to Sundsvall

Ferry

Gulf
of
Bothnia

Kuopio •

Hattuvaara

Outokumpu •

Ilomantsi

Joensuu •

Petkeljärven
National Park

Kristinestad •

Pieksamaki •

Heinavesi •

Varkaus •

Kolovesi
National Park

Jyvaskyla •

Linnansaaren
National Park

Enonkoski •

Juva •

Kerimaki
Savonlinna

Sulkava •

Punkaharju

Mikkeli •

Pori •

Tampere •

Sarkilahti •

Rauma •

Puurijarvi
National
Park

Lahti •

Ladoga

Åland
Islands

Turku

Storby •

Mariehamn •

Ferry to
Grisslehamn,
Sweden

Archipelago
National Park

HELSINKI •

St Petersburg •

Gulf of Finland

Åland Sea

ESTONIA

Finland

www.visitfinland.com

Imagine luscious mounds of clouds mirrored in deep-blue lakes, as in a Monet painting. Then add a silence broken only by the twittering of birds, the skittering of ducks, and the whisper of pines. Breathe in deeply air that is fresh and sweet-scented with the fragrance of earth. True, Finland does not have snowcapped peaks reflected in dramatic fjords. But it does have a jewel-like treasure that is hard to find–a peaceful solitude where tranquility can be regained.

Living in a country with such an extraordinary natural setting, Finns have an ingrained respect for nature and are obsessed with water. Many have a special retreat where they regain peace in their soul. Essential to any Finns getaway is a sauna. When you share one with them at a campground, you share something dear to their hearts. The best are beside a lake. The tradition is to take a break from the steamy sauna by plunging from a diving platform or walking out into the refreshing lake water, which usually has a fine view. Then, you either climb the platform's ladder or walk back again to the wonderfully intense heat.

Finland is located in the northern boreal zone in a climate intermediate between maritime and continental. It is Europe's boggiest country, with shores that are washed by the Baltic's brackish waters. Their lake complex is unique, as are the Ice Age formations of eskers and smooth glacial rocks. Finland's national parks preserve this finery and these unique habitats of international importance. Founding them is a source of national pride. Forests, bogs, lakes, archipelago environments, rapids, scenic views, and heritage landscapes are now networked with trails, interpretive signs, and visitor centers. Boardwalks and bird towers minimize disturbance. Visitor centers have excellent free brochures with maps. Pick one up in Finnish as well as in English to assist in reading signposting and map boards. Visit the Finnish Forest and Park Service, Metsahallitus; www.metsa.fi.

Finns delight in the outdoors and love to camp. It is a tradition to sit around a campfire, listen to the evening's symphony of songbirds and winged insects, and toast *makkara* (sausage), which they affectionately called Finland's national vegetable. To provide for this pleasure, many campgrounds have individual little shelters built picturesquely at the side of the lake. The shelters enclose fireplaces and hold neat stacks of wood. The evening sun has a gentle light and you can watch the sky dress up in queenly colors as the birds trill and the wind hums gently in the pines. Comfortable cabins, lakeside saunas, wonderful cooking and eating areas, canoe, kayak and bike rental, mini-golf, children's playgrounds, and diving platforms all add to the pleasure of these lakeside campgrounds. The best weather for camping is in June, July, and early August, when even after the late sunset the sky retains a pale glow throughout the night and in the early morning the lake is shrouded in mist. The cost for two persons, a tent, and car is less than 20 euros. Renting a cabin will cost about three times more. Campgrounds are well maintained, have hot showers, saunas, often laundry facilities, and a staff person who speaks English. Purchase a reasonably priced Camping Card Scandinavia at your first campground. It acts as a security card against damage and gives you discounts. Finland does not honor Camping Card International.

A paradise for fishermen, Finland's glistening lakes teem with fish. Rental equipment is generally available at the campground. Permits are reasonable and can be purchased at post offices and sometimes at the campground. Much of Finland is either flat or gently rolling terrain, making it perfect for cycling. The roads are excellent and secondary roads have little traffic. Public transportation is bicycle-friendly, and the cities have good cycle paths. Avid boatmen, the Finns drift leisurely on the lakes in seasoned rowboats and cast out with old-style hook and line. But they are also expert fly fishermen. Canoes and kayaks are available for rental. Established signposted hiking routes on certain lakes and rivers have designated campgrounds along the way. Well-informed English-speaking staff at the local tourist office or campground can arrange for guides and reserve equipment ahead from local outfitters.

You will never truly know Finland until you have experienced a sauna (pronounced **sow**-oo-nah not saw-nuh). "Build the sauna first and then the house," an old Finnish proverb instructs. When you check into the campground, ask about sauna schedule. Reserving the sauna and paying ahead means you have a specific private time—usually an hour—for just you and invited guests. During this private reserved time, men, women, and families use the sauna together. Often campgrounds offer a free morning saunas, with separate times for men and women. The sauna usually has three rooms. Outside the first door you are expected to wash your feet in the basin of water. In the first room, you take off all your clothes and hang them on wall hooks. In the second room, you shower to cleanse your body, remove odor or fragrances, and moisten your skin. In the third room—the hot room—you take a towel you've brought to sit on. Upper benches are hotter than lower benches. After sitting for a few minutes, you might want to increase the humidity by throwing water on the stones of the sauna stove. After leaving the hot room, cool off with a cool shower or swim (if it's a public lake, put on your swimming suit before going out). When reentering the hot room, it's correct to beat yourself a bit with a birch branch, if you have one, to increase your circulation. Your body temperature and the humidity should then be right. The hot-cold cycles are repeated usually two or three times. Afterwards, wash in the shower, dry yourself, and dress. Tidy up the sauna, and then sit or lay down somewhere that is peaceful for you. Having a refreshing drink and a salty snack is a popular way to round out this almost sacred ritual.

Finland's roadways are well maintained and signposted. Traffic is light, and it's a pleasure to drive through the graceful, quiet countryside. Gas stations are modern and are enjoyable places to stop for a snack, a few groceries, and tourist information. Automatic pumps with credit card terminals are used when the stations are closed on Sundays and at night. Cash machines are plentiful. Look for them close to a grocery store or ask a local. Grocery stores are well stocked with reasonably priced basics. Museums are often closed on Mondays except in tourist areas. Tourist information offices offer a friendly smile, some one who speaks English, and a host of brochures and maps.

HELSINKI

Four stalwart masculine figures, each delicately holding a glass sphere, grace the façade of Helsinki's railroad station. They represent the spirit of Finland: heroic survivors of prolonged hardship who hold fast to human values and nature. Surrounded by neighbors eager to engulf them, the Finns have excelled in a tightrope balancing act. Today the country proudly hosts international summit meetings.

Leaders in the field of applied art, they incorporate art and nature with impeccable skill, believing that it is wildness that preserves the world. Carved out of a solid piece of granite, Temppeliaukio Church, honors this belief. It has a full calendar of free concerts by visiting choirs so check out their bulletin board; closed Monday. Experiencing Kiasma Museum of Contemporary Art is like walking through a piece of sculpture. The collections are offbeat and often humorous, so take time to read the information about the artists posted in each gallery; closed Monday. The luscious grass in shady, pleasant Sibelius Park is a great place for a picnic. While munching on sandwiches,

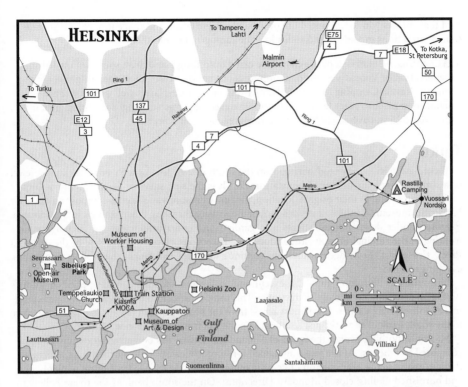

you can study a sensuous, silvery, surreal organ sculpture made from 24 tons of tubing. Look for the lovely benches crafted from birch trees built to honor their beloved tree's natural beauty. Farther down Helsinki's leafy boulevard is the Museum of Art and Design, housing a small but excellent collection; open every afternoon except Monday.

Finland's spirit of nationalism is stirred and kept alive through art. Action-packed scenes from Finland's epic poem, *Kalevala*, and also evocative studies of peasant life painted in the late 19th-century are housed in the Art Museum of the Ateneum and should not be missed; closed Monday. If you are interested in Finnish emigration to America, allow time to wander through the Museum of Worker Housing. Six recreated one-room wood houses depict the tragic home life of the agrarian people who moved to the city in the early 1900s. Finland's independence is relatively new. Travelers should be mindful that she is a youngster compared to her neighbors and has had comparatively few years to pile up collections. Her most impressive possession is the fabulous remoteness, solitude and pureness of her countryside.

Reindeer kebabs, Russian caviar, fresh fish, wild mushrooms, cloudberries, local handicrafts, and T-shirts make a colorful and lively mix for shoppers at Kauppatori, the harbor's morning market. Ferries depart from here for the UNESCO-listed fortress on Suomenlinna Island, for the Helsinki Zoo (it has an outstanding number of owl species), and for the park-like setting of the open-air museum on Seurasaari Island. Don't miss seeing Havis Amanda, the mermaid statue and fountain just west of the market. She embodies the shy, sweet beauty of Finland. Directons: Take the metro from the campground to Rautatientori, the train station. Then use the city map picked up at the campground to find your way around. Tram 3T does a figure eight, passing most of the major sites around the city. Board it at the tram area outside the central train station. Since you'll be using the metro to get to and from the city and the campground, consider buying a Helsinki card that entitles you to unlimited use of urban transportation and free entrance or discounts to tourist attractions in and around Helsinki. The campground sells them.

▲**Camping:** • 16km east of the city. Take exit 4 onto Ring 1 and drive southeast on 101 in the direction of Vuosaari Nordsjo. Camping is on the southeast side of the bridge over the estuary. Rastila Camping (9-321 6551); metro to city closeby; large; well used but convenient; good place to meet fellow international travelers; picnic/sunning/ swimming area on the river; cabins; covered cooking and eating area; open all year; $$.

Turku

Tucked away in a leafy neighborhood on the south side of the Aura River in Turku is a jewel of a *skansen* (open-air museum) Loustarinmaki. It is the sole survivor of 18th-century Turku's ravishing fires. Still in their original location, the tiny workshops and homes compose an open-air handicraft museum. I think it exudes more authenticity than any other *skansen* in Scandinavia. Visitors wander down narrow streets into gardens and courtyards to talk to friendly artisans working in the original homes; closed Mondays. Directions: On the south side of the Aurajoki River. Cross over the bridge on Aurakatu continue south for two blocks then follow signposting east for one block.

Bird-watchers shouldn't miss the exceptional collection of stuffed bird species in Turku's Biological Museum; open daily. Directions: This can be difficult to find because signage is minimal and shrouded by vines. It is almost across from the samppalinnan (swimming stadium), close to the south bank of the river just south and up the hill from the Aaltonen Museum.

Musically, nothing evokes the spirit of Finland more than the evocative symphony *Finlandia* composed by Sibelius. At the museum named for him, strains of his music fill the air, adding aesthetic pleasure to the examination of delicate music boxes, fragile wooden *kantele*, ancient horns, and burnished violins; closed Monday. Directions: On the south bank of the river. Follow the main street to the north end of the old town, watching for the Turku Cathedral—that looms over the river. Park and walk a bit north.

Huge bunches of gloriously golden sunflowers, mounds of brilliantly red currants, baskets of salmon-colored cloudberries, sparkling piles of iced fish, whole grain breads, crispy green peas, as well as succulent crispy fried fish await shoppers at one of the most authentic open markets in Scandinavia. Shoppers at Turku's *kauppatori* (open market) are Finns, not tourists. It's a perfect place rest and indulge in delicious Finnish treats while taking in the local scene.

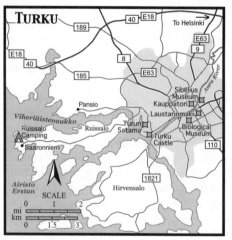

At the mouth of the Aura River, a 13th-century castle still guards the city. Few travelers leave Turku without wandering through its maze of corridors and stairways leading down to dark dungeons and up to sunny sitting rooms. This medieval castle was the seat of power for Finland and, at times, Sweden. Exhibits are supplemented with videos, costumes, displays, and interactive computers to make the historical information come alive for both young and old; open daily. Throughout Turku, you'll find easy street parking close to places of interest. Bring change for meters.

▲**Camping:** • On the tip of Ruissalo Island, 10km west of the city on the bay. Follow signs to Turun Satama, Turku's Harbor.

Drive north in the direction of Pansio for just over a kilometer. Exit for Ruissalo. Follow the road 5km through the park-like area to the end of the pennisula. Ruissalo Camping (258-9249); nice location on the bay; large; covered cooking, barbeque, and eating areas; new café and store; open June-Aug; $$.

Archipelago National Park

Once on the brink of extinction, sea eagles are now seen by the score stretching their wings over Archipelago National Park. The low brackish waters, innumerable islands and twisting shoreline with shallow coastal waters provide a unique habitat for a wealth of life, particularly eiders and red-breasted mergansers. In juniper-dotted meadows, clouded apollo butterflies rest on the bloody cranesbill's rice paper-like dark red petals as they shimmer in the sunshine and barred warblers sing their bubbly song. Prehistoric fisherman sought seals and fish in this land that continues to rise each year. Cattle now graze on some of the islands to maintain the landscape as it looked during the era of sustenance farming and hunting. The Blamuslan Visitor center south of Dragsfjard in the village of Kasnas has a wonderful exhibition of the flora and fauna plus if you call ahead, they can arrange guides for birding; 358 205 64 4620 www.metsa.fi/natural/. Locals provide private ferry service. You might want to pack up a few things and stay overnight at one of the cabins. Directions: From Turku, drive east on E18 for 42km to Salo. Exit south on 52 and continue for 24km. At the fork stay right in the direction of Dragsfjard and drive 34km. Follow signposting in town for Blamuslan and the ferry landing.

Tampere

Set picturesquely between two lakes whose waters are joined by an energetic river, Tampere's roaring rapids provided energy for Finland's most important hub of textile, footwear, metal, and wood industries in the early 1900s. Today its high-tech industries have a global marketplace. In keeping with its goal of excellence, the city built Metso, an architecturally inviting and state-of-the-art library. Visitors are welcome. Directions: Drive over the river on Tampereen Valtatie. Follow the road north for 4 blocks and find parking. It's across from the park and church and signposted Kirjasto. In the same area is the Musuem of Workers Housing and the Tampere Art Museum. To reach the tourist office walk east on the cobblestone Hameenkatu and cross over the bridge to the east bank. Throughout summer, lively festivals give Tampere a festive air. Farther up the river, straddling the rapids, on the west bank, is a huge red brick building that houses the Museum of

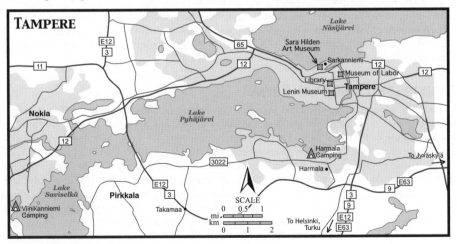

Labor. Changing exhibits center around social and industrial movements. On the shores of Lake Nasijarvi is one of Finland's most prominent modern art museums, the Sara Hilden. Directions: On the bridge of land that separates the two lakes. Exit off 12 for Sarkanniemi, which also hosts and shares parking with an amusement park, aquarium, and zoo. Avoid weekends.

▲**Camping:** • South of the city on Lake Pyhajarvi. Exit west off E12/E63 onto 3 in the direction of Takamaa. Exit 3 almost immediately for Harmala and follow signposting for camping on the lake. Harmala Camping (03-265-1355); older; convenient; beach; cabins; lakeside sauna; simple café; open mid-May-August; $$. • 13km from Tampere in Nokia. Exit off 12 and follow signposting for camping. Viinikanniemi Camping (3 341 3384); newer and nicer; lovely location on the lake recreational area; café; cabins; open all year; $$.

THE LAKELAND

Twinkling silver in the summer sun, Finland's labyrinthine lakes and waterways are decorated along the shoreline with masses of larkspur, phlox, and buttercups. Along roadways, grasslands wave happily in the breeze. This is the summer paradise the Finns love. Here and there, pleasant little towns provide good places to stock up on supplies and experience a hometown ambiance. For urban visitors it is like stepping back in time, when the pace was slower, the impact of people and noise less, and solitude was easy to find.

Savonlinna

Known as the Queen of the Lakeland, Savonlinna's historic castle, Olavinlinna, is known internationally among opera buffs. Arias have been lilting out across the lakes from it since 1912, and today it hosts one of Europe's finest musical festivals. Regally separating herself from commoners, the castle sits on an island in a serene lake. Visitors walk across a floating bridge. She is not large, but rather intimate and pleasing, and graced with lovely courtyards, wood-paneled interiors, and leafy trees; open daily. Buy tickets well in advance for the July opera; www.operafestival.fi. A lively beer festival is held in mid-August and an international film festival later in August. Scenic cruises and cycling are pleasant ways to absorb the scenery.

▲**Camping:** Book ahead if coming during opera season. • Just west of Savonliina exit 14 south and follow signposting. Vuohimaki Camping (015-537-353, fax 09-713-713); wonderful setting on the lake; resort-like; cabins; excellent cooking/eating/shower/toilet area; café; open June-Aug; $$$. • 16km west of Savonlinna exit 14 onto 435 for Sulkava and drive to the lake. Vilkaharju Camping (015-471-223, fax 09-713-713); pleasant location on the lake; not as upscale as Vuohimaki; cabins; open June-mid Aug; $$.

Linnansaari National Park

Sparkling water and sun-drenched islands compose one of Finland's most beautiful national parks, Linnansaari. In castle-like grandeur, Linnansaari Island holds a variety of environments that are a miniature of the whole park. On the little passenger ferry out to the park, you'll see magnificent osprey plunging for prey while tuxedoed gulls and regal loons ride the surf, dipping in for tasty treats. The ferry captain points out platform nests of osprey–the park's symbol–built high in scots pine along the island cliffs. You might see the adults feeding their young. Kayaking is popular, and you can make arrangements for rental on the mainland in Oravi. The company will bring the kayak over the 5 kilometers, of sometimes choppy water, to Linnansaari Island, where you can paddle along its indented shoreline and across to the humpback islands. Directions to Oravi: From Savonlinna, drive east on 71 for one kilometer to the intersection of 71 and 471. Exit north on 471 for 22km to

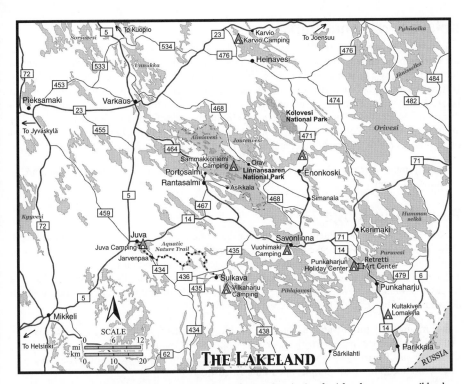

Simanala. Turn west onto 468 and drive another 22km to Oravi. On the island, a nature trail leads to an old tenant farm where the farmstead is kept as an example of heritage landscape. You'll see slash and burn cultivation, rows of tobacco, and cows grazing in forest and meadows. The trail continues across the island through an herb-rich forest, where sunlight filters beautifully through birch onto a carpet of chartreuse ferns. The lovely song of winter wrens tinkles throughout the forest as it forages among the rotting logs. Golden orioles and both wood and greenish warblers are also plentiful. As the trail reaches the cliffs the landscape becomes dark and mysterious with rocky caves and outcrops painted with lichens. A rock-carved stairway leads up to a high rocky ledge where the views over the archipelago are panoramic. If you are going over to the park from the west side, plan to spend some time seeing the Lakeland Center's interpretative exhibits in Rantasalmi. They can make arrangements with excellent local guides for bird-watching from canoes or on trails in the forest. They also have the schedule for the small passenger-only ferryboats that crosses to the island once a day from the dock at Porosalmi. An enterprising local family in Portosalmi retrieved ancient logs buried in the lake's mud and used the wood to build wonderful cabins, which can be rented. The family has lived in the area for generations. It runs the ferry service, and some members are expert nature guides; Hako Apajan Aikhituvat 359 400 939 970. Directions: Drive about 30km northwest of Savonlinna on 14. Then exit onto 467 and drive 14km to Rantasalmi. For the ferry drive 5km farther exiting onto a gravel road signposted for Porosalmi and drive 2km to the dock and parking.

▲**Camping**: • On the island. Pack up some gear and leave your car in the parking area at Porosalmi. Sammakkoniemi Camping (040-275-458); gorgeous location with a friendly ambiance of nature loving people enjoying the incredible scenery; nice cooking and eating house; beautiful lakeside wood-burning sauna (make reservations on arrival); picturesque snack café; large covered campfire/grilling area with plenty of wood; open June-Aug; cute cabins $$; free for tents.

Kolovesi National Park

Elusive like a mermaid, the shy Saimaa ringed seal measures just 1.5 meters in length. It is the world's most endangered seal species and breeds in the narrow coves and straits of Kolovesi National Park, which is accessible only by boat. Lake Saimaa was once connected to the sea. During the Ice Age, glaciers deposited the rocky outcrops that isolated the Saimaa ringed seal in labyrinthine waters. Prehistoric paintings and tar pits prove that there was human habitation here during the Stone Age. You can rent a canoe, join others paddling in a traditional long boat, or arrange a guide with Kolovesi Retkeily, just beyond the village on 471. Directions: Drive east out of Savonlinna on 71 for one kilometer. Exit north on 471 and drive 33km to Enonkoski.

▲Camping: • Free camping is permitted near the boating landing north of Enonkoski; no facilities or water.

Punkaharju Ridge

Formed by glacier movement, this narrow ridge is flanked on either side by beautiful lakes. Drive or join the Finns and take the 7-kilometer walking/cycling path. Just before the ridge exit stop at the Retretti Art Center. Man-made caves gouged out of surrounding rock provide not only galleries but a huge underground concert hall. In the garden, it is fun to watch Disney-like tree trunks and boulders move unexpectedly. The Lusto Forest Museum in the same area is excellent; don't miss it. Directions: Drive 10km east of Savonlinna on 14.

▲Camping: • By the entrance to the ridge off 14. • Punkaharjun Holiday Center (15-739-611); huge; café; cabins; pool with waterslide; game room; popular with families; can be noisy; open all year; $$$. • South of the town of Punkaharju. • Kultakiven Lomakyla (15-15-645); nice location; small; simple; open June-August; $$.

Sarkilahti Bird Lake

Have you ever heard a nightingale sing? Their sweet, melodious, and tender song is a joy to hear. Sarkilahti is known internationally among birders and is one of the finest places to enjoy these night singers. It is one of the best bird breeding lakes in Finland and attracts red-neck grebes, and both Eurasian river and Blyth reed warblers. A guide is an enormous help in viewing.; www.birdlife.fi. Directions: The reserve and visitor center with observation tower are just east of Parikkala, 53km south of Savolinna on 14/6. Camping is allowed in the reserve.

Kerimaki Church

Painted bright yellow like a sunny day the Kerimaki *kirkko* (church) was built in the mid-1800s and claims to be the largest wooden church in the world. It's majestic, but friendly rather than pompous. Directions: Drive east from Savolinna on 14 for 8km. At the fork, exit onto 71 and drive 6km.

Oravareitti Canoe Route and Aquatic Nature Trail

One of Finland's most user-friendly canoe routes, the 52-kilometer Oravareitti, runs from Sulkava to Juva and encompasses level II rapids, smooth flowing rivers, and lakes. There is a 25-meter drop in water level and one portage of 50 meters. Campgrounds and nature interpretive signs dot the route and it is popular with families; www.oravareitti.net. Call ahead and reserve a canoe at Juva Camping, where the route begins.

▲Camping: • Exit 5 onto 14 for Juva and drive one kilometer. Juva Camping (015-451-930); beautiful setting on the river; cabins; covered eating and cooking areas; open mid-

June-mid-Aug; $$. • In Sulkava, on the lake southeast of the village. Vilkaharju Camping (09-6138-3210); lovely setting; small; simple; open mid-June-July; $.

Kuopio

A nice lakeside campground and the world's largest smoke sauna make this campground special for a break in your journey. The huge smoke sauna is only available to the public on Tuesday and Friday nights. On entering, you'll be given a towel to cover yourself during the unisex experience. Buy a birch branch so you can hit your body during the experience and improve your circulation. Breathe in the sweetly smoky aroma as your enter the high heat area. If it seems right, greet your neighbors by whisper, "*tervetuloa*" (terr-vet-tu-lo-a) which means "welcome." They will whisper it back. If you miss the smoke sauna's public use time, the campground's lakeside sauna is also very nice and has a free morning sauna. For either bring your swim suit (hang from wall hooks outside the hot area) because you'll want to run out from the sauna for a refreshing plunge in the public lake several times. See the description of how to take a sauna in the introduction to Finland. Directions: Kuopio is 138km west of Joensuu and 162km north of Savonlinna.

▲**Camping:** • From 5 exit east 5km south of town and following signposting. Rauhalahti Camping (17 473 000); large grassy areas that seem tranquil even in the season; café; lakeside sauna and children's playground; adjacent to forest preserve with trails; cabins; open mid-May-Aug; $$.

Jyvaskyla

Finland's most famous modern architect, Alvar Alto, strove to humanize functional architecture. Collaborating with his wife, he also helped design the famous L-shaped chair and table leg. An account of his life and the time in which he worked are exhibited along with models, photos and drawings in an exceptional building he designed on the grounds of the University of Jyvaskyla.

▲**Camping:** • Drive north of the city on E75/4, exit for the suburb of Taulumaki, then drive north along the lake. Tuomiojarvi Camping (014-624-895); beautiful location on the lake; covered cooking and eating area; cabins; open June-Aug; $$.

KARELIAN REGION

Most of Finland's best national parks are in the northeast. Visit the Finnish Forest and Park Service, Metsahallitus; www.metsa.fi

Joensuu

Music fills the air for most of the summer in this lively city. A deep-rooted love for music has sustained the Karelian region spirits during threats from neighboring Russia. International festivals of rock, gospel, and folk music are held throughout the summer. You'll need to ticket ahead for

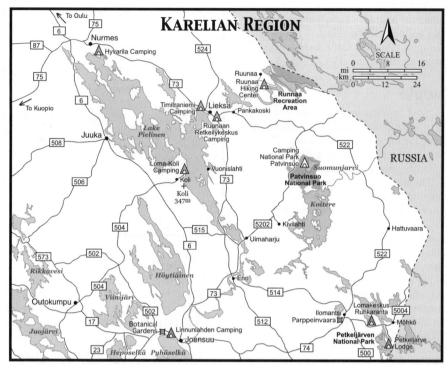

the Ilosaari Rock festival held in mid-July: www.ilosaaiirock.fi and the Gospel Festival which follows the next weekend: www.suomengospel.org. At the University's botanical gardens, magnificent giant butterflies, screeching tropical birds, beetles, and bamboo are housed in exotic greenhouses; closed Tuesday. It's just a half-kilometer west of the campground. For adventure, folks pile into wooden boats in the center of town to paddle the Pielisjoki rapids. The collection at the new cultural museum, the Pohjois-Karjalan Museo, is dedicated to the history and customs of this region so close to Russia; open daily. Directions: Follow signposting for Carelicum and Kauppatori on the west side of the river and north side of the bridge.

▲**Camping**: Book ahead for festival weekends. • West of the town, exit off 6/17 for Areena. Linnunlahden Camping (013-126-272, fax 013-525-486); on a small lake by the festival grounds; older; noisy during a festival; sauna; cabins; very popular; covered cooking and eating area; open June-mid Aug; $$.

Ilomantsi

Before heading to the national parks, stop at the visitor center in this pleasant town. It's easy to access on the town's main street in and has loads of information, trekking and canoeing maps, and can make reservations for guided rafting, canoe, or birding trips all over the region. They even rent equipment. Parppeinvaara, their Karelian theme village, is charming; open daily. Directions: South of town on 74. Stock up on supplies and gas before heading out to the parks. Directions to Ilomantsi: Drive east of Joensuu on 74 for 69km.

▲**Camping:** • South of town on 74, exit onto 5004 in the direction of Mohko and drive 8km. Lomakeskus Ruhkaranta (843 161); nice location in a forest close to lakes; sauna; open June-Aug; $$.

Petkeljarvi National Park

Sitting quietly beside the clear-water lakes and ponds formed from melting Ice Age lozenges in Petkeljarvi National Park, you'll probably hear the black-throated loon's mournful call. You might see it with binoculars. Look for a diving duck with a long neck and white pattern on its dark back. Hiking trails are on long thread-like raised banks dividing lakes and cloud reflecting ponds. They continue into old forests where three-toed woodpeckers drum and then onto boardwalks crossing meadows blanketed with a sea-foam of Labrador tea. An excellent campground and interpretation center/lodge/restaurant make this park one of my favorites. Directions: From Joensus follow signposting east on 74 in the direction of Ilomantsi for 69km. Before entering town exit onto a small road 5004 signposted for Mohko and drive 17km. Turn south at signposting for Petkeljarvi National Park and drive 6km to the park entrance. For a change of pace join the locals in the tiny outpost of Mohko as they sip beer and indulge in delicious homemade pies at Finland's eastern-most lakeside terrace cafe. Directions: Drive 4km further east on 5004 from the turn-off to the national park.

▲Camping: • At the park entrance next to the lodge. Petkeljarvi Lodge (013 520 5700); lovely setting under the pines above a serene lake with diving board; beautiful cookhouse; showers at the adjoining lodge; restaurant; excellent interpretative center; wood-fired lakeside sauna (make reservations when you check-in at the lodge); open June-August; $$.

Hattuvaara

This charming little village hosts the regions very important Taistelijan Talo, or Fighters House Museum. In the Winter War of 1944, Finn's fought heroically against immense odds. The heart-rending story is told through film, photographs, and memorabilia; open daily. The museum is downstairs from the restaurant. Directions: Drive north of Ilomantsi on 552 for 42km.

Patvinsuo National Park

In a mosaic of bogs, old forests, and wilderness lakes, Patvinsuo National Park protects species of international importance. Boardwalks provide walkways into bog areas where white-tufted cotton grass blows gently in the breeze and hikers are greeted by sweet honey-colored cloudberries. Bring binoculars so you can spot the three-toed woodpecker that you'll hear as they hunt for insects in the ancient trees. Brown bears, the park's symbol, still roam, and flying squirrels shriek from treetops. Trails lead through the old growth forests, along the beaches of idyllic lakes, and across the bogs to a bird watching tower. Directions: From Joensuu, drive north on 73 in the direction of Eno for 33km. Stay east at the fork and continue north on 515 in the direction of Uimaharju for 15km. At the fork, follow signposting northeast for Kivilahti for 14km continue on the road for 12km exiting east on a small road signposted for Patvinsuo National Park.

▲Camping: • In the park. Camping National Park Patvinsuo (013-548-506); wonderful location at Lake Suomunjarvi where there is a pristine sandy beach; car parking separate from tents but wheeled carts make taking gear to the campsite easier; excellent interpretative center and knowledgeable English speaking naturalists; canoe rental; open June-Aug; $.

Lieksa

Besides having a pristine setting on Lake Pielinen, Lieksa displays over 70 engaging Karelian wood structures in an open-air museum and has an adjoining regional history museum. Dressed in traditional clothing, museum staff speak English and enjoy chatting about "the old days" as well as the Karelian region. Lieska Brass Week attracts internationally famous brass musicians, and attending one of the exciting events during the last week in July is easy and affordable. www.lieskabrass.com If you are going on to the national parks, stop here for supplies and gas.

▲**Camping:** • In town off roadway 73. Timitraniemi Camping (013-521-780) large; older; on the lake; cabins; covered cooking and eating area; open June-Aug; $$.

Nurmes

Founded in 1876 by Tsar Alexander II of Russia, the terraced Old Town's hillsides still hold fine wooden houses nestled among leafy birch trees. Directions: Follow signposting off 73 northwest of town for Puu-Nurmes. A rousing Bomba Festival in mid-July and a Karelian theme village helps the Karelians to keep their culture alive. Directions: Follow signposting off 73 southeast of town for Bomba House. Paddling the Saramojoki canoe route, hiking the Saramo Jotos, and fishing for salmon on the Lokinlampi are popular Finnish pursuits. The tourist office close to the campground at Hyvarila Holiday Center has loads of information. Taking a leisurely ferry ride on Lake Pielinen is a relaxing excursion. The ferries leave from the harbor close to the train station in Puu-Nurmes.

▲**Camping:** • 2km east of town close to the Bomba House, exit off 73. Hyvarila Camping (013-481-770); nice location on the lake; cabins; covered cooking and eating area; popular with families; open June-Aug; $$.

Ruunaa Recreational Area

Plunging through white water, casting fishing lines into crystal-clear rivers, and hiking the Bear's Path make a perfect combo for many Finns. Guided running-the-rapids trips are even more fun when the guide suggests that you tumble out of the boat and float down the last rapid with your life jacket providing the buoyancy. Afterwards you warm up in a teepee alongside a cheerful fire, sipping tea and dining on a delicious smoked salmon lunch. White water trips are arranged at the Ruunaa visitor center, which has an interesting interpretative nature exhibit, loads of brochures and maps, and a friendly and knowledgeable English-speaking staff. Stop here before going on to the campground. The Bear's Trail runs along the Ruunaanjarvi and Neitijarvi rivers and is dotted with hikers huts and campfire pits. Trailheads are by the visitor center and the campground. A unique and beautiful wood walkway winds out into the rapids. Built for the disabled, it's a wonderful experience for everyone. Well-stocked rivers make fishing popular and fishing gear, licenses, and wishes for "tight lines" are arranged at the campground. Canoeing and kayaking are popular, and equipment can be rented from the campground. Directions: From Lieksa, drive east on 522 for 8km to Pankakoski. Follow signposting north for 14km to the Ruunaa Visitor Center.

▲**Camping:** • On the Neitikoski River, close to the rapids. Drive 4km from the visitor center. Exit east on the road signposted Ruunaa Hiking Center and drive 5km. Ruunaa Hiking Center (013-533-170); large; cabins; great location; all the amenities including laundry; bike and canoe rental; restaurant; popular; open June-Aug; $$.

Koli National Park

From Koli's summit, you look out over what to the Finnish mind is the essence of Finland: a breathtaking view of a sea of jade-green forest surrounding a pristine body of water that shimmers like lapis lazuli and is speckled with tiny islands resembling the backs of whales. In summer, car-ferries cross deep Lake Pielinen, traveling to and from the park via harbors at Lieksa, Joensuu, Nurmes and Vuonislahti. If you don't feel like hiking to the summit a funicular runs from the base of the parking lot. Directions: Almost halfway between Nurmes and Joensuu, on the west side of Lake Pielinen, exit east off 6 onto 504 at Kolinportti and drive 8km to Koli village tourist office. Parking for the summit is just one kilometer farther.

▲**Camping:** • Up the hill from Koli Village at the lake. Loma-Koli Camping (013-673-212); older; large; cabins; covered cooking and eating area; open June-Aug; $$.

LAPLAND AND NORTHERN FINLAND
Oulanka National Park

Suspension bridges span tumultuous rapids, waterfalls thunder, and rugged cliffs enclose shadowy gorges in what is probably Finland's premium park for treking and advanced kayaking. It lies on two billion-year-old remnants of a once high mountain range that stretched from the Russian northwest to Lapland. Oulanka National Park is part of the European Pan Park research network, which makes the visitor center particularly informative. Knowledgeable English-speaking staff is very helpful. Birders might want to arrange ahead for a guide with Kuusamo Bird Touring; www.kuusamobirds.net Interpretive boards dot the nature trail from the visitor center to the Oulankajoki River and the rapids. The visitor center and camping is at Kiutakongas. Directions: Drive north of Kuusamo on 5 for 36km to the intersection of 5 and 950. Exit 5 onto 950 in the direction of Kayla and drive north 10km. At Kayla, exit east onto 8693 and drive 13km on a well-maintained road to the park headquarters and camping.

An easy trail leads for about 2 kilometers through the forest to the waterfalls and rapids of Kiutakongas, which plunges through a canyon of sheer red dolomite. Upon reaching the river, you can cross an exciting suspension bridge above the surging rapids and rugged riverbanks. The

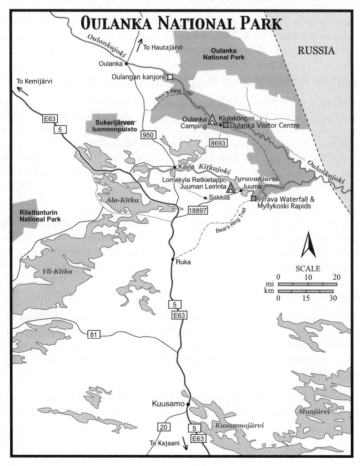

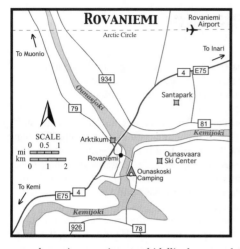

wonderful hikers' hut at the river's edge has picnic tables, maps, and a campfire area so plan to relax and take in the incredible scenery. Directions to the trail: At the north end of the park, exit east off 950, 4km south of Hautajarvi onto a smaller road signposted for Oulangan kanjoni, and drive 11km to parking and trailhead. Almost worth the drive up to Oulanka is the campground's sauna. After placing the "occupied" sign across the forest path leading to the sauna, you walk into the secluded woods hearing only the rustle of leaves and birdsong. The gracious wood sauna building is expertly built and cared for and fits into the natural setting with a sod roof. An artful rock pathway leads from the porch to the diving platform and stairs, where after getting hot in the sauna, you plunge into a private and idyllic deep pond that is just the right temperature.

▲**Camping**: • Close to the visitor center. Oulanka Camping (08-863-429); large; nice setting; fabulous lakeside sauna (make reservations on arrival or try calling ahead); canoe rental; covered cooking and eating areas, campfire, open June to mid Aug; $$.

White Water Rafting the Kitkajoki or Oulankajoki

Advanced paddlers will enjoy the thrill of paddling these tricky and demanding rapids. Some portage is necessary. There are hikers huts along the way. Having a guide is advisable. Tamer, scenic trips are also available. Both are available with Kitkan Sarfarit. www.kitkansafarit One of the best day hikes in the area is the Little Bear's Ring, a 9-kilometers loop that passes the Jyrava waterfall, the Myllykoski Rapids and Lake Jyravanjarvi. Pick up a map at the route at the campground or visitor center. Directions: Exit off 5, 2km south of the interesection of 5 and 950 onto 18897 and drive 14km to Juuma.

▲**Camping**: • Both of these are in the same area by the bridge on 18897, where the road loops northward towards 8693. Both are close to the trailhead and information board at the boat launching and parking and both have equally nice locations by the river. Lomakyla Retkietappi (08-863 218) and Juuman Leirinta (08 863 212). Both have pretty locations along the river; bungalows; canoe rental; open June to mid-August; $$.

Rovaniemi

Dramatically housed under glass, the Arkikum Museum is a fascinating celebration of the people, plants, and animals of the entire Arctic world; open daily. In June, a colorful festival hosted by the Sami, Finland's indigenous people, livens up the town. Reindeer farm visits, Arctic Circle crossings, and Santapark visits are other popular attractions. For a thrill, take the summer toboggan run at the Ounasvaara ski center.

▲**Camping**: • On the river south of town between the two bridges. Exit off E4. Camping Ounaskoski (016-345-304); nice location on the river; convenient for sightseeing; open June-August; $$.

THE NORTHWEST COAST
Oulu Area

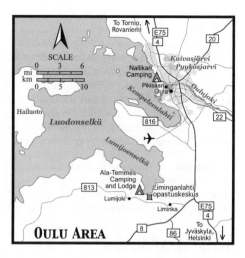

The wetlands at the north end of the Bay of Bothnia is a popular stop-over spot for a wide range of waterfowl and shorebirds refueling and resting before traveling on. At the end of May and beginning of June it is possible to see close to a 100 species at the end of a good day. These months also avoid biting insects and include seeing the midnight sun. Finland is one of the best places in the world to see owls, so if you are a birder you will want to arrange for assistance and take advantage of the rare experience of seeing up to nine species of owls. Both terek sandpipers and yellow-breasted buntings are regularly sighted. Check with the Finnish Tourist Office. www.mek.fi They can provide list of local birding contacts throughout Finland or contact Finnature, a respected company with very experienced guides and popular tours; www.finnature.sci.fi. Get oriented at the Liminganlahti Visitor Center with its terrific interpretative displays. The well-informed-English speaking staff can explain what has been seen recently and where and give you directions on how to get there. Bird-watching towers and boardwalk trails make the adventure fun even for non-birders. Directions: Turn west off 4 south of Oulu onto 6, then almost immediately onto 813. Drive west 6km through Liminka in the direction of Lumijoki, then turn north following signposting for Liminganlahti Opastuskeskus. The path to the tower at Virkkula leads to the visitor center, which is also the best area for sightings of the yellow-breasted bunting.

If you have extra time or want the exercise, rent a bike at the campground or roller blades at Shop 24 at the kauppatori and join the Finns on one of the best networks of cycling/walking paths in Finland. Use the free cycling map available at either place. For an easier pace, to see the sights, hop onto the Potnapekka, a reasonably priced tourist trolley that leaves every hour from the pedestrian street Rotuaari. Don't leave Oulu without sitting down to sample some of the yummy offerings at the kauppatori, and to be serenaded by local musicians.

▲**Camping**: • At Liminganlahti. Ala-Temmes Camping and Lodge (838 4643); wonderful location; new; sauna; excellent cooking/eating/toilet/shower areas; open May-Sept; $$. • At the beach at Oulu. Drive west of town crossing over the bridge in the direction of Pikisaari and follow signposting. Nallikari Camping (558 61350); large; resort-like; cabins; café; open all year; $$.

Tornio

Even a novice golfer won't want to pass up the chance to play 18 holes at midnight on an affordable course where you tee off and play nine holes in one country and time zone and then finish up in another country and time zone. Basic equipment can be rented, but you'll need to reserve ahead for it as well as for playing after 10 PM; www.tornio.fi. Directions: Tornio is 109km north of Oulu at the mouth of the Tornionjoki River and the border with Sweden. The Green Zone Golf Course is well signposted north of town.

▲**Camping**: • Follow signposting off E75/4 2km south of Tornio. Camping Tornio (549 0066); convenient; basic; mid-May- mid-Sept; $.

Vasa

The Bothnia Straits Nature Centre in Vasa's Ostrobothnia Museum has exceptional exhibits of flora and fauna and shows a wonderful video about the Bay of Bothnia; don't miss it. Directions: From the main highway follow signposting for the train station. Cross over to the west side of the tracks. Turn north onto Ratukatu and follow the road to the end and then signposting for the museum; open open daily. Ferries leave from here for Umea Sweden, a 3-hour trip. Directions: Follow signposting through town and across the bridge to the ferry terminal at Vaskiluoto. www.rgline.com The week-long Kaustinen Folk Festival, the Wasalandia Amusement Park, and the Tropiclandia Water Park, bring plenty of vacationing Finns and Swedes to Vasa to relax and have fun with family and friends.

▲Camping: • Follow signposting off main highways for ferry and Vaskiluoto. Cross over the bridge and follow signposting at the fork for camping. Top Camping Vasa (211 1255); resort-like; large; staff directed children activities; can be crowded and noisy; not the best place if you don't have kids; open mid-May-mid-Sept; $$.

SOUTH OF VASA
Solf

Just 15 kilometers south of Vasa the charming village of Solf is hidden in the brilliant fields of mustard and wheat that sweep through the beautiful countryside. The drive to get here is beautiful and on the way you can stop at the Stundars Handicraft Village open-air museum. You'll be served tea with toasts spread with homemade butter and watch artisans work in the traditional buildings brought from surrounding villages. Dressed in traditional costumes, the craftsmen show how it was done in the old days. This is a wonderful detour that shouldn't be missed; open daily. Directions: Drive east of Vasa on E12 for 8km. Exit south onto 673 and drive 7km.

Kristinestad

The very pleasant lakeside campground here is cause enough for a relaxing break in the journey, but the small and idyllic town–with colorfully painted wood houses, an open-market at the town square, a few small but interesting museums, and cafés with terraces from which to enjoy the view–makes it a favorite stop of mine. Directions: 75km south of Vasa take exit 8 and drive west 9km.

▲Camping: • South of town on the west side of the west side of the bay. Drive west of market square two blocks to Staketgatan. Turn south for 3 blocks. Stay west at the fork following signposting for camping. Pukinsaari Camping (221 1484); lovely location on the edge of the bay and small town park; diving board; children's playground; extra nice cooking/eating/toilet/shower facility; bike rental; tranquil; open June-Aug; $$.

VASA AND AROUND
Jakobstad and Around

Motorcycle enthusiasts should zip into this pretty town to admire one man's fascinating collection of more than 120 motorcycles at his Motorcykelsalongen. Homemade versions sit beside vintage Harley Davidsons and Nortons; open daily. Directions: 93km north of Vasa exit 8 west onto 68, and drive 7km. Follow the main road into town. Turn west by the park onto Skolgatan, and drive 4 blocks. If you have kids along, you might want to indulge them with waterslides and arcade games at Fantasea Park at the beach. Directions: Drive north through town, then west towards the beach road at Gamla Hamn, then follow signposting for Fantasea. Several expeditions

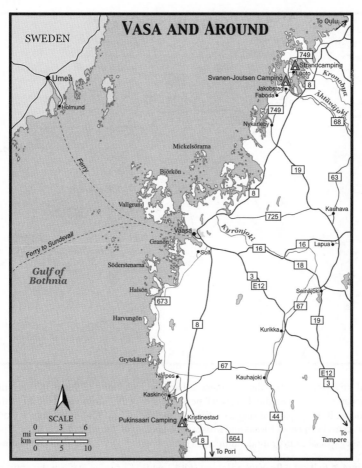

to the Arctic enabled one adventurous Finn to amass a fascinating collection of Arctic-used tools, huts, and other memorabilia. The collection is housed in a tiny Greenlandic peat hut called the Nanoq Arctic Museum; open daily at noon. Directions: Follow the main road southwest of town in the direction of Faboda for 7km. The beach here is extra special with lots of rocky outcrops and inlets so plan to take a walk along the beach and maybe stop for a picnic and a nap.

▲**Camping**: • 6km north of town in Nissasorn. Follow signposting off 749. Svanen-Joutsen Camping (723 0660); large; popular with families; bike and boat rental; open June-Aug; $$. • On a small bay 9km north of Jacobstad, exit east off 749 in the direction of Luoto. Strandcamping (728 5151); small; simple; cabins; open June-August; $.

SOUTHWEST COAST
Rauma

UNESCO listed, Rauma's 17th-century Old Town's wood houses line narrow and winding streets leafy with birch and colorful with well tended gardens. It is one of the most complete and best preserved wood towns in Scandinavia. Noted for its lacemakers, Rauma provided Europe with the beauti-

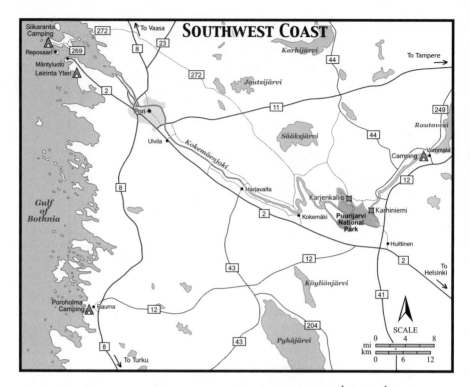

fully crafted, stiffly starched lace that decorated collars and hats in the 17th and 18th-centuries. Even if you think you aren't interested in lace, you'll be impressed by the intricacies of the art in the Rauma Museum and with the displays during Lace Week at the end of July. Also in late July, a Blues Festival features musicians from New Orleans and Mississippi. Located on the edge of a pretty archipelago and featuring a very special campground, Rauma will entice you to linger longer than you planned.

▲**Camping:** • Exit off 8 for Vanha Rauma (Old Town). Continue west on the main street passing through the old town. Cross the bridge, pass or stop at the tourist office, then continue on to a 5-way intersection. Follow signposting west for camping. Poroholma Camping (8388 2500); lovely setting at a tiny harbor; park-like grassy areas wind around the water; lakeside sauna; bike rental; hostel; simple café; open mid-May-Aug; $$.

Pori

World famous jazz performers, invited to express themselves in their music's great tradition, converge on Pori for nine days in mid-July. Fiery and explosive, thrilling and inventive, the music spills out of tents, outdoor stages and old warehouses in more than 100 concerts that attract enthusiasts from all over the world. This festival is held on a park-like island in the town's river. Jazz Street is closed to traffic and a dynamic music scene goes on day and night. Food and beverage stalls line the streets, solo musicians and exciting ensembles play for tips in the lively scene outside the concerts. Leave your car at the campground and take the bus into town during the festival; www.porijazz.fi.

▲**Camping:** • Exit west onto 2 in the direction of Yyteri and drive 20km out onto the peninsula leading to Reposaari Island. • Leirinta Yyteri (634 5700); part of a resort; large; beach;

bike rental; open year-round; book ahead for the festival; $$$; www.pori.fi/va/yyteri. • On Reposaari Island. Drive west of Pori on 2 for 22km to 269 and the bridge connecting the island to the mainland. Siikaranta Camping (638 4120); smaller; beautiful setting; bus to Pori; open June-August; $$.

Puurijarvi National Park

Once an ancient delta where tenant farmers mowed horsetails below the waterline and passed them up to waiting wives and kids in rowboats, Puurijarvi National Park today boasts five fine raised bogs with a periphery of meadow and forest. At the beginning of summer, a cacophony of rasping sedge warblers, whistling goldeneye, and the joyful screams of black-headed gulls fill the air. It is one of Finland's finest bird lakes. There's an observation tower at Karjenkallio. Finding this park is a little difficult because the signage is minimal. Directions: From Pori drive southeast on 2 for 58km. Exit north onto 12 and drive one kilometer in the direction of Huittnen. Exit west onto 12817. Watch for signposting for Karhiniemi, where there is an information board and signposts for the Isosuo nature trail leading out onto the bog and bird watching tower. An additional bird watching tower is found farther north, closer to the road. To reach it, continue northwest on 12817 for 3km to the fork of 12817 and 2481. Stay northwest for 2km watching for signposting and parking for Puurijarvi. Follow the trail posted for the Karjenkallio bird tower.

▲**Camping**: 24km north of the intersection of 2 and 12 in Vammala. Tervakallio Camping (514 2720); convenient; cabins; open May-August; $$.

Aland Islands

Linking Finland with Sweden, this archipelago makes crossing to and from the countries fun and easy. Politically Finnish but culturally Swedish, the residents of Aland like to claim independence of either country. Cycling is popular and one of the best ways to enjoy the archipelago's beauty. An extensive network of cycle paths and inter-island car ferries makes it easy. The shoreline's countless coves and serene waterways make paddling especially enjoyable. Paddling and cycling maps are available, and transport for put-in and take-out can be arranged. Most of the campgrounds are right at the water and have cabins and cafes, so packing some gear for a camping/paddling trip is popular and not overly difficult. Ro-No-Rents is the largest rental company for bicycles, canoes, and kayaks and has locations at the harbors in Mariehamn and also in Eckero Berghamn (358 18 12820).

Attending some of the colorful festivals held throughout the summer will add sparkle to your visit. On the second weekend in July during the Gustav Vasa Days, gaily dressed 16th-century musicians, dancers, marketeers and helmeted soldiers greet visitors to the Castle of Kastelholm on Sund. On the last weekend in July at the Viking Market in Saltvik, handsome Viking costumed craftspeople show off their fine art skills in textiles, ceramics, metal sculpture, and leather goods under colorful tents. Midsummer is celebrated on the third weekend in June around a colorfully decorated pole on each of the islands. It runs throughout the day and night, and is especially spirited. Mariepark in Mariehamn hosts Aland's biggest musical festival, Rockoff a 9-day festival, featuring top performers from Finland and Sweden. Discovering the uniqueness of the each island is part of the allure of Aland. Plan to camp in several locations.

Aland claims to have the more sunshine than any other location in the Nordic so it is a very popular place to take a vacation. It is essential to make your car ferry crossing reservations well ahead. www.visitaland.com www.eckeroinjen.fi;Mariehamn. Ferries leave from Turku in Finland and from both Grisslehamn and Stockholm in Sweden. The least expensive option is Grisslehamn, because from there the crossing takes only two hours.

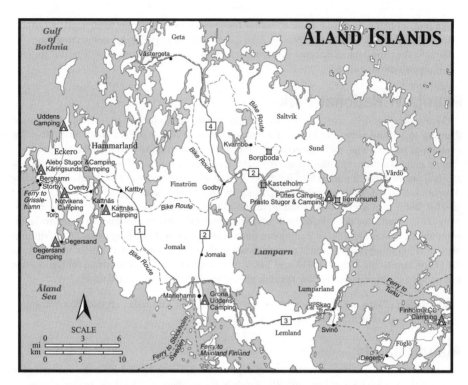

▲Camping: Camping is very popular on Aland. The campgrounds listed have wonderful locations close to the water, a sauna, children's playgrounds, a covered campfire area, laundry facilities, a simple café, and cabins.

Eckero (where the ferry lands from Grisslehamn, Sweden). • From the ferry landing in Bergham, drive east on 1 for 2km to Storby. Turn south in the direction of Torp and drive 9km. Degersands Camping (38592); wonderful location on a small beach away from the crowds; popular with kayakers; good swimming area for families; cabins; open June-August; $$. • Drive east of the ferry landing for 6km in the direction of Overby. Turn south and follow signposting through the forest for 2km. Notvikens Camping (38020); lovely setting on the water surrounded by pines; quiet; minigolf; bike rental; open May-August; $$. • From the ferry landing drive 1/2 kilometer. Turn north, following signposting for the nearby Karingsund harbor and recreational area. These are both next to each other and are similar. Karingsund Camping (38309); open mid May-August, and Aebo Stugor and Camping (38575); open May-Sept. Both are across from the small boat harbor and small family beach; nature trail; Hunting and Fishing Museum; popular with families; $$. • More remote and very tranquil. Just east of Storby exit north for Skag and drive through the forest for 9km. Uddens Camping (38610); lovely setting on the water; quiet; hiking trails; mini golf; open May-September; $$.

Hammarland. • Exit One just east of the bridge between Eckero and Hammarland, and drive south 3km in the direction of Kattnas. Kattnas Camping (37687); lovely location on a boulder strewn hillside beside the beach; quiet; boules court; open May-mid-September; $$.

Aland. • On the east side of Mariehamn. Drive east on Storagatan to the harbor. Turn south, following the coast road for one kilometer. Grona Uddens Camping (21121); very popular and well used; bike and canoe rental; swimming beach; no cabins; open mid-May-Aug; $$.

Sund. • Both of these are close to the Russian fortress Bomarsund on the southeast end of the island. Puttes Camping (44040); pleasant location with small boat and canoe jetty; popular with kayakers; open mid-May-Aug; $$. Prasto Stugor and Camping (44045); pleasant location; nice cook house; canoe rental; open mid-April-mid-Sept; $$.

Foglo. This is my favorite campground in the Aland archepelago. • Drive east of Mariehamn on 3 for 25km to Skag. Turn south following signposting for Svino and the car ferry that crosses back and forth throughout the day from Svino to Degerby. From Degerby, drive east 15km on the main road, then north following signposting for Finholma. CC Camping (51440); lovely location on tiny island in an archipelago; kayak rental; beach sauna; remote; popular with cyclists and kayakers; cheerful owner/host; simple café; open June-August; $$.

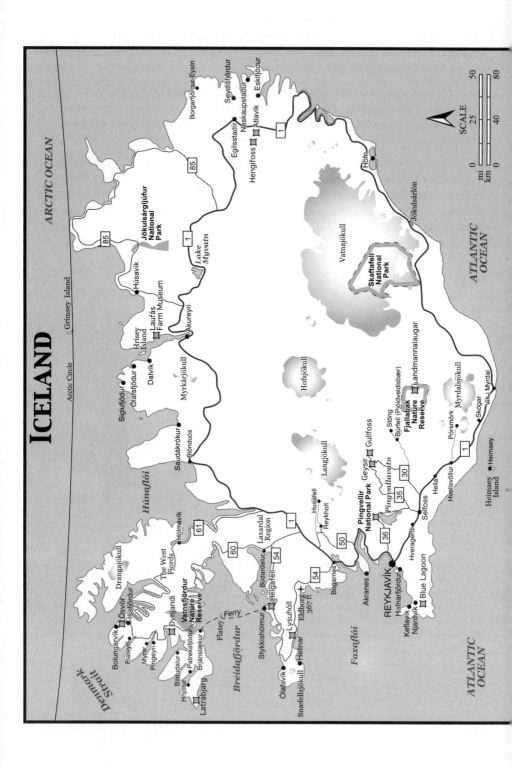

ICELAND

wwwicetourist.is

Iceland is often thought to be covered with ice, but in fact much of it is gloriously green in summer. The country is a superlative combination of lush meadows enlivened with lovely wildflowers, pristine blue-green lakes, steamy hot springs, grandiose and graceful waterfalls, snow-capped glacier-chiseled mountains, massive lava flows, and enormous glaciers. Along the coastline, a fine interplay occurs of little coloring-book towns hugging harbors, farmlands where horses and their foals graze peacefully on succulent grasslands, and ewes with tail-twitching lambs scramble off long grassy slopes. Everything seems fresh and quickens with vibrant new life.

After a long winter, Icelanders love being outdoors and are enthusiastic campers. Not only are there beautiful campgrounds in all the national parks, you'll also find them in almost every town. Always located in a scenic location on a large grassy meadow, they are especially clean and cheerful with plenty of room even at the height of summer. One side of the service building is for cooking and washing dishes. Sometimes it will be enclosed, have tables and chairs, stoves, and even pots and pans. In more remote areas it will have a roof and sides making it covered but not enclosed. Many campgrounds have heated shower rooms with plenty of hot and cold water at no extra charge. Barbecuing is popular and campsites have grills and many have terraces with picnic tables and chairs. Campgrounds in towns are often located next to the public swimming pool and in smaller towns this is where campers shower. Registering for camping, getting tourist information is often here too. Campgrounds are reliably open June through mid September. Expect that for all the listed ones here. Camping cost, throughout Iceland, regardless of amenities, is about 8 euros for two persons, a car, and a tent. These are noted here as $$.

The swimming pool is the town's social hub, and no travel experience to Iceland is complete without experiencing one. You'll get addicted quickly. They are modern, immaculately clean and thermally heated and not expensive. Those in larger towns will have a lap pool, hot tub, sauna, and water slide. No wonder the locals love them. After paying at the front desk, you'll be given a key to a locker. Before entering the dressing room/shower area, you must remove your shoes, and before proceeding to the pool area, you must shower thoroughly using soap. Start up a conversation as you soak with people in the warm thermal waters. Icelanders are very friendly people and enjoy a chat.

Making new friends is easy in Iceland. Most Icelanders speak English, and your fellow international travelers will usually speak English when they converse with them. So you can feel assured that when you speak to a person at the campground, he or she will understand what you are saying regardless of what country they are from. Your fellow campers will be from all over the world. I usually begin a conversation by asking where they are from. Even travelers who are engrossed in what they are doing and not particularly friendly seem to enjoy a conversation once I have started it.

Driving in Iceland is not difficult if you stay on the main roads and, with certain precautions, not hard on secondary ones. Traffic is light. Headlights are required to be on at all times. Secondary roads are usually hard surface gravel part of the time. On narrow roads, slow down or stop and let an approaching car proceed around you. Be aware that the shoulder of gravel roads is often soft, so take care not to pull too far to the side. Always be prepared to stop abruptly. Animals cross the road and sheep in the waysides sometimes jump into the road when they are startled. Drivers who injure or kill an animal are required by law to pay compensation to the owners. It is not always easy to see changes in road surface between gravel and paving. Be careful at all times. Don't let a careless moment ruin your trip. Unless you plan to drive on the more remote roads in the interior, a two-wheel-drive vehicle is fine. Four-wheel-drive vehicles are expensive to rent. Gas is expensive but the distance between sights is not great, and since most roads aren't suitable for high speeds you won't be covering as many miles as you might at home. Gas stations have clean toilets, groceries, fast food, maps, tourist information, friendly English-speaking staff, and sometimes even free use of water hoses for washing off a dusty car. Fill up with gas before going to a remote area. Purchase a quality detailed road map before you start your trip. Then make a habit of stopping in front of the detailed region information maps on main highways throughout the country. Take breaks, enjoy the views, and examine the maps carefully so you don't get lost.

In small towns, look for tourist information–which can be as simple as a desk and computer at the local grocery store, swimming pool, bus stop, or gas station. Knowledgeable English-speaking staff exert real effort to help. They can give you information and for free they will book reservations for horseback rides, rafting, kayaking, special bus rides into hard-to-drive to areas, and ferry crossings. They have plenty of brochures on the local region and sometimes sell books on wildflowers, birds, geology, and history. Car ferries are fun and convenient to use but have limited vehicle space. Reserve space several days ahead with any tourist office. The scenery from a ferry is so spectacular that even the locals pay attention when the great black-backed gulls and Artic terns wheel in the sky and stately snowy peaks sparkle in the sunlight.

I love the small town museums. Not funded by a large corporation, they are careful collections and photographs of local people telling what they think is meaningful. It's easy to imagine the amount of volunteer work that sustains them and it's this effort that makes them meaningful to me. The campground staff or tourist information desk will know when they are open.

Groceries cost about the same as they do in other Scandinavian countries. If you keep your choices simple they aren't overly expensive. The fish caught in the unpolluted North Atlantic waters, is firm and delicious. The free-range lamb is reasonably priced, tender, and flavorful. A wide selection of cheeses, yogurts, and spreads are made from the milk of cows who graze in pollution-free pastures. Stock up on fresh vegetables, fruit, and other supplies in larger towns. Check with the campground or a gas station for the best place to shop. Consider bringing coffee, tea, packaged mixes, nuts, and

dried fruit from home. On arrival, shop in the duty-free liquor store before leaving the airport in Reykjavik. From then on, alcohol must be purchased at a government liquor store.

Purchasing a museum card in Reykjavik and Akureyri is worthwhile because it makes admission cheaper which prompts you to visit more. White gas and bottled propane for camp stoves is available at the camp office in Reykjavik and also in some of the larger gas stations. Get local currency from cash machines located at the banks or grocery stores in larger towns. Iceland's bird-cliffs and lakes, where millions of birds nest, are remarkable bird watching locations. The spring migration and nesting period starts in mid-April and peaks in June. Bring binoculars. The brilliance and beauty of Iceland's wildflowers is outstanding. Consider purchasing a guidebook on arrival.

It can be sunny, rainy, or windy all in the same day or even at the same time. Dress in warm, layered clothing, and bring a waterproof jacket and a hat that ties. Be sure your tent has a quality waterproof rainfly that can be staked securely into the ground. Because the camp cooking areas are so comfortable, most people hang out there and just use their tent area for sleeping and quiet time. Thermal bathing in natural hot springs is lots of fun. Bring water shoes to wear in them because the walk to, and into, the water might have sharp-edged lava stone. The Gulf Stream warms Iceland's coast so that even though it lies within four degrees of the Arctic Circle, it can be colder in the winter in New York City than in Reykjavik. Summer temperatures average 52 degrees Fahrenheit or 11 degrees Celsius, and rainfall averages 2 inches or 50 millimeters.

REYKJAVIK

Even in Iceland's capital–a sophisticated city teeming with poets, performing artists, and avant-garde sculptors–there is a sense of light and wide-open spaces where hues of nature are balanced with a simple palette of full colors. Ringed with splendid mountains, it is built on a narrow isthmus, with a fishing boat-filled harbor on one side and the open sea on the other. One of the city's greatest attributes is its sublime tranquility, something not often found in today's capital cities. Pick up a free city map/guide at the campground and then start experiencing Reykjavik at Tjorn, the town's toy-like lake in the heart of old town. Swans, ducks, geese, and other migratory birds rest here in migratory-transit and are lovingly fed by the locals, so it is a good place to exchange smiles and exclamations. At the north end of the lake, the city hall has a huge raised relief map of Iceland that lets you see your route's landscape. Walk north from here to the excellent visitors' center loaded with information on Reykjavik and the whole of Iceland. Talk with staff about special events. Visit a few museums then just wander through the delightful coloring-book-like town filled with brightly painted turn-of-the-century houses, neatly planted parks and squares, and streets lined with birch trees. Walk up the hill to the church, Hallgrimskirkja. Its bold and dramatic architecture is reminiscent of Iceland's finely carved mountains. From its tower you'll be able to overlook the old town with its patchwork of variegated tin roofs. After 11 PM on the weekends, dancing, drinking, and nuzzling go on until the wee hours of the morning as unrestrained, fun-loving locals and tourists alike live it up. It is a giant club crawl that jams the streets into one big party around Tryggvagata and Hafnarstraeti in downtown Reykjavik.

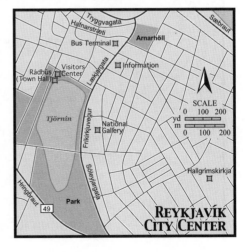

▲**Camping:** • In Laugardalur Park, next to the swimming pool and adjacent to the hostel. From Kelflavik Airport drive 42km northeast on 41 following signposting for Reykjavik. Turn onto Kringlumyrarbraut and drive north to Sundlaugavegur, passing the Grand Hotel Reykjavik. Turn east onto Sundlaugavegur and drive one kilometer to the swimming pool and camping. Laugardalur Camping (553-8110); exceptional cooking/eating areas; warm shower and toilet areas with plenty of hot water; tent camping area separate from caravans; both areas are spacious grassy meadows with shrubs and trees. An experience at the swimming pool should not be missed; open May-September; $$.

AROUND REYKJAVIK
The Blue Lagoon

Great clouds of steam rise off this egg-shell blue natural pool hidden in a rough lava rock field. The Blue Lagoon is even more surreal if the weather is cloudy or cool. A silky silica mud, whose curative effects are so esteemed that it is in skin care products, covers the bottom of the pool. Scoop up some for free, from the basins around the lagoon and apply it to your face. To make you experience as eerie as possible, enter the lagoon through the farthest left-hand door. Walk down the stairs into the soothing warm water, bending to immerse yourself, then enter the cave-like enclosure under the bridge. Gradually move out into the large lagoon. The water becomes warmer and deeper farther out in the lagoon. Try the excellent sauna, built into a lava cave. Directions: From camping turn west onto Sundlaugavegur and drive one kilometer to Kringlumyrarbraut. Drive south on Kringlumyrarbraut to 40, following signposting for the airport. Drive 40km on 41, then turn south onto 43 and drive 8km to the Blue Lagoon. In summer it's open 9 AM to 11 PM and is not overly expensive; 420-8800.

Pingvellir

This is the most important historic site in Iceland. Located in a vast depression of an ancient volcanic fault, the narrow ravine is sided by steep cliff faces whose rocky tops bristle with strange-

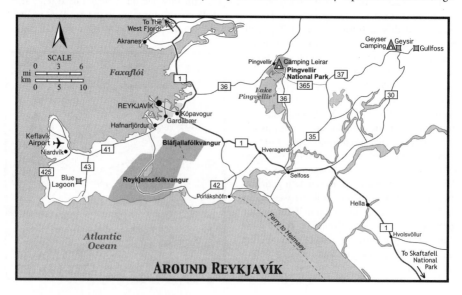

AROUND REYKJAVIK

shaped pinnacles that easily evoke the profiles of ancient gods. This was the setting for the Althing, an ancient judicial assembly. The cliffs face the sun, and wide ledges made it easy to separate the court from the general public. The acoustics are particularly good. Conjure up the colorful scenes that took place here during the Iceland Saga Days when virile men resplendent in fine robes and stunning women with long, flowing hair and richly decorated cloaks gathered to show their strength and beauty. Picture the skirmishes, the duals, and debates. Wander down the river and over to the meadow where the chieftains set up their elaborate stone enclosures, which they roofed with colorful tenting. During two-week summer encampments, they entertained, handled business, established contracts, agreed on marriages, carried out lawsuits and punishments and then returned to their farms located all over the country. A diminutive classic church stands on the sight where a church has stood for ten centuries. Walk behind the church to the small knoll called the Poet's Circle, where Iceland's greatest poets are buried. What a pleasure to find poets honored so finely. Beside the church is a pristine farmhouse, shared today by the rector and the Prime Minister. Walk up to the top of the gorge to stand on the Mid-Atlantic Ridge, where the earth's volcanic rift between the European and North American plates tears longitudinally through the valley. It is eerie to peek into the cracks and crevasses and know that the earth's surface is slowly moving apart. Directions: From Reykjavik, drive north on 41 11km to 36. Turn east onto 36 and drive 33km to the park and visitor's center.

▲**Camping:** • Across from the visitor's center. Camping Leirar (482-2660); pleasant open space along the road; simple covered cooking/washing area; warm water but no showers; picnic tables; $$.

Lake Pingvellir

The plains south of Pingvellir are gashed by many crevasses that carry water to Pingvellir Lake, Iceland's largest. It's a peaceful place with wonderful views of glacial mountains, long sweeps of purple lupine, and bird song. A marked hiking trail leads around the lake. Directions: Drive southwest of Pingvellir on 36 for 16km, and then turn south on 360.

Geysir

Geysir, whose name is generic for all steaming waterspouts, once had an enormous one. Today the Strokkur Geysir slowly develops an intriguing dome in its hot pool every 8 minutes then bursts with a waterspout that erupts with a spray up to 20-meters. In summer, fields of bright green grass cheery with yellow buttercups and dandelions surround this unearthly place, with its bubbling hot springs, steaming vents, and mud pots. Directions: From Pingvellir, drive east 16km on 365. Turn northeast onto 37, and drive 39km to Geysir.

▲**Camping:** • Geysir Camping. Close to the tourist center; all amenities; $$$.

Gullfoss

A deafening roar and clouds of mist greet you as you walk across the grassy cliff to get a closer look at Gullfoss. Gigantic and majestic, the glacier water thunders through the gorge and over a two-level cataract down to a deep chasm below. In mid-afternoon on a sunny day, you'll see a myriad of fairy-like rainbows arched over the falls. Directions: From Geysir, drive 5km to Gullfoss.

SOUTH ICELAND
Heimaey

The puffin–an adorable bird with a clown face, sweet eyes, and a multicolored bill–nests and breeds well on the grassy headlands and cliffs of Heimaey. Some of Iceland's largest puffin colonies are here and on the other Westman Islands. Gregarious, they like to sit on the rocks and ridges in chummy groups and look out to sea. The largest colonies are on the west coast, close to the golf course and camping. Take the walking path along the cliff. Your presence seems to make no difference to them, and you can approach as close as two to three meters.

The Westman Islands, formed by underwater volcanoes, are one of the world's youngest archipelagoes. In 1963, the world watched as sister-island Surtsey began forming from a volcano that continued erupting until 1967. In 1973, Eldfell, the crater at the edge of Heimaey Town, erupted. Spewing tons of molten lava, one-third of the town was eventually buried. Luckily, enough boats were in the harbor to safely evacuate Heimey's 5,000 residents. A clever idea and heroic effort saved their precious harbor: Using fire hoses, cold seawater was sprayed on the molten lava to slow down its movement. The hour-long *Volcano* film at the town's cinema brings this story to life. Hiking trails now weave across the once molten lava.

Allow ample time for the Natural History Museum, one of the best in Iceland; open daily. Fishing and fish-related production are Heimaey's expertise and an important component of Iceland's exports. The ever-present danger that is part of fishing in the North Atlantic waters is something to keep in mind as you admire the fishing vessels, large and small. Pick up the Heimaey brochure, with map of the sights and walking trails, on the ferry. Take precautions for possible seasickness. There is good parking at the harbor if you want to make it a day trip. Directions: Car ferries leave the mainland from Porlakshofn, 20km southwest of Hverageroi, for the almost 3-hour sail.

▲Camping: • On the west side of the island in Herjolfsdalur by the golf course. Camping Herjolfsdalur (481-2075); beautiful but windy; enclosed cooking/eating/washing; hot showers; $$.

Hveragerdi

An easy and spectacular walk starts here. Stop at the tourist office in this small town and get a map of the hiking area, specifically the trail to the hot stream Klambragil. This hike has a thermal stream so bring your bathing suit or wear it under your clothes. Drive up the hill, following the

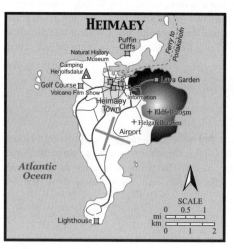

river. Pass the golf course, and then continue to the end of the road and parking. Wade across a wide, but shallow, stream. At the start, the Klambragil route follows the stream but then it leaves the stream to slowly climb up through a verdant valley to the top of a gorge where there is a breathtaking view of a waterfall and mosses so brilliant they look like they were painted with day-glo chartreuse. Farther along the slope you'll see steam vents and hot streams. Soon after, you'll see the stream running through a grassy gorge and, probably, people soaking. To lay relaxed in the stream, peacefully gazing up into the magnificent scenery while the soothing crystal-clear warm water passes over you is an unforgettable experience. This area is webbed with other great trails. In Hveragerdi thermal water is used to warm large greenhouses where vegetables and flowers are grown. To see how this works, take a tour through the Greenhouses of Eden; open daily. Directions: East of Reykjavik 32km on the Ring Road 1.

▲Camping: • Drive north on Breidamork to the swimming pool and camping. Hveragerdi Camping (483-4150); nice town location; new covered cooking/washing/ eating area; hot showers; pay at the tourist office or swimming pool; $$. • Also see Selfoss.

Selfoss Area

Selfoss makes a good stop if you are interested in birding. Concerned local residents created a preserve along the banks of the Olfusa River, now called Floi Nature Preserve. Directions: Drive southwest on 34 for 2km. Turn west on the small road signposted Kaldaoanes and drive through the rich dairy pastureland to the end of the road. Park and walk out to the river where there's a narrow riverside trail. Chances are you'll see families of whooper swans as well as families of pintail, wigeon, and teal ducks. To see Atlantic shorebirds and plant life, drive 6 kilometers south of Selfoss on 34 to Eyrabakki. Park at the school then walk over the embankment to the beach. A periphery of lava extends several hundred meters into the sea, making calm areas for feeding. You'll need to walk carefully on the slippery seaweed-covered rocks. A walking stick is helpful. Godwits, redshanks, and sanderlings all feed in the algae rich mud and the masses of thick bluish-grey oyster-plants are pretty with tiny blue blossoms draping over the rocks and driftwood. On the main street in town there is a large supermarket convenient for picking up supplies.

▲Camping: • Drive halfway through town on 1. Turn south on Bankavegur and drive to the end of the road to the sportsfield and camping. Camping Selfoss (482-3585); nice enclosed cooking and eating area, small pond with ducks, barbeque; sports field; well maintained; $$.

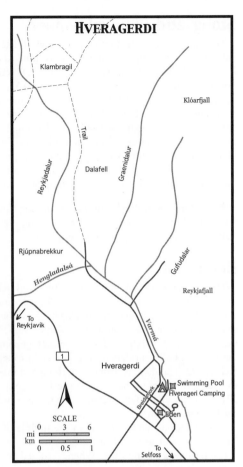

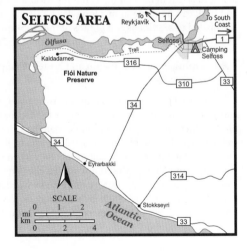

Stong and Pjoldveldisbaer

With meticulous attention to archeological detail, a reconstruction of an ash and pumice buried 2nd-century Viking longhouse, was completed at Stong. This typical medieval Icelandic longhouse is called Pjoldveldisbaer; open daily. Directions: From Selfoss drive 15km east on 1. Exit northeast onto 30 and drive 19km. Exit onto 32, and drive east 33km. Exit onto 327 and follow signposting for Pjoldveldisbaer. After, follow the signposting from the parking area to Stong and the original excavated site. Nestled neatly into the hillside along a pleasant fishing stream, you can enter the ancient longhouse itself, now decorated by moss and wildflowers that found sun in the massive earthen rooms. Along the river's edge, walk the marked 100-meter footpath, lush with blue heath, sage-colored wild thyme, and deep-purple alpine bartsia, towards the Gjain gorge and waterfall. You'll need to climb up then down a few boulders to the natural pool and waterfalls. Protected from wind, it is a perfect place for a picnic and nap.

▲Camping: • At Pjoldveldisbaer. Camping Sandartunga (486-6060); covered cooking/washing; hot showers; $$. • At Arnes. Camping Arnes (486-6048); pleasant location by the river; covered cooking/washing; simple; $$.

Hella Area

Driving across the country it is exciting to watch Iceland's pure bred, masterly horses moving in the *tolt* (a unique fifth gait) that lets the rider move smoothly even in a run. The gallant small horse is full-manned, graceful, intelligent, amicable, is bred to ride, and born to run. Iceland is a magnet for horse lovers, and Hella is a must-stop. Drive out to the Arbakki Horse Farm and lean over the fence to admire some of the best, grazing peacefully in the lush grassland. Their calm temperament allows riders from beginners through equestrians to enjoy a comfortable ride over Iceland's lush landscape. Horseback riding is a major tourist activity, and there are opportunities for riding throughout the country; check with any tourist office. Directions: Exit 1 at Hella onto 271 and drive 7km. Talk to staff at the tourist office in Hella to make arrangements for a tour of the breeding farm.

Mount Hekla stands serenely in the middle of a volcanic belt and is reminiscent of Mount Kilimanjaro and Mount Fuji. Still active, the volcano erupted recently in 1970 and in 1991, spreading ejecta far and wide. When it erupted in 1104, word spread that the entrance to Hell had been located, and so the name. Consider yourself lucky if her summit is visible because very often her head is lost in the clouds. Climbing Mount Hekla is a popular trek, and a climb to the summit and back can be made in one long day by strong experienced hikers. Visit the Hekla Museum in Leirubakki to see videos and photos of the eruptions and for hiking advice; open daily. Directions: Drive 10km west of Hella on 1. Turn north onto 26 and drive 14km to Leirubakki.

▲Camping: • By the museum and hostel. Camping Leirubakki (487-6591); popular with hikers; basic; $$.

Njall once lived in this landscape of tawny plains and grazing lands, with spectacular mountains and glaciers looming from one side of the road and flat sand and river marshes stretching out on the other. A complex and heroic man, he is one of Iceland's most popular saga figures. The *Iceland Sagas* feature blood feuds, Viking excess, lost love, heroism, and brutal killings. They tell the story of a nation that began in the 900s when the Vikings arrived from Norway. Visiting the Njall Saga and Viking Museum to see its dioramas, paintings, maps, and models is lighthearted and fun way to make this history more understandable; open daily. If your interest has been whetted, take a guided tour of the area and stay for a saga feast in the medieval hall. Directions: In Hvolsvollur. Drive 18 kilometers east of Hella on 1.

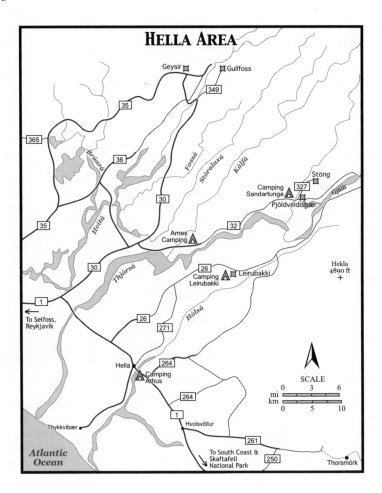

HELLA AREA

Geysir

Gullfoss

349

35

365

36

Stöng

Camping
Sandartunga 327

30

Pjóldveldisbær

35

32

Arnes
Camping

30

26

Camping
Leirubakki

Leirubakki

Hekla
4890 ft
+

1

←
To Selfoss,
Reykjavik

26

271

Hella

264

Camping
Arhus

SCALE

0   3   6

mi
km

0   5   10

264

1

Thykkvibær

Hvolsvöllur

261

*Atlantic
Ocean*

To South Coast &
Skaftafell
National Park

250

Thorsmörk

▲**Camping:** • On the Holsa River in Hella, on the southeast side of the bridge. Camping Arhus (487-5577); one of the best campgrounds in Iceland; scenic location; well maintained facilities; particularly pleasant enclosed cooking/washing/eating area; laundry; cabins; restaurant; good birding along the river; $$.

SOUTH COAST
Skogar

Timber has always been scarce in Iceland, and the indigenous rock is either too hard or too crumbly for a building material. So for centuries people lived in sod-walled houses that were partially buried in the ground. Openings were few and small–for better protection from the cold–and the floors were beaten earth. Beds were short, only four to five feet long so people slept sitting up. Their tiny churches had minimal decoration. At Skogar Folk Museum, visitors duck into the little abodes and comment how charming and cozy they seem today. The friendly curator often plays the farmhouse or church organ and visitors sing along. The adjoining maritime museum is

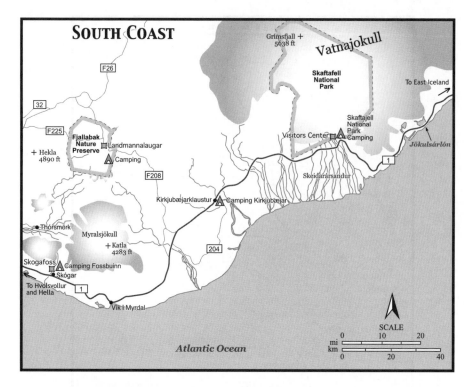

worthwhile. For lack of a harbor, boats–usually made from huge pieces of driftwood that floated from Russia and Scandinavia–were launched straight out into the open waves. Not far from the museums Skogafoss waterfall thunders down from sixty-meter-high cliffs, plunging mightily in a superb curtain of water. Enjoying the perpetual shower, fulmars nest daintily in shallow depressions of the mossy cliffside. A trail leads to the top of the falls. Directions: On the ring road 1, on the southside of the Myrdalsjokull.

▲**Camping**: • At Skogafoss. Camping Fossbuinn (487-8843); beautiful but windy; covered cooking/washing area; toilets but no showers; $$

Thorsmork

Not easy to get to, but a jewel of a place when you do, Thorsmork is a region of grassy alpine meadows bright with the summer glories of buttercups, lavender harebells, and pink cushions of moss campion. Trails lead to mossy caves, flower-filled meadows, and up mountains where views of snow-capped mountains glisten in the sun and seem close enough to walk to in an afternoon. Once held secret by high mountains and the seething ever-shifting tentacles of glacier rivers, today the area can be reached by bus or four-wheel-drive high-clearance truck driven by an experienced Icelander. The glacial rivers here constantly change their route. The high clearance and great weight of the bus enables it to safely ford the rivers, but I still got jittery when it plunged into the turbulent water. Any tourist office can make reservations for the bus and camping. Make them several days ahead and go during the week. On weekends, the park is lively and full of fun-loving, partying people. Park your car at the bus pick-up area in Hella or Hvolsvollur.

▲• **Camping**: • At the national park. The campground is beautiful, and it isn't difficult to take a couple of duffles with a tent, sleeping gear, and easy-to-prepare food on the bus. The cooking/eating/washing area at the campground is fragrant from pine and convenient with pots, pans and a stove. Showers have lots of hot water, and there is even a sauna.

Vik i Myrdal

Verdant mountains, crashing sea, turbulent river water, and long black-sand beaches mesh at Iceland's most southern point in near perfection. Steep cliffs are wild with thousands of shrieking, circling, and diving arctic terns as if they have been shaken roughly from a broom. Standing just offshore is a huge group of rock formations called the Four Horsemen. When the mist is just right, it looks as if the horsemen just rode out of the sea with their swords and shields held high like Vikings. Directions: 35km east of Skogar.

▲Camping: Halfway between Vik I Myrdal and Skaftafell, in Kirkjubaejarklaustur. Camping Kirkjubaejar (487-4612); beautiful view of cliffs and glacier; nice enclosed cooking/ washing/eating; scenic terrace with picnic tables; laundry; hot showers; $$.

Skaftafell National Park

At the base of the immense glacier Vatnajokull, wide grassy meadows welcome you at the entrance to Skaftafell National Park. Here hiking trails lead through springy moss-covered hummocks, up along hillsides where yellow alpine cinquefoil and pure-white saxifrage peek around rocks, and into birch groves where meadow pipits trill. There's a strange electrical-like buzzing from a tiny wren whose wings beat so fast they make a shirring sound. On hilltops, vistas of snow covered ridges beckon hikers to keep going. Waterfalls careen down mountainsides where finely sculpted basalt columns drape like a curtain rising from the stage. Quiet ponds in gardens of moss and fern invite swimming and a picnic. It is no wonder the park is so beloved by Icelanders and visitors alike. Directions: Exit north off 1 and drive 2km to the visitor center.

▲Camping: • Adjoining the national park entrance and visitor center. Skaftafell National Park Camping (478-1627); scenic, large grassy areas separated by hedges; $$. Even though the park is popular its spaciousness permits everyone some privacy even in summer. Stay on a weekday and check out the areas farthest from the visitor center. A few modern coin-operated showers and some picnic tables are located centrally. Free naturalist-guided one-or-two hour hikes plus a good natural history museum encourage learning about the flora, fauna, and geology of the park. $$.

Landmannalaugar

Rhyolite peaks in shades of sun-spilt burnt orange, gold, and shadowy purple inspire an ode to beauty that speaks of stark voluptuousness and immensity. Hikers come from all over the world to experience this austere but excitingly desolate place.

▲Camping: • To experience just a bit of it, reserve space on the bus leaving from Skaftafell to Landmannalaugar in the morning with a pick-up at the Landmannalaugar hut for a return to Skaftafell the next day at 2:30. Pack a couple of duffels with tent and sleeping gear, warm clothes, a swim suit, a stove, and easy-to-prepare-food. The bus stops at interesting places along the way. You won't need reservations to camp, but be prepared for simple facilities and wind. One of the highlights is a soothing soak in the hot springs pool while you watch the mountains change colors. Leave your car parked in the Skaftafell carpark.

Jokulsarlon

This deep glacial lagoon is filled with dramatically sculpted iceberg calves reflecting various shades of blue, pink, and white. It is on Iceland's most popular postcards and promotions. Grab your camera and walk along the shoreline or take the interesting 30-minute lagoon cruise with an accompanying naturalist; open daily Directions: 53km east of Skaftafell National Park entrance; $$$.

EAST ICELAND
Seydisfjordur, Egilsstadir and Atlavik

Ferries arrive from mainland Europe at Seydisfjordur. The tourist office at the ferry dock is a treasure trove of glossy brochures and information for travelers; open weekdays until 5 PM. The ferry landing has a gas station and a bank with a cash machine. The shopping center, just north of the campground in Egilsstadir, makes a good place to stock up on supplies at the large supermarket, get local currency at the bank, and fill up with gas.

▲Camping: • 27km west of 93 in Egilsstadir, on the east side of the river at the tourist information center and bus stop. Egilsstadir Camping (471-2320); convenient but not scenic; covered cooking/washing area; hot showers; well used; ok for one night; $$. • 40km south of Egilsstadir along the east side of the river at Atlavik. Atlavik Camping (471-1774); scenic, grassy meadow surrounded by birch trees; close to the forest preserve, museum of Hallormsstadadur, and Hengifoss waterfall; covered cooking/eating; picnic tables; $$.

Hengifoss

Plunging with a deafening roar through a desolate gorge, Hengifoss is one of Iceland's tallest waterfalls and makes a good destination for a hike. Directions: 7km south of the Atlavik campground cross the bridge over Lagarfljot to the west side of the river. Drive 3km to parking and trailhead.

The Fjord towns

Be sure you get gas, supplies and local currency in Egilsstadir before heading out to the following fjord towns.

Neskupstadur

Paddling is taken seriously in this charming fishing village isolated by water and mountains. Reasonably priced guided kayak trips pass through eerie cliff caves and beside the cliff homes of squadrons of Arctic terns that each year fly 22,000 miles from Antarctic waters. Make reservations through Hotel Egilsbud; (477-1321). A hotly contested rowboat race occurs at the Seamen's Festival on the first weekend in August. Directions: Drive 31km south of Egilsstadir on 92. Continue west on 92 for 17km, pass through Reydarfjordurfor then drive on along the coastal ridge to Eskifjordur. Continue 23km across the isthmus to Neskupstadur passing through a 626-meter tunnel just before reaching the sea and the village.

▲**Camping:** • 2km east of the harbor. Neskupstadur Camping; tranquil and scenic location; hot showers; laundry; free.

Borgarfjordur Eystri

Rhythmical curved lines in natural hues give a sense of the transcendental along the marked walking trails around Borgarfjordur Eystri–home and inspiration for Iceland's famous artist Johannes Kjarval. Rewarding hiking trails are marked and mapped. Pick up the Viking Trail map in town at the Elf Stone rock shop. Directions: From Egilsstadir, drive 69km north and then east on 94.

▲**Camping:** • By the church and nature preserve on the north side of town. Camping Borgarfjordur; simple; scenic; free.

NORTH ICELAND
Lake Myvatn

Wing beats whish as ducks and swans fly overhead, calling to each other in a friendly way, then gliding down to the lake they break the smooth surface with a splash. Year after year they return to breed and nest at Lake Myvatn, one of the largest breeding areas for ducks in the world. Its innumerable inlets, marshes, and pools offer a paradise of reeds, spongy mosses, and peaceful ref-

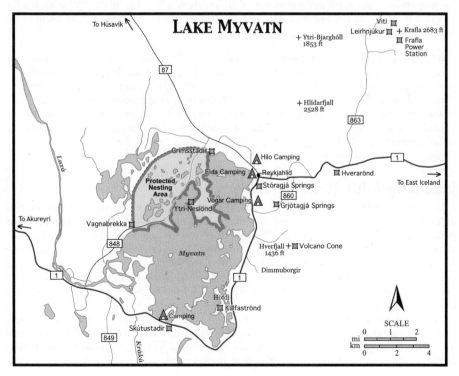

uge. From the shoreline, birders smile behind binoculars as ducks–barrows golden-eye, northern divers, teal, harlequin, merganser, longtailed, and tufted proudly glide by, showing off their fluffy fledgings who paddle furiously to keep up. Directions: Birding is best on the west side of the lake, on both sides of 848 between Grimsstadir and Vagnbrekka, and on the east side among the islets and lava stacks of Hofdi; 4km south of the exit for Dimmuborgir. Much is written about the midges, or small face flies, that swarm around the lake providing food for the abundant bird life, but they aren't any worse here than they are in many USA parks. Face masks can be bought at the local grocery store, or bring one from home. The 35 kilometer level road around the lake is very scenic, and there is little traffic. Lumps of lava stand sculpture-like in meandering ponds and lagoons. The trail into Dimmuborgir leads through a convoluted lava landscape that has the beauty of a nightmare evoking morbid fantasies. Be sure to follow the signs leading out to the large lava cave Kirkjan. Bike rental is available at Elda Camping.

Just east of the lake, steam rises from encrusted lava fields like mist on a warm tarmac. Fissures, like in the skin of an over-ripe tomato, release scalding steam. Gray mud stretches, heaves, and then bursts in devilish mirth. No guard rails offer protection in this unearthly place–just a sign warning you to step only on brown earth, not the white, orange, or yellow. Directions: Drive 2km east of Reykjahlio on 1. Turn south onto 860 following signposting for Hverarond and drive one kilometer. Amid serene, rust-colored low mountains, Mount Krafla blew as recently as 1975 and 1984 and is expected to blow again soon. From the rim above Leirhnjukur, you can look out across the caldera and its flows. Marked paths lead into scary excursions past hot, glittering sapphire lagoons and up into grotesque towers of lava capriciously spewed into monsters. Directions: From Reykjhlio, drive east on 1 for 3km. Turn north for the Krafla power plant, and drive 6km up the steep dirt road towards the power plant to parking. Follow signposting for the walking path heading northwest to Leirhnjukur. Adventurous thermal bath enthusiasts soak in the more-than-warm sulphate-blue waters of an underground spring at Viti. Wear shoes, the rocks are sharp on the descent down into the steep-sided crater. Directions: Drive north to the end of the road to parking.

▲**Camping:** • On the east side of the lake in Reykjhlio. Elda Camping (464-4220); beautiful location along the grassy slopes of the lake; parking separate from tent camping; small but nice gravel parking area for caravans; nice enclosed cooking/eating/washing area; popular but spacious campground; $$. • 3km south of Reykihlio at Skutustadir. Vogar Camping (464-4399); close to Grjotagja ancient bathing springs; good for caravans and tent campers who want to camp next to their car; covered cooking/washing area; $$. • One kilometer north of Reykihlio. Hilo Camping (464-4103); nice hillside view of the lake; good for caravans; no covered cooking area; hot showers; $$.

Jokulsargljufur National Park

Lacking the verdant beauty of Skogafoss and the majestic glamour of Gulfoss, Dettifoss makes up for both in sheer power. Thick and viscous, the rock and sand-filled water of Europe's most powerful waterfall thunders over the cliff and crashes into the canyon's gorge. Viewed from the east side, the cliff side is a basalt spectacle of polished organ pipes gleaming with spray. Directions: At the south edge of the park. From Reykjhlio, drive east 40km on 1. Turn north onto 864 and drive 22km. From the north end of the park on 85 and the main entrance to Jokulsargljufur Park, turn south on 864 and drive 21km. Walking paths from Dentifoss lead to the smaller, but exquisitely, beautiful Selfoss.

At Asbyrgi, birch, willow, and pine trees luxuriate by spring-fed ponds and streams. In boggy areas, miniscule green orchids, marsh violets, and bog bean are delightful finds. Walking paths lead into moist, sheltered hollows alive with a raucous symphony of fulmars and snow buntings nesting in the burnt-orange lichen-smeared cliffs. In a magical pond, red-necked phalaropes and eider ducks are busy educating their fledgings. Easy walking trails lead from here into the moorlands, where golden plovers show off golden-flecked plumage and dunlins sing flute-like. Experienced hikers take the trail up the edge of the canyon wall at Tofugja, using fixed ropes for the ascent, and continuing on loop trails around the gorge. Directions: From Husavik, drive 63km east on 85 to the park's entrance. From Lake Myvatn, drive 33km east on 1. Exit north onto 864 (a good, hard-surfaced gravel road) and drive 53km. Turn west on 85, passing the gas station and then driving directly south into the park entrance.

▲**Camping**: • Asbyrgi National Park Camping (465-2391); pleasant grassy meadow separated by hedges into smaller areas; covered cooking/washing area with outside picnic tables; laundry; hot showers; close to hiking trails and park information office; $$.

Husavik

Whale watching, whether on film or from a boat, involves imagining an animal you see only in bits and pieces at a time. To make the experience meaningful, allow several hours to explore Husavik's award winning Whale Education Center. Five fully reconstructed immense skeletons from 5 species of whale, hang from the high ceiling and ramps allow visitors almost touchable views. You are encouraged to run your fingers through a baleen and across a vertebrae that is as wide as a tree trunk. The museum has remarkable videos, a children's room with interactive material, impressive stories heard from earphones, artifacts from whaling days, a beautiful exhibit of stuffed birds and seals, and excellent descriptive text throughout in several languages –on the whales' feeding habits, ecology, and population–so it isn't a surprise to learn that museum received a U.N. award for environmental tourism in 2000. Directions: Park above the harbor and walk down the steps. The museum is in the old warehouse at the north end of the harbor; open daily. Husavik's handsome whale-watching boats have a good reputation spotting whales, usually minike and humpback who slide in and out of the water as if playing hide-and-seek. The summer's midnight sun gives only a casual bow to the horizon before it rises boldly in flamboyant colors, on the start of new day. Whale watching and viewing the midnight sun can be combined in one excursion. On all trips take warm, layered clothing, gloves, and binoculars. Reservations can be made through any tourist office, or call 464-2350.

In fish processing factories, workers in immaculately clean aprons and caps slice, cut, and pack fish with eye-deceiving dexterity. After taking a guided tour, a purchase of fish at a supermarket has more meaning. For reservations, call the tourist information office; 464-2520. Husavik is the kind of town that makes you want to stay for a while. From lovingly cared for cafes and terraces it is easy to be mesmerized by the view of colorful boats rocking peacefully in the harbor while stately snowy peaks sparkle in the sunshine. Stock up on supplies at the large supermarket just beyond the campground.

▲**Camping**: • Past the swimming pool on 85, on the east side of the road, north of the harbor. Husavik Camping (464-2299); nice, cozy town campground; enclosed cooking/eating/washing area; laundry; hot showers; $$.

Akureyri

As proof of the superb climate, plants from the Mediterranean, Africa, China, New Zealand, and the Americas thrive luxuriantly in Akureyri's large and lovingly cared for botanical garden. This peaceful setting is the perfect place for some down time. Directions: Two blocks south of the campground; free. Akureyri is a pretty town with magnificent views of the mountains that surround it and the fjord on which it is set. Colorful flowers and shady deciduous trees enhance museums, shops, sidewalks, and neighborhoods. Victorian buildings are gay with gingerbread decoration. Climb the long stairway up to Akureyrarkirkja, stopping to enjoy the great view. The architecture of the church is not fussy, but peaceful and soaring implying a tranquil balance in the natural world. Directions: Two blocks down from the campground.

Pleasant little red-roofed clapboard houses, formerly lived in by beloved poets, still have a warm and cozy lived-in look. Letters, original manuscripts, and personal belongings are carefully curated by local citizens and give the visitor a peek at life in the 19th-century; closed Sunday and Monday. Though these people spent their lives laboriously struggling in a harsh environment of snow and lava fields and were isolated from the rest of the world by cold and stormy seas, they produced remarkable poets and historians. Poetry and literature are widely admired by Icelanders. Pick up a walking map and a museum card at the bus terminal tourist office, south of the main hub, on the fjord; open daily. Allow time for a careful examination of the fine collection in Akureyri's Folk Museum. It is cleverly curated so that you come away with admiration for the Icelander's determination, talent, and drive combined with a remarkable resourcefulness for humor and fun; open daily. There's a large supermarket west of the river at the round-about.

▲**Camping:** Drive along the fjord street Drottningarbraut to the hub of the town, Kaupvangsstraeti. Turn west and drive up the hill passing the KEA Hotel and the church. At the fork take Thingvallastraeti further up the hill passing the swimming pool to camping. Camping Akureyri; (462-3379); large; popular with families and well used; covered cooking/washing area with picnic tables; no showers on site; showers are across the street at the pool; convenient; $$. The pool is one of Iceland's best. Choose a site that you will be able to drive out of if the campground becomes crowded because of a local sporting event. • On the eastern side of Eyjafjordur, directly across from Akureyri. Husabrekka Camping (462-4921); on a grassy hillside with a beautiful view; well cared for; covered cooking/washing area; $$. • In the forest parkland Kjarnaskogur, beyond the golf course. Hamrar Camping (461-2264); large sites, picnic tables and barbeques for scout and athletic groups; covered cooking/washing area; $$.

AROUND AKUREYRI
Hrisey Island

Walking paths web this picturesque little island. Interpretive boards covering wild life, plants, geology, and the history of the island, cleverly written to interest both children and adults, are posted along these paths enriching the walks. From all directions there are grand views of the rugged mountains on the mainland. Large colonies of ptarmigan, plump, brown and white freckled birds, cackle cockily on heath covered hillsides. By sitting down and nestling yourself into the soft and mossy tussocks, just like the birds do, you can enjoy the melodious flute call of the whimbrel and the view of the mountains. Peering over the cliff face, you can watch the black guillemots and fulmars looking contentedly out to sea as they rest from feeding. Closer to the quiet little fishing village, whose tidy gardens burst with colorful flower gardens, are lush pockets of blue lupine hiding fresh water springs. Despite the advent of fresh-frozen processing, you'll still find great wooden lattices of old fishing racks in use all along the coastline. At one time, each was hung with thousands of salted, gutted cod drying in the sun and ocean breeze. Typically

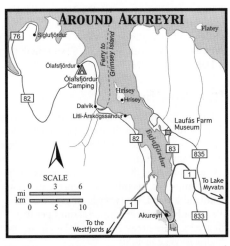

eaten on bread spread with butter, *hardfisku* (dried cod) is so nutritious that one small compressed tablet is enough to satisfy the body's need for protein for a several days. The racks on Hrisey Island, set picturesquely on a buttercup-flecked grassy slope, beg to be photographed. Directions: Drive north of Aukureyri 44km on 82 to Arskogssandur. Park and take the pleasant, reasonably priced, 15-minute, ferry to the island, departing every 2 hours from 9 AM to 9 PM.

Olafsfjordur

Boasting one of Iceland's most outstanding collection of stuffed birds and a large collection of bird eggs, Olafsfjordur at the end of Eyjafjordur, is a worthwhile afternoon drive if you are interested in birds. More than 150 species are represented, almost all collected and preserved by one man. Ask for the English text. The staff is well informed and welcomes questions; 466-2651; open 2-5 PM except Monday. The drive to Olafsfjordur takes you through one of Iceland's longest tunnels–the Mulagong–which is 3 ½-kilometers long. It can be terrifying at first, because the tunnel is only one lane. But cars going to Olfsfjordur have pull-offs to avoid on-coming traffic. Before, the road clung precariously to the edge of the rugged mountain cliff so locals consider the tunnel a piece of cake. The old road is now a popular hike and is a ideal place to see the midnight sun as it makes its curtsey to the horizon. Directions: From Aukureyri drive north on 82 for 77km.

▲**Camping:** • By the swimming pool. Camping Olfsfjordur (466-2363); simple; toilets; showers at the pool; free.

Laufas Farm Museum

Lined up prettily along a slope of Eyjafjordur, these carefully rebuilt sod-roofed and sided-homesteads belonged to 19th-century affluent farmers and are full of good old days paraphernalia. The most impressive feature of the sod-buildings is the painstaking herringbone design of the sod pieces. Directions: On the east side of Eyjafjordur; open daily. Drive 20km on 1 from Akureyri, then continue north along the water on 83 for 8km.

Grimsey Island

To actually be within the Arctic circle and getting a certificate verifying the fact, then seeing large colonies of puffins, with their orange clown-bills, waddling out along the cliff edge, plus sailing across the crown of the North Atlantic, is a memory not easily forgotten. On the 3 ½-hour ferry to Iceland's most northern settlement on Grimsey Island you'll see icebergs, watch for whales, and relax inside to watch a movie. Take precautions for possible seasickness. Directions: Drive 60km from Aukureyri on 82 to Dalvik for the once a day ferry at 11 AM. The ferry returns to Dalvik at 5:30 PM.

The Westfjords

Thrusting out towards Greenland this large peninsula in the northwest corner of Iceland, has some of the deepest and most spectacular inlets in the country. It's a breathtaking drive across the moors where the wrinkled cliffs and plunging valleys exude an isolation that is peaceful and silent. Many of the roads are well-maintained, hard-packed gravel. Few cross over the mountains, instead traversing the edges of the graceful fjords. Plan on averaging 40 kilometers an hour. Relax, enjoy the magnificent scenery, and don't plan to get very far very fast. On west-central mainland Iceland, at Stykkisholmur, a car ferry goes to Bjanslaekur, on the southern coast of the West Fjords. There are two crossings per day. This 3-hour ferry ride is popular and reservations for a vehicle are necessary several days in advance. Book with any tourist office or call yourself to Baldur Ferry; 438-1450.

Isafjordur, the largest town on the West Fjords, has a friendly small-town atmosphere and one of the most scenic campgrounds in Iceland. It makes a good rest stop for several days. A highlight is its Maritime Museum. Climb the stairs to view the video first. It was filmed professionally at the seamen's house just north of Isafjordur and is superb. After viewing the nautical artifacts have more meaning. Throughout the museum, photographs show tough, taciturn fisherman, dressed in drab oilskins and stripped of all pretensions, going about their exacting and dangerous work. Fishing the North Atlantic waters is an occupation that puts not only the fisherman's economic

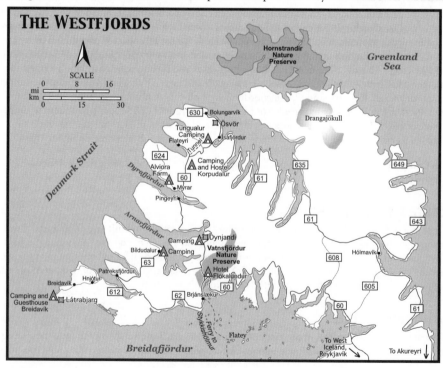

survival, but also his physical survival on the line. Their capacity for hard work is impressive. The museum is inside an old trading house at the edge of the fjord. At its entrance is a carefully built replica of a six-oared fishing boat. Clustered around the museum, 17th-century homes give a cozy, intimate atmosphere to the area; open daily. Directions: At the harbor on the northwest side of the fjord. Stock up on supplies at the supermarket on 61, at the campground turn-off. Fill up with gas before going out of town to the more remote areas and then continue to fill-up when you can.

▲**Camping**: • Just beyond the gold course. Follow signposting for golfing at the southeast end of the fjord. Tungualur Camping (456-5081); next to the golf course; close to a delightful stream and waterfall; hiking trails; covered cooking/washing area; hot showers; pay at the golf course; rental golfing equipment is available; $$. Between the clubhouse and the campground there is a small, well-cared for community garden. Just open the gate and enjoy its loveliness.

AROUND ISAFJORDUR
Bolungarvik and Osvor

Don't miss going out to the authentic and completely restored small fishing station at Osvor. It was one my favorite museums in Iceland. Ducking into the sod building and climbing the ladder to the tiny sleeping quarters, transports you to a different time. Here the fisherman told tales while they combed and spun wool and stitched fish-skin slippers. You can peek into a miniscule cooking area, examine tools in a work area, lean over fish gutting and salting tables, and walk out to the drying racks and boat landing. The video at the Maritime Museum was filmed here. If you are lucky, a smiling fisherman, resplendent in oilskins will be here to explain how the various tools worked and how life was "in those days"; open daily. Directions: Drive 11km north of Isafjordur on 61 in the direction of Bolungarvik. The museum is tucked into an ocean side cliff, almost out of sight, 3km beyond the tunnel on the Bolungarvik side.

Regal and powerful, the polar bear in Bolungarvik's Natural History Museum has pale-yellow fur and black button nose and eyes. He's a tribute to Greenland's superb wild life. The museum also has a first-rate collection of rocks and fine exhibit of stuffed birds; daily except weekend mornings. Directions: Signposted on the main street; upstairs.

Flateryi

Low-sweeping grasses wave in the breeze, calling out a welcome to this little paradise of golden-sand beaches, lagoons, and marshlands. It is likely the only sounds you'll hear will be the call of the whimbrel and the rustle of a light breeze through the grass. It's a nice spot to relax for several days. The lagoon makes kayaking enjoyable for beginners, and the fjord offers a challenge to experienced kayakers. Call several days ahead to make arrangements for kayak rental with Graenhofoi; 456-7762. Easy walking paths make for quiet walks and bird watching. Directions: Southwest of Isafjordur. A new tunnel links the two areas.

▲Camping: • From the tunnel and the intersection of 64 and 60 turn south onto 60. Cross two small bridges. Turn onto a small road that heads southeast towards the head of the lagoon and drive 2km. Camping and Hostel Korpudalur (456-7808); remote, beautiful location; showers and toilet in the hostel; $$.

Myrar and Skrudur

It's hard to beat this majestic setting. Long grassy slopes and pastures strewn with perky dandelions cascade down the hillsides behind a few farmhouses. Picturesque waterfalls tumble down cliffs into inviting narrow gorges. Crystal-clear streams gush forth, exuberant and playful. Small hummocks about the size of watermelons are made soft by thick moss and make comfortable seating in such a beguiling place. As the sun lowers in the sky, the mountains across the fjord resemble ancient Egyptian pyramids. Directions: On the west coast of the West Fjords on the Dyrafjordur.

Anxious to supplement the Icelanders' limited diet, a courageous couple dedicated their lives in 1909 to experimenting with growing vegetables in Iceland's infertile soil and harsh climate. Turning their new knowledge into environmental education, they introduced vitamin-rich potatoes, rhubarb, and turnips. Longing for the beauty of European leafy trees, their experiments included various species of trees. Today the garden is an immaculate, beautiful, and leafy tribute to its founders and to the neighbors who now care for it. Directions: Off 60 turn northwest onto 624 and drive one kilometer in the direction of Myrar; open daily; donation.

▲Camping: • In Nupur, 3km northwest of Myrar. Look for signposting for Alviora Farm; (456-8229). Ask for permission to camp on their property. Then drive down and camp by the stream, which is not only delightful but a source of fresh water. It has exceptional view of the waterfall, mountains and fjord. If the owners are shy to charge, leave a gift as you leave. • Next to the Hotel Edda; (456-8222); good for caravans, pleasant for tents; no covered cooking/washing area; toilets and showers in the hotel; $$.

Dynjandi Falls

In other countries the Dynjandi Falls would be a major attraction, but in Iceland the competition is so tough that they are barely mentioned. Like a cluster of brides gathered to gossip about their future husbands, these wide, lacy falls tumble down over dramatic cliffs painted by lichen in patinas of silver-grey, burnt-red, and gold. Little rivelets race over the granite to join their older sisters, while others hold back forming mirror-like ponds. It's an ethereal landscape of massive boulders, bright yellow-green moss, and glittering water. Directions: On 63 on the Arnafjordur/Borgarfjordur on the mid-west coast.

▲Camping: • South of the falls; spectacular setting; basic; trail head to the falls; free.

Drive from between Pingeyri and Bildudalur

The drive between Pingeyri and Bildudalur on 63–dubbed the Western Alps–is breathtaking. Towering steep cliffs of majestic mountains, layered like a French torte, open to canyons where sheep graze dreamily. The ewes look up as you pass, their enormous coats so tangled they resemble dreadlocks. Blowing quietly in the breeze, cotton grass waves like little white flags. As you descend down to the fjord there is a stillness and purity. Such scenery begs for a picnic.

▲Camping: • On the fjord in Bildudalur; nice location; covered cooking/washing area; toilets; basic; free.

Vatnsfjordur Nature Reserve

The voice of the loon–a superb diving bird–is like that of a lone woman wailing for her lost lover. Heard in the evening, it is spine-tingling and unforgettable. Lake Vatnsfjordur is a favorite nesting area for not only for loons but also finely painted harlequin duck. Directions: On the southern coast of the West Fjords.

▲**Camping:** • In Flokalundur. On the grounds of Hotel Flokalundur (456-2011); convenient; toilets and showers in the hotel; $$.

Latrabjarg

Cradled in the arms of rugged cliffs, stretches of sandy beach look out to swelling and crashing white-capped waves. From the precipitous cliffs, the sea appears brushed with sequins as the sun dances on its surface. You can peer down over hanging gardens of moss to cliff faces, decorously iced with guano and alive with birds. Swimming under water as effortlessly as most birds fly–the razorbill, a member of the auk family–finds Latrabjarg an ideal place to nest and has created the largest colony in the world. Elegantly dressed in black and white with a distinguishing white band along the length of their bill, razorbills fly straight and fast and then suddenly dive directly into the sea. Puffins too, find lodging desirable in this most western point of Europe. Burrowing into the grassy headlands, they carefully build a comfy nest at the end of a chamber then hang out in front of it or waddle over to visit a neighbor. Directions: Exit 62 onto 612 and drive northwest 26km to Hnjotur. At the fork, continue on 612 driving west for 10km to Breidavik. Continue west another 8km to the end of the road, where there is a lighthouse, a good regional posted map for hiking, and parking.

▲**Camping:** • Camping and Guesthouse Breidavik (456-1575); extra-special place; cozy inside and scenic outside; cooking/eating/washing areas; campers welcome to use inside sitting room with a good selection of books about the area; good place to meet other travelers; hot showers; sleeping bag accommodation; simple restaurant; tent campers can have fun staying inside a clean, grassy, rock-walled sheep-shelters; $$$.

Hnjotur

The museum/café at this fork in the road displays a fine collection of fishing, farming, and aviation memorabilia. A stop makes a nice break in the journey to Latrabjarg; open daily.

Brjanslaekur/Ferry to Stykkisholmur and Flatey

Narrow stretches of coastal lowland and sand sheer cliffs, devoid of much vegetation, characterize the southern coast. A 3-hour ferry crosses twice daily, passing an archipelago of tiny islands populated mostly by birds and seals. Vehicle space is limited. Reserve several days ahead with Baldur; 438-1120.

WEST ICELAND
Stykkisholmur

A maze of scattered *skerries* (outcrops of rock) make paddling a kayak here an interesting and wind-protected experience. Birding is terrific. You can float right next to Iceland's "queen of the Atlantic"–the graceful bride-white gannet whose large wings open to display an elegant black cape. For kayaks call ahead to make arrangements with Skolastigur; 438-1535. Walk through town to visit to the carefully restored Norwegian House holding the town's folk museum and the hilltop church–proud and pure in mountain aesthics. A ferry from Stykkisholmur crosses twice daily for the 3-hour sail to Brjanslaekur on the West Fjords. Vehicle reservations are limited so call several days in advance to Baldur; 438-1450. The swimming pool here should not be missed. Where else can you sit in a hot tub, gazing dreamily up at mountains and watch a soccer game at the same time?

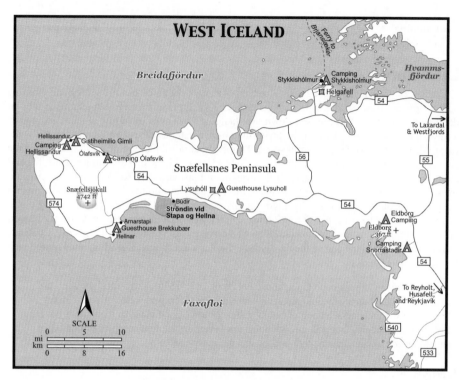

▲Camping: • By the swimming pool and sports field. Camping Stykkisholmur (438-1150); pleasant town campground; covered cooking/washing area; hot showers; pay at the pool; $$.

Helgafell

During the Settlement in Iceland, people held this gently sloping hill sacrosanct. Snorri Godi, one of the greatest and wisest of the chieftans, built his unpretentious and dignified church here. Now restored it still stands. Gundrun, the headstrong and beautiful hero of the *Laxdaela Saga*, is buried just beyond the church. The whole area speaks with unadorned, lonely beauty. Tradition advises that you start your visit at the gravesite north of the church. Then without speaking or looking back, solemnly climb the hill. At the top, face east and look out over the broad panorama and make 3 wishes that will not have any adverse effect on anyone. Return quietly from the east side of the slope without looking back. Directions: Drive south out of Stykkisholmur on 58 for 5km. Turn east onto the second small road signposted Helgafell. Drive 2 km past the small lake to the church and grave.

The sagas tell of lives both stately and simple. The individual characters are developed through their words and deeds, peculiar mannerisms, way of speaking, and clothing. In the sagas, silence is more eloquent than words. Vistas open up between sentences. The romantic, tragic and heart-rending *Laxdaela Saga*, is one of the most beloved.

Olafsvik

Cloaked in the mystery of the sea and leading lives largely removed from the sight of humans, whales have inspired myths, poetry, and wild tales. Graceful and powerful, they are the largest animals on our planet. Whale-watching boats out of Olafsvik often spot humpback whales whose natural curiosity causes them to breach the surface of the sea to take a look around. Rich offshore fishing grounds lure both local and international fishermen. Fishing boats leave daily and equipment is available for rental. Viewing the fishing photos and memorbilia in the warehouse museum at the harbor will make your trip out on the water more meaningful. You can pick up hiking maps and information about Snaefellsjokull and west Snaefellsnes at the tourist desk here. Directions: Northwest end of the Snaefellsnes peninsula.

▲Camping: • One kilomoeter east of town on Dalbraut. Camping Olafsvik (436-1543); covered cooking/washing; hot showers; pleasant site but can be windy; $$.

Snaefellsjokull National Park

In the most fantastic shapes and colors, a ridge of jagged mountains runs down the spine of the Snaefellsnes peninsula. At the end, rising like an ancient pyramid out on the plains, is the ancient volcanic cone Snaefellsjokull. Mystical and powerful, it is often painted, photographed, and written about. This dramatic landscape of strange, convoluted lava formations, basalt cliffs, and deep volcanic caves were the point of embarkation for Professor Lidenbrock his nephew and his courageous Icelandic guide in Jules Verne's classic book, *Journey to the Center of the Earth*. It is also the setting for Iceland's Pultzer Prize winning author Halldor Laxness' book, *World Light*. The tourist information office for the national park is at the post office in Hellissandur. After invigorating hikes in the area, take a soak at the local thermal swimming pool.

▲Camping: • In Hellissandur, at the northwest end of the peninsula. Gistiheimilio Gimili (430-8600); cooking/eating/showers in the guesthouse; simple restaurant; $$$. • Sheltered cove by the river on Utnesvegur. Camping Hellissndur (436-6600); scenic but can be windy; covered cooking/washing area; simple; $$.

Hellnar and Lysuholl

Enthusiastic birders and photographers will want to drive out to this tiny village to enjoy dramatic combination of birds and an azure luminescent sea in the sea cave Badstofa. Directions: Drive 20km on 574 west of the intersection of 54 and 574 on the southwest end of the peninsula at Budir passing the village of Arnarstapi. Exit south off 574 onto the small road steep road signposted Hellnar. Drive to the end of the road and harbor. From the east side of the harbor follow the marked trail signposted Badstofa. There's a snug café at the harbor that makes a comfy and tasty stop after your exertions. See below for directions to the natural swimming pool at Lysuholl.

▲Camping: • In Hellnar. Guesthouse Brekkubaer (435-6820); cooking/eating/showers in the guesthouse; pleasant setting can be windy; $$$. • Ten kilometers east of Budir exit 574 north onto the small road signposted Lysuholl. Drive just over a kilometer to Guesthouse Lysuholl where there is a superb natural swimming pool and hot tubs fed by geothermal mineral water. Guesthouse Lysuholl (435-6716); scenic and fun; covered cooking/washing; basic; $$.

Eldborg

Several campgrounds and views of a symmetrical cinder cone make this a good stop. Directions: Close to the intersection of 55 and 54.

▲Camping: • Drive west of town exiting 567 onto a small road signposted for the hotel, continue 4km. Hotel Eldborg (435-6602);extra nice swimming pool; covered cooking/washing; hot showers; $$$. • 3km east of Eldborg, exit 54 and drive 2km following signposting south for Snorrastadir. Camping Snorrastadir (435-6627); close to the beach; covered cooking/washing; hot showers; $$.

Laxardal Region

Moss-covered hills and verdant valleys characterize the location of Iceland's most romantic and heartrending saga, the *Laxdaela*. Try getting into a heroic and lost-love spirit while you walk the well-marked paths leading to the historical sites that were settings for the tragedies. From here adventurous Vikings set sail in long boats to explore and settle Greenland and North America. Recent archeological excavations of a 1st-century farm thought to be the longhouse of explorers Erik the Red and his son, Leif the Lucky, led to the reconstruction of this replica, called Eiriksstadir; open daily. Directions: On 60 at the southern edge of the town of Budardalur in Haukadalur. At the harbor at Budardalur, see the exhibit of both the saga and the exploration and pick up maps of the walking trails. Directions: 8km north of the intersession of 60 and 54.

▲Camping: • In Laugar, 18km north of Budardalur on 60. Edda Hotel and Camping (434-1265) thermal swimming pool; showers in the hotel; $$$.

Reykholt and Husafell

In the 13th century, master storyteller, Snorri Sturlson, a descendent of powerful and influential parents, wrote some of the most celebrated of Icelandic sagas: Edda, Egill's Saga, and the Heimskringla. Honored and beloved by both Icelanders and Norwegians, his life was filled with love affairs, royalty, politics, and travel but ended with grizzly finality. Both Norwegian and Icelandic funds went into the excellent museum and cultural center in Reykholt. A highlight of the visit to the center is Snorri's soaking pool. It's not hard to conjure up images of him telling riveting tales to friends as they drank and soaked with steam misting the cold night air. On the last weekend in July, the village hosts a music festival with classical concerts featuring talent from

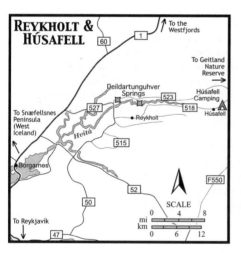

all over Scandinavia and Iceland. Directions: From Borgarnes, drive northeast on 1 for 8km. Exit east onto 527 and drive 14km. Exit east again onto the signposted road for Reykholt and drive 6km. Stop along the way to see the powerful hot spring Deildartunguhver and to purchase some greenhouse-grown fruit and vegetables. Directions: Just off 527, 10km west of Reykholt.

Excellent walking paths in the Husafell area lead to lovely waterfalls careening down mossy rocks, up to mountains with sweeping views of glaciers, and into dark and eerie lava tubes.

▲Camping: • In Husafell, a popular summer cottage area, 26km east of Reykholt. Husafell Camping (435-1550); nice setting; covered cooking/washing area; hot showers; close to an excellent

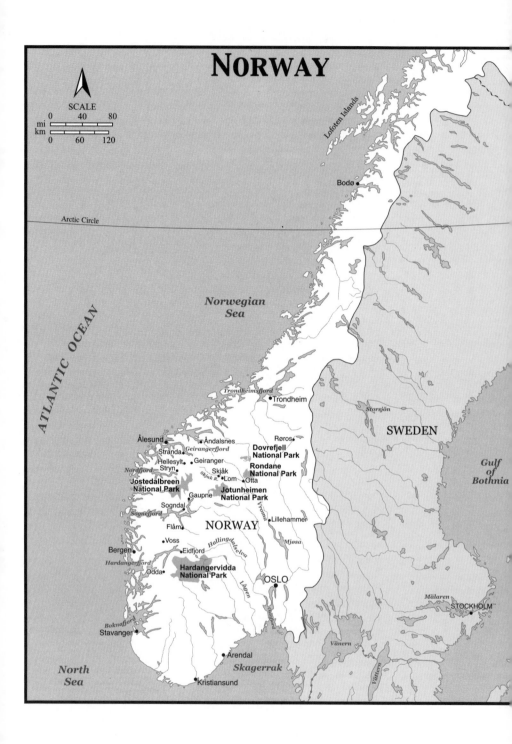

NORWAY

SCALE

mi 0 40 80

km 0 60 120

Lofoten Islands

Bodø

Arctic Circle

Norwegian Sea

ATLANTIC OCEAN

Trondheimsfjord
Trondheim

Storsjön

SWEDEN

Ålesund
Åndalsnes
Røros
Stranda Geirangerfjord
Dovrefjell National Park
Hellesylt Geiranger
Nordfjord Stryn Skjåk Rondane National Park
Jostedalbreen National Park Skjåk R. Lom Otta
Gaupne Jotunheimen National Park
Sognedal
Sognefjord Lillehammer
Flåm Vroma
NORWAY
Voss Hallingdalselva Mjøsa
Bergen Eidfjord
Hardangerfjord
Odda Hardangervidda National Park Lågen OSLO

Gulf of Bothnia

Mälaren
STOCKHOLM

Boknafjord
Stavanger

Arendal Skagerrak

Vänern

Vättern

North Sea Kristiansund

Norway

www.visitnorway.com

Norway is one of Europe's most exotic countries. Velvet-like slopes of apple-green grasses jeweled with brightly colored penstemon, lupine, and asters collar majestic mountains nestling icy blue glaciers. Waterfalls crash and tumble in daring feats while rivers rush and plummet over boulders like laughing children let out for recess. All the while the fjords sit in queen-like elegance. It's a crystalline and intoxicating breath of fresh air and unlike any other place in Europe.

A Norwegian feels truly fortunate if he owns a tiny hut far off the beaten track, perhaps without even running water or electricity. He prefers it to be where no sign of civilization can spoil his view of fjords, mountains, and sky or disturb his longed-for peace of mind and inner harmony. Here in his hytte; he is in his castle. He watches the subtle drama of seasonal change gaining the coveted Norwegian prize: a truce with nature. It is this love of nature that has honed the fiercely individualistic, adventurous, and artistic character of the country's citizens. Norwegians are quiet in their pride of their magnificent country and heroic fight for independence. Their love of the outdoors is evident in the beautiful settings of their camping places. Sharing exclamations about the grandeur of the natural beauty is a good way to start up a conversation with Norwegians. They are relaxed and easy to be around.

Exciting, awe-inspiring, and easy-to-do outdoor activities have been carefully thought out and are readily available. Glacier walks, river rafting, canoeing, kayaking, hiking, biking, and fishing are well-loved sports, and equipment, guides, and advice for enjoying them are at hand. It's a fisherman's paradise. If you are an avid fishermen, consider bringing your own gear so you can stop whenever you want. Otherwise rental gear is available. Relaxing boat rides, fascinating museums, and exciting train trips all add to the fun, but you'll find yourself mesmerized when you take time to just sit and look at the outstanding natural beauty.

The distances and the ruggedness of the terrain mean that every mile of road and every foot of cable are extremely expensive to install and maintain. It is popularly felt that every Norwegian from Kristiansand in the south to Kirkenes at the North Cape should enjoy The Good Life. The roads thread through a countryside that is deliciously beautiful. Driving is a breeze. The roads and tunnels are excellent and well signposted. It's impossible not to be amazed at the skill and perseverance of the Norwegians as your drive through their tunnels. They epitomize their historic ability to withstand and overcome a harsh environment. Many roadways are two lanes so drivers are forced to relax and drive at reasonable speeds. Roadway rest stops are scenic, with picnic tables, toilets, and tourist information. Car headlights must be on at all times when driving. Ferry crossings, both long and short, enable travelers to stop and feast on the magnificence that quietly passes by. Locals stand in awe, too. They are not blase about the beauty of their country. A current road map will indicate where crossings are. Ferries operate on a first-come, first-served basis, except for the longer crossings. When planning your travel for the next day, check with the camping office, tourist office, or gas station about the ferry's schedule. This helps avoid long waits, particularly in remote areas.

Groceries are more expensive than on mainland Europe, so keep selections simple. Dairy and meat prices are reasonable and the quality high. Local produce is reasonable, but imported foodstuffs are expensive. Locals and tourists alike buy a good supply of alcoholic beverages at the tax-free stores on large ferries. Bring coffee or tea from home. Most stores close on Saturday afternoon and stay closed until Monday morning. The mini-markets at the gas stations are open on Sundays and have a surprising array of food, including freshly baked bread—the aroma and taste is a delicious treat. Cash-machines are the most convenient way to exchange currency and are easy to find close to shopping centers.

Camping locations are beautiful, with thick carpets of grass, immaculate toilet/shower areas, and covered cooking areas with an adjoining cozy eating area and laundry facilities. Cabins are also available and generally don't need to be booked ahead unless you are arriving late or are in a popular tourist area. Campground staff usually speaks English, so if inclement weather makes tent camping less fun and you want a cabin, call ahead to reserve. Cabins are cute and cozy and well worth the cost if the weather is stormy. Generally they have two sets of bunk beds without bedding, a cooking and eating area, and a small porch. They don't have plumbing but do have electricity, and the common toilet/shower area and water tap you'll need will be close by. They cost about three times what tent camping does, and you are expected to clean up for the next guest before leaving. A broom, mop, soap, and bucket are provided. The open and closing dates listed are conservative. Call ahead if you are earlier or later than these dates; they might be open.

Camping for two persons with a tent and car will be around 20 euros (Norway has kept its own money system though and doesn't use euros). This is are noted as $$. Larger campgrounds with more amenities will cost 25-30 euros and are noted as $$$. Ask about showers, and purchase appropriate coins or tokens when you check in. If you plan to go out for the evening, check about the night gate opening and closing procedure. If you are departing very early in the morning, pay the night before.

OSLO

Surrounded by forest and fjord, Oslo sits at the end of the blue expanse of Oslofjord like a king in his throne room. Pine-clad hills envelop the city on its other three sides making it feel more like a home town than a metropolis. In full summertime bloom, the fjord is alive with boats. You can board one of the little boats pushing off from shore for Oslo's top attractions, the never to be forgotten museums on the Bygdoy peninsula. Plan to spend the day.

Stop first at the Vikingskiphuset. Until the Viking period, boats were not very seaworthy. The Vikings designed ships that were light in weight and flexible in construction. Their long boat could cut through deep seas and travel easily into shallow waters. Daring to sail beyond landmarks out into uncharted waters, they discovered the Svalbard Islands northwest of Norway and settled the Shetland, Orkney and Faeroe Islands, as well as Iceland and Greenland, which remained under Norwegian influence for centuries. The captivatingly displayed Oseberg ship grave, dates to the 800s, and the ship's skeletons, furnishings, jewelry, and cooking utensils found are in amazing condition; open daily

A host of Norwegians have performed incredible feats. Thor Heyerdahl is perhaps the best-known explorer of the 20th-century. Seeking to prove links between major early civilizations, he built a log raft held together by ropes and wooden pegs in the style of the South American Incas. He sailed the Kon-Tiki, from Peru to Polynesia. Later he traveled on a papyrus reed boat from North Africa to the Caribbean. During his expeditions, he devoted much of his study to the pollution of the oceans and wrote passionately on the subject. The Kon-Tiki Museum is open daily.

Making a Northwest Passage route by sailing across the Arctic Ocean from the North Atlantic to the Pacific occupied the visions of sailors for centuries. In 1903, Ronald Amundsen sailed off in a small ship used for hunting seals. Enroute, the *Gjoa* was locked amid ice deep in the Artic for two years, but Amundsen and his crew survived. Locating the north magnetic pole in a different place than it had been 60 years earlier, he proved that the earth's magnetic poles move. Later, in a race to reach the South Pole, he sailed in a uniquely designed boat called the *Fram* to come within skiing distance to his goal. A terrific combination of a talented husky dog team and his own skiing expertise won him the title of the first man to reach the South Pole. You can experience the close quarters of the *Fram* and pour over the tools, games, and maps that were used on the actual expedition; open daily.

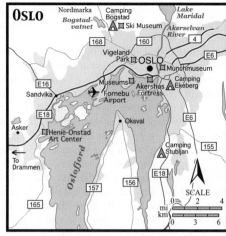

After seeing these museums, stroll through the wooded parkland to the Norsk Folkmuseum. Grouped around a 13th-century wooden church, 140 homes and gardens portray Norway's distinct regions. A harsh climate, mountains, and fjords have made transport and communications between regions difficult. Rural districts, isolated from one another for long periods, were forced to rely on their own resources and to develop their own local identity. This has given rise to a host of cultural traditions, each with its own vitality and clearly recognizable local flavor. When the nation finally emerged and regained its independence from a Danish domination that lasted from the 1400s to 1814, it was the rural areas that were the taproot of the Norwegian character and national values. The rural areas still remain a rich source of Norwegian talent that is anchored in local tradition and identity. Today, these traditions are sustained up to the highest level of society. The Folkmuseum is open daily.

Back on the mainland, the dramatic Akershus Slott and Festning, a castle and fortress, dominate the east side of the harbor. Somber and grim, it symbolizes Norway's long, hard fight for independence. Don't miss its powerful Resistance Museum, Norges Hjemmefront Museet. During World War II, Norway was occupied by the Germans. But the Norwegians fought back like Vikings, mounting an astonishing war effort for such a small-population country. Supplied and directed from their government-in-exile located in London, a heroic underground army sabotaged vital industry and military installations. Photographs and mementos from this heroic effort will leave you emotionally stunned and impressed; open daily.

Oslo's central train station, then board a bus there for Vigeland Park. Heavily influenced by Rodin, Gustav Vigeland gained international fame. He was prodigious and single-minded and he traded the city his sculptural works for a place to live and work. His emotional and touching sculpture, whose main theme is everyday human life, is set amid grand-tree and flower-lined walkways through large expanses of lawn. The park draws a diverse sprinkling of folks who pass the time soaking up the sun, rollerblading gracefully, and licking ice cream cones. In a fascinating museum at one end of the park, you can explore Vigeland's work indepth. Directions: T-bane to Vigeland Park.

Norway's best-known artist, Edvard Munch, painted during the turn of the 20th century. He portrayed the trauma of the modern life through a distortion of color and form and gave the city of Oslo the thousands of paintings that make up the collection seen in the trim white jewel Munch Museum. Directions: T-bane to Toyen and follow signposting.

Oslo's main street, Johansgate, seems more like a park than a street. It's surrounded by the palace, the parliament building, the National Theatre, the old buildings of Oslo University, and plenty of shops and restaurants. Applied-art enthusiasts will want to spend some time in the recently renovated *Kunstindustrimuseum museum* whose masterpiece is the famed Baldishol tapestry woven in the mid-1200s. It has an exceptional collection of textiles, clothing, jewelry, and furniture that includes fine contemporary pieces. Directions: T-bane to Holbergs Plass, then walk three blocks east. The dramatic headland setting and the architecture of the Henie-Onstad Art Center complement its impressive permanent and temporary exhibits of expressionism and modern art. Directions: West of Oslo on E18 in the direction of Drammen.

On the outskirts of the city, it's exhilarating to rent a bike or rollerblades, or just hike, on the oodles of scenic trails winding around Nordmarka. Directions: T-bane #5 or #1. Holmenkollen, one of the mightiest of the thousands of ski jumps in Norway, is a landmark on the outskirts of Oslo. At the top, the skier stands poised like a potential suicide on a wind-swept wooden bridge. Crouching down, he hurtles down the 42-degree slope and shoots into space. For a breathtaking moment, in a picture of pure grace, he is flying man. If you want to peek down over this horrifyingly steep jump to what seems like a minisule bowl at the bottom, buy a ticket to the Skimuseet, where there is access to the millions of stairs. Then enjoy the light-hearted exhibit of the transformation of clothing and equipment over the years, including outfits like the ones Amundsen and Nansen wore on their polar expeditions. Directions: T-bane #1 to Holmenkollen.

Due to increasing number of inhabitants, traffic, and lack of public parking, a toll for motorized vehicles to enter the city was implemented in Oslo. Funds raised go to the nation's roads and public transportation.

▲Camping: • Off E6 southeast of the city center exit Ring Three for Ekeberg and drive up the hill. Camping Ekeberg, Ekebergeien 65 (2219 8568); convenient; wonderful hilltop view; bus to the city center; popular and well used; open June-August; $$$. • On a lake, northwest of the city. Exit Ring Three for Bogstad. Camping Bogstad, Ankerveien 117 (22-51-08-00); public transportation to the city center; cabins; popular with families; well used; open all year; $$$. • 15km southeast of Oslo off the coast road E18, in Hvervenbuka. Camping Stubljan, Ljaruvelen 1250 (2261 2706); tranquil location; easy access to E6; open June-August; $$$.

Lillihammer

Host to the 1994 Winter Olympics, Lillihammer is a must for those who love a full adrenal rush. You can take a terrifying bobsled ride, with guide, down the actual Olympic run in Hunderfossen! It's very popular and very expensive. Less expensive and not quite so terrifying but also very popular is bob rafting. Reserving ahead for either is advised; 6127 7550. Directions: Drive north of town on E6 for 15km and follow signposting.

For a more relaxing pace, wander through the open-air Maihaugen Folk Museum. Displaying the original furniture and accessories inside Mailhaugen's old houses in would not have happened without the heroic efforts of one local citizen, Anders Sandvig, who passionately cared. Experience for yourself the charms of the peaceful pastoral life–so important in understanding the Norwegians–that come alive in the old wood, fine rose-painting, and antique farm equipment. Rose-painting is a rich and complex folk-art which showed off prosperity and social status. Norway's rose-painters traveled from farm to farm carving and painting furniture, walls, and ceilings using pure, bright hues that produced vivid and harmonious effects; open daily. Directions: Exit E6 for centrum, cross over the railroad tracks, then turn south on the first main street, Kirkegaten, and follow signposting up the hill for Maihaugen. If you feel like just kicking back, climb aboard the world's oldest paddle steamer for a scenic ride on Lake Mjosa.

▲Camping: • North of town by the Lake Mjosa. Exit off E6 for Lillehammer-Nord and follow signposting. Lillehammer Motell og Camping (6125 9710); nice location with view of the lake; grassy terraces; open all year; $$$. • 2km south of town by the river. Exit E6 for Lillehammer-Centrum and follow signposting. NAF- Camping Lillehammer (6125 3333); nice location; cabins; open all year; $$$. 15km north of the city by the river in

Hunderfossen. NAG Camping Hunderfossen (6127 7300); nice location by the river; popular with families; cabins; open all year; $$.

RONDANE/JOTUNHEIMEN REGION
Rondane National Park

Noted for sunnier weather than other parts of Norway, this is one of Norway's prettiest river valleys with lush carpets of green grass and fast-moving rivers,. White water rafting trips for both beginners and advanced can be booked with Heidal Rafting in Sjoa; 6123 6037. Book a couple of days ahead. Directions: 11km south of Otta, exit E6 at Sjoa onto 257 and follow signposting.

The alpine part of the park is stark, dramatic, and peaceful with excellent hiking trails of all ability levels. Before hiking, purchase a hiking map and get information and advice at the tourist office in Otta. They can also give you advice about tackling some of the challenging mountain peaks and staying overnight in one of the hiking huts that dot the network of trails. The Mountain Lodge at Rondvassbu, at the southern edge of Rondvatnet Lake, makes a good destination for a short hike or a resting place before hiking farther up the peaks. In July and August, a small boat crosses back and forth to the north end of the lake taking hikers to other trailheads. Directions: Drive 13km northeast of Otta to Mysuster. Drive through the village to the toll road, pay the toll at the post, and continue 5km farther east up the narrow road to the Spranghaugen car park and the trailheads.

▲**Camping:** • At Sjoa, 5km south of Otta, off E6. Saeta Camping (6123 5147); small; beautiful location; cabins; June-August; $$. • At Otta on the west side of the river, one kilometer from the bridge. Otta Camping (6123 0309); large; beautiful location; cabins; convenient for hiking; open June-August; $$$. • 30km west of Sjoa on 257, at junction of 257 and 51. Jotunheimen Feriesenter (6123 4950); popular with rafters; beautiful location; cabins; open June-August; $$.

Dovrefjell National Park

Fokstumyra Bird Reserve in Dovrefjell National Park is considered one of Norway's best. Over 75 species of birds breed here, among them red-necked phalarope, rough-legged buzzards, Eurasian dotterel, red-throated divers, and horned lark. The trailhead is near the Dombas end of the reserve. Visit the new Dovrefjell-Rondane Nasjonalparksenter in Dombas on Sentralplassen, to talk to friendly staff about recent sightings, see the bird exhibit, and examine the informative topographical map of Dovrefjell and Rondane National Parks; open daily.

▲**Camping:** At the south end of the park, at the intersection of E6 and 29, in the village of Hjerkinn. Camping Hjerkinn (6124 2927); close to the river; views of the mountains; small; open June-August; $$. • North end of the park 8km south of Oppdal. Smegarden Camping (7242 4159); view of the mountains; small; cabins; open all year; $$.

Skjak River Region

Located halfway between Rondane National Park and the Nordfjord area, on highway 15, this river area is popular with vacationing families. Horseback riding, hiking trails into river canyons, and river rafting are all popular pursuits. Grassy meadows strewn with colorful wildflowers border the rushing river. Campgrounds have especially nice playgrounds, fishing is good in the river, and there are nice walking/cycling paths the whole family can enjoy. Directions: 100 kilometers north of Lillehammer on E6 exit west onto 15 at Otto. Continue on 15 for 62km to Lom.

▲**Camping:** • In Bismo, 15km west of Lom. Camping Bispen (6121 4130); nice location by the river and road; cabins; grass and trees; open June-mid Seot; $$ • Near the Donfossen

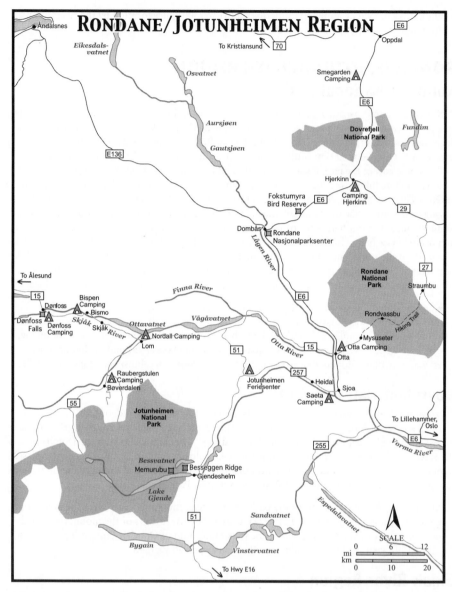

RONDANE/JOTUNHEIMEN REGION

falls in Donfoss. Exit off 15. Donfoss Camping (6121 4898); pool; nice children's playground; cabins; open May-Sept; $$. • In Lom alongside 15. Camping Nordal (6121 9300); large; cabins; simple café; nice children's playground; open May-September; $$$.

Jotunheimen National Park

Norwegians delight in the dramatically beautiful hike across Besseggen Ridge because of the staggering views of emerald-green Lake Gjende on one side and cobalt-blue Lake Bessvatnet on the other. The trail is well marked but you'll appreciate the detail on the purchased map. The hike isn't overly strenuous with plateaus and old glacier rubble fields but the Besseggen ridge part of the hike is very steep and has sheer drops, so those with vertigo be advised. Walking sticks are highly recommended. A boat crosses the Gjende River, taxiing hikers to and from the trailheads. If you take the boat across to Memurubu first–a gorgeous 45-minute ride–you avoid the worry of missing the return boat. The trailhead for this full day hike begins behind the lodge or at the boat dock. Directions: On the eastside of the park, halfway between E6 and E16, drive to Gjendesheim on 51. Beautiful mountain drives, hikes, and summer skiing are available on the west side of the park. Directions: Exit 15 at Lom onto 55, and drive 17 km southwest to Boverdalen.

▲**Camping:** • In Lom alongside 55. Nordal Camping (6121 9300); large; cabins; simple café; nice children's playground; open May-mid Sept; $$. • In Boverdalen, 17km southwest of Lom on 55. Raubergstulen Camping (6121 1800); close to hiking trails; lovely setting; open June-mid Sept; $$.

Roros

The legendary copper-mining mountain town of Roros is one of Norway's finest architectural villages and has UNESCO World Heritage listing. The town's prominent landmark, a black and white church, stands in the middle of the immense, flat, high, and lonely landscape. The two main streets are lined with 17th-through 19th-century brightly-painted houses built for the former mine owners and administrators. Farther up the river, tiny sod-roofed miner cabins hunker down under the shadow of the huge slag-heaps left from working the mine. Townfolk keep the traditions of knitting, carving, and bark wickerwork alive in the artisan shops close to the smelting works. The well-loved epic novels of the heroine *An-Magritt*, by Johan Falkberget, and film starring Jane Fonda were set in and around the mining town. The town is also the location for some of Astrid Lindgren's *Pippi Longstocking* films, and it became Siberia during the filming of Solzhenitsyn's *A Day in the Life of Ivan Denisovich.* A cheerful tourist office lends bicycles. Directions: Close to the Swedish border, 105km south east of Trondheim at the intersection of highways 30 and 31.

▲**Camping:** In Roros. Haneset Camping (7241 0600); cabins; close to hiking trails; open all year; $.

SOUTHERN COAST

Centered by Kristiansand, this idyllic coastline is a favorite vacation spot for Norwegians. The cliffs and seaside pastures are dotted with well-loved wood houses gleaming white, bright red, or yellow. Rocks are polished smooth by the combination of Ice Age erosion and relentless wind and waves, and the water is so clear you can see crabs and starfish on the seabed. You can rent a canoe from the campground, paddle out to one of the small bare islands or reefs, and sunbathe with only the company of seabirds.

In August, the little harbor at Risor teems with boat aficionados who love the sight and sound of finely honed and varnished wood on the water. They've come for Trebatfestivalen the wooden boat contest, and celebrate their saltwater camaraderie exhuberantly. Stop in at the old shrimp factory, Rekefabrikken, a tiny yellow building on a rock inside the Nevlunghavn harbor. Peruse the fine selection of seaside watercolors and crafts and then taste some of their delicious creamy waffles. Directions: 39km north of Arendal at Akland, exit E18 onto 416 for Risor and drive 14km out onto the peninsula.

The small white wood houses built on the rocks along the islets of Lyngor are so striking that an international jury named it the "best preserved place in Europe in 1991." In summer, the port

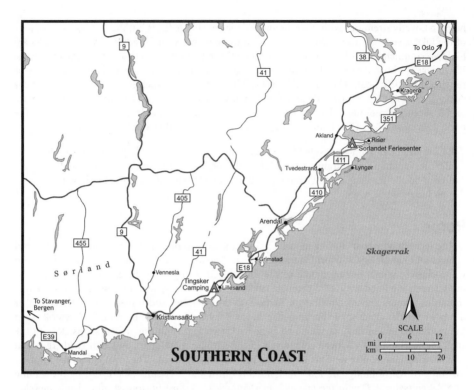

SOUTHERN COAST

swarms with boats as adults and children enjoy precious sunny seaside days. In Norway children are taught at an early age how to handle sea craft, and their bodies quickly become attuned to the sensuous rhythm of the waves. Directions: South of Risor. Exit E18 at Akland and drive 6km to the fork of 416 and 411. Exit onto 411 and drive 30km to Lyngor harbor.

▲Camping: Just south of Risor on 411: Sorlandet Feriesenter (3715 4080); geared for families; cabins; children's program; pool; on the bay; very popular; reserve ahead in season; open mid-April-mid-Sept; $$$.

Stavanger

Once famous for its herring industry, Stavanger now boasts oil and an international ambiance. On the west side of the harbor, explore Gamle Stavanger, where Old Stavanger sparkles with white-picket fences and colorful gardens surrounding its immaculate white-clapboard houses. The old-herring factory museum, Hermetikkmuseet, is in the heart of the old town and is more interesting than you might think. Soon after billions of herring were caught at sea, they were transferred to a freezer ship and delivered to the canneries frozen in slabs of ice. When the cannery was ready to process them, they were defrosted in a shower bath, sorted, cleaned, cooked, and then packed in a flat little tin. The museum's collection of cleverly designed labels is a kick to inspect. On Tuesday, Thursdays and the first Sunday of every month, the museum smokes sardines in a huge oven and offers delicious samples. The tourist office, colorful harbor market Torget, and parking are at located south of Gamle Stavanger at the old harbor.

The Norwegian Emigration Center located just east of the bay at the south end of Gamle Stavanger, helps trace Norwegian ancestry through ship passenger lists and census records. For a

successful search, visit www.emigrationcenter.
com several months before of your trip so you
can provide them with exact information.

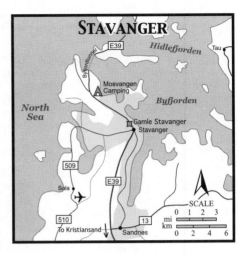

By the mid-1990s, Norway was one of the
world's largest exporters of petroleum, second
only to Saudi Arabia. The Troll Field located
offshore west of Bergen, is one of the largest energy projects in the world. The Troll
A platform was the tallest concrete structure
ever moved. It reaches a height of 472-meters
and is 172-meters long and is expected to be
productive for at least 50 years. The industry's new, sleek Norsk Oljemuseum's displays,
interactive exhibits, simulated helicopter ride,
and diving bell will help you understand the
achievements and occasional disasters of this
important Norwegian industry. Directions: At
the ferry terminal harbor, where there is parking.

▲**Camping**: • At the north end of Stavanger, just before the Byfjordtunnel, exit E39 and follow signposting. Mosvangen Camping (5153 2971); convenient; highway noise; cabins; view
of the water; mid-May-mid-Sept; $$.

Bergen

Nestled into lushly green hills, fjord fingerlings, and waterways, Bergen is a feast for the eyes. Its
900-year-old harbor churns with old and new ships. Ancient and modern buildings lie next to a
backdrop of mountains on whose green slopes tiers of wood houses cling. "I'm not from Norway,
I'm from Bergen," locals say with a pride for the town's past that runs deep. It's an easy-going city,
and smiles come readily. Jokes abound about Bergen's rain, but many are exaggerations for the
sake of a laugh. However, the rain, makes Bergen sparkle like a jewel when the sun bursts from
the clouds, which it does on a regular basis.

At *Torget*, Bergen's fish market at the Vagen harbor, stall tables overflow with freshly cooked
succulent prawns, pickled herring, smoked trout, glistening salmon, piles of cucumbers, and sweet
wild berries. Tasty smoked salmon and crab sandwiches offered by jauntily capped fishmongers
are hard to pass up. Mountains of soft reindeer pelts sit next to potted plants, bunches of flowers,
and colorful T-shirts.

It's a short walk or ferry ride from Vagen to UNESCO-listed Bryggen, the original Bergen settle-
ment. Steep cobblestone steps lead up tiny streets shadowed by overhanging eaves. A mishmash
of ancient wood buildings now house shops and cafes. You don't really understand Bergen until
comprehending its powerful Hanseatic merchant background. The lively Hanseatisk Museum
provides a vivid feeling of the merchant's dwelling and his offices. You'll peer into tiny bed boxes
resembling prison cells, where apprentices were able to rest for only a few hours. Excellent, light-
hearted guided tours of Bryggen are conducted in English at 11 AM and 1 PM daily. Don't miss
the Bryggens Museum on the west end. On-site archeological excavations have unearthed 12th-cen-
tury foundations and artifacts. The lively exhibits are displayed in context with the site's medieval
foundations. Behind the museum is the Romanesque church Mariakirken. The oldest building in
Bergan, it boasts a Baroque pulpit and 15th-century frescos; open weekdays.

For a perspective on how Bergen interlaces with forest and sea, take the Floibanen funicular up
Mount Floyen. Directions: Walk up Vertrlidsalm, the main street between Torget and Bryggen.
Scenic walking paths lead back down. The *Bergen Akvariet* (Aquarium), is one of the finest in

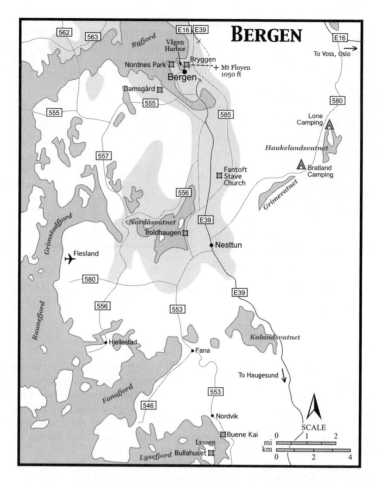

Europe, with realistic nesting cliffs along the pools, and penguins and seals enclosed so close you can almost touch them. Directions: Take the short bus #11 from Torget or the ferry ride from Torget to Nordnes Park on the south end of Vagen harbor.

A string of four museums line up along the southern end of Bergen's city lake, Lille Lungegardsvann. At the eastern end, the Bergen *Kunstmuseum-Samlinger* has an extensive collection of Norwegian painters and a notable sample of Edvard Munch's work. In the Stenersen's collection building, you'll find some nice pieces by Klee, Toulouse-Lautrec, Picasso and Miro. The silversmiths of Bergen were famous for their large baroque designs. The *Kunstindustrimuseum* (decorative arts museum), at the eastern end has some fine pieces from the 17th-and 18th-centuries along with a rich collection of faience and porcelain. Check out the temporary exhibitions; they often focus on contemporary craft and design. All the museums are closed Monday.

The city blossoms every June when an international festival of music is staged in memory of Norway's most famous composer, Evard Greig. He built his home along the quiet shores of Lake Nordas. Choosing a hilltop, he called his home Troldhaugen, or home of the trolls. Bergen was a major trading center and Grieg enjoyed a thriving cultural life. The rambling two-story cream-colored villa was his first permanent home with his beloved wife. Trodhaugen's casual comfort has not changed much since they lived here. At the bottom of a steep path leading to the fjord lies a small wooden hut where Greig found the tranquility necessary to compose. He and his wife are buried nearby. Directions: Drive south on E39 in the direction of Nesttun. Exit at Fantoft, and drive south to Hopsbroen.

Troldhaugen is southwest of the Fantoft Stave Church. A *stave* is a half a tree trunk, that served as the cornerstone of a wall to which slender strips of timber were fastened without nails. This stave technique allowed Norwegians to build churches with several steep roofs that shed snow and made them seem lofty inside. The early churches, still retaining the Viking decorative elements, are small, dark and plain without pews or pulpits. Animals and intertwining decorative lines decorate the doors. The Fantoft Stave Church is especially sweet and photogenic. Directions: Drive south on E39 in the direction of Nesttun to Fantoft.

Norwegians strive to keep their history alive through song and dance. The woodland farm location for Fana Folklore provides an authentic setting. You make advance reservations for the evening program that includes a Norwegian dinner, folk music, and dancing; 5591 5240. Directions: Drive south on E39 in the direction of Nesttun. Exit for Fana/553, and follow signposting for Fanatorget.

Ole Bull's Villa is in the same area. Eccentric and charismatic the violin-virtuoso built his dream house, Bullahuset, in the late 1800s on the lush green hills of Lysoen Island. It has Viking flair, which reflects his lively personality and love for Norway. Directions: Drive south on E39 exiting for Fana/553. Follow signposting for Lysoen, which continues over the mountain to Sorestraumen. Then follow signage to Buena Kai, and take a ferry to the villa. During summer, the 10-minute ferries leave on the hour from 12 to 3 PM weekdays and to 4 PM on weekends. It's fun, go.

If you have some time to spare, go out to Damsgard, three kilometers west of Bergen and stroll through the ravishing gardens and rococo interiors of the manor home. The gardens still remain only with plants cultivated in Bergen during the 18th century.

With all the fjords, lakes and hills tucking in Bergen, it's a confusing city to drive in. Purchase a good city map at a gas station before you come into the city and to help you find your campground. Bergen imposes a toll to entering traffic. Buses go to the city center from the campgrounds. The Bergen tourist card, sold at the campgrounds, includes bus, funicular, short ferry rides, and free or discounted entrance to most of the above sights. Because driving and parking in Bergen is confusing, taking a leisurely and scenic bus ride is advised, making the Bergen tourist card worth buying.

▲**Camping**: • 12km east of the city exit off E16 onto E39/580, and drive two kilometers south to Haukeland Lake. Lone Camping (5539 2960); nice setting; cabins; laundry; open all year $$$$. • Further south on the lake on E39/580. Bratland Camping (5510 1338); cabins; open June-mid-Sept; $$$.

Hardangerfjord Region

You won't forget the majesty of the towering waterfalls thundering exultantly as they leap over boulders tumbling uproariously into the smooth, glassy bed of the fjord. Seductive high mountain plateaus descend to meadows painted flush in Alpine glow. Fruit orchards scent the air. Excellent cycling and hiking trails lace the entire region, as do train and ferry rides. Located between Oslo and Bergen, between E134 and 7, this area is well organized for vacationers.

Taking the "Norway in a Nutshell" excursion makes a great day's outing. There's good reason for it's huge popularity. Don't miss it. Park at the train station at Voss. The trip begins with scenic ride from Voss to Myrdal. At Myrdal the train descends down the steep gorge, passing snowy peaks and tumultuous waterfalls until it reaches the lush valley floor and fjord at Flam. The track, one of the steepest in the world, passes through tunnels that were hand dug over a period of four years in the 1930's. It stops midway at a particularly scenic waterfall so passengers can

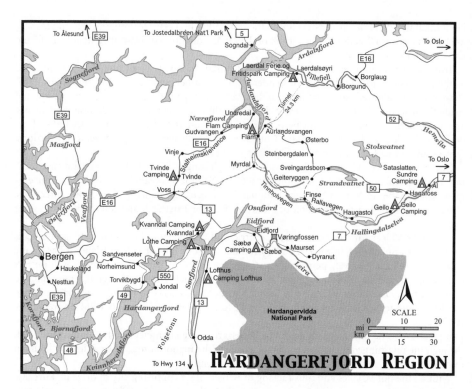

HARDANGERFJORD REGION

get the full impact of the waterfall and snap a photo or two. A tiny museum in Flam highlights the building of the train tracks and early tourism. After enjoying Flam you board a small ferry to slip quietly through the Aurlandsfjord and Naerofjord, a narrow gorge hemmed in by giant, Gothic-cathedral-like mountains. Regal escort is provided by brilliantly white sea gulls. The ferry lands at Gudvangen for an exciting bus ride up the steep Stalheimskleivance and then through the meadow-like countryside back to Voss. Buy tickets at the train station or tourist office in Voss. Alternately, if you have mountain bicycles you might want to put them on the train at Voss, disembark the train at Mydral and cycle down the very steep but exciting old road from Myrdal to Flam. Hikers might want to disembark at Berekvam and enjoy the majesty of the scenery more slowly on a three hour walk to Flam.

▲**Camping**: • Twelve kilometers north of Voss off E16 on a small lake in the village of Tvinde. Tvinde Camping (5651 6919); pretty location on the lake; cabins; laundry; open all year; $$. • In Flam. Camping Flam (5763 2121); gorgeous setting along the fjord; cabins; laundry; open May-Sept; $$$.

Voringsfossen, Norway's most famous waterfall, drops almost 200 meters. The wildly beautiful old road leading into the Mabo Valley and the waterfall is closed to motorized traffic but open to cyclers, walkers, and the Trolltoget, a tourist train on wheels. Hardangervidda Natursenter at Ovre Eidfjord, sparkles with aquariums, an exciting movie, and colorful exhibits. Directions: Drive 25km east of Eidfjord on 7. The walking/bike trail starts at Mabogardane. Park at the top of the tunnel, on the east side, and hike down to the river then back into the valley to the base of the waterfall. For the Trolltoget, park at the Mabo Gard Museum.

▲**Camping:** • At the north end of the park on 7 in Ovre Eidfjord. Saebo Camping (5366 5927); lovely lakeside setting; cabins; open May-mid-Sept; $$. On the west side of the park in Lofthus (5366 1364); gorgeous view of the fjord and mountains; sauna; cabins; laundry; open May-Sept; $$$.

Hardangervidda is northern Europe's highest plateau. Its dramatic stark beauty is quiet and tranquil. Tiny lakes dotted with anglers gleam like burnished disks. Walking and biking trails criss-cross the landscape. One of the most popular hiking trails starts 40km east of Eidfjord. Directions: On 7, exit just west of Maurset at Dyranut for the Tinnholvegen. Rallavegen, a biking/hiking trail, crosses the plateau along the rail line. The trail is 80km long running from Haugastol, 22km west of Geilo on 7, to Flam. (See "Norway in a Nutshell".) Memorials and exhibits of the rail construction pay tribute to the laborious work along its route. Train connections along the way will transport you and your cycle back to your car.

▲**Camping:** • On the eastern end of the park in Geilo, just south of town on 40. Geilo Camping (3209 0733); nice view of the mountains; cabins; small store; open all year; $$$.

Aurlandsdalen valley is Norway's Grand Canyon. The spectacular scenery can be enjoyed close-up by hiking down historic trails to the valley. Directions: Exit 7 at Hagafoss, and drive northwest on 50 for 51km. On the east side of the tunnel at Sveingardsborn, take the small road south for the trail from Geiterygghytta to Finse or Steinberg. From Osterbo, on the west side of the tunnel, a trail leads to the Vassbygdi River.

▲**Camping:** • Nine kilometers east of the intersection of 50 and 7, then one kilometer west of Al near the river. Sundre Camping (3208 1326); pretty location; cabins; laundry; close to hiking trailheads; open all year; $$.

Fillefjell is the gorgeous river valley of the Laerdalselvi River. The mountain road from Laerdal to Aurland, at the western end of 16, is popular with hikers.

▲**Camping:** • By the Laerdal ferry landing on 5. Laerdal Ferie og Fritidspark Camping (5766 6695); in a recreational area; large; nice location; cabins; simple café; open all year; $$.

Folgefonna, the third-largest glacier in Norway, has a summer ski center with skiis, snowboards, and sled rentals. Call ahead for conditions and hours; 5366 8028. Directions: Exit 550 at Jondal and the ferry landing, on the eastside of the Hardangerfjord and follow signposting.

▲**Camping:** • 32km north of Jondal on 550 just west of Utne and the ferry crossing. Lothe Camping (5366 6707); nice location on the fjord, good children's playground; cabins; open mid-May-mid-Sept; $$.

On the west side of the fjord a great hiking/biking trail is carved into the mountainside. The trail goes behind the waterfall at Steinsdalen. Directions: The trailhead is close to Sandvenseter, 19km west of Norheimsund.

▲**Camping:** • In Kvanndal at the ferry landing, 40km from Norheimsund. Kvanndal Camping (5652 5880); nice location with view of the fjord; cabins; simple café; open May-mid-Sept; $$.

GEIRANGERFJORD REGION

Sheer cliffs guard the jewel-like string of brilliant fjords that curve seductively through the narrow Geirangerfjord gorge. Waterfalls plunge dramatically, as if in a bridal veil exhibition.

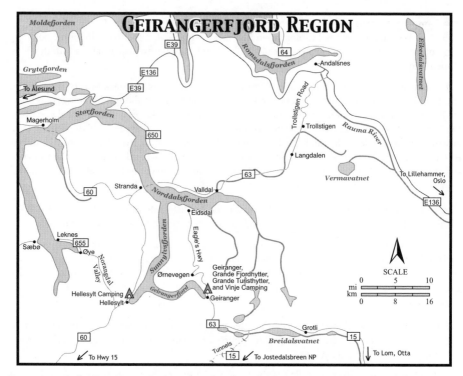

GEIRANGERFJORD REGION

Passengers on ferries gaze upwards and out to the great beauty, awestruck. Directions: From the east, 19km west of Grotli, exit 15 onto 63, the Eagle's Highway, in the direction of Ornevegen. From the west, take the car ferry from Hellesylt. The famous Trollstigen road, Troll's Ladder, stretches in a zigzag up a sheer mountain wall. Most people take the bus, whose expert drivers maneuver the hairpin turns with ease. The Trollstigen bus route runs from Andalsnes to Valldal. Car ferries operate to Valldal from Hellesylt and Gerianger.

▲Camping: This is a very popular area with campers from all over Europe. Call ahead. North of Gerianger on 63. Geiranger Camping (7026 3120); great location on the fjord by the ferry landing near Hellesylt; laundry; open June-mid-Sept; $$$. The following all have cabins, good locations, and laundry facilities. Grande Fjordhytter Camping (7026 1400); open May-September; $$$. Grande Turisthytter Camping (7026 3068); open May-September; $$$. Vinje Camping (7026 3017); open June-August; $$$. From Hellesylt the 19km drive or bike ride through the Norangdal Valley to Oye is bright and sweet-scented and dotted with little farmsteads. Camping: In Hellesylt. Hellesylt Camping (7026 5188); close to the fjord; open May-September; $$.

Jostedalbreen National Park

Queen of the area's parks, Jostedalbreen's blue glacier ice nestles between lofty peaks and ridges, licking its way downward until it finally gives way to the silent, mirror-like glacier lakes. Exuberant cascading streams rejoice in their release, leaping and dancing and then plunging with a weariless roar over the cliffs. Brightly dressed wildflowers watch the show while butterflies sweep silently by. Get off the main trails to fully enjoy it magnificence.

For a fantastic view of the glacier colors, take a guided glacier walk. They vary from easy to difficult. All necessary equipment is provided, including boots if you don't have your own. It's wise to book ahead. Call Briksdal Glacier; 5787 6800. Directions: Exit 60 at Olden and drive 20km south on 724 to park entrance.

▲**Camping**: All of these are beautifully located but rather small because of the mountain and river gorge they are in, so call ahead for reservations. • 20km south of Olden on 724 in Briksdalsbre, closest to Briksdal Glacier and waterfall. Melkevoll Bretun Camping (5787 3864); small; very scenic; terraced; sauna; cabins; very popular; open May-August; $$$. • On the Briksdal-Olden road, beautifully located; open June-August; $$$. Gryta Camping (5787 5936) or Gytri Camping (5787 5934) both have a few cabins. • Closer to Olden. Loken Camping (5787 3268); larger; on the river; cabins; open May-August; $$$.

Glacier walks are also available on Bodalsbreen. Directions: Exit 60 at Loen onto the small road on the eastside of the lake in the direction of Sande, and drive 14km to the carpark. At the Breheimsenteret, glacier walks are arranged on the Nigardsbreen glacier. Directions: Exit 55 north of Sogndal at Gaupne, and drive north on 604 for 35km

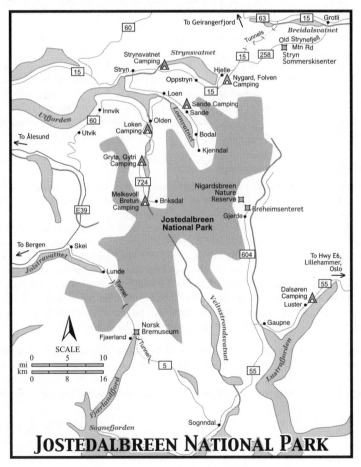

JOSTEDALBREEN NATIONAL PARK

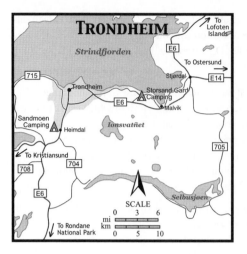

▲Camping: • In Loen I Nordfjord on 60. Sande Camping (5787 4590); beautiful location; terraced; cabins; open all year; $$.. • 16km northeast of Gaupe on 55 at Luster. Dalsoren Camping (5768 5436); cabins; open May-September; $$$.

Cross-country and downhill skiing, and also snowboarding are possible at the Tysig glacier through the Stryn summer skiing center. Call ahead for information on the condition of the slopes; 9455 6110. Directions: 25km east of Stryn at Hjelledal.

▲Camping: • In Hjelledal. Nygard Camping (5787 5258); cabins; or Folven Camping (5787 5340); both popular with young skiiers; open May-September; $$.

East of Stryn on 15. Strysvatnet Camping (5787 7543); beautiful location; large; sauna; simple café; laundry facilities; $$$.

The old Strynefjell mountain road, now a tourist road with picnic areas and tourist information provides magnificent views. Directions: Exit 15 at Grotli onto 258. Excellent park information centers with fascinating videos, Alpine gardens, and cafes enhance your park experience. Directions: At the south end of the park, north of Fjaerland off 5, Norsk Bremuseum has the best information about glaciers. Northeast of the park on 15, east of Styrn in Oppstyrn, Jostedalsbreen National Park Center has a peaceful lakeside setting and an Alpine botanical garden. Southeast of the park, north of Sogndal on 55, Breheimsenteret is architecturally lovely, blending with the stark setting close to the Nigardsbreen.

Trondheim

Founded by Viking King Olav Tryggvason in the late 900's, who was brought up in England and baptized a Catholic, Trondheim, is Norway's historic capital and religious center. In contrast to the beautiful wooden stave churches in the rest of Norway, the Nidaros Cathedral in Trondheim, originally called Nidaros, was built of stone and is the largest and northernmost medieval building in Scandinavia. Gustav Vigeland's beautifully carved figures are on the choir screen and the bas-reliefs on the adjacent font. Directions: At the bow of the river, well signposted. Afterwards cross over the old town bridge, Gamle Bybro, to Bryggen and wander around the splendid old wooden warehouses that lean against one another along the canal bank. The colorfully painted buildings now house inviting shops and restaurants. One of the best things about the Trondheim is the free bikes that are available all around the city center. You release them from their racks just like a shopping cart. Put a coin in to release, then on the return the money is returned.

▲Camping • Drive18km east of Trondheim on E6 in the direction of Storsand and follow signposting. Storsand Gard Camping (7397 6360); resort-like; cabins; beach; ; terraced; open May-October; $$$$. • Ten kilometers south of Trondheim in the village of Heimdal. Sandmoen Camping (7288 6135); large; cabins; well used; close to railraod tracks; open June-mid-Sept; $$$.

Inside the Arctic Circle: The Lofoten Islands

A dentist's nightmare of jagged teeth-like mountains run down the spine of this skeletal-like archipelago. Called the Lofoten Wall, it snuggles in picturesque fishing villages whose hardy locals are laid back enjoying the summer sun. Although quite far north, sunbathing and beach combing are popular pursuits of the Norwegians who come to kick back in an unpretentious setting. The islands are linked by causeways and bridges. Birding is big. Binoculars dangle from the necks of folks from all over Europe who hope to add black guillemot, puffin, and white tailed eagle to their birding life lists. During the summer, sightings of killer, minke and sperm whales are possible on whale-watching boat trips. The village of A, on the island Moskenesoy, the most dramatic in the archipelago, is a photographers paradise with cod-drying racks, colorful rustic fishing huts leaning together, and the unique nordland boats bobbing prettily in the sea. Boat trips called safaris, leave from the various town's little harbors, several times a day, with passengers anxious to see birds and whales. Naturalists on the boats help it happen. Little villages open their doors to tiny museums and local festivals that are heart-warming in local effort and cheer. Directions: Car-ferries leave mainland Norway at Bodo for the three-hour trip to the ferry landing at Moskenes at least once a day. Make your round-trip reservations several weeks in advance with English speaking staff at M/S Rost; 7696 7600.

▲**Camping:** At the north end of Moskenesoy island in the village of Fredvang. Skjaegardscamping (7609 4233); beautiful location on an fjord, laundry; pebble beach; open May-Septermber; $$. On Vestvagoy Island, the next island north, exit E10 onto 815 and follow signposting. Brustranda Sjocamping (7608 7100); nice location on the water; cabins; laundry; sauna; open all year; $$. Other campgrounds dot the islands further north on the archipelago.

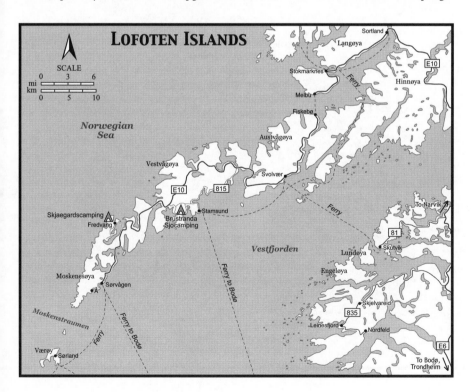

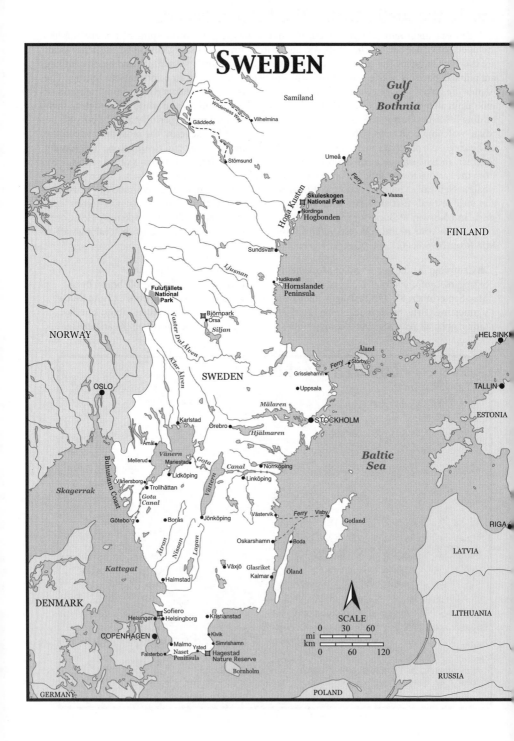

Sweden

www.visitsweden.com

Swedes have striven for perfection from Viking times, when ships were built with mathematical exactness into handsome and highly effective craft. Their azure blue lakes are warm enough for summer swimming and are edged perfectly with leafy forests and sun-warmed boulders. Enticing waterways, ideal for fishing and paddling, wind in and around the archipelagos while craggy coastlines offer tiny secluded beaches perfect for sunbathing. Farmlands roll out in huge blankets of shockingly brilliant yellow mustard or rape edged prettily with the violet bellflowers. Beside clear blue lakes, little red cottages with red trim are tucked neatly near whispering birch trees. These are the symbols of rest and peace that Swedes love.

Swedes are outdoor enthusiasts. They love to be out in nature, particularly if it is close to water. They are prize little nooks and crannies for private, peaceful times in the sun. Owners of campgrounds know that to attract business they must provide well for children and family life so interesting playground equipment, diving platforms, mini-golf, saunas, and barbecues are standard fare. Common cooking areas, with stovetops and scenic eating areas, make it easy to relax and get to know fellow campers. Campgrounds listed are maintained with pride and cost about 20 euros for two persons, a tent, and a car. (Sweden, however, does not use the euro system.) These are noted here as $$. Resort-like campgrounds will cost over 25 euros for the same and are noted here as $$$. Showers require a token or coins; inquire when you check in. Cabins are generally on the premise but need advance booking in popular vacation areas. Simple cabins cost three times what tent camping costs. Many campgrounds have saunas, some are at the lake's edge and some are even in the middle of the lake on a barge. To enjoy this very special Swedish experience, pay to reserve private time at the office when checking in. Sometimes the campground offers free sauna time in the morning with the men and women taking turns. To camp in Sweden, you must purchase a reasonably priced Swedish Camping Card. The open and closing dates listed here are the full-service times. Campground may open a bit earlier and close a bit later but won't have all amenities available. Offices have glossy brochures on local attractions and friendly staff persons who speak English.

The museum schedules listed are summer hours. Many close on Monday. Top sites are open every day with longer hours. Even small towns have a tourist office. Excellent roads with good signposting lace the country. Car headlights are required to be on whenever driving. Gas is expensive, but the distance between destinations is not great except in northern Sweden. Except for Stockholm, parking is easy and costs about the same as at home. Public transportation is efficient and staff is friendly and helpful. English is spoken widely. If you keep your selections simple, groceries aren't overly expensive. Consider bringing coffee, tea, and packaged spice mixes from home. If your travel includes a longer ferry ride, buy a supply of alcoholic beverages in the duty-free store onboard; otherwise it is necessary to buy it in the state-owned *systembolaget* which has limited hours. Fruit and vegetable stands are often conveniently close to a public transportation hub.

Being in Sweden for the *Midsommardag* (Midsummer celebration) the weekend closest to the summer solstice, can be loads of fun. From pagan times it has been a time for rejoicing and merrymaking. Because the days grow shorter after solstice, it was originally feared that the sun would not come back. So bonfires were lit to help drive away evil and encourage the sun to rise again. The tradition remains. A wood midsummer pole–that looks like a giant cross about eight meters high–is laid on the ground. Loops hang off the ends of the crossbeam like a pair of earrings so that people can attach grasses, flowers, and greens they have picked. When the pole is fully decorated, people hoist it into position. Once it is in place, there is a round of applause, traditional songs are sung, and everyone is encouraged to dance around the pole. The long weekend has a free and easy atmosphere–laughter is louder than usual, couples kiss openly and frequently, and music pulsates across the meadows. Every age participates from the young with spiked hair, leather jackets and tight pants to the elderly with mischievous glints in their eyes.

STOCKHOLM

Viewed from Stockholm's highest tower, the city is a dazzling sight of tiny islands scattered as if by a giant who had playfully flung stones into the brilliant blue sea. Below, on what resembles a toy-town island, a somber palace guards a maze of cobblestone streets that were once the nucleus of the city. Leafy trees soften Djurgarden, a nearby island-parkland where smoke rises from ovens baking from bread. On the mainland, contemporary cubes and cylinders of mirror glass punctuate the skyline of a city that prides itself on being up on the latest trends in music, design, and culture. To get this bird's-eye-view and perspective of the city and archipelago, board the elevator to the top of Kaknastornet. Directions: Take bus 69 to Ladugardsgardet. It's just north of Skansen.

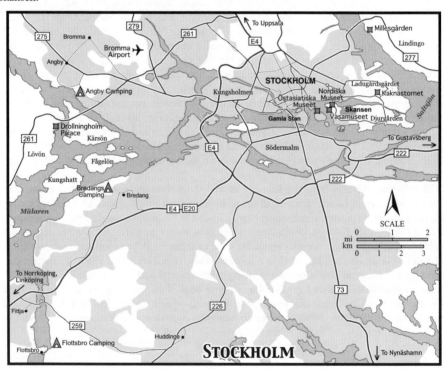

Many jewels await a traveler in Stockholm, but the finest for me is the Vasamusset. The man-of-war ship Vasa, named after Sweden's daring hero and later king, Gustav Vasa I, was fabulous from its very concept. Her uncanny death in front of her admirers was world news. Some tried a resurrection but none succeeded until 1961. Today, a surrounding walkway enables you to have a close-up view of the figures glaring from her gunwales and the monsters sneering from her prow–all proclaiming Swedish might. Her story, from the conceptual beginning to the intricacy of her final resurrection is told in lively exhibits of retrieved items, dioramas of life aboard ship, films of her resurrection, and regularly scheduled tours. Directions: Take bus 47 or 69 or a ferry from Nybroplan or Slussen to Djurgarden.

Skansen, a delightful hillside park also located in Djurgarden, sprouts tiny farms, workshops, and homes bustling with activity of days gone by. Buildings from all of Sweden were brought reconstructed and here. Farmhouses painted in traditional red with windows trimmed in white are cozy with front-porch flower boxes, planted with red, white and purple petunias. Ginger-colored chickens scratch and strut on the lawns, and horses graze peacefully in a fenced meadow. Dressed in period clothing from the region and often involved in an activity from the era, well-informed staff tell stories about what you are seeing. You can watch or ask to participate in the making of *tunnbrod* (a Swedish bread, made for over two centuries from barley flour). A distinctive feature is a hole in the center that made it possible to hang the bread from a long pole hung horizontally from the ceiling, keeping it safe from mice. Baking ovens were waist high so the baker could easily retrieve or deposit the bread on long-handled wooden paddles. Everything displayed in the Sami (indigenous population) exhibit is simple and functional. Sami build *goattiehs*–a type of peat home built with debarked birch trees that provides shelter along the reindeer migration routes. They choose two curved birchs to create the arches that make the *goattieh* spacious. Birchbark is then spread over the outside for waterproofing before being neatly covered with peat. A hearth is centered under a smoke hole, and a large birch beam crossed the hearth where kettles dangle, clothes dry, and fish smoke. The floor of the living and sleeping area is carpeted with generous amounts of birch branches and then covered with reindeer hides, while the kitchen area is covered with more sanitary flat rocks. Everything is within easy reach; it matches its surroundings perfectly. The Skansen is open daily.

To appreciate the Skansen more fully visit Nordiska Museet first. Swedish cultural history is regional, and the museums depict the differences. In Nordiska, the collection is both both contemporary and historical. In addition to a huge statue of Sweden's heroic figure, Gustav Vasa, five centuries of period clothing, tools, and domestic life from each of Sweden's regions is displayed. Seeing the collection gives you a sense of what Swedes value most; open daily in the summer. The museum is at the foot of the bridge in a Renaissance-style castle. For the Vasamuseet, Skansen, and Nordiska, take bus 47 or 69 or a ferry from Nybroplan or Slussen to Djurgarden.

Swedish archeologists have had a long love affair with Asia, so today the Museum of Far Eastern Antiquities, Ostasiatiska Museet, houses one Europe's best collections of ancient Chinese porcelain along with other fine pieces of Asian art. Directions: Take bus 65 to Skeppsholmen. The museum is on the north end, up the hill.

When visiting Gamla Stan, the old town, start with the unique underground museum, Medeltidsmuseum. Foundations of medieval homes were discovered during an excavation. The reconstructed medieval houses depict the life of the average person. Directions: Look for stairs just over the Norrbron bridge, in front of the Riksdag. In Storkyrkam, the church where royalty has been traditionally crowned and married, you are surrounded by theatrical-gilded Baroque. A schedule of free concerts is posted on the bulletin board near the front. At the Royal Palace Kungliga Slottet, which is the world's largest royal palace still in use, it is fun to watch the changing of the guards, resplendent in their shiny brass bobbled helmets. Be there around noon, except on Sundays when the change occurs at 1:00 PM. Sections of the palace can be viewed, but the

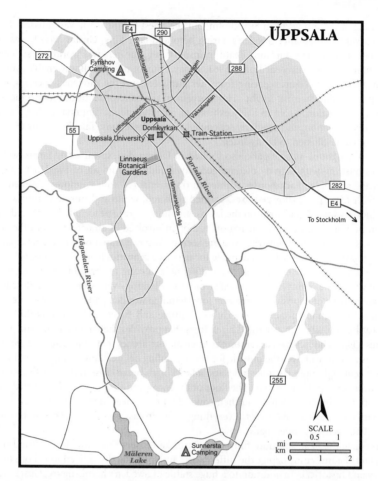

treasury is best. As you lose yourself in the tiny cobblestone streets and alleyways of the old town, note the coats of arms above doorways of the gabled mansions of Hanseatic merchants.

Taking a relaxing boat ride on Lake Malaren to stately Drottningham Palace can be a perfect change in pace. Gustav III, who loved the artistic life, built an elegant court theatre here, and summer performances still take place using 18th-century equipment to change the scenery. The theatre is the oldest in the world still in its original state. It can be toured along with parts of the palace, which is still a royal residence; www.drottningholmsslottsteater.dtm.se. Directions: Ferries leave from Stadshusbron or Kungsholmen, or take buses numbered 301 or 323 from here. To drive, follow directions below for Angby Camping and then signposting for Drottningham.

Hotorget's international open market is aromatic with exotic snacks, flowers, fruits, and vegetables. Munch on a snack on the stairs of the Concert Hall while watching the colorful scene. Then take a short walk to Carl Milles' delightful Orpheus Fountain. Directions: Metro Hotorget. Milles's full sculpture garden, Millesgarden, northeast of the city center on Lidingo Island, is a great place for a picnic and some lazy time. Directions: Take the T-bana to Ropsten, and then the rickety bus over the bridge; open daily. The grotto-like paintings and sculpture that decorate the rough rock walls in the stations of the blue-line are unique to Stockholm and many are humorous. Take a look. Buying a Tourist Card at the metro station pays off in Stockholm, because the campgrounds are out of the city. It gives you unlimited travel on the T-bana (metro), buses, and ferries, and discounted or free admission to many museums and attractions.

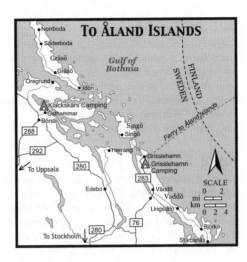

▲**Camping:** • Close to Drottningham Palace, 10km west of the city center on Lake Malern, close to the suburb of Bromma. Drive north of the city, in the direction of Uppsala, exit E4 onto 275 and drive west in the direction of Vallinby. Follow signposting to Drottningham. Just before the bridge to the palace, take the small road north towards Angby and continue 2km. Angby Camping (08-37-04-20); very popular; well used; cabins; metro close-by; open all year; $$. • Southwest of the city, close to Lake Malaren, in the suburb of Bredang. South of the city, exit E4 for Bredang, and drive 3km towards the lake. Bredangs Camping (08-97-70-71); better for caravans; metro close-by; open May-September; $$$. • South of the city on the Bay of Stockholm close to the town of Huddinge. Exit E4/E20 for Fittja. Follow signposting for Huddinge and 259. Flottsbro Camping (08 449 9580); nice location on the water; small beach; sauna; simple café; cabins; public transportation close by; open all year; $$.

Uppsala

Going to Uppsala in Sweden is like going to Oxford when you're in London. Uppsala University, founded in 1477, is the oldest in Scandinavia and is well respected throughout the world. Sweden's largest cathedral, the Domkyrkan, glows gold throughout its immense interior and is worth a walk through, but the highlight for me in Uppsala is walking along the river to visit the Linnaeus botanical garden and adjoining home museum. Binomial classification, developed by botanist Linnaeus, was the foundation stone for scientific classification into family groups. The garden contains more than 1,300 varieties of plants. It is enlightening to examine and compare species.

▲**Camping:** • On Lake Maleren south of Uppsala. From Uppsala drive south on E4 in the direction of Marsta. Follow signposting west to the north end of the lake. Sunnersta Camping (018 27 6084); lovely location on the lake; cabins; open May-Aug; $$. • North of the train station, on the river Fyris next to a sports center with swimming pool. Fyrishov Camping (27-49-60); within walking or cycling distance to historic area; cabins; open all year; $$.

To the Aland Islands

The most economical route to Finland from Sweden is by ferry from the village of Grisslehamn to the charming Aland Islands. Directions: From Stockholm, drive north on E18 in the direction of Norrtalje. Exit onto 76, then drive to Grisslehamn. This part of the Swedish coast is magnificent.

▲**Camping:** • At Grisslehamn. Grisslehamn Camping (175 330 30); nice location close to the water in a very pleasant little town; convenient to the ferry; cabins; sauna; open mid-June-mid-August; $$. • On the coast north of Osthammer, by the yacht harbor. Klackskars Camping (73-331-90); beautiful location; popular with families; cabins; open June-August; $$.

Bothnian Coast

The tranquil and spectacular scenery of the Bothnian Coast with its craggy shorelines, secluded sandy coves, breathtaking fjords, and well-maintained national parks make this part of Sweden my favorite. Here the sea vistas, particularly at sunrise and sunset, are some of the best in the country. Trailheads start at the campground and wind through pine-scented forest, over sandy dunes held down with sandwort and sea holly, and out to pebbly beaches where dunlins probe for worms. Picturesque wharves with terrace cafes are great places to watch the suntanned sailing folks fiddle with their boats.

Hoga Kusten

UNESCO listed in 2000, this strikingly beautiful coast between Harnosand and Ornskoldsvik is probably the most idyllic on the Bothnian Coast. An ice sheet up to 3 kilometers thick once covered this area. Since the land is no longer weighed down by ice, it has risen 286 meters. It's the greatest uplift in the world and is still rising approximately eight millimeters a year. Shimmering fjords that reach deep inland are decorated sweetly with a string of pine-clad pristine islands. Rocky hillsides are studded with gnarled old pines, but in sunny wind-protected spots globe-flowers, harebell,

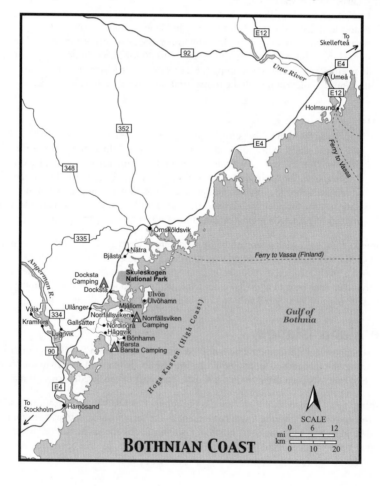

BOTHNIAN COAST

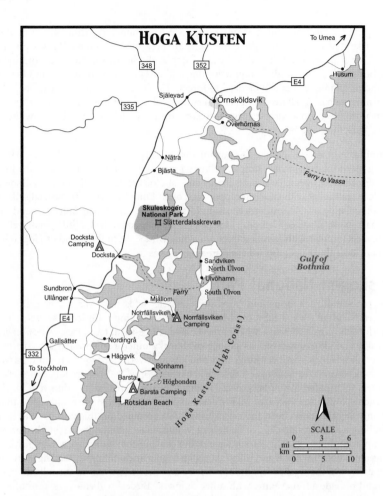

and field gentian luxuriate. Inland, verdant valley pastureland contrasts with sheer seaside cliffs that plunge precipitously into the Gulf of Bothnia. It's a haven of peace and tranquility offering a chance to get away from it all.

Nordingra and Hogbonden

Sweeping views of lush pastureland meet the sea in craggy outcrops in this heartland of High Coast. Vast lengths of smooth-surfaced rocks hide tiny pebbly coves perfect for sunbathing, swimming and enjoying the incredible views of the spectacular sea. Undulating two-laned roads web the hillsides and valleys, where unpretentious little villages offer supplies, art galleries, parish churches, and coffee or tea and sweets in farmhouses. Red and white seaside cottages line the coastline and tiny boathouses on stilts snuggle up eave to eave. Take time to wander through the unusual art colony of Mannaminne in Haggvik. The best beach, with long expanses of smooth stone, is at Rotsidan. Directions: Exit E4 at Gallsater in the south or Ullanger in the north and follow signposting for Nordingra, then southeast for Barsta. Brown road signs indicate the route to Hoga Kusten.

If time permits, take the mid-morning only, pedestrian-only ferry from Barsta or Bonhamn out to the island of Hogbonden, where the views are even more stunning. Pack a bit of gear to camp wild, or make reservations well ahead to stay at the hostel located in an old lighthouse; www,hogboden.se. A star-studded night, evening and early morning birdsong, and the mesmerizing sound of lapping waves will be hard to forget. Don't miss the hostel's extra special seaside wood-burning sauna. You'll need to make reservations ahead and keep the sauna fire going yourself. A great trail leads to a narrow gorge and along the coast. It is a natural place without a cafe or store so pack food and beverage.

▲**Camping:** • In Barsta. Follow signposting east from Nordingra then to Barsta. Barsta Camping (46613 23100); small; simple facilities; lovely setting at the sea; close to the hiking trail for historic miniscule fishing chapel and fabulous rocky sea cliff and beach; next to excellent restaurant with small store; popular; open June-Aug; $$. • In Norrfallsviken. Follow signposting from Nordingra north to Mjallom then east to Norrfallsviken and the end of the road. Norrfallsviken Camping (46613 21255); very large; shady; little grass; well used; no ambiance; popular with families; open June-August; $$. • On the island of Hogbonden (see description above). Camp wild and free.

Skuleskogen National Park

Rocky, pine-studded hilltops and huge stone rubble fields meet the sea in great drama at Skuleskogen National Park, a hilly, road-less wilderness. Hiking trails lead through old-growth forests lush with ferns and moss, where grey-headed, three-toed, and black woodpeckers drum rhythmically, and clear-water brooks plunge over rocky outcrops like waterfalls. In miniscule lakes, water lilies bloom, rustic buntings sing, and it is not overly hard to reach summits where the panoramic views are breathtaking. A dramatic narrow gorge, 200-meters long, 40 meters deep, and 7 meters wide called Slatterdalsskrevan resulted from the erosion of a thin vein of diabase, a type of igneous rock. It is a popular hiking destination. The rough, stony rubble fields that hikers traverse on trails are traces from the ocean waves that pounded on this unique wild landscape. Rock climbing up the granite cliffs of Skuleberg Mountain is popular–there's marked access close to the campground. An excellent park interpretative center, Skule Naturum, has English-speaking, knowledgeable staff, plus maps and information on hiking, rock-climbing, birding, and wildflowers; open daily. On the weekends, outdoor theatre and music festivals on the hillside next to the campground provide a fun evening with other campers. Birders will enjoy the forest next to the campground, where woodpeckers are plentiful. Directions: Almost halfway between Hornoberget and Ornskoldsvik on E4. Stop first at the interpretative and information center, Skule Naturum in Skuleberget, at the south end of the park, just north of Docksta.

A mid-morning, passenger-only, ferry leaves from Docksta for Ulvon Island. Here unusual red granite pebbles, called *rapakivi*, cover a lovely beach a few minutes walk from the ferry landing; just follow signposting for *Strandpromenaden*. You can rent a bike at the tourist office in the village and pedal or hike, 6 kilometers out over a couple of hills to the village of Sandviken and its long and tranquil beach. Sweden's famous *surstromming* (fermented Baltic herring) is produced in the village of Ulvohamn, where the ferry lands.

▲**Camping:** • Adjacent to Skule Naturum. Skuleberget Camping (46613 40055); pleasant and convenient location for enjoying the park; café; enclosed cooking and eating area; cabins; open May-Sept; $$. In Dockstra. Exit off E4 following signposting for the ski-lift. Dockstra Camping (46613 13064); pleasant location in a meadow at the base of the southern slope of Skuleberget; enclosed cooking and eating area; sauna; simple café; open May-Sept; $$.

Umea

It's easy to feel comfortable in this youthful city that feels more like a town. Perhaps it is the fast-flowing river that runs through the town or the abundance of graceful birch trees that give it this pleasant air. It makes a perfect "city" stop. Its museum complex, Gammlia includes a rural open-air museum, a history museum whose collection includes the oldest ski in the world, a good exhibition about the Sami and reindeer-keeping, plus an interesting modern art and photojournalism exhibit. A well-planned cycle/walking route hugs the fast-moving river with places of interest along the way. The tourist office has maps and information on rentals. Gazing into the eyes of a huge tame elk while you stroke its neck is a hard to forget experience at the Elk Sarfari. Diections: In Bjurholm, 70km west of Umea. Unregulated, the River Vindelalven offers plenty of rapids and excitement for paddlers and there is a good canoe route from the campground up into the inner archipelago close to the city and another on the River Savaran with canoe rental at Savar. Ferries cross the Bay of Bothnia from Vasa Finland and Umea, departing from Holmsund, 20km east of Umea. Directions: Umea is 111km north of Ornskoldsvik on E4.

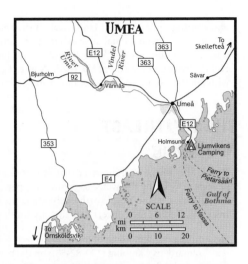

▲**Camping**: • In Holmsund, 3km from the ferry landing on E12, 17km east of Umea. Ljumvikens Camping (46 0 90 417); great location by a popular swimming beach; enclosed cooking and eating area; canoe rental; open mid-May-Sept; $$.

ENROUTE NORTH
Hudiksvall and the
Hornslandet Peninsula

In the old fishermen's town of Fiskarstan, an excellent museum–whose collection includes a 1,000 year old engraved rune stone–plus a nice campground on the beach makes a nice break in the journey before heading up to the High Coast. Directions: Drive 120km north of Gavle on E4. Exit for Hudiksvall. Drive through town to the harbor, following sign-posting for Fiskarsten. Continuing out to the Hornslandet Peninsula will be more back-to-nature experience. The campground out of Holick is adjacent to a picturesque wharf with terrace cafe where sailboats tie up. A trailhead goes out to the Hornslandet promontory where sunbathing is secluded and birdwatching is worthwhile.

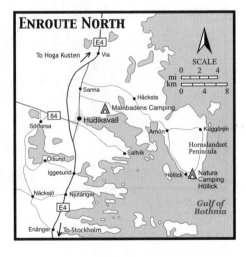

▲**Camping:** • 3km east of Hudiksval on the coast road. Malnbadens Camping (650 132 60); large; in a recreational area; cabins; pub; simple café; enclosed eating and cooking area; open mid-June-mid-Aug; $$. • Exit off E4 for Hornslandet, then follow signposting for Holick driving to the end of the road. Natura Camping Holick (650 56 51 00); large; popular with families; sauna; enclosed cooking and eating area; open mid-May-Aug; $$.

THE SOUTHEAST
Norrkoping

It was this town's rushing river that attracted enterprising industrialist Louis de Greer in the 18th-century. Using the water for power, his paper and textile factories flourished. Today these same factories house note worthy exhibits concerning the average working man and woman. Directions: Behind the concert hall, directly south of the train station, along the river.

▲**Camping:** • 22km north of town on the bay. Exit E4 for Komarden and drive towards the sea. Kolmardens Camping (139-82-50); on the bay; large; popular with families; close to a well-run zoo and dolphin park; open May-Aug; $$. • Southwest of Norrkoping in a recreational area. Exit E4 Norrkoping south and follow signposting for Sportzcentum. Himmelstalunds Camping (460 11 17 1190); smaller; nice location; convenient; cabins; open mid-June-August; $$.

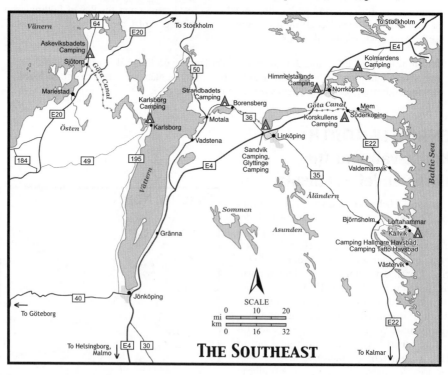

Linkoping

Thought provoking and insightful, the Gamla Linkoping 1920s worker's town open-air museum is worth a detour; open daily. Directions: Gamla Linkoping is on the west side of town, off Maimslattsvagen. Paddling the Stangan river is popular and suitable for paddlers and families of all levels of experience. The Canoe Center at the boat harbor in Linkoping.

▲**Camping:** • North of town on Lake Roxen. Sandvik Camping (460 136 14); nice location; cabins; open all year; $$.

Cycling/walking the Gota Canal

Joining the Baltic Sea with the North Sea via the Gota Canal was one of the world's great civil engineering feats of the 1800s. It took 60,000 soldiers and 22 years to complete, but by linking Lakes Vanern and Vattern the Swedes were able to avoid the costly Danish shipping tariffs on the Oresund. The old tow-path, once used by horses and oxen pulling the barges, is now a popular cycle/walking path. This route along the "Blue Ribbon" is leafy and scenic and passes along the edge of lakes and close to towns that make pleasurable detours. Bike rentals are available throughout the route. Public transportation permits your bike to ride with you back to your car. The route is particularly nice from Sjotorp on the northeast edge of Lake Vanern, to Karlsborg on Lake Vattern, and from Motala on the northeast edge of Vattern to the village of Mem just south of Norrkoping, and east of Soderkoping. Visiting the Canal Museum in Trollhatten will add immeasurably to your appreciation; www.gotakanal.se.

▲**Camping:** • 6km north of Sjotorp close to the canal. AskeviksbadetsCamping (501 514 09); nice location on the lake; enclosed cooking and eating area; cabins; sauna; open April-Sept; $$. • At the lake in Karlsborg, close to the cycle route. Karlsborgs Camping (505 449 16); great location on the lake; enclosed cooking and eating area; cabins; open mid-April-Sept; $$. • 18km east of Motala, on the water, close to the cycle route in Borensberg. Strandbadets Camping (141 403 85); enclosed cooking and eating area; cabins; good place to meet other cyclists; open June-Aug; $$. • South of Soderkoping close to the cycle route. Korskullens Camping (121 216 21); cabins; enclosed cooking and eating area; café; open mid-May-mid-Sept; $$.

Gotland Coast

Pine-scented campgrounds and tranquil canoeing through this archipelago provide a peaceful break in the journey.

▲**Camping:** • 26km north of Vastervik, exit E22 at Bjornsholm onto 213 for Loftahammer and go to the tip of the pennisula. • From Kallvik, drive 3km to Hallamare. Camping Hallmare Havsbad (04 93-613-62); tranquil location on the lake under the pines; canoe and bike rental; cabins; enclosed cooking and eating area; open mid-May-August; $$. • Follow the above directions but continue 3km farther following signposting for Tatto. Camping Tatto Havsbad (04 93-613-30); great location on the water; larger; sauna; cabins; canoe and bike rental; enclosed cooking and eating; pub; open June-mid-Aug; $$$.

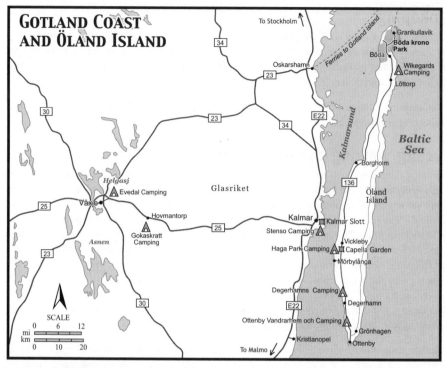

Gotland Island

Sandy beaches, biking paths, picturesque villages, and brilliant red sunsets make this a popular vacation spot with partying folks. Its geographic location has attracted traders since Viking times. Ruins of a medieval castle, tower, and ramparts and especially the Gotland Fornsal Museum, with its exhibition spanning 8,000 years, bears witness to the area's former wealth and importance. Fire-eaters, jesters, jugglers and jousting tournaments entertain throngs of people during

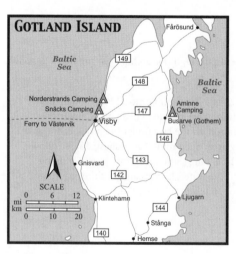

Medieval Week, held in the second week of August. Visby is at its height of gaiety then and an amazing number of locals and visitors dress up in medieval costumes. Brawny competitors hurl tree trunks and compete in other strenuous trials similar to Scotland's Highland Games during the Viking Olympics held in Stanga in July. Directions: Drive south of Visby on 143 for 49km.

A popular cycling route encircles this flat island along its seacoast, passing through charming villages–some with medieval walls and churches–then out to flowering meadows and old farmsteads. Rentals are available in Visby, Hemse, and Ljugarn. Directions: Take the 3-hour car-ferry ride from Vastervik. Make car-reservations for the ferry well in advance; wwwdestinationgotland.se

▲**Camping**: In season reserve ahead. • On the east side of the island. Drive 38km from Visby on 147, exit south onto 146 for 11km in the direction of Gothem. Aminne Camping (498-340-11); nice location on the water; cabins; sauna; enclosed cooking and eating; bike rental; open May-Aug; $$$. • 4km north of Visby on 149. Snacks Camping (04-98-117-50); nice location on the water; large; popular; open mid-June-mid-Aug; $$$. or Norderstrands Camping (04-98-21-21-57); nice location; large; popular; open May-Sept; $$$.

Oland Island

Sandy beaches, outstanding birding, and a network of cycle routes make Oland a popular choice for an island visit. In late May and June, the area around Ottenby at the island's southern tip is busy with birders using the *fagelstation* (bird observatory) and searching in the shrubs around the lighthouse for rare bird migrants. The nature reserve is Sweden's largest sanctuary for migrating birds and has a small but good museum. Capella Garden–an artist colony of weavers, ceramists, and wood carvers who live in picturesque farmhouses surrounded by vegetable and flower gardens–makes a nice stop. Directions: South of Borgholm on 136, in Vickleby. The best long sandy beaches are on the northeast side, with the area north of Lyckesand being the most popular. In June brilliant blue lupine-like flowers carpet Neptune Akrar, a reserve 3 kilometers south of the northwest tip of the island. It's a extraordinary sight. Bring your camera, and include seeing Lange Eric lighthouse located just 3 kilometers farther out on the tip.

▲**Camping**: • Off the southwest coast road, 8km north of Morbylanga, close to the art colony at Vickleby. Haga Park Camping (0495 360-30); nice location close to a recreational park; windsurf rentals; cabins; open May-Sept; $$. • 37km south on 136 to Degerhamn. Not far from Ottenby bird sanctuary, lighthouse, ancient fort, and village of Eketorp. Degerhamns Camping (0485 66 00 75); beautiful location on the water; open May-Aug; $$. Closest to the Ottenby bird reserve. Ottenby Vandrarhem och Camping (0485 66 2062); convenient for early bird watching; small; basic; $. On the north east side of the island there are several resort-like campgrounds. Here's a smaller, less expensive one. • Drive 45km north of Borgholm on 136 to Lottorp and follow signposting. Wikegards Camping (485 251 31); nice location on the beach; simpler than its neighbors; open May-mid-Sept; $$.

Kalmar

With moat and drawbridge, turreted Kalmar Slott stands dignified, as if still mightily guarding Sweden. This Renaissance castle, preserved in great detail, boasts extensive ramparts, casemates, corner bastions and dungeon. Eleven sieges, royal sibling hatred and paranoia make tales about the castle and its ghosts especially colorful; open daily. Directions: Just south of Gamla Stan (Old Town). Follow signposting off main highways for Kalmar Slott. A clever and imaginative walk-through reconstruction of the Kronan, one of the largest ships built in the 17th century, will have you "out to sea with the boys". Gulls shriek, cannons fire, gold coins spill from treasure chests, and fancy officers' hats, and jackets look ready to put on. It a fun and fascinating "on board" experience; open daily. Directions: Located in the Lansmuseum, county museum, five blocks south of the Angobron, the bridge to Oland Island.

▲**Camping**: • Exit Kalmar south off E22 and follow signposting south out to the tip of the peninsula. Stenso Camping (0408 888 03); pleasant location on the water; good birding opportunities; swimming; canoe rental; cabins; open mid-April-Sept; $$.

Glasriket

Watching as air is skillfully blown through a lead tube, turning a glass plug into an artful piece is intriguing. The pleasant forested area from Kalmar to Vaxjo provides the huge amount of fuel needed for this art and tucks in many glasswork studios, factories, and galleries. Whether you are a serious shopper or just want to watch the process, check with the tourist office in Kalmar or Vaxjo to locate the type of glasswork and time of demonstration that works to you.

▲**Camping:** • 26km east of Vaxjo, on 25 in the town of Hovmantorp. Gokaskratt Camping (78-408-07); nice location on a lake; cabins; open June-Aug; $$.

House of Emigrants and the Glass Museum in Vaxjo

Devastating crop failures and immense hardships caused a huge emigration to the USA of peasant families. Placing grand hopes and trust on advertisements for "America, Land of Dreams" over a million Swedes left between 1860 and 1930, many of them settled in and around Chicago. The House of Emigrants Museum's exhibit begins with life in Sweden and covers the crowded steamer crossing and the hardships upon arrival and concludes with some successful and not so successful life stories. Personal and touching the exhibits and audio stories provide a glimpse of the dreams and the realities. If you have Swedish roots, make an appointment ahead at the museum's research center to trace them; info@svenskaemigrantinstitutet.g.se

After a visit to Murano Italy, glassmaking was encouraged and funded by King Gustav Vasa. In the mid-18th century it flourished in the fuel-providing dense forests of Smaland. The Smalands Museum collection of tools and techniques used in early glassmaking foster an appreciation of the art. Artful glass pieces include etched, Art Nouveau, and contemporary. If convenient, before going to individual studios stop at the museum first; open daily. Directions: Both museums are located by the train station.

▲**Camping:** • On the northeast edge of town on the lake. Evedal Camping (46 0 470 63034); pleasant; bike and canoe rental; sauna; covered cooking and eating area; simple café; open mid-June-mid-Aug; $$.

SOUTHERN COAST

Fields of rape in sunburst-yellow edged with blood-red poppies roll out between velvety blue-green wheat fields in this region. Here and there cozy red farmhouses trimmed in white sit proudly against cobalt-blue skies. Grab your camera.

NASET PENINSULA
Foteviken Viking Museum

Full-time residents of Foteviken Viking Museum, some sporting wild beards, make their own homespun garments, bake bread in clay ovens, and build long boats. Guests can set up their own tent, or use theirs, don homespun clothing provided by the museum, and participate in hands-on classes for a back-to-the-earth experience. People from all over Europe come to enjoy this 12th-century experience. On the weekend closest to June 10th there is a reenactment of the Battle of Foteviken, and at the beginning of July there is a very jolly Viking celebration and colorful market. Viking plays and guided tours are scheduled throughout the summer; open daily; www.foteviken.se. Directions: Drive13km south of Malmo on E6. Exit onto 100 and drive 3km in the direction of Hollviken. Follow signposting just before Hollviken for Foteviken.

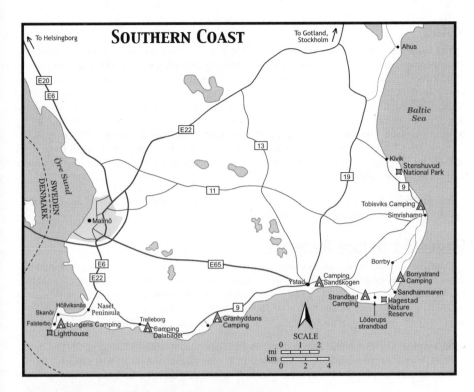

Falsterbo and the Nature Preserves

White sandy beaches border Falsterbo's nature preserves. From late August through October, huge numbers of raptors and passerines heading south for the winter cross the Baltic Sea over the southern tip of Sweden, near Malmo. More than 14,000 raptors have been recorded in one day, and seeing more than 1,000 is not unusual during the peak period. Lesser-spotted eagles are most likely to be seen in late August, and the widest range of species occurs in the first half of September. On fine days with light westerlies, large numbers of raptors–goshawks, buzzards, kites, harriers, and eagles–rise above the heath at Lujungen on mid-morning thermals, and they can be seen at the southwest end by the campground. Many birds often gather along the Falsterbo Canal, but the mass overhead movement of birds is best seen at the lighthouse. Directions: Drive 13km south of Mamo on E6/E22. At the junction, turn onto 100 in the direction of Falsterbo and Skandor, and continue for 13km.

▲**Camping**: • Just east of Falsterbo near Ljunghusen. Ljungens Camping (040 47 1132); convenient for birding; cabins; large; open mid-April-Sept; $$. • East of Trelleborg. Drive south of Malmo on E6/E22 for 26km to Trelleborg. Turn east on 9 and follow signposting to camping just east of the town. Camping Dalabadet (0410 14905); lovely location on the beach; cabins; sauna; open all year; $$. • 15km east of Trelleborg on 9 in the village of Beddinge. Granhyddans Camping (0410 25042); good location on the beach; enclosed cooking and eating area; open mid-April-Sept; $$.

Ystad

The haunting call of a bugle sounds each night from the church's watchtower, still reassuring townspeople that a night watchman is awake checking that no thatched roof is on fire. Three hundred 13th-century half-timbered houses line the twisting cobblestone streets of this pretty town. Start at the Stortorget (town square). Walk over to St Maria Kyrka–a chilling, medieval place. The crucifix of Jesus has real hair, a scary face is carved in the pulpit, and green colored box pews are designated for women who have not been accepted back in the parish since giving birth to an infant. Outside, you'll be warmed as sunlight drifts through the broad leaves of horse-chestnut trees lining the streets where artisans invite visitors to come in and watch them work in their studios. Opera buffs should plan their visit during July when the town hosts an opera festival; www.visitystad.com.

▲**Camping**: • Just east of Ysted on 9. Camping Sandskogen (0411 192 70); cabins, enclosed cooking and eating area; open mid-April-mid-Sept; $$.

Hagestad Nature Reserve

Thousands of pink heather blossoms sway in the gentle breeze amid the gnarled trunks of oaks and sand dunes that border one of the areas most graceful beaches. In an old farmstead up hill from the heathland, Dag Hammarskjold, one of the U.N.'s most famous secretary-generals–spent restful moments surrounded by significant mementos from around the world. He donated the house, his collection, and the surrounding 60 acres for a park; open irregular hours. Check in the village of Backakra or Ystad before you drive in.

▲**Camping**: On the beach 12km east of Ysted at Loderup. Strandbad Camping (0411 526311); great location; café; open April-Sept; $$. 6km farther east on Borrby's beach. Borrystrand Camping (0411 521260); great location; open mid April-mid-Sept; $$.

Kivik and the Apple Growing Region

If you've grown up around apple trees, their blossom-time is extra special to you. A drive through this region permits you to stop to taste cider, devour warm homemade apple pie, and pick up a bag of your favorites. At Applets Hus, a modern eclectic museum dedicated to the tree and its fruit; you will be surprised how much you didn't know about apples; open daily. Directions: Follow signposting in Kivik. From here its not far to Stenshuvud National Park–named for its remarkable rock peak that has been a mark for seaman since ancient times. There is an easy walking trail to it. In midsummer, look carefully in the wooded meadows for the miniscule orchid blossoms. In July one the biggest open market events in Sweden occurs and it is a terrific place to enjoy laughter and fun with locals. Directions: Kivik is 18km north of Simrishamn on 9.

▲**Camping**: 2km north of Simrishamn. Tobisviks Camping (0414 819198); nice location on the water; cabins; open all year; $$.

WEST COAST
Goteborg

Take pleasure in Goteborg by ambling through its graceful gardens, peaceful canals, and lively markets. Tradgardsforeningen Park often lilts with music and street theatre and is a good place to start. Both the Palm House and the Butterfly House here are favorites. At the Rohsska Museum,

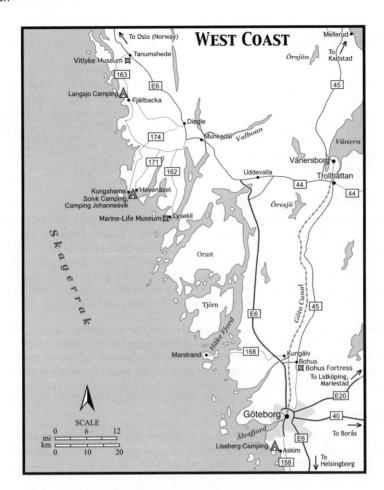

delight in a huge "memory lane" collection of decorative and functional art. Then board a vintage tram winding its way through the city. Goteborg is justifiably proud of its Maritime Center. Besides clever dioramas on how seamen lived and worked, there is an impressive number of ships to climb around on; open daily. Once a church Feskekorka is now a fish market with piles of glistening fish and the raucous calls of the fishmongers; closed Sunday and Monday. Colorful Saluhall market is nearby, so walk over and indulge in some of Sweden's best foodstuffs; closed Sunday. Directions: From the cruise ship harbor follow the southern canal as it winds into the city. To admire first-hand Sweden's enormous technical achievements, watch the robots at the Volvo Factory; closed Sunday and Monday; free. Directions: Drive across the river to Hisingen Island and follow signposting.

▲**Camping:** • 10km south of the city on the Askim Bay and beach. Exit off E6/E20 for Soderleden and following signposting on 158. Liseberg Camping Askim Strand (031 28 6261); lovely location; large; popular with families; sauna; bike rental; enclosed cooking and eating area; open May-Aug; $$$.

HELSINGBORG AREA
Nimis

Sensational and controversial, the "living"–because it is in constant creation–sculpture *Nimis* is a unique attraction to visit. Created by eccentric sculptor Lars Vilks, a professor of art at Oslo University, this immense piece is a creation of driftwood and other odd pieces of this and that which you climb over and walk through. Directions: Drive northwest of Helsingborg on 111 onto the Kullen peninsula passing through for Hoganas for 28km. Turn north on a small road for Arlid–an especially pretty seaside village. Turn northwest here and watch for signposting for Himmelstorp, an 18th-century farmstead open for tours. Park here and follow the yellow "N" signposting down the ridge from Himmelstorp to the beach and sculpture; open daily.

Royal Gardens of Sofiero

These gardens are graceful, with grand trees dressed in myriad leaf color and sculptural grace, rhododendrons blooming in rich colors, and primulas and water-lilies decorating ponds. Founded by the granddaughter of Britain's queen Victoria, these royal gardens exemplify the English concept of natural garden design and hold more than 10,000 plants–500 are varieties of rhododendrons. Be here in May or early June for best bloom. Later in June the air is heavy with the fragrance from an exceptional collection old roses whose names breathe romantic fancies; open daily. Directions: Drive or cycle north from Helsingborg on the coast road for 4km to Sofiero.

▲**Camping:** • 2km south of Hoganas in Lerberget. Lerbergets Camping (42 33 17 05); nice location on the sea; simple; enclosed cooking and eating area; open mid-June-mid-Aug; $$.
• On the tip of the Kullen peninsula 2km south of Molle. Mollenhassle SweCamp (42 34 73 84); resort-like; good location; large; restaurant; pub; cabins; sauna; enclosed cooking and eating area; open May-Aug; $$$.

Bohuslan Coast

Tiny beaches nestle almost hidden in the arms of smooth granite boulders that stretch out to sun themselves along the craggy coastline and archipelago of Bohuslan. Reached by narrow paths through aromatic pine forests, they provide sweet havens for sun lovers. Directions: Directly west of Lake Vanern. E6 runs along its length, and small roads lead from E6 to little villages. For a terrific view of the area, stop

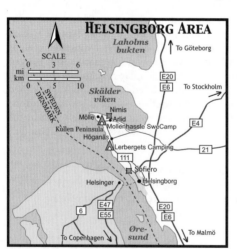

at the ruins of Bohus Fortress and climb the steps to the tower. Directions: 20km north of Gothenburg and east of E6, at Kungalv. You'll feel like an underwater diver as you walk through an 8-meter long tunnel and are surrounded by enormous fish in Lysekil's Marine Museum; open daily. Directions: Exit off E6 24km north of Uddevalla onto 162, and drive 32km out to the tip of the peninsula to Lysekil. The museum is at the end of the village by the sea. The greatest concentration of Bronze Age rock carvings in Scandinavia are found in the countryside surrounding the UNESCO listed town of Tanumshede. The images were carved on the sloping smooth surfaces of rock that was once close to the sea.

Pedaling out to see them is fun and rentals are available in town. Before you go, visit Vitlycke Museum where the images are interpreted and where maps to find them are available. Directions: Almost halfway between Uddevalla and Halden, exit E6 onto 163.

▲**Camping:** In season make reservations ahead. There are many camping places along this coast. Here are a few: • In Kungshamn. Exit E6 at Dingle onto174. Solvk Camping (0523-318-70); nice location; popular; sauna; enclosed cooking and eating area; open mid-May-August; $$$. • In Hovenaset, north of Kungshamn, off 171. Camping Johannesvik (0523-323-87); large; beautiful location; popular; cabins; bike and canoe rental; enclosed cooking and eating area; sauna; pub; open mid-June-mid-Aug; $$$. • Just north of Fjallbacka. Exit E6 onto 163. Langsjo Camping (525 121 16); great location; smaller; popular; enclosed cooking and eating area; canoe and bike rental; open May-mid-Sept; $$$.

CENTRAL SWEDEN
Rafting the Klaralven

Who hasn't longed for a Huck Finn experience? Well you can have one on the Klaralven River located just north of Karlstad. It's even more fun if you build your own raft but you don't have to. The river's slow pace at 2-kilometers an hour, makes its ideal for fishing, swimming, and just lazing about. At night, pull ashore and put up your tent, or moor your raft and put it up on the raft; www.vildmark.se or www.sverigeflotten.

▲**Camping.** • Exit off E/18 for Karlstad and drive towards the lake. Skutbergets Camping (54 53 5139) or Karlstad SweCamp (54 53 50 68); both have great locations; popular with families; enclosed cooking and eating areas; cabins; canoe and bike rental; open end of June-July; $$.

Dalarna and Orsa's Bear Park

Sweden's lake region is perfect for quiet paddling and fishing. Lush pastures strewn with red clover, purple vetch, and gypsy rose daisies surround red-and-white farmhouses making an peaceful idyllic rural landscape. Nine hundred square kilometers of space make Gronklitt Bjorn Europe's largest bear park. The gentle, charming, and mainly vegetarian creatures roam at will, living somewhat like they would in the wilds. Viewing towers and covered walkways provide visitors a chance to observe their often-humorous behavior. Bring binoculars; open daily. Rivers up here run clear, even in runoff. Spilling high, they tumble heedlessly around and over protruding boulders like stampeding cattle. It is a fly-fishing paradise with graylings and brown trout darting in between chartreuse moss covered rocks. Directions: 15km north of Orsa at the north Lake Siljan.

▲**Camping:** • On the lake Orsa-sjon in Orsa. Orsa SweCamp (0250 46 00); very large; popular with families; cabins; simple café; pub; sauna; canoe and bike rental; enclosed cooking and eating area; June-Aug; $$. • At the north end of Lake Siljan in Mora. Mora Camping (250 276 00); nice location on the lake; popular with families; cabins; sauna; enclosed cooking and eating area; open June-Aug; $$. • On a island in the lake, in Solleron, just south of Mora. Solleron Semesterby (0250 290 00); lovely location; no shade; cabins; sauna; open June-Aug; $$.

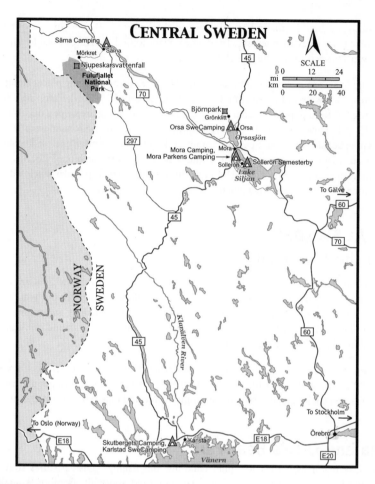

Fulufjallet National Park

From Mt Fulufjallet's sandstone plateau, Sweden's highest waterfall plunges majestically 125 meters into the deep Njupeskar gorge. An easy trail leads up above the tree line, where vast carpets of spongy lichen carpet upland meadows. Newly designated, Fulufjallet National Park boasts 140 kilometers of marked trails. This is genuine wilderness, where hiking trails cross rough boulder-strewn ravines and wind through primeval forests. Directions: From the northwest end of Lake Siljan at Mora, drive northwest on 70 for 122km to Sarna. Turn west and drive 18km to Morkret, then follow signposting for Njupeskarsvattenfall. Just outside of the park, you'll be taken aback by the sight of hundreds of reindeer grazing on the lichen strewn marshlands.

▲Camping: • In Mora. Mora Parkens Camping (0250 276 00); great location on the lake; large; restaurant; pub; sauna; cabins; open mid-June-mid-Aug; $$. • In Sarna. Sarna Camping (0253 108 51); lovely location on the river; enclosed cooking and eating area; sauna; canoe rental; cabins; open June-mid-Aug; $$.

The Wilderness Way

Some of Sweden's most dramatic and spectacular scenery occurs along this very scenic highway. Lush canyons, ancient forests, and fast flowing rapids composed of clear sparkling water seem untouched and pristine. Giant spruce form ceremonial archways where beard lichen hangs spookily from branches and on deciduous tree trunks lungwort lichen grows profusely, both attract Sweden's largest bear population. Squirrels click their tongues and dart up the trees, then stiffen statue-like on a branch. Great contrasts are everywhere: ridged mountains and tiny violets; buff-colored rock and brilliant blue sky; cheery birdsong and softly whistling wind in the trees. The deep and peaceful silence is restoring.

The Wilderness Way, highway 342, begins from Stromsund, 105 kilometers north of Ostersund on 45, and follows the river northwest up to the Norwegian border, the town of Gaddede, and the idyllic Lake Murusjoen. It is a well-maintained two-lane highway, and the journey is 140 kilometers. Get supplies and gas before you head up. Stop at the tourist office on the Stromsund's main street to get the map detailing points of interest on the Wilderness Way and a trail map to the 2,500 year-old *hallmalningar* (Stone Age rock paintings). Farther north, the Wilderness Way hugs the Norwegian border, crosses the steppe-like Stekenjokk plateau, and then turns east towards 45 and Vilhelmina. On the north side of the loop, in the miniscule village of Fatmomakke, Sami huts and cabins cluster around a church and lake. You can visit the *visningskata* (show hut). Look for signposting. Wait outside the door to be invited in. Samis enter their house by crossing over the living area before going to the kitchen, so that the kitchen is kept more sanitary. The living area is carpeted with generous amounts of birch branches covered with reindeer hides, and the kitchen area is neatly covered with more sanitary flat rocks. Everything is simple and practical.

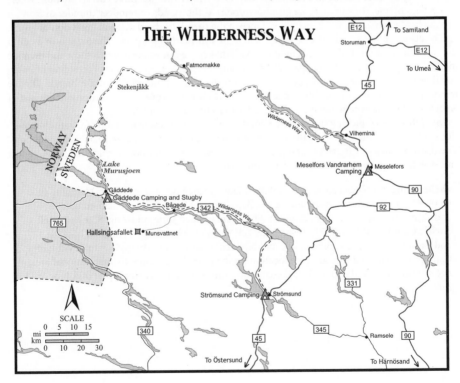

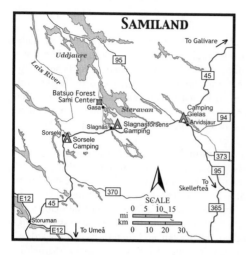

▲Camping: • South of Stromsund on 45 by the bridge. Stromsund Camping (670 164 10); resort-like; wonderful location on the river; cabins; pool; enclosed cooking and eating area; open mid-June to mid-Aug; $$$. • South of Gaddede on the lake. Gaddede Camping and Stugby (672 100 35); small; simple; nice location; cabins; enclosed cooking and eating area; open mid-June-mid-Aug; $$. • 24km south of Vilhelmina on 45. Meselefors Vandrarhem Camping (940 250 89); beautiful location on the river; cabins; enclosed cooking and eating area; canoe rental; open June-Aug; $$. • This is also a popular area for adventurous campers who just set up somewhere that seems especially beautiful.

Samiland

The drama of glaciers, mountains, rushing rivers, and midnight sun lure the hiker, fly fisherman, and paddler to this part of Europe's last wilderness. Huge herds of reindeer still wander about freely looking shabby in summer as they shed winter fur. Reindeer corrals are built where two valleys merge. In summer, the ground vibrates as thousands of reindeer thunder in front of driving herdsmen, dogs, and helicopters. Once in the corral, the herd makes a great dim of grunts and bleats as mothers and calves reunite. Then the calf marking begins. The Sami own a calf if they own the mother. Calves are caught by lassos that curve uncannily beneath them and then are marked with a registered family pattern of slits and notches. At the Batsuoj Forest Sami Center, you'll learn about how this is done as well as how to milk a reindeer and make bread. Try the reindeer barbecue and maybe buy some frozen meat for camp cooking. Directions: 31km east of Sorsele on 45, exit west at Slagnas and drive 16km to the village of Gasa.

Late July is berry-picking time. After a good spring without severe frost look for rare cloudberries while you are hiking. They thrive in moist environments, near water, marshland, and bogs. The distinct cluster of berries is about the size of a raspberry and honey-colored. They are soft and sweet when ripe and drop easily from the stem.

▲Camping: • In between Sorsele and Avidsjaur in Slagnas. Slagnasforsens Camping (960 65 00 93); on the river; convenient for the Batsuo Forest Sami Center; enclosed cooking and eating area, sauna, cabins, canoe and bike rental; open June-mid-Aug; $. • In Sorsele. Sorsele Camping (952 101 24); beautiful location on the river; larger; enclosed cooking and eating area; sauna; cabins; canoe and bike rental; open June-Aug; $$. • In Arvidsjaur. Camping Gielas (960 556 00); nice location on the river; larger; close to a recreational area; enclosed cooking and eating area; sauna; canoe and bike rental; cabins; open mid-June-mid-Aug; $$.

CROATIA

http:us.croatia.hr

Curved like a crescent moon around what the astronauts claim is the bluest sea on earth, the Adriatic, Croatia is fairytale-like stunning. Dubbed the new Riviera, it has more than a thousand picture-perfect islands scattered like marbles out into flat crystalline waters. Little towns and villages cling to steep hillsides that nestle secluded cove beaches. Whitewashed stone houses line a jumble of alleyways and stairways. It's easy to while away an afternoon slouched in a chair well-worn by others who have lost track of what century they are in. Faded-tangerine and mustard-colored houses serve as a backdrop for little fishing boats bobbing up and down in a sea whose waters are warm enough to swim in from late spring to early autumn. Boasting some of the best sun in Europe, it's no wonder that Europeans have been coming to Croatia to camp for years. Tiny villages and towns retain culture from their days as Venetian colonies, and lively seafronts, some with beautiful promenades, stretch along the sparkling sea. The laid-back friendliness of Croatians makes you want time to stand still. It's easy to pitch your tent under the pines at the edge of the sea and take in the gorgeous setting.

Geographically, Croatia lies like a narrow arc margin between Europe and the Balkans, then juts inland into Eastern Europe's mountains and Hungary's farmlands. It's breathtaking beauty makes it a jewel that has been sought after, stolen, and conquered since ancient times, usually by wealthy invaders who wanted to make it an exclusive club where only the chosen few could enjoy themselves. Enduring a thousand years of foreign meddling, subjugation, and outright wars, it was finally recognized as a separate country in 1992.

The modern highways come into Zagreb and Rijeka from Italy, Hungary, and Slovenia are four-lane and divided. The scenery is outstanding. Signage close to the cities is good. The Croatians have a long history of tourism, particularly along the coast, and want to make is easy for their visitors. The new highways planned and being built will make driving a breeze. But on two-lane, busy, inland roads, it is often difficult to pass. Be especially alert when oncoming traffic coming is lined up. Impatient drivers take risks. Avoid passing the car in front of you when you see oncoming traffic lined up with more than 3 or 4 vehicles. When oncoming traffic lets up, you need to pass slower trucks in order to avoid a dangerous line up behind you. On toll roads, drive up to the ticket dispenser and remove the ticket. The bar will lift. You pay when you exit. Be sure to pull into a tollbooth for cars because trucks use ticket dispensers that are too high to reach. Good current maps are available and you need to purchase them before the trip. Don't rely on getting quality maps within the country.

In no other place can you get a better sense of the local people than at the local fruit and veg-etable morning markets. You'll be part of the everyday shopping melee where the price is the best. Vendors are serious when they hand you a plastic bag so that you can select from their produce. Only after they have carefully counted back your change will they burst into a big grin....if you do, first. Be sure to say thank you in Croatian, *hvala*. It always feels good to buy from and share smiles with people who need and appreciate your business. Stop enroute when you see a market going on. They are great places for a break from driving, and the snacks and beverages are cheaper than in more touristy areas. Cash machines can be found throughout the country at local banks and shopping areas.

Although museum hours vary, you can plan on weekday mornings, excluding Monday, as good times for a visit; however, many have longer hours. Churches are open for mass every day at 7 AM and 8 AM and again at 5 PM so you can plan a quiet and respectful visit, properly attired, just before or after. Visas are no longer required for most travelers, but check to be sure. Do bring an international camping card, so you can leave it at the campground office during your stay instead of your passport. Cyber cafes are handy for keeping in touch with friends and family and are now located in many towns and cities; ask at the campground. Excellent books have been written about the Balkans and the former Yugoslavia; check with your library, and do some research so that your visit is more meaningful.

Ferries between the mainland and the islands, and between the islands themselves, are relatively inexpensive. You probably won't need a reservation except when there is only one or two ferry crossings a day. Check with the campground office a day or two before you want to go. Then get there early so you can be sure to get on. The line of cars and trucks can be long. Most of the time it's a first come, first served. It's also easy to take a car ferry for longer trips down the Adriatic coast. The main office for the stately Jadrolinija Lines is in Rijeka, on the waterfront at Riva 16. The friendly and helpful staff speaks English; 385-51-211-444. Good signage to the ferry is provided on the main highways. Public parking is at the south end of the harbor. Stock up on supplies at the morning market held close to this public parking area. You don't need to book a cabin if you don't mind sleeping on deck. There is a charge for deck chairs, but free bench seating is available. Bring blankets, inflatable pillows, and warm clothing. Whether you have a cabin or not, bringing food and beverages makes the trip more fun. Before boarding the ferry, arrange your car so that what you are taking on deck is easy to grab, because parking inside the ferry is tight, and once in it's hard to access your trunk. You won't be able to access your car during the cruise. The carfare will cost the same as one person.

Beaches here are often pebbly rather than sandy, making the sea crystal clear. Bring water shoes and an inflatable air mattress. There isn't much surf, so it is fun to bob around on an air mattress, which doubles as a comfortable resting surface on the beach. At many of the campgrounds,

you'll join lots of other people enjoying the sun and sea in a resort-like setting. Nudity is common, tennis is popular, and there are playgrounds for kids. There's always room for another tent, so you don't have to make reservations ahead for a tent even in the busy season.

There are more than 500 campgrounds in Croatia. Campgrounds close to towns and the resort-like ones often have 24-hour security. Gates at larger campgrounds are locked during the night, and quiet hours are maintained from midnight to 6 AM. It is often required to leave your passport or international camping card at the desk during your stay. Check out time is usually 1 PM. Cost for two persons, a car, and a tent in a non-resort-like setting is 12-17 euros;

indicated here as $$. Resort-like campgrounds cost 18-22 euros; $$$. Croatia has encouraged the development of "mini camps" which are usually in the backyards of people's homes. Hundreds of them are listed in the tourist booklet on camping. They often have special homey touches and are extra welcoming, but they are more difficult to find because signposting is limited. Enlist the help of the local grocery store staff by showing them the name and address.

ZAGREB CENTER

Capitol of Croatia, Zagreb, is graceful with linden tree-filled parks, charming cafes, and clattering streetcars. Movie producers use it to film stories that took place in the late 19th-century. Reflecting five centuries of Hapsburg rule, it feels like Budapest until you notice the orthodox domes. Begin a tour by walking or taking the funicular up to Gradec hill, located northwest of the main square Jelacica. To take the funicular, walk west of the square on Ilica for 200 meters and then follow signposting north for 100 meters. The hill is shady and elegant, with well-maintained mansions lining its cobblestone streets. The symbolic heart of Croatia is Markov trg, a quiet, small square in the center of Gradec hill. It has a cozy medieval feeling rather than one of ecclesiastical power. Its centerpiece, Crkva svetog Marka, (St Mark's Church) has a dramatic multicolor tile roof displaying the provincial coats of arms. The tiny hill is home to many of Zagreb's most interesting museums and churches. Good signage helps you find them but locals also will go out of their way to assist. Write down the Croatian spelling when asking for directions. I particularly enjoy the Mestrovic Atelier–the mansion of Croatia's most famous sculptor Ivan Mestrovic who lived here for 20 years. It has a particularly special lived-in intimacy. In the Galerija naivne (Gallery of Naive Arts), Croatian village life is the subject for most of the colorful works. To understand Zagreb's turbulent past, spend some time in the Mazej grada Zagreba (Museum of Zagreb). A renonovation gave it a classy look and interesting English text. Fruit and vegetable markets are always a good spot to get a feel for a place, and Zagreb's Dolac market is especially lively on Fridays when more vendors are there. It is only a short walk up the hill directly north of the main square Jelacica. Affordable wooden folk art, some engraved with the signature Croatian checkerboard design, make good mementos of your trip. A short walk east of here is the grandiose Archbishop's Palace. Croatian's are proud of their National Theatre and its lavish interior. Built during the Hapsburg Emperor Franz Josef-era, it's located at Trg marsala Tita (Marshall Tito Square).

Simple pleasures and century-old rhythms are experienced in easy day-trips into the countryside around Zagreb. People in these rural areas have a slower pace and live a simpler life that is rooted in the earth. Northwest of Zagreb lie the flat lands and hills of Prigorje. In summer, the hills are lush with orchards, cornfields, and vegetable gardens. Old wood barns and orange tile roofed farmhouses dot the country roads. Tiny chapels are perched on the highest point of a hill and are painted golden in the more prosperous villages. Farmers work in fields of corn and wheat. Chickens and turkeys scratch in the barnyards and beneath trees in plum and apple orchards. Men scythe grassy fields studded with daisies and buttercups. Younger boys and women rake swaths of grass. Wagons piled high with hay, swaying and nearly teetering, creak slowly down country roads. Directions: Drive north of Zagreb on A2/E59 for 6km in the direction of Zapresic. Just after driving over the railway overpass, exit for Zapresic. Follow signposting south and then north for 2km to Zapresic. Continue through town in the direction of Senkovec (the Slovenia border) for 3km to Prigorje. Charming Samobor was built like an Austrian town, with ochre facades and steep slate roofs. Colorful flower and vegetable gardens surround the old brick and wood houses that co-mingle with newer ones. In the market place, you can buy flavorful cheese, savory meat pies, and soft pretzels glazed with salt. On the drive up, the hills are dense with oak, walnut, maple, and beech. Directions: On the outskirts of western Zagreb, exit A2/E59 at Rakitje. Follow signposting for Samobor for 14km.

You'll need a good current map of Zagreb. Roads are still under-construction, and some are only party finished. Signage can be confusing or lacking. Before entering the city, if you haven't already purchased one, purchase a city map at a gas station and examine it carefully. Write down all the exits you'll be passing and the ones you want to use. Draw a simple map showing the major and border towns in all directions and the exits you want to use. A large public parking area is close to the open-air Dolac market, which is a good place to stock up on supplies. It's down the street from St. Stephens Church, on Kapitol. The information office is located on the southeast corner of the main square Jelacica, in the historic area. Use the church's twin spires as a guide.

▲**Camping:** • South of the city, close to the intersection of E65 and E59 and the suburb of Lucko. Because of the netting of the major highways, this campground can be frustrating to enter. It is located on A2/E59, just north of the suburb of Lucko, next to the southbound side of A2/E59 at the reststop called Plitvicka. If you are heading north on A2/E59, it is not easy to exit and get onto the other side of the highway to go south. The intersection of A2/E59 and A1/E65 is a large, very busy toll station and is unforgiving. (You can ask to go in the other direction, but you must pay the toll in both directions and turn around carefully). From the Zagreb airport, near Vel. Gorica, drive north in the direction of Zagreb centrum. Cross over the Sava River bridge and continue north for 4km. Turn west just after crossing the railway tracks, following signposting for Ljubljana (Slovenia). Drive 11km paralleling the railway tracks. Exit onto E59, following signposting for Karlovac. Drive 7km. The campground is part of Motel Plitvicka. Camping Motel Plitivice (01-6530-444); large, restful spot with lots of shade trees even though it's by a major highway; good showers and toilets; friendly English-speaking staff; open April-Sept; $$. Important note: The rest stop store usually has campstove gas but other supplies are limited. Shop before you get to the campground because driving to Lucko for supplies and then getting back to the campground is very confusing.

Duga Resa

This garden-like setting is one of my favorite inland spots in Croatia. A mix of farmlands, hills, orchards, vineyards, forests, and villages hug both sides of the Mreznica River as it flows south-west of Karlovac. Backroads, meandering pleasantly from one village to another, make perfect walking paths. It's a popular area with cyclists, paddlers, picnickers, swimmers, fisherman and bird watchers. Bicycle and canoe rentals are available and in late spring there is enough water for white water rafting.

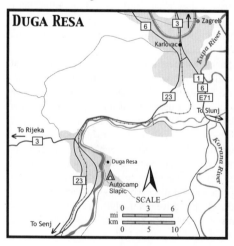

▲**Camping:** • About 46km southwest of Zagreb, exit A1/E/65/71 at the south end of Karlovac for Senj/Rijeka and then Duga Resa. At the fork of 3 and 23, fol-low signposting south for Senj for 4km, mostly along railroad tracks. Then follow signposting for Mreznick Brig. Cross over the one-way wood bridge (okay for smaller caravans) to the campground. Autocamp Slapic (47 854 700); lovely setting on a grassy meadow next to the river; new; beau-tifully built and carefully maintained with many special touches; small café and bar; canoe rental; barbecues; nearby bike rental; open April-Oct; $$$. Important note: Several trains run to and from Zagreb from the village every day. Consider using this lovely campground as a base for seeing the sights around Zagreb.

Plitvice National Park

Shimmering with sapphire lakes and laced with tumbling waterfalls, this sylvan wonderland consists of sixteen interlinking lakes stepping down the face of a gently sloping mountain. Unobtrusive wood walkways thread along countless leaf-fringed waterfalls and across bubbling rivers following the cascading water. Mist-thickened air is ribboned with rainbows and, depending on the season, waterfalls thunder or present just misty veils. UNESCO-listed and protected, the park is shady with beech, fir, and spruce and sweet with bird song. Shuttle buses take walkers to various entrances. Entrance two and hike "H"–my favorite–begins with serene cascades and quiet lagoons that lead to turquoise Lake Kozjak, shrouded on three sides by deciduous trees. The large, grassy meadow at the north end makes a good place to join Croatians and visitors relaxing, picnicking, and swimming. A self-service café, souvenir shop and restrooms are available. Most people catch the little ferry, boarding just off the walking path, to get across Lake Kozjak but a shady walking path also follows along the lake. Beyond here, the cascades become more dramatic, with larger waterfalls falling off the limestone stairways. Gradually everything becomes more dramatic and ultimately climaxes like a Beethoven symphony. The path makes a gradual climb up at the end, with several places to rest and take in the view. Directions: The park has two entrances, 7km apart. Entrance One is located on the north end, closer to Zagreb. Entrance Two is at the south end, closer to Zadar. Both entrances are on the same road, A1/E71. If you buy a ticket at Entrance Two, follow the path that skirts the food and souvenir shops. Walk through the woods and then across the pedestrian bridge over A1/E71. Then follow the path past the hotel to the bus shuttle station. Tell the driver you want hike "H".

Directions from Zagreb: Drive south in the direction of Karlovac on A1/E65 for 41km. From Karlovac follow signposting south on 4 in the direction of Split and Plitvicka for 15km. At the fork continue south on A1/E71 in the direction of Slunj and Plitvicka, and drive 85km to park entrance number one. The drive is particularly beautiful, with lush hillsides hugging meadows cheery with buttercups where farmers and their families carefully tend neat rows of crops. On the weekends, local restaurants spit-roast pigs and lambs on outside barbeques. Your taste buds will tingle as you pass by so plan to take time to join the Croatians in one of their most heartfelt traditions.

Directions from Zadar: Drive east 38km to the fork with the mainland coast road, E75. Continue east, then north for 36km on the new autostrata in the direction of Gracac/Plitvicka. Take the exit for E71, drive 90km in the direction of Korenica/Plitvicka to park Entrance Two.

▲**Camping:** 6km north of Entrance One on the Zagreb road A1/E71. Camping Korana (53-751-015); huge; lovely setting on grassy, tree shaded hillsides; lots of tranquil space; well run; restaurant; store; can be a long walk to shower and toilets; office/security open 24 hours; open May-Sept;. $$$ • 3km north of the Korana campground. Close to Grabovac on E/65/71. ATG Camping (47 784 077); small; on a hill well shaded with trees; simple; small sites; restful; open June-Aug; $$

Istria

Close to Italy and Austria, the northern end of coastal Croatia was settled during the Bronze Age. Since that time, many have claimed the land. Because a protected harbor provided shelter for fishing boats and access for merchant vessels, a lively trade and cosmopolitan atmosphere developed. Fields are fertile and the climate is ideal for growing grapes so wine making prospers. The area is a longtime favorite of European vacationers–particularly Italians–who love its sunny warm weather and crystal clear waters. Thus the Istrian culture has a pleasant sprinkling of the flavors of Venice and Rome. As evidence of their early settlement, Istrians proudly exhibit their ancient Glagolitian script in charming museums and churches. These exhibits are particularly meaningful to a country where their language was once forbidden by various subjugators. On warm summer nights, the seaside towns hum with streams of people and lively music. In the interior, red-roofed towns and villages quietly drape down steep-sided hilltops like orange cake frosting. Park outside the smaller ones and walk in.

Porec has a picturesque setting on the north edge of a fingerling overlooking the sea, halfway down the western side of the Istrian peninsula. Early Christians established themselves here and built the Ephrasian Bascilica, now a main attraction. Byzantine and ablaze with golden mosaics

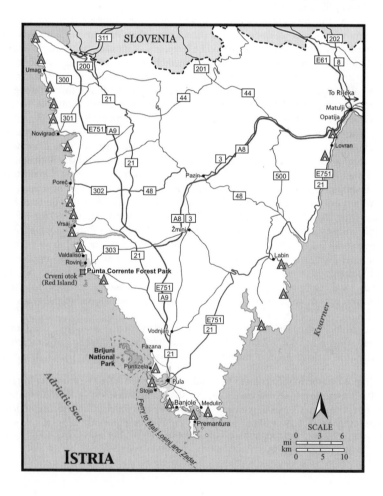

and gracefully sculpted columns, it is the earliest example of a triple-apsed church in Western Europe. UNESCO has listed it as a World Cultural Heritage Site. The Porestina Folk Museum, housed in the Sincic Palace, has a good collection of artifacts, and presents lively summer festivals. Stop by the tourist office on the east side of the old town for information and event ticketing for the whole Istrian peninsula–a large tourist resort area; www.pulainfo.hr. Wind surfing, kayaking, scuba diving, snorkeling, and cycling are all popular sports with rental equipment is available. Check with staff at the campground.

▲**Camping:** The many campgrounds in the area are huge, resort-like places, most with areas for nudist camping. Drive south of Porec on the coastal road and take your pick. Open April-Oct; $$$.

Rovinj rises up dramatically from the edge of the sea in a collage of faded orange and ocher waterfront buildings. St. Euphemia, the largest Baroque building in Istria, sits on top of a hill looming lord-like over a knot of houses lining miniscule alleyways and stairways. Thread your way through these to find charming piazzas that are perfect for resting and absorbing the local scene. The long winding waterfront is lined with cafes spilling out onto the sidewalks and brightly colored market boats sell sponges and affordable shell-adorned mementos. Rovinj is considered the art center for Istria and hosts a well-known open-air art show in mid-August. Artists show off their work on Bregovita ulica, a covered passageway decorated with frescoes. The worthwhile aquarium located along the seawall northeast of town gives you a chance to examine the varied local sea-life. South of Rovinj, the jagged coastline is thick with a rich forest of allepo, cedar, and silver fir pines so sea breezes have a heady pine fragrance. Turn into Punta Corrente Forest Park for a nice place to swim and picnic, or take the ferry to Crveni otok (Red Island) to breathe in air aromatic with myrtle and bay and to explore the 7th-century chapel.

▲**Camping:** The campgrounds here are huge resort-like places. Nudist camping, FKK, is popular, and most have separate areas. • These are both just north of Rovinj close to the village of Valdaliso. Camping Valdaliso (52 805 505) and Camping Porton Biondi (52 813 557); open April-Oct; $$$.

Pula's Arena is sixth in the world in size and is in remarkable condition. Built in 29 BC, it had four stone towers and a reservoir to provide water for the fountains. Although the spectator seats were reused for building material during the Middle Ages, it remains immensely impressive with two rows of 72 arches. Wine and olive production has always been important in Istria, and a pleasant museum here tells that story. Get tickets for a summer evening concert or the July film festival; www.pulainfo.hr. Directions: Northeast end of the main harbor area; open daily. Once a Roman forum, the old quarter's main square holds one of the best Roman temples outside of Italy, The Temple of Augustus. Its tall Corinthian columns celebrated a cult of the emperor and the temple houses a permanent exhibit of Roman artifacts. Climb to the top of the hill to the Venetian Fortress for splendid views. If you have time, visit the historical museum. It concentrates on the People's War of Independence as well as the Istrian struggle with the Italians, Austrians, and Germans. Then walk out onto the ramparts for another superb view; open daily.

An archipelago of 14 islands, beautiful Brijuni has lured the wealthy for centuries. In elaborate gardens and luxurious villas they hosted famous guests who sent back gifts of exotic plant and animal life. Thriving in their protected environment, these gifts now add an extra charm to a visit here. Tito was the last resident, and his fabulous yachts, villa, and sculpture garden are worth seeing. To go, take the morning 3-hour escorted tour of the islands from Fazana, north of Pula; www.np-brijuni.hr or 052 525 888. Excursion boats from the Pula waterfront also ply the waters of the archipelago, making for a scenic 5-hour trip.

▲**Camping:** • Across from Brijuni National Park, north of town in the village of Puntizela. Camping Puntizela (52 517 490); large; lovely setting; rock and pebble beach; April-Oct; $$. • Drive west on the south side of the harbor, almost to the tip. Exit for Stoja. Camping Stoja (52 387 144); huge; resort-like; part stone and part concrete beach area; open April-Oct; $$$.

Cres/Losinj

Besides its beauty and sunshine, the island of Cres is an important nesting place for griffon vultures, peregrine falcons, and both golden and snake eagles. The Eco-Centre Caput Insule (Ornithological Reserve) is just outside Beli, a picturesque little town on the northeastern coast. Your admission fee and interest in the eco-centre help promote the protection of these endangered birds. A seven-kilometer nature trail winds through the forest, pastureland, and an abandoned village. There is a good chance you'll see some raptors so bring binoculars; open daily. Directions: From Cres Town, drive north on a long high ridge. The road descends steeply, winding from one side of the narrow tip to the other. Follow signposting for Beli, located high on a knobby hill–a perfect place for the raptors. As you enter town, follow signposting west onto a narrow rocky road.

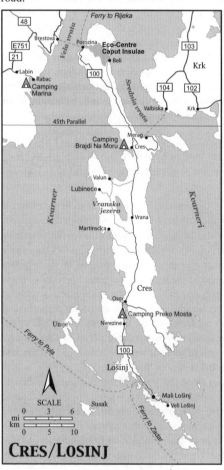

It is a thrill to know you are on the 45th parallel–the line that is equidistant from the equator and the North Pole. It is marked about 5 kilometers from Cres Town, on the east side of the road that runs from the ferry port town of Porozina to Cres Town. The oldest Glagolitic inscription dates from the 11th-century and can be seen on the Valun Tablet built into the wall of the parish church in the village of Valun. Though small and partly in Latin, this inscription is significant to the Işterians. It marks the beginning of their Glagolitian ancestry in Croatia. Directions: Drive south of Cres Town on the main road for 8km, turning west along the Bay to Valun for 6km more. The oldest settlement on Cres is Lubenice. Now almost completely abandoned, it is picturesque and photogenic in its hilltop setting and locals have named it Sleeping Beauty's Castle. Directions: 7km southwest of Valun. The town of Osor, on the southern tip of Cres, hosts summer events and has an interesting sculpture and music exhibition.

Losinj's harbor at Mali Losinj is a blend of pine forests, gardens, and lovely hotels and is considered one of the most beautiful harbors on the Adriatic. Though built up for tourism, it is tastefully controlled. Spend some time cycling or walking on the picturesque path from Mali Losinj to Veli Losinj or cycle on backroads in the countryside, rentals are available. Spend a restful half-day on an excursion boat to the island of Susak.

▲**Camping:** • On the island of Cres: On the bay just west of town. Camping Brajdi Na Moru (51 840 522) smaller; lovely location on the beach; can be crowded; open May-Sept; $$$. • On the island of Losinj: At the northwest side of the bay between Losinj and Cres near the town of Nerezine, by the bridge. Camping Preko Mosta (51 237 350), smaller; shady; pebble beach; $$. • On the mainland, across from Cres. 15km east of Labin on the Bay of Rabac. Camping Marina (052-872-226); small, nice location; $$.

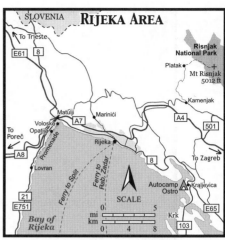

Rijeka Area

Venetians, Austrians, Turks, Hungarians, and Italians have all vied for this important port and gateway to Europe. Shipbuilding, paper manufacturing, and chemical production are important industries. Jadrolinija Ferry Lines has their main office here on the waterfront at Riva 16. The helpful English-speaking staff provides information and sells tickets for ferries up and down the coastline and farther on. A large public parking area is provided on the south end of the port, just north of the bustling open-air market on Veridieva Street, a great place to pick up supplies. The Moorish-style façade of the Capuchin Church found a couple of streets behind the waterfront, is intriguing and northeast of the wide pedestrian street Korzo, the octagonal Baroque Church of St. Vitus is worth seeking out. Built on the site of a 9th-century church, it is squeezed picturesquely into a tiny piazza. To enter the churches, visit in the morning when they are open for worship. The most popular historic site in Rijeka is Trsat Castle. Built on a hill overlooking the harbor, the castle site was built on first by the Romans and followed by Austrians, who hired a Venetian builder. Now the castle hosts art exhibits and summer festivals. Directions: It's signposted off 12/E65. Both the maritime and historical museums are housed in the former Governor's Palace located down the hill from the castle. Royal and wealthy Europeans once flocked to fashionable resorts in this beautiful city, and it is still elegant with lush flower-filled parks and grand hotels. You can enjoy the view of luxury for free by walking on the scenic pathways. The 12km seaside promenade from Volosko to Louvan–a beautiful blending of the sparkling Adriatic, lush vegetation, and colorful flowers–is recommended. It's particularly nice at sunset and sunrise. For a mountain experience featuring panoramic views, pines forests, and hiking trails, drive out of Rijeka for 26km to Risnjak National Park and Platak, the area's recreational center. Directions: Take E65 for 13km in the direction of Zagreb. Exit north onto a smaller road signposted for the park. After 6km, at the village of Kamenjak, drive up the mountain road for about 10km to Platak.

▲**Camping:** • South of the city on the Ostro peninsula in Kralijevica. Drive south of Rijeka on 8/E65 for 19km. Follow signposting in Kraljevic for camping. Autocamp Ostro (51-281-404); older, but pleasant for a short stay; restaurant; open May-Sept; $$.

Krk/Senj/Rab

A huge concrete bridge stretching from the mainland to this island makes access easy for vacationers. An excursion to Krk Town to see the 12th-century Romanesque cathedral makes a nice change of pace from the beach. Park outside the old town and walk south along the narrow main thoroughfare of Strossmayera to the Cathedral of the

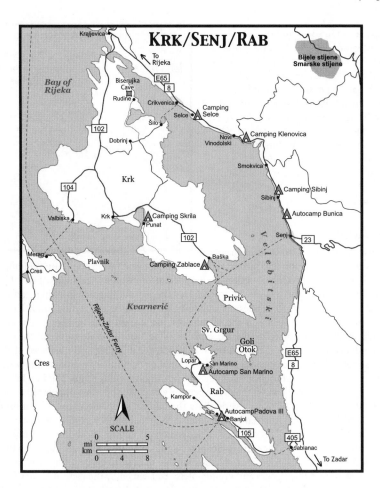

Assumption; open mornings daily. To visit the Biserujka Cave, drive out to a hillside village of Dobrinj, twenty kilometers from Krk Town. The cave is on the bay facing the mainland, 6km northeast of Dobrinj in the village of Rudine.

▲**Camping**: • Midway on the west side of the island, on a small bay in the village of Punat. From the bridge drive 19km south on the main road 102 to Krk Town. Continue on the main road for another 4km. Exit south on a small road for Punat and drive 3km. Camping Skrila (51 844 678); lovely location; popular with boaters; open May-Sept; $$. At the south end of the island, in Baska. Camping Zablace (51 656 111); huge, no trees; no ambiance; popular with families open April-Sept; $$$.

A fishing village in the late 1800s, Crikvenica is now a popular beach and spa town. In August, swimmers flock to town to participate in or watch the Marathon Swim to Silo on Krk Island.

▲**Camping**: • South of town on E65 in the village of Selce. Camping Selce (51-764 038); convenient enroute camping; large; open April-Oct; $$. • 10km south of Novi Vinodolski. Camping Klenovica (51 796 251); convenient enroute camping; open May-Sept; $$.

One of the sunniest places in Europe, Rab Island has attracted sun worshipers and tourism since the beginning of the 19th-century. Mild winters are due to a mountain range that protects it from cold northeastern winds. Although from the mainland it appears barren of vegetation, the island's peaceful roads wind through terraced olive groves and vineyards, and into villages where small white houses with red tile roofs shimmer in the warm sun. The sweet scent of rosemary, myrtle, and pine lingers in the air at campgrounds and along walking trails. The Romans built an important and beautiful port in Rab Town and it's a special treat to watch it turn golden in the sunset from the hillside overlooking the harbor. Seeing the three bell towers, the remains of a medieval wall, and ornate doorways make wandering through the old town's narrow streets and passageways especially interesting. The town's wealth was earned during the medieval period from breeding and raising silkworms. Crossbow enthusiasts will want to be here on July or August when skilled archers don medieval dress to celebrate the ancient skill at festivals. British King Edward VIII swam nude here in 1936, officially sanctioning nudist beaches. Large nudist beaches are found in Kandarola Bay and on the sheltered side of Kamenjak.

▲**Camping:** • At the north end, east of Lopar, exit the main road 29 for San Marino. Autocamp San Marino (51-775-133). • Close to Rab Town, exit 29 south of town for Banjol and follow signposting. Autocamp Padova III (51-724-355); They both are very large; popular with families; separate area for short-stay campers; May-Sept; $$.

At some points in your journey, you just need to take a deep breath of sea air, kick back, and discover unhurried pleasures. Because of a extra nice beach cove campground, Senj is a good place to do just that. The cove is perfect for swimming and snorkeling. The village has a nice morning market, and a fortress on the bluff above the village has a great view and makes a good hike destination. The fortress museum tells the story of the Uskoks, Croatians, and Bosnians who organized themselves in order to repel further encroachment by the Turks in the 16th-century.

▲Camping: • 5km north of Senj watch for signs for Bunica. Pull over into the parking area on the bluff above beach to plan your entrance to the campground. It descends steeply down to the beach. Autocamp Bunica (53 616 718); exquisite setting right at the edge of the sea; very small; tiny beach; beautifully landscaped; small terraced sites; restaurant; open May-Sept; $$. • 2km farther north in the village of Sibinj. Camping Sibinj (51 796 903); easier access for larger caravans; next to the road on the beach; open May-Sept; $$.

Velika/Paklenica National Park/Paj Island

Dramatic cliffs and outcrops tower over the boulder-strewn stream bubbling through this dramatic gorge. A moderately easy trail follows the stream with detours leading to stalactite-packed caverns and more difficult peaks. Plan to spend the day, and take time for refreshing dips in deeper natural pools that are lovely under dappled light. The pleasant streamside mountain hut, Sumarska kuca, sells simple snacks and beverages and makes a good destination for less energetic hikers. More energetic hikers can keep hiking up to Borisov Dom hut, which is the starting point for hikes up to major peaks. Rustic food and lodging are available here, and the setting plus a friendly ambiance will make you want to stay. Book reservations with the national park office; www.rivijera-paklenica.hr or 023 369 202. The cliffs along the gorge entrance are wildly popular with rock climbers from all over Europe. It's fun to hear their calls, echoing off the cliffs in many languages. Arrive early to get parking close to the gorge entrance. Parking attendants keep an eye on the cars and sell simple snacks. Directions: The park is 12km north of the intersection of coast road E65 and the road to the Zadar. Follow signposting at the southern edge of Starigrad. Drive through the village and on to the park entrance/toll booth. Purchase a map. Parking for the gorge is 2km farther on.

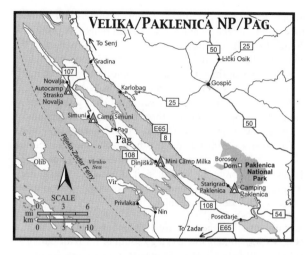

▲Camping: At the southern edge of Starigrad, next to
the Alan Hotel, close to the
park road on E65. Camping
Paklenica (23 209 062); simple;
convenient; pebble beach; open
May-Sept; $$.

The industrious and inventive
natives of Pag Island learned to
support themselves on their bar-
ren rocky isle by creating quality
products. Women made fine lace
and the men raised sheep and
farmed olives. Their distinctive
sheep cheese is carefully soaked in
olive oil and slowly aged in cool
stone. It is pleasant to wander the
grid of stone streets and see the lime, yellow, and white buildings where people are working and chat-
ting to neighbors. The Pag Carnival, held the end of July, is an excellent opportunity to photograph
musicians and dancers dressed in their elaborate traditional outfits. The island is heavily indented
with quiet cove beaches and sun-bleached fields are sprinkled with purple thistle. On hot afternoons
you can rest in the shade to the sounds of the sea and the humming of insects. It's peaceful and less
touristy than neighboring islands. A bridge from the mainland leads to the Zadar penninsula.

▲Camping: • 14km northwest of Pag Town in Simuni. Camp Simuni (23 697 441); partly
terraced; shade trees; large; popular with families; open May –Sept; $$.. • Farther north, just
south of Novalja. Autocamp Strasko Novalija (53-661-226); huge; partly nude; shade trees;
resort-like; open May-Sept; $$$. • 8km north of the small bridge that separates Pag from
Zadar in the minisule village of Dinjiska. Mini Camp Milka (23 691 069); charming 'back-
yard' camping place on the bay; lovely views of the sunset and sunrise; sweet homey touches;
open May-Sept; $.

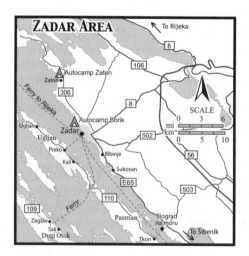

Zadar Area

A leading city on the Adriatic, Zadar has
had more than its share of incidents in which
outsiders took control of the city and the local
population. In the 2nd-century, the Romans
constructed a city wall, built a forum, a the-
ater, thermal baths, and sewers. Then, for
three centuries the Venetians ruled and used
Croatian forests and manpower to maintain
their own position as important ship builders.
In the 19th-century, Austrian rule mandated
that the Croatian language couldn't be spo-
ken. Severely damaged during World War
II, Zadar was raised from ruins by Croatians
and today is proudly free. The main attrac-
tion is round and Byzantine St. Donat, built
in the 9th-century on the site of the Roman

Forum. This drum-like structure has irregularly cross-shaped floors, slanted walls, and uneven angles. It was designed to measure time–in particular the spring and autumn equinoxes and the winter and summer solstices. Musical events are often hosted here; check with the tourist office.

While wandering don't miss appreciating the elegance of St. Mary's Church and the Benedictine Convent. Then head to the harbor to learn more about Croatian history at the National Museum. An exquisite sarcophagus of St. Simeon rests in the church named after him. The beautifully carved cedar burial box is covered with silver and gold plate. Directions: Follow signposting to the old town then pass through the old gate and continue past the five-sided medieval tower. St Simeon is just a bit farther, at the east end of Siroka Ulica. St. Donat and the convent are farther up on the west end of the spit. A colorful morning market is held in the square at the eastern end of the harbor.

KORNATI NATIONAL PARK

▲**Camping**: • In the beach town of Borik, 3km north of the city. Autocamp Borik (23-332-074); nice location on the town's beach; older; warm showers; open May-September; $$. • North of town 10km in the direction of Nin. Exit towards the beach and the town of Zaton. Autocamp Zaton (23-280-280); a sports center; large; popular with families; open May-Sept; $$$.

Kornati National Park

Each of Kornati's 89 islands is isolated and almost barren. Once covered with forest and meadows, the trees were cut for Venetian shipbuilding and the grass was overgrazed by sheep. Today it's crisscrossed by long stone walls that once sheltered the sheep. It's turquoise waters and sheltered coves entice kayakers who come to paddle pristine waters and camp in coves; www.huck-finn.hr or www.adriatic-sea-kayak.com. Excursion boats take day-trippers out to the west side for swimming, lunch and short hikes. Boats leave from Biograd-na-moru and Murter and can be arranged for at the campground office.

▲**Camping**: • On quiet cove beach in Pakostane. Camping Nordsee (23 381 438); pebble beach; shade trees; popular with families; open May-Sept; $$. On the lake next to Pakostane. Camping Crkvine (23 381 433); grass and shade; quiet; open May-Sept; $$.

▲• **Camping Enroute** on E/65 between Zadar and Sibenik.• 28km southeast of Zadar, in Biograd na moru. Camping Crvena Luka, 3km southeast of town, (023-383-106); terraced sites; convenient; open May-September; $$

Sibenik/Krka National Park

Worth a detour, the premier sight in Sibenik is the Renaissance Cathedral of St. Jacob. Built over many years by Italian-trained Croatian artisans, the limestone cathedral is one of Croatia's most beautiful. Enhanced by a majestic dome and finely decorated with sculpture, it has a unique exterior freize of 71 heads. The cathedral also has a notable collection of religious art in its treasury. It is considered one of the largest church ever constructed without the use of brick or wood supports.

ŠIBENIK/KRKA NATIONAL PARK

Directions: At the north end of the harbor and old town; open daily 8 AM to noon and 6 PM–8 PM. The town is well endowed with churches, many with fine organs. Perhaps you'll be lucky enough to catch someone practicing or giving a recital. The Children's Festival held the last week in June and first week in July features parades workshops, music, and theatre and is fun with children or without.

▲Camping: • 20km south of Sibenik just north of the pleasant town of Primosten. Camping Adriatic (22 581 111); shady and peaceful right on the water; medium size; terraced; May-Sept; $$.

Famed for its waterfalls and beautiful lakes, nearby Krka National Park entices one to extend their stay in the Sibenek area. During its flow to the sea, the Krka River has cut narrow, deep canyons into the limestone. Travertine barriers form when the mosses and algae roots became encrusted with calcium carbonate. These *buks* (barriers) have created waterfalls, the most majestic of which is Stradinski Buk. There are two entrances and it is fun to see the falls from both. Start with the Skradin entrance. From here, you can take a 25-minute scenic boat ride through the dramatic canyon and up to the grand Stradinski Buk. At the Lozovac entrance, you walk on wood walkways over gushing rivers and bubbly miniature waterfalls to the concluding sight of multiple cataracts crashing down. Directions: From Sibenik, drive northwest on E/65 to the edge of town, then east into the mountains on 11/20 in the direction of Bilice for 10km. At the village of Tomilja, exit onto a small road sign-posted Skradinski buk, and drive 8km farther. The drive up has panoramic views.

Trogir/Split/Omis Area

Still medieval in appearance, Trogir's engaging small town is a grand achievement in stonework and was awarded a UNESCO listing. The old historic town is on a minuscule island connected to the mainland by a bridge. Visit in the morning to experience the glorious Renaissance, triple-naved Cathedral St. Lovro from the inside as well as the outside. Intricate sculptural work, particularly on the west portal, is a masterful running together of iconography and scenes from legends and folk traditions. Park on the mainland, and walk across the bridge continuing south into the fine-looking Cathedral Square. Stop by the tourist office in the Cipiko Palace to purchase a guide for your walk and to inquire about the town's summer calendar of classical and folk music events. Make the Town Museum, housed in a mansion on the north side of the square, your next stop. With valuable insight gained from the museum and a guide in hand, you will appreciate the fine details seen in the many of well preserved 13th through 15th-century buildings. At the southwest end of the island, Kamerlengo Fortress looms in medieval haughtiness and hosts summer outdoor movies, theater, and musical performances.

▲Camping: • 2kmwest of Trogir, at the west edge of the village of Seget. Camping Seget (21 880 450; older but the areas best for Trogir; on the beach; doable bike ride to Trogir; some shade; open May-September $$.

As you walk through the gates of Split's famous Diocletian Palace that was built by the Roman emperor Dioletian in 245 AD, you pass into antiquity. The intimate town within the castle walls,

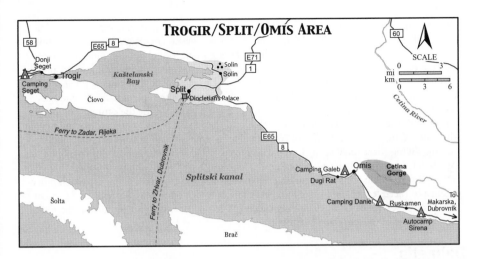

TROGIR/SPLIT/OMIS AREA

still houses 3,000 residents. Shops, cafes, and restaurants are set closely as together as cells in a honeycomb. Purchase a guide from the palace office, and begin your tour at Ivan Mestrovic's enormous and commanding statue of Gregorius of Nin, Croatia's 10th ¯century hero. Don't miss Diocletian's mausoleum, now the Cathedral St Domnius–domed and octagonal on the outside but circular inside and decorated with rows of columns. Throughout the palace-town are remnants of older buildings, weathered porticoes, and Corinthian columns. Directions: From E/65, follow the signs to centrum and then palace, where there is public parking and an information office along the quay. The entrance to the palace is down a narrow passageway on the building's east side.

Split is graceful with colorful gardens and shade trees. Wander behind the palace to Republic Square, where summer music festivals take place. Drive up to Marijan hill to visit the villa of Croatia's most famous sculptor, Ivan Mestrovic. Now a gallery for his work, it is an elegant setting of garden and villa. On the same street, you can visit the Natural History Museum or hike down the hill to the beach.

The archaeological site of the ancient Roman city of Solin is Croatia's most important dig. The settlement was once the Roman governmental headquarters for Dalmatia and still has a working aquaduct. Purchase an English guide. Directions: Drive out of the old town onto E65, heading west in the direction of Trogir. At the webbing of highways 8 and 1 is a grassy divider with a statue of the city's patron saint. At the northwest corner of this intersection, follow the brown and white signposting for Solin.

▲**Camping:** • See Trogir or Omis

Omis is a favorite kick back place for me. One of the campgrounds is so great I could plan a trip around it. The little village has a appealing morning market, a charming labyrinth of alleyways, tiny chapels, little cafes, and enough tourism for you to meet other international travelers. Take the scenic boat ride up the river into the gorge. Lunch or dinner is special at the large outdoor-indoor restaurant Radmanove Mlinice, where the boat stops for a while. Huge quantities of delicious bread are baked in an immense wood-fired oven and the food served is fresh and tasty. Good opportunities for birding occur on the well-marked trail that leads farther east from the restaurant.

Just down the coast, close to Makarska, is a narrow steep road with hairpin turns leading up to Mount Biokovo, Croatia's highest peak. I suggest you drive part way, park, and then walk up as far as you like while enjoying great panoramic views. Directions: Exit E65 south of Makarska onto 512 in the direction of Vrgorac then drive 6km passing through the village of G. Tucepi. Park and hike up the narrow steep road.

▲**Camping** • 8km south of Omis. This campground is very small and very special. Call or e-mail ahead to reserve. The friendly owner speaks several languages fluently, including English. An entrance is found on the either side of a small tunnel but cars move fast here and there is no room to pull off. So note the entrances, pass them, then turn around and come back, giving the drivers behind you plenty of time to realize that you are turning. The campground hangs on a terraced cliff and sites are on individual ledges with just enough space to be comfortable. Turn down hill from E65 and park outside the campground. Check with the office to see what is available, and then make plans to execute driving to your site. Auto Camp Sirena (385 2187 0266 e-mail autocamp-sirena@st.hinet.hr); spectacular setting; diving rock; small sandy beach with grotto; small store; restaurant close by; open April-Oct; $$. • In the village of Ruskamen, 5km south of Omis. Camping Daniel (218-71-400); very small; tents only; parking separate from camping; tents are next to each other along a terraced ledge; good place to meet fellow campers; open May-September; $$. • On the northwest edge of Omis. Camping Galeb (21 864 430); easy to access; next.to the road on a sand/pebble beach; open May-Sept; $$.

Dalmatia

Hugging the sea, the breathtaking coastal drive from Split to Dubrovnik is reminiscent of the drive through California's Big Sur area. Craggy cliffs hug tiny bays with lovely beaches and little red-roof villages cascade down hillsides, acacia in full golden glory spills from mountainside, and the scent of pines perfumes the air. This strip of coast is just across the sea from Italy and is in the same latitude as Tuscany. It has a climate of long rain free summers, and the temperature of the sea is warm enough to swim in from early May until late September. Croatia's side of the Adriatic is usually glassy smooth and because of natural currents is one of the cleanest in the Mediterranean.

The southwestern tip of the peaceful Peljesac pennisula has long stretches of beaches. It's a popular area for vacationing families who come for a week or more to enjoy wind surfing, swimming, and boating. The Franciscan Monastery in Orebic is perched on a hillside overlooking the sea and has long been an important place of worship for the fishing community. To see it, take the walking trail from Hotel Bellevue up the hillside to the monastery, where the views are panoramic. From here, you can walk farther on a marked trail up Mt. Ilija.

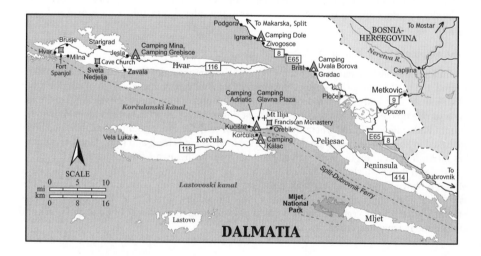

▲**Camping:** • From the main road out of Orebic, drive west in the direction of Kuciste. Both these campgrounds all have nice shady locations on the beach and are open June-August. • Camping Adriatic (20 713 420); medium size; $$. • Camping Glavna Plaza (20 713 399); smaller; $$. There are many others.

Dotted with vineyards and olive trees and aromatic with rosemary and lavender, Korcula Island is less expensive and chic than Hvar Island. Its Old Town seems like a labyrinth in a Moroccan bazaar but the zigzag streets were designed to block the strong eastern winds that assault the town in winter. Gothic arches and Renaissance towers turn golden in the setting sun and add romance to an evening walk. Every Thursday in summer local dancers perform the Moreska, a lively and colorful presentation accompanied by bagpipes and drums. The dance is based on a timeless story–the competition for the love of a beautiful girl–and takes place in the main square. A boat ride to Mljet National Park, a lush island covered with Aleppo pines and home to the endangered monk seals, can be booked for a day's excursion. Renting a bicycle or kayak are good ways to enjoy the island's beauty.

▲**Camping:** • In Korcula Town, close to the ferry landing, follow signage to Bos Repos Hotel. Camping Kalac (20-711-182); partly terraced; convenient to the town; June-Aug; $$.

Surrounded by Romanesque walls and elaborate cathedrals, Hvar Town has the ambiance of Venice without the crowds. It's chic and sophisticated, with picturesque cafes, a palm-lined harbor, and lovely Renaissance architecture. The bells of St Steven chime sweetly. The upper level of the arsenal is one of the oldest theatres still standing in Europe. Hvar has become a top vacation spot for Europeans because of its reliable sunshine and lovely cove beaches. Pedestrian-only alleyways lead through time-polished marble squares flanked by centuries old Venetian mansions. Town stairways overlook the sea and the surrounding archipelago of islands. Walk up the hill through the cool pine forest to the Fortress Spanjol, taking in the cheerful sounds of village life along your way. Inspect the excellent collection of ancient *amphora* (clay vessels used to hold wine or oil) in the old barracks, and take in the sublime view of tiered terra-cotta roofs and the deep blue sea. When you return to the harbor stop at the inviting 15th-century Franciscan monastery and its cypress garden, then examine the priceless collection of medieval books and nautical charts and view a striking painting of the Last Supper. Scenic drives around the island are redolent with the perfume of commercially grown lavender. Renting a moped is popular. Milna Bay, beautiful with sandy beaches and luxurious villas, is located 6 kilometers east from Hvar Town on the beach road. From Starigrad to Brusje, the countryside is blanketed with vineyards. The drive to Zavala on the south coast, located 6 kilometers from Jelsa, is recommended, and the deserted sandy beaches beg you to stop. Six kilometers west from Zavala in Sveta Nedjelja, you can hike up a hill to explore an ancient cave-church.

▲**Camping:** • On the east side of the island close to the village of Jelsa, 10km from Stari Grad in a pleasant little bay with yacht harbor. These are both smaller and are open June-Aug. Camping Mina (21 761 210); $$. Camping Grebisce (21 761 191); $$.

Dubrovnik

Massive, curvilinear 14th-century walls completely enclose graceful historic Dubrovnik, where proud, wealthy, and clever merchants once made lively trade agreements with both Constantinople and Venice. A walk along the top of the city wall is a must. One side of the wall reaches steeply to the sea, seducing your gaze to the azure blue water. The other side of the wall treats your gaze to enchanting gardens, side streets, and red-tile roof tops. Both the tourist office and the stairs leading to the wall are directly across from the Onofrio Well and Fountain. The

Franciscan Monastery features lovely cloisters and has an outstanding apothecary collection dating 15th to the 17th-centuries. The Renaissance palaces and cathedral hint at the wealth of former times. As you walk the wall, note the Lovrijenic fortress just outside. The inscription over the entrance gate reads "*Non Bene Pro Toto Libertas Venditur Auro*" which means "Freedom cannot be sold, not for all the treasure in the world." Use a guidebook to enjoy this historic tiny city in detail. Public parking is nearby, but plan to arrive early in the morning or late in the afternoon to miss the busloads of tourists. From mid-July to mid-August, Dubrovnik hosts a prestigious summer musical festival. Attending the open-air productions in such an ancient setting on a warm summer evening under a canopy of stars is a delight; www.http://dubrovnick.laus.hr or 020-426-354.

▲**Camping:** • 15km north of Dubrovnik just up the hill from Aboretum Gucetic, in Trsteno. Camping Trsteno (20 751 060); small; lovely setting in an olive grove; short walk to the beach; gently sloping terrain; April-Oct; $$. • 13km north of Dubrovnik in Orasac. Camping Rudine (20 891 228); medium size; stairs to pebble beach; partly terraced; shady; May-Sept; $$. • Just outside the historic area in Dubrovnik. Camping Solitudo (20 448 686); new; convenient; level ground; open May-Sept; $$$. • 10km south of Dubrovnik on E80, in the village of Mlini. Camping Kate (20 487 006); smaller; nice location on the mountainside; special touches; solar energy; April-Oct; $$.

▲**Camping Enroute to/from Dubrovnik.** • On E/65 across from the island of Hvar, 18km south of Makarska, in the village of Zivogosce. Camping Dole (21-628-749); large; easy access, pebble beach; open May-Sept; $$. • Four kilometers north of Gradac in the village of Brist. Camping Uvala Borova (21 629 033); medium size; nicely terraced; shady with pines; open June-Sept; $$.

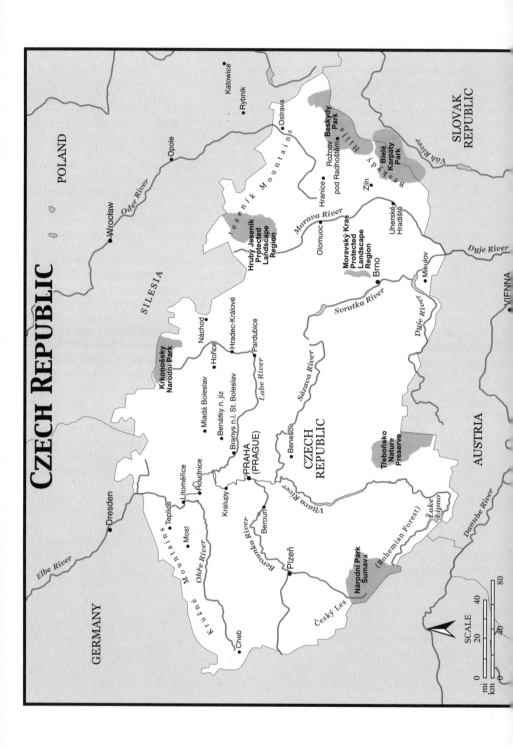

CZECH REPUBLIC

POLAND

SLOVAK REPUBLIC

GERMANY

AUSTRIA

SILESIA

Katowice

Rybnik

Opole

Wrocław

Dresden

VIENNA

Ostrava

Beskydy Park

Rožnov pod Radhoštěm

Hranice

Olomouc

Zlín

Uherské Hradiště

Bielé Karpaty Park

Mikulov

Brno

Beskyd Hills

Bilé Karpaty

Morava River

Moravský Kras Protected Landscape Region

Hrubý Jeseník Protected Landscape Region

Jeseník Mountains

Svratka River

Dyje River

Dyje River

Náchod

Hořice

Hradec-Králové

Pardubice

Mladá Boleslav

Benátky n. jiz

Branýs n.l. St. Boleslav

Litoměřice

Roudnice

Kralupy

PRAHA (PRAGUE)

Beroun

Plzeň

Cheb

Krkonošský Narodni Park

Labe River

Sázava River

Benešov

CZECH REPUBLIC

Třeboňsko Nature Preserve

Teplice

Most

Litoměřice

Krušné Mountains

Ohře River

Berounka River

Vltava River

Český Les

Národni Park Šumava

(Bohemian Forest)

Lake Lipno

Danube River

Elbe River

Oder River

Váh River

SCALE

mi 0   20   40
km 0   40   80

Czech Republic

www.czechtourism.com

Time has beautifully mellowed the texture and color of the Czech Republic. An elaborate succession of nobles and royalty built hundreds of castles impregnating them with romance and legend and testifying to the Czech's bid for "living happily ever after." Many are UNESCO listed and their silhouettes add grace to an already splendid countryside. Weekend folk festivals bring locals out in traditional dress for hotly contested folk dance competitions. Kayakers and canoeists flock to the rivers, where they camp out and sing around campfires. Rock climbers and hikers head north to areas that vie in beauty with Canyonlands USA. A light-hearted ambiance is fostered throughout the country by the production of their world-famous beers. There's more to the richly historic Czech Republic than Praha and thermal bath resorts.

Driving is not a problem. Roads are well signposted, and outside major cities the traffic is light. Fuel is readily available. With the exception of Praha, it is easy to drive into historic areas and to park. Museums are inexpensive. In harvest season, farmers' wives and children sell the fresh bounty along the roadsides. Large shopping malls have found their way to the here and are seen along main roads on the outskirts of major cities. Cash machines located outside banks and in the arcade of large shopping areas provide local currency.

The Czechs adore the outdoors, and you can join them camping happily with their families in scenic areas. Plumbing and maintenance is casual but the scenery and relaxed friendliness are exceptional. Most campgrounds charge under 15 euros for two persons, a car, and a tent, noted as $. Close to major sights, car-camping for two is closer to 18 euros noted as $$. In the Praha area it will be around 22 euros, noted as $$$.

PRAHA

Praha reminds me of a beautiful brooch, carefully treasured and handed down by grandmother to granddaughter. The Vltava River and its ornate bridges are the brooch's finely worked gold edging, the spires of the castle, the dome of St. Nicholas, the intriguing roof of the synagogue, and the curved roof of the National Theatre are the multicolored gems. As you cross the Charles Bridge–a friendly Main Street-like pederstrian bridge it feels like you've entered a country fair. Next to a violinist playing Mozart is an artist painting scenes of the bridge. Farther down, two girls boogy to the beat of a live rock group next to a jeweler selling handmade earrings; while Baroque statues gaze down with grandparent-like tolerance. Passing through the stately castle gate into the grandeur of the Castle District, brings on the sounds and smells of medieval Praha–the clip-clop of horse hooves are still heard, the raucous calls of vendors, the lusty smell of leather. Called the Hradcany, it is a tiny city with museums, galleries, and gardens in a setting of Baroque architecture. In Praha it's not the destination that is the most exciting part; it's little surprises found in nooks and crannies on the way that provide the fun. The tourist office is inside the castle gate.

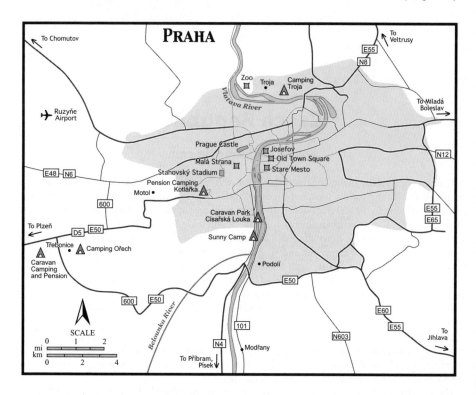

Friendly English-speaking staff can answer questions, and racks bulge with free maps and brochures about sights and cultural events

As you tread up the twisting narrow streets of Castle Hill, suddenly *The Castle*, written by Franz
Kafka, one of the Czech's most famous authors, makes sense. Like a magical kingdom, the romantic castle sprawls gloriously above the river with views of red-tile rooftops, domes, and spires. No
wonder it has become one of Europe's top movie locations. The castle's well-designed gardens grace
the architecture with trees and shrubs of contrasting colors, magnificent rhododendrons and azaleas, and ribbon flowerbeds. If you're here at noon, you'll witness a brass band of smartly dressed
guards parading in the first courtyard. St. Vitus Cathedral's tall, defiant pinnacles reach above a
foundation begun in the 14th-century but the cathedral was not completed until 1929. A long line
of architects left it finished in a variety of styles but the light streaming in through the rosette stain
glass is pure sublime. Be sure to see the world's largest sapphire dazzling alongside other beautiful
jewels in the treasury. What really gives the Old Royal Palace life, though, are the intriguing stories
about the sumptuous succession of royalty that lived there. Walk over to the northeast corner of the
Royal Garden where the *sgraffito* (fine etchings) in the ball court and lovely arcaded summerhouse
personalize its golden era; open daily. Before crossing back across the Charles Bridge, pause for a
rest and the view on Kampa, a slim little island close to the bridge. If you are a Kafka fan, follow the
signposting into the maze of cobblestone streets close to the northwest side of the bridge and find
the Kafka Museum. It's delightfully curated with fog and mystery–like his writing.

In the heart of the city, across the river from the castle, pastel-hued Baroque, Renaissance, and
Gothic buildings outline the Old Town Square. It's an inviting and whimsical stage-set populated
with street theatre, musicians, and vendors. Every 60 minutes for 400 years, Jesus, His Apostles, and
the skeletal figure of Death have paraded out of the tiny trap door of the famed Astronomical Clock
in tower of the Town Hall, reminding town folk to mend their ways before it is too late. Pay homage

to the dramatic Hus Monument by looking for the inscription, "*Pravda vitezi*" which means "Truth prevails." Reflecting on Czech history, you'll understand why the monument is special in the hearts of Czechs today. Try to view the baubles and spires of the Tyn Cathedral from afar, as it's boxed in among the houses. Binoculars will enable you to enjoy fine detail of all of the above.

The Old Jewish Quarter was once one of the most important Jewish centers in Europe. Twenty thousand souls are buried, nine to twelve coffins deep, in a cemetery of less than two acres. Headstones are tilted, fallen, and choked for space. Poignant drawings made by children in the Terezin prison camp cover the walls of several rooms in the Jewish Town Hall. Soft candlelight dimly lights the beautiful ribbed vaulting in the "Old-New" Synagogue–the oldest still in use in Europe today. Admire the exquisite ancient Torah, a parchment scroll of the Five Books of Moses. Jewish communities from all over Europe have donated treasured artifacts to the Quarter, making it a truly an amazing place; closed Saturday. Directions: Choose one of the congenial guides from those who stand at the Astronomical Clock each day.

Praha has long held music close to its heart. Three opera houses, two symphony halls, and many historical settings allow for regularly scheduled performances. Mozart finished *Don Giovanni* during summer visits to Villa Bertamka which was owned by an intimate friend. The piano he played and the rooms and study where he worked and enjoyed himself with his friends are open to wander through. Afterwards, you are treated to a violin-piano recital of his work; open daily. Directions: In the suburb of Smichov, south of Mala Strana. Recitals of Dvorak's operatic arias are performed at Villa Amerika, a Baroque mansion where his museum is located. The tourist office can help a select a performance that suits your taste from jazz to string quartets.

▲Camping:• **On the Plzen/Praha road E50:** • Follow signage to Centrum on Plzenska. Stay left down the hill watching for signposting for Pod Kotlarkou just after the fork with Vrchickeho. Turn north onto Pod Kotarkou. There's a gas station and bus stop at the turn-off. Drive northwest up the hill, and just before the large school on the south side exit onto Kotlarka. Pension Camping Kotlarka, Kotlarka 115, (42 2 5721 0604); my favorite for Praha; country setting in the city; very small and tranquil; part of an old vineyard; affliated with a small hotel; close to public transportation; small restaurant; open all year; $$. • These two camping places are located on the tiny island, Cisarska Louka, on the Vltava River just south of the historic area. Entering from Plizen on D5/E50 take exit 1 east onto 600 and drive 12km. Turn north following signposting for centrum and Smichov, staying right. Just off the major netting of roads watch carefully for signposting east to Cisarska Louka. Caravan Park Cisarska Louka (2 54 5682); open all year; $$$ and Praha Yacht Club Caravan Park; (2 54 5064); $$$. It's tricky to enter the island because of highway netting but the location is excellent except for road noise. It is close to the ferry or metro to historic area; small and popular; arrive early or call ahead; open all year; $$. • In the same area but on the western edge of the suburb of Smichovska. Exit D5/E50 for Stodulky. Drive 2km in the direction of Smichovska and follow signposting. Sunny Camp (251 62 5774); close to metro; road and train noise; open all year; $$$. • In the same area but further south. Exit E50 at exit 5 Rudna drive west for 5km passing through the villages of Chrastany and Orech. Camping Orech (2 471 2339); small; well cared for; close to train to Praha; open June-Oct; $$. In the same area. Camp Drusus (2 651 4391); open May-Sept; $$. • In the suburb of Zlicin. Off the Plzen/ Praha road E50 exit for Zlicin. Follow signposting on the west side of the tracks. Caravan Camping and Pension (2 61223 3223); small; rooms in pension; convenient to bus and tram to historic area; open April-Sept; $$$.

From the Treplice/Praha road E55/8: • Follow roads for centrum . Just before the Vltava River turn west following signposting for Troja and Zoo. • These campgrounds are next to each other with nearby tram to the historic area; open May-Sept; $$$ Autocamp Trojska (2 838 50 487), Camping Sokol Troja (2 838 50 486), and Camping Dana Troja (2 838 50 482).

SIGHTS OUTSIDE PRAHA
Kutna Hora

Once an important, silver-rich city, Kutna Hora's wealthy merchants provided the city with a graceful square, a imposing Gothic cathedral with pinnacles and flying buttresses, and an macabre ossuary (a vault of bones of the dead) with grisly skeletal decorations. You can sip espresso or beer in sidewalk cafe today in the UNESCO-listed square and reflect upon its patina and elegance. Major sites are closed on Monday. Directions: Exit off N12 or N333 about 50 km east of Praha.

▲Camping: • By the train station on the northeast side of town. Camping Transit (327 76 2822); good location for walks to the historic area; open June-August; $.

Konopiste and Pribram

The heady aroma of more than 200 hundred varieties of roses greets visitors to Konopiste Castle, a complex of gardens, terraces, and preserves. Set on a high outcrop of rocks 65 kilometers south of Praha, it is a popular day trip. Archduke Ferdinand–once heir to the Austrian throne, his assassination in Sarajevo in 1914 set off the cataclysm of World War I–built the castle and grounds. His wife came from the area and felt more comfortable here than in Austria. The archduke was an eccentric and passionate hunter. He filled his home with stuffed game heads, keenly polished weapons, and trophies. Huge bear heads, tiger skin rugs with heads still attached, an immense chandelier made with antlers, and an ashtray carved from an elephant's foot are part of the grue-some décor. So it's ironic that the duke's life ended with an assassin bullet. Eager to impress guests

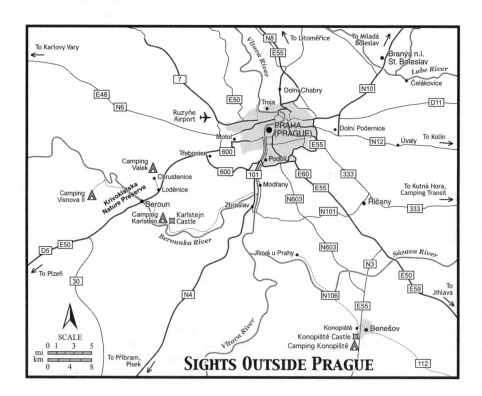

SIGHTS OUTSIDE PRAGUE

he invited to his wife's homeland, he created large terraces and a romantic water garden decorated with fountains and statuary. Today the grounds are a sanctuary for distressed birds; open daily.

Like Kutna Hora, Pribraun was a silver mining town. Today you can don a hard hat and go down into the UNESCO-listed mine shafts; closed Monday. Directions: Drive south of Praha for 44km to Pribraum, then southwest to the suburb of Brezove Hory. Cresting the hillside outside of Pribraun, the lovely domes of Svata Hora create a lovely sight. Devotees reverently admire the frescoes, saintly statuary, and well-loved Madonna and Child. Directions: Drive 50km southwest of Praha on 3 in the direction of Benesov. Both Knopiste and Pribram are well signposted.

▲Camping: • Southeast of Praha. Take N3/E55 in the direction of Benesov. At the fork continue for 2km following signage for Konopiste. Motel and Camping Konopiste (301 22 732); pool; fitness center; tennis; bike rental; open May-Sept; $$$.

Karlstejn Castle and the Krivoklatsko Nature Preserve

Tiny Karlstejn village and its medieval castle are a popular day-trip from Praha, and the village is full of touristy stuff. The hike up to the castle is invigorating but the castle is practically bare of furnishings, so forgo the tour and just enjoy the photogenic fairytale like wedge of towers rising above the castellated walls.

The Berounka Valley is UNESCO-listed biosphere. The walking path along the river twists and turns, heading east and west of the castle through pristine forests of beech and pine. Though the area was once a famous hunting ground, today only the ruins of a 13th-century castle, Krivoklat, stand in memory of the grand hunting events. Directions: Exit southwest of Praha on E50 in the direction of Beroun and drive 28km. Turn east, and follow signposting along the river and rail tracks to Karlstejn.

▲Camping: • One kilometer west of Karlstejn on the road to Beroun. Camping Karlstejn (311 68 4263); on the river; open April-Oct; $.

SOUTHERN BOHEMIA
Tabor and Around

In the 15th-century, Jan Hus believed that all people were equal in God's eye. It was revolutionary stuff for an era ruled by the church hierarchy and feudal-minded nobility. Exiled from Praha, Hus and his followers sought refuge north of the city. Naming their new community Tabor, they established a church founding the Hussite religious movement and bravely fought for their beliefs. Visiting the museum here, with its underground passages and monastery, provides an understanding of their bravery and beliefs; closed Monday. During the second weekend of September, locals dress up in traditional costumes for the Hussite Festival. Directions: Drive south on E55/3 for 61km to Tabor.

There are other interesting side trips in the area. The former home of the sculptor Bilkek features outstanding architecture and houses a gallery of his work. It is worth a small detour. Directions: Drive east of Tabor on 19 for 12km to the village of Chynov. The gallery is signposted Bilkuvdum and is on the south side of the river; closed Monday. For a change of pace, visit Chynovska jeskyne, where a steep descent leads down 50-meters via a spooky narrow stairwell into a stalagmite decorated cave; open daily. Directions: Look for signposting northeast of Chynov, and then drive 3km. Farther east along N19, an entertaining motorcycle museum operates inside the castle in Kamen. If you are in the area in mid-June, stop in Pelhrimov to cheer on hopefuls attempting eccentric feats at the Festival of Records and Performances. Winners appear in the

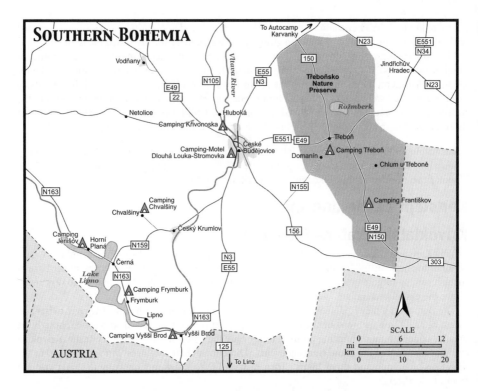

Guinness Book of World Records. At other times visit the Muzeum Rekord a Kuriozit, the amusing museum that commemorates the highly unusual feats; closed Sunday Directions: Drive east of Tabor for 42km on 19 to Pelhrimov.

▲Camping: • 14km south of Tabor, exit 3/E55 at Sobesslav. Autocamp Karvanky (363 52 1003); near a reservoir lake; road noise; open May-Oct; $.

Ceske Budejovice and Around

The main attraction for most tourists in Ceske Budejovice is the Budvar Brewery headquarters, now inside an ultra-modern blue titanium building on U. Trojice, alongside the road to Praha. Save your appetite to indulge in both food and beer here, as they are both inexpensive; open daily. After the tour, the banks of the Malse River await for a walk or cycle ride. Step inside the lively and whimsical atmosphere of the old meat market. Check out the elegant arcades and fountain at the main square. An outstanding 20th-century art collection is displayed in the former riding school of the impressively restored and furnished Hluboka Chateau; open daily. The grounds of the castle make a lovely picnic stop. It's a doable cycle ride from town, and the tourist office has a map of the special cycle path. Directions: Drive west out of town on E49 for 2km. Turn north onto N105 and drive 3km following signposting for Hluboka.

Squeezed into a sharp bend of the River Vltava is the exquisite, rosy-hued Cesky Krumlov. Wooden houses cling precariously to the hillside and rickety bridges cross the river making it a picturesque and popular stop. The tourist office will help with renting a canoe so you can paddle down the river and then return on a mini-shuttle bus. During summer solstice the medieval pageantry of the Five Petaled Rose Festival is a festive celebration.

▲Camping: • 2km south of the historic area of Cesky Budejovice, on the road to Cesky Krumlov. Exit N3/ E/55 at Stomovka. Camping-Motel Dlouha Louka (38 721 0601); nice walk into Ceske Budejovice; pleasant site; playground; cooking area; open May-Oct; $. • 3km north of the Cesky Budejovice exit E49 onto 105 in the direction of the zoo and lake. Camping Krivonoska, in the village of Hluboka (38 96 5285); a recreational area; open May-Sept; $. • 9km northwest of Cesky Krumlov. Exit Cesky Krumlov west on 39 in the direction of Cerna and drive 3km. Turn north onto 166 and drive 6km to the village of Chvalsiny.

▲Camping Chvalsiny (337 88 123); quiet rural setting; playground; open May-Sept; $.

Misty light shrouds the marshy peat bogs of Trebonsko Nature Preserve while reeds nod in the light breeze and the tails of feeding ducks waggle in quiet water. Whistling and chirping birds advertise their presence, and here and there silent fisherman sit patiently waiting for a bite. Birders, binoculars in hand, nudge each other as a sighting is made. UNESCO listed, it is a unique biosphere of fish-ponds, marshy peat bogs, and flat lands. Directions: Drive east of Ceske Budejovice on E49 for 24km to Trebon.

▲Camping: • Exit town southwest on 155 in the direction of Borovany, then drive 2km. Autocamp Trebonsky (333 25 86); good location for birding; cabins; bike rental; open May-Sept; $. • 18km south of Trebon on E49 exit for Kilikov and drive 2km to Franstiskov. Camp Frantiskov (602 109 587); beautiful location close to the woods, good birding; open May-Oct; $.

Lake Lipno and the Vltava River east of it are favorite areas of mine. The countryside beckons with softly rolling hills, gentle forests, and the swiftly running Vltava River. Camping is simple, with festive campfires and singing during the night. The area is popular with kayakers and canoeists, and rentals and guided trips are available. The Orlik and Zvikov castles on the Vltava and the pretty town of Pisek, with its fine medieval stone bridge, make nice excursions.

▲Camping: • On the northeast side of the lake. From Vyssi Brod, drive northwest on 163 for 17 km in the direction of Loucovice/Lipno, then on to Frymburk. Camping Frymburk (337 735 283); scenic location; popular with international travelers; bike rental; open May-Sept; $$. • At the northwest end of the lake, close to Horni Plania. From Ceky Krumlov, drive southwest on 39 for 19km to Cerna. Cross over the bridge, following signposting for Horni Plana for 6km. Autocamp Jenisov (337 738 156); great location on the lake close to the village; open May-Sept; $. • On the north side of the lake, at the junction of N159 and N163 in Cerna. Take the small road to the lake. Camping AMK (337 96 125); cabins; bike rental; open May-September; $. • On the southeast end of the lake, along the river close to Vyssi Brod. From Cesky Budejovice, drive south on E55/3 for 28km in the direction of Freistadt (Austrian border). At the intersection of E55 and 163, turn west in the direction of Vyssi Brod and drive 12km. Camping Vyssi Brod; casual place popular with kayakers; cabins; open May-September; $.

WESTERN BOHEMIA
Karlovy Vary and Marianske

The guest list of the wealthy who have recuperated and played in this quiet, elegant, and well-manicured spa town is impressive. To enjoy the same panoramic view as the rich and famous, walk up behind the Hotel Pupp. From here, take the funicular up the hill to the Peter the Great Monument or just continue walking up the path. In May, the town glitters with cinema stars who have come to see and be seen at the film festival, which some consider as important as the those in Cannes and Berlin.

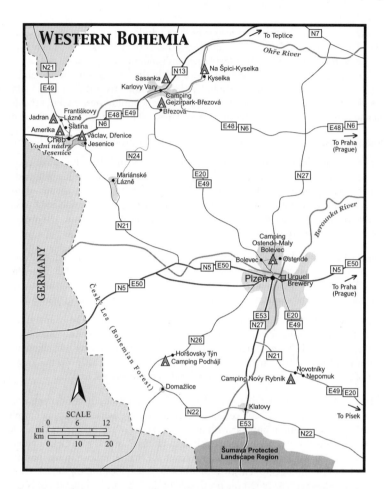

▲Camping: • Northeast of Karlovy Vary. Exit Karlovy Vary on E442/13 in the direction of Ostrov. Drive 7km to Bor. Turn west, and drive under E442/13 in the direction of Sadov and follow signposting. Autocamp Sasanka (353 59 0130); pretty location on a small hill; parking separate from camping; cabins; bus to Karlovy; open April-Oct; $$. • 4km south of town on N20/E49 take the Plizen-Karlovy Vary road, exiting for Brezova. Camping Gejzirpark-Brezova (017-251-01); between the forest and the river Tepla; in a recreational area; pool; open May-Sept; $$. • More remote. Just out of town on N6/E48 in the direction of Praha, turn northeast onto a small road along the river in the direction of Kyselka. Follow the Oder river road for 14 km. It is signposted north of Kyselka. Camping Na Spici-Kyselka (017-394-1152); close to a hotel; cabins; biking/walking paths; open June-Sept; $.

Though less exclusive than Karlovy Vary, Marianske Lazne is also embellished with peaceful and beautiful garden parks and is a user-friendly spa town. Try the mineral baths on the east side of town, just down from the main plaza. Sip water from the superb wrought-iron Kolonada, and relax around the fountain that "sings" to the cascading water every two hours.

The leafy trees and well-tended flowerbeds provide a tranquil setting for walks to springs dotting the park.

▲Camping: • 5km south of Cheb, on the northwest side of Lake Jesinice. Exit Cheb east on 6 in the direction of Karlovy and drive 3km. Turn south in the direction of Podhrad, and following signposting on the east side of the railway tracks. Kemp Vaclav (354 43 5653); great location in a scenic recreational area with canoes and paddleboats; parking separate from camping; popular; May-mid-Sept; $. • In the same area. Camping Drenice (166 31 591); close to the lake; open May-Sept; $. • Drive north out of Cheb on E49/21 in the direction of Frantiskovy, then west on a small road in the direction of Liba. Part of Hotel Jadran. Autocamping & Hotel Jadran (166 542 412); pleasant location close to the lake; toilet & showers in the hotel; pool; cabins; shady with pines; open May-Sept; $. • In the same area. Camping Amerika (166 542 518); open May-September; $.

Plzen

Expert brew-masters have made this appealing town a favorite stop. To see and taste at its most famous pilsner brewery, Urquell, plan to take the two-hour guided tours that leave hourly. Book ahead for a tour in English; www.pilsner-urquell.cz. Directions: The brewery is on the east side of the old town along the river and is well signposted; open daily. You'll be thirsty afterwards, so allow time to enjoy expertly made brews in the Czech Republic's largest pub, Na Spilce, located just beyond the brewery's triumphal arch. A charming brewery museum is just off the main square in a restored malt house; open daily. For even more beer history, stop at Perlova 4 and wander through a maze of medieval underground passageways, some of which display antique brewing artifacts; ask for the English text; closed Monday. The synagogue just outside the town square has been completely restored by the Czech Ministry of Culture. It dates from the 19th-century and is one of Europe's largest.

▲Camping: • 5km north of the city in the suburb of Bolevec by a small lake. Drive north on 27 in the direction of Tremosna. Exit for Bolevec. Cross to the east side of the train tracks and the lake. Camping Ostende (19 520 194); train noise; closeby tram to Pilsen; May-Sept; $. • 22km south of Plzen on a small lake in a recreational area. From Plzen drive southeast on E49/20 for 22km. At the junction of E49/20 and 21, exit onto 21 for Novotniky and drive west to the river. Camping Novy Rybnik (19 859 1336); pleasant location; cycling/walking paths; open May-Sept; $.

One of the best places to mingle with locals is at their festivals. Just 15 kilometers from Germany, the historic town of Domazlice celebrates one in mid-August that's worth a detour. Stubbornly resistant to Germanization, the locals here have determinedly kept their peculiar Czech dialect alive. Proud of their heritage as border guards, they have a rich tradition of costumes and of music played on bagpipes. A stop by the castle to visit the history museum and then at the little Muzeum Jindricha Jindricha to view a collection of traditional clothing and homey goods in a cottage-like setting, is endearing.

▲Camping: • Drive 11km north of the Domazlice on 26 to Horsovsky Tyn and follow signposting. Autocamping Podhaji (188 25 61); lovely rural countryside; small; open June-August; $. • 10km southeast of Domazlice on 22 in the village of Kdyne (189 911 233); pool; tranquil; open May-Sept; $.

NORTHERN BOHEMIA
Ceske Svycarsko National Park

Nicknamed the Bohemian Switzerland, this majestic valley attracts rock climbers in search of a challenge. Its immense sandstone outcrops are weather-carved into amazing shapes. The whole area is riveted with mini-ravines and dramatic bluffs. Climb up the hill behind the village of Tisa so you can look out over this sandstone paradise. Have your photo taken on top of one of the huge boulders which are not overly hard to climb. Pravika Brana, a natural sandstone bridge, is 30-meters long and 21-meters high. It is as impressive as the one in Canyonlands USA and the largest in Europe. The 3-kilometer trail begins behind the Sokolihnizdo restaurant in Hrensko; small entrance fee. Another dramatic and very popular trail goes into Kamenice Gorge. After a steep hike into the gorge, you can float down the narrows by boat; open daily. The trail begins at Mezna, not far from the German border town Hrensko. Trails are clearly marked for various return routes. The high plateau of Decinsky Sneznik permits looking out over the entire region. Directions: Exit off N261 onto N13. Drive north on the small road at Jilove. The northern end of this region is Hrensko, just over the German border. The southern end is in Decin. Both are off N261. Be sure to pick up hiking maps at your campground or in one of the villages.

▲Camping: • In Decin. Close to the railway tracks just off 261. Autokemp Pod Zamken; pleasant location except for the train noise at night; pool; open May-Sept; $. • 28km south of Liberec, southeast of the village of Turnov. 4km southeast of Turnov on E442/25 exit west at the village of Sedmihorky. Cross to the west side of the railway tracks. Autocamping Sedmihorky (436 391 162); close to a small reservoir lake; railway noise; café/bar/shop; open April-Oct; $. • In the same area. Drive northeast of Turnov on 10 in the direction of Tanvald for 5km to tiny village of Mala Skala. Autocamping Ostrov (428 392 157); close to the river; basic but pleasant; open May-Sept; $.

Terezin

In order to convince the world press and visiting International Red Cross that the Jews were being well cared for, Hitler needed a showplace Jewish camp. He used the old fortress Terezin,

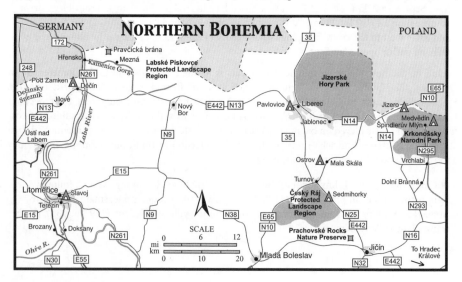

building schools and libraries to show that the confined Jews had a semblance of normal life. But in reality it was just a stopover for Jews on their way to Auschwitz. Cross over the bridge and through the old walls of the fortress onto the crumbling streets. This excursion is made even more sobering if you've seen the hopeful drawings of children confined here that are displayed Praha's Old Jewish Quarter; open daily. Directions: Drive south of Usti nad Labem 21km on N30. Exit for Lovosice, and drive east on N55 for 10km to Terezin.

▲**Camping:** • Along the Elbe River on the north side of the E55 bridge north Terezin. Autocamp Slovoj (416 734 481); close to the sports center with tennis courts; cabins; train noise; open May-Sept; $.

Jablonec and Jizerske hory mountains

An incredible collection of jewelry, including many engaging pieces by Adolf Loos, the famous Secessionist, make a detour into Jablonec to see its glass and jewelry museum a pleasant break in the journey. Directions: Signposted Muzeum skla a bizuterie; its downhill from the town hall; closed Monday. The mountainous area northeast of Liberac bordering Poland is popular for family vacations so it has are nice camping places.

▲**Camping**: • 2km northwest of Liberec. exit 35 for the suburb of Pavlovice. Camping Pavlovice (48 512 3468); it's close to the sports area; bike rental; open May-August; $. • East of Liberec, on the river at the base of the Jizerske Mountain range and the Polish border. Exit Liberec onto N14/10, and drive 25km east to Tanvald. Continue up the mountain road 10 for 11km to Harrachov. Camping Jizero (43 52 9536)); small ; beautiful cabins; pópular vacation area, canoeing; biking, and hiking; cabins; open June-August; $. • 12km south on 14 in Jablonec. Autocamp Zatisi (432 59 1335); use if the Jizero is full; $. • In the Jizerske mountains ski resort at Spindleruv Mlyn. Exit N14/293 at Jilemnice and drive east 7km to Vrchlabi. Continue up the mountain for 18km to Spindleruv Mlyn. a recreational area at the end of N295. Camping Medvedin (048-389-3534); chairlift up to hiking trails; resort-like; $$.

EAST BOHEMIA/MORAVIA
Cesky Raj and Adrspassko-Teplicke Nature Preserves

This twisting labyrinth of sculpted sandstone challenges serious rock climbers and hikers. Trails, some with steps carved into the rock, snake up the soaring rocks and towers. Directions: Exit N10 near Mlada Boleslav, then drive east on N16 in the direction of Jicin. Follow signposting on the west side of town for Prachovske skaly. For a memorable day take a walk along the twisting paths through the "rock villages" of the Adrspassko-teplicke preserve then take a refreshing swim in the secluded lake Piskovna where afterwards you can relax on the warm lakeside boulders. Parking and trailhead are west of the village of Teplice. Purchase a color-coded trail map at the trailheads or a local hotel. Have local change for small admissions on some trails. In late August rock climbers share their videos and prowess at the Festival of Mountaineering Films. Directions: From the Slovak border town Nachod and the intersection of E67 and 303, drive north on 303 for 18km to the village of Police. Turn west on the smaller road in the direction of Teplice, cross over the rail tracks, and then follow them north 7km in the direction of Adrspassko.

▲Camping: • Close to the trailhead for Adrspassko, 2km west of Teplice nad Metuji. Camping Bucnice (447 93 293); great for the rock villages and meeting fellow rock climbers; small; basic; open May-Sept; $. • 2km northwest of Jicin at the intersection of E422 and 16. Kemp Rumcajs (433 210 78); adjacent to a motel; cabins; pleasant spot; open May-Sept; $.

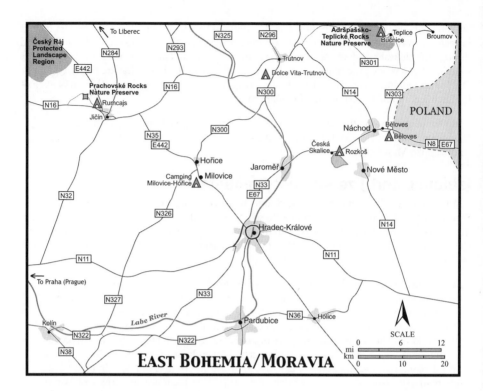

Hradec Kralove and Horice

Cornfields stretch for long distances over this flat terrain, so taking a break in the journey to tour Hradec Kralove's noteworthy modern art gallery, Galerie moderniho umeni, is especially welcome. Housed within a five-story art nouveau building, it is airy and light from a glass-roof atrium and has the Czech Republic's finest collection of modern Czech art; closed Monday. In Horice, 23km northwest of Hradec Kralove, an important school of sculpture was founded in 1884. Today the town hosts international symposiums on contemporary sculpture in July and August. Sculpture beautifies the town, and an exciting collection can be viewed in Galerieplastik; closed Monday. Directions: Drive halfway up the hill on the east side of town.

▲**Camping:** • Southwest of Trutnov. Exit off N16 in direction of Jicin, then follow signposting for Dolce. Camping Dolce Vita-Trutnov (439 81 3065); a recreational area along the river; cabins; biking paths; open year round; $. • North of Hradec Kralove 35km on E67/33. It's on the north edge of Lake Rozkos in Ceska Skalice, a recreational area popular with wind surfers. Camping Rozkos (441 45 1112); boat launch; sauna; cabins; open all year; $. • On the Polish-Czech border crossing of Nachod on 303/E67. Exit just north of Nachod at Beloves. Camping Beloves(44123 014); small; simple; open June-August; $. • 20 km southeast of Hradec-Kralove on N35/E442. Exit 2km north of Holice for Hluboky, a recreational area on a small lake. Camping Hluboky (0456-2233); pleasant area; cabins; basic; open June-August; $

SOUTHERN MORAVIA
Brno and Around

Miles van der Rohe, a famous pioneer in functional architecture was commissioned by a wealthy Jewish family to build a fine villa in line with the style of the day. Vila Tugendhat was finished in 1930. Although it was "modernized" by the Communists who used it for elegant events it is still a shrine for students of modern architecture; closed Monday and Tuesday. Directions: Northeast of town on Milady Horakova, by the Soviet War Memorial. Applied art enthusiasts will also enjoy the UPM, a museum with a particularly outstanding collection of Art Nouveau and Secessionist furniture and glassware; closed Monday and Tuesday. Both the city's main train station and the bus station are also reflections of the city's fin-de-siecle splendor, so include them in your walk. The site where Gregor Mendel, the father of modern genetics, did his research is of particular interest to students of biology. The gardens where he worked and the adjoining museum are located in the Augustinian Monastery, where he was the abbot; closed weekends. Directions: On southwest corner of old town Brno. For a macabre experience, visit Spilberk Castle atop the hill on the western edge of the old town Brno. Its labyrinth of dark hallways are particularly eerie.

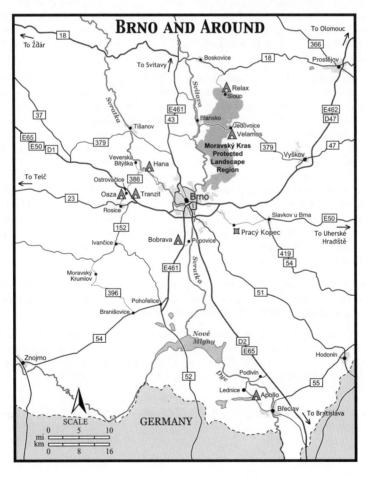

Built as fortress it was famous as a prison,; closed Monday. For photogenic local color and fun visit Zelny trh–an old square with a huge Parnassus fountain. A bustling open market takes place in the mornings, so plan time for sitting by the fountain to munch on a delicious Czech snack.

▲Camping: • 12 km northwest of Brno on E-50 take exit 178 for Ostrovacke. Turn north on 386 on the direction of Veverska Bityska and drive 8km. Camping Hana (504 420 331); lovely location close to the reservoir lake; popular; open May-Sept; $. • In the village of Ostrovacke. Both are small, convenient to the highway. Camping Oaza (502 42 7552); open May-Oct; $ and Camping Transit (502 94 346); open June-Sept;$.

The abyss of the Punkevni jeskyne cave is decorated with a fine array of fantastically shaped stalagmites but it's the boat ride on the underground river in that make this hugely popular detour fun. Get tickets a day ahead from the campground or tourist office; open daily. Directions: In the Moravsky Kras region. 8km north of Bruno, exit E461/43 onto 379 and drive east in the direction of Punkevni for 7km. The main entrance is at Skalni Mlyn. It's more than a kilometer to the entrance, which is a nice walk but consider renting a bike from them and then have a fun ride afterwards pedaling along the forest trails. Many visitors take the little Eko-Train shuttle.

▲Camping: • In Jedovnice. On 377/379 close to the caves. Camping Velamos (506 932 296); close to a lake; south of the village; convenient; open June-Sept; $. • On the north side of the caves. Exit E461/43 for Boskovice and drive east 13 km. Turn south onto 373 in the direction of Sloup and drive 6km. Autokemping Relax (506 43 518); near the football field; open May-Sept; $.

Napoleon outwitted the Austrians and Russians in the fields east of Brno in a battle that led to the disintegration of the anti-Napoleon coalition and the European borders that were observed at the time. Called the Battle of Austerlitz, Tolstoy included it in his novel *War and Peace*. A tent-like monument looks over the hillside's strategic war site. An engaging toy soldier mock-up of the battle is displayed in a nearby museum. Directions: Drive east of Brno on D1 for 12km. Exit southeast onto E50 and drive 5km to Slavkov. In town follow signposting southwest 7km for Pracy kopec and Mohyla miru, outside of Prace.

Twenty enormous canvases in Moravsky Krumlov's Renaissance chateau depict the epic Czech-Slavic history. Artist Alphous Mucha shared a studio with Gauguin in Paris and produced notable Art Nouveau posters, but he felt his real life's work was these phantasmagoric paintings; closed Monday. Directions: 22km south of Brno on E461 exit for Pohorelice. Drive west 2km to 54 and drive south 7km. Turn north in the direction of Moravsky Krumlou and drive 7km. Turn north at Branisovice onto a small road for 9km to Moravsky Krumlov. The museum is on the west side of town. Follow signposting for Zamek.

▲Camping: • 12 km south of Brno. Off D1/E50 take exit 194 onto E461/52 south in the direction of Znojmo. Drive 7km. Take exit for Popovice/Bobrava and follow signposting Bobrava Motel-Camping (502 94 346); convenient; pleasant; open all year; $.

Very powerful landowners built the Gothic, UNESCO-listed extravaganza that is the Lednice Palace. It has rich interiors, stately gardens, reflecting ponds, a huge Islamic minaret, and is a popular day trip. For fun, take the little boat ride or horse-drawn cart out to the minaret, where steps to the top offer fine views; open daily. Directions: 9km north of Breclav exit D2/E65 onto 422 at Podivin. Drive 8km to Lednice.

▲Camping: • 3km south of Lednice by the lake. Camping Apollo (627 20 515); pretty location; open May-Sept; $.

Telc's wedding cake-like palace is romantically bordered by two large fishponds. Both the palace and the Renaissance town square are UNESCO-listed. It is a cheery and enjoyable place to explore and photograph. Cycling is particularly enjoyable and a bike rental outlet operates at the wide end of the main square. Pass through the small gate on the north side of the square to enter an outstanding English-style garden–the perfect place for a picnic lunch. Directions: Exit D1 at exit 112 onto E59/38 for Jihlava. Drive south 4km. Turn west onto19 and drive 6km in the direction of Pelhrimov. Turn south onto 406 and drive 24km to Telc.

▲**Camping:** • On a small lake northwest of Telc. Exit town north and following signposting for Rasna. Camping Velkoparezity (66 96 449); small; casual; nice setting; open May-October; $.

Roznov pod Radhostem

An undulating countryside spreads out before you like a carefully hand-sitched quilt in north Moravia. Before World War II the populace was largely German. Today old-fashioned wood homes and churches still lend a tranquil air. The area is justly known for its open-air museum, the largest and most outstanding in the in country. Located at Roznov Pod Radhostem, the Valasske museum, is separated into three parts. The Wooden Town section's highlights are a graceful 17th-century church and humorous beehives with grimacing faces. In Wallachian Village, farm animals, a schoolhouse, and tidy garden tell of life in sheep-farming settlements. Mill Valley sports an old mill, a water-powered blacksmith, and period dressed workers. Buy a combined ticket, and pick up an English text. Of the festivals held here throughout summer, the best is the Folkloric Dance and Song held in the first week of July. Directions: Directly east of Olomouc, almost to the Slovak Republic border, on 18/E442. Well signposted.

▲**Camping:** .• Close to the open air museum. Camping Roznov (651 64 8001); extra nice facilities; nice walking and cycling area; open June-Sept; $$. • Closeby. Camping Sport (651 55 540); large; pool; tennis; popular; open June-August; $$.

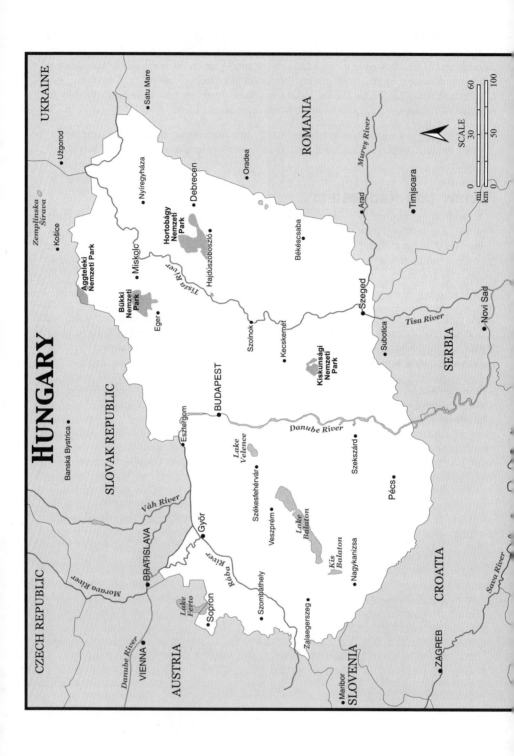

HUNGARY

www.hungrytourism.hu

Hungary's big sky countryside rolls out under a sun lazily ripening fields of wheat, corn, and the fruit of vineyards and orchards. Enormous sunsets explode in a full palate of brilliant golds and reds. Languid rivers are shaded by lacy willows, attracting quiet anglers and thirsty cows. As France is famous for its cuisine, Hungary is famous for its thermal spas. Under vaulted domes built by their Turkish conquerors, the famous and the infamous alike have shed their clothes to soak and gain relief for their aching muscles and weary minds. Having survived a variety of regimes and revolutions, Hungary's music is at once dreamy and high-spirited, and live concerts are inexpensive to attend. Hungarians have a highly developed sense of hilarity and so a musical event can encompass Cossack acrobatics, Viennese waltzes, Gypsy folklore, Yiddish melodies, or a military band. Audiences laugh and vigorously clap their hands in rhythm. At the morning market, red, yellow, and orange sweet peppers are piled astounding high. Luscious peaches, fragrant plums, and spicy sausages are hard to pass up. Farm families do not solicit or plea for a sale but instead stand with dignified simplicity by their market tables. They exchange cheerful smiles with customers and are grateful for a sale. City dwellers are intent on making a living and often have two jobs. They exude the same Horatio Alger energy and strength that was found in America's melting pot. Today energetic young business entrepreneurs provide the lively pulse and tempo to an endearing composition of Old-World classics.

Hungarians have been in the tourist business for a long time and know how to keep their customers happy. Vacationing Austrians, Germans, and Dutch come for a relaxing, unpretentious good time and to shop where prices are lower than at home. Highways are well paved, and signposting is good. Maps are excellent and up to date. Gas is plentiful. Locals are helpful. Parking is no more difficult than at home. With the exception of Budapest, it is easy to drive into the city center and find parking close to the historic area. Farmer's markets are held daily except Sunday and are easy to find in the small towns and villages. They are usually held close to the main square and begin closing at noon. Big chain supermarkets are open every day including Sundays. Food is plentiful, of excellent quality, and inexpensive. Cycling is good with many quiet secondary roads and picturesque little towns so consider bringing your bicycle from home or use rentals close to the tourist areas. You are required to keep your passport on your person at all times.

Many campgrounds have outdoor thermal pools. Besides being a great way to relax at day's end, they are great places to meet fellow travelers. There is always space for a tent and car or a small caravan, so don't hesitate to travel in high season, when the weather is better and the festivals are happening. Hungarian campground owners want to appeal to an international clientele and take pride in maintaining comfortable and homey campgrounds. Many have good cooking areas and nice children's playgrounds. Most campgrounds charge around 20 euros for two persons, a tent, and a car and are noted as $$. Those close to popular tourist destinations may cost more and

441

are noted here as $$$. (Hungary does not use the euro, however.) You don't need to call ahead unless the campground is very popular or it is at the edge of the season and want to make sure they are open. A Camping Card International is required at most campsites. See appendix for information.

BUDAPEST

Budapest is a grandiose and cinematic city steeped in Old World ambiance. Its 19th-century architecture reflects a sense of glory from the Austrian-Hungarian monarchy. The city's wide boulevards and Baroque wedding cake-like buildings have been the background for such Hollywood films as *Evita, Casablanca, A Star is Born* and *My Fair Lady*. The city courts filmmakers with tax incentives, professional crews, and large studios.

Eight beautiful bridges span the wide and powerful Danube River, connecting once imperial Buda to commercial Pest. Varhegy–a tiny Baroque city known as Var–is UNESCO listed and is now a castle-like open-air museum, on the Buda side. It has been reduced to rubble and rebuilt with devastating regularity. Gothic archways, fancy ironwork, and stone carvings take you back 7 centuries. Styles of music from jazz to folk tunes ring from the Mary Magdalene tower, adding lightness to your step. Let the music direct you to the beautiful Matyas Church, one of Hungary's most sacred shrines. Light streams in through the rose windows, gently lighting up the elaborate embellishments of geometric motifs. The acoustics are excellent and choral and organ concerts are held on Fridays and Saturday nights during summer. Use your guidebook or information from the tourist office or a nearby hotel to enlighten your stroll through this fascinating area. Don't miss the Museum of Commerce and Catering. Its reconstructions of shops, coffee houses,

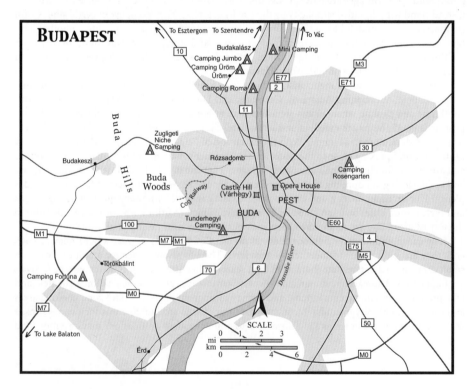

and hotel rooms bring smiles. Music is part of everyday life in Hungary so the outstanding Music History Museum has an evocative setting in a Baroque palace where Beethoven was a guest and Bartok had a music-studio. It's not hard to imagine its days of great splendor. To get to Castle Hill, take the Metro to Moszkva ter. Walk across the bridge over the square and continue on Vartok utca until you come to a large junction of streets and see the Vienna Gate just beyond. If you'd rather not walk there is an inexpensive tourist bus marked "Budavari Siiklo" at the bridge which goes to Clark Adam ter near the Chain Bridge, from there a cable car will take you up to the top.

Be sure to ride the Cog Railway up to the top of the Buda Hills. Then stroll through the tranquil Buda Woods to enjoy the views. In August folk-artist wood-carvers, jewelers, and sculptors display and sell their work. To catch the Cog Railway, walk from Mozkva ter to the circular highrise Hotel Budapest; the station is just opposite it. It's popular to take bikes on the cog railway to pedal along the leafy paths.

All of the world's great opera and ballet stars have performed in Budapest's sumptuous and famous opera house. The BudaFest Opera Festival takes place in summer, and a lively Jewish Festival that presents music from jazz to klezmer occurs at the end of August. Watching the flamboyant and intricate footwork of handsome men and the swirl of embroidered skirts and petticoats worn by their lovely partners as they dance to the indefatigable finger work of Hungarian gypsy music is touristy fun. It's easy to purchase same evening tickets at the Municipal Cultural House or tourist office. Hungarian composers Bartok and Liszt both have sentimental museums that present small concerts featuring talented young musicians. The biggest crowd gatherer is the Sziget Festival, a huge rock festival held on a tiny island-park just north of the Magrit Bridge; @www.sziget.hu. On August 20, the city gets lively as it celebrates St Stephen's Day with craft fairs, fireworks, and a river parade. A much larger parade with elaborate floats occurs the following weekend. Check the calendar of events on the web before you leave home; www.musicmax. hu. To reach the main tourist office, take the metro to the Deak ter. Here you can get a wealth of information not only about Budapest but all of Hungary. The friendly staff can tell you about the festivals and special events throughout the country.

Public transport in Budapest is excellent and inexpensive. Purchase tickets at the campground, and validate tickets on boarding. Inspectors are strict and fines are expensive. Day-passes and three-day passes are available that include all public transport, including the Cog Railway. Consult your fellow campers or campground staff to decide what is best for you. Sunday is a great day to cycle around Budapest. You can stop at a couple of museums, have a picnic on Sziget Island, and watch the traffic on the Danube from one of the bridges.

Don't leave Budapest without soaking in one of their famous thermal baths. Popular with an international clientele, they are easy to experience. Take your bathing suit if you want to use the large communal men's and women's pool as part of your experience. You can rent a cap if you don't have one. In the foyer, pay for what you want: hot tub-like thermal bath; sauna; massage; large communal pool. You'll be assigned a locker. Undress and go into the misty massage room for a dousing and vigorous rub if you have chosen to include a massage, then to the shower, sauna, and hot tubs. Donning your bathing suit, enter the communal pool area for a cool down. It's a very pleasant custom to indulge in elaborate ice cream concoction afterwards. The baths vary in atmosphere. Some have an elegant Old World atmosphere, others are old with exotic Turkish touches, and some are high-tech modern. The tourist office can help you make a selection and provide directions on how get there on public transportation.

▲Camping: • **Coming from the north on 11, the Szentendre-Budapest road**. On the river side of the road. • 10km north of the city, just before the railroad tracks. Camping Roma (36 86 260); easy to find; large; popular with caravans; close to the Danube; close to public transportation; swimming pool; open year round; $$. • 15km north of the city. Watch for signposting before the traffic light and gas station. Follow signposting towards the river to Kiralyok. Mini Camping (302 00 3752); small; close to ferry to Budapest; open; May-Sept; $$.

• **Coming from the north on 10, the Esztergom-Budapest road.** These are both 10km north of Budapest in the vicinity of the suburb Urom. Follow signposting east off 10. Drive through Urom towards Budakalaszi. • Camping Jumbo (26 35 1251); nice location with view of the bridge; bus to city; open April-Oct.; $$. • At the north end of Urom. Camping Urom (26 350 556); nice cooking area with barbeque; bus to city; open April-Oct.; $$.

• **Coming from the west on MI or M7.** • 14km southwest of Budapest in the suburb of Torokbalint. Exit M7 at exit for Torobalint. Drive to Torobalint. Where road bends follow signposting in the direction of Erd. Drive 3km up the hill. Adjacent to the vineyard. Fortuna Camping (23 33 5364); lovely terraced location; thermal pool; bus to Budapest; open all year; $$. • 8km from Budapest. Watch for signposting at the end of M1 and traffic light. Drive up the hill. Tunderhegyi Camping (60 336 256); small; thermal pool; bus to the city; open April-Sept; $$. • 5km northwest of Budapest. On M1, before the intersection of M1 and M7, exit in the direction of Budakesi and follow signposting to Zugligeli. Zugligeli Niche Camping (1-200-8346); in a wooded area at the bottom of the Buda Hills, close to the Cog Railway; popular; open all year; $$$.

• **From the east on 30/M3.** • 6km east of the city. On Kerepesi (highway30), by the overhead railway bridge and MacDonalds, follow signposting. Camping Rosengarten (26 19 537); convenient to bus and metro; traffic and railway noise; popular; open all year; $$$.

Danube Bend Area

In this area north of Budapest, friendly little towns steeped in history sport a wide variety of little shops and galleries that add interest to walks and bike excursions. Consider splurging on a boat excursion ride to or from Budapest and taking the train or bus the other way. Camping here is more tranquil than in the city, and you can take moonlight walks or bicycle rides along the Danube from the campground. Close to the main square in each town you'll find a tourist office with a cheerful English-speaking staff that will take time to assist you. Become part of the coming and going of people heading to the open-air markets with baskets. The old-fashioned conviviality and shared smiles with farmers in weather-worn hats and women in colorful scarves feels good.

Charmingly atmospheric, Szentendre has attracted artists since the early 1900s. Settled by Serbians fleeing Turkish rule, it has a Balkan flair. Along sloping narrow streets and stone stairways, you'll find tiny, intriguing Serbian Orthodox churches and artistic museums. Don't miss the Magrit Kovacs Museum. Her ceramic sculpture captures Hungary's struggle in a heartwarming way and Hungarians consider her one of their greatest sculptors and ceramists. Directions: Off the northeast corner of the square. Throughout summer, the historic main square is a natural setting for concerts ranging from classic to folk and rock. Up on a hillside outside of Szentendre, thatched-roofed farmhouses from all the regions of Hungary are filled with old-fashioned household furniture and tools. In summer, there are craft demonstrations and school children present traditional folklore shows at the *skansen* (open-air museum). It's a treat to watch the proud parents who are keeping Hungarian heritage alive in their children. Directions: Follow signposting off 11 in Szentendre, and drive west up the hill 5 kilometers.

▲**Camping:** • At the north end of Szentendre on the river side. Follow signposting at kilometer 22.3 on 11. Camping Papsziget (26 31 0697); convenient to the village; cabins; large; open May-Sept; $$. • On the east side of the Danube from Szentendre, in Dunakeszi. Take

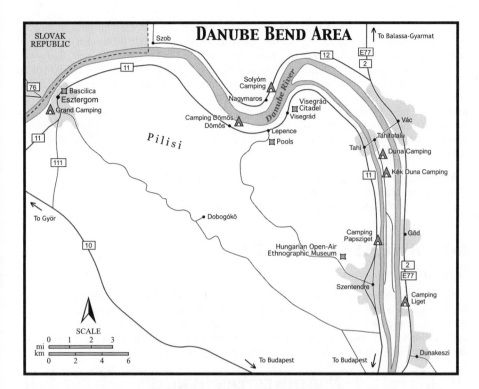

the car ferry, or drive north of Budapest on 2/E77for 18km. Camping Liget (20 41 5912); small; simple; pleasant; near a sand beach; open May-Sept; $$.

Farther north, Visegrad sits on a hill looking down on the Danube Bend. Its mighty Citadel should not be missed. Artifacts from the 14th and 15th-centuries establish an old glory and can be examined in the museum in the Solomon Tower located close to the palace ruins. In July, you can join the locals cheering on their favorite combatant dressed in period costume and competing in a medieval tournament. A series of pools carved into the hillside provide some memorable soaking time with fine views of the Danube. Directions: From Visegrad, drive 4 kilometers further on 11. Exit at Lepence, and drive up the hill.

▲Camping: • On the island of Szsentendre, close to the village Tahitotfalu. Both of these have scenic locations, but the facilities aren't as good as some others. Duna Camping (26 38 5216); open May-Sept; $. Kek Duna Camping (26 39 8102); May-mid-Sept. • Across the river from Visegrad, in Nagymaros. Take the car ferry across the river. Solyom Camping (27 59 4320); nice view of the river and Visegrad; part of a motel; some shade; open May-September; $$. • North of Visegrad, at the Danube Bend in Domos. Exit 11 in Domos. Domos Camping (33 48 2319); good location; pool; biking and walking trails; cabins; public transport to Budapest; open May-August; $$.

At the end of the Danube Bend, Estergom's Bascilica gazes serenely down from its hilltop location by the river. It is the country's ecclesiastical and historical heart, with altars and a treasury that are impressive. A large and important collection of medieval religious art–rich with gold leaf and intricate carvings–is housed in the Christian Museum; closed Monday. As you stand on the parapet looking down on the Danube River, imagine Charlemagne's–and later the Hapsburg's–troops coming down the river. Then turn and imagine the Roman and Ottoman Empires coming up the river. While camping on the edge of the river, Marcus Aurelius wrote his famous *Meditations*, and it was here over 1,000 years ago that Hungary's first king Stephen I was crowned. Today you can see the ruins of a small bridge that connected Hungary to Slovakia before it was blown up by the Nazis. One day there will be another bridge, but in the meantime a small car ferry makes crossings. To get the full impact of the strategic location, park at the town square in Estergom and walk up the hill. Directions: Follow signposting off 11. Dappled light drifts through the leafy woodland called Pilis where hill trails lead to sweeping vista points above Esztergom. Trailheads are marked from the excursion center in the village of Dobogoko. Directions: Follow signposting in town up the hill for 14 kilometers.

▲**Camping:** • In Esztergom, just at the edge of town. From the ferry landing and tourist parking area, drive to the river road and follow signposting. Gran Camping (33- 402-513); swimming pool; view of the Basilica; within walking distance of town; June-September; $$.

NORTHWESTERN HUNGARY
Sopron

The wealthy Hungarian Eszterhazy family chose Sopron for the location of their lovely palace. Set in a small wooded area, it is weathered but still evocatively elegant. Liszt was enticed to live in the palace, and for many years he conducted symphonies, wrote music, and gave music lessons to the children. Even Beethoven was persuaded to conduct the premiere of his *Mass in C* in 1807 here. So attending a weekend concert here is pretty heady stuff; open daily. Directions: 27km east

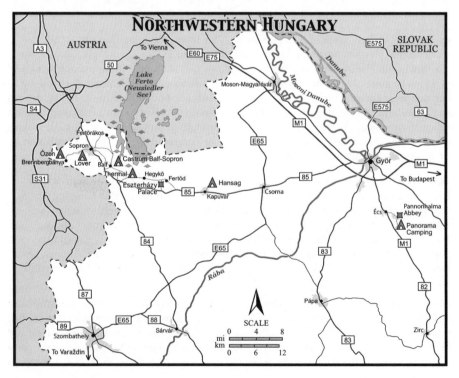

of Sopron, exit off 85 for Fertod. The town of Sopron has an easy charm. Wandering or pedaling past the Baroque facades and stopping at little museums, sweet-smelling bakeries, and well-placed monuments are extra special. Sopron is noted for its fine theatre and music. A highlight is the thrill of hearing operatic love songs lilt through the acoustically perfect cave in nearby Fertorakos. During Festival Weeks, something is happening every evening at Fertorakes, the Petofi Theatre, and the Liszt Cultural Center; www.prokultura.sopron.hu.

▲Camping: • On the southwest edge of Sopron on 84, follow signposting for Hotel/ Camping Lover (Szamia) over the railway tracks then up the hill for 2km. Camping/ Hotel Lover (99 31 1715); tiny, but very charming; open May-Sept; $$$. • Close to Brennbergbanya. Follow signposting from the bus station in Sopron. Camping Ozon (99-331-144); nice location; thermal pool and sauna; cabins; open May-Sept; $$$. • South of Sopron in Hegyko, west from the Eszterhazy Palace, exit the Sopron-Gyor road 85 at km 60.2 for Hegyko. Drive north 3km. Thermal Camping (99- 376-818); thermal and regular pools nearby; open May-Sept; $. • East of Eszterhazy Palace, off Gyor-Budapest road 85, northeast of Kapuvar. Hansag Camping (96- 241-524); thermal and regular pools nearby; sauna; open June-Aug; $

Lake Ferto/Neusiedler Sea

Naturalists fond of quiet cycling or walking time, love this area. In the early morning, great herons are seen taking wing from reed beds and then cranking up over the misty sea. Swans, with wings arched like the skirt of a prima ballerina, float close to admirers. It's a vast marshland forming a 240-kilometer network of reed-lined canals. The wind surfing and fishing from a rowboat are allowed; rentals are available in Fertorakas. A 110-kilometer cycle path circles the lake. Directions: Southeast of town 7km, exit 84 in the direction of Balf and drive 12km. Much of the lake is in Austria. Austrians call it the Neusiedler Sea.

▲Camping: • In Balf. Camping Castrum Balf-Sopron (99 33 9124); nice views of the lake; thermal and regular pools nearby; open all year; $.

Pannonhalma Abbey

Honored by a visit from Pope Paul II, who came to compliment the monastic community on their support of spiritual values, the peaceful and unpretentious Pannonhalma Abbey sits on a small hill overlooking fertile farmlands. Excellent guided tours are given by students. If your visit coincides with an organ or choir recital in the basilica, don't miss it; closed Sunday and Monday. Directions: 20km south of Gyor, exit off 82 (Gyor-Veszprem) at Ecs and follow signposting.

▲Camping: • In Pannonhalma, on the south side of the Benedictine Abbey. Panorama Camping (96 471 240); extra special tiny restaurant; restful and popular spot; grand sunset views; terraced, grassy slope; open May-September; $$.

Lake Balaton Area

For wind surfing or just soaking up the sun, this is the place. Only an hour from Budapest, the huge silvery lake is a hugely popular getaway. The picturesque setting of the Tihany peninsula and its lovely Abbey Church draw camera-toting crowds. But you can have tranquility if you hike up to its inner lake, a favorite haunt for bird watchers. Drive north from Keszthely to Heviz to see an astonishingly large thermal lake. For a small admission fee, you can spend a few hours or an entire day soaking up its warm therapeutic waters amidst water lilies. Directions: At the west edge of the lake at Keszthely, exit for Heviz and watch for signposting for Parkerdo.

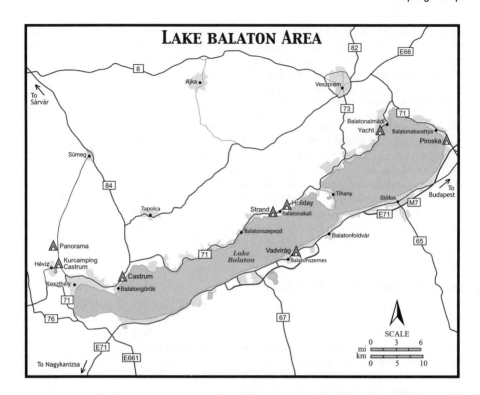

The water of Lake Balaton is warm enough to allow swimming with the swans. Wind surfing or just floating on an inflatable mattress are popular pastimes. Rentals are available for most water sports. Inflatable mattresses or tubes and swimming gear are easy to purchase. Scenic cycling/walking paths edge the shoreline. Bike rentals are available in the little villages. Campgrounds are plentiful; many are low-key resorts. Train tracks and roads circle the lake, so those noises are unavoidable. You get used to it.

▲Camping:

• **Northeast end of the lake**: • In Balatonakaratty, exit onto the Lake road 71. FKK Camping Piroska (88 54 4401); great location; separate nude sunbathing area; resort-like; parking separate from tent; open June-Aug; $$$. • In Balatonalmadi, at the northeast end of lake at the yacht harbor. Yacht Camping, at km 25.5 (88 43 8906); great location; diving platform; close to boat launch and cycle path; open June-Sept; $$$.

• **Halfway down the lake on the west side**: • 4km south of the Tihany pennisula, in Balatonakali. • All 3 are resort-like with scenic locations at the water's edge and are open June-Aug; $$$. Strand Camping (87 54 4021) and Holiday Camping, (87 44 4093). Farther west in Balatonszepezd. Venusz Camping (87 46 8048)

• **Northwest end of the lake**: • In Balatongyorok. Castrum Camping (83 31 4422); resort-like; open June-Aug; $$$.

• **South side, midway of the lake.** • In Balatonszumes, west of Balatonfolder. Camping Vadvirag (84 36 0114); good location; open June-July; $$.

• **On the thermal lake Heviz**: These are less expensive than those on Lake Balaton. • 3km north of Heviz. Panorama Camping (83 31 4412); good location; open April-Oct; $$. • Just east of town. Kurcamping Castrum (83 34 31 98) large; good location; parking separate from tent; open April-Oct; $$.

NORTHEASTERN HUNGARY
Aggetelek Nemzeti Park

Deep inside the amazing caves of Aggetelek Nemzeti park you are in almost complete silence. The sound of dripping water and the swooshing of passing bats, not to mention the popular pastime of searching for darkness-loving salamanders with a flashlight, make for an eerily fun experience. Considered some of the largest and most spectacular caves in all of Europe, they harbor waterfalls, rivers, lakes, countless stalactites, and almost 300 species of life. The main 22-kilometer long Baradla cave passage twists and turns, passing stained, convoluted formations glittering with crystals. As you enter the "Concert Hall" in a little boat from the "River Styx," Bach's *Toccata in D minor* is played to create a *Phantom of the Opera* experience. The park is UNESCO listed; open

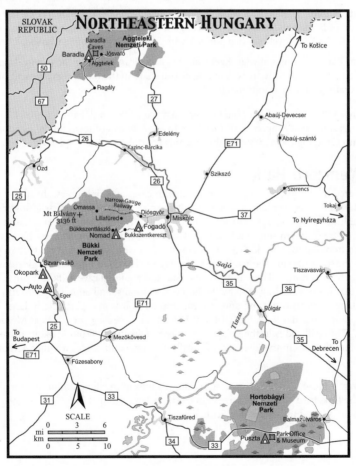

daily. The most popular tours are one or two hours long; longer tours are available. They start at both ends. From the Aggtelek end, the experience is more errie because the passage is more twisted and convoluted than at the Josvafo entrance. The park is nice for cycling. There is a bike rental is in Josvafo. Purchase supplies and gas in a large town before setting out. Directions: From Miskolc, drive 14km north on 26 to Kazincbarcika. Continue on 26 for another 20km. Just before the border into the Slovak Republic, exit north for Ragley. Drive north 21km to Ragley. Continue northwest for 9km to Aggtelek and the park entrance.

▲**Camping:** • In Aggtelek. Camping Baradia (48 343 073); cabins; simple; pleasant; open May-Sept; $.

Eger and Miskolc

Music is a vital force in Miskolc. In the first week of July an international festival of Dixieland jazz and classical music gets things hopping at the 12th-century Queen's castle in nearby Diosgyor. A week later, the Kalaka Folk Festival draws an international crowd to one of the most prestigious festivals of folk music in Central Europe. In mid-June, promising new international opera stars sing in the Bartok International Opera Festival.

▲**Camping:** • 16km southwest of Miskolc. Drive southwest out of Miskilc on a small road in the direction of Bukkszentkereszt. Drive through the village, continuing another 4km. Fogado Camping (46 390 370); lovely setting; popular with families; cabins; open May-Sept; $.

Hungarian Baroque comes alive in Eger's old town and castle during the last week in July and first part of August. The locals are welcoming as you share in the fun and excitement of dancers, comedians, crafts, and tasty traditional food.

▲**Camping:** • 7km north of Eger on 25 near Szarvasko. Oko-Park Panzio (36 35 2201); small; newer; some shade; open April-Oct; $. • In Eger. North of town follow signposting off 24. Auto Camping (36 41 0558); cabins; tennis court; large; basic; open May-Sept; $.

Bukki Nemzerti Park

Once covered by the sea, this region is riddled with caves and sink-holes. In spring and early summer, its hillsides are painted gaily with wildflower color so bring your wildflower book. If you take the little narrow gauge, 30-minute train ride up to the trailheads at Omassa (it leaves from the Tiszai train station at the eastern end of Miskolc), you might meet some Hungarians and perhaps even hook up for a walk. The trails are easy and well marked, but it's wise to pick up a trail map at the train station. Named for the beech trees (*bukk*), its hillsides are glorious anytime but particularly in autumn. There is a pristine lake and a guided cave walk just outside the village of Lillafured. On your way, stop by the home of naturalist and ethnographer Otto Herman. His painstaking work in collecting and stuffing animals, birds and particularly large beetles is remarkable. For a nice day hike, make Mount Balvany and the *Nagymezo* (Great Meadow) your destination. The trailhead is in the village of Omassa. Directions: From Miskolc, drive west out of town up into the hills in the direction of Lillafured, then continue for another 4 kilometers to Omassa.

▲**Camping:** • From Miskolc drive west up into the hills in the direction of Lillafured for 4km. At the fork, turn south and drive 6km to Hollosteto. Nomad Camping (46 39 0183); close to trailheads; cabins; open May-Sept; $.

Hortobagy Nemzerti Park

Steppe-like, this grassland area–now a nemzeti park–is known as the Puszta. It is an important nesting area for migrating herons, great white egrets, black-headed gulls, and spoonbills all nesting in strictly protected fishponds. Due to the wide variety of habitats, birders find it relatively easy to see 40- to 50 species on a spring day. During late summer and early autumn, red-footed falcons hunt together in large, loose flocks. It's Europe's most spectacular setting for the autumn gathering of common cranes. Stop by the park office to pick up a map, a visitor's pass, and information on what species were recently sighted and where. Directions: Off 33 at km 79.

An action-filled experience in this huge–730 kilometer–nemzeti park is provided by a living heritage museum with roaming cattle and cowboys, a Herdsmen's Museum, a Rare Breeds Park, and a Nature Reserve. Plan ahead to be part of the goulash competition, a horse show, or the Bridge Fair featuring leatherwork and barbecue.

▲**Camping:** • Behind the park office in Horotobagy. Puszta Camping (52 369 300) great location; large; thermal pool; open May-Sept; $.

SOUTHEAST HUNGARY
Kiskunsagi Nemzerti Park

In this environmentally fragile area of dunes and grassy desert, horse and man appear fused as one and ride like phantoms of their steppe-born Magyar forebears. Hawks perch on fence posts, and owls hoot during the night and predawn hours. It's fun to join into touristy activities offered in the park. In barnyards filled with the savory aroma of barbecues, you'll hear colorfully dressed Gypsies fill the air with music trembling with sorrow and hardship. Get into a saddle and head out over the seemingly endless plains, or just enjoy looking into the big eyes of the beloved Hungarian horses. Directions: Drive to the entrance out of Bugac at Bugaci Karikas Csarda, or take the narrow-gauge train from the Kecskemet KK station. On the train, it's about a one-hour ride to the Bugugac felso station and then a short walk to the park entrance. From the park entrance, take the horse-pulled wagon ride to the Herder Museum, horse stables, and horse show. In July street food and music abound at the Szeged Festival. Salami lovers will want to visit the famous Pick Salami factory in Szeged.

▲**Camping:** • South of the entrance to Kiskunsagi Nemzerti park, on a small highway between highway 53 and 5/E75. Exit for Kiskunmajsa, and drive northeast of town. Camping and Motel Kiskunmajsa (76 32 9398); thermal resort; cabins; open all year; $.

SOUTHWEST HUNGARY
Pecs/Wine Region

With softly rolling farmlands and ancient vineyards, this corner of Hungary invites you to relax in thermal pools and to sip its famous Villany wines. In the cosmopolitan city of Pecs, you can wander through an exotic Turkish mosque, visit a memorable Jewish synagogue, and then absorb its lively university atmosphere at a sidewalk cafe. After Budapest, this is Hungary's most fascinating city. It is filled with art and culture. The canvases of Kosztka Csontvary burst with vivacious and powerful landscapes in the same sumptuous colors of his contemporary, Vincent Van Gogh. Picasso challenged Chagall to paint as well. Don't miss this exciting collection in the museum named after him; closed Monday. Directions: Walk southeast of the main square and cathedral to Janus Pannonius, and followsignposting to Csontvary Museum. Another highlight is the elegant synagogue, the first in Hungary to be restored with contributions from both the state and abroad; closed Saturday. Directions: Follow signposting for Zsinagoga, on the south side of the historic area, just inside its perimeter, on Timar utda..

▲**Camping:** • North of Pecs, exit the northeast end of Dombovar and drive in the direction of Hogyesz for 3km to km 90. Kurcamping Castrum Bad Gunaras (74 46 5523); adjacent thermal and regular pools; cabins; open April-Oct; $. • North of Pecs on highway 66, exit west at Magyarszck and drive west on a small road along the rail tracks to the village of Magyarhertelend. It is on a small lake. Camping Forras in Magyarhertelend (72 71 9175); adjacent to thermal pool; open May-Sept; $. • In Pecs, north of town in the suburb of Misna, go in the direction of the TV tower. Vidam Park and Zoo are nearby. The road is steep and not recommended for large caravans. Mandulas Camping (72 23 2132); cabins; shade trees; basic; open May-Sept; $. • South of Pecs in the grape-growing area of Villany, exit at Harkany from highway 58 at km 25.3. Camping Harkany (7 48 0117); affiliated with a motel; thermal pool adjacent; near the park; open May-Sept; $.

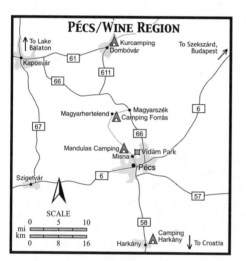

PÉCS/WINE REGION

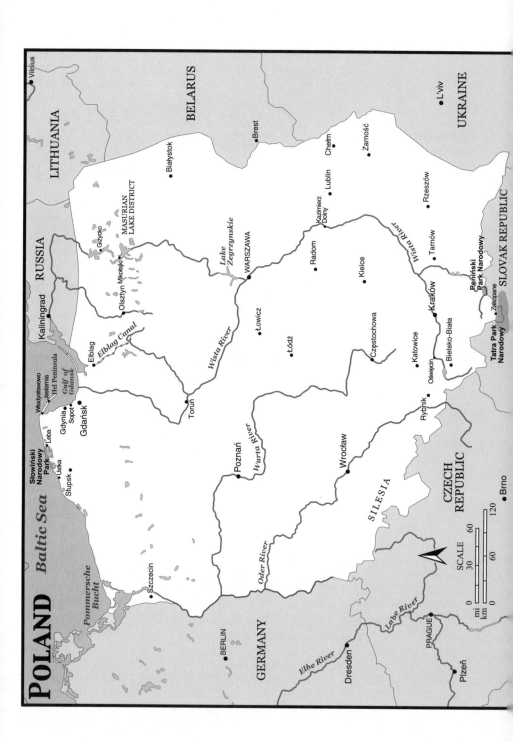

POLAND

Baltic Sea

Pommersche Bucht

Słowiński Narodowy Park

Słupsk
Ustka
Łeba
Władysławowo
Jastarnia
Hel Peninsula
Gulf of Gdańsk
Gdynia
Sopot
Gdańsk

Kaliningrad

RUSSIA

LITHUANIA

Vilnius

Elblag
Elblag Canal
Olsztyn
Mikołajki
Giżycko
MASURIAN LAKE DISTRICT

Białystok

BELARUS

Brest

Szczecin

Toruń

Poznań
Warta River

Oder River

Wisła River

Łowicz

WARSZAWA
Lake Zegrzynskie

Łódź

Radom

Kielce

Lublin
Kazimierz Dolny

Chełm

Zamość

UKRAINE

L'viv

Rzeszów

Tarnów

Wisła River

Pieniński Park Narodowy

Kraków

Zakopane
Tatra Park Narodowy

SLOVAK REPUBLIC

Częstochowa

Katowice
Oświęcin
Bielsko-Biała

Rybnik

Wrocław

SILESIA

CZECH REPUBLIC

Brno

Elbe River

Labe River

PRAGUE

Plzeň

Dresden

GERMANY

BERLIN

SCALE
mi
0 30 60
km
0 60 120

Elbe River

POLAND

www.gopoland.com

The Poles have a contagious vigor and enthusiasm. There is liveliness in their step and a gay, easy laughter that rubs off on everyone around. They are justifiably a proud and courageous nation and offer a rich variety of experiences to the traveler. At the historically important port of Gdansk, you can join both Poles and fellow international travelers marveling at the meticulous restoration and buff up on the port's history as you study the lively exhibits. Boating enthusiasts from all over Europe are drawn to the Masurian Lake region, where they paddle and sail quietly by a profusion of elegant swans. Naturalists revel in being in Europe's last major primeval forest, Bialowieski Park Narodowy, and are thrilled when they see the last surviving European bison. Serious birders put Biebrzanski Park Narodowy at the top of their list. It is one of Europe's most extensive and unspoiled wetlands and is a breeding habitat for the rare singing aquatic warbler and almost 200 other species. Supported by the Worldwide Fund for Nature, guides lead wildlife enthusiasts in canoes and along wooden walkways in season. At golden Krakow, the past glories of nobles and wealthy merchants seep from the buildings. UNESCO has named its Rynek Glowny (main square) one of the most significant cultural sites in the world. A pilgrimage to the haunting Auschwitz-Birkenau concentration camps is unforgettable. In Warsaw you'll be impressed by the indomitable spirit of the Poles, who never lost hope in all their years of oppression. In Renaissance Zamosc, you'll feel like you're entering an 18th-century painting, and at Czestochowa, you'll be impressed by the worshipers revering their most precious icon, the Black Madonna. High up in the sophisticated mountain village of Zakopane, you can hike up into the magnificent Tatras by cable car, be transported to high ridge trails and a pristine blue lake. Along the Baltic coastline, you can share the sea with locals, climb large sand dunes, and spot aquatic birds. You'll find yourself wanting to stay in Poland longer than planned.

Poles love to camp, and there are hundreds of places. The cost of the camping place reflects its amenities and maintenance. They are friendly places, and the Poles are happy you have chosen to visit their country. Simple places can cost as little as 8 euros for 2 persons, a tent, and a car. Those close to major historic areas are around 18 euros indicated as $$ but most cost around 15 euros indicated as $. (Poland does not use the euro however) Many campgroungds have cute little cabins that are cozy when it is rainy or cold. You use your own bedding and the common campground toilet/shower area and they cost about 3 times what tent camping costs. Call in the morning to reserve one for the evening. Roads are good and well signposted, and the countryside is gorgeous. Designated car parks and plenty of street parking make parking close to historic areas simple. Cities are easy to get around in, and it's pleasant to join the locals cycling. If you learn some Polish words, you'll have more fun.

Car rental is more costly in Central Europe than in Western Europe. Make arrangements from home to pick up a car, in perhaps Germany, and drive into Poland. It's important to tell your rental company that you will be driving into Poland. They will rent you a car that the Polish/Russian car-theft groups are not interested in. You'll be much more relaxed in a modest vehicle.

Let it get dirty and look like a local owns it. Also reread the section on car/property insurance in the appendix. Don't use the car rental firm's insurance. In Warsaw in particular, car theft is a problem. One thing that is great about camping in Poland is that your car is safely next to your campsite. In Warsaw, leave your car at the campsite and use public transportation. Read and follow the suggestions in Traveling Safe and Smart at the beginning of this book while traveling in the Poland's larger cities, but especially before entering Warsaw.

Summers are pleasantly warm with some interlacing of rain, which keeps the forests and hillsides green and bountiful with wildflowers. Food is plentiful, of excellent quality, and inexpensive. The Poles love to eat, and their markets reflect this. Outdoor markets are common in most towns of any size and occur in the main squares every morning but Sunday. The vendors are grateful for a sale. Eye contact, smiles, and simple greetings of "hello" and "thank you" in Polish are always heartwarmingly appreciated. Large shopping malls are found on the outskirts of larger towns. Ask for directions to them at the campground.

The rich tradition of art and crafts is evident in the museums, restorations, festivals, and open-air museums. Check the festival schedule and then arrange your trip to join the Poles attending these colorful and lively events. They will welcome you warmly. Museums are closed on Monday and are inexpensive unless indicated otherwise.

KRAKOW

Once called "Golden" Krakow because it was the home of royalty, historic Krakow bursts with ancient legacy and sits like a jewel on the grassy banks of the Vistula River. It has one of the oldest universities in Europe and is home to many well-known intellectuals, including Karol Wojtyla once Krakow's outspoken Archbishop later the beloved Pope John Paul II. Art, beauty, and religion are foremost in Krakow.

The heart of the old town is the Rynek Glowny, an elegant medieval market square that is one of the largest in Europe. It's like a subdued St Mark's Square in Venice. In spite of its size, it feels intimate; perhaps it's the flower stalls, the sidewalk cafes, the birds, and the trumpet's call which always halts mid-note in deference to a 13th-century trumpeter who climbed the tower to warn of invading Tartars (a Tartar arrow stopped his alarm mid-way). The Cloth Hall, set picturesquely in the square's center, almost glows from all the golden amber on sale inside. Showcasing the works of hometown 19th-century Polish painter Matejko, the Gallery of 19th-Century Paintings is impressive. The

entrance is up an outside stairway on the east side of the Cloth Hall; closed Monday. But the city's masterpiece is splendid St. Mary's Church on the east corner of the square. Its grand high altar is a pentaptych–a central panel with two pairs of side wings–measuring13 meters high and 11 meters wide. It is the world's largest piece of medieval artwork and is considered the greatest piece of Gothic art in Poland. It is opened slowly and solemnly at noon each day. After paying a small admission, tourists enter through a door on the south side into the dark and soaring interior. The intricately carved 15th-century altar, by Veit Stoss, is an exuberant scene of Mary ascending to heaven attended by angels. Bring binoculars. English guidebooks are available at the ticket booth.

As you wander through the streets, you'll find them loaded with atmosphere. Ul. Florianska is a popular walking street lined with lovely shops, galleries, bookstores, and aromatic cafes. It's part of the Royal Way and leads to the Florian Gate. The home of Matejko, the famous painter who documented Polish history with such large and powerful canvases, is on the way. He lived on this street for 20 of his most fruitful years, and it's interesting to see the mementos from his life; closed Monday. After soaking up the ambiance at the Florian Gate, turn west and follow the main street to Sw. Jana. There you can examine the Czartoryski Museum's impressive collection of art, including *Lady with the Ermine* by Leonardo de Vinci and *Landscape with the Good Samaritan* by Rembrandt. The collection was established by Princess Czartoryski in 1800; closed Monday. A significant collection of religious art is displayed in the Szolajski House, located in the northwest corner of the old town across from the parking area on Ssczepanski. Jagiellonian University's Collegium Maius is a short walk from the Town Hall Tower. Located on the southwest corner of Rynek Glowny, it houses a good collection of ancient astronomical devices in tribute to Copernicus–the sagacious Pole whose theory of planetary rotation revolutionized man's view of this world. One of the world's oldest globes–from 1510–is remarkable to examine; closed Sunday.

Grassy embankments along the Vistula grace the walls of Wawel Hill, where Krakow's famous castle, crowned with graceful turrets and spires, beckons. Intricately woven tapestries and exquisite furnishings decorate the Royal Chambers with quiet elegance. Don't miss the Exhibition of Oriental Art, where sumptuous Turkish tents are just part of the fascinating collection amassed at the Battle of Vienna. Take a few minutes in the rooms of the Crown Treasury to examine the famous13[th]-century Jagged Sword, used in all of the country's coronations. Arrive early in the morning, when there is still mist on the rose-filled gardens. The ticket booth is in the passageway leading to the castle's courtyard; closed Monday. After descending the steps to the Dragon's Cave (there's an addition small admission) next to the Thieves Tower, you emerge on the grassy banks of the Vistula–the perfect place for a relaxing picnic lunch.

From here, continue walking south to explore the Kazimierz area that was once home to thousands of Jews. Ul. Jozefa leads to the Old Synagogue, a simple low-slung building now housing the Museum of History and Culture of Krakow. Here Jewish culture through the centuries is artistically celebrated; closed Saturday. Don't miss the touching cemeteries, and note the tribute to Rabbi Moses Isserles, an important philosopher (it's behind the Remu'h Synagogue). Although Kazimierz was not the actual setting for Spielberg's *Schinder's List*, the film brought world attention to Krakow Jewry. Consider taking one of the popular reasonably priced tours of the area which include a Schinder's List tour. Ticket ahead by calling Jarden Jewish Bookstore; 421 7166. The Ethnographic Museum here displays a carefully crafted a peasant cottage interior as well as meticulously stitched traditional costumes from all over Poland. It's straight down from the bridge on Krakowska.

Krakow is full of summer festivals, so you'll likely see Poles dressed in elaborately embroidered traditional costumes dancing to fiddlers' free-spirited music as you gorge on freshly grilled sausage and sip flavorful beer. The friendly locals will gladly make room for you at their table and you'll have fun smiling and complimenting them on their beautiful country. Zwierzyniec–an enormous green space where colorful parachutes often float down from the sky and where musical groups perform–is an all-around nice place to be. Kosciuzko–a very large mound of earth handbuilt by thousands of Poles to pay tribute to their hero–is nearby. Entry to it is through a little chapel. Directions: Bus 100 from Plac Matejki.

▲**Camping:** • 4km west of the historic area, exit off 4/7 west onto 780 in the direction of Oswiecim, on the north side of the Vistula bridge▲. Camping Smok (012 429 7266); one of my favorites; country setting; across from the Vistula; closest to the historic area; close to public transportation; doable by bicycle to the historic area; homey ambiance; open all year; $$.

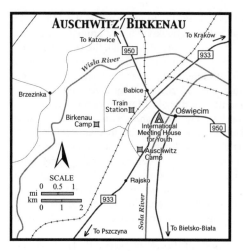

• 6km south of Krakow. Exit the city on 7/ E77 in the directions of Cieszyn. Turn west following signposting for Borek Falecki and Hotel Krakowianka, Camping Krakowianka, (012 268 1417); associated with a hotel; cabins; close to public transportation; pool; playground; open May-Sept; $$. • 5km northwest of the historic area in the direction of Katowice. Close to the round-about-intersection of E40, 914, and E77, next to Motel Krak. Camping Krak (012-637 2957) large; close to public transportation and supermarket; road noise; open mid-May-Sept; $$. • 4km north of Krakow on 7/E77 in the direction of Warsaw. Close to a pool complex Clepardia Basen. Camping Clepardia (012 415 9672); medium size; bus to historic area; some shade; open May-Sept; $. • 10km south of Krakow off 7/E77 in the suburb of Gaj. Camping Korona (012 270 1318); small; nice country location; friendly ambiance; communal BBQ; some shade; Open May-Sept; $.

Auschwitz/Birkenau

It is said he who forgets history, may relive it. Your pilgrimage to see the death site of almost 2 million people will be a sobering experience. Start at Auschwitz. Pick up the free brochure then view the 15-minute documentary film in the museum. Don't wait for the English showing; it's easily understood in another language. After passing through the gate inscribed *Abeit Macht Frei* (Work Makes Free), go to the prison blocks to see the moving exhibitions presented by all the major European countries. Then go on to the crematorium and gas chamber. After a break, take the shuttle bus to Birkenau, or drive the 2 kilometers. Softened only by poppies, wild sweet pea, and green grass, this death camp remains vast and sinister. Walk reflectively down the train tracks to the monument at the end. Before leaving, climb the stairs at the entrance gate to view the complex in its entirety; open daily; free.

▲Camping: • Close to the museum. Center for Dialogue and Prayer (033 843 1000); meadow next to the center; basic; $.

Wieliczka Salt Mine

This subterranean labyrinth of tunnels, immense halls, altars, monuments, and figures all carved from salt is like an underground castle. The delicacy of the chandeliers, altarpieces and statues in the immense chapel is breathtaking. Renown for its microclimate and health-giving properties, the mine features a sanatorium at the depth of 211 meters where severe cases of allergies are treated. It's a 2-hour tour and 2-kilometer walk, so wear comfortable shoes. Arrive early; it's UNESCO listed and popular; open daily. Purchase an English brochure if your tour is in Polish. Directions: Drive to the southeast edge of the city. Signposting is good for exiting off highway 4.

Czestochowa

The Jasna Gora Monastery might be the most important place of religious pilgrimage in Central Europe. Devotees come to pay homage to the sacred Byzantium-style icon of the Black Madonna, painted on lime-tree wood and measuring 122-centimeters by 82-centimeters. It is ancient, but the date of its creation is unknown. For six centuries the icon has been revered in the hearts and minds of the Poles as a miracle worker for the devoted and for the country itself. It rests on a high altar, below which many kneeling people pray. For many, it's an icon they have waited a lifetime to see. The tiny mother and baby are elaborately dressed in jewel-studded robes. Adding to the drama, a screen is slowly raised and lowered throughout the day to the call of a trumpet. Poland is an intensely religious country and the devoted here are not just the elderly–teenagers are part of the faithful. Quiet and sacred, Jasna Gora is located on the top of a hill at the west end of the wide, tree-lined main boulevard, Al Najswietszej. On your walk up, quiet Poles,

many in traditional dress, will accompany you. You won't pass any tacky souvenir stalls. The main entrance is on the south side, through four successive fortress-like gates. Follow signs for the separate chapel, Kaplica Cudownego Obrazu. Buy an English guide, and bring binoculars. Major holidays attract masses of people (May 3, August 15, August 26, and September 8th). Directions: West of the railway tracks. Follow signposting from all roads to the town's main boulevard, al, Najswietszej, abbreviated NMP.

▲**Camping:** • West of the monastery's car-park. Camping Olenka 76 (034 365 5799); excellent location; cabins; open all year; $.

Zakopane

Magnificent mountains, grassy meadows sparkling with daisies and colombine, and tumbling crystal-clear creeks beckon as you breathe in the fresh air and absorb the ambiance in charming Alpine Zakopane, located in the Carpathian Mountains bordering Slovakia. Outdoor stalls offer for sale mounds of thick wool sweaters, neat rows of wooden shoes, and intricately molded and smoked sheep cheese. Jump onto a reasonably priced horse-drawn wagon filled with Polish families laughing and having a good time, and take a pine-scented ride up to Morskie Oko, the largest and most pristine Alpine lake in the Tatras. A trail loops around the lake, and at the far end another trail leads up to deep-blue Lake Czarny Staw. Experienced trekkers will want to climb farther up to Mt. Rysy, where there's an incredible view of over 100 peaks on a clear day. Hikes from hut to hut can be arranged at the PTTK office in Zakopane. Directions: Drive to the car park at Kuznice or take the PKS bus from the bus terminal. No motor vehicles are allowed beyond Kuznice.

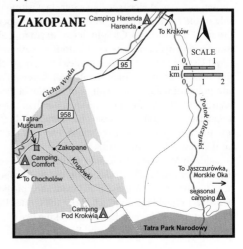

The heart of the mountains is most easily reached by the cable car from Kuznice to Mt Kasprowy Wierch, where the pinnacles seem dramatically nearby. A round-trip-ticket permits one and one-half-hours to enjoy the excursion. Or you can purchase a one-way ticket and hike down. Several marked trails lead down. The most popular one is about 4 to 5-hour hike. From Mt Kasprowy Wierch, follow the yellow trail to Dolina Gasienicowa Hostel where you can stop for a rest and lunch. From there take the trail to Dolina Jaworsynka, which is initially blue-coded then yellow to Kuznice. For a longer hike, take the red-coded trail down to Lake Morskie Oko. It first traverses the ridge, then descends down to Zawart (where there is a hostel) on a blue-marked trail passing through the lovely Dolina Pieciu Stawow (5 Lakes Valley) down to Lake Morskie Oko, where you can continue down on foot or take the wagon to Kuznice. Plan to stay at the hostel at Zawart or get an early start because it's a 6 to 8-hour hike. In summer, the lines for the cable car are long. If you plan to hike down book a ticket ahead from a local travel agency so you can get an early start. Kuznice is not far from the campground.

In late August, a gargantuan tent fills with families who have come to applaud the highly spirited dance troupes from all over Eastern Europe at the Zakopane Mountain Music Festival. The joyful music and dancing have kept alive the hopes of many during their country's troubled history. Tickets are inexpensive and easy to buy that day. Performances are scheduled for both afternoon and evening, so you still have time for hiking.

▲Camping: • South of town, follow signs to Kusznice. At the roundabout, turn west onto the road just beneath ski slope. Camping Pod Krokwia, (018-201-2256); great place to meet other travelers; close to hiking and cable car to Kuznice; cabins; cozy café with terrace looking at mountains; open all year; $$. • At the north edge of town on 95, stay west at the round-about. Turn south to cross the bridge onto a divided road following small signs up the hill through a residential area. Make a U-turn to return to the campground entrance on the other side of the divided road. Camping Comfort, ul. Kaszelewskiego 7a (018-149-42); tricky to find; close to town; lovely terraced hillside with view of the mountains; small and tranquil; open May-Sept; $$$. • Follow signposting on 95 driving north 5km in the direction of Nowy Targ. Camping Harenda (018 201 4700); large open area with little shade; nice view of the mountains; May-Oct; $$. • On the road to Lake Morskii Oka and Jaszcurowka there are several seasonal camping places; small; more remote but tranquil and scenic; watch for signs; $.

Warszawa

After being almost totally destroyed during World War II, Warsaw's restoration is amazing. It's authentic 17th to 18th-century appearance after restoration was acknowledged when it was chosen as a World Heritage Site. Start by visiting the Historical Museum of Warsaw, on the north side of the main square at number 42, which documents the town's destruction and restoration. Listen to the music of Chopin, a countryman, being played by talented street musicians. If you wander down the narrow cobblestone streets, you'll invariably come to Castle Square and the Royal Castle; buy the English guide. The exquisitely beautiful cathedrals and small churches dotting the old town are solemn with worshipers. Pay tribute to Marie Curie, discoverer of radium and polonium, and twice winner of the Nobel Prize in a tiny museum. She lived her adult life in France, but her family home was just north of the immense Gothic Barbakan church topped with a Renaissance parapet. Warsaw has a wide and interesting array of museums, palaces, and galleries. Buy a map at a magazine stand, and visit the tourist office at Pac Zamkowy. The old town is on the west side of the Vistula River.

Saddenly Warsaw has become victim to organized crime. Thieves work in highly skilled groups that blend in well. They operate on public transportation, around gas stations, and parking areas near tourist areas. Although for insurance purposes you'll need a police report, regretfully the police seem unable to do much about the crime. Retrieving stolen goods is highly unlikely so drive a modest car and keep it dusty and looking like a local owned it. Reread and follow closely the suggestions in "Traveling Smart and Safe" in this book, and you shouldn't have a problem.

▲**Camping:** • 5km west of Krakow. On E67 from Wroclaw, turn west at traffic light by the Warsaw monument and follow sign-posting. Camping Astar (022-254 4391); small; cabins; pool; playground; close to public transportation; good security; April-Oct; $$. • In the same area. Follow directions above but turn east at the light by the Warsaw monument then north at the T intersection. Camping Gromada (022-254-391); close to the airport and public transportation; cabins; May-Oct; $$. At both campgrounds pack everything back into your vehicle before leaving for the day.

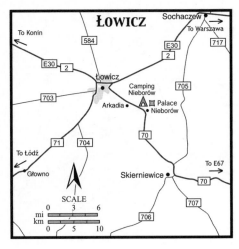

Lowicz

Long ago aristocratic Poles, caught up in memories of travels to France and Greece, were anxious to impress their wealthy friends with lavish palaces and gardens. The landscaped park Arkadia and nearby Nieborow palace in Lowicz are fine examples of their success. The palace grounds make a nice place to stretch your legs, enjoy a nap, and take some photographs. The restored palace is pleasant to tour and has an especially fine collection of world globes; closed Monday. Grounds are open daily. Conceived in the 18th-century by Princess Helen Radziwill after extensive travels in Greece, the reproductions of temples and pavilions in the gardens she named Arkadia have been left evocatively unrestored. Directions: Drive 100km west of Warsaw to the small village of Nieborow, and then continue 10km southeast to Lowicz.

▲**Camping:** • One kilometer west of the palace park, on the road to Skierniewice. Camping Nieborow (046 838 5692; nice location; cabins; open June-Aug; $.

Lodz

Lodz was the center of Poland's celebrated textile industry from its beginning. The city produced vast fortunes but abject poverty was rampant and was described in 1899 by Nobel Prize-winner Wladyslaw Reymont in his novel, *The Promised Land.* Pianist Arthur Rubinstein was born in Lodz and memorabilia from his life is just part of an eclectic collection housed in Poznanski Palace, set picturesquely next to an old mill; closed Monday. Directions: From the roundabout in the center of town, drive north on Piortrkowsa one block. Turn west onto ul. Ogrodowa and drive another block. A replica of a Renaissance palace museum houses one of Poland's best art collections. Works by Chagall, Mondrian, Ernst, and Leger hang in Muzeum Sztuki, along with contemporary works by lesser-known Polish artists; closed Monday. Directions: Drive south of the roundabout 2 blocks. Turn west onto Wieckowskiego and drive 3 blocks.

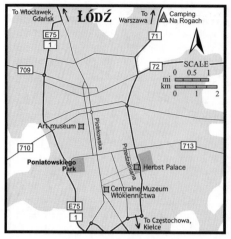

▲**Camping:** • 4km northeast of the city off 71 in the direction of Warsaw. Camping Na Rogach, (042 659 7013); cabins; close to highway; small and basic; open June-Aug; $.

Zamosc

Zamosc was designed by the Italian Bernardo Morando of Padua for the dynamic and aristocratic Jan Zamoyski, who hoped to build a perfect city both culturally and economically. The town attracted wealthy international merchants whose presence is still embedded in the architectural details of the old center. Miraculously unscathed by war, the 16th-century historic area is UNESCO listed. Take some time to absorb the atmosphere of the lovely square, then go into the Regional Museum at number 24 to exam the meticulous model of the town in its heyday. As you wander through the old town, note the exquisite details of doorways and vaulted ceilings. Street music and open-air concerts occur all summer. The horrific story of mass executions of both Jews and Poles by the Nazis and Soviets is told in tiny cells of the Rotunda in a 19th-century arsenal; closed Mondays. Directions: On the south side of the railway tracks. Walk south from the main square Rynek Wielki following signposting for Rotunda. Opposed to the usual kind of game reserve for sportsmen, Jan Zamoyski bought a huge tract of land to protect game and botanical species. Now a national park, Roztoczanski is shaded by immense beeches, and along the banks of its tranquil river storks and cranes stand statue-like while thousands of summer butterflies flutter as if in a dream.

▲**Camping:** • Just outside the northwest corner of the fortified walls, next to Hotel Sportowy. Camping Tenis Zamosc (084-39-24-99); in a sports park; basic; $.

Kazimierz Doly

Picturesque in its setting between the Vistula River and surrounding wooded hills, this small town boasts a Gothic hilltop castle on the hill and an especially attractive market square. It has always

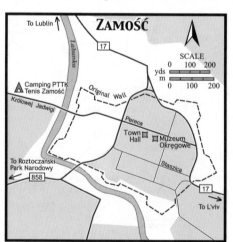

been a haven for artists who still make up a good portion of the populace and sell their work from stalls on the main square. The town provides a welcome break from larger cities and cycling is easy and scenic. Don't miss the small Museum of Goldsmithery. Located on the main street west of the square; it is a real gem. The reasonably priced ferry ride from Kazimierz to Janowice on the Vistula River makes a nice break in the journey.

▲**Camping:** • On the west side of the square, drive up the small hill toward the tiny church. Stay right, taking the narrow road closest to the Vistula River, ul. Krakowska. Drive west for one kilometer. Camping Dom Turysty (081-810-036); lovely setting on the river; small; open June-August; $$$.

Bialowieski National Park

In the early 1900s extinction threatened the European Bison, the biggest mammal on the continent. The citizens of Bialowieza attempted to save their beloved wild animal in 1929, by bringing zoo-kept animals to their vast forest and breeding them, and the once royal hunting grounds was designated a national park with strict entry regulations. The experiment was so successful that today the park supplies bison to zoos all over the world and almost 300 roam the park itself. At this park you'll also see tarpan, a small wild horse that is indigenous to the Ukrainian steppes and distinguished by a dark stripe running from head to tail. With selective breeding, the Poles have been able to preserve the animal with its original traits. Park breeders have also created a new animal–a cross between a bison and a cow they call a "zubron". Ancient trees here, some more than 4-centuries old, are named after monarchs. You can lean back and look way up at them in the Royal Oaks Way. The park can only be entered with a guide. To arrange an English-speaking guide, call the park office a day ahead; 085-12-295; open daily. Cycling is a popular way to get around in the park and rentals are available. Your guide will also ride a bike. Horse-drawn carriage is another option. Visit the excellent natural history museum first to bring more meaning to your experience. A self-guided English brochure of the museum is available if you are taking a tour in Polish; closed Monday. Directions: 52km south of Bialystok on 19, exit at the village of Bielsk Podlaski onto 689, and drive 44km east to the park entrance.

▲**Camping:** • One kilometer south of the park entrance in the village of Grodek. Camping Grodek (085-12-804); simple; open June-August; $.

Masurian Lakes District

Canoeists, yacht enthusiasts, and kayakers put this extensive waterway of rivers, lakes, and canals at the top of their list. The Krutynia Kayak Route is popular for those wanting to spend a week paddling and camping. All types of boating equipment are readily available for rental. To book an organized trip for the Krutynia Kayak route, call the OZGT office in Olsztyn a couple of weeks in advance; 089-275-5156 To do it on your own, stop in Olsztyn at the outdoor equipment store, Sklep Podroznika, to purchase a map and get advice. Both businesses are in the old town behind the tourist office, close to the High Gate.

The excursion boat down the Elblag Canal is an unusual trip, with five slipways and dry land, rail-mounted trolleys. Call first to check the schedule. In Elblag; 089-50-324-307 in Ostroda; 089-88-463-871. The open-air farming village museum in Olsztynek is particularly pleasant; with hollyhocks, heartwarming little cottages, and old-fashioned tools. Directions: Northeast corner of town.

For a break from nature, spend an hour or so seeing the massive concrete ruins of Hitler's Headquarters at Wolf's Lair. It is a bizarre place. The shadowy paths leading to the ruins of huge concrete bunkers can be cycled, but most people walk. Purchase an English guide. Directions: Take the main road 592 in the direction of Gizycko for 8km. Drive northeast of town, then turn onto the small road signposted for Gierloz. It's located in the forest east of Ketrzyn. The admission and carpark costs are expensive for Poland.

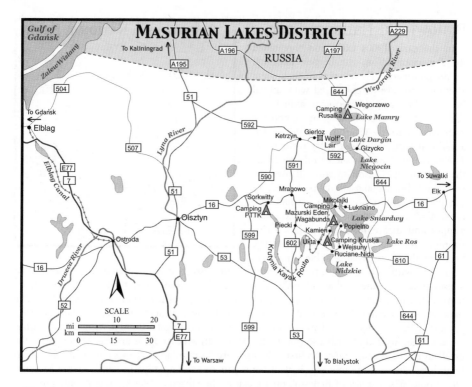

The elegant and enchanting swans at the Luknajno Reserve glide regally by as if they were Parisian models posing for a photographer. Directions: Drive northeast out of Mikolajki for 5km on a small dirt road paralleling 16 on the south side, to Lake Luknajno. Follow the sign to *wiezy widokowej* (viewing tower). Popielno Tarpan is a fascinating breeding station research institute. If time permits go there to see if you can join a pre-booked tour group to see and learn about the small wild horses. Directions: From Ruciane, head north on a small road in the direction to the tiny village Wejsuny. Take the road heading north in the direction of Popielno. Cycling or walking along the lakes and through forests is refreshing and tranquil.

▲Camping: • In Sorkwitty (a stop in the road about 10km west of Mragowo) cross the railway tracks and small bridge on 16, turn south onto a small road. Camping PTTK (89 742 1025) on the lake; cabins; boat rental; open June-Aug; $. • Drive 11km south of Mikolajki on 609 in the direction of Ruciane. Turn east and go for about 6km on a small narrow dirt road in the direction of Nowy Most and Iznota. Camping Mazurski Eden (089 231 669); remote; lovely location on the lake; open June-Aug; $$. • In Mikolajki, on 609 in the direction of Ruciane. Camping Wagabunda, (089 816 018); on the lake; close to town and excursion boats; boat rental; cabins open May-Sept; $$. • South of Mragowo on 602, exit east onto 610 at Piecki. Drive north on a small road for 4km in the direction of Wygryny and Kamien. It is east of tiny village Ukta. Camping Kruska (089 231 597); remote; beautiful location on the lake; quiet; open June-Aug; $$. • North of Gizycko about 22km on 644, just south of Wegorzewo on the lake. Camping Rusalka (089 772 191); large; cabins; boat rental; close to excursion boats; open June-Aug; $$.

Gdansk

Being the key port in Eastern Europe has given Gdansk a tumultuous history. Meticulous and complex restoration has brought this city, once in state of rubble, back to its 16th-century elegance. Home to heroes of the Solidarity Movement as well as to famous authors, scientists, and artists, it enchants and awes. Follow the signs for Glowne Miasto, the historic town. Parking is not difficult. Use the brick tower of St. Mary's Church to orient yourself. Pick up a "*What, Where, When Guide*" at any hotel to check for special scheduled events in this lively, interesting city.

The bustling waterfront is a hub of activity with ships entering the canal way of the Motlawa River. At its northern end, look for the Gdansk Crane, it was the largest loading crane in the world during the 15th and 16th-centuries. Now meticulously rebuilt, the crane is part of the captivating Maritime Museum housed in old granaries and a freighter across the waterway. Ride the shuttle boat over, or take a leisurely stroll or bike ride by crossing the waterway via the bridge at the Green Gate. Take an excursion boat out to historic Westerplatte, where World War II began. Boats leave from the wharf by the Green Gate.

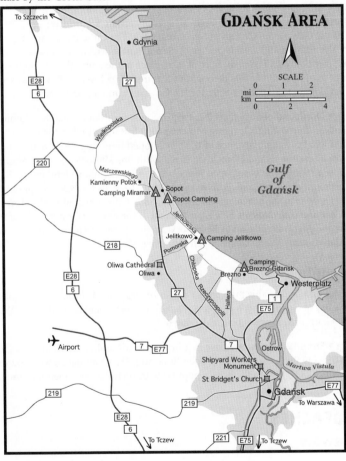

The Green Gate is the entrance to Gdansk's old marketplace, a festive place with rousing music, entertaining street theatre, and enticing aromas. The marketplace is most lively during the Dominican Fair held in the first weeks of August. Rest at Neptune's Fountain and marvel at the gilded figure of King Zygmunt August situated atop the pinnacle of the tower. The town hall now houses the Gdansk's Historical Museum, where you can climb to the tower for a great view and then examine the second floor photo exhibit of the city's destruction and restoration. The Red Room has a richly ornamented ceiling and pictures detailing Polish life. Back on the square, just behind the fountain, view the giant Renaissance tile stove in Artus Court. Then walk east from the immense St Mary's Church and find ul. Mariacka–a street that was painstakingly restored to the tiniest detail. For Solidarity history, go a few blocks north of St Mary's Church to just south of the Radunia Canal and St Bridget's Church. The clergy and parishioners of St Bridget risked their lives when they gave their strong support to the dockyard workers. Touching bas-relief works depicting Solidarity's history are on its north aisle. Cross over the canal to spend time at the touching Moument to the Shipyard Workers, who gave their lives in protest, and reflect on Czeslaw Milosz's poem at the base.

In the suburb of Oliwa is a famous cathedral well known for its lavishly decorated organ. You can hear its rich and sonorous tones at short recitals given throughout the day. In July and August, during the International Organ Music Festival, special recitals are held on Fridays. Directions: Drive north of the Gdansk on 27. Exit at Spacerowa/ 218. The cathedral complex is at this fork.

In August, the fashionable seaside resort of Sopot, just north of Gdansk, is alive with the International Song Festival. The main festival takes place in the amphitheater at Opera Lesna, on the west side of town, but music lilts throughout the area. Jazz lovers will want to arrange being in Gdynia, a few kilometers farther north, for the Gdynia Summer Jazz Days.

▲Camping: • North end of Sopot, off 27. Exit east, just south of the exit for Kamienny Potok and follow signposting. Camping Miramar (058 518 011); best in the Gdansk area; good location within walking distance of the beach; open June-Aug; $$. • South end of Sopot, exit off 27 for the Grand Hotel, then drive south one kilometer. Sopot Camping (058-516-523); close to the beach; basic; open June-Aug; $. • In the suburb Jetitkowo, 10km north of Gdansk, exit east off 27 onto ul. Pomorska and drive towards the Bay. Camping Jelitkowo (058 553 2731); close to the beach; open June-Aug; $$$. • Just north of the old town exit, go towards the Bay and shipyards on E75/1. At the end of the road, drive north along the main road, passing the port tram station to Brzezno. Camping Brzezno-Gdansk (058 435 531); closest to Gdansk; some shade; cabins; open June-Aug; $$.

Hel Peninsula

Unique in size and beauty, this picturesque finger of clean, sandy beach juts out of the north-west end of the Bay of Gdansk and is a perfect place to rest, swim, and lay in the sun. Wind surfing is popular. Stock up with supplies before driving out.

▲Camping: • From Wladyslawow, drive east in the direction of Jastarnia on 216. Camping Na Skarpie (058 749 095); nice location; open June-Aug; $$. Camping Nowa Maszoperia, ul. Mickiewicza (058 752 348); on the beach; popular with surfers; basic; open June-Aug; $.

BALTIC BEACHES
Wladyslawow

If your schedule doesn't allow enough time to go out to the Hel pennisula, this lovely little port town makes a nice substitute.

HEL PENINSULA/SŁOWIŃSKI NATIONAL PARK

▲**Camping:** • West of town 3km on the beach road. Camping Kaper (058 674 1486); nice location in a pine forest; open June-Aug; $$. • Farther west on the beach road near Chlapowo. Camping Roza Wiatrow(058 674 0544); nice location; close to the beach; smaller; cabins; open June-Aug; $$. In the same area but west of Chlapowo on the road to Wladyslawowo. Camping Male Morze (058 674 1231); good location; some shade; open June-Aug; $$. • In Puck, overlooking the Bay. Camping Omega (058 673 2980); good location; within walking distance to the beach; open June-Aug; $$.

Slowinski National Park

The vast 40-meter high dunes of Slowinski National Park, a UNESCO-listed biosphere, make for a mini Sahara Desert-like experience. South of the dunes, a reed-lined lagoon, Jezioro Lebsko, lists 250 bird species that migrate through or live there permanently. Directions: Drive west from the seaside resort town of Leba to Rabka. For big dune exploration drive 3km farther or take a mini-bus shuttle.

In the village of Smoldzino, the park's Museum of Natural History exhibits the local flora and fauna. Walk up Rowokol Hill, west of the village, and climb the steps of the observation tower for a panorama of the whole park. Directions: Drive southwest of Leba on 213. Exit the graceful tree-lined road, and drive north on a small, scenic road to Smoldzino.

In the hamlet of Kluki, you can meander around the best of the country's open-air farm village museums. Warmly welcoming visitors, the staff maintains the authentic old gardens, houses, and barns with pride. Directions: From Smoldzino, drive east on the small road to Kluki.

▲Camping: • West of Smoldzino on the Baltic coast, take the small road west of the lagoon Gardno in the direction of the tiny village of Objazda. Continue to the coast road at Debina, and go a bit farther north to the village of Rowy. Camping Rowy Przymorse (59 141 940); close to the beach; cabins; open Jun-Aug; $. • Out of Slupsk drive north to the Baltic and Ustka on 21, then follow signs to Przewloka. Camping Morski (144 789); cabins; within walking distance to beach; well cared for; open June-Aug; $$. • In Leba follow the main road 214 into town. The area around Leba is a popular seaside resort with plenty of campgrounds. All the camping places are open June-August. On the west side of the river. Intercamp (661 380); $$. Camping Rafael (661 972); $. Camping Lesny (661 380) $$. • In town. Camping Przymorze, (661 304); $$. Camping Ambre (662 472); $.

Western Baltic Coast

For some beach time on the Baltic Sea, these are good places to soak up the sun and salt air with the locals; open June-August.

▲Camping: • Southwest of Miedzyzdroje. Drive north on 3/E65 north and then on the beach road 102. Camping Miedzyzdroje (097 80 275); within walking distance of the beach; $$. • Farther east on 102, close to Dziwnow. Camping Wiking (091-813-493); close to the beach; cabins; $$$. • In the same area, Camping Korab (091 381 3205); within walking distance of the beach; $$. • North on 109, exit on 103 for Pogorzelica and drive 2km west of the town. Camping Liwia (096-163-111); close to the beach; cabins; $$. • 15km west of Kolobrzeg drive west on the beach road to Dzwirzyno. Camping Biala (096-585-402); cabins; $$.

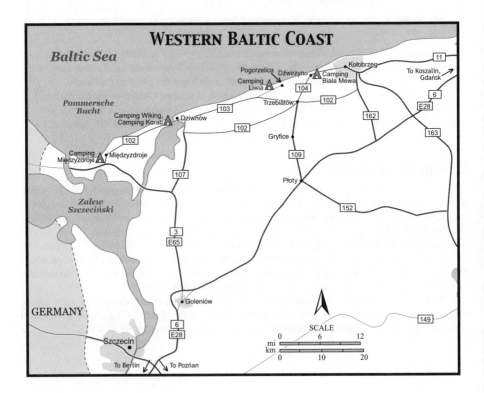

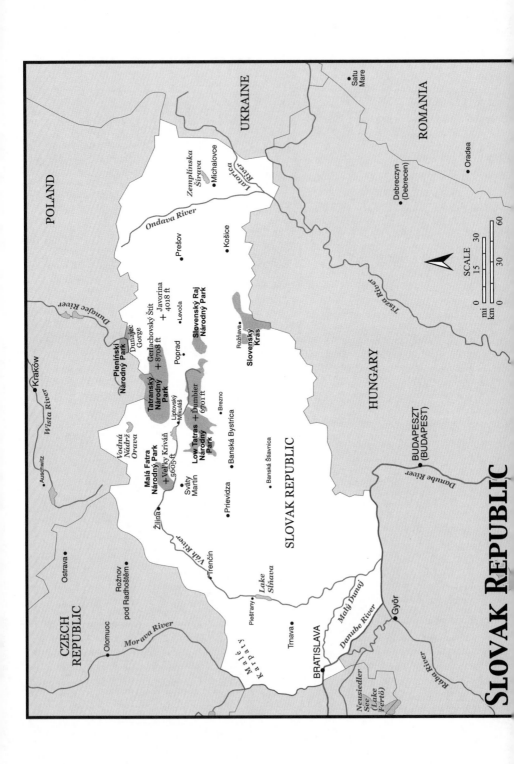

SLOVAK REPUBLIC

Slovak Republic

www.sacr.sk

At a fraction of the cost of visiting Western Europe's Alps, oudoor enthusiasts can visit Slovakia's saw-toothed, brooding High Tatras. A primeval exhilaration of being at the top of the world is felt at their summits. Difficult and challenging, their granite sides are slashed by glacier-carved ravines, and there are large areas of slippery scree. But Slovakia's mountaineering clubs have built 35-meters of rope climbs on fixed chains to summits where long-range vistas are heart-stopping. In the both the High and Low Tatras, trails pass serene alpine lakes as well as waterfalls tumbling wildly over boulders. Creeks skip through quiet valleys, and blankets of red and yellow clover enhance its grassy meadows. On undulating hills dense forests of beech and pine are interspersed with fields of corn, wheat, and potatoes. Slovakia entices you to linger longer than you had planned in its easy, low-key, unpretentious atmosphere.

You'll share your campgrounds with Slovaks having an old-fashioned good time. They are outdoor enthusiasts, proud of their country and happy to have you enjoying it with them. Campgrounds are found throughout the country. Some are just basic with casually maintained, but the easy friendliness of the local people is always there. The cost of the campgrounds reflects the amenities. Most cost about 12 euros for two persons, a tent, and a car and indicated here as $. (Euros are not used in Slovakia though) Driving is relaxing and scenic. Freeways are few, but roads are in good condition. Horse-drawn carts and small tractors on the rural roads are not uncommon. There are few toll roads and parking is readily available except in Bratislava. Fill up with gas, get supplies and local currency before going to smaller towns.

Open markets found in the morning close to a town's main square. Generally shops are open 9 to 5 weekdays. Many close by noon on Saturday and remain closed until Monday morning, so check your supplies on Friday or Saturday morning. Slovakia is an inexpensive place to visit. Museum entrance fees, food in the markets, and campground cost, won't add up to very much. Get local currency from cash machines outside banks in larger towns. Museum and historic sites, except Jewish ones, are generally closed on Monday, while the Jewish ones are closed on Saturday. They are generally open from 10 AM to 4 PM and usually close for lunch noon to 1 PM. Ask for an English text for museum tours, which are generally obligatory but not usually given in English.

Tatra National Park

Slovakia's national anthem, Thunder Over the Tatras, sounds with pride over these peaks that soar abruptly from grassy meadows. Electric trains, picturesque villages, and campgrounds have been carefully built to protect the natural beauty from over-development. Chair lifts whisk people to high trails and panoramic views. It's like visiting Kitzbuhel Austria before it became an expensive resort. For long hikes, be sure to take a good trail map, wear sturdy shoes for the rocky terrain, and include in your day pack: extra warm waterproof clothing, plenty of energy food, a whistle for emergencies (Blow 6 times in a minute to call for help), and water. Serious hikes should not

be attempted without consulting the weather forecast and getting advice from the mountain rescue service at the park's office at the eastern end of the park; people die every year in these mountains, usually from getting stranded in a sudden storm. Rock climbing, as opposed to hiking up to the summits, requires a membership in a recognized climbing club (you'll need proof of membership) or hiring a guide; www.horska-sluzba.sk. Visiting the Tatra Park Museum makes a stay more meaningful. Not only are the natural and geological history exhibits well done, but the way of life of the people who live in the Tatras is colorfully presented. Just outside, a botanical garden permits examining species you'll see tucked away in the granite and limestone high up in the mountains. The main Tatra tourist information office is northwest of the train station in the village of Stary Smokovec. The Tatra National Park Office and Museum is at the eastern edge of the village of Tatranska on 540. Both have English-speaking staff, and are excellent sources of information, maps, and booklets; open daily. Tatra National Park attracts an international clientele. In pleasant little cafes, shops, and park gardens, people relax and soak up the mountain air. It's easy to meet other travelers and perhaps link up for some hiking; www.tatry.sk

The most popular chairlift is in Tatranska Lomnica. It whisks you up for an easy walk to the alpine lake, Skalnate Pleso, and to the trailheads of other hikes. Trails meander back down to the valley through forests where you can smell the pines and hear the happy chatter of birds. For more adventure, continue on the chairlift going up from Skalnate Pleso for an exciting 2632-meter high ride to Lominicky stift. The stunning panoramic view from here includes southern Poland and eastern Slovakia. For an easy loop hike park in Tatranska Lomnica. Take the chair lift to Skalnate Pleso. Follow the red trail west to Hreblenok. At the waterfalls you can rest on massive warm boulders lacing the falls, breathe in the clear mountain air–and thrill to the thundering sound. At the mountain cafe at Hreblenok, buy a snack and join others relishing the view of sharp and craggy mountains on an outside terrace. To return to the base of the mountain, board the funicular train at Hrebenok for a scenic ride down to the village of Stary Smokovec. The electric train will take you back to the village of Tatranska Lomnica and your parked car. For a shorter trip, take the funicular railway from Stary Smokovec up to Hreblenok. Directions: At the northeastern corner of the village of Tatranska Lomnica, follow the road up through the park-like setting of the Grand Hotel Praha. The cable car station and car park are below the hotel.

▲Camping: • From Stary Smokovec, drive south on 534 for 2km in the direction of Poprad. Tatracamping; lovely setting along the river; small; basic; open July-Aug; $. • From Tatranska Lominica, drive south on 540 for 3km in the direction of Velka Lominica. Eurocamp (052 446 7741); large; cabins; popular with caravans; café; open all year; $$. • Drive 20km west of Stary Smokovec. Exit south onto 50 (a winding mountain road), in the direction of Tatranka Strba. Camping Tatranska Strba; tranquil location; affiliated with a hotel; small; open June-Aug; $. • 2km east of Tatranska Lominica near the intersection of 540 and 537. Intercamp Tatranec (052 446 7092); little shade; cabins; close to the bike trail and cable car to hiking trails; open May Oct; $$.

Mala Tatra National Park

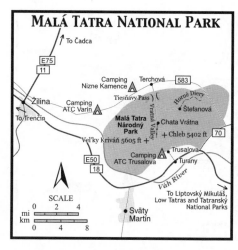

Considered to be Slovakia's most beautiful valley the Vratna Valley is the birthplace of their national Robin Hood-like hero, Janosik. Trails lead up and down rocky cliffs, through leafy forests, along gurgling creeks, and past charming wood houses. The clear mountain air is laced with the delicate aroma of pines whispering in the breeze and is rich with the whistles and squeals of birdsong. Gold and purple gentian and larkspur decorate the rock garden setting. Fishing in the bolder-strewn rivers, walking up to alpine meadows with bubbling creeks, and cycling along designated forest paths are popular pursuits. The trail from Krivanska to Stefanova passes by a limestone region of bizarrely shaped columns and into a narrow gorge where ladders cling over small waterfalls, then finishes with picturesque views of the shingled roofs of wood houses in Stefanova. Trail maps are essential in the area, as logging markers can be mistaken for trail markers. Bring energy food, water, and warm waterproof clothing for changeable weather. Directions: Located on the western edge of Tatra National Park. From Zilna, drive east on 583 for 25km to Terchovca. Turn into the magnificently beautiful Tiesnavy Pass. At a fork about 3km from the Terchovca turnoff, take the road signposted for Stefanova. Pick up trail maps at the mountain rescue service signposted Horska sluzba. Then return to the fork, and take the other road signposted for Chata Vratna. A year-round chair lift here goes to Snilov sedlo–saddle between the peaks of Velky Krivan and Cheb–where there are pleasant walking paths along the ridge and back down to Vratna. In late July, a particularly enjoyable festival of music and dance in Terchovca makes visitors feel welcome among the fun-loving Slovaks.

▲Camping: • At the turnoff to Branica on 583, about 3km west of Terchova. Camping Nizne Kamence (69-5151); nice location; basic camping; open July-Aug; $. • 15km east of Zilna on 583. Camping Varin (69-2410); cabins; open June-Aug; $. • On the south side of the Tatra National Park, close to Martin take E50/18 for 12km towards Turany. Exit north in the direction of Trusalova onto a small road along the river for 2km. Camping Trusalova; lovely location; basic; open July-Aug; $.

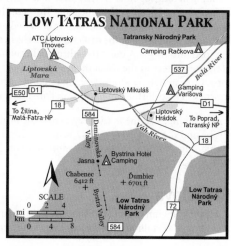

Low Tatras National Park

Beneath the towering peaks of the High Tatras lie the tree-covered hillsides of the Low Tatras. Here you can take walks through the pristine valleys along delightful creeks and rushing rivers. Stop and wave to a farmer working in one of the tiny villages, explore deep caves, and camp along the lake with other Slovaks. This is the homeland of some of Slovakia's best-loved heroes: Kral, poet of the Slovak

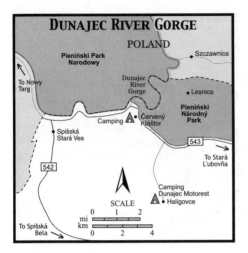

revolution; Razusova-Martakova, biographer of Slovakia's hero Janosik; and Martikan, canoeist and Olympic Gold Medal winner. At Liptovska Mare, a large reservoir lake, you'll join Slovakians and their families at the campground and on the trails. Bikes, canoes, and paddle boats are available to rent. Farther up the road, in the tiny hamlet of Pribylina, Slovaks proudly show off life in the olden days at the Liptov Open Air Village; open daily. Directions: From Liptovska Mikulas, turn north onto 584.

In Demanova Valley, in the village of Jasna, a chair lift ascends to high peaks and a ridge trail. Visit the subterranean ice cave of Demanovska Jaskyna and the Demanovska Cave of Freedom. They are signposted off the road between Jasna and Liptovska Mikulas; closed Monday. Directions: At Liptovska Mikulas, turn south onto 584 and drive south 15km to Jasna.

▲Camping: • North of Liptovsky Hradok exit D1 or E50 for Lipt Peter and drive north 3km. Autocamp Vavrisovo (044 527 1087); associated with a hotel; pretty location close to the river; open May-Sept; $. • 4km farther north on the same road to the village of Pribylina. Autocamp Rackova Dolina (044 529 3274); small; close to hiking trails and river, lovely remote setting; open June-Aug; $. • On the west side of the Tatras, exit off D1 or E50 for Lipt. Mikulas, and drive north 6km to the lake. Autocamp Liptovsky Trnovec (044 559 8459); nice setting on the lake; paddle boats, canoes, and bikes for rent; playground; café-bar; close to bike trail; open May-Oct; $$. • South of Lipt Mikulas. Exit off of E50 or D1 on 584 and drive 6km to Bystrina. Autocamp Bystrina (044 554 8163); nice setting along the river; some shade; close to the bike trail; open all year; $.

Dunajec River Gorge

There is a festive and fun-loving air among the boatmen–dressed in traditional costumes and standing in long log rafts–as they steer their way down the Pieniny River. The boat is reminiscent of Venetian gondolas as they meander through the scenic Dunajec Gorge. The photogenic 1 ½-hour trip passes small villages, hillside churches and pasturelands. Boat trips leave from both the Cathusian Monastery at the east end of the river road, and at the intersection of the river road and the road into town. A quiet tree-shrouded trail follows the river into the gorge. Cross the bridge at the monastery to the reach the trailhead. Boat trips and the trail end in Lesnica. Your choices for return are taking a bus, taxi, or walking. The museum in the monastery has some notable frescoes. The colorful Eastern Slovak Folk Festival occurs in mid-June.

▲Camping: • At the monastery, across the bridge in the park by the gorge trail. Car entrance is behind the monastery on 543. Dunajec River Camping; lovely setting; basic; open June-Aug; $. • 3km south of the monastery on 543, exit for Haligovce. Camping Dunajec Motorest; cabins; open June-Aug; $.

Bratislava

Historically important Bratislava was a coronation city for centuries. Eleven royal crownings, including Maximillion's, took place here. Let your imagination evoke the pomp and rituals of the crowning pageants as you stand on Castle Hill taking in the panoramic views of the Danube River and the Cathedral of St. Martin. On a clear day, you can see three countries: Hungary, Austria, and Slovakia. The castle fortress houses parts of the Slovak National Museum. Of the several museums within the castle walls, my favorite is the Folk Music Museum signposted Hubobne muzeum. Music has kept alive the Slovaks' pride in their history and culture, and visitors to this museum are treated to recordings of the ancient pipes, whistles, and drums on display. Descriptive text is included in English. Directions: In a separate building, north of the main castle. Just inside the main castle entrance, in a spotlighted glass case, is the museum's most unique artifact—the figure

of a woman carved—in the Paleolithic era—from a mammoth tusk found by the Vah River. The museum has an impressive collection of furniture and crafts including Art Nouveau glassware and a set of bedroom furniture decorated with peacock feathers that elicits giggles. The grounds and the ramparts of the castle walls are good places for a picnic, or opt for a snack at the terrace cafe; closed Monday. Directions: Exit west off E65—the main road coming into the Stare Mesto—and follow signposting up the hill to the Hrad (Castle Hill) on Zamocka ul where there is a car park.

At the bottom of the cobblestone path from the castle is Zidovska (Jewish Street). Walking north along it, peek into the tiny clock museum inside a colorful, wedge-shaped bugher's house at Zidovska 1; the collection is pure kitsch. The decorative arts museum is located across from it; both are closed Tuesday. Don't miss the Museum of Jewish Culture, signposted Muzeum zidovskej kultury, just a little farther on at Zidovska 17. Everyday life, festivals, and objects of religious importance are explained in English; closed on Saturday.

Retrace your steps back past the clock museum, and walk toward the street that crosses under the main highway, continuing a little farther to Gothic Dom sv Martina cathedral. The steeple with a golden crown commemorates 250 years of royal crownings. From here, head up Kapitulska, one of the city's oldest streets. When you reach Bastova, continue east until you come to Michalska veza tower. Climb the stairs for a panoramic view of the castle and old town. Back on the ground, you can rest here in the quiet garden, which was once a moat, and reflect on what you've seen. The passageway to the garden is in front of the tower between the tower gates.

Just south of the tower, at Michalska 28, is the exceptional Exozicia farmacie (pharmaceutical museum) attesting to Bratislava's rich herbalist past; closed on Monday. Continue down Michalska to Sedlarska, heading southeast and follow signposting for Stara radnica, the old town hall. The beautiful passageway and Renaissance courtyard are sedate and elegant. At the information office here, pick up the local map and then continue your explorations. Torture chambers and instruments used from the Middle Ages to the 19th-century are displayed in the Municipal Museum at the Town Hall. Just behind the courtyard is the Primatial Palace, where Napoleon and Emperor Franz Josepf signed a peace pact. Paintings of peasantry—the backbone of the Slovaks—are in the Town Gallery.

Consider taking a cab back to your car rather than walking. Cabs are metered and fairly inexpensive. Use your tourist map to show the driver where you want to go. For a relaxing excursion boat trip, take a ferry to the ruins of the watchtower of the Danube, Devin Castle, just 9 kilometers west of Bratislava. The boat landing is across from the Slovak National Museum. Check with the tourist office or a hotel for the ferry's operating hours before walking down to the esplanade. It's also an easy drive to Devin Castle along the Danube River.

▲Camping: • East out of the city on E751/D61 in the direction of Trnavka and Piestany, just beyond a large chemical factory on the small recreational lake, Zlate piesky. Camping Zlate Piesky (744 257 373); grassy field with trees; tennis courts; playground; public transportation to the city center; open June-Aug; $.

ALONG THE VAH RIVER
Trnava

Trnava sits at the intersection of the ancient roadways to Prague, Vienna, Budapest, and Krakow and is Slovakia's oldest town. For a time it was the religious center for the Hungarian Empire. The University Church here is the Slovak Republic's finest and boasts a magnificent Italianate Rococo carved-wood altar. Stop by the Slovakian Museum south of the church

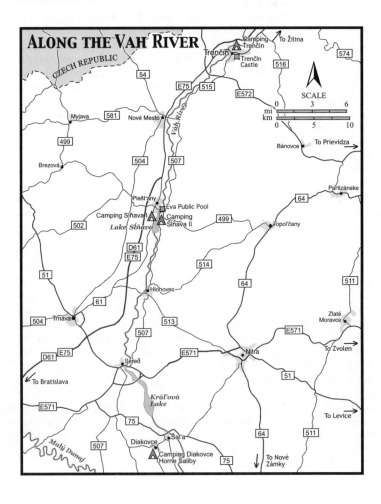

to view a notable collection of folk art. Easy parking is found close to the church. Directions: Enter through the old town walls, and follow signposting.

▲Camping: • South of Trnava, exit E751 at Sal'a and drive west on 573. Cross the railway tracks and follow signage to Diakovce and Horne Saliby, a large recreational area. Camping Diakovce-Horne Saliby (0707-932-50); cycling trails; cabins; open June-Aug; $$.

Piestany

Considered Slovakia's queen of spa towns, Piestany is a nice spot for a recuperative soak in thermal water. On the narrow strip of land in the middle of the Vah River, called Spa Island, you can enjoy old-fashioned and inexpensive fun in the public pool Eva. Directions: After crossing the river to the island, drive north on the west side of the island. The pool is just north of the luxurious Thermia Hotel. After your soak, relax in the large garden area just north of the pool.

▲Camping: • Exit D61/E751 on the east side of the river. Camping is south of town. Camping Slnava II (0838-235-63); basic; open May-Aug; $. • On the west side of the reservoir, follow 61 south along the river. Camping Slnava I (0838-943-29); cabins; basic; open May-Aug; $.

Trencin

Like the king in a chess set, the tower of Trencin's castle stands high above the town on a steep and craggy cliff. In summer, it is illuminated and festive with fun-filled performances given by actors dressed as sword fighters.

▲Camping: • From 61 on the east side of the river, cross under the train tracks and follow signage to Na Ostrova. It's on the southern tip of the island. This is a popular day use area for boating and swimming. Camping Trencin (831-340-13); good view of the castle; cabins; $$.

CENTRAL SLOVAKIA
Banska Stiavnica

Picturesque because of its lovely setting and Old World ambiance, this silver-mining town is now UNESCO listed. Besides seeing the mining camp, with its workshops and church, you can take a trip down into the labyrinthine mine; closed Monday. Directions: 2 kilometers south of town on 524, in the direction of Levice.

▲Camping: • On 524, 4km south of the old mining town, follow signage to Pocuvadianske jazero, a small recreational lake. Camping Pocuvadlo (94-112); basic; open July-August; $.

Kremnica

A very large gold vein was found here in the 12th-century. Since then, famous commemoratives coins have been minted here, including ones for both Churchill and Stalin. The collection of exquisitely decorated money is enlightening. At night the town is illuminated and inviting with narrow cobblestone streets and sidewalk cafes. Directions: On 65, west of Banska Bystrica.

▲Camping: • Southwest of town on the narrow road in the direction of Lucky. Camping Caravan (92-587); small; basic; open July-Aug; $.

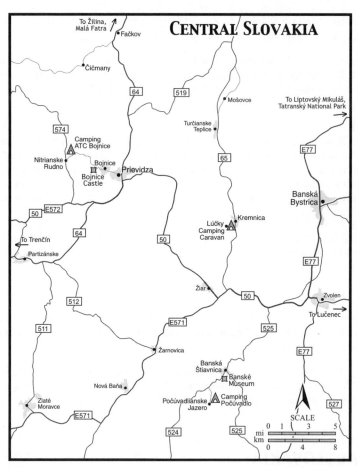

Cicmany

Folk art enthusiasts are fond of this town nestled deep in the mountains of northwestern Slovakia and virtually isolated from other parts of the country. During the 1800s, men farmed and herded sheep and cows while women spent time after chores carefully embroidering clothing. Eventually the villagers began decorating their houses with the handcrafted designs. Today Cicmany is a national monument, and you can tour and photograph the old-fashioned wood cottages decorated with lacework in the designs of snowflakes, flowers, and crisscrosses. Directions: Halfway between Zilna and Prievidza, exit west off 64 following the Rajcanka River. The turnoff for the small road to the village is just south of the village of Fackov on 64.

Bojnice

When you visit this Gothic, fairytale-like castle, it's not hard to conjure up visions of knights in shining armor, beautiful maidens with silky long tresses, and noble kings draped with fur. It sits atop a small hill and is reminiscent of castles seen in the Loire Valley in France. As you approach, you'll see the Gothic turrets rising above the trees, providing a good photo. Tours are conducted by guides in period costume; closed Monday. Directions: West of Prievidza, follow signage to Bojnice, then go farther west to Bojnicky zamok.

▲Camping: • Farther down the road in the direction of Nitrianske Rudo. Camping Bojnice (0862-33-845); pleasant location; open June-August; $$.

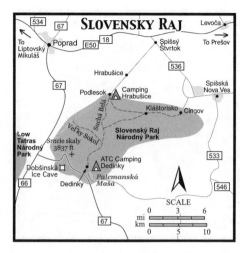

EASTERN SLOVAKIA
Slovensky raj National Park

Ladders have been carefully slipped down through cracks in gorges here to enable thrill-seeking hikers to climb over waterfalls. Fallen timber has been carved with footholds to bridge difficult gaps on the trail and chain bridges built to cross over river rapids. On the Hornad river gorge trail, a chain bridge spans a gorge where the river is 15 meters below. Not all the trails are this exciting. Many are pleasant walks through leafy oak, beech, and pine forests. It's important to get a map of the area before hiking. Trail markers aren't always evident. Pick up trail maps and information at the mountain rescue stations at Cingov or Dedinky. The map you want is *VKU Slovensky raj*. Purchase supplies and gas, and secure local currency before you come into the area. You'll need a warm jacket if you want to descend the slippery steps of the Dobsinska Ice Cave, where mysterious tunnels of slick, smooth ice lead to giant ice halls glistening with fragile stalactites. It's well signposted off 67 as you enter the national park.

▲Camping: • In Podlesok at the northwest end of the park, exit 536 onto a narrow road heading southwest in the direction of Hrabusice. The exit is at the junction of 18 and 536 at the village of Spissky Stvtok. It's in a pretty location that is close to the trails and the river. Camping Hrabusice in Podlesok (90-281); low-key family resort; café/bar; tennis; close to hiking and cycling trails; open all year; $S. • At the southern end of the park. At the intersection of 66/67 exit onto 66 and drive 7km to Stratena. Continue on 66 for 9km. Exit east off 66. Cross railway tracks. Turn immediately north and drive up the narrow mountain road for 2km to Dedinky. Autocamp Dedinky (058 798 1212); pretty location; close to a hotel and pension; swimming, boating, and cycling; open June-Sept; $$.

Levoca Area

Breathtaking in detail and sensitivity, the finely carved figures of the Madonna, St. James, and St. Paul seen in the masterpiece wood altar in St James Cathedral were carved by Pavol in the 16th-century. Each is over 2 meters tall; open daily. Resplendent in Old World grandeur, Levoca's old town has a quiet ambiance and makes a nice break in the journey. If you're traveling east on E50, turn into Spisska Kapitule, 18 kilometers east of Levoca, and stroll through the tiny, completely enclosed fortress and peek into the lovely cathedral. Continuing farther east on E50, after 2 kilometers you'll see the ruins of

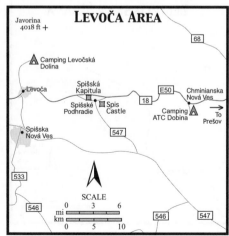

neo-Baroque Spis Castle, founded in the 12th-century. It is a rewarding photo stop. Directions: Levoca is 41km east of Poprad.

▲Camping: • Exit 50/18 at Levoca drive north out of town up a narrow mountain road that runs along the river in the direction of Levocska Dolina. Camping Levocska Dolina (053 451 2701); beautifully located at the base of the Levocske Vrchy Mountains; low-key family resort with cabins, sauna, café/bar; playground; open all year; $$. • About 16km west of Presov, just off E50/18, exit at Chiminanska Nova Ves, drive south one kilometer. Camping Dubina (0966-951-90); convenient; affliated with a hotel; open year round; $$.

Slovensky Kras

Limestone canyons and caves riddle the Slovensky Kras region. At 22-kilometers Domica jaskyna is one of the longest caves in the world. Stretching to the Hungarian border, it joins Hungary's Aggtellek cave. The one-hour tour includes a short trip down the underground river Styx; open daily. Directions: South of Roznava about 20 km take exit 50 at the small village of Plesivec and drive southeast on a small road for about 12km. For a dramatic, narrow, wooded ravine walk, detour to Zadielska dolina. At one point, the trail's width is only 10 meters. The red-marked trail is an easy 2-kilometer walk. Directions: Halfway between Roznava and Kosice on E571, exit onto the small road heading north in the direction of Zadiel. The trailhead is at the end of the road, about 6km from E571.

Stories of intrigue and romance embellish Krasna Horka Castle, making it an interesting castle stop. Restored in a Renaissance style, it is classical on the outside but highly ornamented on the inside, with gorgeous marble throughout. It also has a notable Art Nouveau mausoleum. Directions: Exit E571 east of Roznava. Drive 10 kilometers to the village of Krasnohorske Podhradie, exiting north onto the narrow road and driving 2 kilometers. The well-designed garden setting of the regal hunting lodge in Betliar makes a nice break in the journey. Souvenirs from the owner's adventurous travel include a mummy, elephant tusks, and warrior apparel from Samurai and African tribes. Directions: 10 kilometers north of Roznava on 67.

Zemplinskavv Sirava

▲Camping: • Exit E571 west of Kosice at Moldava, and drive north on 550/548 for 12km. It's on the north side of the village Jasov. Camping Jasov (056-649 2234); close to a reservoir; cabins; cycling/walking trails; open all year; $$. • Almost to the Ukraine border, 5km east of Micalovce, at the large reservoir lake and recreational area, Zemplinskav Sirava. There's little shade at any of the campgrounds. • Close to Vinne. Camping Horka (056 649 2123); tennis; disco; open June-Aug; $$. • In Kalusa. Autocamp Kaluza (056 649 2848); resort-like; cabins; café/bar; store; playground; open May-Sept; $$. • In Klokocov. Autocamp Klokocov (056 649 2110) smaller; open May- Sept; $.

Camping Enroute to Hungary:

Between Lucenec and Zvolen. On E571/50 exit 16km north of Lucenec in the direction of Divin. Autocamp Divin (047 439 7267); close to the railway tracks; simple and basic but convenient; little shade; open May-Oct; $.

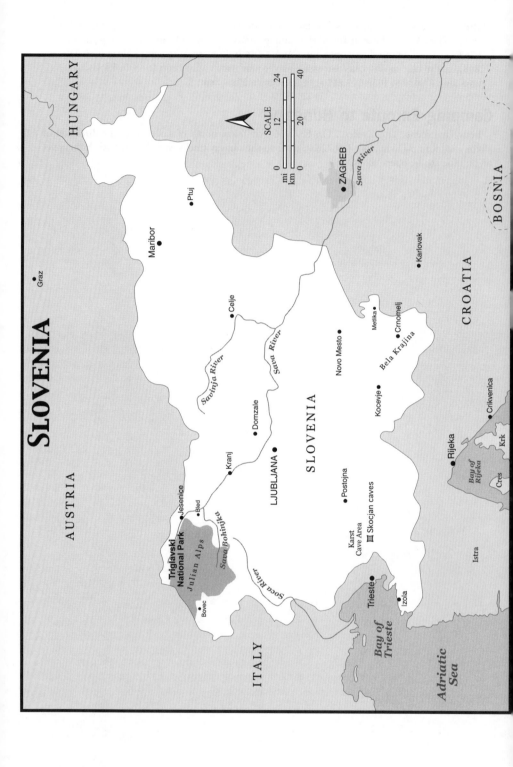

SLOVENIA

- Graz

AUSTRIA

HUNGARY

ITALY

Triglavski
National Park
Julian Alps

Bovec

Soca River

Sava Bohinjka

Jesenice
- Bled

Kranj -

LJUBLJANA -

- Domzale

Savinja River

Sava River

Celje -

Maribor -

- Ptuj

SLOVENIA

Novo Mesto -

Metlika -
- Crnomelj
Bela Krajina

- Kocevje

- Postojna

Karst
Cave Area

□ Skocjan caves

Istra

Izola -
- Trieste

*Bay of
Trieste*

*Adriatic
Sea*

Rijeka -

*Bay of
Rijeka*

Cres

Krk

CROATIA

Karlovak -

- ZAGREB

Sava River

BOSNIA

Crikvenica -

SCALE

0   12   24
mi
0   20   40
km

N

Slovenia

www.slovenia-tourism.si

With countryside noted for being the greenest in Europe, Slovenia is like a big park. Easy walking paths traverse lush grassy meadows so full of wild flowers it's like walking through a bouquet. High peaks, rain forest-like mountain gorges, and tumultuous waterfalls treat the hiker. Crystal clear rivers and quiet lakes invite the paddler and fisherman. Driving is pleasurable through such beautiful countryside, and highways are excellent and well signposted. The secondary roads are well maintained and excellent for cycling. Locals are very friendly and do all they can to make your trip enjoyable.

Camping in Slovenia is expensive compared to other central European countries, but the campgrounds are modern and well equipped. Standards are high. Tennis is popular so bring your racket. Most campgrounds will cost about 20 euros for 2 persons, a car, and a tent; note as $$. Beautifully landscaped resort-like campgrounds will cost closer to 25 euros; noted as $$$. Slovenia uses the euro for their money system.

JULIAN ALPS

Situated on the edge of an emerald-green lake boasting a jewel-like islet in its center, this picture postcard-perfect town is a major tourist resort with the accompanying crowds and prices. But for very little you can enjoy the manicured gardens, take an inexpensive boat ride out to an island with a tiny church, visit Bled Castle, and take a walk or cycle around the lake. It's an easy walk into the bottom of the Vintgar Gorge in Podhom, just over 4 kilometers north of Bled. The trail into the gorge is a wood walkway that hugs the cliffside, passing over the river rapids several times. Ferns, tiny primroses, and crystal-clear waterfalls hurtling past rocks robed in chartreuse-green moss make good material for photographs. Bring a waterproof jacket and wear shoes that don't slip. There's a small entrance fee. Consider extending your walk by parking in Podhome, a quintessential eye-catching Slovenian village, that features steep-sloping tile roofs hanging over immaculate white stucco houses decorated with carefully tended flower and vegetable gardens. Stop by the tourist office by the lake on the main road coming into Bled from 1, next to the Park Hotel. They speak English and can give you details on interesting things to do in the area.

Next, take the road along the lake and river heading into the national park. Bordered by lush green forests and meadows on one side and the Bohinjka River on the other, the valley drive is so beautiful you might want to stop at the first campground but continue on. In the village of Ribcev Laz, stop at the tourist office and then visit the miniscule church of St John the Baptist. Inside, the brilliance of the frescoes brightens the tiny arches and ceiling; open daily. Directions: Just across the stone bridge on the north side of the river. While you're in the village, check with Alpinsport in the kiosk next to the bridge. They can help you with adventures that include renting a canoe or kayak for the lake and rafting through the Mostnica Gorge. Housed in a charming cot-

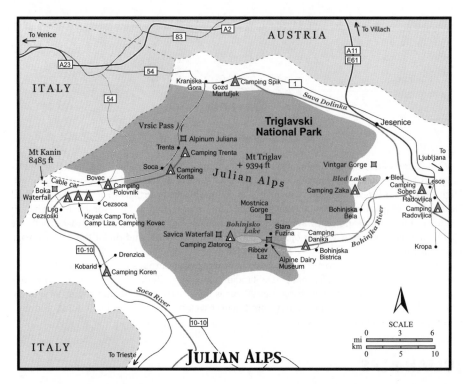

tage, the Alpine Dairy Museum has some interesting photographs and artifacts; closed Monday. Directions: Just north of Ribcev Laz, on a small road on the east end of the lake in Stara Fuzina. Allow time to walk to the impressive 60-meter Savica Waterfall, one of the most important sights in the park. You will be sprayed by a veil of water, so wear appropriate clothing. Directions: The trailhead begins close to the Zlatorog Hotel. It's an easy 4-kilometer walk, and there's a small admission fee. The tourist office has excellent maps for longer hikes in this area. Stops in the tiny picturesque villages guarded by the majestic Julian Alps add to the pleasure of driving and cycling in this beautiful countryside.

▲Camping in Triglav National Park: Take the river road out of Bled in the direction of Bohinjska Bela. • In Bled. Stay right at the fork and continue up the narrow winding road Camping Bled (64 74 1117); garden-like setting; open May-Sept; $$. • West of Bohinjska Bistrica. Camping Danica (64 72 1055); pretty location near the village; open May-Sept; $$. • At the west end of lake Bohinj. Camping Zlatorog (64 72 3441); natural setting on the lake; in a pine forest; popular; large covered common areas; great for meeting fellow hikers; open May-September; $$.

Soca River Valley and Bovec

The pristine beauty of the Soca River has made it a mecca for rafting and kayaking. It is one of Europe's last undammed rivers and has some excellent white-knuckle class V rapids. Trips, guided or unguided, can be arranged in Bovec with Soca Rafting. They also rent mountain bikes and guide canyoning trips. You can make arrangements ahead with the Bovec Tourist Center, the adventure sports capital of Slovenia; www.Bovec.si.

If the weather is clear, take the cable car up to the top for views stretching to Trieste and the Julian Alps. Directions: Drive southwest out of Bovec in the direction of the Mt. Karin Funicular; it's signposted. The trailhead for Boka Waterfall is about 5 kilometers farther on the road. Park by the restaurant, Gostilna Zikar. It's a steep hike. If you don't have the time or energy, continue down the road and get a view of it after parking close to the bridge.

Declared the European Museum of the year in 1993, the Kobarid Museum is a don't miss. Its exhibits tell the story of the Soca (*Isonzo*) Front–the same battle described by Ernest Hemingway in *A Farewell to Arms*. Drawings by Erwin Rommel, also known at the Desert Fox, depict the lines of battle during the fall and winter of 1917. Touching memorabilia and photographs have descriptions in four languages including English and fill three floors. Little cemeteries dot the entire area, and an ossuary under the Church of Saint Anthony holds the bones of unburied soldiers. A path to the Kozjak Waterfall passes trench lines, observation posts, and a shelter cave; open daily.

Between Bovec and Kranjsha-Gora, a spectacular drive through the Vrsic Pass takes you either to or from Triglav National Park. Directions: 4 kilometers northeast on the main road out of Bovec, look for the narrow road heading east in the direction of Kal-Koritnica/Kranjsha-Gora. It runs right along the Soca River. Coming from Kranjsha-Gora, drive directly south in the direction of Bovec. This road is under snow in the winter. Allow plenty of time for this drive because there are interesting stops along the way. From Bovec it is 12 kilometers to the graceful village of Soca. Here, inside the 18th-century Church of St Joseph, note the fresco portraying St Anthony struggling with Mussolini and Hitler; open daily. In the village of Trenta, 8 kilometers farther, stop at house 34, Dom Trenta, and go through the Trenta Museum which is dedicated to the mountain guides who first ascended the Julian Alps. The museum is also an information center for Triglav Park, with exhibits of the flora, fauna, and pioneers of this alpine area. Maps are available for some spectacular hikes in the area; open daily. Take time to visit the Alpinum Juliana botanical garden, just 4 kilometers farther. From there the road winds up to the Vsic Pass, passing a Russian Chapel dedicated to 400 Russian POWs who were buried here in an avalanche in 1916. The descent is steep and winds sharply. At the base of the mountain, pass through the village of Kranjska-Gora and then stop for a rest and view the deep-blue Lake Jasna.

The jagged limestone peaks of the Slovenian Alps are considered the most pristine in Europe and their hut-to-hut trekking trails are still pleasantly free of the trappings of mass tourism. The comfy huts are dorm-style and include a full breakfast, packed lunch, dinner, beer, and bedding at very reasonable price. So you might consider packing up a little gear to enjoy this incredible mountain experience alongside some of Europe's wildest peaks. Arrange ahead at Bohinj Tourist Office close to where the trail begins. www.bohinj.si

▲Camping: • Exit off 10 at Bovec, and drive south on the small road11/301 in the direction of Cezsoca on the Predel Pass. Camping Polovnik in Bovec (658 6069); good location; small and basic but nice; open May-Sept; $. • For a more remote place, ask in Bovec at the Alp Hotel for directions to Vodence. There are three camping places on the river in this area. Kayak Camp Toni (658-6454), Camp Liza ((658-6073), or Camping Kovac (658-6831); basic but good; wonderful locations on the river; open May-Sept; $. • 2km north of Bovec, exit east onto the narrow and winding Bovec/Kranjska-Gora mountain road and drive 12km to the village of Soca. Camping Korita; in a lovely village; basic; open July-Aug; $. 7km farther east in the village of Trenta. Camping Trenta; simple and very pleasant; open July-Aug; $. • In Kobarid. Camping Koren (658 5312); beautifully located close to the river; bike rental; open April-Sept; $$. • From the Kranjsha-Gora/Bled Road 1 at Krankska Gore follow the road for 4km, passing under 1 to the river and the village of Gozd Martuljek. Camping Spik in Gozd Martuljek (648-80120); affiliated with Hotel Spik; convenient; pretty location; road noise; swimming pool; open all year; $$.

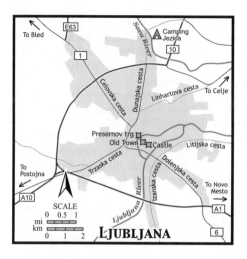

From Bled to Ljubljana

A side trip from Bled to one unusual museum and a unique village makes an interesting half day. In the Beekeeping Museum folk art panels and exhibits, with English labeling, tell the story of beekeeping–an important part of Slovenia's agriculture; closed Monday. Directions: 5 kilometers south of Bled on E651 in Radovljica. The museum is in a cream and white manor home on the north side of the street in the center of the historic area. You might not think you are interested in foundry work, but after visiting the charming little village of Kropa, noted for its metal work during the 17th and18th-centuries, you'll begin to appreciate the craftsmanship; closed Monday. Directions: Take the small road south of Radovljica in the direction of Kropa.

▲**Camping:** • South of Bled 4km on 1, along the Save Dolinka River, exit at Lesce. Camping Sobec in Lesce (471 8006); wonderful location along the river; large; popular with families; open June-Aug; $$. • In the same area, exit 1 at Radovlija. Camping Radovlijica (471 5770); close to the public pool; road noise; open June-Aug; $$.

Ljubljana

This beloved city has handsome little pedestrian bridges crossing its canals that are bordered by willow-lined walkways and extra friendly cafes and parks and gardens around every corner. It's an easy city to drive into and park. Follow the signposting to the historic area and make your first stop the tourist office to get the schedule of free performances in the historic area and a list of its wide variety of museums. It's southeast of the triple bridge and well signposted. Peek into the little shops and courtyards on Stari trg. Walk up to the castle, where you can look down into the old town and out over the city from the ramparts. Walk down through Pogacarjev trg, a colorful open-air market and stock up on just picked fruits and vegetables and freshly made cheeses. The market for meat, fish, and dairy products is on the southwest corner. Then wander over to Presernov trg to rest in either the pleasant ambiance of one of the cafes or on the steps at the monument to Presernov. Both the International Summer Festival of music, theatre, and dance and the Summer in the Old-Town run throughout July and August, making a visit during these months particularly lively and fun; www.ljubljana-tourism.si.

▲**Camping:** • North of the city in the suburb of Jesica, exit off 10/E57. Camping Jezica (1 168 3913); cabins; playground; some road noise; open all year; $$.

Velika Planina

In this gorgeous highland meadow contented cows graze and friendly cow-herdsmen sell white cheese from cone-roofed huts. An exhilarating cable car ride takes you up 1,420 meters. Directions: Drive northeast of Ljublijana on 10 in the direction of Domzale. Exit north on a smaller road for Kamnik. Stop at the tourist office here if you want a hiking trail map. The cable car station is 11 kilometers north of Kamnik. Popular hiking trails to waterfalls and caves start at the old world village of Kaminiska Bistrica, 3 kilometers beyond the cable car station.

▲**Camping:** • In the Old Town of Kamik. Camping Resnick in Kamik (61-83 1233); close to the river; tennis; open June-Aug; $.

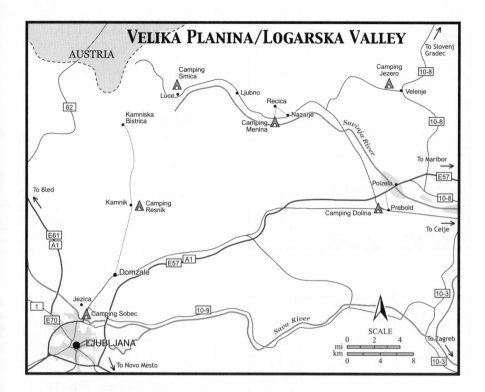

Logarska Valley

This is a popular area for kayaking, rafting, paragliding, and tennis, and equipment rental is available. Directions: Exit A1 west of Sempeter onto a smaller road in the direction of Nazaeje, then continue west on the same road for 3 kilometers in the direction of Ljubno.

▲**Camping:** • In Recica. Camping Menina (383 1787); a recreational area; nice location on the Savinja River; open July-August; $$. • Farther on the Savinja River Road up into the mountains for 19km to Luce. Camping Smica (384 4330); beautiful location; tennis; open June-Aug; $$.

▲**Camping Enroute from Ljublijana to Maribor:** • Halfway between the two cities, exit A1 south onto the road just west of Sempeter in the direction of Prebold. Camping Dolina in Prebold (637-24501); pretty location; pool; cabins; $$. • On a reservoir lake. Exit 2km east of Sempeter, and drive north on 10/8 in the direction of Velenje. Pass through Velenje, and drive northwest along the river road towards the reservoir. Camping Jezero in Velenje (638-63400); a recreational area; wind surfing and catamaran rental available; open June-August; $$.

Ptuj Thermal Area

Noted for its thermal water, Ptuj is Slovenia's oldest town. Its small but interesting historic area is perfect for walking or cycling. A castle, whose rooms house a small museum, looks down on the old town; closed Monday. Directions: 22 kilometers south of Maribor, along the River Drava on 3/E59.

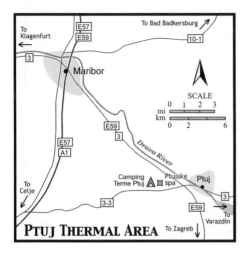

PTUJ THERMAL AREA

▲Camping: • In Ptuj, on the small road between E59 and 3. Camping Terme Ptuj (2 78 3777); resort-like; thermal pool; sauna; playground; cabins; open May-Sept; $$$.

Bela Krajina

On Slovenia's southeastern border with Croatia, the Kolpa River is warm, clean, and popular with locals. It's a good place to relax with kids. You can join folks taking scenic kayak runs from Stari Trg to Vinica, or fish for carp and trout with rented equipment. There are horses for rent and easy walking or cycling routes in Lahinja Regional Park and the surrounding vineyards. In Adlesici, museum farmhouses promote an appreciation of folk culture.

BELA KRAJINA

▲Camping: • Exit 4 at Novo Mesto-Metlika, just south of Metlika, and drive southwest in the direction of Podzemeji. Camping Podzemelji (68 69 572); on the Kolpa river; open from June-Aug; $$. • In the village of Adlesici, southeast of Crnomeli 12 km. Take the small road in the direction of Tribuce and Dolenjci. Camping Jankovic in Adlesici (68 622 877); nice location on the river; open June-Aug; $$. • In the village of Vinica. Drive south on the Crnomeli-Vinica road for 18km. Camping Vinica (68 64 018); on the river; basic; open May-Sept; $$. • Close by. Camping Katra in Vinica (68-64-319); on the river; basic; open May-Sept; $$.

Bay of Trieste

Slovenia's little nugget of a Mediterranean seaside is just south of Trieste Italy, making it a popular destination for the locals. The strip of coastline is bordered on the north by Ankaran and on the south by Portoroz.

▲**Camping:** • In Ankaran. 3km south of the Italian bordering crossing at Muggia, at the junction of 10 and 2, continue west on 10 for 8km to Ankaran.

▲**Camping Adria** (666 8322); on the
beach; popular; open June-Aug; $$.
• Farther south along the coast road, close
to Izola. Camping Jadranka (666 1202);
popular; cabins; open June-Sept; $$.

Karst Cave Area

The Skocjan caves are among the deepest
and most picturesque in the world and have
been tagged by UNESCO as a World Heritage
site. This captivating place is more natural
and less touristy than the caves at Postojna.
The Reka River still rushes through, racing
down in a spectacular waterfall and filling
the silence with the sounds of gushing whirl-
pools. Directions: Just east of Trieste drive 2
kilometers south of Divaca on 10 and follow
signposting. While you are in the area stop in Lipica to admire the famous Lipizzaner horses at the
Lipica Stud Farm; open daily. If you are here on Tuesday, Friday, or Sunday you can watch them
perform their complicated paces to Viennese waltz music at 3 PM. Horses also can be rented for a
guided ride in the countryside or in the ring. Directions: From Divaca, drive 12km southwest to
Lipica and follow signposting. For small chil-
dren, the caves at Postojna are more enjoyable.
Disneyland-like, an electric train ride passes
by the colorfully lit stalactites and stalagmites
making good material for story telling later.
Predjama Castle provides another story telling
setting. It looms gloomily from a gargantuan
rock cave in the center of a 123-meter rock
face and its 15th-century history tells of Robin
Hood-like tales. Directions: From the caves,
drive northwest in the direction of Bukovje.
Pass through the village, continuing in a west
for the Predjamski grad.

▲**Camping:** • From Postojna, take the road
heading northwest in the direction of Pivka
Jama. Camping Pivka Jama (386-6725-382);
in a forested area; cabins; pool; playground;
open May-September; $$.

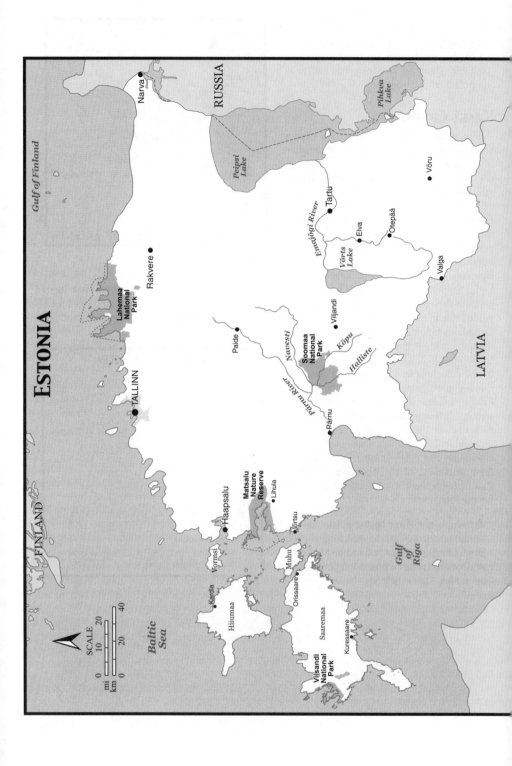

ESTONIA

estoniatourism.com

Estonia can proudly boast that it has one of the highest percentages of protected lands in Europe. These large areas are of biological importance, protecting species that are rare in Western Europe. During Russian occupation, coastal areas were out of bounds. The reward today is vast tracts preserved and protected in their natural state.

About half of Estonia is covered by forest and woodlands; scots pine stands are threaded with silver and downy birch, gray and common alder, and aspen. When the woods are wet and warm, it's a special pleasure for Estonians, basket in hand, to wander through the woods gathering berries and mushrooms. Although the country is tiny, it is larger than Switzerland or Slovenia. But its population is one of the smallest in the world, and most of it resides in Tallinn, leaving the countryside marvelously quiet and peaceful. You'll share main highways with local cyclists and walkers on their way to work or to shop. Parents stroll nonchalantly down the road pushing baby strollers, stopping occasionally to pick berries or wave a greeting. The remains of old manor homes stand towering above grass and wild flowers. White storks peer down from huge nests along roof edges and strut with elegance in search of frogs in rural pastureland.

The Estonian language belongs to the Finno-Ugric language family, which includes Finnish and Hungarian. However, even in the countryside someone will speak English, especially the younger generation–members of which are usually manning the front desk at tourist sites. Reestablishing their native language, in the schools after independence affirmed Estonian nationhood. It's not hard to learn to say a few words such as: hello (*tere*; te-rre), thank you and you're welcome (*tanan*; ta-nahn), goodbye (*head aega*; head ae gah), excuse me (*vabandage*; vah bahn dah ge), yes/no (*jah/ ei* yah/ay), where is (*kus on*; kus on). (The first syllable is usually accented.) They will be surprised and appreciative of your efforts.

Estonians have a huge legacy of song. They began their Song Festivals in 1869 and have continued them through the years, even under the watchful communist eye. After being declared almost nonexistent as a nation by various occupiers, the country's song festivals encouraged people to stand up for themselves–to feel united and strong. During the time of National Awakening in the mid-19th century, it was the song festivals that kept the people's sense of personal pride alive. After the compulsory Soviet songs were sung and duly applauded, the Estonians sang their own songs from their hearts. In 1980, one-third of the Estonian population came to the Song Festival Grounds in Tallinn. They held hands and sang out courageously for freedom. In 1990, at the first non-Soviet influenced festival since their first independence from 1920 to 1939, they madly waved their formerly banned flag and sang their formerly banned national anthem with hope in their hearts. Song festivals are held every year in every town–many are in June–and competition is intense. The winners from small towns sing at the Song Festival Grounds, held every four or five years in Tallinn. UNESCO listed the Song Festival as "Masterpieces of Oral and Intangible Heritage to Humanity" in 2004. Try to time your visit to one of these inspirational events.

Manor homes built by wealthy families between the 15th and 17th-centuries and restored in the 19th, have their own significance in Estonian history and culture. European Union monies have helped to restore many of them as sites for interpretive centers and museums. Set behind well-maintained lawns and flower gardens shaded with magnificent old trees, they are especially graceful. Some that have been left to ruins emit a decayed beauty in the midst of natural garden where purple bellflowers, pink rosebay, and golden vetch bloom wild.

Access to Finnish television from 1970, the reestablishment of the ferry service from Helsinki in 1965, and the Olympic Games in 1980 gave Estonians a good look at the lifestyle towards which they aspired. This was a head start that resulted in a higher quality of goods in their shops, better housing, and a more dependable social infrastructure than the other neighboring republics of Russia. Estonians are environmentally conscious and work towards the high standards of their Finnish neighbors, who are also a goodly portion of their tourist market. Owners of tourist-oriented businesses are enterprising. You won't find them "letting grass grow under their feet." They realize that a friendly and knowledgeable staff, a clean and pleasant environment, and clever marketing tools are keys to developing Estonia as a tourist destination. Progressing towards this goal, the tiny nation has left the Soviet era behind and set its sights on European Union membership and a western-style democracy and economy.

Roads are clearly marked and have been resurfaced in recent years. Most are two-lane with light traffic. A few four-lane divided highways are being built around larger cities. Modern gas stations with mini stores are scattered along the main highways, but fill up if you are going to a remote area. Secondary roads are sometimes well-maintained gravel, forcing you to slow down and enjoy the scenery. If your driver's license includes a photo, you don't need to bother with an international driver's license. Headlights need to be on at all times and driving beyond the speed limit or after drinking is cause for ticketing by watchful police. A road atlas or map with an expansion of 1:500 000 is essential if you are going to explore beyond the main towns and cities. Excellent road maps and atlases are available.

Many tourists from Scandinavia and Europe arrive in Estonia with their caravan (camper van). They want pleasant, well-maintained sites with hot showers and clean toilets. They are pleased by a sauna, an enclosed cooking/eating area, and a lovely location. Most Estonian campground owners work hard to provide this in hopes that their investment in time and money will pay off. I was impressed by their ingenuity in thinking up clever ways to entice campers and keep them returning. You'll find one or two of these features at the best campgrounds I list: an immense swing, a diving board, canoe or bike rental, volleyball court, fresh bread brought to the campground, national flags of the camping guests hung, and interesting locals giving evening talks. Camping at a well maintained campground will cost about 10-15 euros for two persons a car and a tent; listed as $$.

TALLINN

A signature of the centuries has etched the Old Town of Tallinn, a UNESCO World Heritage Site since 1997. It's a compact maze of medieval beauty, with picturesque turrets, tower ramparts, and red-tile rooftops. Because its natural harbor is able to guard the narrow passage between the Gulf of Finland and the Baltic, it lured rulers from other countries who followed one upon another until the city was accepted in the Hanseatic League with the other Northern European port cities. Each era has left its mark, but somehow Tallinn miraculously managed to save its thousand-year-old beauty. As you wander through the pedestrian-only Old Town, passing brightly colored buildings in the shades of shell-pink, lime-green and cerulean-blue, you experience a Middle Ages ambiance.

The 13th-century defense wall, one of Tallinn's most striking features, is 75% original. Leave your car at the campground and take bus 34 or 38 (they stop right outside the campground) to the Town Square. The campground has maps of the Old Town. Start your exploration on Toompea Hill, where a circular limestone wall and watchtowers still loom over the city. From here you will get a perfect view of the city's red-tile rooftops, the massive St Olaf's spire, and the swan-like

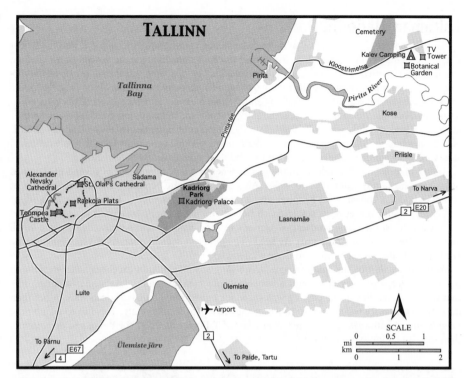

cruise ships berthed in the harbor. In the castle square, the elaborate mustard-colored and delib-erately powerful Russian Alexandre Nevsky Cathedral, almost diminishes the classically graceful pink Parliament House. Its pleasurable to wander down the hill through the maze of cobblestone streets and alleyways to the *Raekoja plats* (town hall square), where you can rest and conjure up images of finely dressed merchants and noblemen haggling the price of goods.

The tourist office here has plenty of information and maps of the Old Town to fine-tune your exploration. Ask what's happening during your stay. Concerts are reasonably priced and add enormously to the pleasure of a visit. Estonia has many noted glassblowers, weavers, and cera-mists so their *Tarberkunstimuuseum* (applied art museum)–hidden away in an old granary off Lai Street, a couple of blocks northeast of Town Hall Square–is especially good; closed Monday and Tuesday. Bird-watching in the countryside is greatly enhanced by spending some time first at the *Loodusmuuseum* (natural history museum). Directions: Close to St Olaf's Cathedral. Entrance is through a lovely courtyard. Built in 1721 by Russian Emperor Peter the Great who was inspired by Italian architecture, Kadriorg Palace is one of the best-preserved works of Baroque architecture in Northern Europe and its huge duck pond is a perfect place for a picnic. Directions: 2 kilometers east of Old Town, on Narva mantee. Medieval fare, street markets, and outdoor entertainment make visiting in June during the Old Town Days Festival especially fun.

▲**Camping:** • On the top of the hill by the TV tower and next to the Botanical Gardens. Follow the coast road Pirita tee, which curves northeast from the harbor along the Tallinn Bay to Pirita. Cross over the small bridge, turn east onto Kloostrimetsa, and drive about 3 kilometers. After passing the cemetery, following signposting for the botanical gardens. There is no signposting for camping. It's next to a motorcycle shop at the top of the hill. Kalev Camping (372 623 9191); convenient; friendly; good place to meet other international travelers; bus to the city; pleasant setting but can be crowded; toilet/shower/cooking areas run-down; open May-Sept; $$.

Lahemaa National Park

Named after the sheltered bays that dip between craggy promontories jutting out into the Bay of Finland, Lahemaa National Park is a very special place. It's magical to stand far out in the shallow, warm Baltic at sunset. The sea shimmers in a kaleidoscope of colors, and the silhouette of the surrounding forest mimics a castle wall with turrets. Woodlands cover two-thirds of the park. Extensive marked trails, appropriate for both walking and cycling, meander along the forest floors carpeted in ferns and moss. Lichen paints enormous boulders in coral and mustard, soft green moss drapes over fallen trees, and sprightly waterfalls and beaver dams add even more beauty to the landscape. Lush lilac bushes line the walking paths and gardens in villages that are visitor-friendly with cafes and stores. Several carefully restored manor homes and their gardens are open to visitors.

Palmse manor home's brightest moment was when it was the residence of several generations of an eminent family from 1677 to 1923. After that the estate became a German then a Soviet command post, a convalescent hospital, and a pioneer camp for youth. Today it houses a bright and cheery visitor center in its stable/coach house, and the manor house itself is a lovely period piece open for tours. The landscaped gardens include a pond where swans float, and a small amphitheatre where musical events are held. The gift store sells local crafts at reasonable prices. Directions: Exit E20/1 at Viitna and drive 9 kilometers north.

Vosu, the liveliest of the small villages, has a long sandy beach, an excellent bakery/cafe with outside terrace, a grocery store, and a couple of nice campgrounds. Lilacs line walking paths that wind through the village passing well-cared for homes and gardens. Locals walk rather than drive from one place to another, so much of the town is pedestrian-only. It is fun to wander the neighborhood pathways. Directions: 70km east of Tallinn, exit E20/1 for Kolga and drive north, then east, on 85 for 29km to Vosu.

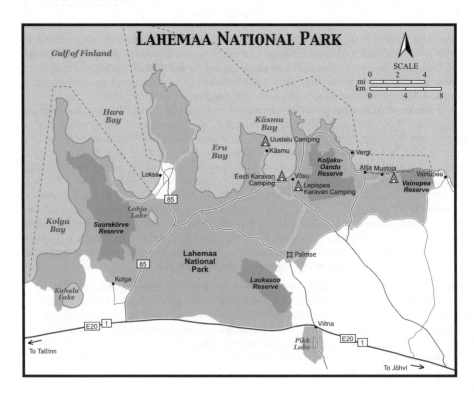

▲**Camping:** • In Vosu signposted on the road coming into town. Lepispea Karavan Camping (372 564 75 663); small; family-run; homey atmosphere with large vegetable and flower garden; wood-fired sauna; beach access; one cabin; large separate lawn next to the beach; open June-August; $$. • In the same area. Eesti Karavan Camping (372 505 2053); large; popular with caravans; little ambiance; playground; sauna; beach access; open June-August; $$.

Kasmu, known as the Captain's Village, is impressive with fine homes and manicured gardens. A naval training school opened here in 1884 and for almost 50 years prepared men to navigate. Ships were built to export timber and bricks and to smuggle salt and liquor. After WWII, the Soviets built a barbed wire fence along the coast to prevent people from escaping to Finland. It was only after 1991 that the fishermen could go freely out to sea. Today their guardhouse houses the *Meremuuseum* (maritime museum). The collection of memorabilia was surreptitiously gathered, mostly by one man. Local artists and craftsmen display their work, and it has an expanding exhibit on marine life; open daily. At the end of Kasmu village, a hiking trail leads out along the coastline picturesquely scattered with boulders. Wild rose bushes, yellow tansy, and wild sweet pea decorate the walking path and here and there are cozy patches of sand perfect for picnics and sunning. Directions: From Vosu drive 10km north west of town to Kasmu. Continue to end of the road to trailhead and car-park.

▲**Camping:** • On the bay next to coastal trailhead in Kasmu. Uustalu Camping (372 3252 965); elegant setting with manicured lawn to the bay; new; sauna; cozy enclosed eating area with nice views; hotel rooms; good for tents but not appropriate for caravans because campsites are on a garden lawn; open June-Aug; $$$. In the forest at a designated camping place (pit toilet, no water) just off the coastal trail about 500 meters from parking; free.

Morning glory vines wrap around vintage thatch-roof houses, cats sleep on window sills, and women chat over weathered fencing in Altja. In the park along its coast, old fishing huts drip with fish line, and on a grassy hill an immense swing awaits. A good hiking trail leads east along the coast from Altja to Vainupea. From Altje the coast road goes 3 kilometers farther north to Vergi. Small yachts and fishing boats dock here. There's a café with tables out on a terrace which makes a nice place to watch the going-ons and an old fishing boat that kids can climb on and pretend they're captain of the ship.

▲**Camping:** On the hiking trail, halfway between Altja and Vainupea just east of the village of Mustoja. Designated camping area with pit toilet; no water; free.

Haapsalu

Haapsalu was once a spa-town of such repute that even Tsar Nicholas I visited in 1852, and Alexander II visited several times. A glamorous railway station was built for the Tzar's arrival in 1905. The station is now a museum and wonderfully photogenic. Tchaikovsky also enjoyed the spa in 1867, drawing inspiration for several works, including his 6th symphony. He has a commemorative bench at the old harbor. Memorabilia from this time is part of the Laanemaa Museum's collection. A castle built in the 13th-century served as both a fortress and a cathedral. Take a walk on the ancient walls for a nice view of the town and its community vegetable gardens. Today

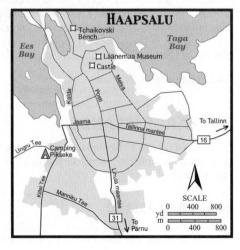

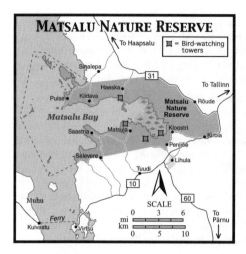

the cathedral is used as a concert hall and for exhibitions. Above a touching memorial to islanders deported to Siberia is the Window of the White Lady whose local legend has given rise to an annual festival, they are found in the side chapel. The sea is shallow here and protected from high winds by the bay. Directions: Drive south of Tallinn on E67 for 8 kilometers in the direction of Parnu. Exit onto 16 in the direction of Haapsalu and drive 71km.

▲Camping: • On the southwest edge of town. Drive south of town on Lihula maantee, the road to Saaremaa and Parnu. Turn west onto Manniku Tee, then right onto Kiltsi, then left at the Neste gas station then drive 100 more meters. Camping Pikseke (372-4755 779); popular, pleasant spot; sauna; covered cooking area; fresh bread brought to campground from local bakery in the morning; laundry facilities; open June-August; $$.

Matsalu Nature Reserve

The rocky and sandy shores of Matsulu Nature Reserve are relatively undisturbed and provide important resting and feeding areas for migrating birds. Protected since 1957, it is recognized as a Birding Area of Global Importance. In spring, the vast coastal meadows are flooded by melting snow. These wet areas offer plentiful food for the greylag geese, cranes, dunlin, bewick's swans, avocet, lapwing, and godwit. Oyster catchers search for worms along the shores, and artic terns whirl and shriek. Thousands of bewick and whooper swans drift gracefully, occasionally filling the air with their haunting call. Bird life is at its peak from the end of April to the beginning of July. Guided small boat trips into the reed beds are prearranged through the reserve's office; e-mail muuseum@matsalu.ee 047-24236. Marked walking paths through the coastal meadows have observation towers. European Union's Life-Nature funding provided funds for an excellent new interpretive center located in a beautiful manor home at Penijoe; don't miss it. Knowledgeable and enthusiastic staff is fluent in English. The tourist office in Haapsalu also has walking maps and information about Matsulu Nature Reserve. Directions: Drive southeast of Haapsalu on 31 for 52km. Turn southwest on 10 and drive 10 kilometers in the direction of Lihula, exiting north onto a small road for Penijoe and drive one kilometer.

▲Camping: • See Haapsalu.

THE LARGE ISLANDS

Estonia has about 1,500 islands scattered along its northern and western shores. Most are tiny, in fact mere humps, but several are sizable. The most attractive and easy to visit are Saaremaa and Hiiumaa.

Saaremaa Island

During the 1930s, Saaremaa Island was an idyllic health resort popular with the Germans, British, and Scandinavians. But from 1944 to 1989, when the Soviets occupied Estonia, it was classified as a security zone. Thus the island was saved from industrial and residential development. Today it is

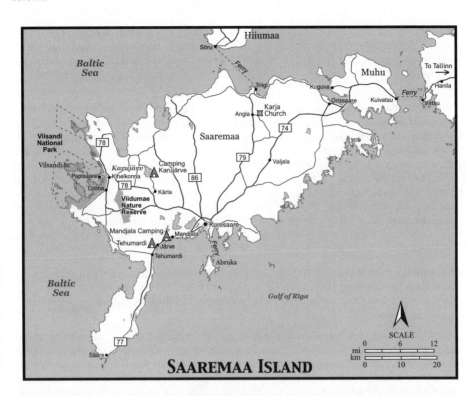

blissful place to visit. Lush grassy parks surround restored manor houses, churches, and a castle that were left by the wealthy from more powerful occupying nations. Ferries leave every hour for a half-hour ride to Muhu Island where there is a causeway over to Saaremaa. Book car space for the ferry ahead with English speaking staff at Virtsu Ferry Terminal; 372 45 350 Directions to the ferry landing: From Tallinn, drive south in the direction of Saue on 4 for 14km. At the fork, exit onto 9 in the direction of Haapsalu and drive 40km. At the next fork, exit onto 10 in the direction of Lihula and drive 95km to Virtsu and the car-ferry to Muhu Island. From Haapsula drive southeast on 31 for 52km. Turn south on 10 and drive 40km to Virtsu. From the ferry landing on Muhu Isalnd drive 18 kilometer to the causeway connecting Muhu Island with Saaremaa Island.

Kuressaare–the only town of any size–is charming with a main street lined with carefully tended wooden homes from the 18 and 19th-centuries. Flower baskets dripping with color hang from lampposts, terrace cafes are filled with people relaxing, and interesting handicraft stores sell lovely souvenirs carved from juniper wood, hand-knitted woolen goods, and items decorated with traditional embroidery (locals make these during the long winter months). In the old town hall, friendly English-speaking staff assists travelers and dispense color brochures of the area. At the west end of the street, surrounded by a park and moat, is the Baltic nation's only entirely preserved medieval castle, Kuressaare Castle. Built of white-grey dolomite quarried in Saaremaa, its corners each have a tower crowned by a turret. After crossing the castle's bridge, you enter a tiny court-yard. Stone steps lead down to musty rooms and up to a vaulted cloister. A drawbridge connects to the watchtower on the southeast corner, and a honeycomb of stairways and some gruesome castle tales make visiting extra fun. Take time to see the rooms housing the Saaremaa Regional Museum. The collection includes intriguing photographs and memorabilia from Estonia's first independence period that were hidden during the Soviet occupation. Directions: From the cause-way and Orissaare it is 76km to Kuressare.

▲**Camping:** • On the beach, 16km southwest of Kuressare at Mandjala. Mandjala Camping (372 52 25300); large; older; sauna; cabins; tent and caravan camping on the beach under the pines; open May-Sept; $$. • 2km farther west on the north side of the road just past Jarve. Tehumardi (372 45 71 666); new; beautifully built; lovely setting under the pines; enclosed cooking area; sauna; small pond; hotel rooms; open May-Sept; $$.

Vilsandi National Park, on the west coast, is designated as a Bird Area of Global Importance. Large flocks of migrating common eider duck and barnacle geese are carefully monitored here. The park is located halfway between hibernation areas of Central Europe and nesting grounds farther north and during the spring and autumn migration many species rest and feed here before continuing on. Vilsandi, the largest of the islands that make up Vilsandi National Park, is a short boat ride away. You can go on your own or pre-arrange for guide (staff is fluent in English) at the park office in Loona; fax/phone 372 46 554 A boat crosses to the island from Loona twice a day on Tuesday and Friday. The best time for birding is May through mid-June. Directions: From Kuressaare drive 33km west on 78 to Kihelkonna. Boats to Vilsandi leave from the harbor at Papisaare 2 kilometers farther north. The park office is in Loona, 5 kilometers south of Kihelkoona.

▲**Camping:** • On the east side of Lake Karujave, 21km from Kihelkoona. From Kuressare drive 20km northwest on 78. Exit for Karla, and then drive 8km on a gravel road to Karujarve. Kamping Karujarve (372 42 034); nice setting on the lake under the pines; basic; open June-August; $.

Allow time to or from the mainland ferry to visit the Koguva Outdoor Museum on Mulhu island. It is not far from the causeway connecting Muhu Island and Saaremaa Island. Smuggling liquor was an important source of income along Estonia's coast. You can examine some early 19th-century brandy vats here, along with some nicely preserved homes of affluent farmers. The touching contributions from the locals that make up a collection upstairs at the Hanila Museum, along with beautifully tended vegetable and flower gardens will make your smile. It's located and signposted just east of Virtsu and the ferry landing on the mainland.

Hiiumaa Island

With fewer tourist attractions then neighboring Saaremaa, Hiiumaa Island's natural wildness makes a get-away-from-it-all destination where the sweet fresh fragrance of pine and juniper mingles with the sea breeze. Proud of their commitment to ecology, the islanders have developed their own "green label." Luckily they were pretty much untouched by Soviet immigration or industrialization, leaving the surrounding waters clean and the population almost all native Estonian. Cycling is popular and many campgrounds rent bikes. For a good loop ride, start at Luidja, pedal to Kopu and stop at the lighthouse, then go out to tip of the pennisula to see another lighthouse at Risna, then down to the southern side of the peninsula, and back to Luidja. Bike rental is available at Camping Kardla Puhketalu. It is a 1 ½-hour ferry ride from Rohukula (the Haapsalu ferry landing) to Heltermaa (Hiiumaa Island ferry landing). Ferries run back and forth all day but reserve car space ahead with English-speaking staff; 372 452 4444

Kardla, the island's main town, is shady and pretty with deciduous trees and carefully kept gardens and parks. The enthusiastic staff at the tourist office speak English, and you can pick up brochures, an excellent map of the island, and chat with them about birding, lighthouses, nature trails, and cycling. Don't miss visiting the homey, family-run Vaelma Wool Factory (*Hiiu Vill*) close to the tourist office. It's enlightening to see how wool fabric is made from start to finish in a small factory using old-fashioned equipment. Plan to treat yourself to a slice of their café's delicious homemade pie. Directions: From the ferry landing at Heltermaa drive 6 kilometers. At the fork stay north, and follow signposting to Kardla for 20km.

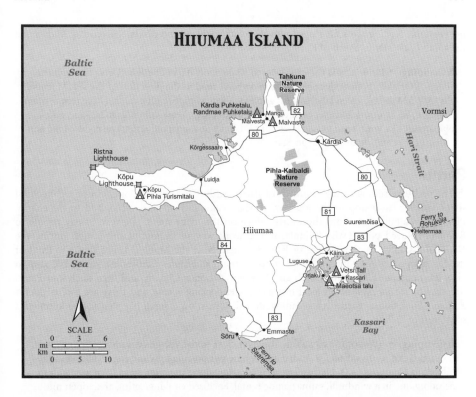

HIIUMAA ISLAND

▲**Camping**: • On the Tahkuna pennisula. Drive west of Kardla on 80 for 5km. Exit north for Malvaste, and drive one kilometer. Continue west on a small road for half a kilometer to Mangu. Kalda Puhketalu (372 462 2122); wonderful location close to the sea; bike and boat rental; campfire pits; pool; cabins; open May-Sept; $$$. • In the same area. Randmae Puhketalu (372 5691 3883); good location close to the water; large grassy area with pines; cabins; open May-Sept; $. • Close to the Mihkli Farm Museum. Malvaste (372 469 1901); convenient; cabins; café; open May-Sept; $$.

The island's shore is mostly shallow, with endless shoals making it a treacherous approach for boats. Lighthouses dot the island. The one in Kopu is one of the oldest continually used lighthouses in the world. It was originally lit up with wood-burning fires, but an electric light was installed in 1900 and proudly exhibited at the Paris Exposition that year. Climb up the narrow staircase for the highest view of the island. Take time to visit a few of the lighthouses; each is unique. The tourist office in Kardla has a driving/cycling lighthouse tour map.

▲**Camping**: • In Kopu. One kilometer from the lighthouse. Pihla Turismitalu (372 469 3491); green label award; large grassy area with pleasant farm house with rooms and pre-arranged group dining; campfire pit; close to walking trails; open May-Sept; $$.

Kaina Bay is cut off from the sea and considered an internationally important wetland. Its huge reed fields and coastal meadows are an important nesting and resting area for birds. Birders can look for sedge warblers, laughing gulls, mute swans, and reed buntings. Flocks begin to arrive in mid-August. 10,000 to 15,000 birds stop to rest here every year. Spring is also good with more than 60 to 70 species staying to nest. On the east side of Kassari the sea is shallow and clear, making favorable feeding areas for ringed plovers, avocets, eiders, and divers. Directions: Midway on the south coast. Drive south of Kardla on 81 for 19km.

▲**Camping:** • Drive across the causeway to Kassari, off 83, at Luguise. Drive through the village of Orjaku. Follow signposting onto a gravel road in the direction of the sea. Maeotsa talu (372 524 4820); green label award; good location; campfire pits; cabins; bike rental; open May-Aug; $$. • One kilometer farther on the main road. Vetsi Tall (372-462 2550); cute cabins built like wine kegs; grassy lawn for tents and caravans; old style tavern/café; bike and fishing gear rental; open May-Sept; $$.

Parnu

The park-like setting of the old town of Parnu, with its eclectic combination of architectural styles, makes a nice stop in the journey. Terrace cafes and sidewalk tables add to the charm. Pick up a walking map from the tourist office on the main street. Be sure to pay tribute to Estonia's beloved poet, Lydia Koidula, whose work was an important inspiration during the National Awaking. A tiny park is dedicated to her. Note the headless Lenin statue in front of the Contemporary Art Museum then see its current exhibition. Continuing your walk, stop to view the Lutheran Elizabeth Church and Russian Orthodox Church, and then duck into Parnu Museum to see its exhibits on local history. Street parking is easy, and there are nice parks for a picnic. Directions: Parnu is in southwestern Estonian on a small bay that is 130 kilometers southwest of Tallinn.

▲**Camping:** • West of the city along the river close to the village of Audru. 10km west of the Parnu, exit south off 60 for Audru and follow signposting for camping. Kullimanniku Puhkekula Camping (372 4440 169); lovely location along the river, large lawn area, cabins including one in a windmill, sauna, canoe rental, enclosed cooking/eating area; open mid May-mid Sept; $$.

Soomaa National Park

Many of the rivers in Estonia are still unregulated in their course. This results in a remarkable amount of flood plain, much of which is preserved in its natural condition. The evolving marshes rise into what is called a bog, which consists mostly of spongy peat mosses. The Parnu River and its tributaries flood several areas, producing bogs that are now protected in Soomaa National Park. Walkboard trails lead out over thick sphagnum moss prettily decorated with cottongrass, cloud-berries, and heather. It is wonderfully silent place except for the occasional call of a crane feeding here during migration. The tourist office in Viljandi has information about the park, including guided boat trips during spring. Well-written interpretive signs in English are at trailheads. Directions: The park is located northeast of Parnu and west of Viljandi. From Parnu, drive north on 5 for 25km. Exit east for Tori. Drive 11km then follow signposting for the park for another 12km, passing through the village of Joesuu. From Viljandi, drive southwest on 56 for 19km, exiting onto a small road at the village of Kopu. Drive 15km to Tipu.

▲**Camping:** • Close to the park trailhead on the west side. Follow directions above from Parnu. Pass through the village of Tori. It's just east of the village. Ritsutalu Kasesalu Puhkelaager (051 48 751); a special place; scenic location right on the bend of the river; part of a prosperous farm; cabins, tiny entrance road; barbecues, diving board; big swing; canoe rental including shuttle; open June-Aug; $$.

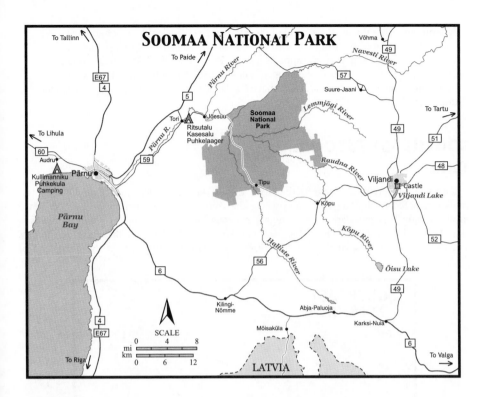

Viljandi

The ruins of an old castle surrounded by a lovely park and a tiny picturesque old town make a stop here a pleasant break. It sits prettily atop a green hill overlooking the north shore of Lake Viljandi. Park trails are shaded with trees and grassy slopes are carefully tended. A bright red-and-white suspension footbridge passes over the castle's moat. Climb the stone wall for a wonderful view of the little lake. Directions: Viljardi is in the south-central region of Estonia.

▲Camping: • See Soomaa National Park.

Otepaa

Softly rolling grassy hills decorated with tiny mirror lakes and woodlands invite a stay. Lake Puhajarve, just south of the Otepaa, is considered one of Estonia's prettiest lakes. It is dotted with five minute islands and was consecrated by the Dalai Lama in 1992, when he was part of a conference of unrepresented nations here. Alexander Solzhenitsyn, recovering from his Siberian imprisonment, wrote the *Gulag Archipelago* here. In winter it is the country's ski area but during the summer its walking/cycling paths–that weave around the woods and lake–make a pretty route for roller blading, cycling, and skate boarding. Rentals are available in town. The ski museum received an award by the Ski Federation. Canoe rental and horseback riding are available. You are enticed to linger. Directions: Drive 41km south of Tartu on 3. Exit east onto 71 and drive 18km.

▲**Camping:** • On the northwest end of the lake close to the lakeside park and large hotel. Follow signposting across from the hotel for Pedajamae. Neitsijarve Kulalistemaja (37 250 97 918); small and homey; rustic ambiance; pretty location on the lake; sauna; wood paneled eating area; cozy rooms upstairs; open June-Aug; $$. • At a trailhead for hiking and mountain biking on the west side. Annimatsi Puhkekula (5110317); run down; large; open June-Aug; $$.

SOUTHEAST ESTONIA
Tartu

Locals proudly refer to Tartu as the "real" Estonia because it was here that the song festivals originated in the late 1800s and where the voice of the national awakening was heard most strongly. Its population has a high percentage of native Estonians. Tartu University was the intellectual force behind the National Awakening and is still the pulse of the city. The Old Town and a sprinkling of the University's main buildings are at the north end of

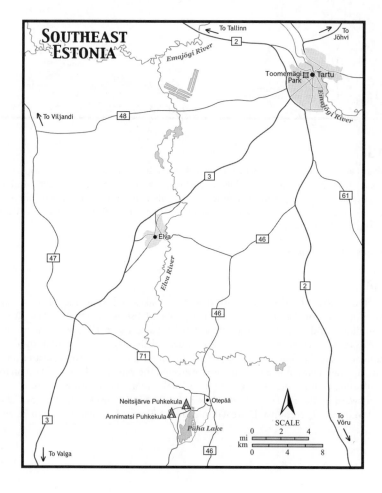

the Emajogi River. University students often meet in front of the graceful pinkish Town Hall beside a charming statue of a kissing couple under an umbrella. The atmosphere at the university is a blend of Oxford and Berkeley, with plenty of optimism for the future. All of Estonia's most famous scientists, writers, and activists spent their formative years here. If you wander a couple of blocks west off the Town Hall Square towards the hill, you'll come to the main university building. Six white columns enhance the impressive pale-yellow neoclassical building built in 1809. Before independence in 1991, the Soviets didn't allow students any contact with western culture. Today professors and students come from many parts of the world. Perusing the bulletin boards, you'll be astounded at the pace of the transformation. Stock up on supplies at the outdoor market and at the indoor market hall just off the south side of the town square, and then take your picnic supplies to shady Toomemagi Park, behind the Town Hall. Directions: Follow signposting for centrum, then Raekoja Plats (town hall square).

▲**Camping:** • See Otepaa.

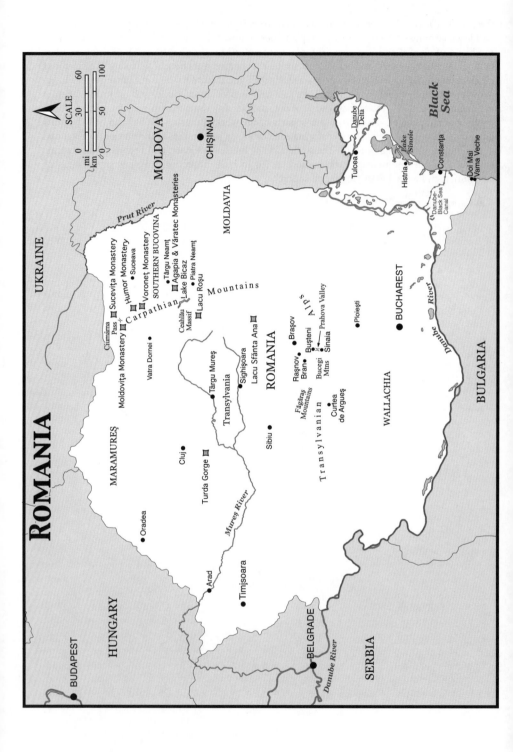

ROMANIA

www.romaniatourism.com

Vast areas of spruce and beech forests flank the Carpathian mountain range dominating Romania. They are one of Europe's most important regions for wildlife and have the highest concentration of bears, wolves and lynx. In the dappled light of beech forests, birdsong is strong, and wild flowers vivid. Scattered here and there, pastoral villages nestle in the alpine meadows below towering summits, vast forests, and stunning limestone gorges. Marked walking trails lead into gorges, up mountains, and along ridge lines.

The Danube Delta, on Romania's southeastern corner, is one of Europe's most isolated and inaccessible regions. Now protected as a biosphere reserve, it can rightly claim to be one of Europe's richest locations for birds. Extensive reedbeds–the world's largest–tuck in 400 freshwater lakes and a tangled web of channels. More than 300 birds rest here during their migration, and 175 of these species nest and raise young here as well. Guided boat tours with knowledgeable bird experts make exploration appealing.

Poor road conditions ensure a slower pace that affords the chance to appreciate plains shimmering with ripening wheat, corn, and sugar beets. Slowing down in villages for waddling geese cackling down dusty side streets, for cows ambling slowly home, and for children playing ball makes a nice change of pace from life in a faster lane. Enormous stork nests, often with the long-legged owners hovering over their young, can often be seen on top of power poles and chimneys. Attractive village wells–with carved trellis roof and bench–beg to be photographed. Villages have electricity but not every resident has running water. Hay and corn are harvested the old-fashioned way, by hand and scythe. Wagons pulled by trusted horses, lovingly dressed up with red tassels on their harness, bring in the harvest without the cost of gasoline or the possibility of a break-down. In the evening, young and old sit on benches attached to the street-side of their fenced yard–playing games, enjoying a rest and chat with neighbors, or just watching the world go by.

Two-lane roads often elegantly tree-lined and usually with little traffic pass through vast stretches of rich farmland. Beehives, colorfully code-painted, make extra splashes of color. Roadside stands with honey and local produce make nice stops. Although many of the roads are potholed, roadwork is in progress. The E-highways are well paved and maintained with good signage. Getting gasoline is not a problem. Petrom brand stations are often new and usually have clean toilets. Romanians are aggressive drivers and take chances passing one another. Driving demands a mix of constant alertness, quick reflexes, caution, and aggression. Driving at night is not recommended. There are usually no more than two or three main roads going in and out of the larger towns, so finding your way isn't difficult with a good map and navigation skills. Even little villages are signposted. Locals are friendly and enjoy going out of their way to help if you ask. See this book's section *Finding Your Way* in the Introduction.

Campgrounds are safe. Gates are closed in the evening, and security personnel often are posted throughout the day and night. Located out of the town center, often in a recreational area, they don't suffer from polluted air. The grounds are usually kept tidy, but the grass, which is only watered when it rains, is often dry and scratchy. Bring a ground cover and collapsible table and chairs because there are rarely any common cooking areas except on the Black Sea Coast. Toilet/ shower facilities are rarely modern. Plumbing is often rudimentary, old, and falling apart. Throw used toilet paper in the small garbage can provided. Do not flush it, as the rudimentary plumbing cannot process it. When you register, ask when the water is warm. Sometimes it is only warm a few of hours a day. Showers are always included and don't require tokens. Don't expect warm showers in simpler campgrounds. Bring a bag shower from home and let the sun warm the water as you drive during the day. Hang it from a tree or car door and take sponge baths. Singing and talking around the campfire is a popular part of Romanian camping. You'll find remnants of campfires that are convenient to use again. Keep an eye out for firewood then stay up to stargaze. Popular rough camping places can be scruffy with trash. Romanians are just beginning to learn to be environmentally conscientious. Taking a few minutes to clean up the area around your campsite will make you more comfortable.

Most campgrounds have cabanas (cabins). Many are relatively new and equipped with single beds with clean sheets, pillow and blanket, a table, and a couple of chairs. Outside is a small porch. Toilet-shower facilities are in the common building the tent-campers use, too. They cost about double what you pay for a tent, a car and two persons but they are very cozy when it is raining. Usually the campground will have a simple café/bar. Vacationing Romanians like to listen to music long into the night, so bring earplugs and sleeping aids. Camping will cost just over 10 euros in the larger towns for 2 persons, a car and tent. In the smaller town it will cost under 10 euros. Both are noted here as $. Food is inexpensive in both markets and restaurants. Larger towns and cities now have mega-markets located on the main highway just outside the center. You need to register with your passport, at these mega-markets but it is easy to do and doesn't take long. They are huge and offer almost anything you need, just like at home. Ice is not available even though you can buy ice chests so you need to shop everyday for perishables.

BUCHAREST

Underneath the noise and chaos of traffic in Bucharest lie tree-lined boulevards, statues, parks, and historic sights. Although it won't be your favorite city, spending a day seeing its most famous sites is valuable to understanding the country itself. The campground is pleasantly located in a large, shady park not far from the airport and is easy to find. A bus runs from the campground to the center of the historic area and leaving your vehicle at the campground is safe due to gates and 24-hour security guards. Although you need to be on guard for the usual pickpockets and scams, particularly on public transportation, Bucharest is no longer rife with them. Reread the section *Safe and Smart* in this book before venturing into Bucharest.

One of the best museums in Bucharest is the *Muzeu Taranului Roman* (Museum of the Roman Peasant). Its collection of icons, woven rugs, traditional tools, costumes, and ceramics is outstanding. Don't miss the wood church, typical of the Marmares, at the back of the museum. The museum is a good introduction to further travels out to the rugged and richly forested Carpathian Mountains, the broad hillsides with sheep grazing, and with rich farmland; closed Monday. Directions: Northeast of Piata Victoriei on Blvd Mihalache. In the same general area you can visit the delightful Storck Museum, which was once the workshop of one of Romanian's most famous sculptors, Frederic Storck; closed Monday. Directions: From Piata Victoriei walk southeast on Blvd Lascar for a long block. Turn west onto the first street going west. Continue west for 2 blocks, and then turn south on Str Alecsandri to #16.

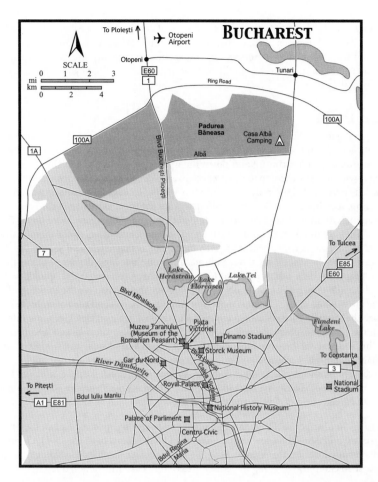

The National History Museum's exhibits start in prehistoric times and extend to World War I, but its most riveting collections are from the Roman occupation. The Romans arrived late in the 1st-century and imposed their harsh discipline and Latin tongue on the native Dacians. You'll see plaster casts of various battles. Don't miss the fascinating collection of jewelry and weapons unearthed at archaeological sites; closed Monday and Tuesday. Directions: At Calea Victoriei 12, on the north side of the river. The restored National Art Gallery houses a collection of international artistic work, but its most important collection is of its own artists. Here you'll see the most famous works of Grigorescu and Aman, two of Romania's favorite painters who studied in Paris with the Barbizon group painting *en plein air*. One of the finest sculptors of the 20th-century was Romanian Constantin Brancusi. His strong and simple works were revolutionary for his time. The collection is impressively curated and presented; closed Monday and Tuesday. Directions: At the south entrance of the Royal Palace, on the southwest corner of Piata Revolutiei.

With a megalomaniac stomp, Romania's now dead but unlamented dictator, Ceausescu, scarred the city as well as the countryside. Today his enormous white elephant of a building called the Palace of Parliament attests to his unrelenting use of public funds for his own self aggrandizement. For a close-up view, take the 45-minute guided tour of ten of the enormous hallways; open daily. Directions: In the Centru Civic.

▲**Camping:** From Otopeni Airport drive south on E60/1 for 4km to Alba. Turn east onto Alba and drive one kilometer through the park. • Camping Casa Alba (230-5203); restful and pleasant with trees; cabins; modern toilets and showers; friendly and helpful staff; popular with international travelers; bus to the historic area; 24-hour closed gate and security guards; open all year; $$.

Danube Delta

Like the great game parks in Africa, the Danube Delta is so remarkable for its richness in wildlife that it attracts visitors who have only a faint knowledge about what they will see. The Danube Delta has no roads. Ferries run up and down the main channel but like in the game parks, the best viewing will be with a company that specializes in small boat trips with a knowledgeable naturalist. The overnight (and more) trips into this World Heritage Site take you into the maze of channels whose reed beds of 2,700 square kilometers are the most extensive in the world. Birding is the highlight, with more than 300 species sighted throughout the year. More than 175 species breed here. They are often bright and colorful, and watching and listening for them is absorbing. Huge flocks of enormous white pelicans glisten in the sun as they circle and soar in the thermals. Great-crested grebes hold their regal head plumes high on their long slender necks as they swim and dive not far from their bulky, reed-hidden nests. Perhaps you'll hear the "quokk" before you see the stocky black-crowned night heron, or the "whoosh" before you see the slow dignified wing beats of the great-white egret. Cuckoos make you smile as they call and the naturalist teaches how to recognize the strongly melodic fluted whistles and trills of nightingales. Get more information at the Danube Delta Biosphere Reserve Authority; www.ddbra.ro or at largest and perhaps best operator, Ibis Tours; www.ibis-tours.ro I enjoyed touring on a small boat and staying in one of the Delta's villages overnight (arranged by Ibis) but floating hotel-boats are also an option. It is easy to book reservations ahead. Delta tours begin in Tulcea. Directions: Drive east out of Bucharest on 3 in the direction of Constanta for 188 km. Turn north onto E87 on the western outskirts of Constanta in the direction of Tulcea and drive 102km.

▲**Camping:** In Murighiol. Drive through town and follow signposting east in the direction of Nufaru and Murighiol for 36km. Camping Hotel Pelican (040-51-43-41); beautiful area and a terrific location for birdwatching; no toilet-shower facilities to speak of; pay at the hotel desk then camp rough along the grassy areas along Lake Murighiol; open May-Sept; $.

Tulcea

It's the setting along the Danube River that makes Tulcea charming. As the sun sets over the river, you can join in an evening stroll with lovely dark-eyed women, handsome men, kids on roller-blades and skate boards, babies in strollers, and toddlers on trikes. Folks stop for snacks along the quay. You'll be warmly welcomed in the Ethnographic Museum, which displays the heritage and culture of the delta region; closed Monday. Directions: From the Piata Republicii and the Delta Hotel walk southeast on Str 9 Mai. It's in an old manor house on the southwest side of the street. Tulcea's art museum holds an interesting collection of both traditional and Avant-Garde Romanian works; closed Monday. Directions: Just east of the Delta Hotel on the east side of Str 9 Mai. Viewing the exhibits in the Museum of the Danube Delta will give you a hint of what you will see in the Delta; closed Monday. Directions: From Piata Civica, walk southwest on Str Babadag for 2 short blocks. Turn west onto a small street and walk one block. The museum is in a lovely tree-shaded white building notable because of its exterior grand stairway.

▲**Camping:** In Murighiol. See above.

Cetetea Histeria and Lake Sinoie

In the 7th century, merchants from Greece founded Histeria and established it as a key port for trade. However gradual silting of the harbor led to its decline. Today, in a fine airy museum, relics from archaeological digs are artistic exhibited with English descriptions. From the museum, paths lead out to the remains of thermal baths and public buildings, open daily.

Along with the Danube Delta, this is one of Europe's most important birding areas. The best birding is a stretch of marshy land, reedbeds, and pools between the freshwater Lake Nuntasi and the brackish lagoon Lake Sinoie. You're likely to see black-winged stilts walking in the mud, swinging their bills from side to side as they feed in the soupy water. Chummy groups of little plovers run over the sand flats, stopping suddenly, almost in unison, and then run again. Standing alone, the little or great egrets–stunning in their white plumage–wait stiffly. Then, without warning, they suddenly spread their long broad wings, utter a deep rasping "croak", flap ponderously, and glide gracefully down to a new vantage point. Directions: From the north: Exit E87 30km south of Babadag at the village of Miha Viteazu. Drive east through the village in the direction of Sinoie, following the main road as it turns south for 6km to Istria and Cetetea Histeria. From the south: Drive north from Mamaia on the spit of land that separates Lake Siutghiol from the Black Sea for 30km to Istria and Cetetea Histeria.

▲**Camping**: North of Mamaia on the coast road. Camping Hanul Piratilor (831-454); nice location close to the beach; hot showers/modern toilets; open all year; $.

BLACK SEA COAST

Beaches, sun, and a festive ambiance draw crowds of Romanians and other Europeans on inexpensive package tours, to the coastal resort towns up and down the Black Sea Coast. It is easy to find a well-maintained campground close to the beach with modern toilet/shower facilities and a common cooking area. Besides enjoying the beach you can while away some time at terrace-cafes, discos, and shops. Slightly warm saline springs feed shallow Lake Techirghiol. Black, mineral-rich mud forms on its northern shore. Relaxing in the mud is popular and fun and touted to be therapeutic for tired bones. Most people indulge in it as part of one of a hotel's therapeutic package. Directions: From Eforie Nord drive west, following signage for Techirghiol village along an elevated bank on the north shore. There are some fine views south across of the lake, and before development this was the best place for birders to see black-neck grebes in Romania.

▲**Camping**: South of Constanta: • 12km south of Constanta. at the north end of Eforie Nord close to the beach. • Camping Meduza (742-385); shade trees and grass; extra friendly staff; smaller than some of the others in the area; close to the mud baths; cabins; open May-Sept; $$. • 43km south of Constanta at the south end of the artificial lake Neptun II. Camping Neptun (701-244); nice grassy location with shade trees, quiet; common cooking area; modern toilets/hot showers; cabins; open April-Oct; $$. 40km south of Constanta. At the north end of Olimp Camping Olimp (731-314); nice location with grass and trees; disco; open April-Oct; $$. North of Constanta: 8km north of Constanta in Mamaia. On the beach side of the coast road between Mamaia and Navodari. • Camping Hanul Piratilor (831-454); nice location close to the beach, grass with shade trees; common cooking area; hot showers/ modern toilets; open all year; $$.

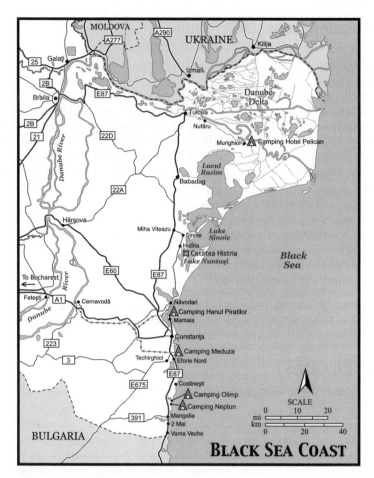

Vama Veche and 2 Maia

Semi-nude or nude sunbathing, beach cafes, and a wildly popular Callatis-Fest with rock bands and art shows brings hordes of young Romanians to the beautiful beaches close to the Bulgarian border. The festival is held in the town 2 Mai in August. The most popular place to sunbathe is north of Vama Veche along a blue lagoon separated from the Black Sea. Directions: From the beach in Vama Veche walk north towards 2 Mai on a narrow strip of sand for 2km.

▲Camping: Camp wild or in the very scruffy campground in Vama Veche. There is little water so bring your own.

PRAHOVA VALLEY/BUCEGI MOUNTAINS

Some of the most spectacular and accessible mountain terrain in the Carpathians is found between the towns of Sinaia and Brasov. A stunning valley snakes its way along the Prahova River, which froths beneath the gigantic Bucegi Mountains. Sheer escarpments of over 600-meters recede into grandiose slopes covered with fir, beech, and rowan trees punctuated here and there with capricious Karst rock formations. Clusters of tiny white-flowering saxifrage, drooping mountain bluebells, and lemon-colored violets grow along creeks beneath a canopy of leafy trees. Sunny open meadows lie green and lush. Hikers climbing up through the woods on the network of marked trails are treated to the drumming of woodpeckers as they feed on wood-boring insects. Reasonably priced cable cars provide easy access to panoramic views at summits. The cable cars run reliably in July and August from 8:30 AM to 4:00 PM. Directions: Drive north of Bucharest in the direction of Ploiesti for 112km on D1/E60 to Sinaia. D1 is an excellent, well-maintained highway.

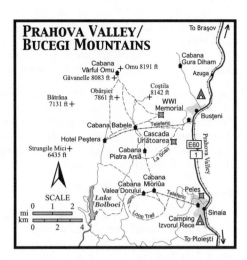

Sinaia

Exuding an elegant, but not exclusive, mountain resort atmosphere, Sinaia is home to the striking Peles Castle. It is set on a grassy hillside above a lovely forest of beech, where dappled light floods through chartreuse leaves. Enamoured by castles seen on trips to Western Europe, Carol I built the richly decorated castle in the late 1800s. Stained-glass windows, finely carved ebony and walnut inset with mother-of-pearl, and a Renaissance weapon collection are highlights of the tour; closed Monday and Tuesday. Directions: Follow signposting off D1 north of town. To enhance your enjoyment of the flora and fauna you'll see while hiking, drop into Muzeul Rezervatiei Bucegi. It has a small, but good collection of stuffed birds and animals plus an exhibit on wild flowers. Directions: Exit D1 in the center of town onto the road signposted for the Hotel Parc and Hotel Palace, or park and walk up the stairs across from the train station. The museum is in the center of the park between the two hotels; open daily.

Many hikers take the *teleferic* (cable car) up to mountaintop hiking trails. Directions: Follow signposting for Hotel Montana at the south side of the bridge just before you enter town at the south end. Buy tickets to Miorita Cabana. From here, one of the more popular trails heads southwest through the lovely Dorului Valley to La Lacuri, a picturesque mountain pond. It's a loop trail that takes 3 to 4 hours and is signposted with yellow crosses with red stripes. For a more exciting hike, go north towards Cabana Arsa and follow the blue triangles down towards Busteni on La Scari–a spectacular stairway hewn in the rock. From Busteni, catch the bus back to Sinaia.

▲**Camping:** • On the hillside along D1 south of Sinaia, by the souvenir stands in Izvorul Rece. Camping Izvorul Rece. Pleasant grassy, terraced sites backing up to the nature preserve; older facilities; cabins; open May-Sept; $.

Busteni

A pleasant unpretentious little town, Busteni is an easy place to spend some time. For hiking, follow signposting for Hotel Silva at the south end of town. Turn onto Str Telecabinei and drive up the hill where there is car park. From here, hikers take the blue cross-marked, hour-plus hike up from the base of the cable car to Cascada Urlatoarea, a lovely waterfall. It's a nice enough area to stay for several hours. The waterfall is off the main trail and not signposted. Watch for a smaller trail when you hear the falls. The cable-car ride to Cabana Babele goes up 2206-meters. Many take the red cross-marked trail to enjoy the view of the valley and to see the giant cross built in the 1920s. For more mystical ridge after ridge views of the Carpathians, plan at least a half-day of hiking and take the yellow-marked trail from Cabana Babele to Mount Omu at 2505-meters. Kestrels–small colorful falcons–are commonly seen in the area hovering and then diving for prey. Continuing on the cable car to Hotel Pesters shortens this hike.

▲**Camping**: Close to Cabana Gura Diham. • At the north end of town follow signposting west on a dirt road for Cabana Gura Diham. Drive 3km on a stream-sided road into a valley whose meadows in summer are aglow with yellow vetch, white daisies, and owls' clover. Camp rough on the grassy meadows east of Cabana Gura Diham. Use a plastic water bag for warm water and bring bottled water for drinking and cooking. It's a pleasant place that is popular with picnicking Romanians.

Brasov

Brasov makes a good spot to camp for several days. The city is within easy driving distance to hiking in the Bucegi Mountains. It has an interesting Baroque historic area and an extra nice campground. To enjoy its medieval ramparts and the Brasov's famous Black Church, drive east out of the campground on the main road into town. Cross over the train-bridge and follow signposting for Piata Sfatului. Watch for the massive Black Church's soaring needle-like steeples on the south side of Strada Baritiu. On Wednesdays at 6 PM organ music from 400 pipes fills the enormous space decorated uniquely with Turkish rugs.

▲**Camping**: Turn south off DN1/E60 8km southwest of Brasov, at a car showroom. The entrance to the campground and the car showroom share the same drive. The showroom is next to the campground and restaurant. • Camping Darste (068-339-967); pleasant views of the mountains; quiet; shady; English-speaking staff; cabins; recommended restaurant; open May-Sept; $$.

Rosnov

Built in the 13th-century, Rasnov *cetate* (castle), successfully protected the local population against both the Tartars and the Turks. Its dramatic hilltop location and careful restoration make it an enjoyable stop; closed Monday. Directions: From Brasov, drive west on DN1/E68 in the

direction of Fagaras for 7 kilometers. Turn south onto 73 and drive 15km to Rasnov. From Predeal, turn west off DN1/E60 onto 73A and take the winding road down 21km to Rasnov. Follow signposting in town for *cetate*. The spectacular *Cheile Rasnoavei* (Rosnov Gorge) between Predeal and Rosnov is worth taking the time to drive through. Sheep graze along the forest edge, and there are superb views of some of Bucegi's highest summits.

▲**Camping**: • In the park just below the castle. Camping Valea Cetatii (068-230-266); field with little shade but next to a shady park; quiet; adjacent to forest road through the Rosnov Gorge to Brasov; basic; open June-Aug; $.

Bran

Tiers of towers rise above the mountain crags and pines, giving the Bran castle a fairytale look. Inside the castle is softened with flowers, balconies, and pleasant furnishings suiting the tastes of the remarkable Queen Marie of Romania, the granddaughter of Queen Victoria. Rebelling against the confining royal life in Bucharest, the feisty queen loved the nooks and crannies and the secret spiral stairways. Inside the castle gate, the grounds have a few restored farm buildings and a well-manicured garden. Billed as Dracula's castle, outside the castle gates Dracula souvenirs, Romanian crafts, and postcards delight shoppers. Directions: Drive 8km south of Rasnov. Park close to the park in the center of the village. The street to the castle is off the northeast corner of the park where the shady trees and grass make for a good picnic and rest stop.

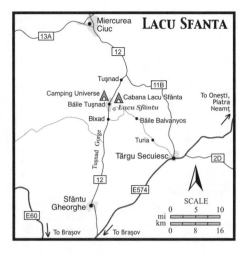

Lacu Sfanta

High above the magnificent Tusnad gorge, the volcanic crater lake Lacu Sfanta and the thermal spa Baile Balvanyos make a jewel of a camping and hiking area. Here lush grassy meadows share the mountainsides with pine-scented woods. Buttercups, yarrow, penstemon, birdsong, and fresh mountain air make you want to linger longer than you planned. The campground has a lovely mountain setting–but campers spread themselves beyond it onto the surrounding grassy hillsides. Instead of turning on a faucet, everyone walks to the well to draws clean cool water with a bucket. Both a marked walking path from the campground and a short toll-road lead to the lake–which has a perfect temperature for swimming. Moonlight swims touched with the fragrance of pine are unforgettable. People set up barbeques, sunbathe, play volleyball, read, and relax. A walking path edges the lake and it is large enough to not feel crowded. Directions: Both the 26 km from Targu Secuiesc or the 24km from Sfantu Gheorghe on 12 are scenic climbs up through the Tusnad Canyon. Shady trees and grassy meadows invite picnics and rest stops along the bubbly Olt river. Directions: From Targu Sceuiesc, drive west out of town in the direction of Turia for 9km. Continue up the winding mountain road for 11km to Baile Balvanyos. The campground and road down to the lake are 5 kilometers farther. From Stantu Gheorghe, drive north on 12 in the direction of Miercurea-Ciuc for 41km to Bixad. Turn east on the small road and drive 10 kilometers to the campground and road to the lake.

▲**Camping:** • Just above the lake. Follow directions above. Cabana Lacu Stanta Camping; lovely setting; run-down facilities; good café; friendly staff; open May-Sept; $. • In Baile Tusnad near the narrow gauge train tracks. Follow directions above from Stantu Gheorghe. Camping Universe (116-319); nice location shady with pines by the river; large; popular with families; cabins; older; open May-Sept; $.

EASTERN ROMANIA
Lacu Rosu/Chelle Bicazului

For many Romanians, Lacu Rosu is a favorite place to camp. Many spread themselves out beyond the campground and you can too. A nice day hike south of the lake is marked with

red bars in the direction of Cabana Piatra Singuratica. It ascends to high cliff top, across a sheep-grazed grass hillside, and through bits of forest. Bring your own water, food, and supplies. The road from Lacu Rosu continues east through the canyon for several kilometers to the dramatic narrow gorge of Chelle Bicazului, where the Bicaz river thunders through a stunningly beautiful red rock defile. Directions: From Lacu Sfanta (Lake Anne), drive west in the direction of Bixad to 12 and then north in the direction of Baile Tusnad. Continue on 12 for 30km to Miercurea Ciuc. Drive through the city following signposting for Gheorgheni. Continue for 65km to Gheorgheni, then turn east onto 12C and drive 25km in the direction of Lacu Rosu.

From the other direction, drive west on 15 from Piatra Neamt in the direction of Bicaz for 28km. Exit 15 onto 12C in the direction of Gheorgheni, and drive 30km southwest on 12C for 15km to the gorge of Chelle Bicazului and then kilometer more to Lacu Rosu.

Lake Bicaz/Ceahlau Massif

The Ceahlau Massif's eroded crags and vigorous mountain trails lead through dramatic, pillar-like outcrops to high summits where eagles soar. On your way up, water pipits, nutcrackers, and woodpeckers provide pleasant company. The best place to start hiking is from Durau. At the trailhead, there's an office where you pay a fee for use of the trails and can purchase a trail map. At least one person on the friendly staff will speak some English, so you can chat and get a few tips. From here, take the steep, red bar-marked, one-hour hike up to the Fantanele Cabana set picturesquely on a high meadow and featuring lovely views, or take the easier two-hour yellow triangle-marked route. There is also a two-hour red cross-marked trail to the dramatic Duruitoarea Cascade, which forks from the yellow triangle-marked trail. From Fantanele Cabana,

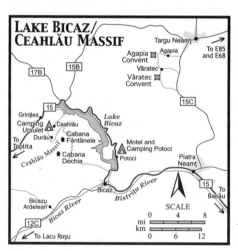

red bar-marked trail climbs up to a dramatic craggy outcrop softened only by cliff clinging wild flowers and ferns. If you have the time and energy, hike on up to the Dochia Cabana which is above tree line and close to the summit. On the way up a high plateau area provides the views of the dramatic, rugged Panaghia crags and the Toaca Peak. Here you can rest and spend the night. (Check with the park office before you begin your hike). From the summit, the trails descend to the village of Bicazu Ardelean and the Bicaz Gorge or Cheille Bicazului. Directions: From Bicaz, drive north for 44 kilometers then continue west on 15 in the direction of Toplita for 6 kilometers to the tiny village of Grinties. Turn onto a small road towards Ceahlau and Durau.

▲**Camping:** • In Ceahlau. Camping Ursulet. New; lovely setting on the river; recommended restaurant; cabins; open May-Sept; $$. • At the east end of Lake Bicaz in Potoci. Motel and Camping Potoci (672-236); wonderful view of the lake but steep slope makes finding a tent site difficult; doable sites behind bungalows; very old toilet/shower facilities; recommended restaurant with modern toilet; open May-Sept; $$.

Varatec and Agapia

Outside the walled convents of Varatec and Agapia potted geraniums drip in bright pinks and oranges from the veranda of the nuns' eye-pleasing little homes. Novices greet you with sweet smiles. At prayer times, nuns make the call with panpipes, bells or an ancient wood toaca. Both have fine icons in their sanctuaries and small museums. Directions: Drive 3 kilometers southwest of Targu Neamt on 15C. Follow signposting west on a small road towards the village of Agapia, then continue to the monastery. The Varatec monastery is directly south and can be reached on the little forest road from the Agapia monastery or from 15C just 5 kilometers south of the turn-off for Agapia.

▲**Camping:** • In the woods between Varatec and Agapia; a doable rough camp place if you are discrete. Set up later in the day, break down early, and leave no trace of your stay.

Southern Bucovina/Painted Monasteries

The remarkable painted monasteries of Southern Bucovina are one of the finest examples of Byzantine art in Europe. Visiting Romania just to see these monasteries is enough to justify a trip. The thriving monastic communities and their surroundings remain as they were when they were founded in the 15th and 16th-centuries. The frescoes on the outside walls still look upon fortifica-

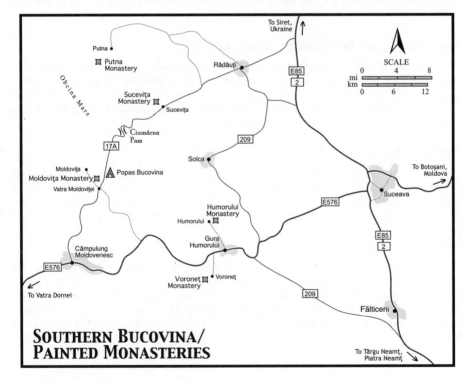

SOUTHERN BUCOVINA/
PAINTED MONASTERIES

tions, beyond which are quiet hay-meadows and forests. Though many are over 400 years old, the frescoes and enlivening Biblical stories still burst with color and vitality. To hear the swish of the nuns in black habits scything hay as birds call from fruit trees in these almost silent, sacred places is ethereal. Gardens overflow with roses, daisies, and peonies in carefully tended flowerbeds, and at the well nuns whisper and exchange smiles as they draw water to carry in buckets to the monastery. Each monastery is unique so seeing three or four isn't repetitive.

Bucovina comes from the word *Buchenwald* (beech-covered land). In these misty valleys, the deciduous forests allow large patches of open meadows to be painted vividly with the oranges, yellows, and greens of wild flowers and grass. Because the farmland and forest are monastery-owned, the area is protected from development.

Voronet and Humor Monasteries

The story of humanity being brought to judgement is vividly told in the extraordinary frescoes on the outside west wall of Voronet Monastery. Jesus sits in judgement while gruesome devils and trumpeting angels accompany Moses and St Paul escorting souls to their appointed destiny. Inside, the still colorful frescoes relate exciting stories of martyrs and miracles. Brochures, small guidebooks, and nun-guided French or Romanian language tours provide a more detailed understanding; open daily.

In hues of reddish-brown with rich blue and green highlights, interior frescoes are still astonishingly fresh and continue to instruct devotees at the Humor Monastery. The portico is particularly impressive, with a magnificent fresco of the Last Judgement. Inside, the three dimly lit small chambers are entrancing. The first room is largest and brilliant with frescoes of martyrs that have been carefully restored with UNESCO funding. The ceiling in the tomb room, where the treasury was hidden, is low, giving it a cave-like feeling. Inside the *naos* (altar room) the ceiling rises and an *iconostasis* (precious gilded partition) shields its sacred eastern end; open daily.

Sucevita and Moldovita Monasteries

Almost completely covered with frescoes, the Sucevita Monastery is the most impressive of all the monasteries. Two brothers painted the walls in 1596, giving them first an undercoat of emerald green and then painting the landscape, figures, and animals in reds and blues. Enormous eaves have helped protect them. With a backdrop of brilliant blue on the south wall, the Tree of Jesse arranges the genealogy of prophets culminating in the Holy Family.

Moldovita

A charming village surrounds the well-defended Moldovita monastery. Here walls dripping with ivy and roses beg to be photographed. Climbing the defensive tower provides a view of the meticulous gardens beyond the walls. Well-tended gravesites make a walk through the nearby cemetery extra nice. Afterwards, stop in the little park for a picnic.

Ciumarna Pass

The road between the Moldovita and Sucevita monasteries, highway 17, goes through the Ciumarna Pass–an extensive area of mature spruce and beech forest accented by sunny meadows carved here and there by tributary streams. Opposite the Sucevita monastery, a spruce forest path goes through the Putnisoara Valley to the Putna monastery. The entire area is popular with birders who relish seeing the hazel hens and black and white backed woodpeckers that are common here.

Directions for the Monasteries: The monasteries are in the area between Suceava and Campulung Moldovenesc, in north-central Romania. Coming from the south, drive east of Targu Neamt on 15B for 16 kilometers, then north on E85 for 22 kilometers. Exit E85 onto 209 just south of Falticeni to enjoy a drive through the villages for 32 kilometers. Turn west for Gura Humorului, where both the Humor and Voronet are located. There is good camping farther west on 17A north of Campulung Moldovenesc, where the Sucevita and Moldovita monasteries are located.

▲**Camping:** • 3km east of Moldovita on 17. This is one of my favorite campgrounds in Romania. Popas Bucovina (030-565-389); tiny lawns, fruit trees, wood piles and flowers surround the beautifully built wood cabana and cabins; cozy restaurant; open May-September; $$.

▲**Enroute Camping:**

Piatra Neamt: • Along the Bistrita River in a recreational area. Follow signposting in town for the train station. From the station drive south one kilometer on Bule 9 Mai to a small bridge. Cross over the bridge, and follow the road north along the river on Str Aleea Tineretului to the recreational park. Camping is at the west end of the park. Cabana Strand (033-217-835); cabins, tents pitched on grassy area close a fenced horseback riding track; toilets but no showers; disco nearby; open May-Sept; $$.

Vatra-Dornei: • On a hillside on the northwest end of town. Follow signposting at the west end of Str Eminescu or on the road that runs along the train tracks (Str Dornelor) up the hill. Camping Runc (030-371-892); modern toilets and showers; cabins on a terrace above a narrow gravely strip where caravans and tents squeeze together; café; open April-Oct; $$$.

Suceava: Follow signposting for Gara Nord at the northeast end of town, then follow signposting for camping on Str Cernauti. Camping Suceava (030-217-048); noisy from trains and disco; not recommended; open April-Oct; $.

Marmures

Valleys and meadows of Arcadian beauty are tucked among small-scale hay meadows and orchards, and villages with wood churches spill down the flanks of the mountainsides into valleys carved by the Iza and Viseu Rivers in the Marmures. Picturesque farmhouses, surrounded by kitchen gardens and fruit trees, huddle together for company in idyllic villages where water is still carried from wells or rainwater cisterns. Cows coming home from the fields walk through the village and into their own barnyards without direction, like pet dogs. Charming old wood churches with bulbous steeples, four-corned pinnacles, carved doorways, and painted walls are carefully maintained. Newer, larger churches, whose spires are often clad in metal for protection against lightning, retain the traditional asymmetrical rooflines and give testament to the skill of fine local carpenters who donate their work. Market days are especially photogenic and fun with squealing pigs and piglets, carefully brushed and decorated horses, fluffy peeping chicks, and leather horse halters sharing space with tables of succulent strawberries, yellow peppers, and pale green cabbages.

On festival days the villages are lively with friends and relatives celebrating. Before Mass, villagers exchange chatty greetings then move slowly towards the church in a priest-led procession. Afterwards, food and wine are shared. Later, perhaps, a band will play and people will dance.

During the summer hay harvest, an enormous amount of work must be done by the whole family while the weather is good. Scything, raking, and hay stacking are all done by hand. At mid-morning, the workers gather under shade trees to rest, gossip, and eat. Later, the hay cutters and rakers return to the village with their tools resting over tired shoulders, minding little the cars

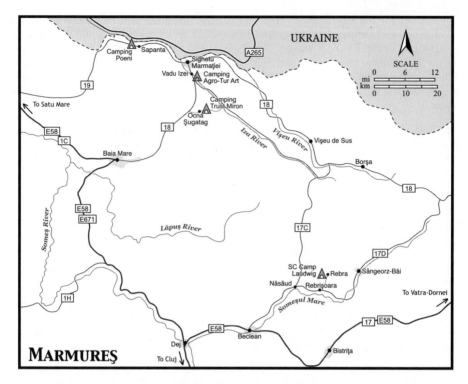

going by. It's fun to exchange waves and smiles with the village folks as they drive their horse-drawn carts piled high with sweet-smelling hay. Guided tours of the workplaces of artisans in the area can be arranged in Vadu Izei with Agro-Tur-Art, opposite the Casa de Cultura. They are an excellent source of information for the whole area and can arrange visits to the local farmsteads, the most outstanding of the wood churches, and agro-farm-camping. In mid-July, village fiddlers come from surrounding villages to entertain at the four-day Maramuzical Festival. It is well worth attending. Call or fax ahead to Agro-Tur-Art for information; 062-330-171. Directions: Vadu Izei is 6 kilometers south of Sighetu Marmatiei on 18, near the Romanian/Ukraine border.

A popular stop for visitors is the unique Merry Cemetery in Sapanta. With wit and skill, woodcarver Patras spent much of his life carving and painting unique headstones that told about the life of the deceased villager. Souvenir stalls selling traditional wool blankets hug the road into town. In the Sighetu, you can pay tribute to courageous intellectual prisoners at Sighet's notoriously cruel prison, now the Museum of Arrested Thought. Get directions at the museum for a short walk to the former home of Nobel peace prize-winner Elie Wiesel, who wrote the first account of the horrors of the Nazi concentration camps in his autobiography *The Night*.

▲**Camping:** • 50km northeast of Baia Mare, exit 18 onto a small road for Ocna Sugatag and drive 3km. Camping Trust Miron; in Ocna Sugatag; newer; convenient for exploring the Maramures; restaurant; $. • Drive north and then west on 19 for 18km passing Sighetu Marmatiei and continuing to Sapanta. Camping Poeni; cabins; open June-Sept; $. • In Vadu Izei; arranged with Agro-Tur-Art to camp in a farmer's field; $ • On the southwest corner of the Marmures close to Nasaud. Drive 7km east of Nasaud on 17D to Rebrisoara. Pass through the village exiting onto a small road and drive 3km in the direction of Rebra. SC Intercamp Ludwig(367-150); small; nice location along a creek; open year round; $.

Cluj

A university always gives a city a certain lift and excitement. Pleasant terrace and courtyard cafes, live music, a national theatre, an opera house, a philharmonic orchestra, and a national art museum make Cluj well worth a stop. Dominating the center of the historic area is the monumental St Michael's Church, where services are held daily and the immense organ is often played during evening services. Across the street, on the east side of the *Piata Uniri* (main square) is the National Art Gallery. Its collection is rich in art celebrating the essence of peasantry, painted by artists strongly influenced by 19th and 20th-century French artists. Romania's most well-known artists,

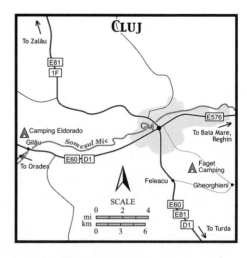

Grigorescu and Aman, are both well represented. Afterwards spend some time in the museum's delightful courtyard café where musicians often entertain. Walk west of St Michael's along Str Memorandumului to one of Romania's best ethnographic museums. Bold, complicated designs burst from the fine collection of carpets, jackets, aprons, and pottery; closed Monday. The open air museum on a the small hill northwest of the town center has an interesting collection of peasant homes, water mills, and churches restored and rebuilt on the museum site. Museum staff proudly unlocks doors and stand back while you admire. It is difficult to find, so get detailed driving directions from the Ethnographic Museum or tourist office. You'll find the tourist office by walking a bit farther from the Ethnographic Museum on Str Memorandumului. Inquire about tickets and what's happening in Cluj and the surrounding area.

▲**Camping**: 4km south of Cluj exit D1 east onto a small road across from the Liliacul Hotel and drive an additional 2km south. Faget Camping (116-227); lovely setting on a quiet hillside; little shade; simple café; open May-Sept; $ 21km west of Cluj exit D1 for Giliau and following signposting. Camping Eldorado (351-446); lovely location on the river; modern toilet/shower facilities; recreational area; some shade; open May-Sept; $$.

Turda Gorge

The Apuseni Range is a complex tangle of rather low mountains that snake along narrow valleys in Transylvania. Here and there the limestone has been dramatically slashed, forming gorges. The *Cheile Turzii* (Turda Gorge) is the most spectacular. It has been a nature reserve since 1939 and in summer it's a popular spot for picnicking and camping. An easy path leads along the bottom of the gorge, and another more challenging one leads along both rims. As you hike, look up occasionally. If you're lucky, you'll see one of the golden eagles–recognized by their immense dark wing-span–who soar regularly over the gorge. At the west end, the gorge opens up to grassy hillsides where sheep

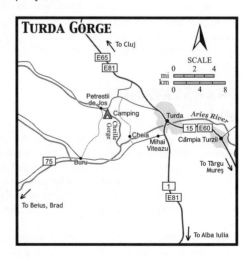

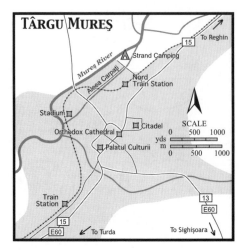

graze and drink from the creek. It's a fine, quiet place for a picnic and snooze. Walking farther, you can explore the charming village of Petrestii de Jos before returning through the gorge. Directions: 31km southeast of Cluj, drive through the town of Turda on E60/81. Exit west onto D75, and drive 8km to the village of Mihai Viteazu. Pass through the village, continuing on D75 for another 2km. Exit north to the village of Cheia. Drive through the village, then uphill passing the quarry. When you get to the top of the ridge, there is a nice view of the gorge. Stop here and use your binoculars to view raptors–especially the golden eagle–as they soar over the gorge.

▲Camping: • Camp rough with everyone else along the river or up on the hillside. Little shade. Not too far from a lively bar with a very old pit toilet.

Targu Mures

A very pleasant campground close to the Mures River makes a stop here worthwhile. The town gets an extra lift in spirit from its university students. A sports center with tennis courts and a swimming pool is close to the campground. Under the Ceausescu regime the city teemed with tension between Romanians of Hungarian background and other Romanians forcing many Romanians of Hungarian background to emigrate.

For me the highlight of a walk in the historic area is the *Palatul Culturii* (Cultural Palace) at the south end of Piata Trandafirlor. Its rooftop glitters with polychromatic tiles set in geometric patterns. Inside, intricate stained-glass windows–with scenes from folktales–cover a large hallway. Concerts are often held here so try to get tickets for one or perhaps just sit in on a rehearsal; closed Monday. At the other end of the square, the immense Romanian Orthodox Cathedral makes an interesting stop.

▲Camping: • Follow signposting in town for the Nord train station, cross over the river and drive north on Aleea Carpati in the direction of the swimming pool. • Strand Camping; very pleasant location with grass and shade trees, modern toilets and warm showers; nice café with terrace; friendly staff; open May-Sept; $$.

TRANSYLVANIA
Sibiu

In the 14th and 15th-centuries, the prosperous citizens of Sibiu, ever mindful of the possibility of invasion, fortified their town with four rings of defensive walls and 40 towers. Within the walls, the lower and upper sections of town were linked with tunnels and stairways. Today much of the medieval city remains, making it one of Romania's most picturesque and intriguing cities. Pick up a tourist map from the campground or a hotel. Parking is not hard a block off the historic area, but you can also take trolley #1 from the campground to the train station and then walk northwest a few blocks to Piata Mare.

The Brukenthal Art Museum is one of Romania's best. It is housed in a lovely Baroque palace on the northwest corner of Piata Mare. Although its most outstanding collection is paintings, the museum also has collections of silverware, religious sculpture, and icons that are note worthy; closed Monday. Stop in the square at the monument in front of the church and take some time to study the 15th-century facades. From here it's just a few steps to the Evangelical Church, in front of which in a dramatic moment in 1510 Vlad Tepes' son was stabbed to death. Walk up the aisle of the sanctuary to examine the fresco of the Crucifixion, painted in 1445, on the north wall of the choir. Then turn around to see the impressive organ. It is Romania's largest. Check the bulletin by the front doors for scheduled organ recitals. If the tower is open, climb up the stairs for a fine view of the historic area. From the church walk north towards Piata Mica, taking note of

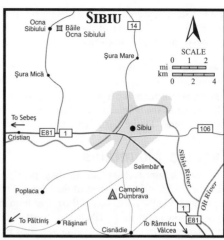

the little bridges and the cheery pastel-colored 15th-century buildings. Stop for a snack at one of the outside cafes to rest and absorb the scene. Several appealing little museums are along the walk so use your guidebook or map to seek them out. In the evening, join the locals at the funky and fun Cinema Tineretului. It's a kick to watch the Romanians respond to a Hollywood blockbuster film. The films are in English with Romanian subtitles. You'll find it down the hill from the historic area, on the west side on Str Odobescu. Romanians love to sunbathe, barbecue, and play with friends and family around the thermal lake area of Baile Ocna Sibiului. Well used for years and still popular, the campground there is too scruffy for me but the thermal area can be a nice change of scene. Directions: Drive west out of town on 1 in the direction of Sebes for 9 kilometers. Exit north onto a small road in the direction of Baile Ocna and drive 12km.

▲**Camping** • In the Dumbrava forest park 4km south of the city. Follow directions for Paltinis then Motel-Restaurant Dumbrava. Enter the parking area for the motel and you'll see a sign for the campground. Camping Dumbrava (214-022); in a peaceful recreational area; large flat area with little shade; cabins; convenient to town; older; open May-Sept; $$.

Sighisoara

World Heritage listing has given Sighisoara's citadel a place on the Romanian tourist map. Built by merchants during the 14th and 15th-centuries, it sits on a hill behind a 30-foot wall punctuated by nine defensive towers. In the evening its silhouette peers menacingly over the town, making it particularly impressive and photogenic as the sun sets. Visitors enter on cobblestone street passing under a massive clock tower whose seven figurines can be examined in its Muzeul de Istorie. Take the walkway all the way up to the seventh floor so you can look out over the town's beautiful buildings and stately towers; closed Monday. From the main square, Piata Cetatii, walk southwest on Str Scolii and climb the steep,

covered *scara acoperita* (wood stairway) up to the *Biserica in Deal* (restored church). Most tour groups also stop in front of the birthhouse of Vlad Tepes–now Restaurantul Cetatea–just off the southeast corner of Piata Cetatii.

▲**Camping**: • 4km west of town on 14 in the village of Danes. Hula Danes Cabana and Camping (771-052); basic; open May-Sept; $. • On the hill behind the train station, on the northeast corner of the historic area. Cross the river on Str Liberatatii then turn west onto Str Sefan. Cross the railroad tracks, then turn east on Str Primaverii, and follow signposting for the campground. Dealul Garii Restaurant and Camping (771-046); run-down; open May-Sept; $.

Fagaras Mountains

In the Carpathian chain, only the high peaks of the Tatra Mountains in Poland and Slovakia surpass the height of the long crest of the Fagaras. The road over the summit is only open from June to September. On the north side of the ridge, dramatically steep escarpments of crystalline schist rich in mica give way, only occasionally, to pine forests. On the south face, the mountains are carved with deep valleys softened by pines and mountain streams and at the base is the beautiful 16 kilometer-long Lake Vidraru. The drive is very steep and narrow, particularly on the north side. At the windswept sum-

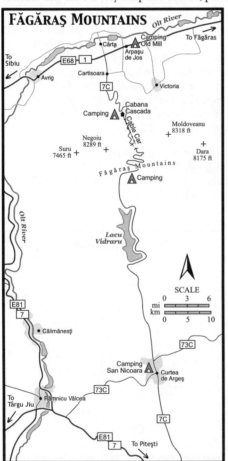

mit the views are exhilarating. It is doable in a regular car. Near the tunnel at the top is a one-hour trail to Balea Lac, which you can also access either by cable-car–which usually operates in July and August from Cabana Cascada–or by driving and parking on the north side of the tunnel. Experienced mountain hikers enjoy the challenging red stripe-marked ridge trail from Piatra Craiului in the east to the Olt Valley in the west. If you're up to the challenge, be aware that even though it's sunny and warm below it can be cold, rainy, and very windy on the ridge. Carry food, water, and emergency supplies. Some of the cabanas (hikers' huts) shown on maps are no longer functioning; get advice ahead. Directions: From the north side of the Fagaras highway, between Sibu and Brasov: On E68 drive 17km east from Avrig to Carta. Turn south on 7C in the direction of Cartisoara. Drive 35 kilometers to the summit. From the south side of the mountain road: Drive north of Curtea de Arges on 7C, passing Lake Vidraru. The road becomes steeper as it winds up to the summit. It is 107km from Curtea de Arges to the summit.

▲**Camping**: • On the north side: 4km east of Carta in Arpasu de Jos. Camping Old Mill; lovely setting on the river; artistic-friendly owners; small; homey, farm-like atmosphere; open May-Sept; $$. • On the meadow behind Cabana Cascada; no facilities unless you arrange with Cabana Cascade; rough camp in a beautiful

meadow with view of the waterfall; hiking trails nearby; cafe; open June-Sept; $.
• Along the river at the base of the winding mountain road north of Lake Vidraru. Wonderful setting, reminiscent of the Rocky Mountains in Colorado; rough camp in small meadows along the river; scenic hiking trails made by grazing sheep. • In Curtea de Arges. See below.

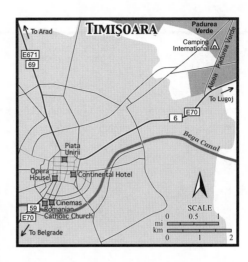

Curtea de Arges

In the 14th century, Curtea de Arges was the home of the region's prince and so it has several noteworthy things to see. The imposing *Manastirea* (monastery) now an Episcopal Church—was masterfully built in the 16th-century with marble and mosaic tiles from Constantinople; open daily. Directions: One kilometer north of town on Str Basarabilor. The original frescoes in the small graceful *Curtea Domneasca* (church) have been restored. The individuality and motion of the figures is particularly intriguing; open daily. Directions: Near the center of town and park in an area surrounded by large boulders, signposted.

▲**Camping**: In Curtea de Arges. From the park in the center of town, drive northeast up Strada San Nicoara following signposting. • Camping San Nicoara (722-126); nice location with shade trees; cabins; simple café and terrace; open May-Sept; $.

Timisoara

This lovely city is close to the Hungarian border. Its historic area is ringed with quiet parks belying the tumultuous uprisings in 1514 and 1989. Take a memorial walk/drive to examine the plaques and sculpture that are placed throughout the city in memory of the martyrs. They include: Martyrs' Fountain behind Cinema de Vara on Blvd CD Loga; outside Romanian Catholic Church at the south end of Piata Victoriei; on the front of the Opera House at the north end of Piata Victoriei; and outside the Continental Hotel. They are noted in the tourist map of the city in the magazine *What, When, Where Timisoara* which you can pick up at the campground or in a hotel. Walk along the canal and stop at one of the terrace cafes. Watching an action-packed Hollywood film in English while the Romanian's read subtitles is particularly fun in the outdoor Cinema de Vara on Blvd CD Loga.

▲**Camping**: 3km east of the city in the forest park Padurea Verde. Follow signposting off D6/E70. Camping International (208-925); pleasant setting in a recreational area; bus to town; cabins; decent toilet/shower facilities; café; open all year; $$.

▲**Camping enroute**: Close to the Hungarian Border:
Arad: • 2km from the center of the city. Follow signs to the immense citadel (*cetate*), cross the Mures river then drive south on Str 13 Generali. • Camping Sub Cetate (285-256); run-down but perhaps doable for overnight; open May-Sept; $. **Oradea:** • 9km south of Oradea on E79 in the direction of Deva. Camping 1. May (318-264); by a thermal bath hotel and restaurant; older; road noise; open May-Sept; $. **East of Timisoara:** • 170km east of Timisoara on 7. In between Deva and Simeria by the river and train tracks. • Touristic Komplex Strei (26-0581); in a recreational area; some shade; parking separate from tents; cabins; disco; open May-Sept; $$.

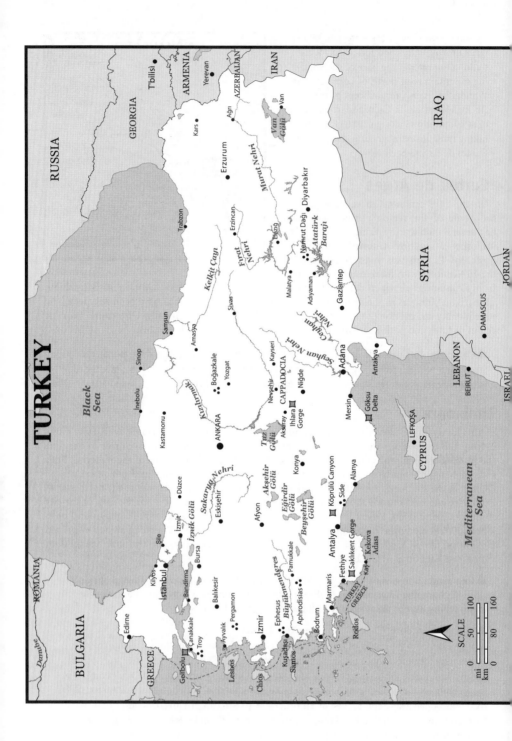

TURKEY

wwwtourismturkey.org

Turkish history is a maelstrom. Once known as Asia Minor, it is here that the Greeks fought the Trojans, where Homer was born, where Alexander the Great rampaged, where Anthony and Cleopatra met, where the Apostles preached, and where the Romans threw Christians to the lions. The Byzantine Greeks held sway here until the Turks began to come from Central Asia in the Middle Ages. The Turkish invasion's climatic moment came in 1453, when the last Byzantine emperor, Constantine XI, perished in battle, leaving Sultan Mehmet the Conqueror master of the multinational empire that would eventually stretch from Persia to Central Europe.

Turkish nomads from Central Asia moved into Asia Minor, now Turkey, and merged Byzantine culture with their own. Ottoman sultans were in effect latter-day Byzantine emperors, whose mosques imitated the architectural style of early Byzantine churches. Ataturk's Turkish Republic succeeded the Ottoman sultanate following World War I. A visionary statesman, he ruled as a benevolent dictator and led the country towards Westernization with astonishing boldness and drastic reforms. Time has done little to dilute the reverence Turks have for him. Respect and grateful admiration bordering on mystical attachment are widespread and genuine. Visitors are wise to take note and be respectful.

Turkey is a big country–the size of a combined Britain and France. Its treasure-trove of ancient sites is great. Many are remote, and you have an excellent chance of having some almost to yourself. Relics of some of the oldest civilizations known to the world have been found in Anatolia in central Turkey. Greeks settled along the Aegean coast in the second millennium BC. The Hittite Empire predates these Greek city-states by 8,000 years. There's a rich diversity of ancient sites-Hittite, Phrygian, Persian, Greek, and Roman.

Once you've had a hamam (Turkish bath) experience you'll want another. Bring your own soap, scrub brush, and shampoo. At the desk when you enter and pay, tell them whether or not you want an attendant to scrub you and whether or not you want a massage. You'll be directed to a dressing room and handed a towel. Put your clothes in a locker, wrap the towel around you, and go into the "hot room," where scrubbing basins ring the room. The basins with water taps must be kept free of soapy water. Use the small scoops provided to rinse, and avoid splashing anyone else. Before leaving the basin area, rinse it down so it is clean for the next person. After scrubbing, relax on the platform that is usually in the middle of the room under a domed roof. This is also where massages are done. Turkish people are devoted to cleanliness, and joining them in this tradition gives you a taste of their culture. In medium priced hamams, entrance fee, scrub, massage, and tip totals around 20- to 25-euros.

The pace at Turkish tea cafes is slow. Time seems plentiful. There is not much sound except the click of dice as backgammon is played. Conversation is soft, with long pauses. Some patrons work on a crossword puzzle others are lost in reverie. The regulars share a companionship that is at once solitary and convivial. Tea is delivered on trays, with a saucer of sugar cubes on the side. Include backgammon when you pack for your trip, so you can pleasantly while away some time in a tea café yourself.

If you leave the main tourist track, your experiences in Turkey will overflow with warm and generous hospitality. It is natural for them, and a gift they give with pleasure and without strings attached. When I think of Turkey, it's not the beautiful beaches, the carpet-like rolling steppes, the fascinating underground churches, the exquisite mosques, or the haunting call of the muezzin that I remember first. It's Mustafa in his tiny produce store demonstrating how to cook green beans and insisting that we stay for a delicious dinner of the beans, bread, and olives. It is camping along the river unknowingly close to a goat corral, and hearing the tinkling of bells coming over the hill just as we began to eat. In this case, the sweet old shepherdess couldn't understand why we would want to cook and sleep outside, but she smiled and graciously excused herself from sharing our dinner. It is the young girl who rescued us when we couldn't find a camping place, insisting that we camp in the garden of her lakeside condominium and then asking us to join her for a barbecue dinner on her porch. And it is the words "Is there anything more I can do for you?" said seriously and with dignity.

With 5,500 kilometers of coastline waters—the Mediterranean, Aegean, Marmara, and Black Sea—Turkey has plenty of waterside campgrounds that Europeans have enjoyed for years. The Turks love to camp with the whole extended family. During dinner hours, barbecue aromas fill the air. The relaxed ambiance includes swimming, cards, and singing. You don't need reservations; there's always room for a tent. The cost will reflect the amenities. Pleasant campgrounds are found close to tourist areas throughout Turkey. They have scenic locations, warm showers, and usually a choice of western or eastern toilet styles. Medium-priced campgrounds are under 16 euros for two persons, a car, and a tent; indicated here as $$. The more expensive campgrounds are around 18 to 20 euros; indicated here as $$$. Fancy resorts can cost up to 25 euros; indicated here as $$$$. Note that Turkey does not use the euro money system. I don't bring my camp stove from home when I camp in Turkey. Instead, I buy the smallest returnable propane gas canister available from the local gas store and an inexpensive screw-on burner. For not more than 25 euros, I have plenty of gas for the entire trip and can cook on a burner that is as good as the ones I use in my restaurant kitchen. (If I return the canister and get the deposit back, it only costs 12 euros.) The canister fits easily behind the passenger seat.

The roads and signage in Turkey are very good all the way to eastern Turkey and from the Black Sea to the Mediterranean. Excellently constructed highway and road improvements are underway. There are a few toll roads. Truck drivers are courteous and often give signals when it is safe to pass. This big country has a varied landscape. Fields of cotton, sunflowers, and a wide variety of vegetables make a colorful mosaic. Shepherds herd their sheep and goats are quick to return a smile and wave. Yellow and black highway signs mark sites of historic interest. Bazaars are usually closed on Sunday, and museums are often closed on Monday. Cash machines are found outside of banks and shopping areas. Make it a habit to fill up with gas, purchase supplies, and obtain local currency before leaving more populated areas.

ISTANBUL

Where else in the world can you visit an exotic, richly decorated palace and dazzling treasury, step inside a Harem shrouded in mystery, get pleasantly lost in a covered bazaar, get squeaky clean at a Turkish bath, and absorb the holiness and beauty of a great mosque. It's one of the great cities of the world. Start your visit in the Sultanahmet area, where Istanbul's most famous sites are concentrated. As you walk through the doors of the Aya Sofya Museum you are taken aback by the seemingly endless space. In the golden light of sunset, it's like walking into the sunset itself. The dome rises to the height of a 15-story building and exerts a remarkable energy and

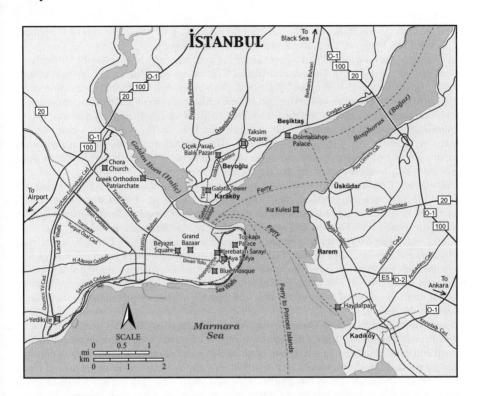

serenity at the same time. Built in the 6th-century by architects Anthemius and Isidore, it stunned the Byzantine world with its size, decorations, and technical achievements. The color from the original mosaics and gold leaf was dazzling. Use your guidebook and binoculars to appreciate the figurative mosaics.

The sprawling, 175-acre Topkapi Palace complex was the consecutive home for 25 Ottoman sultans who ruled for over 400 years. It is perched strategically on a hilltop overlooking the confluence of the Golden Horn and the Bosporus. Dazzling treasures include gem-encrusted Koran covers with richly illuminated manuscripts, intricate music boxes with rotating scenes, exquisitely worked jewelry, and ornately embroidered caftans–are just tokens to what is on view. Look for the gold-on-silver cradle in which newborn sons were presented to the sultan and for the 18th-century solid-gold hookah. The hilt of the renowned dagger is ornamented with enormous emeralds, and on the scabbard there is an enameled basket of flowers surrounded by diamonds. In richly decorated rooms, thrones are bejeweled with gold and gemstones, walnut is inlaid with mother-of-pearl and tortoise shell, and quotations from the Koran are set in gold. In the *harem* (private place) lived the *Valide* (sultan's mother), the sultan's hundreds of concubines, black eunuchs who guarded them, and female slaves. The grand audience room and the domed salon, with it's bronze chimneypiece and calligraphic freize, are stunning. The palace kitchen displays a collection of treasured porcelain along with gigantic ladles and cauldrons. After 1826, the sultans lived in the new palace, Dolmabahce, which was built with an eye to Versailles and French extravagance rather than Turkish. After World War I, Ataturk had the good taste to convert Topkapi Palace to a museum for all to enjoy. Tickets for the harem are separate from the main entrance tickets and can be purchased from the booth on the corner on the far left, after the main entrance. Interesting audios can be rented for both the main palace and treasury and another for the harem. Plan to spend at least half a day. Bring a picnic lunch to enjoy in a garden–the museum's café is expensive;

closed Tuesday. As you walk down the hill from the palace, stop for the iconic view of the famous six minarets and domes of the Sultanahmet Camil (Blue Mosque).

As you cross the long formal park known as the Hippodrome, which separates the Sultanahmet Camil from the Museum of Turkish and Islamic Culture, imagine the excitement and chaotic sounds of chariot races that once took place here. Stop by the tourist office at the north end; it's the city's best. The Museum of Turkish and Islamic Culture displays a outstanding collection of Turkish carpets, a fine exhibit from the Selcuk Empire, and exquisite Persian miniatures.

Almost in theatrical darkness, the 336 columns that hold up the Yerebatan Sarayi (Basilica Cistern or "Sunken Place") seem to go on forever. The columns were gathered from abandoned temples. Those not needed for the Aya Sofya were used here. It is ghostly and fun; open daily. Directions: Southwest corner of the Aya Sofya, close to the tram stop.

Sultanahmet Camili is known in the West as the Blue Mosque because blue is the predominant color of the luscious Isnik-produced tiles inside. This is a sacred, quiet place where devotees still pray in the magnificent space undaunted by the thousands of tourists. Both men and women need to cover their arms and legs and women also their heads. Wraps are available.

Using your imagination, try to peel back the years as you walk down Divan Yolu, the road that connected the Aya Sofya to the Theodosian walls and the Topakapi Palace. Try to picture the Janissaries, the Crusaders, and the armies of Mehmet the Conqueror parading along it. The Janissaries were a corps of elite soldiers taken from Christian families when they were children and brought up in the imperial court as Muslims and guards. In time they became the most feared soldiers in the empire.

From Sultanahamet walk up Divan Yolu to Beyazit Square, where the 15th-century mosque of Sutan Beyazit towers over the Grand Bazaar–a several-kilometer-long shoppers delight with a domed and vaulted ceiling. In a labyrinth of alleyways, a vast number of shops display perfectly arranged goods, both glorious and kitsch, that look as if the owner spent hours arranging. Gold, brass, and silk shops sit next to those with CDs and T-shirts. Rug salesmen unfurl their wares with a twist of the wrist that produces a showy snap. Incense smolders. It is touristy, cinematic, and fun; open daily.

For locals, the pedestrian street Istikal Caddesi is a favorite. Lined with shops selling every-thing from inexpensive souvenirs to diamond-studded watches, it attracts shoppers as varied as the goods behind the glass. Although you can take a tram across the Galata Bridge, it is more interesting to walk. On the Karakoy port side, you can take either take the Karakoy Tunel train (the entrance is just across the bridge) or walk up through the Beyoglu area to Istikal Caddesi. I suggest that you do both, one each way. An antique tram runs the 1^1/2 kilometer length of Istikal Caddesi to Taksim Square. Tickets can be purchased at the kiosks at either end or the halfway point. At the northern end, you can walk through the famous and touristy Cicek Pasaj (Flower Passage). Afterwards, continue on to the Balik Pazari (fish market) and then to Nevizade Sokak street which is popular with locals and lined with lively cafes and bars with outside terraces. At the end of Istikal Caddesi, Taksim Square offers benches, leafy trees, and open-air teahouses. On the east side of Taksim Square, the Ataturk Cultural Center is the home of the State Opera and Symphony Orchestra, which is also the venue for numerous festivals. The box office is open daily, and ticket prices are reasonably priced because of government subsidies. At the other end of Istikal Caddesi, the panoramic views from the Galata Tower are unbeatable. Seeing the confluence of the Sea of Marmara, the Golden Horn, and the Bosporus edged by the minarets of the ancient acropolis' mosques is a heady concoction, particularly if you've timed it right for a call to prayer that echoes from minaret to minaret.

The extravagant Dolmabahce Palace is located on the edge of the Bosporus, where Mehmet the Conqueror launched his attack on Constantinople. Surrounded by elegant gardens with grand magnolia trees and playful fountains, it has a stunning setting. An enormous crystal chandelier–a gift from Queen Victoria and reputed to be one of the largest ever made–fits right in with the rest of the incredibly lavish décor. English tours of the interiors are on the half-hour; closed Monday and Thursday. Directions: Take the tram over the Galata Bridge to Besiktas, then walk to the palace.

A scenic ferry ride up the Bosporus makes a nice change of pace. Bring a jacket and lunch. Directions: Ferries leave frequently from the Galata Bridge harbor. Istanbul's tram system is efficient and user-friendly. Buy tickets at a kiosk near major tram stops. To board, insert the ticket into the turn-style and pass out onto the waiting area.

▲**Camping:** There is no longer a campground in Istanbul. The closest one is in Kilyos. Use your guidebook, and stay in one of the many reasonably priced hotels or pensions.

ISTANBUL AREA
Kilyos

Only 30 kilometers from Istanbul, the beach town of Kilyos provides a nice break from the hubbub of the city. The campgrounds here are the closest ones to Istanbul. Directions: Off E80 or 100, drive north in the direction of Saiyer. After passing Ottman Park, you'll see signage to Kilyos. Follow the mountain road up to Kilyos.

▲**Camping:** • Drive west out of the center of town on the beach road for 3km.. At the fork, turn down towards the beach. Mistik Camping (212 201 1077); pleasant; quiet; common area with terraced shaded tables; not far from a pay beach; open all year; $$$.

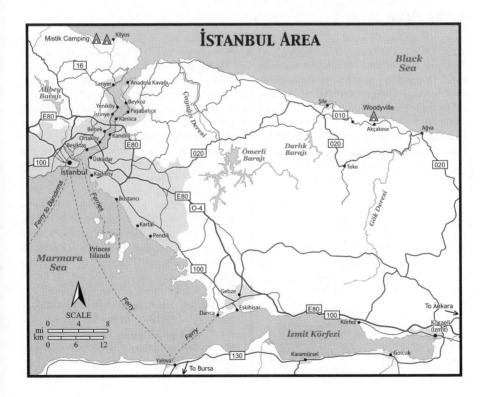

Sile

Only about 120 kilometers from Istanbul, this popular vacation area manages to keep a low-key, relaxed atmosphere. The beach is beautiful and serene. Happily catering to weekend tourists, Sile has a town square with shops where you can buy supplies. Directions: From Istanbul, take E80 east. After crossing the bridge over the Golden Horn, stay on E80 and follow signage to Umraniye. Drive east in the direction of Alemdar. Turn north to Omerli on 020 and then to Sile. Coming from east of Istanbul, exit E80 for Samandira. Follow signage to Omerli. From Omerli, drive northeast on 020 to Sile.

▲Camping: • This resort is unique. Called Woodyville (Akcakese in some guidebooks), it is located on a secluded private beach with a large grassy meadow. Covered wagons, tree-houses, and log cabins–all carefully knitted out with what you need for a good night's sleep–are separated spaciously on terraces. In the meadow, a few sheep and horses graze peacefully. An elaborate pool winds around a lounge chair-studded terrace overlooking the sea and an inviting bar features all sorts of American Indian and wild-west décor. Dining areas are tucked here and there and have a variety of decors to suit the weather or guests. The friendly owner assured me campers with tents and caravans are welcome. Directions: 16 km east of Sile. Drive east out of Sile in the direction of Aqua. At the fork, stay left driving in the direction of Akcakese. Follow signage for Woodyville (0216-727-7010); on a secluded private beach; cabins; pool; restaurant; lovely setting; open all year; $$$.

AROUND THE SEA OF MARMARA
Bursa Area

Famous spas nestle along a river beneath the Uludag Mountains in the town of Bursa, first set-tled in 200 BC. The raising of silk worms has been an important industry in the area for centuries. Every year silk cocoons are brought to the auction at the Silk Cocoon Caravanserai, a park-like, graceful old inn that now houses shops selling bolts of fine silk, scarves, and ties. Mosaic tiles and intricate wooden filigree decorate the opulent city's mosques and tombs. A covered food market and large car park are both close to the historic area. If you're going to Bursa from Istanbul take the car ferry from Eskihisar to Yalova because the traffic is heavy on the highway and the scenery is boring. On the ferry, transport yourself back through history as you cross this stretch of water that has been so important through time. You can purchase tickets just before boarding. Directions: Follow signage on 100 to Darica, and then to Eskihisar/Feribot.

Thermal waters springing from the Uludag Mountains have been enjoyed here for centu-ries, so it is a great place to indulge in a *hamam* experience. Directions: Drive west out of Bursa toward Muradiye and Cekirge. The Yeni Kaolica (New Bath) is on the northwest side of Kultur Park. Look for a steep accessway opposite Celik Palas Hotel. For an experience in a beautifully restored old *hamam*, drive a bit farther. Just before entering Cerkirge, on the eastern side next to the Kervansary Thermal Hotel, is Eski Kapicalari (Old Bath). The experience here will be more expensive because of the careful restoration but the aesthetics are outstanding. The baths here have large pools where you can soak in the hot thermal water. If you prefer an outdoor pool experience, go to the beautiful one at the Kervansary Hotel.

▲**Camping:** • In Uludag Mill Parki, about one hour south into the mountains behind Bursa. Drive west out of Bursa on E90 for 5km in the direction of Cekirge/Uludag. Take the scenic road–reminiscent of the Sierra foothills in California–up to the village of Sarialan and the Milli Parki. Camping Sarialan; popular with Turkish families; close to hiking trails; open June-Aug; $.

▲**Camping:** • Between Bursa and Canakkale. Exit off E90 for 10-09/Edincik and drive 8km. Continue north for 15km to Erdek Camping ANT (0266 855 7044); small; pretty location; shady with pines; open May-Sept; $.

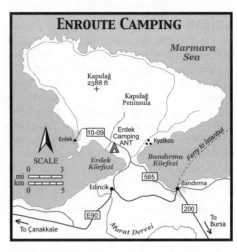

Gelibolu Peninsula

When Winston Churchill planned the Allied assault on Gallipoli, he was confident of victory. The ragged Turks will we defeat, he thought, and we will put an end of the Ottoman power. Australians and New Zealanders, who made up a good portion of the Allied troops, were eager to show their worth to the world. To their surprise however, the Turkish defenders were astonishingly tenacious and willing to take staggering casualties. The two armies fought, sometimes from trenches only yards apart, for most of 1915. Finally, the invaders were forced to leave in defeat. In poignant letters and diaries now in the museum, they tell of new found respect for the Turkish fighters. Visitors read this message from Ataturk on a memorial stone, "Those heroes that shed their blood and lost their lives, you are now lying in the soil of a friendly country. Therefore rest in peace. There is no difference between the Johnnies and the Mehmets to us, where they lie side by side in this country of ours. After having lost their lives on this land, they have become our sons as well." Softened now by grassy rolling hills and quiet beaches, the poignant reminders of grim military history– particularly of World War I when there was an enormous loss of troops on both sides–are kept fresh in the touching and beautiful museum, battlefields, and cemeteries. Directions: Take the car-ferry from Canakkale to Eceabat. Turn north upon exiting the ferry, then follow sign-posting west for Kabatepe for 9km. South of the battlefields, the beach around the village of Kum Limani is a wonderful setting for camping.

▲**Camping:** • After getting off the car-ferry from Canakkale to Eceabat, turn north, and then west, following signposting for 9km to Kabatepe. Turn south, and drive 6km. Mocamp Kum (0286 814 1455); beautiful setting on the beach; pool; cabins; restaurant; open May-Sept; $$.

Edirne

Continuing in its role as part of Via Egnatia (the route from Roman Rome to Byzantine Constantinople), Erdirne is Thracian Turkey's main town. Bordering Greece and Bulgaria, it is a popular entryway for travelers coming from other parts of Europe. One of Turkey's finest mosques, the Selmiye Camii was designed by the renowned Mimar Sinan and is the city's icon. Visiting it is a good break in the journey. Hoping to surpass the Aya Sofya in Istanbul–which he did by several centimeters–Sinan supported the celestial dome with eight-twelve-sided columns. Inside delicate sunlight streams in through upper windows and intricate calligraphy proclaims the glory of Allah. Devotees chanting prayers in Arabic sound like the cooing of doves are almost hypnotic in such a space. For a complete change in mood, see the exhibition of photographs and memorabilia from the 600-year-old sport of oil wrestling in the mosque's Museum of Turkish and Islamic Arts, located in the northeast corner. The big event for the sport is the annual Kirkpinar Festival held outside Edirne on Saray Ici islet. To add to the fun of this mid-summer event (date depends on religious holidays), the Romany population sets up a carnival and also presents a very colorful competition and parade.

▲**Camping:** • Take exit 31 off E80 onto 100 in the direction of Kirklareli, and follow sign-posting 6km. Omur Camping (0284 226 0037); large; popular; pool; open Apr-Oct; $$. • In the same area. Fifi Lokanta MoCamp (0284 226 0101); rooms, restaurant; pool; popular; open Apr-Oct; $$$.

NORTHERN AEGEAN
Troy

When Homer composed his epic the *Iliad*, 27 centuries ago, he described his walled city of Troy as being at the edge of a cape overlooking the southern entrance to the Dardanelles and said that the strait was called the Hellspont and that it stood on the edge of a flood plain. Xerxes came to the site before he set off for Macedonia to pray to his hero Achilles, and it is thought that Alexander the Great kept a copy of the *Iliad* with him on his campaigns.

Whether or not you believe that the ruins that Homer told of in the *Iliad* are what you are look-ing at, archeologists have found evidence that a great battle was fought at the archeological site named Troy. They believe the battle took place around 1250 BC–exactly the period of Homer's Trojan War. So knowing that Achilles, Odysseus, and Agamemnon might have gazed on the same walls you are looking at is a thrill. In ancient times, sailors had to wait for a favorable wind to put ashore at the southern entrance to the Dardenelles. Troy was on the coast then. Silting has moved it 11 kilometers inland.

The excavation was made famous by amateur archeologist Heinrich Schliemann. Passionate to uncover evidence of the Trojan War he instead uncovered a fabulous cache of jewelry he named Priam's Treasure. Since then, archeologists have reliably dated the hoard of jewelry a thousand years earlier. Nine successive settlements have been distinguished; the seventh corresponds to Homer's Troy. An outline of a fortress, gateways, and fortified walls have been exposed and reconstructed, as they might have existed in the 13th-century BC. Directions: 17km south of Canakkale, exit off 550 and drive west for 5km. At the entrance is a replica of the wooden Trojan horse with lookout tower.

▲**Camping:** • South of Canakkale 10km on 550/E24, on the beach road at the village of Dardanos. Karol Mocamp (0286-263-5452); nice location; cabins; open May-Sept; $$. • Close to the ruins of Troy. Drive 12km south from the Canakkale exit on 550/E87 to the beach at the village of Guzelyali. Trova-Mocamp (0286-232-8025); affiliated with a motel; all year; $$

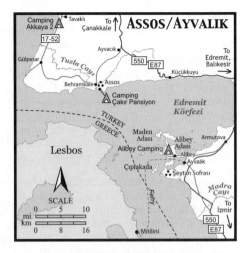

Assos

Minor ruins are being excavated in this out-of-the-way, blissful setting. If you have extra time, this is a nice excursion. Directions: 73km south of Cankkale, exit off 550 for the small town of Ayvacik (not to be confused with the larger town of the same name, located farther down the coast south of Edremit). Drive west 19 kilometers on a winding road with panoramic vistas and high desert landscape. Just before you get to the village of Behramkale, note the lovely 14th-century humpback bridge. There is a Friday morning market in the village of Kucukkuyu, on 550 just as the road meets the sea on the north side of the Bay of Edremit.

▲Camping: • Next to the harbor. Cakir Pansiyon (0286 721 7148); some shade; great views; basic; open Apr-Oct; $ • In the same area but farther south on the west coast of the promontory. From Ayvacik, drive west in the direction of Gulpinar for 28km. Turn north at the fork onto 17-52, and drive 14km in the direction of Tavakli. Camping Akkaya 2 (0286 647 0016); remote; beautiful setting; café; open Apr-Sept; $$.

Ayvalik

Picturesque Ayvalik is popular with international campers and is a good place to relax on the beach, cook, share stories, and watch the sunset and the night sky as it fills with stars. The morning market at the main square is excellent. Ferries leave from here for the Greek Island of Lesbos.

▲Camping: • On Alibey Island. Cross the bridge to the island on the north end of Ayvalik, then drive to the northwestern edge of the island. Ada Camping (0266-327-1211); lovely beach; shade trees and palapas; restaurant; cabins; open May-Sept; $$.

Bergama Area

Almost completely enclosed by mountains and a fertile plain, Pergamon was once self-sufficient. Its setting for an acropolis was ideal. Rising high above the plain, the isolated rock disposed itself to rocky terraces perfect for the curves of a theatre. Spectators looked beyond the stage to a fertile plain and distant sea. The Altar of Zeus, its most famous antiquity, stood on an enormous stone plinth supporting a double colonnade of Ionic columns separated on one side by a 20-meter stairway. A four-meter-high freize decorated the sides with furious battle scenes between the Titans and the gods. Remains of the altar and freize were taken to Berlin and dramatically restored and are now in the Pergamonmuseum, a highlight of any trip to Berlin. Pergamon was a powerful ally of Rome, and in the 2nd-century AD its kings ruled 5 million subjects. The Egyptians, concerned that Pergamon's 2,000-volume library would lure scholars from Alexandria, refused to supply more papyrus. So Pergamum developed parchment from animal skins (*pergamena* means parchment in Latin).

The Archeological Museum is on the main street coming into Bergama. As you drive the 6 kilometers up to the Acropolis, you'll pass the Red Basilica. Behind the museum, next to the army camp, are the ruins of Asclepion, where the famous physician Galen practiced.

▲**Camping:** • In Bergama, 2km west of town on the main road. Berksoy Mocamp (0232-633-5345); affiliated with a motel; convenient to ruins; pool; open all year; $$. • Halfway between Bergama and Aliaga, on 550 and the Candarli Bay. Camping-Motel Afacan, (0232-628-7030); beautiful location; pool; restaurant; open April-Sept; $$$. • In Yenifoca, south of Alaga, exit 550 and drive 12km west. Pass through town, and continue west for another 2km. Azak Restaurant and Camping; nice setting; basic; $.

Sardis

The setting at the base of the beautiful Boz Daglari mountains, amid vine-covered fields, is what is most impressive about these ruins. The broad valley that they sit on is immensely fertile and made the city a perfect apex for trade. Lydian houses and the tombs of 12-century BC (Mycenean levels) have been uncovered, including a structure identified as an installation for refining gold. Herodotus wrote of the Lycian invention of gold coinage, and Croesus, their peaceful and celebrated ruler, gave great golden gifts to the treasury at Delphi in Greece. The main ruins are on the north side of the main road. The walking path to the Temple of Artemis is on the south side of the road by the teahouses. Directions: It is 90km east of Ismir on E96/300, just west of the town of Salihi. Look for signs in the village of Sartmahmut, just west of Salihi.

CENTRAL AEGEAN AND AROUND
Izmir/Cesme Peninsula

Izmir is a big, western-style city whose focal point is a carved clock tower at the *konak* (main square). Its archeological museum has notable collections from excavations in the area, and the ethnological museum has a beautiful replica of a Turkish wood house, a merchant's house, and dioramas showing felt and pottery production. Upstairs are re-creations of a nuptial room and a circumcision celebration room. If you are here close to sunset, climb the stairs to the fortress and watch the sky gradually twinkle with stars. Directions: Follow signposting to centrum, then Konak. The exit for Konak is where the freeways net, and traffic is heavy. Watch closely for signs so that you are in the correct lane to exit. Off the freeway, drive toward the harbor and bus terminal. Turn into Turgutreis Park just south of the bus terminal and follow signposting to the museums and car park.

▲**Camping:** These are all on the Cesme Peninsula, a popular international resort area. The freeway out has a toll, but it is excellent: • In Uria, 40km west of Izmir. Take exit #3 at Uria. UCamp (0232-755-1021); resort-like; open May-Sept; $$$. • In Alacati, 85km west of Izmir. Exit at #6 for Alacati, and follow signs for Sorf Cenneti. Camping Surf Paradise; on the beach; open May-Sept; $$ • In Ilica, 85km west of Izmir. Exit at #6 off Ilica/Alacati highway and drive north to Ilica then out to the end of the spit. VeCamp (0232-723-1416); resort-

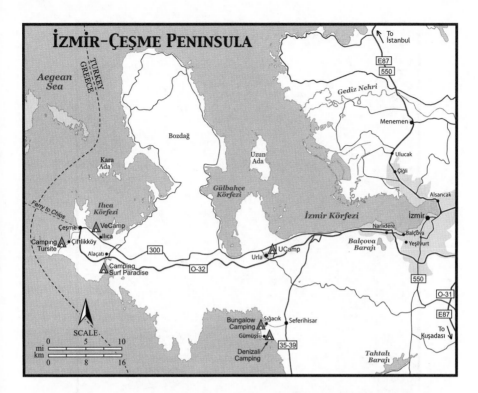

like; lovely setting; natural thermal springs; private beach; open May-Sept; $$$. • At the west end of the spit, 11km south of Cesme in Ciftlikkoy. Camping Tursite (0232 722 1221); resort-like; can be windy; open May-Oct; $$.

Coast Route to and from Ephesus

For remote beach camping with an archeological dig thrown-in, exit Cesme/Ismir expressway at exit #2 and drive south on 35-39 in the direction of Seferihisar for 21 kilometers. This is a scenic route through farmlands where rocky hills hug the shore and roses and bougainvillea engulf the houses. When you arrive at the beach, take the small road west to Sigacik and the archeological site of Teos, once a site for a Temple of Dionysos.

▲Camping: • On the cape of Sigacik in the village of Akkum, adjacent to the Neptune resort. Bunglow Camping; basic; $. • Farther south on the southeast side of the promontory in Gumussu. Denizati Hippocampus Holiday Village (0232 798 9191); full resort; program for children; pool; restaurant; open Apr-Sept; $$$$.

Ephesus

Because it is one of best-preserved ancient cities on the Mediterranean, Ephesus is a major tourist sight in Turkey. Even though the town where it rests, Selcuk, is loaded with tourists, it retains a Turkish feel. It has a good open market, an excellent archeological museum, and pleasant sidewalk cafes. The Archeological Museum is on the main road into Selcuk and is a good first stop. Artifacts are artistically displayed, and it's an airy, pleasant place; closed Monday. Visit the tourist office in

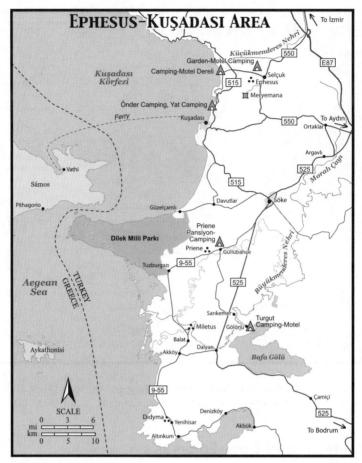

front of the museum. Then drive up to Ayasoluk Hill, where you can look out over the entire setting and see the colonnades of the Basilica of St John and his presumed tomb and baptistery; open
daily. Ephesus was the capital of Asia until the 3rd-century AD. Built on the outskirts of a modest temple dedicated to the Asiatic cult of Artemis, it has a long history. After liberating the city,
Alexander the Great promised to rebuild the exuberant and ostentatious temple if the citizens
would rename it after him. "It's unseemly for one god to dedicate a temple to another god," was
their polite refusal. The citizens themselves rebuilt the temple 22 years after its destruction in the
form that later gave it the title of one of the Seven Wonders of the World. In Roman times, Saint
Paul came to the great theatre to preach. Many churches were built within its walls, most notably
the Bascilica of St John. Its 24,000-seating capacity theatre was a scene of anti-Christian riots.
More than anywhere else along the Turkish side of the Mediterranean, the ruins evoke the daily life
of the people who lived and worked here. It's hard to believe that Ephesus was completely buried
under clean alluvial sand before the middle of the last century. Much is still buried. Locals say that
in the 1930s it was difficult to reach and rarely visited. To experience Ephesus, come either very
early in the day or late in the afternoon, and bring a guidebook, water bottle, and snack or picnic.
In your mind, replace the tourists with attractively robed Romans, talking and gossiping.

If you have extra time, consider an additional trip to the Cave of Seven Sleepers to view the
now fenced catacombs where the martyrs slept. Meryemana is the presumed site where the Virgin

Mary lived her last years and died. It's a shady, quiet place with lots of tourists. Directions: Take Ataturk Caddesi south out of Selcuk, then drive 8km up the hill on a winding road with panoramic views. The expressway from Izmir to Selcuk is excellent but heavily trafficked with large tour buses. Consider taking the Coast Route to and from Epheus described in the previous section.

▲**Camping:** • In Selcuk, west of Ayasoluk Hill. Signposted on the north side of the Isa Bey Camili. Garden Camping (0232 893 1205); garden-like setting; small sites; popular; walking distance to town sights; cabins; open all year; $$$. • On the beach in Pamucak, 7km directly west of Selcuk. Camping-Motel Dereli, (0232 893 1205); large and popular; on the beach; restaurant; cabins; tennis; open April-Nov; $$$.

Kusadasi Area

Once a lovely seaside town, this is now a port stop for cruise ships and ferries to the Greek island of Samos. A walk to the ancient wall and tower–peering into the courtyards off the narrow winding streets along the way–provides a pleasant break in the journey. A car park is close to the tourist area.

▲**Camping:** • Just north of town, close to the discos and shopping. They both have pools and restaurants are located near the beach, and are open May-Sept; $$. Onder Camping (0256 618 1590) and Yat Camping, (0256-618 1516).

Nearby Sights

Dilek National Park is a restful day spot with a beach and pine forest. A large part of the park is a well-signposted military zone that includes the tip and the summit, but the beaches and pines provide a respite from the crowds in Kusadasi. Directions: Drive southeast out of Kusadasi on the main road for 8km, then exit onto a smaller road and drive 18km in the direction of Guzelcamli. The park entrance is 2km farther on the west side of town; open daily.

The setting of awe-inspiring Priene is reminiscent of Greece's Delphi. Try to be here at sunset; open daily. Directions: Drive southeast out of Kusadasi on the main road for 21km in the direction of Soke. Exit south onto 525 and drive 5km. Exit onto a smaller road and follow signposting west to Priene, passing through the village of Savulca.

▲**Camping:** • On the road to Priene. Priene Pensions-Camping (0256-547-1249); basic; open May-Sept; $$.

For a view of the entire area, climb to the top of the mammoth theater at Miletus. The sea has now receded, but imagine it long ago when it was at the edge of the sea. Afterwards, drive farther on to see the huge columns still standing at the Temple of Apollo. It's not hard to recreate in your mind the Temple's magnificence and religious importance. Directions: Follow the directions to Priene above, but drive west 9km, exiting south at Tuzburgazi. Then drive 19km farther through cotton fields and olive groves. Miletus is just north of the village of Balat. The Temple of Apollo is just south on the same road, in the direction of Akkoy and Didim. If you're not visiting Priene, take 525 south of Soke for 25km, exiting west onto a small road in the direction of Yenikoy and Akkoy. Miletus is about 4km north of Akkoy, and the Temple of Apollo is 15km south of Akkoy.

▲**Camping:** • On the Bafa-See, exit 525 at Sarikemer and head east to the village of Golonu. Turget Camping-Motel (0521-224-4075); nice shady location on a small lake; open May-Sept; $$.

Aphrodisias

Set in a valley of pines and tobacco fields, this is one of Turkey's most important archeological sites. Its isolated location keeps crowds away. In the 1st-century AD, it was a flourishing city and remained so for the next 600 years. Chalk-white Ionic columns, 12 meters high, outline the Temple to Aphrodite. The stadium is one of the best preserved in the world. In the museum, compare the classical beauty of the statuary with photos in today's body building magazines. Directions: 55km southeast of Nazilli. Get gas on E87 before driving out. After passing through Nazilli and Kuyucak on E87, exit on the smaller road 505 and drive south following the Menderes River for 38km. At the village of Karacasu, the road turns east towards the village of Geyre. The site is just beyond.

▲**Camping:** • West of the site on the main road. Aphrodisias Hotel-Camping (0256-448-8132); basic; open May-Sept; $.

Pamukkale

Pamukkale isn't the experience it once was. The beautiful travertine terraces that glisten like the insides of abalone shells in the gold and pink of sunset are still there, but the terrace area is smaller than it used to be. People can no longer walk out to soak their feet in the warm thermal waters, and the travertine terraces are now viewed from paths above. The new restrictions are certainly merited, but considering the time it takes to drive here it can be a disappointment. If you drive to the north entrance, it's a shorter walk to the springs, museum, and archeological site; open daily. Directions: Driving out on E87 is pleasant but time-consuming. It's 195km from Selcuk or 215km from Kusadasi. The good two-lane road has a third lane for passing. The rocky mountain landscape is studded with olive trees, and the divider strips are ablaze with roses, zinnias, and oleanders. Go into the town of Denizli, exiting north on 320 for 14km to Pamukkale. For a shortcut to Pamukkale, instead of going into Denizli take a small road off 320 south of the village of Saraykoy. Watch for a road heading east then follow signposting east for 15km to Akkoy/Karahavit.

▲**Camping:** • South of Pamukkale, just before you enter town, on road 320. Camptur Camping; pool; large restaurant catering to busloads of tourists; nice view of vineyards; open May-Sept $$. • 5km north of Pamukkale, in the village of Karahayit. Camping-Motel Termotes (025-271-4066); pool; better for caravans; open all year; $$$.

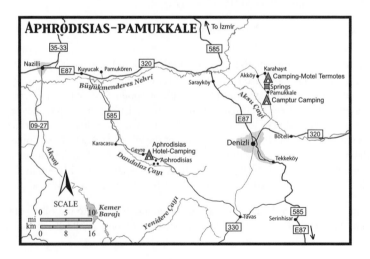

Bodrum Peninsula

This is a hip resort town with plenty of places to hang out and meet other international travelers. Its icon landmark is the Castle of St Peter, built by the Knights of St John and finished in 1437. It rises with the natural slope of a hill on the edge of the sea and today houses the Museum of Underwater Archeology featuring fragments of amphorae, tools, and vases as well as plates with the octopus design of concentric circles–all brought up from underwater explorations. Walking across a moat and through a courtyard populated with peacocks, adds fun to visiting the towers and dungeon. Direction: Park outside the tourist area and walk in. Car parks are expensive, but street parking is carefully ticketed and car impoundment is prompt. Ferries go to several Greek islands from here. The drive to Milas on the main road 303 passes through pleasant pine forests with picturesque views of Bodrum, the yacht harbor, and the castle.

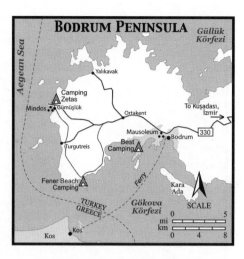

▲**Camping:** • Closest to town. On the main road heading west from Bodrum, exit toward the beach at Bitez. Best Camping (0252-316-7688); part of the hip scene; open May-Sept; $$$$. • At the end of the main road at Turgutreis, 25km from Bodrum, drive north on the beach road to Gumbet. Camping Zetas (0252-316-2231); nice location on the beach; open all year; $$$$. • From Turgutreis, take the beach road south 5km to Akyariar, passing through the village to the lighthouse. Fener Beach Camping; lovely location; open May-Sept; $$.

Turquoise Coast

The panoramic views from the highway along this beautiful coastline are spectacular. When the road turns inland, the air becomes filled with the scent of pine, while on flatter areas your eyes are treated to colorful small fields of corn, beans, and citrus. The sea here turns the color of gemstones–sapphire, turquoise, and lapis lazuli. When you swim, there is a sensation of being suspended between the matching blues of the ocean and sky. Quiet bays are surrounded by pine and low, shrub-covered hillsides, and leaves of tamarisk trees rustle in the wind. Ancient Lycian tombs are carved into steep rock walls and the crumbling stone ruins of once vibrant cities reflect early morning and evening light.

▲**Camping:** • South of Mula, exit 550 onto 400 and drive south in the direction of Marmaris for about 10km. Pass through the village of Cetibeli, watching for a small forest road close to the bridge. Drive 2km on this road. Naturcamp Boncuk (0252-495-8116); beautiful location; small; Apr-Oct; $$$. • Take 400 west out onto the finger-like pennisula for 71km to Resadiye, then follow the road south 4km to Datca. These are both resort-like, with stunning locations, and are open May-Sept; $$$$. Aktur Datca Mocamp (0252-724-6168) and Ozil Mocamp (0252-712-3149).

Koycegiz Golu

Silting deposits created a lake here out of what was once a bay open to the Mediterranean. Now herons and storks feed among the reeds where the ruins of ancient Kaunos still stands, remote and

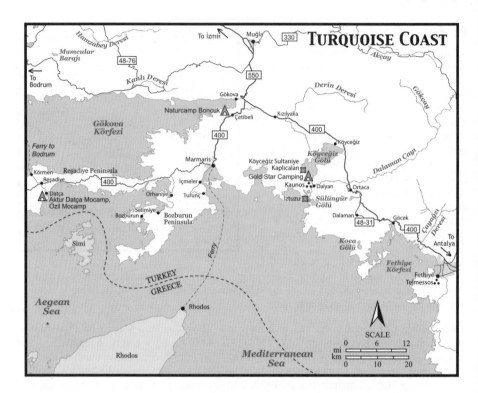

mostly unearthed. Cliffside tombs elaborately carved into the vertical faces of mountains look like the great doors of classical buildings slipped into the mouths of caves. The series of open-air mud pools and the more luxurious dome-sheltered thermal pool with marble sides and rocky bottom that are south of Koycegiz are particularly fun. Directions: Exit 400 south, and drive along the west side of the lake for 14km to Koycegiz Sultaniye Kaplicalari; open daily to 10 PM. The popular resort of Dalyan and the nearby Iztuzu sand beach use a turtle motif as their icon because the beach is a breeding ground for loggerhead turtles. Swathes of reeds line the banks of the Dalyan Cayi, the river that connects the lake Koycegiz Golu to the Mediterranean. You can rent a canoe or rowboat to paddle up the river into the lake or you can board an evening rowboat ferry from the river end of Yali Sokagi near Daylan.

▲**Camping:** • 38km southwest of Koycegiz on the east side of the bay at Ekincik. Gold Star Camping (0252 266 0241); lovely setting on a sandy beach; good for bird and turtle watching; open June-August; $$$

Fethiye Area

Lycian rock tombs from ancient Telmessos hide in the hillside above the bazaar in Fethiye, bits of the ancient theatre nestle behind the tourist office, and a medieval knight's castle looms on the hillside overlooking the harbor. Today the city is the business hub for the region. For a break in the journey, consider the locally popular half-day boat ride out into the Bay of Fethiye. Wear your swimsuit, because when you stop in a scenic cove for lunch it is fun to jump or dive from the boat into the beautiful turquoise water. Directions: Buy tickets at the harbor in the morning. The ruins of mountain-top Kadyanda provides an interesting hike with scenic with views. Directions:

3km north of Fethiye, exit 400 onto 48-27 at Gunlubasi. Drive 13km. Exit east for Uzumlu and drive 6km, passing through the town. Follow signposting for the Kadyanda car park up the hill for 7km. Then walk the signposted trail up through the pines to the ruins. During the population exchange of 1923 after the War of Independence, Greeks were forced to leave their village of Kaya Koyu. After paying a small admission charge, you may wander through the government-protected ghost town and reflect on the plight of the 6,000 people who were forced to leave their homes. Directions: Drive southeast of town in the direction of Ovacik for 12km. Drive through Ovacik to Hisaronu. Exit west, following signposting for Kaya Koyu for 4km. One of Turkey's most popular resorts is the area around the sapphire lagoon of Oludeniz, located 10 kilometers south of Fethiye. You can rent a kayak at the national park entrance, but if you just want some restful time go 3 kilometers farther south to the forest service campground of Kidrak. Directions: Drive 3km east of Belcekiz. The long-distance Lycian Way Trail runs parallel to the Turquoise Coast. It begins in the mountains above Oludeniz in the village of Ovacik and ends in Antalya. Inaugrated in 2000, it is still in the infant stages of clearing trail and signposting. Like the Pacific Coast Trail, it is a backpacking experience; wwwthelycianway.com.

▲**Camping:** • South out of Fethiye 11km, take the small road to Oludeniz and the beach. Bambus Camping (0252-617-0694); small; beautiful location; cabins; restaurant; Apr-Sept; $$$.

Termessos

To sit as high as an eagle in the spectacular Termessos' amphitheatre, while practically alone, is delightfully eerie. From the parking area a 20-minute walking trail climbs up to the ruins. There clearly marked trails wind down the hillside to various sections of the site. Wear walking shoes and bring water and a guidebook. A small museum and picnic/camping area are under the pines at the base of the mountain. Directions: From Antalya, exit 400 north in the direction of Burdur/Afron-Denesli/Mugia. Where the road forks stay left, driving in the direction of Korkuteli on 350/E87. Drive 20km on 350/E87 to Gullukdagi Milli Parki and road to Termessos. From the park entrance, the road winds up another 9km through aromatic pines.

▲Camping: • At the park entrance. Gullukdagi Milli Parki Camping; a forest service campground; tranquil setting under the pines; basic; open June-Aug; $$. • 14 km from Antalya, in the direction of Burdur on 650. Parlar Mocamp (0242-332-6601); popular with caravans; open May-September; $$$.

LYCIAN COAST
Sakikent Gorge

Hiking into the Sakikent Gorge is like hiking through a vast marble sculpture. The water-carved chasm goes in for 18 kilometers, however most hikers don't go that far. Young guides can assist less able hikers up into the chasm. Wear shoes that can get wet and aren't slippery and bring your camera. Outside the gorge, it's great fun to float down the river for several kilometers in an inner-tube. Directions: From Fethiye, take 400 east, but instead of following 400 south continue east on 350 for 3km. Watch for a small road heading south and signage for Sakikent Gorge. It's a picturesque route through small farmlands. Little roadside cafes have outside dining and serve grilled trout right off the outdoor barbecue. They are terrific places to rest and absorb more of the Turkish countryside ambiance.

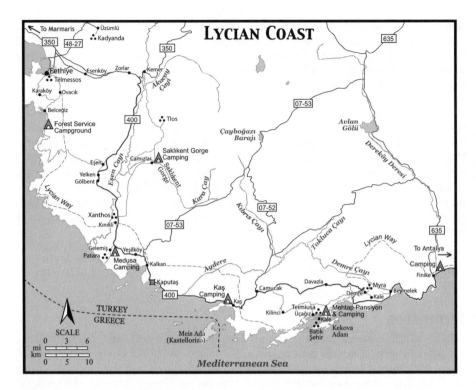

▲**Camping:** • Close to the gorge, along the river. Saklikent Gorge Camping (0252 659 0074); pleasant; basic; inner-tube rental; café; open May-Sept; $$.

Xanthos Ruins

In 2,000 BC, a race of Indo-Europeans populated this region. They were courageous and bravely fought off intruders. Called Lycians, they established Xanthus as their capital. For great views of the river valley where many important ancient Lycian towns were located, take a small detour off 400 to the ruins of Xanthos. Its 4th-century Nereid Monument, a highly decorated Ionic temple, is now in the British Museum. Directions: Exit 400 by the bridge in the village of Kinikli. Once an important port for Lycia, the village of Patara located southwest of the ruins is now known for its long white-sand beach. It is 9 kilometers from the access road and car park to the beach, so consider taking a beach shuttle.

▲**Camping:** • In Gelemis. 6km south of Kinikli, take exit 400 for Patara and drive 2km. • Medusa Camping; very basic; open May-Sept; $.

Kas and Kekvoa

The gorgeous coastline from Kalkan to picturesque Kas should be savored. Take time to stop at viewing areas to enjoy the postcard panorama scenes. Kas is a stopping place for yachts on the Turquoise Coast, but what was once a sleepy fishing village is now a holiday metropolis. Bougainvillea shrouds stores and cafes and colorful awnings cover tiny passageways to the water-front. The best way to see Batik Sehir, the sunken city off Kekvoa Island is by kayak. Peering at the remains of stairs, house foundations, and a long quay wall is eerie. In an attempt to prevent lose of the antiquities, swimming or being directly in the water is not permitted. If you are an experienced kayaker, go on your own; otherwise book with a tour group. The kayak rental can include a motorized tow from Ucagiz to the start of the ruins. Scuba diving is also popular. The visibility and variety of underwater scenery is considered the best in Turkey; www.bougainville-turkey.com. If you don't want to kayak, drive to Ucagiz and hire one of the local boatmen to take you out. You'll get much closer to the ruins than in the larger boats from Kas. As part of your boating experience, stop in Kale and clamor up the hillside to see the ruins of the Knights of St John and ancient Teimiusa. The village of Ucagiz is delightful, particularly at night when most of the tourists have left and the castle and small restaurants overlooking the bay twinkle with lights. Directions: Drive east out of Kas for 11km on 400. Exit onto the small road, and drive south 8km in the direction of Kilici. Follow the road east for 12km to Ucagiz. If time permits, stop at ancient Myra to see the house-style rock tombs. Directions: 24km east of the exit for Ucagiz, exit at Kale for Myra and drive 2km following signposting.

▲Camping: • Off 400, one kilometer west of Kas. Kas Kamping (0242 836 1050); nice location at the beach; shade trees; cabins; disco nearby; open May-Sept; $$$. • 50km east of Kas on 400, on the wide and long beach east of Finike. At the southeast end of the tiny harbor at Ucagiz, close to the ruins of ancient Simena in Kale. Mehtap Pension and Camping (0242 874 2146) great location; open all year; $$$.

Cirali Olimpos Area

Beneath dramatic mountain gorges where wild thyme, bay, and mint fill the air with refreshing aromas, the ruins of Olimpos lay half-hidden by leafy trees. A cool stream, whose banks are daubed colorfully with wild cyclamen and oleander, accompanies a walk to the beach. Tree house pension-cafes that are popular with backpackers line the road along the beach. Directions: Exit 400 at the southern exit marked Olimpos11, Adrasan ad, and drive 12km to the car park. The *chimera* (perpetual flame) in the foothills of the Tahtali Dag is fed mysteriously from underground natural gases. As the sun is setting, it is fun to walk up the 30-minute trail and peer down through the rocks to the flame. Directions: Exit 400 just north of the Olimpos for Cirali 7, Chimira (Yanartas). Drive down to the village of Cirali, and then continue south on a small road to the car park and trailhead. Directions: 18km east of Kumluca, exit off 400 for Olimpus or go 800 meters farther for Cirali.

▲Camping: • In the Olimpos canyon just north of the mouth of the river. Olympia Tree House (0242 825 7351); tents only; tree-house cabins; basic; open May-Sept; $$.

Phaselis

Alexander the Great wrote while in Phaselis that it was an extraordinarily beautiful town with three harbors, straight avenues, plazas, and a theatre. But what astonished him most was that roses were blooming in winter. Cleopatra is said to have visited Phaselis, so when you look at the ruins of the classically proportioned theatre imagine her there. Plan for a stop here for a swim and picnic. The mountains tumble right down to the edge of the sea, making secluded little coves. You can drift off to sleep smelling the pines and listening to lapping waves. Directions: Halfway between Finike and Antalya, exit off 400 for Phaselis and drive 3km to the beach. The morning market at Kemer is good, and you can browse through the town's ethnographic exhibit of nomad life. Directions: Kemer is 15km east of the exit for Phaselis.

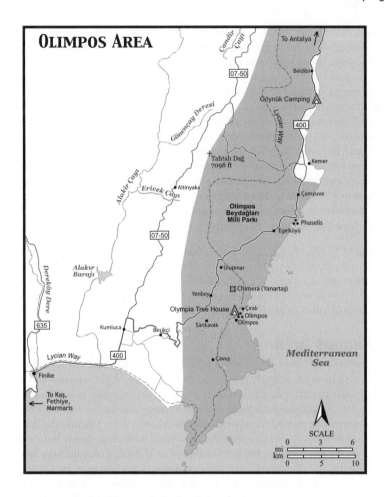

▲Camping: • 10km north of Kemer on 400. Goynuk Kamping (0242 815 3141); nice location; grass and shade; open all year; $$.

Antalya

Antalya's Archeological Muzesi is considered one of the country's best. The chronological exhibit begins with the Stone and Bronze ages, proceeds through the Mycenaean and Hellenistic periods, and goes on to the Seljuk and Ottoman periods. Start with the Roman Floor Mosaics exhibit on the first floor. It's one of the finest such collections in the world, and the themes are full of fun and frivolity. Exhibits are artistically designed and include labels in English. Directions: Exit off 400 on the west side of Antalya, and drive to the beach road. The museum is on Kenan Evren Bulvari, across from Ataturk Park on the west side of the river; closed Monday. Walking or cycling into old town Kaleici is doable from the campground. Proceed through Hadrian's gate into the shady and low-key neighborhood of old Ottoman houses. The modern city is vibrant and prosperous with Europeans who have bought retirement property. Large, well-stocked supermarkets and shopping malls are readily available. Frequent flights from Istanbul to Antalya make it a good choice for beginning a journey along Turkey's southern coast.

▲**Camping:** • In Antalya, on a bluff overlooking Bambus beach; at the south end
of the narrow parkland that lines the sea
bluff south of the old town, just northwest of Dedeman Waterpark. It is tricky
to find among high rises. Bambus Beach
Restaurant and Camping (0242-321-5263);
open to the public, who are charged admission for use of a very scenic slope of tiered
terraces to the sea; campers terrace use is
included in camping fee; wonderful diving
and swimming area; toilets are near camping area, but showers are farther away on
the public terrace area; open all year; $$.

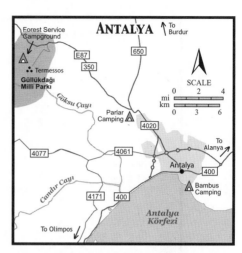

Perge

The elaborate theatrical productions, gladiator displays, and chariot races once staged here were famous. Built into the side of the hill, the theatre seated 14,000 people on 42 levels. The massive stadium was the largest in Asia Minor. Perge was a beautiful, luxurious city with a fine Byzantine basilica, spacious Roman baths, a lengthy colonnaded street, and a *nymphaeum* (spring-fed orna-mental water fountain); open daily. In the café outside the ruins, Turkish women roll out bread dough on a small round table, tossing it several times to stretch it until it is very thin. After a sprinkling of cheese and fresh herbs, it is folded over and placed in a brick oven. Don't miss this fresh-from-the-oven treat. In the car park women hunker down under shady trees like colorful birds in their *salvar* (wide trousers) and spread out their goods for sale. Directions: 21km east Antalya, exit 400 north following signposting for Perge.

Aspendos

One of Rome's best engineering feats in 200 AD, Aspendos' elaborate aquaduct brought water from the Taurus mountain 18 kilometers way. Built during the reign of Marcus Aurelius, the ancient theatre's acoustics are marvelous and it is still used for performances today. Check the calendar of events before coming to the area, so you can time your visit to coincide with a starlit performance. The Aspendos Opera and Ballet Festival, held from mid-June until mid-July is cel-ebrated but other performances are held regularly. Check with the English-speaking tourist office; 0242 243 4384. Watch for the lovely humpbacked Seljuk bridge that crosses over the Kopru River just west of the exit for Aspendos. Directions: 55km from Antalya. Exit off 400 just east of Serik, and drive 4km north.

▲**Camping:** • 15km east of Serik on 400. Beypet Camping (0242-617-205); convenient location; open May-Sept; $$.

Koprulu Canyon

This is one of my favorite areas in Turkey. Wood cottages are draped in colorfully blooming vines, gardens burst with flowers, and there is a joyful symphony of humming insects and song-birds. The Turks who live here are friendly and welcome visitors. To jump off boulders and swim in the inviting Koprulu River, stop at the new bridge. Rafting is popular on both sides of the river. Competent boatmen accompany paddling groups on four to six-man boats. Arrange for a paddle at 8:30 AM, and you'll have the river and boat pretty much to yourself. Though not a challenging

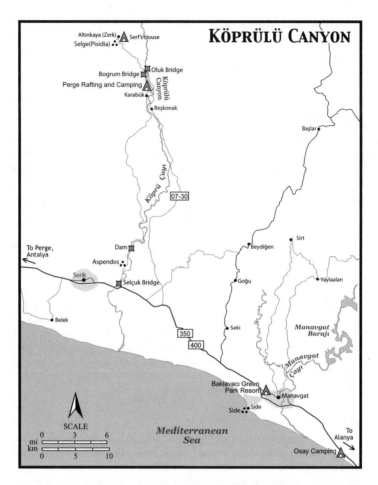

river for experienced paddlers, it is still fun and scenic. Stop to see the old Seljuk bridge which is so pretty in the dappled light then continue north to the modern Bogrum bridge. On the west side, a precipitous cliff-side trail leads back to the mouth of the river. Hiring a local guide ensures safety for this adventure and helps support ecotourism.

Visiting the Roman ruins of the Selge is a dramatic mountaintop experience. The road to the ruins winds steeply up through arid mountains dramatically juxtaposed with chimney-like sculptures carved by the wind. Fuchsia-colored oleander blooms are a welcoming touch along with pine-scented pull-outs offering stunning views. At road's end is the village of Zerk, a artist's canvas of green wheat and yellow daisies accented with slate-roofed farm houses. Your experience here will be part village and part ruins so park outside the village and walk in quietly, immersing yourself in the tinkle of goat bells and the fragrant mountain air. Local guides will be eager to lead you through the ruins, but you might choose best to just trek around on your own. Directions: 5km east of the exit for Aspendos, exit 400 for Koprulu National Park. Drive 31km to Beskonak, staying west at the fork to the bridge for Karabuk Koyu. From here, you either continue up to Zerk or cross over the Bogrum bridge and drive down the east side of the Koprulu River. Both sides have campgrounds and rafting.

▲**Camping:** • This is my favorite. 8km from Beskonak, on the west side of the river. Perge Rafting and Camping (0533 475 8108); wonderful location beside spring-fed ponds and a creek that flows into the Koprulu River; part of a popular trout restaurant with picturesque terraces stretching out into the spring-fed pond; camping on large field adjacent to restaurant; nice toilet and shower areas; practically free if you also raft; open May-Sept; $. • Most of the other rafting companies on both sides of the river will also let you camp if you book a raft trip. • In Zerk, at the entrance to the ruins of Selge. Serf's House (0242 765 8091); field or terrace depending on the weather; basic; $.

Side/Manavgat

The twin temples to Apollo and Athena here overlook the old harbor, and visiting them makes a nice sunset walk. Vines and flowering shrubs partially shroud the ruins of white marble fountains, ornamental public latrines, and a large theatre. Once an important port based significantly on slave trade, the city is now a booming tourist resort.

▲**Camping:** • 20km east of Manavgat on 400. Osay Camping (0242 748 2878); pleasant setting with shade trees, grass, and flowers; sand beach; cabins; open April-Sept; $$. • On the west side of Manavgat. Baklavaci Green Park Resort (0242 756 9141); large resort; nice location among other resorts; open all year; $$$$.

MEDITERRANEAN COAST
Alanya

Greenhouses filled with bananas, tomatoes, and strawberries line the highway coming into Alanya, a major beach resort and harbor. In town, the medieval red-stone defensive tower at the harbor houses an ethnographic museum. Inside the walls, a castle-fortress looms over the old town from its hilltop location.

▲**Camping:** • Just west of town on 400. Perle Camping (0242 526 2066); small; nice location with private beach; reed screen shade; café; simple; basic; $. • 20km east of town on 400. Sedre Camping (242 516 1111); good location on the beach; larger; shady with pines; open all year; $$.

Drive from Alanya to Silifke

Undulating hills along this coastal road are a terraced patchwork of fields embroidered with wind-breaking pines. The road winds up and down the mountain's sea-cliff edge and is reminiscent of California's Big Sur Coast. It is dramatic, pine scented, and slow moving. On the lowlands, a sea of greenhouses decorated with hollyhocks, yellow daisies, and purple thistle provides roadside stands with bananas and strawberries.

Anamur

On the eastern side of the headland–Turkey's most southern point–and just southwest of town, the partially excavated ruins of ancient Anemurium sweep down the mountain-side and make for an interesting view from a nearby campground terrace.

▲**Camping:** • On the west side of town, on the beach just beneath Anemurium. After coming down the mountain to Anamar, exit 400 south onto a small road heading to the beach.

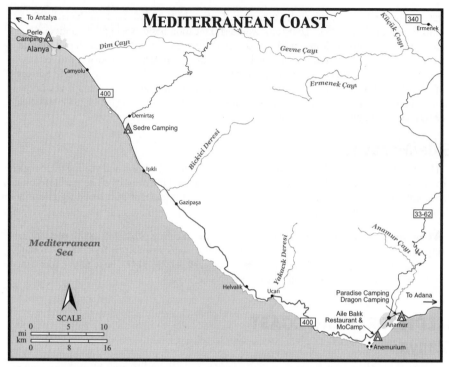

Stay left at the fork at the beach road. Aile Balik Retaurant and Mocamp (324 835 1666);
nice setting on a grassy lawn just above the beach, with fine views of the sea; recommended
restaurant; $$. • Just east of Anamur on the beach on the west side of the castle Mamure
Kalesi. Paradise Camping (324 827 1775); great location just beneath the castle; good snor-
keling around large rocks; recommended restaurant; shady with palms; sites are small; can
be crowded; open all year; $$. • Nearby. Dragon Camping; shady with eucalyptus; use if
Paradise is too crowded; open all year; $$.

Goksu Delta

Two immense natural lagoons enclosed
by a sand spit make up the Kuscenneti Bird
Reserve in the Goksu Delta. Well-maintained
gravel roads wind through fertile fields punc-
tuated by minute villages where storks nest on
power poles. Akgol, on the west lagoon, is a
popular starting point. Park at the last village,
and walk out on the trail to see Dalmatian
pelicans, pygmy cormorants, spoonbills,
egrets, herons, and purple gallinule. The
nesting and migrating season between late
March and early April is best. The drive out
can be confusing. Stop first and pick up
the informational brochure with map at the
delta's protection agency (Ozel Cevre Koruma

Kurumu) at the DSI waterworks west of Silifke. They can arrange for an English-speaking guide if you call several days in advance; 0324 713 0888. Directions: Exit 400 on the curve of the road west of the bridge; 4km from Akcakil Camping. A 22-meter-high tower, a monumental gateway, and a theatre are highlights when you visit the ruins of the ancient city of Uzuncaburc, originally a Hittite settlement. It's sits on a restful, wildflower-strewn hilltop, and is worth a detour. Directions: 3km northeast of Silifke exit 400 for Uzuncaburc and drive north 24km.

▲**Camping:** • 11km west of Silifke in Tasucu. Akcakil Camping (324 741 4451) nice location on the beach, convenient for birding; restaurant; cabins; open March-Sept; $$. • 27km east of Silifke on 400. Kizkalesi Mocamp (324 523 2149); large; good location on the beach; cabins; open May-Sept; $$.

Drive from Mersin to Adana

The E90 autostrada paralleling highway 400 has six lanes, little traffic, and only a moderate toll. The scenery is reminiscent of Tuscan Italy, with patchwork fields of wheat, sunflowers, and grapevines interspersed between orchards of fruit trees. Rest stops with large, modern gas stations are called Welcome Centers and have shaded picnic tables, small stores, and cafes.

▲**Camping:** • East of Adana on 400. Camping Motel Green (0322 321 2758); convenient; pleasant, with shrubs and shade trees; open Apr-Sept; $$.

CENTRAL TURKEY/ANATOLIA

The Seljuk tribes that migrated from the east took what they liked from Armenia and Persia and welded it into a style of their own. Their beliefs were originally animistic but they converted to Islam. You'll smile when you see that Seljuk lions sometimes have a tail ending in a snakehead, that horsemen sometimes fly on their steeds, and that mythical beasts peer from behind masses of flowers. From the mid-11th-to the mid-12th-century, their courts ruled an immense region that included Anatolia, Iran, and Mesopotamia. The lovely stone bridges, *caravanerais* (hostels), and fine mosques with conical domes that still survive across Anatolia attest to their greatness and sense of style. The Chinese taught them to glaze tile employing a double painting and firing that resulted in many brilliant colors, but they were particularly fond of a turquoise reminiscent of Lake Van.

A Late Stone Age mound known as Catalhoyuk was found on the Anatolian plain near Konya in the 1950s by British archaeologist James Mellaart. It contained wall paintings of hunters and bulls and mirrors made of volcanic glass. The excavation included looking at the DNA structure of bones buried 9,000 years ago. Succeeding inhabitants came in wave after wave, and the austere-looking Hittites left their formidable stone lions to guard their fortresses and Assyrian traders bequeathed storehouses full of order books written in wedge-shaped cuneiform script.

Konya

Located in the middle of the country's Anatolian bread-basket, Konya is authentic Turkey. It is an important place of pilgrimage for the Muslim world and was the adopted home of the mystic Mevlana, who founded the Whirling Dervish sect. It is a uniquely memorable town. All the museums are within walking distance of the round Alaeddin Parki in the center of town. Parking is available. An excellent market/bazaar area is between the intriguing museums around Alaeddin Parki and the Mevlana Muzesi (Whirling Dervish Museum). Pilgrims are tearful and

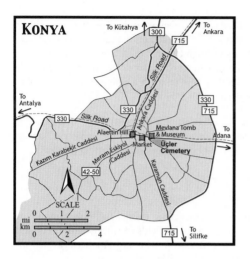

solemn as they pay homage to Mevlana, whose teachings promised deliverance from the cares of the world. The tombs of the mystic and his son are shrouded in elaborately brocaded velvet and topped with majestic turbans. Seeing this enhances your explorations of the town's fabulous tile work, exquisite portals, and lovely mosques. Museums are closed on Monday. Bring a guidebook. Directions: From the center of the historic area and the round Alaeddin Parki, look for the fluted turquoise dome that embellishes the Mevlana Muzesi.

▲**Camping:** None. Use your guidebook and choose one of the reasonably priced hotels.

Between Konya and Aksaray

▲**Camping Enroute between Konya and Aksaray:** • On 300 at the south end of the enormous salt lake, Tuz Golu, in the village of Sultanhani. These both have grassy sites with some shade; cabins; open all year; $. Kervan Pansiyon and Camping (0382 242 2325) and Camping Pansiyon Kervansaray (0382 242 2008).

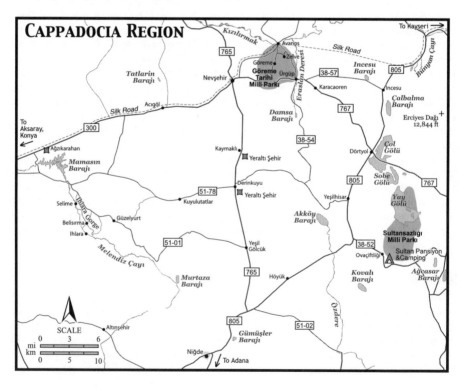

Cappadocia Region

In a fantastic explosion a millennia ago, Erciyas Dagi–one of Turkey's highest peaks–sent out a volcanic explosion that blew tufa and granite rock throughout an entire region. Gradually, water and wind sculpted out river valleys, caves, and fantastically shaped pinnacles. In 2000 BC, the Hittite Empire ruled from today's Ankara to the Black Sea, the Tarus Mountains, and the Mediterranean. Early Christians and some Muslims carved monasteries, churches, and mosques into the hills and the ground. The tufa rock is easy to carve but hardens when it is exposed to air. Some were simple, others more elaborate. These sanctuaries were deliberately hidden from the great sweeps of armies and nomads that passed over this high steppe land.

Ihlara Valley

In this valley songbirds trill, trees whisper, and the sun peers through leafy branches, dappling soft, grassy areas. All through the gorge, the clear creek bubbles along delighting walkers. It's an easy walk. Allow time to rest, picnic, and dangle your feet in the water. If you start by 8AM, you'll miss the tour groups who have discovered its beauty. There are three entrances: Selime at the north end, Belisirma in the middle where the campgrounds on the creek are located, and Ihlara at the south end–the official entrance. Admission is charged at all three entrances. At Ihlara, a long staircase leads down to the gorge. At the bottom, you can visit the remains of monastic churches tucked into mountainside caves. Directions: Aksaray is at the southeast corner of Golu Lake, south of Ankara. Drive east from Aksaray on 300 for 11km in the direction of Nevsehir. Exit south on a small road in the direction of Ihlara, and drive 31km. Exit this small road onto a smaller road in the direction of Ihlara.

▲**Camping:** • In Ihlara Village, on the road to the main entrance of the gorge. Anatolia Pansiyon (0382-453-7128) and Akar Pansiyon (0382 453 7018); both allow tent camping in the garden of their pensions; open May-September; $. • In Belisirma, mid-way along the river in the gorge. From Ihlara, take the small road heading north to Yaprakhisar. One kilometer south of the village, turn onto the road going towards the river and otopark. • Both of these are along the river in the gorge. Valley Anatolia Restaurant and Camping (0382-213 3780) and Tandirci Restaurant and Camping (0382 457 3110); you must park at the otopark and carry your camping gear across the walking bridge to the campground. Both are scenic and peaceful places; basic; open June-August; $. • In Selime. Piri Motel and Camping (0382 454 5114); pleasant location in an interest-ing little village; open May-Sept; $.

Derinkuyu

The fascinating underground dwellings here were used by the Hittites and are in remark-able condition. Rooms are more airy and light than you might imagine. Ventilation shafts, kitchens, deep wells, and storage jars were all painstakingly carved. Round sculpted stones were used as doors to close off sec-tions in case of attack. The passageways between rooms are narrow and low. Wait for those ahead of you to move to the next room before you start through. Printed guides can be purchased, but everything is clearly labeled in English. Directions: Derinkuyu is about

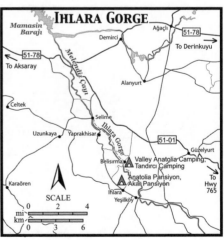

halfway between Nevsehir and Nigde. From Ihlara, take the small road directly east to Guzelyurt, then follow signage east in the direction of Kuyuluttlar and Derinkuyu. Once in town, the underground city is signposted "Yeralti Sehri" on the east side of the road.

Cappadocia

Unique in the world, this landscape of soft rock sculpted by wind, rain and snow is an environment totally different than anywhere else. The ancient caves have been refuges since the days of the Hittites. Colorful Byzantine frescoes decorate the tiny cave churches; bring a guidebook to learn the fascinating stories connected to some of them. Besides an entry fee, some of the churches have additional charges. The Valley of the Fairy Chimney's thickly clustered reddish cones are more dramatic with the shadows that come early or late in the day. Directions: Out of Goreme, drive east in the direction of Avanos/Cavusin to Yeni Zelve. From Zelve, drive 2km farther. For an adventure that requires strength, agility, and nerve, explore the monastery complex in Zelve. It requires rock climbing through a honeycomb of rooms and has a long, winding, completely dark tunnel in one part. Bring a flashlight and water and hire a local guide. Ambling along the Dovecote Valley walking trail, which winds between Goreme and Uchisar is a pleasant way to escape the crowds and enjoy the stark beauty of this high desert area. Directions: Goreme is about 300km southeast of Ankara. From Nevsehir, drive east on 767 for 5km. Exit for Goreme. It's well signposted. Drive 8km to Goreme.

▲Camping: • In Goreme, within walking distance of the open-air museum. Both have some shade; a pool; open Apr-Sept; $$$. Panorama (0271-2396); and Berlin Camping (0384 0271-2249). • 3km from the open-air museum, on a bluff with views of the area. Kaya Camping (0384 343 3100); some shade; pool; open Apr-Sept; $$$.

Goreme Valley/Sultansazligi

The open-plain landscape of this protected bird marsh area is reminiscent of Montana in the USA. Staying in the village is like stepping back into old Anatolian Turkey. The stars are brilliant, and you might be lulled to sleep by shepherd's flute. In the early morning, as the sun begins to paint Mount Erciyes a brilliant crimson, flat-bottom tourist boats are pushed by long poles into the marshes and inner ponds. The experience is silent except for the rustle of wind in the reeds and the flutter of birds' wings. Arrangements for the trip are made at the small museum, where you can study the

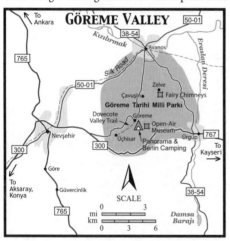

birds you'll see in the marsh. Bring binoculars and a camera. Directions: Sultansazligi Milli Parki is 85km southeast of Goreme. The scenic drive from Goreme to the park passes through groves of poplars and willows to a plateau with ochre-colored escarpments. As you wind down from the plateau, you pass through a dramatic valley of flat lands with tidy plots of vegetables and wheat fields. From Urgup, 5km east of Goreme, drive east on 767 for 30km to the village of Dortyol and 805. Turn south in the direction of Yesilhsar, and drive 11km south of Yesilhsar. Turn east on a small road and drive 12km to the village of Ovaciftlik and Sultansazligi Milli Parki.

▲Camping: • At the end of the village's main road, across from the museum. Look for the bird-viewing tower. Sultan Pansiyon and Camping, (0352-658-5549); lovely location on the plains beneath Mount Erciyes; within walking distance of the marsh area; basic; open May-Sept; $.

BOGAZKALE AREA
Bogazkale/Hittite Ruins

In 1907, a vast archive of cuneiform tablets (Assyria script pressed into terra cotta) were found in a huge buried city whose fortress was called Buyuk Kale. Their contents identified the city as Hattusas, and among the texts was a treaty between Ramesses II of Egypt and the King of Hattusas. The archive revealed that for five centuries, starting about 1700 BC, a great nation called Hatti, whose leaders were Indo-European, occupied much of central Anatolia and contested for territories as far south as Egypt and Assyria. The remnants of the Great Temple, the Sphinx Gate with its 70-meter tunnel cutting straight through to the outer wall, a rock-cut shrine decorated with a carved procession of mythical gods, and six kilometers of ponderously constructed fortifications convinced archeologists and historians that this had been a home to a great imperial people.

Start your visit at the little museum in Bogazkale where you can examine some cuneiform tablets, clay pots; and primitive tools; closed Monday. Buy an informative brochure or use your guidebook. Directions: Drive about 200km east of Ankara on E88. Exit E88 at Yozgat, and drive north on 66-77 for 33km.

▲**Camping:** • In Bogazale, on the road to Yazilikaya. Baskent Hotel-Restaurant-Camping (364 452 2037); nice location on the hillside, with view of the Great Temple; open all year; $$.

Amaysa

Dramatically set in a beautiful gorge alongside a rushing river, this is where more than 2000 years ago the Pontiac kings carved their tombs out of cliffs above the river. Strabo, the western world's first historian, was born here. Ataturk spent time here planning the Turkish independence. Now, half-timbered homes border the river, and an easy, relaxed alpine village-like ambiance prevails. The museum, just west of the Sultan Beyazit Canii, has an excellent collection and displays a re-created Ottoman home with wood-carved walls. Benches built neatly along the walls are covered with colorfully designed carpets and embroidered pillows. In the evenings, the wall of the castle and the rock-faced tombs are softly lit. The glow is romantic to locals and visitors alike, who stroll along the river to enjoy this graceful, quiet, and gorge-hidden city. Directions: Amaysa is about 80km south of the Black Sea, almost due south of Samsun.

▲**Camping:** • The closest is on Lake Borabay 63km from Amasya. Drive east of

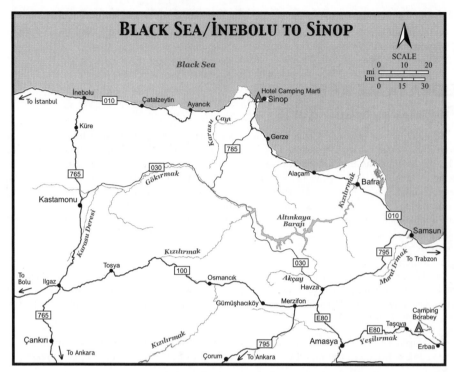

Amaysa on E80 for 63km in the direction of Tasova, and exit north following signposting for Lake Borabay. Camping Borabay (358 218 7428); nice setting in a pine forest at a reservoir lake; basic; open May-August; $. Or use your guide book to stay in a pension in Amaysa.

Black Sea/Inebolu to Sinop

This drive here is stunning. In the fall, the forests are tipped like newly painted fingernails with red, gold, and ochre, and in summer, they are lacy, green, and lined with masses of wild berry bushes. Stately vintage Ottoman homes stand on the hillsides, looking down on lowland fields of wheat that stretch to the sea. Fushia-colored oleanders blooms decorate the meridians of small towns. At tiny harbors, fishermen throw out lines from half-moon breakwaters. At street markets, scarved women haggle with mustachioed vendors. The wide paved road from Ankara to the Black Sea cuts through Tyrolean-like mountains thick with forests and dramatic rock faces.

▲Camping: • In Sinop. West of town follow signposting in the direction of Ayancik. Exit towards the small airport, and drive to the beach. Motel/Camping Marti (368 287 6214); across from the beach in a large meadow; open May-Aug; $$.

ANKARA

Turkey's capitol and most modern city is Ankara, but on a hill above the modern city you'll step into another time. At its base, in a labyrinthine of alleyways, prospective buyers carefully inspect tall stacks of eggs, lettuce, and tomatoes. Farther up, fine old Ottoman houses are still lived in, and tiny ferns peek out of rocky ancient citadel walls. Ankara is home to the famous Museum of Anatolian Civilization, whose collection tells the story from the first settlements to ancient cities of cultural sophistication. The collection is labeled in English and includes tomb-found weapons and jewelry, ceramic vases in the forms of birds, and the original lion and sphinx figures from the city gates at Hattusa. A highlight is the Royal Buttress at Carchemish–a touching 800 BC basalt relief depicting a royal family; closed Monday. Directions: Follow signs on Ataturk Bulvari to Hisar, the citadel on top of the hill. The museum is at the hill's base. Ataturk's Mausoleum (Anit Kabir) is a quiet, spacious, and beautifully green place. On the east side of the courtyard, a museum exhibits the personal effects of this remarkable man whose fierce secularism created a Turkish state from the carcass of the multinational Ottoman

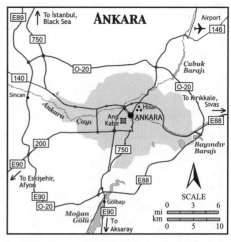

empire. Directions: The Anit Kabir is on the south side of the rail tracks, southwest of the museum. The historic museum areas are well signposted and have good parking.

▲**Camping:** • None. Use your guidebook to find a reasonably priced hotel.

Istanbul to Ankara

▲**Camping Enroute between Iasanbul and Ankara:** • Just west of Akcakoca, on the coast road 010. Camping Tezel (0374-611-4115); grassy terraces with lovely views of the sea; restaurant; cabins; open April-November; $$.
• 12km west of Akcakoca. These are both in the same area and have grassy areas on the bluff above the sea, are basic and open June-Sept; $. Hello Camping (053 5680 4989) and Nejat Camping (0380 611 4335).

EASTERN BLACK SEA COAST

   Mountain ranges running parallel to the shore leave a narrow coastal strip along Turkey's eastern Black Sea Coast. Deep gorges cut through here and there, relieving water from snow-covered mountains. The climate is cooler and rainier than the Mediterranean coast. Hazelnuts and maize farmed in fertile deltas supply important exports.

Trabizon to Sinop

▲**Camping:** • 45km east of Samsun in Unye. 3km east of the intersection of 010 and 850. Uzunkum Restaurant-Paj-Camping (0452 323 2022); good location on a small bluff overlooking the sea; shady with pines; open Apr-Sept; $$.

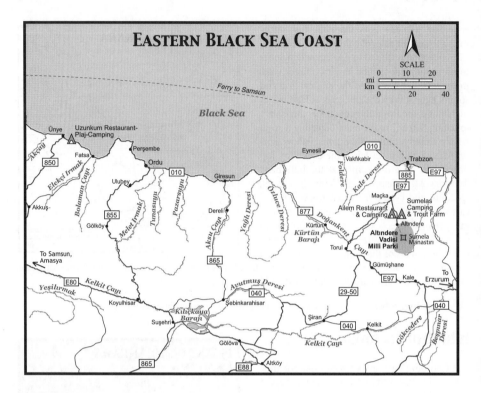

EASTERN BLACK SEA COAST

SCALE

Black Sea

Ferry to Samsun

Ünye   Uzunkum Restaurant-
        Plaj-Camping

Perşembe   Eynesil   010

Akçay   Fatsa   Vakfıkabir   Trabzon

850   Ordu   885   E97

Elekçi Irmak   Bolaman Çayı   010   Giresun   E97

Ulubey   Maçka   Sumelas
                                                                     Camping
Akkuş-   Dereli   877   Ailem Restaurant   & Trout Farm
                                                  & Camping   Altındere
        855   Kürtün
Gölköy Melet Irmak Tunasuyu Pazarsuyu Yağlı Deresi Doğankent Kürtün Altındere
                                           Baraji   Torul Vadisi   Sumela
To Samsun,   Milli Parki Manastırı
Amasya   865
                                                       Gümüşhane
                                                                          To
E80   Kelkit Çayı   E97   Kale   Erzurum
Yeşilırmak   Avutmuş Deresi
       Koyulhisar   040   Şebinkarahisar   29-50

       Suşehri Kılıçkaya   Şiran   040   040
                Baraji
                       Gölova   Kelkit Çayı   Kelkit   Gökçedere Başpınar Deresi

       865   E88   Altköy

Trabizon

Protectively set between two mountain gorges, Trabizon was once a Greek Christian city and held out against Mehmet the Conqueror for eight years after the fall of Constantinople. Steep streets lead up to the old town from the harbor, whose port once sent exotic goods from India and China to Western Europe. The towers of Trabizon stand along the protecting seawall and are the city's icon. A narrow strip of parkland prettily edges the sea with walking paths and parking, providing a perfect place for picnics, evening strolls, and easy parking for walks into the old town. Byzantine headstones, Roman-carved stelae, and Ottoman tombs are softened by a fragrant rose garden surrounding Hagia Sophia, Tabizon's romantic and graceful church set on a bluff overlooking the sea. Inside the apse, portals, and narthex, bright frescoes adorn the walls and ceilings. In the 14th –century, Byzantine painters gave more warmth and fluidity to their subjects, and works here attest to that Renaissance; open daily. Directions: Drive west on the coast road 010, passing the ancient walls. Follow signposting south up the hill, staying right for the church's free car park.

Both here and in Greece monks sought out wild high retreats. The huge cave-monastery of Sumela clings tenaciously to a cliff more than 1,000 feet up from the floor of a canyon here, looking out over a vast range of mountains thick with forests. A narrow stairway leads up into an inner courtyard surrounded by the sanctuary, kitchen, monks' cells, and guest rooms. Only fragments of frescoes were found before restoration, but they are sweet and appealing so bring binoculars for a close-up view of expressions. Directions: Exit 010 onto E97, and drive south for 27km to Macka. Turn east into the town, and drive up the hill through the forest and along the river for 16km. Park and take the somewhat steep woodland trail, allowing 30-60 minutes. A narrow, steep road winds up beyond the trailhead to a parking area used by staff, but most people walk up the more atmospheric pine-and-fern adorned trail.

▲**Camping:** • 11km from the monastery. From the junction of E97 and Macka, drive 5km. Turn onto a narrow road that hugs the river on the west side. Drive one kilometer. Cross over the small bridge to camping. Sumelas Camping and Trout Farm (0462 531 1176); great location on the river; picturesque picnic chalets at the edge of the tumultuous river; grassy meadow in the mountain gorge; quiet; open all year; $$. In the same area but closer to Macka. Ailem Restaurant and Camping (0462 512 4062); along the road to the monastery; playground; cabins; open all year; $$.

Nemrut Dagi

A 50-meter-high burial tumulus of stone rises from natural rock at the isolated peak of Nemrut Dagi. Colossal statues–the detached heads alone are up to 2-meters high–depict a hierarchy of gods and heroes. The colossus was built in the 1st-century BC by Antiochus I Epiphanes whose vanity seemed to own no bounds–he claimed he was a descendent of Darius the Great from Persia, but his rule over a small territory called the Commagene was short-lived. As you climb the path leading up to terraces of the tumulus–best done a few hours before sunset–it is hard to imagine the grueling work that was necessary to built such a tribute. On the eastern-facing terrace 6 decapitated seated statues sit on an altar above their remarkable heads. At dawn, Antochus' people would trudge up the mountain then onto the tumulus to witness a sacrifice and present offerings at the altar. After seeing this amazing remote site, it is a relief to be greeted warmly at hotel-camp-grounds with panoramic views of the mountains in the village of Karadut, just below the site. Directions: Drive east on autostrada 052 to Sanliurfa. Exit northwest on 360 in the direction of Adiyaman, and drive 96km on a scenic highway overlooking the huge reservoir lake. Exit north in the direction of Kahta, and drive 55km. At the fork, stay north, passing through Karaku, then east to Narince for 17km. Continue up the hill to Karadut. From the village, it is 8km to the mountain top sanctuary. This is a national park so an admission is charged at the entrance, about 7 kilometers from the top.

▲**Camping:** • The mountaintop settings here are hard to beat anywhere and being so remote makes them even more special. You'll want to linger. These are both just beyond the village of Karadut, on the way to the national park. Karadut Pansiyon-Restaurant-Camping (0416 737 2169); campsites are along the edge of the mountain with dramatic views of a mountain gorge; open all year; $$. Hotel Kervansaray-Restaurant-Camping (0416 737 2191); grassy meadow with panoramic views of the mountains; pool; open all year; $$.

Appendix

PERSONAL DOCUMENTS
Passport

A passport is required for entering a foreign country, reentering your own, and boarding a flight out of the country. If you already have a passport, check the expiration date. Make sure it is valid several months beyond your return from your trip out of the country. Applicants for new passports need their birth certificates, identification cards such as driver's license and social security card, and two passport photos. Check ahead on how payment can be made: personal check, charge card, or cashier's check. Use your phone book or the web to access where to get a new passport or renew an existing one. Make copies of the photo and information pages on your passport. Take one copy with you and leave one copy with someone at home. This copy will help expedite a new passport at an embassy or consulate overseas if necessary. Processing for new or renewed passports can take up to 8 weeks.

Visa

A visa is a stamp that entitles you to visit a country for a particular reason-tourism. A tourist visa is usually valid for three months from entry to exiting the country. Most European countries don't require a visas but a web check at the country's website could save time later. Allow six weeks for processing.

Discount Cards

With the following cards you can often get discounts on museum and historic site entrance fees and transportation:

International Student Identity Card (ISIC)
Available to students studying in the past year. Contact the school office or in USA 800-2-COUNCIL.

Federation of International Youth Travel Organization (FIYTO)
Available to persons under 26. Call USA 800-2-COUNCIL.

Senior Citizen Card
If you are 65 or over show your passport.

Other Documents and Cards

International Driver's License (IDP)
Not necessary if you current driver's license has your photo.

Cash Cards

This is the easiest way to obtain local currency. Your card will need to be linked to Cirrus, Maestro, and Plus networks. Pin numbers need to be numerical with four digits. Cash machines are found in all over Europe in the larger towns and cities, including Eastern Europe and Turkey. Directions for use are in major languages and they are user-friendly. Before leaving a city always get enough local currency to carry you through to the next city. They are located in the same places you find them at home: outside banks, shopping malls, grocery stores, and tourist areas. It's safest and more economical to use bank cash machines during business hours. Airports and shopping malls often have higher transaction costs. Order new cards if the magnetic strip is worn.

Credit Cards

In Western Europe and Scandinavia you'll be able to use a Visa credit card at major gas station, large shopping malls, and major tourist attractions in larger towns and cities. In the rest of Europe and all small towns and villages in all of Europe, this won't always be the case. Many accept only credit cards issued in their own country.

Driver's License

Be sure to bring it. Make sure the expiration date is several months beyond your departure from Europe. You'll need it to pick up your car and to be legal on the road.

Auto Club Card

Most European countries have reciprocal agreements with other countries' auto club. Bringing yours eases problems on the road.

International Camping Card

Often when you check into a campground you'll be asked to leave your passport for security against damage or nonpayment. However, many campgrounds will take your International Camping Card instead. Some campgrounds give a small discount with it. For this reason alone it is worth getting. It is a different card from the regular membership card. Be sure to specify that you want the international camping card. Contact: USA Family Campers and RV's 1-800-245 9755 or ficcnorthamerica@ol.com. or www.fcrv.org. In Scandinavia they usually only honor their own card. Purchase it at your first campground.

Vehicle Rental/Leasing

Rental rates very from country to country. The least expensive rates are in Germany, Switzerland, The Netherlands, Britain, Belgium, and Luxembourg. When you call to inquire about rentals get the rental rate of the neighboring countries too. If the neighboring country's rates are lower consider picking up the car there. See Getting Vehicle Rental/Lease Information in the introduction.

Vehicle Rental/Lease Firms:
www.autoEurope.com
www.europcar.com

www.Avis.com
www.NationalCar.com
www.Kemwel.com

Insurance

Collision Damage Waiver (CDW) covers you for loss or damage of the vehicle you are renting. It is compulsory in most countries. Loss damage waiver (LDW) and theft protection (TP) are often included in CDW insurance, but verify this is writing. Be certain vandalism, attempted theft, and theft are included in your collision and damage policy. See Arranging Insurance in the introduction.

Insurance Agencies

Travel Guard Insurance www.buy.travelguard.com 1-800-826-4919

Arrangement for the insurance must be done 24-hours before picking up the vehicle. They are open 24-hours a day, everyday of the week. Rates are very reasonable and making a claim is easy.

Credit-Card Insurance. Check on the limitations and conditions carefully and have them verified in a contract.

Personal auto insurance. Check the limitations and conditions carefully and have them verified in a contract.

Car-Rental Company Insurance

Expensive and not advised. See Arranging Insurance in the introduction.

Theft Insurance. You will want insurance that covers personal effects left unattended in a locked vehicle. Verify the maximum coverage. Your homeowner's policy may also include theft coverage while traveling. Otherwise check with your auto club, the vehicle insurance agencies above, or your travel agent.

Medical Insurance. Check your own medical insurance carrier to find out what is deductible and how reimbursement is made for expenses incurred. USA Medicare does not cover expenses out of the country.

Comprehensive Insurance. For coverage of medical, baggage, trip cancellation, and emergency flight home Travel Guard Insurance offers an inexpensive policy.

To make a claim . Call your insurance carrier as soon as possible after the accident. Get a claim number when you call. They will mail you a claim form. Your insurance will probably cover you for damages to the car that did not involve another vehicle or persons and did not need a police report. Give the claim number to the car rental firm when the car is returned. Give the car rental firm a few days then fax them for a request for a copy of the bill so you can submit it to the insurance carrier within the limited time frame.

Road Signs

The word stop, the colors green, red, and yellow indicate the same meaning as at home. No turn may be made on red, even after stopping. A sign with a border, a red color, or a round shape indicates a prohibition or warning-no parking, no entry, or danger. The graphics inside tell what is prohibited. A round sign with a border and "X" indicates no stopping. A round sign with a border and slash indicates no parking. Blue and green background and rectangular shapes indicate something is available–a rest stop, a cycling path, or information. Camping signs are rectangular with a tent.

As at home, roadways marked with solid lines mean no passing while dashed lines indicate a passing zone. Other passing rules are also what you are used to a home. When two roads of equal size intersect, the vehicle on the right has the right-away. Otherwise the larger road has priority over the smaller road. On round-abouts the vehicles already on the round-about have the right-away. Once you enter the round-about, use your turn blinker to change lanes or exit.

Truck drivers will often use their turn-blinker and wave their arm to indicate that it is safe to pass on them on that side. On-coming drivers might flash their headlights to warn you to slow down because of something ahead. To thank them beep twice and wave.

When you are entering a city to see the sights exit at the signs for "center" in the local language. Tourist offices or boards are usually signposted with a "I". To exit the city follow signs for "all directions" in the local language or the place name of where you want to go. Street signs are usually posted on the corner building and can change names even though the route hasn't. Keep your car registration and insurance papers easily accessible.

Website Information

Go to www.visiteurope.com, the official European website that links to 30 individual country websites. Here you'll find updated information on their cultural, musical, and festival events. They are lively and fun to visit. Additional links will lead you to information on advanced ticketing.

INDEX